Life

TEACHER'S BOOK | UPPER INTERMEDIATE

NATIONAL
GEOGRAPHIC
LEARNING

MIKE SAYER

Australia · Brazil · Mexico · Singapore · United Kingdom · United States

LEARNING

Life Upper Intermediate Teacher's Book
2nd Edition
Mike Sayer and Rachel Godfrey

Vice President, Editorial Director:
  John McHugh

Executive Editor: Sian Mavor

Publishing Consultant: Karen Spiller

Project Managers: Sarah Ratcliff and
  Laura Brant

Development Editor: Helen Holwill

Editorial Manager: Claire Merchant

Head of Strategic Marketing ELT:
  Charlotte Ellis

Senior Content Project Manager:
  Nick Ventullo

Manufacturing Manager: Eyvett Davis

Senior IP Analyst: Ashley Maynard

Senior IP Project Manager:
  Michelle McKenna

Cover: Lisa Trager

Text design: Vasiliki Christoforidou

Compositor: Lumina Datamatics Ltd.

Audio: Tom Dick and Debbie Productions Ltd

DVD: Tom Dick and Debbie Productions Ltd

For product information and technology assistance, contact us at
Cengage Learning Customer & Sales Support, cengage.com/contact

For permission to use material from this text or product,
submit all requests online at **cengage.com/permissions**
Further permissions questions can be emailed to
permissionrequest@cengage.com

ISBN: 978-1-337-28630-5

National Geographic Learning
Cheriton House, North Way, Andover,
Hampshire, SP10 5BE
United Kingdom

National Geographic Learning, a Cengage Learning Company, has a mission to bring the world to the classroom and the classroom to life. With our English language programs, students learn about their world by experiencing it. Through our partnerships with National Geographic and TED Talks, they develop the language and skills they need to be successful global citizens and leaders.

Locate your local office at **international.cengage.com/region**

Visit National Geographic Learning online at **NGL.Cengage.com/ELT**
Visit our corporate website at **www.cengage.com**

CREDITS

Text: Test 1 Adapted from 'National Geographic's Genographic Project', www.nationalgeographic.com; Test 2 Source: from 'A Quiet Passion reviewed', https://www.spectator.co.uk/2017/04/cynthia-nixon-is-terrific-as-emily-dickinson-a-quiet-passion-reviewed/Reprinted by permission; Test 3 Adapted from 'Historic Solar Flight Shows Promise', www.nationalgeographic.com; Test 4 Adapted from 'Cave Walls Record Early Encounters Between the Old World and the New', www.nationalgeographic.com; Test 5 Adapted from 'Cities', www.nationalgeographic.com; Test 6 Adapted from 'Stay at National Geographic Lodges', www.nationalgeographic.com; Test 7 Source: from 'Do whales have culture?', http://www.natgeoeducationvideo.com/film/455/barcelona-street-life; Test 8 Adapted from 'Are we evolving?', www.nationalgeographic.com; Test 9 Adapted from 'Treasure Trove of Ancient Human Footprints Found Near Volcano', www.nationalgeographic.com; Test 10 Adapted from 'The Science of Superheroes', www.nationalgeographic.com; Test 11 Adapted from 'Are you ready to learn a new language?', www.nationalgeographic.com; Test 12 Adapted from 'The Journey of Humankind: How Money Made Us Modern', www.nationalgeographic.com

Cover: © John Harrison/500px.

Illustrations: Lumina Datamatics Ltd.

DVD Videos: Unit 1 National Geographic; Unit 2 National Geographic; Unit 3 Sky News/Film Image Partner/Getty Images; Unit 4 Sky News/Film Image Partner/Getty Images; Unit 5 National Geographic; Unit 6 © Sertac Yuksel; Unit 7a © Isaac Blencowe; Unit 7b © Mark Watts; Unit 8a Feature Story News – Footage/Getty Images; Unit 8b Anadolu Agency/Footage/Getty Images; Unit 8 Music 1 © Audiojungle; Unit 8 Videos 1–27 © Videohive; Unit 10 National Geographic; Unit 11 National Geographic; Unit 12 © Gary Breece; Videos 18–19 © Videohive.

DVD Photos: Unit 9 © twphotos/Getty Images; Karina Walton/Alamy Stock Photo; © Creatas/Jupiterimages; © Konrad Mostert/Shutterstock.com; © PhotoDisc/Getty Images; © Corel Images; © Natalia Macheda/Shutterstock.com; © Creatas/Jupiterimages; © idreamphoto/Shutterstock.com; © ziiinvn/Shutterstock.com.

Printed in China by RR Donnelley
Print Number: 01   Print Year: 2017

Contents

Contents

Listening	Reading	Critical thinking	Speaking	Writing
three people talking about important relationships in their lives an extract from a radio programme about animal friendships	an article about changing attitudes in China an article about immigrant families in New York	evaluating conclusions	friendships differences between generations family influences	text type: an informal email writing skill: greetings and endings
an interview with a film critic an interview with a professional photographer	an incredible story of a Formula 1 racing driver an article about the Brothers Grimm	the main message	a key moment the stories pictures tell storytelling	text type: a story writing skill: using descriptive words
three people making predictions about the future a lecture about overpopulation an interview from a radio programme about 3D printing	a lecture about overpopulation an article about appropriate technology	supporting examples	predictions the future technological solutions	text type: short email requests writing skill: being polite
a conversation about two people who are creative in their free time an extract from a radio programme about what's on in Melbourne	an article about unusual street art an article about how music helps us	identifying opinions	art and music participation in the arts music playlists	text type: an online review writing skill: personalizing your writing
someone talking about the development of the Belo Monte dam in Brazil an interview with a journalist about social development in southern India	an article about urban development in Dubai an article about the teenage mind	ways of arguing	changes in your town a happy society stages of life	text type: an opinion essay writing skill: linking words
someone describing their stay at a mountainside guesthouse an interview about volunteer vacations	a blog about holidays at home an extract from a travel magazine about historical hotels	analysing tone	planning a staycation a volunteer holiday ideas for an unusual hotel	text type: a letter/email of complaint writing skill: formal language

Contents

Contents

Introduction

National Geographic

The National Geographic Society is a leading nonprofit organization that pushes the boundaries of exploration to further our understanding of our planet and empower us all to generate solutions for a healthier and more sustainable future. Since its beginning in 1888, the Society has funded more than 12,500 exploration and research projects. *Life Second Edition* uses *National Geographic*'s content and principles to inspire people to learn English. A portion of the proceeds of this book help to fund the Society's work.

National Geographic topics

The topics are paramount and are the starting point for the lessons. These topics have been selected for their intrinsic interest and ability to fascinate. The richness of the texts means that students are so engaged in learning about the content, and expressing their own opinions, that language learning has to take place in order for students to satisfy their curiosity and then react personally to what they have learned. This element of transfer from the topics to students' own realities and experiences converts the input into a vehicle for language practice and production which fits the recognized frameworks for language learning and can be mapped to the CEFR scales. (Full mapping documents are available separately.)

People and places

Life Second Edition takes students around the globe, investigating the origins of ancient civilizations, showing the drama of natural forces at work and exploring some of the world's most beautiful places. These uplifting tales of adventure and discovery are told through eye witness accounts and first-class reportage. For example, Unit 7 of the Upper Intermediate level includes a radio feature about the unusual diet of the indigenous people of northern Alaska and Unit 9 tells the true story behind the famous 'Afghan girl' photograph.

Science and technology

Students learn about significant scientific discoveries and breakthroughs, both historic and current. These stories are related by journalists or told by the scientists and explorers themselves through interviews or first person accounts. Students see the impact of the discoveries on our lifestyles and cultures. Because much of the material comes from a huge archive that has been developed and designed to appeal to the millions of individuals who make up *National Geographic*'s audience, it reflects the broadest possible range of topics. For example, Unit 3 of the Upper Intermediate level examines the risks and benefits of 'appropriate technology', and the exciting applications of 3D printing.

History

History can be a dry topic, especially if it's overloaded with facts and dates. However, the *National Geographic* treatment of historical events brings them to life and there is often a human dimension and universal themes that keep the events relevant to students and to our time. History – or the re-telling of historical events – can also be influenced by a culture or nation's perception of the events. *National Geographic*'s non-judgemental and culture-neutral accounts allow students to look behind the superficial events and gain a deeper understanding of our ancestors. For example, Unit 6 of the Upper Intermediate level looks at how the hotel industry is capitalizing on historic buildings to offer guests an unusual experience, and Unit 9 examines the legacy of the controversial Hatshepsut, a fifteenth-century female pharaoh who ruled as 'king'.

Animals

The animal kingdom is exceptionally generative in terms of interesting topics. *Life Second Edition* provides astonishing photos that give a unique insight into the hidden lives of known and lesser-known animals, offering rare glimpses of mammals, birds, bugs and reptiles in their daily struggle for survival. It also informs and surprises with accounts of animals now extinct, species still evolving and endangered species which are literally fighting for their existence. For example, Unit 1 of the Upper Intermediate level presents some unlikely friendships between members of the animal kingdom.

Environment

It isn't always possible to find clarity in texts on the environment and climate change, or trust that they are true and not driven by a political agenda. *National Geographic*'s objective journalism, supported by easy-to-understand visuals, presents the issues in an accessible way. The articles are written by experts in their fields. It's often true that those who have the deepest understanding of issues are also able to express the ideas in the simplest way. For example, Unit 4 of the Upper Intermediate level is based around an article about an environmentally friendly form of graffiti.

National Geographic photography

We live in a world where images are used more than ever to reinforce, and at times replace, the spoken and written word. We use our visual literacy – the ability to look at and understand images – every day of our lives. In particular, photographs tend to prompt emotive memories and help us to recall information. For this reason, the use of photographs and pictures in the classroom is a highly effective learning tool. Not surprisingly then, the *Life* series makes maximum use of the great photographs which are at the core of *National Geographic* content. The photographs in *Life Second Edition* add impact and serve as an engaging starting point to each unit. Then, in each lesson, photographs form an integral part of the written and recorded content and generate meaningful language practice in thoughtful and stimulating ways.

There are photographs which:

- tell a story by themselves
- draw the viewer in and engage them emotionally
- support understanding of a text and make it memorable
- provoke debate
- stimulate critical thinking by asking you to examine detail *or* think about what is NOT shown *or* by questioning the photographer's motives
- are accompanied by a memorable quotation or caption
- help learners to remember a lexical set
- help to teach functional language
- lend themselves to the practice of a specific grammar point

As a first exercise when handing out the new book to your students, you could ask them to flick through the book, select their favourite photograph, and then explain to the class what it is they like about it. You will find specific suggestions in the teacher's notes for using the photographs featured within each unit, but two important things to note are:

- pictures of people or animals can capture a moment, so ask students to speculate on the events that led up to this moment and those that followed it
- pictures of places aim to capture their essence, so feed students the vocabulary they need to describe the details that together convey this (the light, the colours, the landscape, the buildings)

National Geographic video

Student's visual literacy and fascination with moving images means that, in addition to the use of photographs and pictures, video is also an extremely effective tool in the classroom. Each unit of *Life Second Edition* ends with a *National Geographic* video. These videos, which can be found on the DVD at the back of the Teachers's Book, the Student's App and on the *Life* website, are connected to the topic of the unit and are designed to be used in conjunction with the video lesson pages. Typically, a video lesson is divided into three parts:

Before you watch

This section leads students into the topic of the video and engages them in a pre-watching task. It also pre-teaches key vocabulary so that students can immediately engage with the video without being distracted by unfamiliar words and the need to reference a lengthy glossary.

While you watch

These tasks assist with comprehension of the video itself, both in terms of what students see and what they hear. The exercises also exploit the language used in the video.

After you watch

There are two parts to this section. The first is an on-screen exercise called Vocabulary in context, which focuses on useful words and expressions from the video. The second allows students to respond to the video as a whole and take part in a discussion or task that leads on from the context and theme of the video.

The videos are designed to form part of your lessons. However, if there is insufficient time in class to watch them all, you can ask students to watch the videos and complete many of the exercises on the page in the Student's Book at home. This can form a useful part of their self-study. Students can also watch the videos again after seeing them in class. This is useful for review and enables students to focus on parts of the audio that particularly interest them.

For further variation with the videos, here are some more ideas you can use and develop:

- Play the video with the sound down. Students predict what the narrator or people are saying. Then play with the sound up and compare.
- Play the sound only with no video. Students predict where the video takes place and what is happening on the screen. Then play the video as normal and compare.
- Show the first part of the video, pause it, and then ask students what they think happens next.
- Give students a copy of the video script and ask them to imagine they are the director. What will they need to film and show on the screen? Afterwards, they present their 'screenplay' ideas to the class, then finally watch the original.
- Write a short text on the same topic as the one in the video. However, don't include the same amount of information and leave some facts out. Students read the text and then watch the video. They make notes on any new information and rewrite the text so it includes the new details.
- With monolingual groups, choose part of the video in which someone is talking. Ask students to listen and write down what they say. Then, in groups, ask them to create subtitles in their own language for that part of the video. Each group presents their subtitles and the class compares how similar they are.

National Geographic and critical thinking

Critical thinking is the ability to develop and use an analytical and evaluative approach to learning. It's regarded as a key 21st Century skill. *Life Second Edition* integrates and develops a learner's critical thinking alongside language learning for the following reasons:

- critical thinking tasks such as problem-solving and group discussion make lessons much more motivating and engaging
- developing critical thinking skills encourages an enquiring approach to learning which enables learners to discover language and become more independent in their study skills
- language practice activities that involve critical thinking require deeper processing of the new language on the part of the learner

In *Life Second Edition* you will see that there is a graded critical thinking syllabus that starts at Elementary level and runs through all later levels. The sections entitled 'Critical thinking' always appear in the C lessons in each unit and are associated with reading the longer texts. These lessons begin with reading comprehension activities that test students' understanding and then may ask them to apply their understanding in a controlled practice activity. Having understood the text at a basic level, the critical thinking section requires students to read the text again more deeply to find out what the author is trying to achieve and to analyse the writing approach. For example, students may have to read between the lines, differentiate between fact or opinion, evaluate the reliability of the information, assess the relevance of information, or identify the techniques used by the author to persuade the reader or weigh up evidence. Activities such as these work particularly well with the C lesson texts in *Life Second Edition* because the texts used in these lessons are authentic. These authentic texts, which have been adapted to the level where necessary, tend to retain the author's voice or perspective, so students can work to understand the real argument behind a text. Naturally, these kinds of reading skills are invaluable for students who are learning English for academic purposes or who would like to take examinations such as IELTS. In addition, life in the twenty-first century requires people to develop the ability to assess the validity of a text and the information they receive, so this critical thinking strand in *Life Second Edition* is important for all students.

As well as applying critical thinking to the reading texts, *Life Second Edition* encourages students to apply critical thinking skills in other ways. When new vocabulary or grammar is presented, students are often expected to use the target language in controlled practice activities. Then they use the language in productive speaking and writing tasks where they are given opportunities to analyse and evaluate a situation and make use of the new language both critically and creatively. In this way, students move from using 'lower-order thinking' to 'higher-order thinking'; many of the lessons in *Life Second Edition* naturally follow this flow from exercises that involve basic checking and controlled practice to those that are productive, creative, and more intellectually engaging. This learning philosophy can also be seen at work in the way in which photos and videos are used in the book. Students are encouraged to speculate and express their opinions on many of the photographs or in the 'after you watch' sections of the video pages. Finally, on the writing pages of the units, students are asked to think critically about how they organize their writing and the language they choose to use. They are also guided to think critically to establish criteria by which their writing can then be judged.

Central to the approach to critical thinking in *Life Second Edition* is the premise that students should be actively engaged in their language learning. Students are frequently invited to ask questions and to develop their own well-informed and reasoned opinions. The overall combination of text analysis (in the C lessons), a guided discovery approach to language, and the way in which the book makes use of images in the classroom effectively supports this aim.

Life Second Edition methodology

Memorization

An important role for teachers is to help learners commit new language to longer-term memory, not just their short-term or working memory. According to Gairns and Redman (*Working with Words*, Cambridge University Press, 1986), 80% of what we forget is forgotten within the first twenty-four hours of initial learning.

So, what makes learning memorable? The impact of the first encounter with new language is known to be a key factor. *Life Second Edition* scores strongly in this area because it fulfils what are called the 'SUCCESS factors' in memorization (Simplicity, Unexpectedness, Concreteness, Credibility, Emotion and Stories) by engaging learners with interesting, real-life stories and powerful images. *Life Second Edition* also aims, through motivating speaking activities that resonate with students' own experiences, to make new language relatable. What is known is that these encounters with language need to be built on thorough consolidation, recycling, repetition and testing. It is said that a new language item needs to be encountered or manipulated between five and fifteen times before it's successfully committed to longer-term memory. With this in mind, we have incorporated the following elements in *Life Second Edition*:

a) more recycling of new vocabulary and grammar through each unit and level of the series

b) activities in the Classroom Presentation Tool (CPT) that start each new lesson with revision and recycling of previous lessons

c) progress tests and online end-of-year tests

d) activities in the Review lessons at the end of each unit, marked 'Memory booster'

These 'Memory booster' activities are based on the following methodologically proven principles:

- Relatability: learning is most effective when learners apply new language to their own experience.

- A multi-sensory approach: learning is enhanced when more than one sense (hearing, seeing, etc.) is involved in perception and retention. (Language is not an isolated system in memory; it's linked to the other senses.)

- Repetition and variation: learners need to frequently retrieve items from memory and apply them to different situations or contexts.

- Guessing/Cognitive depth: making guesses at things you are trying to retrieve aids deeper learning.

- Utility: language with a strong utility value, e.g. a function such as stating preferences, is easier to remember.

- No stress: it's important that the learner does not feel anxious or pressured by the act of remembering.

- Peer teaching: this is an effective tool in memory consolidation (as in the adage, 'I hear and I forget. I see and I remember. I do and I understand. I teach and I master.')

- Individuality: we all differ in what we find easy to remember, so co-operation with others helps the process.

Introduction

You probably already use revision and recycling in your teaching. Our hope is that these exercises will stimulate ideas for other fun and varied ways you can do this, which in turn may lead students to reflect on what learning and memorization strategies work best for them as individuals.

Treatment of grammar

Target grammar is presented in the first two lessons of each unit in the context of reading or listening texts. These texts are adapted for level as necessary from authentic sources which use the target language in natural and appropriate linguistic contexts. Such texts not only aid comprehension, but present good models for the learner's own language production through a variety of 'voices' and genres. In general, reading texts have been used in the first lesson and listening texts in the second. Where a presentation is via a listening text, written examples of the grammar structures are given on the page, for example in content comprehension tasks, so that the student gets the visual support of following the target structures on the page. In both types of presentations, the primary focus is on the topic content before the learner's attention is drawn to the target grammar structures. Learners are then directed to notice target structures by various means, such as using highlighting within the text, extracting sample sentences or asking learners to locate examples themselves. Tasks which revise any related known structures are given in the Student's Book, Teacher's Book or via the CPT package.

At the start of each grammar section is a grammar summary box with examples of form and use from the presentation text, or paradigms where this is clearer (for example, in lower levels). This supports the learners and is a 'check point' for both teacher and learner alike. The grammar box summarizes the information learners arrive at through completing discovery tasks and it also acts as a focus for tasks which then analyse the form, meaning and use of the grammar structures, as appropriate. A variety of task formats have been used to do this, usually beginning with accessible check questions. This approach is highly motivational because it actively engages learners in the lesson and allows them to share and discuss their interpretation of the new language. Each grammar box gives a cross reference to two pages of detailed explanations and additional exercises per unit at the back of the Student's Book. These are suitable for use both in class and for self-study, according to the needs of the learner. They are also presented as video tutorials for extra support in the Online Workbooks.

The grammar summary box is followed by grammar practice tasks. Depending on the level, the grammar practice exercises have a differing emphasis on form and use. In all levels, however, the practice exercises in the unit favour exercises which require students to think more deeply over those involving mechanical production. Where appropriate, contrastive and comparative formats are used. The first practice exercise is usually linked to the topic of the lesson and is content rich. Subsequent exercises move into real-life contexts and particularly to those which the learner can personalize. This gives learners an invaluable opportunity to incorporate the structures in the context of their own experiences. The practice exercises are carefully designed to move from supported tasks through to more challenging activities. This anchors the new language in existing frameworks and leads to a clearer understanding of the usage of this new or revised language. Frequently, the tasks provide a real and engaging reason to use the target structure, whether by devices such as quizzes, games and so on, or by genuine exchanges of information between students.

Each lesson ends with a 'My life' speaking task. This personalized and carefully scaffolded activity enables students to create their own output using use the target grammar as well as other target language in a meaningful context. Typical formats for this final task include exchanges of information or ideas, 'gap' pair work, personal narratives, discussion and task-based activities (ranking, etc.). The emphasis from the learner's perspective is on fluency within the grammatical framework of the task.

Treatment of vocabulary

Life Second Edition pays particular attention to both receptive and productive vocabulary. All of the authentic input texts have been revised to reduce above-level lexis while retaining the original 'flavour' and richness of the text and providing an achievable level of challenge.

Lexis is effectively learned via carefully devised recycling and memorization activities. Target vocabulary is recycled continually throughout each level – for example the writing and video lessons provide the ideal opportunity to incorporate and review lexis in meaningful contexts. Memorization (see page 10) is a key feature of exercises within the unit and in the Review lessons.

Life Second Edition teaches vocabulary in a range of different ways. This eclectic approach takes account of recent research and builds on tried and tested methods. There is further practice of the vocabulary input (apart from words occurring in glossaries) in the Workbook and also in the photocopiable Communicative Activities, which can be found in this Teacher's Book. There is also frequent practice of useful expressions, collocations, idioms and phrasal verbs as well as everyday lexis.

The specific sections dealing with new lexical input are:

1 Lexical sets

Some of the benefits generally associated with teaching words in lexical sets are:

- learning words in a set requires less effort
- retrieving related words from memory is easier
- seeing how knowledge can be organized can be helpful to learners
- it mirrors how such information is thought to be stored in the brain
- the meaning of words can be made clearer by comparing and contrasting them to similar words in the set

Each unit usually has two or more lexical sets. The lexical sets also cover commonly confused words. There is evidence to suggest that once students have learned one or more of the words that belong to a group of commonly confused words (e.g. *job* and *work*), it's useful to compare and contrast these words directly to clarify the differences (or similarities) in meaning. *Life Second Edition* focuses on these groups of words as and when they come up.

2 Wordbuilding

There are at least eight of these sections in each level. The independent wordbuilding syllabus offers students another opportunity to expand their vocabulary. The wordbuilding boxes in the units focus on areas such as prefixes, suffixes, parts of speech, compound nouns and phrasal verbs, and they highlight contextualized examples in the reading or listening texts. The box gives a brief explanation and some examples. It's followed by one or two practice activities. Each wordbuilding focus is followed up and extended in the Workbook and CPT – giving more practice and introducing more words that belong to the same morphological area.

3 Word focus

The word focus sections take high-frequency words and give examples of the different meanings they can have according to the contexts in which they appear and the different words they collocate with. At higher levels there is increased exposure to idioms and colloquial usage. The Workbook and CPT expand the range of phrases and expressions generated by these key words and provide further practice.

4 Glossaries

Occasionally, words are important to the meaning of a text but are above the level of the student. In such cases they are glossed. Students aren't expected to learn these words, but the short and simple definitions provided on the page prevent them from being a barrier to understanding.

5 Word lists

Each level has a comprehensive word list which covers all of the vocabulary either at the level, or above the level, of the student. The rich headword entries include phonetics, definition, part of speech, examples, collocations, word family and word family collocates. These are available on the Student's App and on the *Life* website as pdfs.

Learning skills

There is a comprehensive learning skills syllabus in the Workbook. This covers traditional learning skills, such as recording new vocabulary, using a dictionary, remembering new vocabulary, planning study time and assessing your own progress.

Assessment

Students and teachers can assess progress in the following ways:

- Each unit in the Student's Book finishes with a Review lesson where students do the exercises and complete a number of 'can-do' statements linked to the objectives of the unit.
- There are photocopiable progress tests in the Teacher's Book.

- There are end-of-year tests that follow the format of international exams on the *Life* website.
- There is a *Check!* section at the end of each unit in the Workbook for students to check what they have learned (general knowledge as well as language).
- There are IELTs practice tests at the end of the Workbooks. These have been graded to the level of the course, but follow the format of the test. These allow students to benchmark their progress against the course objectives, whilst becoming familiar with a global test format.

Lessons in a Student's Book unit

Opener: a one-page introduction to the unit that gets students interested in the topic

A and B: double-page lessons that teach grammar and vocabulary through reading and listening texts

C: a double-page lesson that focuses on reading comprehension and critical thinking

D: a one-page lesson that teaches functional/situational language

E: a one-page lesson that teaches a writing skill and the features of a text type

F: a double-page video lesson

Review: a one-page lesson of practice activities, memory booster activities and 'can-do' check statements

Components

- Student's Book
- Workbook + audio CD
- Teacher's Book + DVD + class audio CD
- Student's App
- Student's eBook
- Online Workbook
- Website: www.NGL.cengage.com/life
- Classroom Presentation Tool

Lesson type

Unit opener

This single page introduces the unit topic and lists the unit contents.

Unit 4 Art and creativity

An impactful photograph serves as an engaging starting point to the unit and provokes class discussion.

A woman sits arranging flowers – a performance artwork, Lima, Peru.

The unit lesson headers let students see what they will be studying and stimulates their interest.

FEATURES

46 Reverse graffiti
Art that carries a message

48 All about Melbourne
Art and culture in Australia's second city

50 Why do we need music?
How music helps us

54 Art for the people
A video about the work of the graffiti artist 'Banksy'

1 Look at the photo and the caption. What is unusual about this artwork? Can you describe any other performance art you have seen?

2 Work in pairs. Look at these words about artists and performance. Put them into three categories: who, what and where. Then write four sample sentences describing who does what and where.

an actor   an artist   a band   a busker   a circus performer
a classical concert   a comedian   a concert hall   a dancer
an exhibition   a gallery   a gig   a live music venue
a musical   a (night)club   an orchestra   a performance
a play   a show   the street   a theatre

Who	What	Where
a dancer	a performance	a theatre

You can see dancers give a performance in a theatre.

3 ▶ **31** Listen to a conversation about two people who are creative in their free time. Answer the questions.

1   What does each person do as their normal job?
2   What creative thing does each person do and where do they do it?

4 Do you (or does anyone in your family) do anything creative? What is it? When and where do you/they do it? Tell your partner.

Warm-up exercises get students talking about the topic and introduce them to key vocabulary.

Each unit opener lesson contains a Listening exercise that further develops the topic.

my life   ART AND MUSIC   ▶ PARTICIPATION IN THE ARTS   ▶ MUSIC PLAYLISTS   ▶ LIKES AND DISLIKES
▶ AN ONLINE REVIEW

45

Lessons A and B

Grammar and vocabulary

These double-page lessons focus on grammar and vocabulary, presented through listening and reading texts.

The primary focus is on the topic content before the learner's attention is drawn to the target grammar structures.

Target grammar is presented through texts in the first two spreads of each unit. These texts are authentic reading and listening texts, adapted for level as necessary, which use the target language in natural and appropriate linguistic contexts. Such texts not only aid comprehension, but present good models for the learner's own language production through a variety of 'voices' and genres. The main input alternates between reading and listening on these first two spreads.

Clear paradigms or examples of form and use are given on the page in a simple summary box. This supports the learners and is a 'check point' for both teacher and learner alike as it summarizes the information learner will have arrived at through completing the discovery tasks. A cross-reference is provided to more detailed information and additional exercises at the back of the book. These are suitable both for use in class and self-study, according to the needs of the learners.

---

reading **unusual street art** • vocabulary **art** • grammar **determiners** • speaking **art and music**

4a Reverse graffiti

Reading

1 Is there any graffiti or street art where you live? What do you think about graffiti in cities? Do you think it improves or damages the appearance of a town?

2 Look at the photo and title of the article. What do you think *reverse graffiti* is? Read the article and check your ideas.

3 Use the information in the article to complete these sentences. Use one word in each space.

1 Most city authorities say that graffiti is wrong because it is done without _____ .

2 Reverse graffiti works by cleaning away the _____ on walls.
3 The aim of the reverse graffiti artists is to highlight the problem of _____ in cities.
4 In removing soot from the car tunnel, Alexandre Orion wasn't actually guilty of a _____
5 The only solution the São Paulo authorities could think of was to clean every _____ .

4 Work in pairs. Cover the article.

Student A: Retell the story from Alexandre Orion's point of view.

Student B: Retell the story from the city authority's point of view.

R E V E R S E G R A F F I T I

▶ 32

The idea of graffiti is to find a blank wall and spray-paint an image on it that expresses a particular message. Some graffiti artists use pictures, some use words, some both. But because the images are usually painted on walls
5 which the artist has no permission to paint on, the policy of most city authorities is to remove such graffiti where they find it (although they tend to leave it in certain places, such as old industrial buildings which are going to be demolished anyway).
10 The principle of 'reverse graffiti', a growing movement in the last fifteen years, is different. Reverse graffiti artists take a dirty wall and make images by removing the dirt. Each artist has their own style but they all share a common aim: to draw attention to the pollution in our
15 cities. Brazilian artist Alexandre Orion turned one of São Paulo's many car tunnels into a rather scary mural by scraping away the dirt caused by pollution from cars.

Made up of white skulls, the artwork reminds drivers of the effect that their pollution is having on the planet.
'Every motorist sits in the comfort of their car, but they 20 don't give any consideration to the cost that has for the environment and ultimately for them too,' says Orion.

The city authorities in São Paulo were annoyed. Since Orion hadn't committed any crime, they had only two choices: to remove the graffiti or to leave it. Either 25 option seemed unsatisfactory, but in the end, they decided that any graffiti was wrong and that they should remove Orion's work. In other words, they chose to clean all parts of the tunnel that Orion had already 'cleaned'. Encouraged by this, Orion continued making 30 reverse graffiti on both sides of the tunnel. The city officials then decided to take drastic action. They not only cleaned the whole tunnel, but also every other car tunnel in São Paulo.

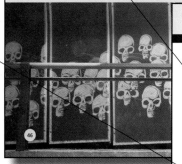

46

---

listening **what's on in Melbourne** • grammar **expressions of quantity** • pronunciation **weak form of** • speaking **participation in the arts**

4b All about Melbourne

Listening

1 Work in pairs. Ask and answer the questions.

1 What cultural or arts events for visitors and tourists are there in your country?
2 Which events do you enjoy? Is there an exhibition or performance that you've enjoyed recently?
3 What type of cultural activities do you think Australia offers visitors and tourists?

2 ▶ 34 Listen to a feature about Melbourne on a weekly radio programme. Answer the questions.

1 What is the main difference between Melbourne and Sydney?
2 What does Melbourne offer visitors?
3 What events do local people enjoy particularly?

3 ▶ 34 Listen to the radio programme again. Are the sentences about Melbourne true (T) or false (F)? Correct the false sentences.

1 Melbourne always has sunny weather and has many places of natural beauty.
2 It is known as the architectural capital of Australia.
3 The arts are enjoyed by a small number of art lovers.
4 Festivals in Melbourne only take place in the summer.
5 Melbourne's Formula 1 motor race and tennis tournament are world famous.
6 Not many visitors know about the local sports.

4 Would you like to visit Melbourne after hearing this radio programme? What would you like to do there?

5 Look at the grammar box. Which words or expressions of quantity indicate:

a a large number/amount?
b a small number/amount?
c neither a large or small number?

6 Look at audioscript 34 on page 183. Find and underline as many expressions as you can that mean:

1 'many' or 'much'
2 'not many' or 'not much'
3 'some'

7 Choose a word to replace the underlined words in the sentences.

a She has <u>many</u> friends.
b There is <u>a lot of</u> pollution.
c I <u>don't</u> have <u>much</u> time.
d There <u>aren't many</u> good shops.
e I have <u>some</u> ideas.
f Do you want <u>some</u> help?

Grammar expressions of quantity

▶ **EXPRESSIONS OF QUANTITY**

+ plural countable noun: *(not) many, (a) few, a (small/large) number of, several*
Several festivals take place in the winter months.
+ uncountable noun: *not much, (a) little, a bit of, a large/huge/small amount of*
Cricket enjoys a huge amount of support.
+ plural countable or uncountable noun: *a lot of, lots of, plenty of, loads of, a lack of, (almost) no, (not/hardly) any, some, enough, the majority of*
A lack of natural attractions has meant that Melbourne ...

For further information and practice, see page 162.

48

The independent wordbuilding syllabus offers students another opportunity to expand their vocabulary. The wordbuilding boxes in the units focus on areas such as prefixes, suffixes, collocations, parts of speech, compound nouns and phrasal verbs, and they highlight examples from the reading or listening texts. The box gives a brief explanation and some examples. There is an activity for further practice and a reference to an activity in the Workbook which introduces more words that belong to the same morphological area.

The grammar practice tasks within the unit are linked to the presentation text and topic and are thus content-rich in the same way. They move from more supported exercises through to more challenging tasks.

A variety of task formats are used to lead learners to analyse the form, meaning and use of the grammar structures, as appropriate.

A final task on each spread allows the learners to create their own output and is structured so that learners have the opportunity to use the target grammar as well as other target language, for example vocabulary, in a meaningful and personalized context. This final task has a variety of formats such as discussions, personal narratives, task-based activities (ranking, etc.) and the emphasis from the learner's perspective is on content and fluency rather than grammatical accuracy.

Vocabulary art

▶ WORDBUILDING word families

When you learn a new word, try and learn other words from the same family at the same time e.g. *artistic, artwork*

For further practice, see Workbook page 35.

5 Work in pairs. Complete the sentences using these words and phrases related to art.

| art exhibition | art gallery | artists | artistic |
| artwork | arty | fine arts | street art | the arts |

1 We went to see a great _____ at the weekend in the new _____ in town. It was by a group of local _____ .
2 If you walk around the city, you will see lots of examples of _____ . For example, the station wall is covered with _____ by local graffiti artists.
3 '_____' is the term for painting, drawing and sculpture, whereas the expression '_____' describes creative areas like poetry, music and dance.
4 I'm quite an _____ person in that I enjoy going to see art, but I don't really have any _____ talent myself.

Grammar determiners

▶ DETERMINERS

+ singular noun: *each, every, the whole, either, neither*
Each artist has their own style, but they all share a common aim.
They cleaned **the whole** tunnel.
Either option seemed unsatisfactory.

+ plural noun: *all, both, most*
The policy of **most** city authorities is to remove such graffiti where they find it.

+ singular, plural noun or uncountable noun: *any, no*
The artist has **no** permission to paint on the walls.

+ a plural or uncountable noun: *all, certain, some*
Some graffiti artists use pictures, **some** use words.

For further information and practice, see page 162.

6 Look at the grammar box. Then underline the examples of determiners in the article. What type of noun is used with each determiner?

7 Rewrite the sentences using the word in brackets.

1 Every motorist sits in the comfort of their car. (each)
2 Either option seemed unsatisfactory. (neither)
3 Orion hadn't committed any crime. (no)
4 They decided that any graffiti was wrong. (all)
5 They chose to clean all parts of the tunnel. (the whole)
6 In certain places, like old industrial buildings, they tend to leave it. (some)

8 Choose the correct determiners to complete this text about another 'reverse graffiti' artist.

The UK's Paul Curtis, known as 'Moose', who works in Leeds and London, has had some trouble with the authorities. He was paid by [1] *any / certain* companies to make reverse graffiti advertisements for their products in [2] *either / both* cities. Leeds City Council said, 'We view [3] *all / each* advertising of this kind as environmental damage and will take strong action against [4] *some / any* company carrying out such campaigns.' In fact, [5] *no / any* action was taken against the companies, but Moose himself was ordered to clean up the graffiti. But how was he supposed to do this? By making [6] *all the / the whole* buildings he had cleaned with his reverse graffiti dirty again? [7] *Most / Every* people agree that this would be a ridiculous solution.

9 ▶ 33 Work in pairs. Read the sentences about art and discuss which determiners could go in each space. Then listen to an interview with an artist and complete the statements.

| all | any | certain | either | no | some |

1 _____ art should contain something pleasing for the viewer.
2 Art should involve _____ hard work on the part of the artist.
3 To be an artist, you need to possess _____ technical skills.
4 Art should make a social or a political point; without _____ message it's not true art.
5 The viewer shouldn't have to make _____ effort to understand a work of art.
6 There is _____ such thing as 'bad' art.

10 Work in groups. Discuss which of the statements in Exercise 9 you agree with.

Speaking my life

11 Complete the sentences about art or music in your own words. Then discuss your sentences with a partner.

1 I like certain …
2 Some … is really difficult to understand.
3 Tastes in art? I don't have any …
4 Both … are musicians.
5 All … should have free entrance.
6 At my school, we had no …
7 Some people say that all … is the same, but I think that each …

---

8 Look at these sentences. Is there any difference in meaning between the words in bold in each pair of sentences. Is there any difference in the way they are used in a sentence?

1 a Melbourne has **a few** grey days a year.
 b Melbourne has **few** natural attractions.
2 a There are **hardly any** tickets left for the Australian Grand Prix.
 b There are **almost no** bad coffee shops in Melbourne.
3 a There is **a lot of** information on what to do in Melbourne on the website.
 b There **isn't much** information about where to eat on the website.

9 Choose the correct options to complete the sentences.

1 A visit to the opera can cost *much / a lot of* money.
2 A reasonable *number / amount of* winter festivals are free.
3 There is almost *no / any* rain in Melbourne at Christmas time.
4 There are *few / a few* tickets for the tennis available on the day – if you get there early.
5 We saw *several / some* interesting street art at the Sweet Streets festival.
6 *Almost / Hardly* anyone attended the afternoon performance.
7 Most visitors show a *little / little* interest in Australian Rules football – and why should they?
8 There aren't as *many / much* differences between Melbourne and Sydney as people say.

10 Pronunciation weak form of *of*

a ▶ 35 Listen to these phrases. Notice how *of* is pronounced.

1 a bit of relaxation time
2 a lot of information
3 a huge amount of support
4 lots of people
5 a huge number of galleries
6 a lack of natural attractions

b Work in pairs. Practise saying these phrases.

- as a matter of fact
- just the two of us
- first of all
- most of the time
- in spite of that
- of course
- instead of me
- that's kind of you

Speaking my life

11 Work in pairs. Look at the infographic showing Australians' participation in the arts. Then complete the sentences. Use one word in each space.

1 Overall quite a _____lot_____ of Australians take an interest in the arts, and a small _____ of them also participate creatively.
2 _____ of Australians read literature and a _____ of them also write creatively.
3 There is certainly not a _____ of interest in the visual arts, with a quarter of the population being involved in some way.
4 _____ Australians attend live performances and _____ anyone said they never listened to music.
5 The main reason for not participating is having too _____ time. But the _____ of money it costs to be involved and not having _____ opportunities close are also important factors.

12 Work in groups. Research how much your classmates participate in the arts (both creatively and receptively) and then report your findings. Follow these steps:

- Each group should research ONE of the following: visual arts and crafts, theatre and dance, reading and writing, music.
- Make questions about the items in the infographic.
- Circulate around the class asking and answering questions (get reasons for not participating).
- Work in your group again. Put your results together and make conclusions, using expressions of quantity.
- Present your findings to the class.

A lot of students read books but very few do any creative writing.

Australians' participation in the arts

Participation by art form

Creative participation only (making and doing) %   Receptive participation only (watching, reading, etc.) %   Both receptive and creative participation

Visual arts & crafts
Theatre & dance
Writing and books
Music

Participation in music: Reasons for non-participation

It's difficult to find the time
I'm not really interested
It costs too much
There aren't enough opportunities close to where I live

Lesson C

Reading

This is a double-page reading lesson. The reading text is always on the right-hand page, and the activities on the left.

The mini contents section at the beginning of every lesson sets clear targets.

reading **how music helps us** • critical thinking **identifying opinions** • word focus *spend* • speaking **music playlists**

4c Why do we need music?

Reading

1 Write down the names of two of your favourite songs or pieces of music. Then work in pairs and answer the questions.

   1 What kind of music is each one: pop, traditional/folk, classical, rock, R&B/soul, hip-hop, etc.?
   2 Where and when do you usually listen to this piece of music?
   3 Why do you particularly like this piece of music?

2 Look at the title of the article. Do you think we need music? Why? / Why not? Then read the article and compare your ideas.

3 Cover the article. Work in pairs and see how many of these details you can remember in three minutes. Then compare answers and see which pair remembered the most.

   1 how much time we spend listening to music
   2 what 'motherese' is
   3 why we listen to sad songs when we are sad
   4 what rap music around the world is about
   5 how music is like language

4 Look at the expressions in bold from the article and choose the correct meaning. Look at the article again to help you.

   1 music has the power to excite or **soothe** us (line 12)
      a calm   b inspire   c please
   2 can give you **goosebumps** (line 16)
      a a feeling of pride   b a feeling of excitement
      c a feeling of sadness
   3 sad music seems to help us **regulate** negative feelings (line 26)
      a prevent   b get rid of   c control
   4 western pop music follows very different **patterns** to traditional Chinese music (line 44)
      a repeated structures or forms
      b musical rules   c historical influences
   5 we've made a kind of intellectual **conquest** (line 53)
      a victory   b progress   c solution

Critical thinking **identifying opinions**

The word focus sections take high frequency words and give examples of the different meanings they can have according to the contexts in which they appear and the different words they collocate with.

Critical thinking activities require students to engage with the reading texts at a deeper level, and require them to show real understanding – not just reading comprehension. This training – in evaluating texts, assessing the validity and strength of arguments and developing an awareness of authorial techniques – is clearly a valuable skill for those students learning English for academic purposes (EAP), where reflective learning is essential. However, it is also very much part of the *National Geographic* spirit which encourages people to question assumptions, and develop their own well-informed and reasoned opinions.

5 Read the article again and look at these opinions. W... opinion are they: the author (A), Valorie Salimpoor (an unknown source (U)?

   1 Music is not something we need to survive.
   2 Music stimulates us emotionally and intellectual...
   3 We listen to sad songs because it helps us feel so... is sharing our sadness with us.
   4 Music can make a verbal message more powerfu...
   5 Music stimulates us intellectually because we use brains to predict the direction of the music.
   6 Music satisfies key human needs.

50

6 Answer the questions. Then discuss your answers with a partner. Which of the opinions in Exercise 5:

   a are supported by clear evidence in the article?
   b need more evidence to be convincing?
   c are convincing because they reflect our experience?
   d summarize the main argument of the article?

Word focus *spend*

7 We use *spend* with expressions of money or time as in 'We spend many a fifth of our waking lives listening to music.' Complete these sentences with the correct word (*money* or *time*).

   1 He spends _____ like there's no tomorrow.
   2 It was great to spend _____ together and catch up on news.
   3 How do you like to spend your free _____?
   4 In business, you've got to spend _____ to make _____ .
   5 We all need to spend _____ alone sometimes.

8 Complete these sentences in your own words.

   1 I spent hours trying to …
   2 I've spent a fortune on …
   3 Once I spent a night in …
   4 I don't spend a lot on …

Speaking **my life**

9 Imagine you are making a playlist for the following situations. Think of one song or piece of music for each situation. Then compare your list with two other students.

Unit 4 **Art and creativity**

WHY DO WE NEED MUSIC?

▶ 36

Humans, on average, spend a fifth of their waking lives listening to music. It is deeply rooted in all cultures across the world and yet, unlike food or shelter, it is not something we actually need in
5 order to survive. So, why is it so important to us? Valorie Salimpoor, a neuroscientist at Montreal's McGill University, who has researched the effects of music on the brain, believes that the answer lies in music's ability to stimulate us both emotionally
10 and intellectually.

On an emotional level, music has the power to excite or soothe us and it can do this more effectively than any other way humans have come up with so far. Think how a rousing theme – for example, the Welsh national
15 anthem sung by 70,000 rugby fans before a match – can give you goosebumps. Or how a calming lullaby can stop tears or help babies to sleep. The musical way of speaking to babies, known as 'motherese', is a feature of every culture around the world.
20 Music produces emotions that we immediately feel and understand, but that we find difficult to explain. Why, for example, do we like listening to sad songs when we have experienced loss or are feeling down? You would imagine they would make us feel even more unhappy.
25 But actually sad music seems to help us regulate negative feelings and even lift us out of them. Some people say the reason is a sense that someone else is sharing our loss with us; others say we are comforted by knowing that someone is suffering more than we are.
30 But no-one really knows the answer.

Music's emotional power also comes from the fact that it can make a verbal message stronger. Rap and hip-hop began in America as songs with a social message: they described life for people who lacked the same
35 opportunities as the rich. These days, most commercial hip-hop artists in America rap about the things that fame and money have brought them, but in other parts of the world, rap music is still a powerful tool for expressing the injustice that people in poor communities feel.

On an intellectual level, Salimpoor says that music
40 challenges our brains to understand and recognize certain systems and patterns. Just as with languages, music has patterns that are culturally specific. Western pop music, for instance, follows very different patterns to traditional Chinese music. But when we figure out a new system
45 works – in other words, when we 'understand' the music and are able to predict the direction it will take – we find this incredibly rewarding, intellectually. We experience exactly the same satisfaction when we begin to understand a new language and its patterns. Interestingly,
50 says Salimpoor, we enjoy new music most when it moves in an unpredictable, but still understandable, direction. In that situation, she says, 'we've made a kind of intellectual conquest'.

Humans have various needs – physical, emotional and
55 psychological – and while music may not fulfil the first, it clearly plays an important role in satisfying the others. You probably didn't think of this when you first heard your favourite song, but perhaps it explains why you have listened to it so often since.
60

my life ▶ ART AND MUSIC ▶ PARTICIPATION IN THE ARTS ▶ MUSIC PLAYLISTS ▶ LIKES AND DISLIKES
▶ AN ONLINE REVIEW

51

Lesson D

Real life

This is a one-page functional lesson focusing on real-life skills.

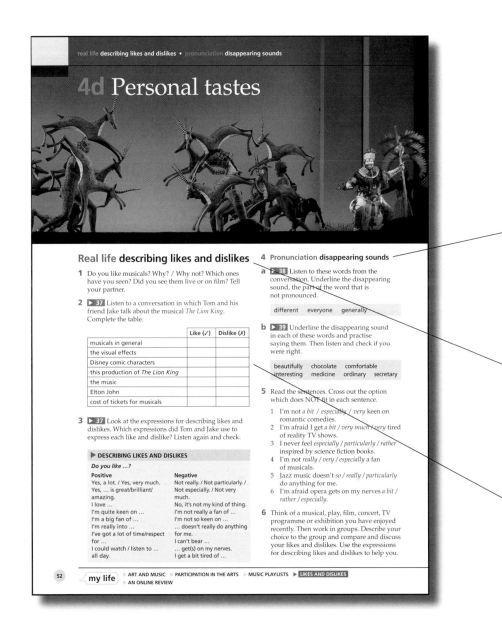

The pronunciation syllabus covers sounds and spelling, connected speech, stress and intonation.

The D lessons have clear 'Real life' functional aims.

The key expressions are made memorable through an activation activity.

Lesson E

Writing

This is a one-page writing lesson. All the text types that appear in international exams are covered here.

Every E lesson focuses on and explores a specific text type.

Every writing lesson includes a model.

A different writing skill is presented and practised in every E lesson.

Students always finish with a productive task.

Students are encouraged to take part in peer correction.

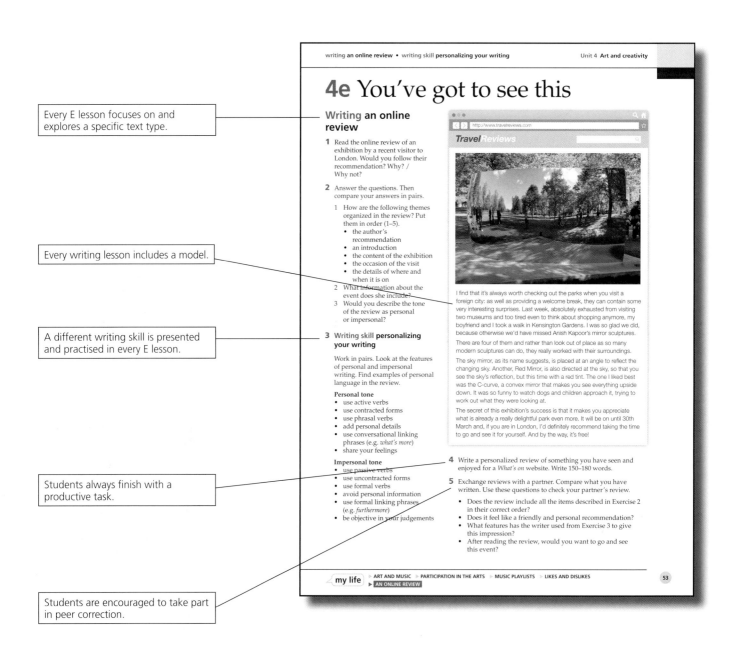

writing **an online review** • writing skill **personalizing your writing**   Unit 4 **Art and creativity**

4e You've got to see this

Writing **an online**
review

1 Read the online review of an exhibition by a recent visitor to London. Would you follow their recommendation? Why? / Why not?

2 Answer the questions. Then compare your answers in pairs.

1 How are the following themes organized in the review? Put them in order (1–5).
   • the author's recommendation
   • an introduction
   • the content of the exhibition
   • the occasion of the visit
   • the details of where and when it is on
2 What information about the event does she include?
3 Would you describe the tone of the review as personal or impersonal?

3 Writing skill **personalizing your writing**

Work in pairs. Look at the features of personal and impersonal writing. Find examples of personal language in the review.

Personal tone
• use active verbs
• use contracted forms
• use phrasal verbs
• add personal details
• use conversational linking phrases (e.g. *what's more*)
• share your feelings

Impersonal tone
• use passive verbs
• use uncontracted forms
• use formal verbs
• avoid personal information
• use formal linking phrases (e.g. *furthermore*)
• be objective in your judgements

*Travel**Reviews***

http://www.travelreviews.com

I find that it's always worth checking out the parks when you visit a foreign city: as well as providing a welcome break, they can contain some very interesting surprises. Last week, absolutely exhausted from visiting two museums and too tired even to think about shopping anymore, my boyfriend and I took a walk in Kensington Gardens. I was so glad we did, because otherwise we'd have missed Anish Kapoor's mirror sculptures.

There are four of them and rather than look out of place as so many modern sculptures can do, they really worked with their surroundings.

The sky mirror, as its name suggests, is placed at an angle to reflect the changing sky. Another, Red Mirror, is also directed at the sky, so that you see the sky's reflection, but this time with a red tint. The one I liked best was the C-curve, a convex mirror that makes you see everything upside down. It was so funny to watch dogs and children approach it, trying to work out what they were looking at.

The secret of this exhibition's success is that it makes you appreciate what is already a really delightful park even more. It will be on until 30th March and, if you are in London, I'd definitely recommend taking the time to go and see it for yourself. And by the way, it's free!

4 Write a personalized review of something you have seen and enjoyed for a *What's on* website. Write 150–180 words.

5 Exchange reviews with a partner. Compare what you have written. Use these questions to check your partner's review.

• Does the review include all the items described in Exercise 2 in their correct order?
• Does it feel like a friendly and personal recommendation?
• What features has the writer used from Exercise 3 to give this impression?
• After reading the review, would you want to go and see this event?

my life   ▸ ART AND MUSIC ▸ PARTICIPATION IN THE ARTS ▸ MUSIC PLAYLISTS ▸ LIKES AND DISLIKES
▸ AN ONLINE REVIEW

53

Lesson F

Video lesson

This is a double-page video lesson. A large, engaging introductory photograph is always on the left-hand page, and the activities on the right.

4f Art for the people

Spy Booth: an artwork by graffiti artist, Banksy, next to a public telephone box in Cheltenham, UK

This section leads students into the topic of the video and engages them in a pre-watching task.

There are two parts to this section. The first is an on-screen exercise called Vocabulary in context which focuses on useful words and expressions from the video. The second allows students to respond to the video as a whole and take part in a discussion or task that leads on from the context and theme of the video.

These exercises assist with comprehension of the video itself, both in terms of what students see and what they hear. The tasks also exploit the language used in the video.

Unit 4 **Art and creativity**

Before you watch

1 Look at the photo and caption. Then read the background to the video below. Explain to your partner in your own words what GCHQ does.

> **Background**
> The video is about an artwork in Cheltenham in the UK. Cheltenham is home to GCHQ, the British Government Communications Headquarters. GCHQ is a government agency that checks communication on the internet and other electronic media to protect national security.

2 Key vocabulary

a Read the sentences. The words in bold are used in the video. Guess the meaning of the words.

1 You don't see many public phone **booths** these days, because most people have mobile phones.
2 There is a **campaign** by local residents to stop the authorities turning the park into a car park.
3 James Bond is probably the world's most famous **spy**.
4 They removed the carpet to **expose** the beautiful wooden floor underneath.
5 I bought this table at an antiques **auction**. No one else was interested so I got it for $20.
6 We wanted to thank the person who gave us the money, but they wished to remain **anonymous**.

b Match the words in bold in Exercise 2a with these definitions.

a to reveal or show something which is hidden
b small enclosed compartments or cubicles
c when the name of the person (who did or said something) is unknown
d a sale where the item is sold to the person who offers the most money
e a person employed to secretly collect information (often for their government)
f a series of planned actions to achieve a particular goal

While you watch

3 ▶ **4.1** You are going to watch a video about a public work of art. Watch the video and answer the questions.

1 Where is the work of art and what is around it?
2 What is it a picture of?
3 Who are the people you see in the video? What do they want?
4 What is the other work of art you see by the same artist?

4 ▶ **4.1** Read the statements. Then watch the video again and choose the correct options to complete them.

1 The man at the beginning of the video is trying to *remove / put on* boards that cover the mural.
2 The mural tries to make a *serious / funny* point about GCHQ and government surveillance.
3 The owner of the building wants to *sell / move* the mural.
4 The mural will go to *a local gallery / wherever the collector decides.*
5 Local campaigners want it to stay because it is about *Cheltenham / an important issue.*
6 One resident believes that people *should / shouldn't* pay to see it.
7 Another Banksy mural in *London / Cheltenham* was sold for £750,000.
8 Banksy himself *is / isn't* involved in the debate.

After you watch

5 Vocabulary in context

a ▶ **4.2** Watch the clips from the video. Choose the correct meaning of the words and phrases.

b Work in pairs. Complete the sentences in your own words.

1 There has been a lot of protest about …
2 My ideal place to live would be …
3 My favourite discount store is …

6 Work in groups of three. Act out two short interviews about the Banksy mural.

Student A: You are the news presenter. Ask each resident questions about what they think of the mural.

Students B and C: You are residents of the town. Answer the presenter's questions.

7 Work in small groups. Your town or city would like to commission an artwork that would a) improve the appearance of an area in the city centre; b) be fun; and c) attract visitors.

• Discuss what kind of artwork you would like to have.
• Decide who you would like to make the artwork.

8 Exchange your suggestions from Exercise 7 with another group and evaluate their ideas.

> **elusive** (adj) /ɪˈluːsɪv/ difficult to find or catch
> **epitomize** (v) /ɪˈpɪtəmaɪz/ to sum up perfectly, be a perfect example of
> **scaffolding** (n) /ˈskæfəldɪŋ/ a metal and wooden structure for workers to stand on when repairing a building
> **surveillance** (n) /sɜːˈveɪləns/ the act of watching very closely

55

Review lesson

This is the one-page review lesson found at the end of every unit.

Grammar and vocabulary from the unit is clearly signposted and systematically reviewed to reinforce students' learning.

Engaging images from the unit aid the recall of key vocabulary.

Memory Booster activities are specifically designed to enable students to recall and activate new words more easily.

'Can-do' statements give students the opportunity to assess their own learning.

Every review lesson concludes with a 'Real life' activity that allows students to consolidate the functional language from the unit.

UNIT 4 REVIEW AND MEMORY BOOSTER

Grammar

1 Complete the text about the Edinburgh Festival Fringe using these words.

| a few | a lot | both | every | lack | no |
| many | much | number | whole | | |

The Edinburgh Festival Fringe is the world's largest arts festival. It takes place [1] _____ year in August and for the _____ month the city is taken over by actors, street performers, comedians, artists, musicians, etc. There is certainly no [3] _____ of variety. The festival attracts a huge [4] _____ of visitors from all over the world and two million tickets are sold for over 2,000 different shows. The tickets don't cost [5] _____ – £10 or £15 typically – but if you go to [6] _____ of shows, then the costs can add up.
[7] _____ artists just come to perform for the fun of it, but [8] _____ are young performers hoping that this will be their chance to be noticed by critics and producers. The festival has launched the careers of several famous actors and comedians, but there is [9] _____ guarantee of success. [10] _____ the famous and the unknown can succeed or fail.

2 Are these statements true (T) or false (F)?

1 It's cheap to visit the festival even if you see a lot of performances.
2 The Edinburgh Festival has a mixture of amateur and professional artists.

3 **>> MB** Make two sentences about a festival in your country using at least one of these words or phrases in each sentence. Then rewrite the sentences with the words from the box missing. Ask a partner to guess what the missing words are.

| amount | any | each | enough | a little |
| loads of | most | several | the whole | |

I CAN
| use determiners | ☐ |
| use expressions of quantity | ☐ |

Vocabulary

4 Match each person or performance with a place to make six pairs of words. Use one place twice.

an artist	a busker	a concert hall
a gallery	a gig	a live music venue	a musical
an orchestra	a play	the street	a theatre

5 **>> MB** Work in pairs. Describe the type of art or artist that you see in each photo. Add any details that you can remember (what, where, who, etc.).

6 **>> MB** Work in pairs. Each write down as many words or two-word phrases as you can from the root word **art**. Then compare your lists.

I CAN
| talk about art and artists | ☐ |

Real life

7 Complete the exchanges. Use one word in each space.

A: Do you like watching live comedy?
B: No, not [1] _____ . It doesn't really do [2] _____ for me.

C: I'm not so [3] _____ on this music. Can I change radio station?
D: Sure … it's not really my [4] _____ of [5] _____ either.

E: I'm a big [6] _____ of Kurosawa's films.
F: Me too. I have a lot of [7] _____ for him.

G: Don't you [8] _____ tired [9] _____ watching musicals?
H: No, I could watch them [10] _____ day.
G: Really? I couldn't. They really get on my [11] _____ .

8 **>> MB** Work in groups. Use the first four words of each exchange in Exercise 7 to begin a conversation about TV programmes that you like and dislike.

I CAN
| describe likes and dislikes | ☐ |

56

Unit 1 Relationships

Opener

1

- Ask students to look at the photo and the caption. Ask them to work in pairs and choose the phrase that best describes the photo. Elicit a few ideas from the class in feedback, and check the meaning of the phrases (see Vocabulary notes below).

- **Optional step** Once students have completed the task, ask them to use dictionaries to check any words they aren't sure of.

> **EXAMPLE ANSWERS**
>
> a faithful companion, a strong bond
> Students may also argue that 'true friends' and 'an odd couple' are possible.

Vocabulary notes

a faithful companion = a companion is someone you spend time with, perhaps on a journey, and 'faithful' means that this is a friend who will always be there to help and support you

blood relatives = people who are related by 'blood' (i.e. genetically), e.g. your father or daughter, but not your wife or mother-in-law

a passing acquaintance = an acquaintance is someone you know, but not very well – 'passing', here, means for a short time (e.g. someone you meet on holiday or on a journey)

mutual respect = when two people feel similar admiration for each other and treat each other politely and kindly

a strong bond = a very close relationship

true friends = friends who will always be together and will always support each other

an odd couple = two people you don't expect to be together, perhaps because they look very different or have very different personalities or interests

Background information

Rajasthan is India's largest state, and borders Pakistan. It's located on the north-western side of the country. A large part of it is made up of the wild, inhospitable Thar Desert, where camels are common.

2 [1]

- Read the words to the class and check their meaning. You could use definitions, synonyms and antonyms, or concept check questions (see Teacher development below).

- Tell students they are going to listen to three people talking about important relationships in their lives. Play the recording. Students listen and put the number of the speaker next to the person they are talking about. Let students compare answers in pairs before checking with the class.

> **ANSWERS**
>
> 1 husband   2 old friend   3 colleague

Audioscript [1]

Speaker 1

It's a bit odd because I see him almost every day at work. He works in the marketing department on the fourth floor and my office is on the fifth floor and occasionally, just occasionally, we attend the same meetings. Umm … it's strange seeing someone you're so close to in a different context. We've been married for seven years, and colleagues for about nine, but we try not to discuss work at home …

Speaker 2

We were really good mates at school and then in our early twenties we went travelling together, but we see each other very rarely now. John lives in Birmingham with his wife – she's a friend of my sister's – and I still live in London. The funny thing is, it doesn't matter how little we see each other – we're still great friends. Actually, he never calls me – and every time I call him he says 'Oh, I've been meaning to call you for ages'.

Speaker 3

We've always got on very well at work, but we never see each other outside the office. He's one of those people that can always make you laugh, which is really important in a stressful work environment. He's very good at his job too and I'm always asking for his help with stuff.

Teacher development

Checking new words

Instead of asking students to use dictionaries or translation when checking the meaning of new words, use some of the following techniques:

1 Put the new word in a sentence to provide context: *My **fiancé** and I have been engaged for six months and we're getting married in November. / Joe is a **colleague** at work – we are in the same department, but he's not a friend.*

2 Use a synonym, antonym or hyponym. You could say the first part of the sentence and elicit the missing new word (shown in brackets) from the class: *My sister's husband is my (**wife**); Jill's my wife and I'm her (**husband**); My grandmother and grandfather are my (**grandparents**).*

3 Use concept check questions instead of definitions: ***an old friend** – Have I known him for a long time? (yes) Do I know him very well? (probably); **a flatmate** – Do I live in the same place with him? (yes) Do we share the rent? (probably, but not necessarily).*

3

- Ask students to work with a new partner to look at the sayings (a–d) and discuss the questions (1–3).
- **Optional step** Ask pairs to choose just one of the sayings and discuss questions 1 and 2. Set a five-minute time limit. At the end, ask different pairs to present what they think their saying means to the class.
- In open-class feedback at the end, discuss question 3 and find out what other sayings students can think of.

ANSWERS

1

a 'Blood is thicker than water' = family relationships and loyalties are the strongest and most important ones

b 'A friend in need is a friend indeed' = a friend who helps you when you really need help is a true friend

c 'Like father, like son' = you can expect a son's personality or behaviour to be similar to that of his father

d 'No man is an island' = nobody is self-sufficient – people need the company and support of other people (this is a quote from a poem by the sixteenth-century English poet John Donne)

2/3 Students' own answers

1a Unlikely friends

Lesson at a glance

- vocabulary: describing character
- listening: animal friendships
- grammar: present tenses: simple, continuous and perfect
- vocabulary: friendships: phrasal verbs
- speaking: friendships

Vocabulary describing character

1

- Ask students to work in pairs or small groups to complete tasks 1 to 3. The aim here is for students to show what they know and to personalize the words, so encourage students to discuss words first before checking in dictionaries.
- **Optional step** Focus on pronunciation by asking students to listen to you say some of the longer words. Tell students to listen and mark the strong stress for each of them (see Pronunciation notes below).

EXAMPLE ANSWERS

1 Positive: considerate, dependable, energetic, good fun, outgoing
Negative: selfish, unreliable
Either positive or negative: laid-back, serious, shy

2 (near) opposites: considerate/selfish; dependable/unreliable; energetic/laid-back; outgoing/shy; good fun/serious

3 Students' own answers

Pronunciation note

Note the strong stress on the longer words: con*si*derate, de*pen*dable, ener*ge*tic, *out*going, *sel*fish, *se*rious, unre*li*able

---

Extra activity

Get students to personalize and practise the words by putting them into sentences about family and friends. Provide some examples first: *My sister Jo is very* **considerate** *– she never forgets people's birthdays; My young son Harry is* **energetic** *– he's always running around.* Then ask students to create personalized sentences of their own.

Listening

2

- Ask students to discuss questions 1 to 3 in pairs or small groups.
- In feedback, elicit answers to questions 1 and 2 briefly from the class. Ask different pairs and groups to suggest adjectives. Ask students if they can think of any other adjectives they might use (e.g. *intelligent, playful, caring, hard-working*).

ANSWERS

1 an orang-utan: they are rarely found working, but are sometimes used in tourism; they are sometimes kept as pets in people's homes; in the wild they are found in the forests of Indonesia and Malaysia

a dog (labrador): they are often used by farmers, hunters and also as guide dogs for the blind or helping dogs for those with disabilities; they are frequently kept as pets; domesticated dogs do not usually live in the wild

2 Students' own answers – possible characteristics of orang-utans may include *laid-back* and *shy,* and of dogs: *dependable, energetic, good fun* and *outgoing.*

3 💿 [2]

• Tell students they are going to listen to an extract from a radio programme about the two animals in the photo. Ask students to predict the unlikely things the dog and orang-utan might do together. Elicit ideas.

• Play the recording. Students listen and note answers. Let them compare their answers in pairs before checking with the class.

ANSWERS

They hug and play together; the orang-utan shares his food.

Audioscript 💿 [2]

This week we're looking at the subject of animal friendships. We know that animals often co-operate in their own social groups, helping each other to hunt or raise their young. Some highly intelligent animals, like elephants, go even further than this, and sometimes help other elephants who are not in their own family group. But co-operation between animals of different species is unusual, so that's why the story of Suriya, the orang-utan, has attracted a lot of interest.

Suriya lives with his keepers at The Institute of Greatly Endangered and Rare Species in Myrtle Beach, South Carolina, which is a kind of sanctuary for rare animals. Recently this orang-utan has been spending time with a local hound dog – an unlikely friend. Now most dogs avoid apes, because they are scared of them basically, but these two have formed a strong bond. Each day the dog comes into the compound and searches out Suriya.

When he finds him, they carry on like long lost friends, hugging and playing together. They've been doing this every day since they first met and over four million viewers have watched them since their video was put up on YouTube. The founder of the institute, Dr Antle explains: 'It's clear they are having the time of their lives. Suriya is really good fun, but what's more striking is how considerate he is. His understanding of the hound dog's character is growing day by day. For example, he has noticed that the dog is often hungry and so he regularly shares his monkey biscuits with him. Orang-utans are very generous creatures. If you give one a piece of candy, often they will break it in half and hand one piece back to you.'

So how does he explain the fact that their relationship has a lot of the characteristics of what we call 'friendship'? Antle says that the two animals have recognized a basic social need in each other that we don't normally associate

with animals. 'Animals need fun and interaction just like us and these two are not getting this from other animals in their group.'

Extra activity

Before playing the recording a second time, check some of the difficult words or phrases in the audioscript (see Vocabulary notes below).

Vocabulary notes

co-operate = to work together with other people to achieve something

hunt = to find and follow animals in order to kill them

(zoo) keepers = people who look after animals at a zoo

rare species = types of animals that aren't common

sanctuary = a place where people (or, here, animals) go to be looked after and to find peace

hound dog = any of several different breeds of dogs that are often used for hunting

compound = here, an area, usually with a fence or wall around it

just like us = similar to us (people)

4 💿 [2]

• Read questions 1–5 to the class. Point out *ape* (= large, intelligent animals that are similar to monkeys but don't have tails – an orang-utan is an ape, and so are gorillas and chimpanzees).

• Play the recording. Ask students to listen and write short answers to the questions. Let them compare their answers in pairs before checking with the class.

ANSWERS

1 co-operation
2 they are scared of them
3 they have a strong bond
4 as very generous
5 a basic social need for fun and interaction

Background information

Myrtle Beach is a city on the east coast of the United States. It has a warm sub-tropical climate, which makes it a popular tourist destination and an ideal location for The Institute of Greatly Endangered Rare Species.

Grammar present tenses: simple, continuous and perfect

5

• Ask students to look at the sentences in the grammar box and match the tenses with the uses. Go through the answers with the class.

ANSWERS

1 present continuous
2 present simple
3 present perfect (simple and continuous)

Refer students to page 156 for further information and practice.

ANSWERS TO GRAMMAR SUMMARY EXERCISES

1a

1 are becoming	5 She's staying
2 has bought	6 is always
3 have known	7 It's raining
4 I often meet	8 I'm learning

1b

a 6   b 4   c 7   d 8   e 1   f 5   g 2   h 3

2

1 are/'re	5 's looking *or* he's been looking
2 he's been going *or* he goes	
3 haven't seen	6 have moved
4 doesn't like	7 'm
	8 's ringing

3

1 've been waiting	5 have they been
2 've had	6 've been looking
3 's been	7 've seen it
4 've been working	

Grammar notes

The difference between the three tenses is down to aspect (aspect expresses how an action, event or state, denoted by a verb, extends over time, so perfect aspect connects past to present, and continuous aspect has duration and temporariness).

The tenses can be expressed in short, simple terms and as concept check questions (see Teacher development below).

1 Simple (simple means it has no aspect): *Is it permanent/ always true?* (Yes) *Is it a fact?* (Yes) *Is it a habit or routine?* (Yes)

2 Continuous aspect: *Is it temporary?* (Yes) *Does it have duration?* (Yes) *Does it happen over a period of time?* (Yes) *Is it temporary and happening now?* (Yes) *Is the situation changing?* (Yes)

3 Perfect aspect: *Did the action start in the past and continue to now?* (Yes) *Or did it happen in the past but the result is evident or important now?* (Yes)

Teacher development

What are concept check questions?

Concept check questions (CCQs) are simple questions you can use in open class to check the meaning of grammar or vocabulary (see checking new words in the development section earlier in this unit).

Form a concept check question by taking a simple grammar rule (e.g. we use the present perfect to talk about an action that starts in the past and continues to now) and turning it into short, simple questions, e.g. *Did the action start in the past?* (Yes) *Did it finish in the past?* (No) *Does it continue to now?* (Yes). Note that the answer to CCQs is usually *Yes* or *No*.

6

* Ask students to match the tenses in each sentence in the grammar box with the specific uses in Exercise 5. Let them compare their answers in pairs before discussing as a class.

ANSWERS

Suriya lives with his keepers. – something seen as permanent

Most dogs avoid apes. – a fact

Each day the dog comes into the compound. – a habit or routine

It's clear they are having the time of their lives. – something happening around the time of speaking

His understanding of the dog is growing day by day. – a changing situation

This week we're looking at animal friendships. – something happening around the time of speaking

The story of Suriya has attracted a lot of interest. – a past event that has relevance in the present

Over four million viewers have watched them since their video was put up on YouTube. – something that started in the past and continues into the present – it has an impact on or relevance in the present

They have recognized a basic social need in each other. – it has an an impact on or relevance in the present

Recently, he has been spending time with a local dog. – something that started in the past and continues into the present – it has an impact on or relevance in the present

They have been doing this every day since they first met. – something that started in the past and continues into the present – it has an impact on or relevance in the present

---

7

* Ask students to answer the question individually.

ANSWER

present perfect continuous

Grammar notes

The difference in use between the present perfect simple and present perfect continuous forms is down to aspect. If the speaker chooses the continuous form, they see the action as having duration and/or as being temporary. Very often, both the simple or continuous form could be used depending on the speaker's intent. Compare:

The story of Suriya has attracted a lot of interest.

= here, the speaker sees the event as completed and with a result in the present (i.e. many people are interested now).

The story of Suriya has been attracting a lot of interest.

= here, the speaker emphasizes the duration and repeated nature of the activity – different news agencies or Twitter feeds have been talking about Suriya repeatedly over a period of time and are still active now.

It's important to emphasize that the uses aren't right or wrong, but are dependent on the message the speaker is sending.

Note that the continuous form cannot be used with stative verbs (*The two animals ~~have been recognizing~~ a basic social need*).

8

* **Optional step** Ask students to read the text quickly for general understanding without worrying about gaps. Set a focus task: *Which three animals are mentioned?* (dogs, elephants, giant pandas).

* Ask students to work individually to choose the correct options to complete the text. Elicit the first answer to

---

get them started. Let students compare answers in pairs before feedback. In feedback, ask students to justify answers by referring to the uses listed in Exercise 5.

ANSWERS

1 have been	5 are now asking
2 have been discussing	6 have been living
3 show	7 has provided
4 has recovered	8 live

Grammar notes

The aim of this controlled accuracy practice is to make sure that students fully understand the uses of these forms. You can deal with any confusion that arises either by correcting individuals as they work, or with the class as a whole.

1 *have been* = present perfect simple: a past event that has an impact on or relevance in the present (*be* is a stative verb)

2 *have been discussing* = present perfect continuous: expresses a repeated activity that began in the past and continues to now

3 *show* = present simple: fact, always true

4 *has recovered* = present perfect simple: a completed past event that has an impact on or relevance in the present

5 *are now asking* = present continuous: happening at or around the time of speaking, including currently changing situations

6 *have been living* = present perfect continuous: expresses a prolonged activity that began in the past and continued to now

7 *has provided* = present perfect simple: a completed past event that has an impact on or relevance in the present

8 *live* = present simple: fact, always true, permanent

Vocabulary notes

extraordinary = very unusual

solitary = in a place or situation where there are no other people or animals, alone

9

- Ask students to work individually to complete the sentences. Elicit the first answer to get them started. Let students compare answers in pairs. In feedback, ask students to justify answers.

- **Optional step** Ask students who finish quickly to rewrite three or four similar sentences that are true for them. Explain that personalizing language makes it more memorable.

ANSWERS

1 'm living; has	6 has always stood
2 've just been learning	7 have been teaching, 're writing
3 've been	
4 do you know; 've known	8 never see
5 often hangs; never comes	

Grammar notes

1 *'m living* (temporary – happening around now); *has* (stative verb, permanent)

2 *'ve just been learning* (repeated activity over a period of time up to now – seen as temporary)

3 *have been* (stative verb – began in the past and continues to now)

4 *do you know* (stative verb – permanent fact); *have known* (stative verb – began in the past and continues to now)

5 *often hangs* (*often* suggests habit or routine); *never comes* (habit or routine)

6 *has always stood* (*always* true over a period of time beginning in the past)

7 *have been teaching* (repeated activity over a period of time beginning in the past); *'re writing* (happening around now)

8 *never see* (habit or routine)

Extra activity

Read out the list below, pausing after each one so your students have time to think and write brief notes. Ask students to write the following:

1 something you've never done

2 something you've been doing since the start of the lesson

3 something you do every day

4 something you haven't done for a while

5 something people you know are doing now

Put students in pairs or groups to share and talk about what they wrote. Monitor as students are talking and note any errors of form or use that you hear. Give feedback to the whole class on one or two of the most common errors at the end of the activity.

Vocabulary friendships: phrasal verbs
10

- Tell students to find and underline the phrasal verbs in Exercise 9. Then ask them to work in pairs to discuss each verb, the number of particles, and what the verb means.

- In feedback, check the meanings of the verbs. Ask students whether the meanings are literal (e.g. *come round* = it makes sense that you 'come' to a friend's house and that it involves going 'round' other houses to get there) or non-literal (e.g. *get on with* = individually, *get, on* and *with* give no clue as to what the whole phrase means).

ANSWERS

get on (with) = to have a good relationship with

stand by (someone) = to support and be friends in difficult times

hang out (with) = an informal way of saying to spend time with (e.g. go for a coffee, to clubs or parties together)

hang around = to stay in a place doing nothing or waiting for something to happen

meet up = to come together with someone, either as planned or unexpectedly

keep up (with) = to stay in contact and share news

come round = to visit (when a friend comes to visit you at your house)

go round = to visit (when you visit a friend at their house)

Phrasal verbs that contain two particles: *get on (with)*, *hang out (with)* and *keep up (with)*

Vocabulary notes

'Phrasal verb' is a term used to describe the three combinations below. Strictly speaking, the verb + adverb combination is a particle verb, and the verb + preposition combination is a prepositional verb, but the term 'phrasal verb' tends to be used to refer to all three variations.

1 verb + adverb or particle

I'll **come round** tomorrow; We'll just **hang around** here = intransitive phrasal verbs (no object)

2 verb + preposition

Joe **stood by** me = by is a preposition that introduces the prepositional phrase *by me*

3 verb + adverb + preposition

I **get on with** Frank = on is an adverb that qualifies *get*, and *with* is a preposition that introduces the prepositional phrase *with Frank*

11

- Ask students to work individually to complete the sentences. Let them compare answers in pairs before feedback.

- **Optional step** Ask students to write personalized sentences with the phrasal verbs, e.g. *My cousins often* **come round** *at the weekend; My parents* **stood by me** *when I left university.*

ANSWERS

1 get on	4 come round
2 hang out/around	5 stand by
3 kept up	6 meet up

Speaking ⟨ my life ⟩

12

- Start by writing a brief note on the board for each bullet point to show what you as a teacher might say about one of the students in the class, e.g. *Anna – met Sept 2016.*

- Then ask students to use the points to prepare similar notes about a friend. Encourage students to make notes rather than write whole sentences or a script. Monitor and help with ideas and vocabulary.

13

- Organize the class into new pairs. When students have finished describing their friends, ask them to work with a new partner so that they get lots of practice at using language from the lesson.

- **Optional step** As students speak, monitor and note down errors you hear (see Teacher development below). Concentrate on errors with the use of the present tense forms. At the end of the activity write up five or six sentences containing errors you heard. You can present them as 'common' or 'typical' mistakes and therefore avoid attributing errors to specific students. Ask students to work in pairs to correct the errors.

Teacher development

Error feedback

It's important to give feedback on your students' language performance after a free speaking activity in which one of the aims is to practise language recently learned or revised. Here are some tips for carrying out useful feedback on errors:

1 Decide what type of errors you are listening for. As you monitor students' language performance, have a clear idea of what type of errors you will focus on. You could set a clear aim, e.g. *I will listen for form and pronunciation errors with present perfect simple and continuous.* You could prepare a notepad page with different sections or categories for errors (e.g. form, pronunciation, meaning). Carry it with you and note down errors under each of the headings as you monitor.

2 Explain your role. Tell students that you are going to listen to them and note errors. Students usually welcome this constructive personal feedback when they understand the process.

3 Monitor each pair or group equally. Note down just one or two things you hear before moving on to listen to other students. It's important to show you are listening, but to be unobtrusive, too, so that students keep talking.

4 Feedback on content before errors. Find out what information students shared, problems they solved or conclusions they reached, before correcting. This is important because, from the students' point of view, they need to feel a sense of purpose and conclusion in the task.

4 Let students correct the errors collaboratively. At the end of a speaking activity, write up no more than six short sentences with errors in them on the board. These should be errors that you noted as you monitored. Then put students in pairs to discuss and correct them. Never say who made the original error. Encourage students to see correcting errors in feedback as a collaborative exercise that they do to help each other collectively to learn from their mistakes.

1b A confused generation

Lesson at a glance
- reading: changing attitudes in China
- wordbuilding: forming adjectives
- grammar: past simple and present perfect
- pronunciation: auxiliary verbs *have* and *has*
- speaking: differences between generations

Reading
1
- Organize the class into pairs to discuss the photo and questions.
- In feedback, elicit ideas and encourage students to share personal experiences.

> **ANSWERS**
> 1 It shows a girl who is sitting at a table with her parents, her head in her hands.
> 2 She is possibly having an argument, or she has been told off by her parents for something she has done. In any case, she doesn't look happy.
> 3 Students' own answers

2 [3]
- Ask students to work in pairs to discuss what they know about modern-day China. You could ask them to think of three facts and three opinions.
- **Optional step** If you feel your students may have little to say about China, write the following phrases from the text on the board before they read and ask them to say how they relate to China: *economic boom, old values, duty, western brands, rebellious teenagers.*
- Ask students to read the article. In feedback, ask students to share any new information they learned.
- **Optional step** The reading text is recorded. You could play the recording and ask students to read and listen.

3
- Ask students to read the article again and find examples of how the new China and the old China are different for each of the areas listed.
- Let students compare answers in pairs before checking the examples with the class.

> **ANSWERS**
> Caring for the old: caring for aged parents has always been a child's duty, but now families are putting their older relatives into care homes
> The relationship between parents and children: *'Once parents taught children, but now we learn from them.'*
> Standard of living and shopping: the family can buy many more things these days; Bella wants to buy the 'right' western brands
> Experience and knowledge of the world: in spoken English Bella has overtaken her parents; she has already, in her short life, learned more about the outside world than her parents have

4
- Discuss the question with the class. Ask students to give opinions and reasons for their opinions.
- Alternatively, you could organize the class into pairs or small groups to discuss the question. Encourage them to justify their opinions.

> **ANSWERS**
> Bella's parents are finding the changes difficult (*Her parents are part of a confused generation in a confused time.*; *I suppose our child-raising has been a failure.*).
> Bella is part of the 'new' generation, so is finding the changes more natural.

Extra activity
Ask students to discuss how things are changing for younger and older people in their country, and to say how their situation is similar to or different from China.

Vocabulary notes
Check that students are familiar with the following vocabulary:

economic boom = a period when the economy improves very quickly

material benefits = higher salaries, a broader range of products on sale and a better standard of living generally

duty = a duty is something your family or society says you must do

(don't want to be a) burden = a burden is a heavy load – here it is used in a fixed expression meaning that somebody doesn't want to make life difficult for somebody else (compare: *a financial burden*)

latest slang = most recent phrases used by young people in the street

glare = to look at somebody angrily

Wordbuilding forming adjectives
5
- Ask students to read the information in the box. Elicit other words students may know with similar endings (e.g. *hopeful, active, childish*).
- Ask students to work individually to find adjectives in the article that come from the root words in the box. Let students compare their answers in pairs before checking with the class.

> **ANSWERS**
> painful, selfish, dutiful, supportive, rebellious

Refer students to Workbook page 11 for further information and practice.

6
- Ask students to form adjectives from the words. Elicit the first answer to get them started, and point out that they may have to change the root word a little as well as add a suffix. Let students compare their answers before checking with the class.

ANSWERS

1 ambitious	4 helpful
2 childish	5 respectful
3 decisive	6 successful

Extra activity

Ask students to write personalized sentences using the adjectives they have just formed.

Grammar past simple and present perfect

7

- Read the information in the box to the class. Ask students to tell you how the present perfect forms are made (present perfect simple: *have* + past participle; present perfect continuous: *have + been* + present participle or *-ing* form).

- Ask students to choose the correct options to complete the sentences. Let them compare answers in pairs before checking answers with the class.

ANSWERS

1 present perfect	3 past simple
2 past simple	4 present perfect

Refer students to page 158 for further information and practice.

ANSWERS TO GRAMMAR SUMMARY EXERCISES

4

1 from 2012 to 2014	5 since
2 twice this week	6 over the last few months
3 in 1998	7 for
4 for a few days	

5

1 have been arguing	4 helped
2 I've tried	5 have given
3 's not spoken *or* hasn't spoken	6 didn't teach
	7 've been working

Grammar notes

The aim of this section is to provide revision of when to use the past simple and when to use the present perfect. A simple way to establish this is to ask whether we say 'when' or not. If 'when' is important, then it is a past event (past simple). If 'when' is not stated or important, then there is a link between the past and now (present perfect).

8

- Ask students to work in pairs to find and underline three sentences with the past simple and five with the present perfect in the article. In each case, ask them to say which tense is used and why. In feedback, ask students to explain and justify answers by referring to the rules given in Exercise 7.

ANSWERS

Examples of the past simple:

1 *A few months ago, Bella's family put Bella's grandfather into a nursing home.* – refers to something at a specific time in the past and uses an adverbial of finished time (*a few months ago*)

2 *It was a painful decision ...* – refers to something at a specific time in the past

3 *When she told us that ...* – refers to something at a specific time in the past

4 *Once parents taught children, but now we learn from them.* – refers to something at a specific time in the past

5 *... they gave up helping with Bella's homework some time ago.* – refers to something at a specific time in the past and uses an adverbial of finished time (*some time ago*)

Examples of the present perfect:

1 *In the last twenty years, China's economic boom has brought enormous material benefits ...* – (present perfect simple) impacts on the present or is relevant now

2 *Have new possessions made our lives richer?* – (present perfect simple) impacts on the present or is relevant now

3 *... in China, caring for aged parents has always been a child's duty.* – (present perfect simple) a situation which started in the past and is continuing now

4 *This is something my daughter has been trying to teach us.* – (present perfect continuous) an action which started in the past and is continuing now

5 *'I suppose our child-raising has been a failure.'* – (present perfect simple) impacts on the present or is relevant now

Pronunciation auxiliary verbs *have and has*

9 🎵 [4]

- Ask students to look at the present perfect sentences they underlined in Exercise 8.

- Play the recording. Students listen and note the pronunciation. Let them practise saying the sentences in pairs.

- **Optional step** Model and drill the sentences or play the recording and ask students to repeat each sentence in turn.

Audioscript 🎵 [4]

1 In the last twenty years China's economic boom has brought enormous material benefits.

2 Have new possessions made our lives richer?

3 In China, caring for aged parents has always been a child's duty.

4 This is something my daughter has been trying to teach us.

5 'I suppose our child-raising has been a failure.'

Pronunciation notes

In natural speech, *has* and *have* are reduced to /həz/ and /həv/. Because these words are generally unstressed, the schwa sound /ə/ is used.

When practising the sentences, encourage students to reduce other unstressed sounds in the sentences to /ə/, and reduce *been* to its short unstressed sound /bɪn/. For example, in sentence 4, students should stress *try* in *trying*, but reduce the sounds in *has, been* and *to*: /həzbɪn**traɪɪ**ŋtə/. In sentence 5, *has been a* becomes /həz**bɪn**ə/.

10

- Ask students to read the conversation once without trying to complete the gaps. To make sure they understand the content in general, ask: *Does the child want the parent's help?*
- Ask students to work individually to complete the conversation. Monitor and prompt as students write. Let them compare in pairs before checking answers with the class.

ANSWERS

1 Have you done	5 asked
2 didn't do	6 've been looking
3 was	7 haven't studied
4 've studied	8 've already arranged

11

- Ask students to underline the time expressions in Exercise 10 and complete the table. Let them compare answers in pairs before checking with the class.

ANSWERS

Time expressions in the text: *yet, yesterday, before, a few days ago, all morning, since I was a child, already*

Past simple: *yesterday, a few days ago* (finished time)

Present perfect simple: *yet, before, already, since I was a child* (unfinished time)

Present perfect continuous: *all morning* (unfinished time)

Grammar notes

Note that the unfinished time expressions in the table could be used with both the present perfect simple or continuous. The exceptions are *ever* and *yet*, which are almost always used with just the present perfect simple.

ever: *Have you ever been to France?* – used in questions to mean 'at any time'

just: *I've just left home* – used to say 'very recently'

not ... yet: *I haven't done that yet* – used to say something hasn't happened, but will in the future

already: *I've already left* – used to say something has happened earlier than expected

since + point in time: *since Wednesday / 1999 / last August*

for + period of time: *for two weeks / a hundred years / ever*

12

- Ask students to work in pairs to prepare and act out conversations. You could ask students to brainstorm ideas of things to say for one minute before improvising conversations, or you could ask students to work together to write a dialogue before acting it out.

13

- Ask students to work individually to choose the correct options to complete the sentences. Let them compare answers in pairs before checking the answers with the class.
- Ask students to discuss the statements in pairs or in groups of four (put two pairs together). Tell them to choose three or four statements they are interested in rather than discussing all of them.

ANSWERS

1 have been growing	5 had
2 has left	6 has replaced
3 probably worked; didn't have	7 rebelled; were
4 have already retired	8 have spoilt

Speaking ⟨ my life ⟩
14

- In the same pairs, ask students to work together to list the ways in which their parents' lives have been different from their own. Monitor and help with ideas and vocabulary.
- Ask students to work with a new partner or in groups of four. When students are ready, ask them to discuss which generation has had a better life.
- As students speak, walk round and listen to how well your students are using the present perfect and past simple forms. Note down some errors as you monitor. At the end, write several errors on the board and ask students to work in pairs to correct them.

EXAMPLE ANSWERS

Here are some possible differences from a UK perspective about the previous generation's experience:

upbringing and school: stricter rules; wore uniform, ate simple school meals, strict discipline

work opportunities: more jobs in factories, jobs for life, fewer opportunities in high tech industries, fewer opportunities for women

free time: more time outside, less time on computers, holidays at home not abroad

standard of living: less money to spend, fewer electronic gadgets – no smartphones

Extra activity

Ask students to write a blog entry based on their ideas about how life has changed over the years. This could be done for homework.

1c Bloodlines

Lesson at a glance
- reading: immigrant families
- critical thinking: evaluating conclusions
- word focus: *sense*
- speaking: family influences

Reading

1
- Pre-teach *emigrate* (= to go and live in another country) and *first-generation immigrants* (= people who go and start a new life in a new country).
- Ask students to work in pairs to discuss the questions. Elicit a few ideas from the class in feedback.

EXAMPLE ANSWERS

Reasons for emigrating: work opportunities, better quality of life, friends and family, better education, escaping war or poverty

Difficulties: learning a new language, getting used to local customs, finding work and housing, not having family and friends, racism or hostility from local people

Students' own answers

2 💿 [5]
- Ask students to look at the photo and read the three article headings on page 15 of the Student's Book. Check the meaning of *ancestors* (= people in your family who lived before you). Ask students to predict what the article might be about and what information it might include.
- Ask students to read the article individually. Then ask them to cover the page and work in pairs to try to remember the details of Richard and Tanja's stories.
- **Optional step** The reading text is recorded. You could play the recording and ask students to read and listen.
- **Optional step** Ask students to write notes from memory for each bullet point before they talk about the details of Richard and Tanja's stories.

ANSWERS

Richard:
1 His grandfather came to America (from Poland) when he was fifteen. He wanted to run away from his stepmother.
2 Richard is a builder.
3 He has a strong sense of belonging to a group that has struggled and fought together to succeed in America.

Tanja:
1 Her parents came to America from Jamaica. Her father wanted to be a doctor in the US.
2 Tanja is also a doctor.
3 She has a desire to get ahead.

3
- Ask students to read the article again and decide whether the sentences are true or false. Let them compare answers in pairs. In feedback, ask students to justify answers by quoting from the article.

ANSWERS

1 T (*a common feeling of pride in their American identity*)
2 F (*their ancestral roots; tracing back your family tree*)
3 F (we infer he is unhappy: *Tomas didn't like his new stepmother*)
4 F (he saw an announcement in the paper by chance, but they arranged the meeting in New York: *Tomas got in touch and the two had an emotional reunion in New York.*)
5 F (we infer this as she worked as a nurse and was very involved in her children's lives)
6 T (*Both my sister and I have followed them into the medical profession and now I'm working as a doctor*)

Background information

Queens is the easternmost and largest in area of the five boroughs of New York City.

First generation means people who are born in one country and emigrate to live in another. So, second generation means their children and third generation means their grandchildren.

4
- Ask students to find the words and phrases in the article. Students work in pairs to discuss the meaning of each word or phrase. Encourage students to look at the context of the surrounding text to help them work out the meaning of each item.

ANSWERS

1 a place where different people mix together
2 where they came from
3 look for a way to get rich
4 a necessity
5 a belief that hard work is important

Vocabulary notes

There are other words and expressions in the article that may be new to students. You could ask students to underline three or four more words or phrases in the text and try to guess them from context.

trace your family tree = to find out about the people in your family who lived before you

descendant = person in your family who lives after you

settle = to start living permanently in a particular place

identity = how you see or define yourself

Critical thinking evaluating conclusions

5

- Ask students to work individually to read the conclusions (a–e) and decide which ones the author wanted the reader to draw. Briefly elicit which conclusions your students think are correct but don't confirm or correct answers at this stage.

6

- Ask students to work in pairs to compare their answers to Exercise 5. Encourage students to find evidence in the text to support their ideas.
- In feedback, ask students to justify their choice.

ANSWERS

Exercise 5

Students' own answers, but c and d are the main points of the article.

c: *... how their grandparents and great-grandparents arrived in America what brought them there in the first place, and how they – their descendants – can best honour their memory; she never forgets family details. This has meant that all of us ... now have a strong sense of belonging*

d: *a group that has struggled and fought together to succeed here; I don't know if that kind of dedication is genetic or just something that you learn from your parents, but that desire to get ahead ... we've certainly both inherited it.*

Exercise 6

d is the author's main conclusion.

Word focus sense

7

- Read the example sentence to the class and draw their attention to the phrase 'sense of belonging'. Ask students to choose the best option to complete each sentence. Let students compare answers in pairs.

ANSWERS

1 make	4 duty
2 common	5 direction
3 humour	

Vocabulary notes

The word *sense* has many meanings and uses and, depending on the context, may mean a strong feeling or belief, an ability, a meaning or a purpose.

make sense = to be practical or sensible

common sense = the ability to use good natural judgment about everyday things

a sense of = here, it's used to describe a feeling for or understanding of something, e.g. sense of humour/duty/direction/loss/helplessness, etc.

Extra activity

Ask your students to research *sense* in a learner's dictionary to find its different meanings and collocations. They may find other interesting phrases, e.g. *talk sense, see sense, business sense, a sense of identity/well-being/optimism.* Ask students in pairs to choose three of these new collocations and write sentences that show their meaning.

Put each pair with another pair and ask them to read out their sentences, but say '*beep*' instead of the collocation with *sense*. The other pair must guess the missing collocation.

Speaking my life

8

- Ask students to read the questionnaire individually and note their own answers to the questions.
- Ask students to work in pairs or small groups and take turns to ask and answer the questions. In feedback, ask students to summarize what they found out about their partners.

Extra activity

Do a class survey. Organize the class into groups of three. Ask groups to choose three questions to ask from the list on the page. Tell students to mingle individually and interview different class members using the questions they chose, and to note responses. Then put students in their groups of three again, and ask them to collate their information and produce a report for the class on their findings.

1d What have you been up to?

Lesson at a glance
- real life: meeting people
- pronunciation: word boundaries

Real life meeting people

1
- Students work in pairs to discuss the questions and categorize the phrases. Elicit the first answer to get them started.

EXAMPLE ANSWERS
a How do you do? Pleased to meet you.
b How are you?
c How are things? How are you? How's it going?

Background information

You could ask your students, especially if they are studying in an English-speaking country, whether they have heard other informal ways of greeting. *Hi!*, *Hiya!*, *Hello!*, *What's new?*, *What's up?* and *Whatcha?* are all informal greetings used by British English speakers.

2 [6]
- Tell students they are going to listen to a conversation in the street between two friends. Ask them to read the three listening questions.
- Play the recording. Students listen and note answers. Let students compare answers in pairs before checking with the class.

ANSWERS
1 a long time ago
2 Tim has been working abroad (in India) for the last eighteen months doing some teacher training for the British Council; Greta has been doing a course and studying for her law exams.
3 They are going to meet up for a drink the next time Tim is back in the UK, in two months' time.

Audioscript [6]

G = Greta; T = Tim

G: Hi, Tim! This is a surprise. How are you?

T: Oh, hi Greta. Yeah, I'm doing fine, thanks.

G: Oh, that's good to hear. I haven't seen you for ages. What have you been up to?

T: Actually, I've been working abroad for the last eighteen months.

G: Really? Anywhere exciting?

T: Yeah, in India. I've got a contract with the British Council, doing some teacher training.

G: Well, it obviously suits you: you're looking very tanned and relaxed.

T: Thanks – it's been a lot of fun. And you? You're looking very well too. How are things?

G: Oh, you know, busy as ever. I've been studying for my law exams.

T: Oh yes, of course – I remember. Is the course going OK?

G: Well, you know, it's a lot of work. But it's going well, generally, thanks.

T: Good. And what about Amanda? I haven't seen her for ages either. How's she getting on?

G: Yeah, she's well. We still meet up from time to time. She was asking after you the other day, actually.

T: Oh, well, I'm only back for a few days, but please give her my best wishes when you next see her.

G: I will.

T: And the next time I'm back, perhaps we can all get together for a drink.

G: That'd be great. How long will you be away for?

T: Well, I've got to do another two months over there. Then I'll be back in the UK for a while, I hope.

G: OK. Well, give me a call when you're back. You've got my number, haven't you?

T: Yeah, if it's still the same one.

G: Yeah, it is. I'll look forward to that. Well, I don't mean to be rude, but I need to get back to college – but it was really nice to see you. I hope the journey back goes well.

T: Thanks. Well, it was great to see you too, Greta. Take care … and good luck with the exams.

3 [6]
- Tell students to read the expressions in the language box and to work in pairs to discuss which of the expressions were used in the recording.
- Play the recording. Students listen, check and tick the expressions they hear.

ANSWERS
The following expressions should be ticked:
How are things?
What have you been up to?
I'm doing fine, thanks.
Busy as ever.
I've been studying for my exams.
You're looking very relaxed / very well.
It obviously suits you.
How's she getting on?
She was asking after you the other day.
Please give her my best wishes.
I don't mean to be rude, but I need to …
It was really nice to see you.
It was great to see you.
Good luck with …

4

- Check meaning by asking students to match the expressions in the language box that they ticked with the functions (1–5). Explain *mutual friend* (= a friend that you both have).
- Elicit the first answer to get students started. Let students compare their answers in pairs.

> ANSWERS
> 1 What have you been up to?
> 2 You're looking very well.
> 3 Busy as ever.
> 4 She was asking after you the other day.
> 5 I don't mean to be rude, but I need to (get back to college).

Vocabulary notes

Busy as ever. = I'm as busy as I always am

to ask about someone = to ask whether someone is well or what their news is

it suits you = here, this means that a job / a lifestyle / a relationship, etc. is good for someone because they appear happy or confident

Pronunciation word boundaries

5a 🔘 [7]

- Start by reading through the information in the instruction with your class. Explain what a word boundary is (see Pronunciation notes below) and why they can be difficult to hear in fast speech.
- Play the recording. Students listen and write expressions 5 to 8.
- Play the recording again and ask students to listen and repeat.

Audioscript 🔘 [7] (and answers)

1 How are things?
2 How's everything going?
3 What have you been up to?
4 I haven't seen you for ages.
5 Busy as ever.
6 I'm in a bit of a hurry.
7 That'd be great.
8 Give her my best wishes.

5b

- Organize the class into pairs. Students take it in turns to practise saying each expression.

Pronunciation note

Linking and word boundaries

The term *word boundaries* refers to where words begin and end, so *been* begins with /b/ and ends with /n/. In fast speech, these word boundaries become compromised. Often, it may sound as if a word begins with the consonant sound of the previous word, for example.

When one word ends with a consonant sound and the next begins with a vowel sound, the consonant sound appears to join the next word: *How severything? It's bee nages.* We can show this with a linking line: *It's been‿ages.* When a word ends with a vowel and the next begins with a vowel, an intrusive, or extra, consonant sound may be introduced: *How‿w‿are things? Busy‿j‿as ever.* This makes it easier to say.

In fast, natural speech, unstressed sounds are often reduced to /ə/: *What have* becomes /wɒtəv/.

Sometimes sounds are lost or changed. For example, the /d/ in *That'd be great* is lost or reduced to a glottal stop, a sound made when air is blocked and released in the throat.

6

- Ask students to read the task. Then tell them to stand up, walk round and practise meeting and greeting each other. You could start by modelling the activity with one student: *Hi, Anna. How are things? What have you been up to? Are you free on Sunday?* etc.
- In a very large class, divide the class into groups of about six, and ask them to meet and greet people within their group.
- As students speak, listen for errors, and prompt students to use expressions correctly.

Extra activity

Here are two variations on the activity:

1 Play music. Students walk round. When you stop the music, they chat to a person they are near. When you start the music again, they say *I'm in a bit of a hurry* and move on to someone new.

2 Students move round the room until you say stop. Before they chat, you tell them what their relationship is to the person they are talking to, e.g. an old friend, a colleague, an acquaintance, someone you didn't like at school.

1e News from home

Lesson at a glance
- writing: an informal email
- writing skill: greetings and endings

Writing an informal email

1
- Discuss the question with the class or ask students to discuss the question in pairs or groups. Elicit ways of communicating: letters and postcards, special occasion cards, emails, instant messaging, texts, social networking sites, Facebook, Twitter and tweets, telephone calls, video conferencing, etc.
- **Optional step** Ask students to say how they communicate with different people, e.g. emails and video conferencing for work colleagues, phone calls for older relatives, Facebook for cousins.

2
- Ask students to read the email and answer the focus question. Let students compare answers in pairs.

> **ANSWERS**
>
> Mateo is in Sri Lanka (in the hills outside Kandy). He's there to try and get experience as a freelance journalist and photographer.

3
- Ask students to read the email again and work in pairs to discuss how the listed things are expressed in the email.

> **ANSWERS**
>
> 1 *I hope all's well with you; Do send everyone my love.* (at the beginning and end)
> 2 *How's the family? Is Sarah still … ?* (3rd paragraph)
> 3 *I'm now … ; At the moment I'm … ; I'm trying to …* (2nd paragraph); *my plan is to …* (3rd paragraph)
> 4 *It would be great to get together with you then.* (3rd paragraph)
> 5 *I've been meaning to write with my news …* (1st paragraph)

4
- Read the differences between formal and informal written English to the class. Then ask them to find and underline as many examples of informal language as they can in the email. Let students compare answers in pairs before checking with the class.

> **ANSWERS**
>
> Contracted verb forms: *all's well; I've been meaning to,* etc.
> Informal linking words: *but my work … ; But I have to … ; So, my plan is to …*
> Conversational words: *for ages; or so; get a plane; go and chat to; great to get together; working for that awful estate agent*
> Idiomatic expressions: *I hope all's well with you; you wouldn't believe it; Fingers crossed!; Do send everyone my love; I'll write again soon; All the best*

Writing skill greetings and endings

5
- Ask students to work in pairs to discuss which phrases are appropriate for an informal email.

> **ANSWERS**
>
> *All my love, Best wishes, Hello, Hi John, Love.*
> Note that *Kind regards, Regards* and *Warm regards* are too formal for a close friend, but might be used with, for example, an elderly relative.

Extra activity

The verb *get* is used often in spoken or informal written English. There are five phrases or sentences in the letter where it is used. Ask students to work individually to find and underline the five phrases with *get* in the email. Then ask students to work in pairs to discuss what *get* means in each case. Follow up by asking students to work in small groups to give recent news about themselves using *get*.

> **ANSWERS**
>
> *getting quite homesick* = becoming
> *get experience* = to gain, achieve
> *get an interview* = to receive, obtain, be given
> *get a plane* = to catch, travel on
> *get together* = to meet up

Vocabulary notes

Get is a very common verb in English, and is used informally, especially in spoken English, with a wide range of meanings. In some ways, it's a verb native speakers use because it is so versatile. What unites the many meanings of *get* is the idea of 'change':

Change of state: *get homesick/experience* (*get older, get tired, get ill, get thinner*)

Change of possession: *get an interview* (*get an email, get a new car, get a job, get some shopping*)

Change of position: *get a plane / get together* (*get home, get in a car, get up, get on a train*)

6

- Read the imaginary situation to the class and ask individuals to decide who they want to write to.
- Ask students to make brief notes under each heading in their notebooks. Be available to help with ideas and vocabulary. Ask students to share their notes in pairs and to suggest possible ways of adding to or improving the notes.
- Ask students to work individually to write the email. This could be done in class or for homework.

Extra activity

Give students alternative scenarios to write about, e.g. an email to a person you secretly want to date; an informal email to an old friend who owes you money; an informal email to a family member who you dislike.

7

- After students have written a first draft of the email, ask them to work in pairs and exchange emails. Each student reads their partner's email and uses the questions in the Student's Book to check it and make suggestions for improvement.
- Students rewrite their emails in response to the feedback. Put the emails on the classroom wall for others to read.

1f 'Lady Liberty' and Ellis Island

Before you watch

1

- Ask students to read the description of the video and work in pairs to answer the questions. Refer students to the glossary at the bottom of page 19 for the meaning of *stewards*.

> **ANSWERS**
> 1 because of significant damage from Hurricane Sandy
> 2 stewards and visitors

Background information

Liberty Island and Ellis Island are in Upper New York Bay, and can be visited as part of a boat trip that leaves regularly from Manhattan, New York. They are separate islands, but both form part of the Statue of Liberty National Monument.

On Liberty Island stands the Statue of Liberty, the iconic symbol of New York, which was erected in the 1880s.

Between 1892 and 1954 Ellis Island was the nation's busiest immigrant inspection station and during this period was the gateway for over 12 million immigrants to the United States. Today there is a museum of immigration at the Statue of Liberty National Monument.

Hurricane Sandy hit New York City on 29th October 2012, flooding streets, tunnels and subway lines and causing power cuts in and around the city.

Key vocabulary

2a

- Ask students to guess the meanings of the words in bold and either make notes, or discuss in pairs.

2b

- Tell students to match the words in bold in Exercise 2a with the definitions (a–e).

> **ANSWERS**
> 1 d   2 b   3 a   4 e   5 c

While you watch

3 ◼️ [1.1]

- Ask students to watch the whole video. Tell them to make notes to answer questions 1–3 as they watch. Let students compare answers in pairs before discussing as a class.

> **ANSWERS**
> 1 immigrants from all over the world
> 2 tourists
> 3 no

Videoscript ■◀ 1.1

Part 1

0.00–0.30 David Luchsinger I don't know if that's something to be proud of, but I have the dubious distinction of being the last resident of Liberty Island, yes. Walking around the island at night and looking up at the Statue of Liberty, it's quite an experience seeing all the different ways she changes. Some nights she's actually a little bit blue, as opposed to green.

0.31–0.44 I had two sets of grandparents that came through Ellis Island. I wonder what they would think if they found that their great grandson was going to be the steward of the Statue of Liberty on Ellis Island.

0.45–0.49 Welcome to the Statue of Liberty.

0.50–1.15 It's about going to a different country, they may not speak the language. And they show up; everything that means the world to them is in this one or two bags that they are carrying. And they are told to drop those bags and go upstairs to be processed, and they never even know if they are ever going to see that picture of their parents or their children that they left behind. They are relying on their faith that everything is going to be OK because this is a country that they want to come to.

1.17–1.25 It's been reported that we've never lost a bag on Ellis Island. I guess the folks today could learn a thing or two about keeping tabs on bags.

Part 2

1.28–1.37 Judith Leavell Everybody came from some place in America, except the native Americans. And it's important to keep that alive, I think.

1.38–1.47 I don't know that our generation would be as gutsy as they were, to come. My grandmother was twenty, and she never went back to Italy.

1.48–2.14 Pablo Cachón I don't know why, but I got emotional when I saw it for the first time I was crossing. I think it was just part of history, it being there, and it was an emotional moment. I mean, even me being born here, I guess I put myself in the emotion of all the people that came by boat, and the first thing they saw was this statue, in a sense welcoming them to a new world, to freedom.

2.15–2.14 Peter Wong Right here, at Ellis Island, this is where my family became 'American'. My parents immigrated here from Hong Kong in China. To be able to tell their story by using the site as a focus. I just love it, I mean, there's just no way around it.

2.33–2.45 Raea Hillebrant Our ancestors came over in 1914 from Lithuania. When we walked up the steps it gave you the chills down your spine, kind of what they went through when they came on the boat and came up here.

Part 3

2.50–3.03 David Luchsinger During our peak immigration period at Ellis Island, we would average between eight and ten thousand people a day. In our biggest visitation we processed over twelve thousand people.

3.04–3.25 Today, our visitation during the summer is between eighteen thousand and twenty-two thousand people a day, so we welcome quite a few more people. Of course, we don't process these people, other than putting them through security.

3.26–4.10 October 29 2011, we had closed down to do some life safety renovations. Fortunately when Sandy hit, none of those upgrades were damaged. But our entire infrastructure were all destroyed. While it was a very sad day for us, we quickly realized it was also an opportunity to make this a more sustainable park. It was also kind of moving, in this devastation, to see the statue standing there, the flag still flying, proud and defiant. No storm was going to bother her.

4 ■◀ [1.1]

- Ask students to read questions 1–5 and complete any answers that they remember.
- When students are ready, play the first part of the video (0.00–1.25) again. Let students compare their answers in pairs before discussing as a class.

> ANSWERS
>
> 1 resident
> 2 His two sets of grandparents came through Ellis Island (as immigrants).
> 3 'everything that means the world to them'; pictures of their children or parents
> 4 drop them
> 5 They have never lost a bag on Ellis Island.

5 ■◀ [1.1]

- Play the second part of the video (1.28–2.45) again. Ask students to make notes to complete the table. Let students compare their answers in pairs before discussing as a class. Note that the word *gutsy* is checked in the vocabulary exercise later, so there is no need to explain the word here.

> ANSWERS
>
> 1 Judith: Italy; –
> 2 Pablo: – ; emotional
> 3 Peter: Hong Kong; loves it
> 4 Raea: Lithuania; gave her the chills

6 ■◀ [1.1]

- Play the third part of the video (2.50 to the end) again. Ask students to choose the correct options to complete the facts. Let students compare their answers in pairs before discussing as a class.

> ANSWERS
>
> 1 a day
> 2 up to
> 3 the infrastructure
> 4 the park

Vocabulary notes

over 22,000 = more than 22,000

up to 22,000 = 22,000 or fewer than 22,000

After you watch

Vocabulary in context

7a ■◀ [1.2]

- Explain that students are going to watch some clips from the video which contain some new words and phrases. They need to choose the correct meaning of the words.
- Play the clips. When each multiple-choice question appears, pause the clip so that students can choose

the correct definition. You could let students compare answers in pairs before discussing as a class.

ANSWERS

1 c   2 a   3 b   4 a   5 c   6 b

Vocabulary notes

Note: son – grandson – great grandson – great-great grandson

show up (at a party/wedding) = to appear unexpectedly or without invitation

means the world to me = e.g. *My children mean the world to me* or *This promotion means the world to me* = nothing is more important

keep tabs on = an idiomatic expression which means to follow or watch something or someone very carefully so as not to lose them

gutsy = compare to *have guts* = be brave

devastation = is similar to, but stronger than, destruction – it means everything is destroyed

Videoscript ■◀ 1.2

1 ... if they found that their **great grandson** was going to be the steward ...

   a wonderful grandson
   b son of a son
   c son of a grandchild

2 ... and they **show up**.

   a arrive
   b feel nervous
   c present themselves

3 Everything that **means the world to** them is in these one or two bags.

   a belongs to
   b is very important to
   c is necessary for

4 I guess the folks today could learn a thing or two about **keeping tabs** on bags.

   a knowing where something is
   b treating something carefully
   c putting labels on something

5 I don't know if our generation would be as **gutsy** as they were ...

   a emotional
   b strong
   c brave

6 It was also kind of moving in this **devastation** to see this statue standing there ...

   a bad weather
   b destruction
   c rebuilding

7b

• Students work individually to complete the sentences in their own words. Elicit one or two ideas for the first sentence to get them started. Let students compare sentences in pairs.

EXAMPLE ANSWERS

1 My job/promotion/family means the world to me.
2 I showed up late for work / my wedding / my daughter's performance.
3 It was very gutsy of my brother to run a marathon / admit he was wrong.

8

• Give students one minute preparation time individually first, then ask them to work with a new partner. Ask them to take turns to describe their place or monument. Monitor and prompt students as they speak.

EXAMPLE ANSWERS

Stonehenge is an ancient monument in the UK. It is made of ancient stones that are arranged in a circle. The huge stones make you feel small and thoughtful. It means the world to British people. They are proud of its history and it makes them feel connected to their ancestors. I was disappointed when I visited because there were a lot of tourists and it is close to a busy road.

Extra activity

As an alternative, you could ask students to describe a famous place or monument without saying its name. Their partner must guess which place or monument it is.

Another alternative is to get students to prepare and give a presentation on the place or monument they choose. The preparation could be done for homework.

9

• Ask students to prepare key points individually or in pairs. Monitor and help with ideas and vocabulary.

• **Optional step** Once students have thought of some ideas, ask them to write them down in a formal way. Tell them to produce a guide entitled 'A Guide for Immigrants'. Tell them to use the imperative form to write six clear bulleted points.

10

• Organize the class into groups. Ask students to compare their six key points in the guides they have produced. Ask students to find out which points are similar or different.

• Ask students to discuss the questions.

EXAMPLE ANSWERS

Reasons why it is hard to adapt to a new life: language barrier, missing family and friends, having to learn new customs and ways of doing things, having no money or contacts, racism or distrust from people already in the country

UNIT 1 Review and memory booster

Memory Booster activities

Exercises 3, 5, 6 and 9 are Memory Booster activities. For more information about these activities and how they benefit students, see page 10 of this Teacher's Book.

I can ... check boxes

As an alternative to asking students to simply tick the *I can ...* boxes, you could ask them to give themselves a score from 1 to 4 (1 = not very confident; 4 = very confident) for each language area. If students score 1 or 2 for a language area, refer them to additional practice activities in the Workbook and Grammar summary exercises.

Grammar

1
- Ask students to work individually to complete the article by choosing the correct verb forms.

ANSWERS

1 need	6 were
2 means	7 are choosing
3 has been decreasing	8 have changed
4 relied	9 are losing
5 We shared	10 have lost

2
- Ask students to read the article again and answer the questions.

ANSWERS

1 A nuclear family is just the parents and children; an extended family is all the people who are related to us by blood or marriage, e.g. grandparents, cousins, aunts and uncles.
2 help with childcare, being looked after in old age, sharing domestic chores, cheaper living costs

3 >> MB
- Ask students to work in pairs to answer the questions.

ANSWERS

1 3 *Has been decreasing*: it's still continuing
4, 5 and 6 *relied, shared, were*: things that happened in the past
7 *are choosing*: it's a trend
8 *have changed*: (recent) past event with an impact on the present
2 *for some time* = since the 1950s, for many years, in recent years
In the past = 50 years ago, last century, in my grandparents' time

Vocabulary

4
- Ask students to complete the words and phrases individually, then check with a partner.

ANSWERS

1 companion	4 flatmate
2 close	5 acquaintance
3 mutual	6 blood

5 >> MB
- Ask students to talk about the people in pairs. Encourage them to use words and phrases studied in the unit.

ANSWERS

Students' own answers

6 >> MB
- Ask students to look at the photo and the list of adjectives Then ask them to work in pairs to answer the questions.

ANSWERS

Students' own answers

Real life

7
- Ask students to work individually to complete the phrases using a preposition or particle. Check answers with the class.

ANSWERS

1 in	4 with
2 for	5 together
3 on	6 up

8
- Ask students to put the sentences in the right order to make a conversation. Check answers by inviting individual students to read the lines to the class in the correct order.

ANSWERS

The sentences in the Student's Book should be numbered as follows: 1, 9, 3, 7, 5, 11, 10, 6, 4, 8, 2

9 >> MB
- Students work in pairs to act out the conversation from Exercise 7. You could then ask students to find a new partner and act out the conversation again, from memory if possible.

Unit 2 Storytelling

Opener

1

- Ask students to look at the photo and the caption. Explain that, in the past, a *watermill* used water to drive machinery. Ask them to discuss the questions in pairs. Elicit a few ideas from the class in feedback. Don't give any further information about the photo at this stage as students will find out more in Exercise 3.

> **EXAMPLE ANSWER**
>
> It could be a fantasy film, because it doesn't look like a real house/place. It looks very rural and idyllic.
>
> Students may also suggest a historical (or period) film because the watermill is very old and the scene is very rural, or even a romantic film because they can imagine two lovers meeting there.

Background information

Note that the watermill is a location for a scene in the film *The Hobbit: An Unexpected Journey*. New Zealand director Peter Jackson used locations in his native New Zealand for the majority of scenes in his epic fantasy film trilogies *The Lord of the Rings* and *The Hobbit*.

The films are based on classic fantasy books by J.R.R. Tolkien. *Lord of the Rings* tells the epic story of a journey by a short, fur-footed human-like hobbit called Frodo, and *The Hobbit* tells a similar story about a different hobbit called Bilbo.

2

- Ask students to match the adjectives with the types of film. Elicit the first match as an example. Let students compare answers in pairs before discussing with the class.
- **Optional step** Once students have completed the matching task, ask them to use dictionaries to check any words they aren't sure of before you go through the answers.
- The answers below are the most likely answers, but if students disagree, and can give reasons why, accept their explanations.

> **EXAMPLE ANSWERS**
>
> 1 d   2 e *or* a   3 a   4 f   5 c   6 b

Vocabulary notes

touching = you feel sad for somebody in the film

creepy = you feel uncomfortable or scared

gripping = you can't stop watching

convincing = you believe the story

Pronunciation note

Note that the strong stress is on the first syllable of the adjectives, except for: *ori*ginal, i*ma*ginative, con*vin*cing

3 💿 [8]

- Read the questions to the class and check students understand *location* (= place in a film) and *successful* (= something that has done well). Play the recording. Students listen and answer the questions. Let them compare answers in pairs before discussing with the class.

> **ANSWERS**
>
> 1 *The Hobbit*
>
> 2 He remained true to the spirit of the book and captured the heart of the story; visually stunning; feels like the book; fast-moving and gripping

Audioscript 💿 [8]

P = Presenter; M = Mark Mowlam

P: Take a bestselling book with a great storyline and add a great cast, an experienced director and a large filming budget. And what do you get? A box office success, you would think. Think again. Successful books don't always make good films. Some film adaptations have worked, others haven't. So what's the secret? That was the question I put earlier to film critic Mark Mowlam, who recently wrote about the making of Tolkien's *The Hobbit*.

M: Well, the key is to make a film that remains true to the spirit of the book, and that captures the heart of the story, even if it doesn't include every detail. Peter Jackson's *The Hobbit* is a fantastic example of this. The writer of the book, which is basically a fantasy novel, J.R.R. Tolkien, created a very original imaginary world and Jackson had somehow to reproduce this, in a way that satisfied the millions of people who had read the book and loved it. I think he did a fantastic job. For a start, it's a beautifully filmed movie. Jackson used the varied scenery of his native New Zealand for the film's locations: the soft countryside where Bilbo, the Hobbit, lives – which you can see in this photo – the dark scary mountains that he has to travel to. The result is a film that is visually stunning. It also feels like the book. Sometimes the story is very fast-moving and gripping; at other times it goes more slowly and gently.

4 💿 [8]

- Ask students to read the phrases and guess or remember the missing adjectives.
- Play the recording again. Ask students to listen and complete the phrases.

> **ANSWERS**
>
> 1 original   3 scary
>
> 2 beautifully filmed   4 fast-moving, gripping

5
- Start by telling the class what films you like and why. Recycle some of the adjectives used in the lesson. This provides a model for students.
- Organize the class into new pairs to discuss films. In feedback, ask a few individuals to tell the class what types of films their partner liked and why.

Extra activity 1

You are at the start of a new course, so use this opportunity to get students to meet and get to know classmates they haven't met before. Ask students to stand up, walk round and talk to as many different students as they can in five minutes. Tell them to find somebody who likes similar films.

Extra activity 2

Ask students to work in pairs to think of examples of films in each of the categories in Exercise 2 (e.g. *X Men* = science fiction / fantasy). Tell them to choose films they have seen on TV or in the cinema in the last year.

2a A key moment

Lesson at a glance
- vocabulary: describing stories
- reading: an incredible story
- grammar: narrative past tenses
- pronunciation: /æ/, /ʌ/ and /ɒ/
- speaking: a key moment

Vocabulary describing stories

1
- Ask students to match the words in list A with the words with a similar meaning in list B. Elicit the first answer to get students started. Let students compare their answers in pairs before checking with the class.

ANSWERS

1 d   2 f   3 a   4 c   5 b   6 e

Extra activity

A good way of making sure that students know all these words is to check during feedback by setting the vocabulary items in a context (see Teacher development below). Read out the following 'extracts' from stories and ask students to say which word is being described:

Tall, brave Captain Jones set out on his journey. (hero / main character)

It was an old castle with high walls by the sea. (setting)

Suddenly, Clara shot Captain Jones. (key moment / turning point)

The story was about how love is the most important thing. (theme)

Aliens landed. Then there was a war. They discovered a secret weapon. The aliens left. Tom and Clara fell in love. (plot)

It was 1915 and the country was at war. (background)

Teacher development

Using context to show meaning
Putting words into sentences provides context and allows students to see not just what words mean but how they are used, and what other words they collocate with. Here are three ways of using context in an upper intermediate classroom:

1 Produce sentences with the key word missing. For example: *The _____ for the drama was an old castle by the sea.* Students have to work out the missing word from the context.

2 Ask students to produce their own sentences that show the meaning of key words. The sentences could be from students' own experience. Other class members say whether the meaning of the word is clear. This could involve some research using dictionaries or digital aids.

3 Ask students to use online corpus material. They type in a key word (e.g. *setting*) and select useful sentences that the word appears in which best show its meaning and use.

2

- Ask students to think of a film or TV drama that they have seen recently and answer the questions. Point out that *key moment* and *turning point* both describe the specific part of the story when things change.
- **Optional step** You could set up this activity by briefly describing a film or TV drama you know. This provides a teacher model, which is both a useful live listening activity and an incentive for students to produce fuller descriptions of their own.
- Once they have prepared descriptions of films or TV dramas, you could ask students to describe and discuss them in pairs or small groups.

ANSWERS

Students' own answers

3

- Ask students to look at the poster for the film *Rush*. Ask: *What can you see on the poster? What do you think the film is about? Have you seen the film? If so, what do you know about it?*
- Ask students to read the description quickly and say what the film is about (the rivalry between two racing drivers). Check the meaning of *rivalry* (= when two or more people compete with each other – e.g. the rivalry between Nadal, Djokovic and Federer in tennis) and *mutual respect* (= the positive feeling competitors have for each other).
- Ask students to read the description again and complete the gaps with words from Exercise 1. Let them compare their answers in pairs before discussing answers with the class.

ANSWERS

1 story/plot
2 main characters / heroes
3 themes / central ideas
4 key moment / turning point

Reading

4 💿 [9]

- Ask students to read the questions. Point out that the Nürburgring is a famous Formula 1 race track in Germany. You could ask students to predict the answers to the questions.
- Ask students to read the account and find the answers. Let them compare their answers in pairs before checking answers with the class.
- **Optional step** The reading text is recorded. You could play the recording and ask students to read and listen.

ANSWERS

1 The track was narrow and bumpy, and in poor condition, and many people, including Lauda, considered it unsafe – in places, cars actually took off into the air.
2 He came out of a left-hand corner too fast and lost control of the car.
3 Three other racing drivers stopped and pulled him out of the car.
4 He suffered extreme burns and was fighting for his life immediately after the accident. He survived, but needed to have serious plastic surgery. Six weeks after the accident he began racing again. The Nürburgring race was restarted and Hunt won, but it was the last Formula 1 race at the Nürburgring track.

Vocabulary notes

bumpy = not smooth; a bumpy road is one where the car goes up and down as it drives along

pits = the place where cars stop to refuel or get repairs during a race

bounce back = to hit something and come back – like a ball hitting a wall

burst into flames = to suddenly be on fire

marshall = a person who works on and around the race track – they go on to the track to remove cars and debris and wave flags to slow drivers down

trapped = unable to get out of a place

pull free = to pull somebody away from a place where they have been trapped

Background information

Niki Lauda was F1 World Champion in 1975, 1977 and 1984. He went on to start the airlines Lauda Air and Niki, and today is still involved in Formula 1 as a commentator and team manager.

James Hunt won the Formula 1 World Championship in 1976 after Lauda's accident robbed the Austrian of the chance to win the Championship. Hunt also went on to become a commentator on Formula 1. He died of a heart attack in 1993 at the age of 45.

The film *Rush* was directed by Ron Howard and was released in 2013. It tells the story of the rivalry between the serious Lauda and the wild Hunt between 1970 and the fateful 1976 season. The word *rush* has layers of relevant meanings to the film. It means 'go fast' but also 'in a hurry' (both drivers were in a hurry to be at the top of their sport), and is used in expressions like *a rush of adrenaline*.

The Nürburgring is a historical race track near Nürburg in Germany. After Lauda's accident, the track was rebuilt. Today, F1 races are held there once more, but the track is completely different to the one used in 1976.

Grammar narrative past tenses

5

- Ask students to read the grammar box and match the verb in bold in each example with the descriptions (a–e). Let students compare answers with a partner.

- Check the answers with the class. Then ask students to look at the account again and find other examples of each tense.

ANSWERS

a past simple
Examples: *the cars* set *off; the race* progressed, *the track* began *to dry and the drivers* came *into the pits; he* began *to push harder; It* hit *a bank ... ,* bounced *back and immediately* burst *into flames; three of them* stopped *and* ran *to help; They* managed *to pull him free; a helicopter* arrived *and* transported *Lauda to hospital; his wife* fainted *when she* saw *his face; the organizers* restarted *the race; Hunt* went *on to win; Lauda* got *back into his racing car ... and* finished *fourth*

b past perfect simple
Examples: *Lauda* had tried *to ... ; James Hunt* had argued *for it to go ahead and* had won*; He* had suffered

c past continuous
Examples: *other drivers* were following *Lauda's car;* was fighting *for his life*

d past perfect continuous
Examples: *It* had been raining*; he* had been sitting

e past simple
Examples: *It* was *July 1976; The next race* was*; The track* was *narrow; Lauda,* considered *it unsafe – in places, cars actually* took *off; parts of the track* were *still wet; There* were *few safety marshals; that* was *the last Formula 1 race held there*

Refer students to page 158 for further information and practice.

ANSWERS TO GRAMMAR SUMMARY EXERCISES

1a
1 e   2 i   3 b   4 g   5 a   6 f
7 d   8 h   9 c

1b
she'd left – e
had completely forgotten – b
had – a
was sitting – c
'd been waiting – d

2
1 it had been raining all night.
2 he hadn't been sleeping well.
3 We hadn't been waiting for long ...
4 I had been studying all morning ...
5 Had you been looking for a new job for a long time ...
6 he had been trying to pass the exam for years.
7 I had been singing all morning.
8 Had Maria been working at the company for long ...

3
1 was reading
2 saw
3 decided
4 received
5 had received
6 didn't understand
7 had printed
8 wrote
9 developed
10 had sent

Grammar note

Timelines are useful ways of showing tense usage (see Teacher development below). Draw these timelines on the board and ask students to match them to the example sentences in the grammar box.

A general state in the past:

Past |——————————| Now
an old track that **ran** *through the forest*

A sequence of events in the past:

Past   X   X   Now
He **came** *out ... and* **lost** *control*

An activity in progress in the past:

Past   ～～～   Now
He **was leading** *the ... championship*

Something that happened before:

    lost time   began to dry
Past   X   X   Now
The track **began** *to dry but Lauda* **had lost** *time.*

An activity in progress before the main event:

    raining   set off
Past   ～～～   X   Now
The cars **set off** *... It* **had been raining**.

Teacher development

How to draw a timeline

Timelines are useful when the difference between two forms is about time, order or duration. It provides a visual representation which is clearer for visual learners than a verbal or written explanation. Draw them as follows:

1 Start with a line and show past, present and future:

Past   Now   Future

2 Show single actions or events with a X on the line: X

3 Show repeated actions with a series of Xs: X X X X X

4 Show events or states that are always true with a continuous line: |——————|

5 Show events that are temporary and have duration with a wavy line: ～～～

Compare the following:

Past |———|　 Future
      Now
I **live** *in London.*

Past   ～～～   Future
      Now
I'm **living** *in London.*

Past   ～～X～   Now
I **was living** *in London when I* **met** *Mike.*

6

- Ask students to cover the text and work together to remember and retell the story. Tell students to use the questions in Exercise 4 to prompt them to recall the story.
- **Optional step** Write word prompts on the board to help students retell the story. For example, write: *July 1976, Nike Lauda, James Hunt, German Grand Prix, Eifel Mountains, unsafe, one vote, first position, wet-weather tyres, difficult, halfway, bank, helicopter, burns, plastic surgery*.

7

- Ask students to read the summary briefly and answer a gist question. Ask: *In what ways were Lauda and Hunt different?* (Lauda usually prepared carefully the night before a race, but Hunt was often out at a nightclub.)
- Ask students to read the summary again more carefully and choose the correct options. Elicit the first answer to get students started. Let them compare answers in pairs before checking answers with the class.
- **Optional step** You could ask students to match the correct past tense options in the summary with the rule descriptions in Exercise 5.

ANSWERS

1 drove	4 refused
2 was preparing	5 returned
3 knew	6 had been lying

Grammar note

The aim of this controlled written accuracy practice is to focus on the uses of the narrative tenses.

1 *drove* – a general state in the past

2 *was preparing* – an activity in progress in the past, which is a background to the main story or to an event within it – here, *while* tells you that the action has duration

3 *knew* – a general state in the past – note that you can't use a continuous form with this stative verb

4 *refused* – a general state in the past

5 *returned* – an event in a sequence of events in the past

6 *had been lying* = *had* + *been* + present participle or *-ing* form – an activity in progress before or up to the main event(s) in the past

Vocabulary notes

Note the verb + adverb collocations *drove hard* and *play hard*, which are similar to *work hard*, a collocation students will know.

drove hard = drove in an aggressive and competitive way

play hard = go to parties, stay up all night, drink, take drugs, in a way that is very extreme

Pronunciation /æ/, /ʌ/ and /ɒ/

8a [10]

- Play the recording. Students listen and notice the pronunciation. Model the lip and tongue position required for each sound (see Pronunciation notes below) and ask students to copy you.
- Play the recording again. Students listen and repeat.

Audioscript [10]

/æ/	crashed, ran, sat
/ʌ/	run, stuck, suffered
/ɒ/	got, lost, stopped

Pronunciation note

/æ/: Stretch out and open your lips, place the tongue low and at the front of the mouth, and make a short sound.

/ʌ/: Open and round your lips, place the tongue low and between the middle and front of the mouth, and make a short sound.

/ɒ/: Open and round your lips, place the tongue low and to the back of the mouth, and make a short sound. Push your lips slightly together as you make the sound.

8b [11]

- Ask students to work in pairs to write the past forms. Then play the recording. Students listen and check.
- **Optional step** You could play the recording a second time and ask students to listen and repeat.

Audioscript [11] (and answers)

become	became	become
begin	began	begun
drink	drank	drunk
forget	forgot	forgotten
go	went	gone
shine	shone	shone
sing	sang	sung
strike	struck	struck
win	won	won

Extra activity

Write two sentences on the board using three of the vowel sounds in each sentence. For example, *Jan crashed the van*; *Tom got lost*. Ask students to listen and repeat the sentences. Then put students in pairs to write their own sentences using the vowel sounds and to practise saying them.

Other possibilities:

/æ/: *Stan ran madly*; *Adam sacked his gran*

/ʌ/: *Her son loves fun*; *Another Monday in London*

/ɒ/: *What a lot of cloth*; *Bob washes boxes*

9 🔘 [12]

- Ask students to read the story briefly to answer a gist question: *Does the story have a happy ending?* (No). In feedback, check the meaning of difficult words (see Vocabulary notes below).

- Ask students to read the story again and to write the correct past tense form of the verbs. Elicit the first answer to get students started. Let students compare answers in pairs.

- Check the answers with the class, then ask students to take turns to read out the story to their partners. Monitor and correct errors of form and pronunciation.

- Once students have finished telling stories, play the recording. Ask students what they noticed about the speaker's pronunciation. Give them a chance to practise reading out the story or parts of the story again.

- **Optional step** Ask students to close their books after they have had a chance to read out and listen to the story. Tell them to work in pairs to recreate as much of the story as they can remember.

ANSWERS

1 were driving (longer, background action to the main story)

2 fell (one of a sequence of events)

3 landed (one of a sequence of events)

4 had escaped (event that happened before another event)

5 had been grazing (long action happening up to the main event)

6 plunged (one of a sequence of events)

7 were suffering (longer, background action to the main story)

8 had (one of a sequence of events)

Audioscript 🔘 [12]

Mr Charles Everson and his wife Linda were driving home from church one Sunday when a cow fell from the sky and landed on the bonnet of their van. The cow, which had escaped from a local farm, was grazing too close to the edge of a cliff next to the road, when it slipped and plunged seventy metres to the road below. The Eversons were not hurt, but they were taken to hospital because they were suffering from shock. The cow was not so lucky and had to be put to sleep.

Vocabulary notes

bonnet = the part of a car that covers the engine – you can open it

graze = to eat grass

cliff = the steep side of an area of high land

plunge = to fall a long way down

put to sleep = to give an injection to an animal to kill it

Speaking ⟨ my life ⟩

10

- Ask students to read the first sentence of the beginning of the story and ask them: *What do you think the news story is about? Do you know this story? If so, what happens?*

- Ask students to work in pairs to read the story and write an ending. Monitor and help students with ideas, vocabulary and with forming past tenses.

ANSWERS

Students' own answers. The actual ending will be heard in the recording during Exercise 11.

Vocabulary notes

emerged into = came out into

collapsed = fallen in/down suddenly

blocking = stopping someone from moving forward or getting out

11 🔘 [13]

- Put pairs together to form groups of four. Ask pairs to take turns telling their versions of the story.

- Play the recording. Students listen and check. In feedback, ask students what differences there were between their story and the actual story.

Audioscript 🔘 [13]

As the sixteenth miner, Daniel Herrera, came out, for Melanie, it was love at first sight. He had a beautiful smile and she knew he had a good heart. So she contacted him on Facebook and they started writing to each other. Daniel wasn't married and was living with his mother. After some months, they began speaking on the phone and Melanie helped Daniel to overcome the trauma he had experienced. In 2012 she flew to Chile to meet Daniel. He fell in love with her too and in 2014 they got married.

Background information

This is a true story. The Copiapó mining accident occurred in August 2010 in the Atacama Desert in Chile. It attracted worldwide attention as Chilean and international rescue teams kept the men alive and eventually rescued them all. The rescue was shown live on TV and the internet.

12

- Ask students to work in pairs to describe a key moment in their lives. Tell them to talk about the events before and after it. Encourage them to use each past tense at least once.

2b Visual storytelling

Lesson at a glance
- vocabulary: communication
- wordbuilding: collocations
- listening: visual storytelling
- grammar: the passive
- pronunciation: weak forms in passive verbs
- speaking: the stories pictures tell

Vocabulary communication

1
- Ask students to say what they think the title of this section ('visual storytelling') means. Elicit ideas.
- Ask students to match the verbs with the nouns in Exercise 1. Elicit the first match to get students started. Let them compare answers in pairs before checking with the class.
- In feedback, read the information in the wordbuilding box to the class, and check meaning (see Vocabulary notes below).
- **Optional step** After they have done the vocabulary matching task in Exercise 1, ask students to discuss the title again, using the collocations they have just matched.

Refer students to Workbook page 19 for further information and practice.

ANSWERS
a share / sum up / tell
b express / share / sum up
c present/share
d engage/reach/tell
e share
f bring
g express

Vocabulary notes

Some of these verbs have similar meanings in these contexts. You could ask students to look up words they don't know in dictionaries and to explain them to their partner using examples. Alternatively, use the ideas below to check meaning:

tell a story (*to*) (= one person speaks, others listen) but *share a story* (*with*) (= if somebody shares a story, it means he/she tells a story about or personal to themselves, and it was generous to do so because it was personal)

pre<u>sent</u> = to speak to a group of people

sum up = to give a summary of something

engage an audience (= to make them interested) and *reach an audience* (= to get the interest of people who weren't interested before)

bring a story to life = to make a story interesting and real

Extra activity

If students in your class share the same first language (L1), ask them to say which collocations in English are different in their first language. By comparing L1 to English, students can see where there are differences and where they may make errors unless they learn the correct collocations.

2
- Start by asking students to look at the photos. Ask: *What can you see?* Elicit ideas briefly from the class. Pre-teach *life jackets* (= the orange vests in the picture).
- Ask students to work in pairs to discuss the questions. Encourage students to use vocabulary from Exercise 1 in their answers. Elicit ideas in feedback, and write any new or interesting words, phrases or collocations students came up with during their conversations on the board.

EXAMPLE ANSWERS
1 The first photo aims to engage its audience by expressing emotions such as happiness and togetherness / bringing a story to life. The second photo aims to bring a story to life / sum up or express an idea / express a sense of loss.
2 Students' own answers. The first photo may make the viewer think of many things depending on their own culture and context – childhood, education, happiness, etc. The second may have more impact and make the viewer think of dangers at sea – losing lives, rescuing people, perhaps refugees escaping to Europe on life-rafts.

Listening

3 🔊 [14]
- Tell students that they are going to listen to an interview with a professional photographer, Olaf Paulsen. Ask them to read questions 1–3. Play the recording. Students listen and note answers. Let students compare their answers before discussing with the class.

ANSWERS
1 using an image or series of images to convey what is really happening in a place, or to a person
2 because anyone can do it from anywhere (via the internet)
3 the first photo captures an emotion (boys' delight at hearing a joke); the second photo brings the migrant crisis to the world's attention by conveying the idea of refugees who risked their lives by crossing the sea to Greece

Audioscript 🔊 [14]

I = Interviewer; O = Olaf Paulsen

I: Olaf, for a long time you didn't call yourself a photographer, because it was still just an interest rather than a full-time paid job.

O: Yes, that's true, although whenever I went travelling with my camera I sort of treated it like a job. I acted like I had been paid by a magazine or newspaper to get some great photos to go with a story.

I: Well, that's what I wanted to ask you, because more recently you've been called a 'visual storyteller' – rather than a photographer. Can you explain what people mean by that?

O: OK, for me, a good photographer *is* a storyteller. Visual storytelling means using an image – or a series of images – to communicate what is *really* happening in a place, or to a person. A good photo immediately engages the viewer emotionally. It pulls you into the story behind the image.

I: And we see images used everywhere now to tell stories and to express ideas … not just photos, but icons, video animations, infographics, and so on.

o: Absolutely. Visual storytelling is definitely a phenomenon of our time. As you say, a lot of factual information is presented visually now. Obviously, in the past photos were used in magazines, in newspapers, on TV to bring stories to life. The difference now is that it is not just the media companies that are in control of this. Stories can be shared by anyone in the world from anywhere, simply by uploading a photo or sharing a link to an infographic or a striking image. So it's an amazing time for anyone who takes photographs – because it doesn't matter if the photo is taken with a professional camera or just an ordinary mobile phone; you have a way of reaching thousands of people with it very quickly.

I: And do you have any examples of visual storytelling that you particularly like?

o: Umm … there was all the good work that John Stanmeyer did in helping to bring the migrant crisis to the world's attention: for example, his photos of life jackets left on the beach by refugees who risked crossing the sea to get to Greece. But it doesn't have to be about, so to say, big stories like that. There was a wonderful photo I saw the other day – I don't remember the name of the photographer – but it's of some boys laughing at a joke they've just heard. The joy of the moment, their youthful delight, is captured wonderfully in the picture. It sums up an emotion in a way that words cannot do.

4 🎧 [14]

- Ask students to read the sentences and decide if they are true or false. Tell them to remember what they can and compare ideas with a partner.
- Play the recording again. Students listen and check their answers, before checking answers with the class.

ANSWERS

1 F (*whenever I went travelling with my camera I sort of treated it like a job. I acted like I had been paid by a magazine or newspaper to get some great photos to go with a story*)

2 T (*A good photo immediately engages the viewer emotionally.*)

3 T (*not just photos, but icons, video animations, infographics*)

4 F (*Stories can be shared by anyone in the world from anywhere, simply by uploading a photo or sharing a link to an infographic or a striking image; it doesn't matter if the photo is taken with a professional camera or just an ordinary mobile phone; you have a way of reaching thousands of people with it very quickly*)

5 T (*the good work that John Stanmeyer did in helping to bring the migrant crisis to the world's attention: for example, his photos of life jackets left on the beach*)

Vocabulary notes

Point out these words and expressions from the listening:

treat it like a job = to do it in the same way as a real job

act like = to pretend (note the use of the preposition *like* meaning 'in the same way')

pull someone into a story = to make somebody very interested in a story

a phenomenon = an event or situation that is happening

Notice the computer language collocations: *take* or *upload a photo, share a link/image*

Background information

Olaf Paulsen is fictional.

John Stanmeyer is an award-winning American-born photographer and filmmaker who has a particular interest in political and human rights issues. He worked for *Time* magazine before working almost exclusively for *National Geographic* magazine.

The Migrant Crisis refers to the European migrant crisis which began in 2015. A rising number of refugees and migrants started crossing the Mediterranean Sea to the European Union (EU) to seek asylum. They came from areas such as Western and South Asia, Africa, and the Western Balkans, and many were escaping conflict in Syria and Afghanistan.

Grammar the passive
5

- Ask students to look at the grammar box and compare the passive sentences with the active versions. Then ask students to tell you how the passive forms are made. Elicit some or all of the following: the object goes at the start of the sentence, the subject is omitted or becomes the 'agent' using *by*, and the appropriate form of *be* + past participle is used.

- Ask students to choose the correct options to complete the sentences. Let them compare answers in pairs before checking with the class.

ANSWERS

1 object; subject

2 *be* + past

3 *by*

4 you don't always have to (because either it's obvious or you don't know exactly who the agent is)

5 has (In addition, we occasionally use the passive because putting the agent after the action gives more emphasis to it, e.g. *The television was invented by Vladimir Zworykin, not John Logie Baird.*)

Refer students to page 158 for further information and practice. In addition, an irregular verb list can be found on the inside back cover of the Student's Book.

ANSWERS TO GRAMMAR SUMMARY EXERCISES

4

1 It can be seen in the British Library in London.

2 It was written and performed by Pharrell Williams.

3 In 2024, they will be held in Paris.

4 It had been stolen two years earlier from a gallery in Oslo.

5 They were never found …

6 While you're reading this sentence, about 1,000 messages are being sent every second.

5

1 was made

2 being read

3 has been downloaded

4 had already been taken out

5 be seen

6 to be awarded

Grammar notes

Form

The form follows a clear rule. We use the auxiliary verb *be* in the same tense as the verb in the active form and add a past participle (so, *presents* becomes *is presented*). Some forms can seem complicated (for example, the present perfect simple passive – *has been done*), leading to slips by students. Irregular past participles can also be difficult for students to remember (see the inside back cover of the Student's Book). Make sure you do lots of written accuracy practice if your students have such problems (see page 156 of the Student's Book).

Meaning and use

Many languages use passive forms less frequently than English. They may use reflexive forms or phrases beginning with the equivalent of the rare and more formal English use of 'one' (as in, *One may share stories with others*). It's a good idea to explore why the example sentences in the grammar box use passive not active forms: *Recently you have been called a 'visual storyteller'.* = the passive is used here because we don't know or care who called Olaf a storyteller.

Obviously, in the past photos were used in magazines. = here, we want to make *photos* the main subject, but we also want to emphasize the list of places that follow.

I acted like I had been paid by a magazine to do a job. = here, because we are talking about 'I' – 'I' has been mentioned before and we are following what happens to it.

Pronunciation weak forms in passive verbs

6a 🎵 [15]

• Ask students to look at the sentences in the grammar box. Tell them to underline the stressed part of the verb and circle the unstressed or contracted forms. Write *presented* with the relevant part underlined on the board as an example to make it clear.

• Play the recording. Students listen and underline and circle. Let them compare answers with a partner.

• **Optional step** Model and drill the sentences or play the recording and ask students to repeat them.

Audioscript 🎵 [15] (with answers)

1 A lot of factual information is pres**ent**ed visually now.
2 Recently you've been called a 'visual storyteller'.
3 Obviously, in the past photos were used in magazines.
4 I acted like I'd been paid by a magazine to do a job.
5 Stories can be shared by anyone from anywhere in the world.

Pronunciation note

Contracted forms are pronounced as short, weak sounds in natural speech: *you've* is pronounced /jʊv/ or /jəv/ and *I'd* is pronounced /aɪd/.

The schwa is used when auxiliary verbs are unstressed: *was* /wəz/, *were* /wə/, *are* /ə/, *can* /kən/.

When unstressed, *be* becomes /bɪ/, and *been* becomes /bɪn/.

6b 🎵 [16]

• Ask students to work in pairs. Tell them to discuss which sounds are unstressed and which are stressed before they practising saying the sentences.

• Play the recording. Students listen and compare their pronunciation. Play the recording again. Students listen and repeat.

Audioscript 🎵 [16] (with stress patterns marked)

1 The story was first pub**lish**ed in 2012.
2 She has been given permission to tell her story.
3 More photos are being shared online.
4 It will be seen by people all over the world.
5 The joy of the moment is captured wonderfully.

7

• Ask students to read the text about infographics and ask them a gist question to check comprehension: *What does the text tell you about the history of infographics?* (William Playfair probably created the first infographic in 1786, but Edward Tufte became the true father of the infographic in 1982).

• Now ask students to rewrite the text using the passive form of the verbs in bold. Elicit the passive form of the first example, *combine*, to get them started (*data and images are combined*). Remind students that they may need to make other changes, such as moving, or removing, the agent.

• Monitor and prompt students as they write. Let students compare with a partner before checking answers with the class.

> **ANSWERS**
>
> In infographics, data and images **are combined** to communicate information. The data **can be presented** using numbers or words. The first infographics **were** probably **created** by William Playfair in his book of 1786, *A Commercial and Political Atlas of England*. However, Edward Tufte, a teacher at Princeton University, **has been called** the true father of the modern infographic. His book, *Visual Display*, **was published** in 1982. Today, infographics **are being created** by non-experts too, with simple web design tools.

8

• Ask students to read the text once for comprehension before doing the task. Students could read and think of a title for the text (e.g. *Reasons behind the rise of visual storytelling*).

• Ask students to choose best options to complete the text. Let them compare answers in pairs before checking with the class.

> **ANSWERS**
>
> 1 a or b   2 b   3 a   4 a or b   5 b   6 a

Speaking my life

9

- Ask students to work in pairs to complete the questions. Explain that these questions could be used to talk about any photo. Check the answers with the class.

ANSWERS

1 Where was this photo taken?
2 What is (being) shown in the photo?
3 What story does the photo tell?
4 What emotions or ideas are expressed in the photo?

10

- Ask students to work together in pairs to talk about the two photos. First, students decide who is A, and who B. Give them two or three minutes to read the information on either page 153 or 154 and prepare things to say.

- When students are ready, they take turns to ask and answer the questions. As students speak, walk round and listen to how well your students use passive forms. Note down some errors as you monitor. At the end, write some of the errors on the board and ask students to work in pairs to correct them.

EXAMPLE ANSWERS

A 1 It was taken in the Maasai Mara National Reserve in Kenya.
   2 The picture shows a Kenyan chef. He's waiting to serve breakfast to tourists on safari in the Maasai Mara National Reserve.
   3 It tells the story of how tourists in Kenya pay over $300 per day for a hot air balloon safari. Included in the safari is a champagne breakfast.
   4 One idea that is expressed is that some tourists enjoy luxury there.
B 1 It was taken in Ontario, Canada.
   2 The picture shows twin girls, Lily and Gillian, who were born in China. They are meeting each other after a long separation.
   3 It tells the story of Lily and Gillian. They were adopted when they were less than one year old by two different families in Canada. Now the families meet regularly so the girls can spend time together.
   4 Happiness at being reunited is expressed, and the strong bond between twins is shown.

Extra activity

Ask students to work in groups. Tell students to find a photo on their phone that is interesting to talk about. Tell them to show the picture to their group. The group asks questions from Exercise 9 and the student describes their photo.

2c Once upon a time …

Lesson at a glance
- reading: the Brothers Grimm
- word focus: *keep*
- critical thinking: the main message
- writing and speaking: storytelling

Reading

1

- Ask students to work in pairs to discuss the question. You could model this activity first by describing one of your favourite stories or books. In feedback, elicit what students found out about their partners.

ANSWERS

Students' own answers

Background information

In the UK, favourite picture book stories for very young children include *The Very Hungry Caterpillar*, *Where the Wild things Are* and *Guess How Much I Love You*.

Children's classics include *Alice's Adventures in Wonderland*, *The Wind in the Willows*, *The Tale of Peter Rabbit* and *The BFG* by Roald Dahl.

Classic fairy tales that are well-known in the UK include *Cinderella*, *Sleeping Beauty*, *Beauty and the Beast*, *Jack and the Beanstalk*, *Snow White*, *Hansel and Gretel*, *Red Riding Hood* and *The Princess and the Pea*.

Extra activity

Write the classic fairy tales listed above on the board (some are referred to in the reading text on this spread). Ask students to say what they are called in their language and what they remember about the stories.

2 [17]

- Ask students what they know about the Brothers Grimm. Read out questions 1–4 and ask the class if they know or can guess what the answers are.

- Ask students to read the article. Then tell them to close their books or turn them over. Let students compare what they remember with a partner before discussing with the class.

- **Optional step** The reading text is recorded. You could play the recording and ask students to read and listen.

ANSWERS

1 in Germany, in the late 1700s to 1800s
2 people who told them stories / (oral) storytellers
3 they were 'students of local folklore, who were trying to save the stories … from disappearing'
4 (from final paragraph): 'Some suggest that it is because they are about our struggle for happiness'; 'an escape from the hard realities of daily life, but also hope for a better future'

3

- Read the questions to the class and check they understand all the words (*lack* = not have). Ask students to read the article again and find answers. Let students compare their answers in pairs before discussing with the class.

ANSWERS

1 while at school   *3*
2 We infer that it sells very well – it has been 'translated into more than 160 languages' and is a 'global publishing phenomenon' and it 'competes with the Bible' (*competes* = sells as well as).   *13*
3 illustrations   *23*
4 scholarly footnotes   *24*
5 for over 45 years (from before the first publication in 1812 to the publication of the final edition in 1857)   *38*
6 morals – 'In an effort to make them more acceptable to children's parents, he stressed the moral of each tale.'   *39*
7 unpleasant details   *43*
8 'poor to rich', i.e. a story of someone who is poor and then becomes rich   *53 - 54*

4

- Ask students to work individually to find the words and expressions in the text. Tell them to check their answers in pairs.
- **Optional step** As well as the words in the glossary section, there are other words and expressions students may not know (see Vocabulary notes below). You could ask them to underline three or four in the text and try to guess them from context (see Teacher development below).

ANSWERS

1 Once upon a time
2 villain
3 wise
4 faraway lands
5 the moral
6 cruel
7 witch
8 ever after

Vocabulary notes

(*folk*)*tale* = (traditional) story

humble = not rich or important

oral storytellers = people who tell, but don't write down, stories

untouched = not changed

beast = a wild, dangerous animal or a cruel, unpleasant person

Background information

Jacob (1785–1863) and **Wilhelm Grimm** (1786–1859) popularized many fairy tales including *The Frog Prince* (*Der Froschkönig* in German), *The Goose-Girl* (*Die Gänsemagd*), *Rapunzel*, *Rumpelstiltskin* (*Rumpelstilzchen*) and *Sleeping Beauty* (*Dornröschen*), as well as those mentioned in the text: *Cinderella* (*Aschenputtel*), *Snow White* (*Schneewittchen*) and *Hansel and Gretel* (*Hänsel und Gretel*).

Beauty and the Beast (*La Belle et la Bête* in French) is a traditional fairy tale written by French novelist Gabrielle-Suzanne Barbot de Villeneuve and published in 1740. It wasn't in any of the Grimms' collections.

In the opening and closing paragraphs of this article, the writer uses the language of fairy tales. Traditionally, they open with phrases such as 'Once upon a time …', 'Long, long ago' and 'There lived a poor tailor/washerwoman, etc. …' and they finish with the reassuring '… and they all lived happily ever after'. Note also: 'a wise man', 'enchanting', 'faraway lands', 'humble' and 'cruel' (words which are all associated with fairy tales).

Teacher development

Using context to guess meaning

Developing the skill of being able to work out meaning from context is important. Train students to do this confidently by following this procedure when modelling how to do the task in Exercise 4:

1 Ask students to look at the first synonym, antonym or definition (here, *a long time ago*) and ask if they already know any words or phrases that mean the same.

2 Ask students to look at the text and find a phrase that has a similar meaning. They can check that it is right by looking at the whole sentence and seeing if it helps define it, or by replacing it with the synonym or definition and seeing if the sentence still makes sense.

Word focus *keep*

5

- Organize the class into pairs. Ask students to complete the phrases with 'keep' by finding the missing words in the article. Encourage them to use the context surrounding the phrase to help them discuss what each phrase means.

ANSWERS

1 *keep each other entertained* = here, tell lots of stories over a period of time so that people didn't get bored
2 *keeping records* = storing or maintaining records (e.g. by writing them down and putting them in a library)
3 *keep your promises* = do what you promise; not break your promises

Vocabulary notes

The verb *keep* has many meanings and uses, and, depending on the context, may mean stay, stop, continue, look after, delay or store.

1 *keep (somebody)* + adjective / past participle. Here, *keep* is used to say that you maintain a situation over a period of time, e.g. *I'll keep you informed* (= give pieces of information over a period of time); *It kept us warm* (= it helped us stay warm over time).

2 *keep* + noun. Here, *keep* means store or maintain.

3 *keep* + noun. Here, *keep* means you do what you say you will do. Compare *keep your word* (= keep your promise).

6

• Organize the class into pairs or small groups to discuss the meanings of the phrases in context. At the end, ask different groups to provide explanations or definitions.

ANSWERS

1 watch / be aware of
2 stay positive
3 not telling people
4 record or have a system to record
5 delay or stop (someone) from leaving
6 write down your experiences each day (in a book, or digitally)

Extra activity

Use learner dictionaries to research these phrases. Ask students to find out which category of definition each phrase is filed under. Ask them to find other phrases and collocations with similar meanings.

Critical thinking the main message

7

• Ask students to work in pairs to discuss the messages and decide which one expresses the main message of the article. In feedback, ask students to justify their choice.

ANSWERS

b is correct

a is not true – the brothers didn't know or expect they would be popular: 'early editions were not even aimed at children. They had no illustrations, and scholarly footnotes (were included)' and 'they were just keeping records of tales'

c is not true – it wasn't 'an academic book about the history of folk tales', but a 'story collection'

8

• Ask students to read the article again to find evidence for the ideas. You could ask students to work in pairs to compare their answers before discussing with the class.

ANSWERS

1 paragraph 1 – 'a treasure'
2 paragraph 3 – 'trying to save the stories of oral storytellers from disappearing'

3 paragraph 3 – 'During their lifetime the collection sold only a few copies' and paragraph 2 – 'As a global publishing phenomenon it competes with the Bible' and paragraph 7 – 'they ensured that Grimms' fairy tales would live happily ever after'

Extra activity

It's important to develop your students' ability to read between lines, or look for meaning which is implied but not explicitly stated. Ask them to explore the writer's intent in choosing particular language in the text. Write the following short extracts from the text on the board, and ask students to say (a) what they mean and (b) why the writer chose the words used:

At school they met a wise man who led them to a treasure
a) a well-educated teacher introduced them to traditional folktales;
b) the writer uses words typically used in fairy tales to be clever and to make the story more interesting and 'magical'

millions in faraway lands
a) people all over the world;
b) because they sound dramatic and refer, again, to the style of fairy tales

Some suggest that it is because they are about our struggle for happiness
a) some people say;
b) the writer uses *Some suggest* to imply that this is not the writer's opinion, nor an opinion held by the majority, but merely an idea

Writing and speaking my life

9

• **Optional step** Start this task with a class brainstorming activity. First brainstorm five or six classic stories students might tell. Then brainstorm useful words and phrases on the board. So, for *Cinderella*, stepmother, prince, ball, golden shoe, etc. would be key words.

• Ask students to work individually or (if you think they may struggle for ideas) in pairs. Ask them to think of a story and prepare to tell it. Break this down into two stages:

1 Students think of a classic story and brainstorm words and expressions to use. Introduce *Once upon a time, there lived …* and *They all lived happily after*. Let students use dictionaries to find key words.

2 Students prepare their stories, ideally with a modern setting. Set a time limit of four or five minutes and keep students focused. Monitor and help with ideas and vocabulary.

10

• Once students have prepared, ask them to share their stories with a new partner. Monitor and note examples of good language use as well as errors as students speak.

• Once students have completed the task, ask them to say what they can remember of their partners' stories. Give feedback on errors and write examples of good language use on the board.

Extra activity

For homework, ask students to write their fairy tales and add an illustration. Collect the tales and put them in a folder for the class to share and read.

2d What a nightmare!

Lesson at a glance
- real life: reacting to stories
- pronunciation: linking and elision

Real life reacting to stories

1

- Ask students to work in pairs to discuss day-to-day things that often go wrong. Start by eliciting two or three examples from the whole class, or by providing your own example of something that you have recently experienced.

> **EXAMPLE ANSWERS**
>
> Computers: computer crashing, accidentally deleting data, programs freezing, batteries on laptops running out, forgetting a power cable
>
> Transport: missing the bus/train, heavy traffic, getting on the wrong bus/train, delays, cancelled services, losing a ticket, missing your bus/train stop
>
> Things in the house: appliances breaking down, water leaks, accidentally dropping or breaking something, power cuts
>
> Forgetting things: not buying someone a birthday card or present, leaving a wallet/phone on the bus or train, forgetting where you put your car/house keys, missing a meeting/appointment, forgetting to pay a bill or renew insurance

2 [18]

- Start by reading the extracts to the class. Check the meaning of *door handle* (= the thing you turn to open the door); *bump* (= a small area in the road surface which is higher than the surface around it). See Vocabulary notes below for other words which occur in the audio script.

- Organize the class into pairs or small groups to discuss what they think happens next. In feedback, elicit ideas, but don't give any answers.

- Play the recording. Students listen and check. In feedback, find out how the stories were different from your students' ideas.

> **ANSWERS**
>
> 1 Another bus came within about fifteen minutes and they all transferred to that one.
>
> 2 He had to walk right across the restaurant back to his table with his hands over the hole.
>
> 3 She went to the neighbours' house, but they weren't at home. So she just had to wait for someone else to come home.
>
> 4 The lights in the lift went off and one of the other two people in the lift started screaming.
>
> 5 She fell off the bike and cut her hand. Luckily there were no cars behind her.
>
> 6 He had lost about four hours' work, but when he rebooted the computer he searched for some of the key words in the document and then found a temporary file which had most of the document in it.

Audioscript [18]

Conversation 1

A: The bus broke down on the motorway, so we were all left waiting until help could arrive.

B: What did you do?

A: Luckily another bus came within about fifteen minutes and we all transferred to that one.

B: That must have been a relief.

Conversation 2

A: My trousers got caught on the door handle and as I walked away, they tore.

B: Oh, that's awful.

A: Yes, I had to walk right across the restaurant back to our table with my hands over the hole.

B: How embarrassing!

Conversation 3

A: I bent the key trying to force it into the door lock and when I tried to straighten the key, it snapped.

B: How did you get in?

A: I went to the neighbours', but they weren't at home. So I just had to wait 'til someone came home.

B: Yeah, a similar thing happened to me once.

Conversation 4

A: The lift got stuck between the eighteenth and the nineteenth floors and two people completely panicked.

B: What a nightmare!

A: It was. Then the lights in the lift went off and one of them started screaming.

B: Yeah, I think I would have done the same thing.

Conversation 5

A: The tyres on my bicycle were badly worn and when I hit a bump in the road one of them burst.

B: Poor you!

A: Well, I came off and cut my hand. Thank goodness there were no cars behind me.

B: That was lucky.

Conversation 6

A: My computer froze without any reason while I was working.

B: Really? How strange!

A: Yeah, I thought I'd lost about four hours' work, but when I rebooted the computer I searched for some of the key words in my document and I found a temporary file which had most of the document in it.

B: That was good thinking.

Vocabulary notes

Check the meaning of the following words, which are connected with things going wrong.

break/broke down = when a machine stops working or moving

get/got caught = here, when something becomes accidentally connected to something and prevented from moving

tear/tore = to pull something so that it accidentally separates into pieces or has a hole in it and is damaged (you could mime this)

bend/bent = to become curved and not straight (a piece of metal, for example)

snap(ped) = to break into two pieces suddenly

get/got stuck = here, be unexpectedly prevented from moving

worn = not in good condition because they have been used a lot

burst = (a tyre, balloon, ball) suddenly loses all its air

my computer froze = all the open programs stopped and opening files or writing anything was impossible

reboot my computer = to restart a computer after it has crashed, or been turned off

3 🎧 [18]

• Tell students to look at the expressions in the language box. Ask them to work in pairs to discuss which expressions were used in the conversations in Exercise 2.

• Play the recording again. Students listen and check their answers.

> ANSWERS
>
> 1 That must have been a relief.
> 2 Oh, that's awful. / How embarrassing!
> 3 Yeah, a similar thing happened to me once.
> 4 What a nightmare! / Yeah, I think I would have done the same thing.
> 5 Poor you! / That was lucky.
> 6 Really? How strange! / That was good thinking.

Pronunciation linking and elision

4a 🎧 [19]

• Play the recording. Students listen to the responses and notice the linking and elision (see Pronunciation notes below).

• Play the recording again for students to listen and repeat.

4b 🎧 [20]

• Organize the class into pairs. Students work together to underline the linked or elided sounds.

• Play the recording. Students listen and check then practise saying the sentences with their partner.

Audioscript 🎧 [20] (with linking and elision marked)

Linked:

1 What‿a nightmare!
2 Oh, that's‿awful. Poor you!
3 How‿embarrassing!
4 Really? That's‿odd.

Elided:

5 That was good‿thinking.
6 A similar thing happened‿to me.

Pronunciation note

Linking is when the consonant sound at the end of one word is followed by a vowel sound at the start of the next. It's as if the consonant sound joins the next word: so *That's awful* becomes 'That sawful' /θat 'sɔːfʊl/. When a word ends with a vowel sound and the next word begins with a vowel sound, a linking, or extra, sound is inserted: so the sound /w/ is inserted between *How* /haʊ/ and *embarrassing* /haʊ(w)ɪmˈbarəsɪŋ/. This makes it possible to link the mouth and lip positions more smoothly.

Elision happens when sounds disappear into each other. It's used with the sounds /t/, /d/, /ð/ and /θ/. It's hard for the mouth to switch from a hard, voiced /d/ sound to unvoiced /t/ or /θ/ sounds. Similarly, in English, if the sound at the end of one word is the same as the sound at the start of the next, it is pronounced only once, so there is only one /d/ sound in *good doctor*, for example.

5

• Ask students to work individually to choose one of the topics and prepare a story. Focus students' attention on the situations and the task and pre-teach key words (*stranded* = left behind, alone and with no way of getting home; *panicked* = suddenly feel so afraid or worried that it is difficult to think calmly and clearly). Monitor and help with ideas and vocabulary as students work.

• When students are ready, organize the class into groups of four. Ask students to take turns telling their stories in these groups. Remind students to use as many of the 'reacting to stories' expressions as they can when listening to the other students' stories.

• Monitor and listen for errors, and prompt students to use the key expressions correctly.

2e A real-life drama

Lesson at a glance
- writing: a story
- writing skill: using descriptive words

Writing a story

1
- **Optional step** With books closed, write the following words from the story on the board and ask students to check them in dictionaries: *stuck, painful, moaning, sore, jungle, hiking, camp, thorn, free, trap*. Ask students to work in pairs to predict what the story is about from these words.
- Ask students to read the opening paragraph and answer the questions. Let them compare answers in pairs before discussing with the class.

> **ANSWERS**
> 1 He got his foot (right ankle) caught in a metal animal trap.
> 2 They are both tired and want to return to the camp before it gets dark.

2
- Ask students to work in pairs to order the events. Point out that while the story begins with Rowan crying out, this isn't in fact the first event. The writer uses the past perfect form to refer back to earlier events.
- In feedback, ask students why the writer chooses to begin with Rowan crying out.

> **ANSWERS**
> 1 d   2 c   3 b   4 a   5 e   6 f
> The writer probably chooses to begin with Rowan crying out because it is the most dramatic point in the story and is likely to immediately engage the reader's interest.

Writing skill using descriptive words

3a
- Ask students to look at the highlighted words and phrases in the story. Ask: *Which words and phrases describe movement and which describe a way of speaking?* Ask students to work in pairs to decide whether each word or phrase describes movement or a way of speaking, and to discuss what each one means.

> **ANSWERS**
> Movement: *struggling* (= finding it difficult to do something); *hiking* (= walking long distances at a good speed); *walking back slowly* (= returning on foot slowly)
> A way of speaking: *cried* (= here, shouted); *moaning* (= complaining in a miserable voice); *said encouragingly* (= said to try to help somebody feel better or try harder)

3b
- Organize the class into new pairs. Ask students to try to work out meaning of the bold words from context before checking in dictionaries.
- **Optional step** Use mime to elicit or check these words.

> **ANSWERS**
> Speaking:
> 1 screamed = shouted in a loud voice because the person was angry, in pain or, in this case, trying to get people's attention
> 2 muttering = speaking quietly and in a low, slightly angry voice because the person is unhappy with the situation
> 3 mumbled = spoke in a quiet and unclear way that made it difficult for others to understand
> 4 said with a sigh = said with a deep, slow outward breath that shows the person is sad, disappointed or upset
> 5 said bravely = spoke with a strong, firm voice even though the person was scared
> Moving:
> 6 moved cautiously = moved in a very careful way
> 7 leapt = jumped suddenly
> 8 tripped = fell over something small or low because the person hit a foot against it
> 9 hurried on = continued going in a quick way because they wanted to get somewhere sooner
> 10 turned anxiously = changed the position of her head or body in a worried way, so that she was facing in a different direction

Vocabulary note

Note the use of adverbs after the verb (*walk slowly*, *said bravely*), and the use of expressions using *with* (*said with a sigh*, *walked with a limp*).

3c
- Ask students to suggest other verbs that describe a particular way of speaking or moving.

> **EXAMPLE ANSWERS**
> Speaking: shout, call, whisper, grumble
> Moving: run, jump, race, hop, step, stride, walk, hike

Extra activity

Ask students to work in groups. Students take turns to mime words or phrases from the vocabulary section. The rest of the groups must guess the word. Alternatively, ask students to grade the speaking verbs (from soft/slow to loud/fast) and the moving verbs (from slow/minimal to fast/expansive).

4

- Ask students to look at the list of main events of a story on page 153 of the Student's Book. Check the meaning of *rhino/rhinoceros* (= a large African animal with a single horn on its nose), *horn* (= a hard, pointed growth on the side, or in the centre of the head of some animals, e.g. cows, goats and rhinos) and *jeep* (= a car with no roof that can drive over all types of land).

- Ask students to work in pairs to discuss how best to order the story. Remind them how the example story used the past perfect and a earlier event in the sequence to start the paragraph.

- Then ask students to work individually to write their story. Remind them to use the checklist.

5

- Tell students to exchange stories with their partner. Ask them to make notes on each other's work and to give feedback about how to change or improve their story. Tell them to use the checklist in Exercise 4. Monitor and be available to help or advise at this stage.

- **Optional step** Ask students to pass their stories round the class so everybody can read each story, or put the stories on the walls so students can walk round and read them all.

- In feedback, ask students to say what they liked about their partners' stories.

2f How not to climb a mountain

Before you watch

Key vocabulary

1

- Ask students to work in pairs or small groups to explain the features of a mountain.

> ANSWERS
>
> *peak/summit* = both can mean the top of a mountain, but *peaks* can refer to a series of high points as you go up a mountain, whereas *summit* is the very top of a high mountain (e.g. the *summit* of Everest, not the *peak*)
>
> *ridge* = a flat section up in the mountains
>
> *vertical face* = the face of a mountain is the part that 'faces' out – if it's 'vertical' it's straight up and down and difficult to climb
>
> *base* = the bottom – base camp is the place from which mountain climbers start

2

- Ask students to work in pairs to look at the title of the video and discuss what mistake the two climbers made.

- Ask students to think of two further possible mistakes in pairs. In feedback, check *equipment* (= here, the things you need when you climb a mountain) and elicit ideas, but don't comment on any of the statements.

> EXAMPLE ANSWERS
>
> Possible additional mistakes:
>
> They set off without checking the map/route.
>
> They wore the wrong clothes.
>
> They didn't take enough food/water.
>
> They didn't have enough / the right experience.

While you watch

3 ■◀ [2.1]

- Check that students understand the meaning and pronunciation of the words in the glossary section at the bottom of the page.

- Ask students to watch the whole video and answer the question. Let students compare answers with a partner.

> ANSWERS
>
> They climbed the wrong mountain.

Videoscript ■◀ 2.1

0.00–0.29 Cedar Wright   So this one time we were trying to climb Middle Pallisade, which is one of the 14,000-foot peaks in California, with my good friend, and climbing partner Alex Honnold. We basically were very ill-prepared. We had read the description of how to climb the mountain on our phones, and so we'd get to the base of this, like, really big-looking peak and we were like, that's for sure got to be it, I mean, it's, like, the biggest mountain here.

0.30–0.42 We start heading up the peak, and it's kind of vertical and it's getting kind of hard, and I'm like, I don't really remember, like the description of this route, like, having such difficult climbing on it, but I'm like, 'maybe we're just a little off-route'.

0.43–0.58 At the summit of each of these peaks there's a summit register, and so, you know, we were signing all the summit registers, and so we get up there and we're like, 'Yes, that was awesome!' and we go to look at the summit register and Alex opens it up and he's like …

0.59–1.04 Alex Honnold We just climbed the wrong mountain. What a tragedy.

1.05–1.07 Cedar Wright Just still emotionally recovering from the fact that we climbed the wrong mountain.

1.08–1.24 Yeah, it was a big bummer. And then, like, to make matters worse, we're like, 'Oh, there's the mountain.' And we were looking out, like, into this huge, like, treacherous ridge, just like, just looks like death – like death on a stick.

1.25–1.50 We start out across this ridge and it is terrible. It is … the rock is just peeling off, like, just like sheets of paper. You know, it's like, one false move, if you go off of that rock, you're dead. We pick our way up, get to the top of Middle Pallisade, it's like twelve hours later, I'm completely exhausted.

1.51–1.52 Alex Honnold What a horrible, horrible ridge.

1.53–1.54 Cedar Wright It was awful.

1.55–1.56 Alex Honnold Yeah, it was awful.

1.57–1.59 Cedar Wright Yeah, good times, you should totally do it. You should get out there and try it, it'll be terrible, yeah.

4 ▪◀ [2.1]

- Ask students to read sentences 1–8 and choose the correct option for any they can remember.
- When students are ready, play the whole video again. Let students compare their choice of options in pairs before checking with the class.

ANSWERS

1 14,000-foot	5 the summit register
2 had already read	6 walk along
3 really difficult	7 thin pieces
4 route	8 twelve

5

- Ask students to work individually to complete the sentences with the words. Elicit the first answer (*biggest*) from the class to get them started. Point out that recognizing the part of speech and the context of the sentence will help them find the answers.
- Let students compare answers in pairs. In feedback, use check questions to confirm answers (see Vocabulary notes below).

ANSWERS

1 biggest	5 paper
2 vertical	6 false
3 awesome	7 exhausted
4 treacherous; stick	8 Good

Vocabulary notes

Check questions are a good way of checking students have understood in feedback to a vocabulary task. So, for example, ask, *awesome – is it really good or really bad?* (really good); *treacherous – is it very dangerous or quite dangerous* (very).

Note the use of American slang terms typical of the sort of young, adventurous climbers in the clip:

like = young Americans (notably those from California) regularly use 'like' as a redundant discourse marker – it has no meaning, but reflects the fact that the speaker is thinking about how to express something

In contrast, when the speaker says *like death* or *like sheets of paper*, *like* is used to form a simile, and means 'similar to'.

kind of vertical/hard = an example of understatement – it means 'absolutely vertical / incredibly hard'

Using understatement is a common way that adrenaline junkies make what they do sound cool rather than scary.

Good times = It was really enjoyable!

death on a stick = a very high likelihood of death – this is a made-up, jokey expression

horrible, awful, terrible = these are words used to mean 'challenging, but really exciting'

awesome = American teens frequently use this word to describe something that is seen as very positive

After you watch
Vocabulary in context
6a ▪◀ [2.2]

- Explain that students are going to watch some clips from the video which contain some new words and phrases. They need to choose the correct meaning of the words.
- Play the clips. When each multiple-choice question appears, pause the clip so that students can choose the correct definition. You could let students compare answers in pairs before discussing with the class.

ANSWERS

1 b   2 a   3 c   4 b   5 c

Vocabulary note

It was a big bummer = it was a very disappointing experience – this is a very informal expression

Videoscript ▪◀ 2.2

1 We basically were very **ill-prepared** …
   a well prepared
   b badly prepared
   c over-prepared

2 We start **heading up** the peak …
   a making our way
   b moving quickly
   c walking in a line

3 Yeah, it was **a big bummer**.

   a an interesting experience

   b an unexpected shock

   c a disappointing situation

4 ... the rock is just **peeling off**, like, just like sheets of paper.

   a becoming very thin

   b coming away in layers

   c falling off in large pieces

5 We **pick our way** up, get to the top of Middle Pallisade ...

   a go quickly

   b go slowly

   c go carefully

6b

- Students work individually to complete the sentences. Let students compare sentences with a partner before inviting a few students to share their sentences with the class.

> **EXAMPLE ANSWERS**
>
> 1 The house was in a bad condition. The paint was peeling off *the walls in all the bedrooms* and *the roof was falling down*.
>
> 2 I was very ill-prepared for *the examination / having to go into hospital.*
>
> 3 For our summer holidays we are heading *to the beach / the mountains / my grandmother's villa.*

7

- **Optional step** Ask students to read the list of prompts and take a minute to think individually about how they will use the prompts to retell the story from the video.

- Ask students to work in pairs to retell the story together. Monitor and prompt students as they speak.

- As an alternative, ask students to tell the story from the point of view of a climber who may have been nearby and watching the events.

8

- Ask students to read situations 1–4 and think about what could go wrong in each case.

- Read the example sentence for situation 1 to the class and elicit one or two other possibilities for that scenario. Then ask students to work individually or in pairs to prepare ideas for situations 2–4. Monitor and help with ideas and vocabulary.

- Organize the class into groups. Ask students to compare ideas and decide which of the mistakes they thought of would be the worst.

> **EXAMPLE ANSWERS**
>
> 2 Your car breaks down or you get stuck in traffic. You realize you have forgotten your passport.
>
> 3 You wrote the wrong name on the card. You lose the card and present. You go to the wrong place.
>
> 4 Your car breaks down or you get stuck in traffic. You go the wrong way or go to the wrong place.

UNIT 2 Review and memory booster

Memory Booster activities

Exercises 3, 4, 6 and 7 are Memory Booster activities. For more information about these activities and how they benefit students, see page 10 of this Teacher's Book.

I can ... check boxes

As an alternative to asking students to simply tick the *I can ...* boxes, you could ask them to give themselves a score from 1 to 4 (1 = not very confident; 4 = very confident) for each language area. If students score 1 or 2 for a language area, refer them to additional practice activities in the Workbook and Grammar summary exercises.

Grammar

1

- Ask students to work individually to complete the story using the correct past tense of the verbs in brackets. Tell them that they will need to use both active and passive forms. Let students compare answers in pairs before eliciting answers from the class.

> **ANSWERS**
>
> 1 have heard   8 has even played
> 2 was published   9 were called
> 3 had just bought   10 had reported
> 4 revealed   11 were not expecting
> 5 had been working   12 had been made
> 6 were flying   13 stepped
> 7 was picked

2

- Ask students to read the article again and answer the questions.

> **ANSWERS**
>
> a The 1989 incident where the police were called to sightings of a UFO.
>
> b The 2011 story that Branson had just bought the planet Pluto.

3 ≫ MB

- Ask students to work in pairs to find the four passive verbs in the story in Exercise 1. Then tell them to discuss why passive forms are used rather than active forms.

> **ANSWERS**
>
> 1 *an article was published*: we are interested in the article, not in who published it
>
> 2 *the story was picked up*: the object is the focus of the sentence, not the subject, so it is placed first
>
> 3 *they [the police] were called*: the action was happening *to* the police, it wasn't being done *by* them
>
> 4 *a hot air balloon that had been made*: we do not know who performed the action

4 >> MB

- Ask students to work individually to write two sentences about something that happened to them last week, using the passive where possible.

- Students work in pairs to read out their sentences and ask each other questions.

ANSWERS
Students' own answers

Vocabulary

5

- Ask students to work individually to choose the correct options to complete the description of a film. Let students compare answers in pairs before checking with the class.

ANSWERS	
1 gripping	4 told
2 setting	5 bringing
3 plot	6 engaging

6 >> MB

- Ask students to look at the photos and answer the questions. You could ask students to work in pairs or you could ask the whole class.

ANSWERS
Students' own answers

Real life

7 >> MB

- Ask students to work in pairs and decide who is Student A and who is Student B. Students take it in turns to make statements and respond using the phrases in the box. Monitor, encouraging students to use appropriate intonation and a range of phrases.

Unit 3 Science and technology

Opener

1

- Discuss the questions with your class. Elicit ideas from students and find out which students depend most on technology.

EXAMPLE ANSWERS

I'd lose the contact details of friends and people I work with; I'd lose hours of work on my computer; I might not have access to documents for a meeting; I couldn't work at all; I'd lose photos, diaries; It really gets to me when my phone runs out of battery; I'd literally panic if I lost my phone; I wouldn't mind actually.

2

- Ask students to look at the photo and the caption. Read the areas in the box to the class and explain any new words (*breakthrough* = an important discovery which usually happens after a lot of work or research; *artificial intelligence* = not real intelligence, so the intelligence of a computer or robot).
- Discuss the questions with the class.

EXAMPLE ANSWERS

The areas of technology represented in the photo could be: artificial intelligence and communications.

Students will have their own ideas, but breakthroughs could include bionic body parts (medicine), fuel in cars (energy use) and integrating information on the internet with our surroundings (communications).

Pronunciation notes

Read the words in the box to the class, and have them repeat them chorally and individually. Check the words where the stress is not on the first syllable: arti*fi*cial, intelligence, communications, explo*ra*tion.

Note also the elision in *medicine*: /ˈmedsn/.

3 🎵 [21]

- Read the predictions (1–3) to the class. Ask students to say what reasons the speakers might give for each prediction. You could put students in pairs to do this. The more students think about what they may hear, the easier it will be to hear and understand what the speakers say.
- **Optional step** Ask students to predict what specific words or phrases they expect to hear from each speaker (possibilities include: *getting older, living longer, medical breakthroughs, robots, technology, new inventions, ozone layer, rising temperatures*).
- Play the recording. Students listen and note the reasons the speakers give. Let students compare their answers in pairs before discussing as a class.

ANSWERS

1 Quite a few people are already living to be 100 and those numbers are predicted to increase.
2 The technology already exists (chatbots).
3 The benefits are great so someone will work out a way of controlling the weather.

Audioscript 💿 [21]

Speaker 1

I expect that most of my generation will live to be around a hundred years old. There are already 12,000 people in the UK aged over a hundred and it's predicted that by the year 2060 that number will have risen to about one million.

Speaker 2

I think people in the future will be interacting with intelligent machines even more than they do now. I read this article about things called chatbots which are programs that can hold intelligent conversations with people in chat rooms on the internet. These programs already exist.

Speaker 3

I don't think global warming is going to be the problem that everyone says it is. By the middle of this century I think humans will have discovered ways to control the weather. If you think about it, the benefits, commercial and otherwise, are so great – for agriculture, for stopping natural disasters and so on – that it's only a matter of time before someone works out a way.

4

- Organize the class into new pairs to discuss the predictions in Exercise 3. In feedback, find out which predictions a majority of students think may come true.

Extra activity

Ask pairs to think of their own future prediction for the next fifty years. Ask different pairs to briefly present their idea. Have a class vote on which prediction is most likely to come true in the future.

3a Is technology the answer?

Lesson at a glance
- reading and listening: overpopulation
- pronunciation: /r/ and /t/ in American English
- grammar: future forms
- speaking: predictions

Reading and listening

1

- Check the meaning and pronunciation of the words in the box, pointing out word stress (see Vocabulary notes below).
- **Optional step** Ask students to repeat the words chorally and individually.
- Organize the class into groups of four to discuss the question. Point out that there may be more than one possible answer. Ask students to explain or justify their ideas.

> **EXAMPLE ANSWERS**
>
> Congestion is the most obvious answer: the taxis can hardly move because the streets are crowded.
>
> Students may also suggest pollution (from the traffic) and poverty (this is a photo from a developing country).

Vocabulary notes

congestion = too much traffic – nothing moves

epidemic = the rapid spread of a disease

overpopulation = too many people in one place or area

pollution = harmful or poisonous substances introduced into an environment

poverty = a situation in which someone doesn't have enough money to pay for their basic needs

starvation = a situation in which someone suffers or dies because they don't have enough food to eat (verb: *starve*)

Background information

Kolkata /koʊlˈkɑːtɑː/ (formerly known as Calcutta), which is shown in this photo, is the capital of the Indian state of West Bengal. It has India's oldest operating port and a population of about five million.

2

- Ask students to discuss the question in their groups. Monitor and note interesting ideas to pick up on in feedback (see Teacher development below).
- In feedback, elicit ideas from the class.

> **EXAMPLE ANSWERS**
>
> Congestion: better information on traffic with GPS systems; robot traffic police officers; improved road building to ease traffic; advanced computer software to predict and solve traffic problems; improved or new public transport methods
>
> Epidemic: new medicines; new hygiene solutions; cheaper drugs; genetic modification to improve resistance to disease
>
> Overpopulation: improved contraception; better education and family advice
>
> Pollution: new methods to monitor and treat pollution; new technologies to create clean energy
>
> Poverty: computer technology enables people in poor countries to work online; improved agricultural techniques help poor people grow food; new technologies to create 'free' energy, e.g. from solar and wind power
>
> Starvation: improved agricultural techniques; technology to build infrastructure such as dams and wells; GM (genetically modified) foods that are more resistant to drought, disease, etc.

Extra activity

Ask students to provide examples of the problems in the box in Exercise 1 from current news stories.

Teacher development

Monitoring and noticing

When students are talking freely in pairs or groups at a lead-in stage of a lesson, it's advisable to just allow them to have fluency practice. However, by monitoring what they say discretely, and noticing what ideas they have and what language they use, you can gather useful information to help you develop the lesson. Here are some things to listen for:

1 Interest: If students are motivated and interested, and have things to say and questions to ask, consider spending more time on this topic, and including more debate and personal response to the topics raised. If they don't seem interested, think about how to make the topic more relevant, personalized and engaging.

2 Knowledge: If students already know a lot about the topic, take advantage of that knowledge by getting students to predict or comment on content. Ideas include asking students to say what they think will be discussed or saying how they would answer questions put to a speaker. You could ask a particularly knowledgeable student to talk about a topic in detail at the lead-in stage.

3 Language: Find out what words students are trying to use, but aren't sure of, during the lead-in stage. This is language that can then be actively introduced at this stage, or later in the unit. Encourage students to paraphrase what they want to say, but note better ways of saying it as you listen. Then, in feedback, write up any useful phrases for students.

4 Previewing language: Often a lead-in activity will naturally preview vocabulary and grammar from the unit. For example, in the lead-in discussion in Exercise 2, students need to speculate using modals and future forms. Listen out for how well and naturally students use language you aim to teach later, and listen to the type of errors students make. If you note what they naturally say to communicate, it will help you recognize how good they already are at future forms, which forms they naturally use and what errors they are most likely to make.

3 🎧 [22]

- Ask students to read the three opinions. Ask: *Which of the opinions is positive?* (3).
- Play the recording. Students listen and read and then match the opinions with the correct person or group. Let them compare their answers in pairs before checking them with the class.

ANSWERS

1 b   2 a   3 c

4

- Read sentences 1–5 to the class. Point out *limited space* (= a space with boundaries), *conflict* (= wars, fighting or disagreements between people) and *consuming* (= buying and using – the noun is *consumption*).
- Ask students to read the transcript again, decide whether each sentence is true or false, and correct any false sentences. Let students compare their answers in pairs before checking them with the class.

ANSWERS

1 F (*overpopulation … is a situation where there are more people than there are resources*)

2 T (*people might even begin to fight over the limited resources*)

3 T (*Paul Ehrlich wrote … that … we were keeping too many people alive*)

4 F (*the population … at the current rate, is going to reach nine billion by 2050*)

5 T (*The real question is: have we now reached a point – with incomes rising and the world's middle classes expanding – where we cannot simply rely on science to provide the answers?*)

Background information

Paul R. Ehrlich (born 1932) is a professor at Stanford University, New York. His views are controversial. He has been criticized by some for being overly pessimistic, but praised by others for encouraging countries to take action to avoid disaster.

Thomas Malthus (1766–1834) was a cleric as well as a scholar. His views contradicted the idea in his time that society was improving. The 'Malthusian Trap' is the theory that wealthy societies don't result in wealth for everybody, but a growth in population until the weaker members of society are in poverty again.

Pronunciation /r/ and /t/ in American English

5a 🎧 [23]

- Play the recording. Students listen and note the pronunciation. In feedback, ask students to say how the speaker's pronunciation differs from British English (the accent most prevalent in this course).

ANSWERS

She pronounces a rolled /r/ sound clearly (British English speakers don't pronounce the /r/) and changes the /t/ sounds to something closer to /d/ sounds in the words. See Pronunciation notes below.

5b 🎧 [24]

- Play the recording. Students listen and complete the phrases. In feedback, ask students to say how the pronunciation differs from British English. If you are a native speaker, model how you would say the phrases.
- **Optional step** Give students time to work in pairs to practise saying the phrases with an American or British accent. Find out if their partner can recognize if they are attempting the American or British pronunciation.

ANSWERS

1 eight (UK: /eɪt/)

2 Internet (UK: /ˈɪntənet/)

3 twenty-first (UK: /ˈtwentiˈfɜːst/)

4 poverty (UK: /ˈpɒvəti/)

5 energy (UK: /ˈenədʒi/)

6 reality (UK: /riˈæləti/)

Audioscript 🎧 [24]

1 eight billion

2 an internet site

3 a twenty-first birthday

4 great poverty

5 generate energy

6 another reality

Pronunciation notes

/r/

American English is mainly rhotic – speakers generally say every written /r/. So, the /r/ in *bird*, for example, is pronounced /bɜrd/, whereas in British English, which is non-rhotic, the /r/ is not pronounced and a long vowel sound is used instead: /bɜːd/. In standard British English, /r/ is only pronounced when followed by a vowel sound (compare *brain* /breɪn/ and *mother* /ˈmʌðə/).

/t/

In both British and American English, a 't' at the start of a word is usually pronounced /t/. However, after vowel sounds, in the middle of a word, while British English generally retains the /t/ sound, American English changes to something closer to a /d/ sound. The soft 't' sound of American English is usually described phonetically as a 'flap' or 'tap'.

Grammar future forms

6

- Ask students to look at the sentences in the grammar box and answer questions 1–4. Go through the answers with the class.

ANSWERS

1 1 is the most definite prediction; 2 is the least definite

2 be about to

3 3

4 5; 6

5 8; 7

Refer students to page 160 for further information and practice.

ANSWERS TO GRAMMAR SUMMARY EXERCISES

1
1 won't
2 going to
3 might
4 it's about to
5 isn't going to
6 we might not
7 I'll

2a
1 I'm flying to Canada next month!
2 I'll have some coffee, please.
3 We're going to visit Tom's parents some time next month.
4 I'll make you a sandwich.
5 They're eating out tonight.
6 … so she's going to look for her own place soon.

2b
a 3, 6   b 1, 5   c 2, 4   d 4

3
1 are you going to come *or* are you coming
2 're going
3 'm meeting *or* 'm going to meet
4 'll call
5 'll pick
6 's going to come

Grammar notes

The choice of future form is often dependent on the point of view of the speaker. *I'm playing tennis tomorrow, I'm going to play tennis tomorrow* and *I'll play tennis tomorrow* are all correct, but a speaker might choose to say the first to emphasize that it is arranged and in the diary, or the second to emphasize that this is his or her intention, or the third to emphasize that the decision has just been made at the moment of speaking – it is spontaneous or instant. To simplify the area for students:

1 The intention of the speaker

Is it a plan? (the speaker intended this before speaking) – use *going to*

Is it an arrangement? (the speaker has arranged this – it's in the diary) – use present continuous

Is it instant? (the speaker just decided this) – use *will*

2 Making predictions

Is there evidence for the prediction? – use *going to*

Is it a personal opinion? – use *will*

Note that *about to* can be used for a plan as well as a prediction (e.g. *We're about to head off on a round-the-world trip*). It emphasizes that something will happen very shortly.

Teacher development

Using concept check questions (CCQs)

Using concept check questions, for which the answer is *yes* or *no*, is a useful way of checking lexical or grammatical meaning, especially in multilingual classrooms where you cannot use the students' L1.

To form a CCQ, start with a contextualized example or target sentence (e.g. *We're going to look at the question of overpopulation.*). Then take the grammar rule that explains its use (e.g. *We use 'going to' when we express a plan.*) and turn it into a simple question: *Is it a plan?*

By asking questions instead of 'delivering' rules, you keep students engaged and active. It's also a way of finding out if they have fully understood the rules.

Use concept check questions as you introduce and practice forms. For example, to check the uses connected with the intention of the speaker (see above), ask:

Is it a plan? (Yes) *Did the speaker know he/she was planning it before speaking?* (Yes)

Is it an arrangement? Is it in the 'diary'? (Yes)

Is it an instant decision? (Yes) *Did the speaker decide to do it at the moment of speaking?* (No) *Did the speaker decide to do it at the moment of speaking?* (Yes)

To check the uses connected with prediction, ask:

Is there evidence now for the prediction? (Yes)

Is it the speaker's opinion? (Yes)

To check the use of *about to*, ask:

Will it happen quite soon, very soon or in the distant future? (very soon)

7
- Ask students to work in pairs to discuss what future form is used in each sentence and why. Let them compare their answers in pairs before checking as a class.

ANSWERS

1 *be going to* for plans
2 *will* for fairly definite predictions
3 *be about to* for predictions about something happening very soon
4 *will* for offers
5 *might* for less definite predictions
6 the present continuous for arrangements
7 *be going to* for predictions based on some evidence
8 *will* for decisions made at the time of speaking

8
- Ask students to read the introduction to a presentation and choose the correct options for 1–8. Elicit the first answer to get them started. Let students compare answers in pairs. In feedback, ask students to justify their answers.
- The aim of this controlled accuracy practice is to ensure that students fully understand the rules. You can deal with any confusions that arise by correcting individuals as they work, or by asking CCQs to prompt students. Check difficulties with the whole class during feedback. See it as an opportunity to voice concerns rather than a test.

ANSWERS
1 I'm just going to wait   5 (both are possible)
2 I'll begin   6 you'll find
3 I'm going to speak   7 she's going to speak
4 (both are possible)   8 I'm going to show

Grammar notes

1 *I'm just going to wait* (a plan – but not an arrangement)
2 *I'll begin* (a decision made at the time of speaking)
3 *I'm going to speak* (a plan – speaker knew topic before speaking; we use *about to* in order to emphasize the imminence of something happening, not a plan, so it would be odd to announce a speech as an imminent happening)
4 both are possible (*might be* is more tentative and less likely as 'I hope' already conveys less likeliness so it isn't necessary to repeat this)
5 both are possible (depends on whether you wish to emphasize what she plans to do or has arranged to do)
6 *you'll find* (personal prediction)
7 *is going to speak* (plan)
8 *I'm going to show* (plan)

Vocabulary notes

seminar room = a room designed to be used for discussions, typically by university students to enable them to exchange ideas

9 [25]

• Ask students to work in pairs to act out the conversations, putting the verbs in brackets in an appropriate future form as they do so. Students then listen to compare their answers.

EXAMPLE ANSWERS

All possible answers are given, but the answers given in the recording are given first and are underlined in the audioscript below.

1
A: are you doing / are you going to do
B: might go / 'll go / 're going to go
A: 're just going to stay
2
A: 'm going to go; are going travelling / are going to travel
B: Are you going to show / Will you show
A: 'll let
3
A: Will you help; won't take
B: 'll just finish
4
B: 'm about to start / 'm going to start
A: 'll be
5
A: 's just going to carry on
B: will probably reach

Audioscript [25]

Conversation 1
A: What <u>are you doing</u> this weekend?
B: I'm not sure, but we <u>might go</u> to the seaside if the weather stays nice.
A: Sounds like a good plan. We<u>'re just going to stay</u> at home and relax.

Conversation 2
A: <u>I'm going to go</u> shopping for a wedding dress on Saturday. Jen and I <u>are going to travel</u> up to London to choose one.
B: How exciting! <u>Are you going to show</u> it to anyone else before the wedding?
A: <u>I'll let</u> you see it, if you want.

Conversation 3
A: <u>Will you help</u> me move this table? It won't take a moment.
B: Sure. <u>I'll just finish</u> writing this email.

Conversation 4
A: Have you started your new job yet?
B: No, but <u>I'm about to start</u>. Next Monday is my first day.
A: Good luck. I'm sure you<u>'ll be</u> fine.

Conversation 5
A: Another rise in the population, I see! Do you think it<u>'s just going to carry on</u> going up and up?
B: No, I think at some point soon it <u>will probably reach</u> a peak.

Grammar notes

Conversation 1:
Here the speaker uses the present continuous to ask about arrangements already made. Speaker B uses *might go* because he/she hasn't made an arrangement and isn't sure. Speaker A uses *going to* for an intention or plan.

Conversation 2:
Both speakers use *going to* for plans and arrangements already made. Speaker A then switches to *will* (*I'll let you see it, if you want*) because this is an instant offer.

Conversation 3:
Speaker A uses *be about to* to say that something is happening in the near future. Speaker B uses *will* to make a personal prediction.

Conversation 4:
Both speakers use *will* to make predictions that are personal opinions.

Conversation 5:
Speaker A uses *will* to ask for a prediction. Speaker B uses *will* to give a personal prediction.

10

• Organize the class into new pairs. Ask them to have five brief conversations with each other using future forms and the list of prompts on the page. Mix pairs two or three times and then repeat the exercise so they get lots of practice at using language from the lesson.

- In feedback, ask students what they found out about classmates.

- **Optional step** As students speak, monitor and note down errors you hear. Concentrate on errors with future forms. At the end, in feedback, write up five or six short sentences containing errors you heard. There is no need to say which students made the mistakes. Ask students to work in pairs to correct the sentences.

Extra activity

Write a checklist of future forms on the board. Ask students to stand up and walk round the class. Say stop. Tell students to find a partner and imagine they have just met this person in the street. Tell them to have a conversation for one minute in which they try to include as many of the future forms on the board as they can. After one minute, say stop and ask students to walk round again. Say stop. Students meet a new partner and have another conversation.

Alternatively, ask volunteer pairs to come to the front to act out conversations in front of the class. Each individual in the pair has to compete against other pairs to use as many future forms as possible.

3b Just press 'print'

Lesson at a glance
- vocabulary: materials
- listening: 3D printing
- wordbuilding: compound nouns (noun + noun)
- grammar: future continuous and future perfect simple
- speaking: the future

Vocabulary materials

1

- **Optional step** If you think a lot of these words will be new to students, pre-teach them. Point to items in the classroom and ask: *What material is this made of?* You could drill the words for pronunciation: note that they all have stress on the first syllable.

- Refer students to the words in the box and the list of items (a–f). Ask them to choose two possible materials for each item. Let students compare their ideas in pairs.

- In feedback, elicit ideas and check students know what all the materials are.

> EXAMPLE ANSWERS
>
> a a chair: leather, metal, plastic, wood
> b a wall: brick, concrete (wood, glass, metal and plastic possible)
> c a shirt: cotton, nylon
> d a box: cardboard, plastic, wood (possibly glass)
> e a pair of shoes: leather (possibly rubber or plastic)
> f a screen: glass, metal, plastic (possibly wood depending on the type of screen, e.g. to separate areas in a room)

Listening 3D printing

2

- Ask students to work in pairs to discuss the questions. In feedback, ask students to share information they have with the class.

- **Optional step** If you feel your students may have little to say about 3D printing, write the following phrases from the audioscript on the board before they listen and ask them to say how they relate to the topic: *design, a range of materials, body parts, new houses.*

> EXAMPLE ANSWERS
>
> 1 3D printing is designing then printing objects in three dimensions. It can be used for making simple objects like cups as well as more complex things like body parts or homes.
> 2 Students' own answers

3 🎵 [26]

- Tell students they are going to listen to a radio programme about 3D printing. Ask them to read questions 1–7 carefully. Play the recording. Ask students to listen and make notes.

- Let students compare answers in pairs. Elicit answers in feedback.

ANSWERS

1 a machine that can make different kinds of three-dimensional objects
2 It prints like an ink-jet printer does and you also connect a 3D printer to a computer just like an ordinary printer.
3 A 3D printer uses a range of materials like plastic or metal or wood. Each layer comes out as a liquid or paste or as powder. They then set or are bonded together using heat or light.
4 You can make individual things cheaply. In the future, anyone with a 3D printer will be able to make what they want.
5 body parts
6 3D printers are still expensive and they don't mass-produce things, so the cost of each item you print is high.
7 A lot of people will have bought their own 3D printer and we'll be making parts for things at home that have broken or can't easily be replaced.

Audioscript [26]

Welcome to today's edition of three-minute science. This morning, we're going to take a closer look at 3D printing. It's a technology that's arrived and that most people have heard of. But not everyone understands it. So, here we go:

Firstly, what is a 3D printer?
Well, '3D printing' means three-dimensional printing. So, a 3D printer is a machine that can make different kinds of three-dimensional objects – coffee cups, sunglasses, replacement car parts – not just printing on paper. And it uses different materials, like plastic, metal, glass, concrete … even chocolate.

And why is it called a printer?
Because it makes things in thin slices, building them up layer by layer. Imagine an ordinary ink-jet printer which prints letters on a page. If you let the printer go over each letter again and again, soon you'd build a letter that comes up from the page in 3D.

Is that the only similarity to an ink-jet printer?
No, you also connect a 3D printer to a computer just like an ordinary printer. You create the design for an object on the computer and then you just press print.

How do the layers of printed objects stick together?
A 3D printer uses a range of materials like plastic or metal or wood. Each layer comes out as a liquid or paste or as powder. Some materials just naturally set; others are bonded together using heat or light.

And what are its advantages over traditional construction?
It means you can make individual things cheaply. You can already make standard products in a factory cheaply, but customized products are very expensive. In the future, anyone with a 3D printer will be able to make what they want. There's a Dutch architect who's printing a house next to a canal in Amsterdam. He thinks in the future his firm will be building a lot of houses this way, using designs that they create with the customer exactly as the customer wants them.

What's the most amazing thing 3D printers can print?
Perhaps the most interesting area is the printing of human body parts made of real cells and electronic components. Some, like new 3D-printed ears, already exist, but I expect twenty years from now scientists will be making all kinds of body parts.

And what are its disadvantages?
3D printers are still expensive and they don't mass-produce things, so the cost of each item you print is high. But in ten years' time the cost will have come down a lot.

So, lastly, where will 3D printing be fifteen years from now?
A lot of people will have bought their own 3D printer and we'll be making parts for things at home that have broken or can't easily be replaced: a light switch, your favourite bottle opener or an old phone charger. And a bit like with any technology, like computers or smartphones, in time we will all have forgotten what life was like before 3D printers existed.

4 [26]

- Ask students to make a list from memory of objects mentioned by the speaker.
- Play the recording again. Students listen and check.

ANSWERS

coffee cups; sunglasses; replacement car parts; a house next to a canal in Amsterdam; human body parts made of real cells and electronic components; new 3D-printed ears, all kinds of body parts; parts for things at home that have broken or can't easily be replaced: a light switch, your favourite bottle opener, an old phone charger

Extra activity

Ask students to work in pairs to think of what they would most like to reproduce with a 3D printer and why. Ask different pairs to present their ideas to the class.

Wordbuilding compound nouns
5

- Read the information in the language box to the class. Elicit other compound nouns (noun + noun) students may know (e.g. *cell phone, shopping bag*).
- Ask students to match words from box A with words from box B to make compound nouns. Let students compare their answers before discussing as a class.

Refer students to Workbook page 27 for further information and practice.

ANSWERS

can opener, coat hook, coffee cup, cup holder, credit card, phone charger, printer cartridge, replacement key/charger

Vocabulary and pronunciation notes

Although the examples here are of two separate words, note that noun + noun compound nouns can also be one word (e.g. *lighthouse*).

Stress is usually on the first word in a compound noun.

6

- Ask students to form more compound nouns from the words in box B. Let students compare their answers before discussing as a class.

EXAMPLE ANSWERS

ID card, library card, phone card, ink cartridge, battery charger, fish hook, hotel key, room key, bottle opener

---

Extra activity

Ask students to research words in dictionaries to find compound nouns. Allocate specific words from box A to different groups or pairs, and ask each group to present findings in feedback.

Grammar future continuous and future perfect simple

7

- Read the information in the grammar box to the class. Ask students to tell you how the forms are made (*will + be +* present participle or *-ing* form; *will + have +* past participle).

- Ask students to choose the correct options to complete the sentences. Let them compare answers in pairs.

ANSWERS

1 an action in progress
2 before

Refer students to page 160 for further information and practice.

ANSWERS TO GRAMMAR SUMMARY EXERCISES

4
1 will have increased
2 will be using
3 will have started
4 will be producing
5 will have become
6 will be selling
7 will be using

5
1 won't be sitting; will have started
2 'll be teaching; won't have finished
3 won't be driving; will have stopped
4 'll be passing; won't have got
5 Will you be using; won't have fixed

6
1 will have started
2 won't have finished
3 'll be having lunch
4 won't be talking
5 will be working out
6 will have been

Grammar notes

The future continuous is used with an action in progress before, during and possibly after a future point in time:

~~~~~~~~

_____X_____
Past   Now   Future point in time

*His firm **will be building** a lot of houses this way.*

The future perfect is used with an action that happens after now, but before a stated future time:

X? X? X?

_____X_____
Past   Now   Future point in time

*In ten years' time the cost **will have come down** a lot.*

8

- Ask students to work individually to complete the sentences using the future continuous or the future perfect simple. In feedback, ask students to explain and justify their answers by referring to the rules in Exercise 7.

ANSWERS

1 will be making (happening around the time of 'twenty years from now')
2 will already have bought (happening after 'now', but before 'fifteen years from now')
3 'll be making (happening around the time of 'fifteen years from now')
4 'll all have forgotten (happening after 'now' but before 'fifteen years from now')

9

- Ask students to read the text quickly, without attempting to complete the gaps, and say what it is about.

- Ask students to read again and complete the text with the correct forms. Elicit the first answer to get students started. Note that answers will be checked as part of Exercise 10.

ANSWERS

1 will have learned/learnt
2 will be wearing
3 'll be eating
4 will have found
5 will have come
6 will be making
7 will be trying

10

- Let students check their answers to Exercise 9 in pairs.

- Ask students to discuss the predictions in pairs. You could ask them to think of negative as well as positive developments.

EXAMPLE ANSWERS

Students may feel 3D food printing, which would allow us to create new, healthier foods, is the most positive of those mentioned.

Other positives: people can be creative, people won't need to go to shops, you can replace things that are important to you, it is cheaper than buying things

Some negatives: bad for manufacturers and designers, people will illegally copy products, some will make things that are illegal and/or dangerous such as guns or drugs

Speaking _my life_

11

- Ask students to work individually to prepare questions from the prompts. Then ask students to work in new pairs to ask and answer the questions.

- As students speak, walk round and listen to how well your students use future forms. Note down some errors as you monitor. At the end, write several of the most common errors on the board and ask students to work in pairs to correct them.

EXAMPLE ANSWERS

1 How many more years do you think you will be studying English?

   I'll be studying for a few more years. / I'll be taking my exams this year, so I won't be studying after that. / I think I'll always be learning new words.

2 What things do you hope you will have achieved by the end of this year?

   I'll have passed my exams / got married / bought a house, etc.

3 What do you think you will be doing in five years' time?

   I'll be working for a multinational. / I'll be living on a beach. / With any luck I'll be earning lots of money.

4 Ten years from now, which of your friends or colleagues do you think will have enjoyed the most success in their careers?

   My friend Karen – she's very clever and ambitious. / I think Mark will have worked his way to the top of his company by then. / Sue will probably have made a fortune and will have already retired!

5 When do you think you will have earned / will be earning enough money to retire?

   I hope I'll have earned enough by the time I'm 50. / I don't think I'll ever have enough to retire! / Hopefully I'll be earning enough after my next promotion.

Extra activity

Ask students to write a blog entry about what they will be doing and what they will have achieved five years from now. This could be done for homework.

3c Appropriate technology

Lesson at a glance

- reading: technology
- critical thinking: supporting examples
- vocabulary: describing technology
- speaking: technological solutions

Reading

1

- Discuss the questions with the class. You could ask students to work in pairs first to share information. In feedback, elicit students' ideas.

EXAMPLE ANSWERS

smartphone – it's useful for keeping in touch with people, keeping informed about news, listening to music, providing travel directions, taking photographs, etc.

computer – it's useful for my work, for storing and finding information, for keeping in contact with friends and family, etc.

digital alarm clock – it gets me up in the morning

ebook reader – it's useful for reading on my way to work, it's a good way of taking lots of books on holiday

2 ⊚ [27]

- Organize the class into pairs and ask students to look at the devices and answer questions 1 and 2. Check answers with the class and ensure that students understand all the words (*purify* = to make something clean and pure with no bad things in it; *shelling corn* = taking the cover off corn).

- Ask students to read the article and answer the questions. Let them compare answers in pairs.

- **Optional step** The reading text is recorded. You could play the recording and ask students to read and listen.

ANSWERS

1 a sewing machine: India, where people are poor

   a solar-powered lamp: rural communities in developing or less industrialized countries / areas with no electricity

   a water purifier: rural communities in developing or less industrialized countries

   a central heating system: Sweden, a busy train station and a nearby office building

   a machine for shelling corn: Guatemala, poor women working in villages

2 They are all examples of 'appropriate technology', or at least they are initiatives that intended to be 'appropriate technology'.

3

- Ask students to read the article again and tick the correct ideas. Let them compare answers in pairs. In feedback, ask students to justify their answers by quoting from the article.

ANSWERS

a ✓ it does not cost a lot ('affordable', 'takes into account … cost considerations', 'expected to bring down central heating costs in the building by up to twenty per cent')

b ✓ it is easy for the user to understand ('suits the needs and abilities of the user', 'needs to fit in with people's customs and social practices')

c ✗ it is only used in developing countries (Sweden)

d ✗ it uses very simple ideas ('it did not matter whether the technological answers to people's needs were simple or sophisticated')

e ✓ it is good for the environment ('takes into account environmental … considerations')

f ✗ it is a new form of technology (sewing machine / bicycle 'It's old technology – a system of pipes, water and pumps')

g ✗ it does not upset people's way of life (Guatemalan village)

Background information

Mohandas Karamchand Gandhi /'gɑːndi/ (1869–1948) led the Indian independence movement in British-ruled India. He used nonviolent civil disobedience, or peaceful protest, to achieve his goal, and inspired movements for civil rights and freedom across the world. *Mahatma* is special title meaning 'high-souled'. He was a Hindu and lived a simple, modest life.

E. F. 'Fritz' Schumacher (1911–1977) was an influential economic thinker in Britain in the 1970s. His 1973 book, *Small Is Beautiful: a study of economics as if people mattered*, was among the 100 most influential books published in the second half of the twentieth century.

4

• Ask students to work individually to delete two words in each of the sentences to make them true. Elicit the first answer to get students started. Tell them to check their answers in pairs.

ANSWERS

1 rich and
2 and by
3 the station's
4 successful in

Critical thinking supporting examples
5

• Ask students to match the types of technology (1–4) with the examples (a–d) which support them. In feedback, ask students to justify their choice.

ANSWERS

1 b   2 c   3 a   4 d

6

• Discuss the questions with the class. You could ask students to work in pairs or small groups to discuss the questions before presenting their views to the class.

EXAMPLE ANSWERS

It could be argued that all the examples were effective for the following reasons:

1 b: It's cheap because it doesn't require the user to pay for electricity; it is eco-friendly because it uses the sun not carbon fuels.

2 c: It's in Sweden; it uses people's body heat (eco-friendly) and reduces costs by 20% (cheap).

3 a: It's faster than walking and can be used to go to work or from village to village.

4 d: The Guatemalan villagers preferred the manual labour as it was part of their daily lives and gave opportunities for social interaction.

Vocabulary describing technology
7

• Ask students to complete the sentences with adjectives from the box. Do the first one with the class as an example to get students started. Let students compare answers in pairs.

ANSWERS

1 appropriate
2 efficient
3 long-term
4 useful
5 old
6 easy
7 recycled
8 little

Vocabulary notes

1 *neat* = it looks/works well and simply; *appropriate* = it's correct for its purpose

2 *efficient* = it uses time, energy and/or money in the best way

3 *a quick fix* = a short-term solution that won't last long

4 *handy* = useful and practical (often used to describe small things that do a job)

5 *cutting edge* = new, modern, the latest thing

6 *labour-saving* = you don't have to work so hard or so long

7 *recycled* = used again

8 *economical* = here, it costs less to run than other cars

Extra activity 1

Ask students to think of examples of technology that could fit some of the phrases in bold in the sentences, e.g. a penknife is a *handy* gadget, the latest smartphone is *cutting edge*, a vacuum cleaner is a *labour-saving* device.

Extra activity 2

Ask students to describe a possession using some of the terms in this vocabulary section. Partners must guess what they are describing.

Speaking ⏤ my life

8

- Ask students to work in pairs to complete sentences 1–8 with the phrases in the box. Tell students to compare their answers. Once the phrases are complete, ask students to take it in turns to use the phrases to describe something they own. Their partner guesses what the item is from the description.

ANSWERS

Product 1:

1 It can hold up to 6 people.

2 It's made of strong nylon.

3 It can be put up in a few minutes.

4 It weighs only 2 kilos.

This product could be a tent, a trampoline or even a hammock of some kind.

Product 2:

5 It runs on solar power.

6 It lasts up to 6 hours.

7 It costs only £1.90.

8 It provides light and a little heat.

This product could be a light, a torch or a lamp.

9

- Read the instructions to the class. Organize the class into groups of four or five. Mix students so they have new partners to work with. Ask groups to read and follow the instruction on page 153 of their Student's Book.
- As students prepare, monitor and help with ideas and vocabulary if necessary.
- Ask students to take turns to present their products. Encourage other groups to ask questions in feedback. You could have a class vote on which was the most effective presentation.
- You could take the opportunity to give some general feedback on any errors you heard from students.

Extra activity

Ask students to work in groups to design a device which solves a particular problem students in their group may have. For example, if one student has trouble getting up in the morning, others could design a device to help him or her.

3d I can't get the TV to work

Lesson at a glance

- real life: dealing with problems
- pronunciation: stress in two-syllable words

Real life dealing with problems

1

- Discuss the questions with students. You could ask students to work in pairs to think of as many problems as they can in two minutes. Elicit problems in feedback from the pair who claim to have the longest list.

EXAMPLE ANSWERS

noise from other guests

no Internet connection or having to pay extra for the connection

not enough hot water

unpleasant smells

no room service

uncomfortable bed

dirty sheets

empty mini bar

rude staff

noisy fridge or air conditioning

problems with the room key

the wrong type of room or the room not being ready in time

2

- Ask students to match the sentence halves. Elicit the first match to get students started. Let students compare answers in pairs before discussing as a class.

ANSWERS

1 d   2 h   3 g   4 a   5 f   6 b   7 c   8 e

Vocabulary notes

flickering = when a light or screen is flickering, it goes on and off or the brightness of the light goes brighter and duller

adjust = to change something a little to make it better, or more accurate, or more effective

blocked = water can't go out of the basin, bath or shower because something is stopping it

---

3 💿 [28]

- Tell students they are going to listen to three conversations in a hotel between guests and a receptionist.
- Play the recording. Students listen and complete the table. Let students compare answers in pairs before checking answers as a class.

ANSWERS

Problem	Resolved? Yes / No / Partly
1 The window won't close and there's a lot of noise coming from the street.	Yes
2 The guest can't (seem to) connect to the internet.	Partly ('… you're welcome to come down here to the lobby where there's a stronger signal.')
3 The guest has locked her wallet and passport in the security box and now can't get it open again.	No

Audioscript 💿 [23]

R = hotel receptionist; G1 = first guest: G2 = second guest;
G3 = third guest

Conversation 1

R: Hello, madam. Is everything OK with your room?

G1: Actually, no, it isn't. The window won't close and there's a lot of noise coming from the street. I keep shutting it, but it just opens again.

R: Have you tried turning the handle at the side of the window to close it?

G1: Handle? No, I didn't know there was one.

R: Yes, if you look on the right-hand side near the bottom, there's a handle that opens and shuts the window.

G1: Oh, no, sorry, I didn't see that. I'll give that a try then. Thanks.

R: Not at all, madam. My pleasure.

Conversation 2

R: Yes, can I help you?

G2: Um, yes. I'm in room 768 on the seventh floor. I've got the wi-fi code, but I can't seem to connect to the internet.

R: Are you using the guest wi-fi?

G2: Yes.

R: Oh, I'm sorry. Sometimes the connection isn't so good up there. I'm afraid there's not much I can do about it … but you're welcome to come down here to the lobby where there's a stronger signal.

Conversation 3

G3: Excuse me, I need some help.

R: Of course. What can I do for you?

G3: Do you have any idea how I can get back into the security box in my room? I've locked my wallet and passport in there and now I can't get it open again.

R: Did you key in a code?

G3: Yes, I did. But now I can't remember the number I used. Is there some way you can open it?

R: I believe we have an override code, but I'll need to get the manager for that.

G3: Umm, could you possibly do that now? I'm going out for the evening.

R: OK. One moment, please … I'm afraid she's not answering, but I'll keep trying. When I speak to her, I'll ask her to call your room directly.

4 💿 [28]

- Ask students to work in pairs to read the expressions and discuss which were used in the recording. Then play the recording. Students listen and mark the phrases they hear according to who said them.

ANSWERS

Asking for help:

Do you have any idea how I can turn off the … **G3**

Can you tell me how to … ?

I don't know if it's just me, but …

Explaining problems:

I can't seem to open / turn on / connect (to) the … **G2**

I can't get the … to work / open / switch on. **G3**

The … won't close/open/work. **G1**

The … is broken/blocked/stuck/faulty.

There's no … in the room/bathroom.

There's a lot of noise / a bad smell coming from … **G1**

Responding to a problem:

Have you tried turning/putting/switching … ?

                          R (conversation 1)

I'll send someone to look at it.

I'm afraid there's not much I can do about it.

                          R (conversation 2)

OK. Thanks / I'll give that a try. **G1**

Pronunciation stress in two-syllable words

5a 💿 [29]

- Play the recording. Students listen and note on which syllable the stress falls in each word. Let them compare answers in pairs before checking with the class.

- Ask students if they can see a general pattern (see Pronunciation note below). Ask them to identify which words do not follow the rule.

- **Optional step** Play the recording again for students to listen and repeat.

ANSWERS

Verbs: the stress usually falls on the second syllable of a two-syllable verb. *Open* doesn't follow the rule.

Nouns: the stress usually falls on the first syllable of a two-syllable word. *Control* doesn't follow the rule.

Audioscript 🔵 [29]

Verbs

ad<u>just</u>   be<u>lieve</u>   con<u>nect</u>   for<u>get</u>   <u>open</u>
re<u>pair</u>   sug<u>gest</u>

Nouns

<u>basin</u>   <u>bathroom</u>   con<u>trol</u>   <u>cupboard</u>   <u>mirror</u>
<u>signal</u>   <u>window</u>

5b 🔵 [30]

- Organize the class into pairs. Ask students to work together to decide where the stress falls in each word.
- Play the recording. Students listen and check.

> **ANSWERS**
>
> Verbs: in<u>tend</u>, <u>man</u>age, pre<u>fer</u>, pro<u>vide</u>, re<u>place</u>, un<u>do</u>
> Nouns: <u>carpet</u>, <u>curtain</u>, <u>entrance</u>, <u>pleasure</u>, <u>shower</u>, <u>wall</u>et, <u>wardrobe</u>

Audioscript 🔵 [30]

<u>carpet</u>   <u>curtain</u>   <u>entrance</u>   in<u>tend</u>   <u>man</u>age
<u>pleasure</u>   pre<u>fer</u>   pro<u>vide</u>   re<u>place</u>   <u>shower</u>
un<u>do</u>   <u>wallet</u>   <u>wardrobe</u>

6

- Organize the class into new pairs. Ask students to read the task and choose one of the problems in Exercise 2. Then tell them to act out the problem. You could start by modelling the start of the activity with one student.
- **Optional step** Give pairs some preparation time before they improvise dialogues. You could ask them to think of the phrases they want to use in their conversation or you could ask them to script the conversation in note form.
- As students speak, listen for errors and prompt students to use expressions correctly.

> **Extra activity**
>
> Ask students to work in new pairs. Tell them to think of another problem of their own devising to explain. Encourage them to use a dictionary if necessary to prepare what to say.

3e Technical help

> **Lesson at a glance**
> - writing: short email requests
> - writing skill: being polite
> - word focus: *out of*

Writing short email requests

1

- **Optional step** As a lead-in, ask students to think for a moment of something they bought which was faulty or caused them a problem. Organize students into small groups to discuss the following questions (write them on the board): *What was the problem? What did you do about it? What happened in the end?*
- Ask students to match the emails (1–4) and replies (A–D), and put the correct name in each reply email. Discuss with the class how each person offers to help.

> **ANSWERS**
>
> A 4 Sophie – He/she suggests a place to take the bike which is very good and not too expensive.
> B 2 Kevin (Lyons) – She attaches some tips on how to make the printer run faster.
> C 3 Nathan – He suggests looking at the discussions boards on the Internet for the particular model of car.
> D 1 Kate (Winslow) – She suggests downloading a user manual and gives the link to do this.

Writing skill being polite

2a

- Explain to students that how polite you need to be depends on both your relationship to your correspondent, and what you are asking for. Ask the class: *In what situations do we need to be more polite?* (if you don't know the person, if the person is in a position of authority, in a formal business-like context, if you are asking for something which is demanding to do, or where the person you are asking is more likely to say no).
- Ask students to underline the phrases used to make polite requests in emails 1–4, and the polite forms used to apologize in emails A–D. Let students compare answers in pairs before checking with the class.

ANSWERS

Polite requests

<u>I wonder if you can</u> help me.

<u>Could you please tell me</u> where I can find one?

<u>Please can you advise me</u> how to go about this?

<u>do you know</u> what kind of oil is best to use with an old car?

<u>can you</u> drop me a line and let me know?

<u>Would you mind</u> popping over to have a look at my bike some time?

Apologies

<u>Sorry,</u> Sophie, <u>I'd normally say yes, but</u> I'm going on holiday tomorrow for three weeks.

<u>I am sorry,</u> <u>but</u> an exchange is not possible.

<u>My apologies again.</u>

<u>I'm afraid</u> I've no idea.

<u>I regret to say (that)</u> we …

2b

- Discuss the questions with the class. You could ask students to discuss the questions in pairs first before eliciting answers.

EXAMPLE ANSWERS

1

1 D customer and customer care operative or store/ company manager

2 B customer and customer care operative or store/ company manager

3 C two friends

4 A two friends, or perhaps a customer who is very friendly with local bike shop owner

2

1 D is quite small, so although the situation is formal, the writer does not use very formal language.

2 B is a bigger, more demanding request in a formal context.

3 C is small – hence the chatty language used.

4 A is quite big – Sophie is asking a real favour from Jim – that's why she uses the more polite *Would you mind*, even though she is generally using more informal language that friends use – *popping over*.

3

Phrases only used formally: *Could you please tell me …*; *Please can you advise me …* ; *My apologies again*; *I regret to say …*

Phrases only used informally: *do you know …* ; *can you drop me a line*; *Sorry, I'd normally say yes, but …*

Phrases that are polite and neutral: *I wonder if you can …* ; *Would you mind …*

Vocabulary notes

In order to be polite, as well as distant, impersonal or tentative, English uses the modal verbs *would* and *could* (*can* is used more informally), longer prefacing fixed expressions (*I wonder if*), and less common verbs and nouns (*I regret* or *My apologies* instead of *Sorry*).

Word focus *out of*
3a

- Ask students to find and underline expressions with *out of* in the emails.

- Ask students to work in pairs to discuss what the phrases mean. Put each pair with another pair to discuss and confirm their ideas.

ANSWERS

a shop … which has since gone out of business = a shop that has closed and is no longer trading

Just out of interest … = it's not important, but I am interested in knowing

Please don't go out of your way though. = a friendly way to say don't do anything extra or make a lot of effort to do this

3b

- Ask students to work individually to complete the expressions using the words in the box. Let them compare their answers in pairs.

ANSWERS

1 practice

2 order

3 date

4 time

5 luck

Vocabulary notes

out of practice = I haven't done this for a long time

out of order = (this machine) isn't working

out of date = it's old and no longer relevant or useable

out of time = we have taken too long and there is no more time (see: *run out of time*)

out of luck = unlucky (often used to say that you can't do or get something which, in other circumstances, you could)

Extra activity 1

Ask students to write sentences that are true for them, using the expressions. This could be done for homework.

Extra activity 2

Extend the work on *out of* with a dictionary task. Ask students to find more expressions that contain *out of*. For example, *run out of petrol/ink/food/energy* (= to use all of something and not have any left), *out of your depth* (= it's too hard), *out of the question* (= it really cannot be allowed/done).

4

- Read the situation to the class and ask students how formal their email should be (answer: fairly formal and business-like as it is a formal situation and quite a big request – the 1 D email exchange from page 41 is the best model for this).

- You could tell students to establish the name of the person or company they are writing to, or they could choose *Dear Sir or Madam.*
- Ask students to write their email individually.

5

- Tell students to exchange emails with a partner and to use the questions to comment on the email.
- Tell students to write replies and 'send' them to their partners. In feedback, ask students whether they are happy with their replies or not, and why.

> **EXAMPLE ANSWERS**
>
> **Email request:**
>
> Dear Sir or Madam,
>
> I wonder if you can help me. I bought two ink cartridges for my printer online, but when they arrived I noticed that the best-before date on them had already passed. Could you please send replacements for these cartridges?
>
> Tom Smith
>
> **Email reply:**
>
> Dear Mr Smith
>
> I am sorry that we sent you cartridges which are out of date. We will send new ones in the post immediately. Our apologies again.
>
> Kind regards
>
> Sophie Wilson
>
> Manager

Extra activity

Brainstorm true situations students have faced in which they have had a problem with a purchase (refer back to the lead-in if you did it). Ask students to write an email exchange (in class or for homework) about one real situation they faced.

3f   3D-printed prosthetic limbs

Before you watch

1

- Ask students to discuss the question in pairs. In feedback, elicit ideas from students.

> **EXAMPLE ANSWERS**
>
> Five-year-old children typically enjoy: playing games, playing with toys, drawing pictures, watching animated cartoons and films, listening to stories, playing running/jumping/skipping games, talking to friends, craft activities, etc.

2

- Ask students to look at the photo and the caption. Tell them to discuss the questions with a partner. Do not check answers at this stage as they will find out more when they watch the video.

While you watch

3 ◼◀ [3.1]

- **Optional step** The video deals with a sensitive subject: children with disabilities. You could introduce it by having a discussion on what type of challenges people with different disabilities might face generally in life.
- Ask students to watch the whole video and answer the questions. Let students compare answers in pairs before discussing as a class.

> **EXAMPLE ANSWERS**
>
> 1 brave, independent, resourceful
> 2 They are cheap, easy to make and can affordably be changed every year.

Videoscript ◼◀ 3.1

Part 1

0.00–0.17   For a girl with no hands, her dexterity is remarkable – her drawing skills on a par with other kids her age. Charlotte lost both hands and both legs to meningococcal septicaemia. But hers is not the sad story you might expect.

0.18–0.44 Mother   I think some people are surprised when they see her, like, how mobile she is, and how she can write and draw and … you know, her sort of, the fine motor skills she's still got, even without her hands. You know, even though, like I said she's so independent and so able, she does need help with things.

Charlotte   I do not.

Interviewer   You don't need help?

0.45–0.49 Charlotte   Definitely not. This one is my old leg.

0.50–0.59 Interviewer   Charlotte shows me the false limbs she's had so far. Prosthetic legs – basic, yet do the job, but for hands it's not so simple.

1.00–1.03   'Does it go on this arm or this arm?' 'That one.' 'That arm. And then this goes round the back.'

1.04–1.12   This crude hook will be little use as she grows up and has to fend for herself. Though anything more sophisticated costs the earth.

1.13–1.20 Mother   An adult bionic hand was £40,000 for one hand.

1.21–1.27 Interviewer   And at the rate children grow, she'd need a new, bigger one every year.

Part 2

1.28–1.35   But this could be the answer. And at a target price of £1,200, it's within range of normal families.

1.36–1.42 Joel Gibbard   If I flex my muscles, the hand in response will open and close all of the fingers.

1.43–1.58 Interviewer   First a 3D scan is made using a tablet computer. Then a 3D printer constructs it bit by bit. For the first time these techniques are being combined to custom-build a robotic hand.

1.59–2.20 Joel Gibbard   At the moment, children are a bit under-served by the prosthetics industry, in the realms of robotic hands, so this project can really help them, because as a child grows, they need to have a new prosthetic every year or so, ideally, and that's where the cost component really, really helps out.

2.21–2.35 Interviewer   It's still at the prototype stage, but this new advance means that for Charlotte, a working hand is not far off in the future. The wait now, not decades or years, but maybe only months. Nick Ravenscroft, Sky News.

4 ■◀ [3.1]

- Ask students to answer any questions they can remember.
- When students are ready, play the first part of the video again (0.00–1.27). Let students compare their answers in pairs before discussing as a class.

ANSWERS
1 She is mobile and has fine motor skills – writing and drawing.
2 She doesn't need any – definitely not.
3 The legs are basic, but do the job. The hands are crude and of little use as she grows up.
4 The image suggests she operates it by stretching the limb to make the two parts of the hook grip.
5 £40,000
6 every year, because she is growing

5 ■◀ [3.1]

- Tell students to read sentences 1–5 carefully before they watch part of the video again. Play the second part of the video (1.28 to the end). Ask students to choose the correct option. Let students compare their answers in pairs before discussing as a class.

ANSWERS
1 £1,200; normal   4 prosthetics
2 muscles   5 working
3 tablet computer; bit by bit

After you watch
Vocabulary in context
6a ■◀ [3.2]

- **Optional step** You may wish to ask students to look at the words in the glossary on the page and check that they understand the words.
- Explain that students are going to watch some clips from the video which contain some new words and phrases. They need to choose the correct meaning of the words.
- Play the clips. When each multiple-choice question appears, pause the clip so that students can choose the correct definition. You could let students compare answers in pairs before discussing as a class.

ANSWERS
1 c   2 a   3 b   4 c   5 b   6 a

Videoscript ■◀ 3.2

1 ... her drawing skills **on a par** with other kids her age.
  a better than
  b worse than
  c at the same level as
2 ... as she grows up and has to **fend for herself**.
  a manage on her own
  b defend herself
  c find a job for herself
3 Though anything more sophisticated **costs the earth**.
  a is bad for the environment
  b is very expensive
  c is very complicated to make
4 And at a target price of £1,200, it's **within range** of normal families.
  a expensive for
  b cheap for
  c affordable for
5 If I **flex** my muscles ...
  a relax
  b bend
  c exercise
6 ... these techniques are being combined to **custom-build** a robotic hand.
  a make something for a particular individual
  b make something at home
  c make something in a factory

6b

- Students work individually to complete the sentences. Elicit one or two ideas for the first sentence to get them started. Let students compare sentences in pairs.

EXAMPLE ANSWERS

1 I'd say that my *language* skills are on a par with *my DIY skills*.

2 I recommend buying a *bike*. They don't cost the earth and they *are a way of getting around and keeping fit*.

3 It would be great if someone could custom-build a *walk-in wardrobe* for me. Then I could *use the odd-shaped corner in my bedroom for storing clothes*.

7

• Organize the class into new pairs. Ask students to work together to summarize the report. At the end, ask students to pass their summaries around the class for others to comment on.

EXAMPLE ANSWER

Charlotte's a young girl who had an illness that affected her limbs when she was younger. In spite of this, she is independent and mobile, and has fine motor skills. Currently, the prosthetic limbs she uses are basic and crude, but her family can't afford more sophisticated prosthetic limbs. Hopefully, in the future, a new 3D technique will allow children like Charlotte to have inexpensive but useful prosthetic limbs that they can change every year as they grow.

8

• Organize the class into small groups. Ask students to look at the photo and description of the device and discuss the questions. Elicit ideas in feedback.

EXAMPLE ANSWERS

1 Benefits: it's easy to use, it's quicker to speak instructions than to type, you could use it hands-free, it's a single device which can control a number of things

  Most useful for: children to research or to find the answer to a question; people who travel a lot to find directions while driving, traffic alerts or for other information while travelling; elderly people to set reminders, or carers could set up reminders for them, automatically switch on/off heating, lights, etc.; (There are many possible answers.)

2 Other things the device could be used for in the home: to do research or to find the answer to a question; to give traffic alerts or for other information before setting out on a journey (e.g. business addresses, restaurants); give reminders for appointments, to pay bills or check smoke alarms; it could be linked to an intelligent burglar alarm system; it could play music in different rooms; control pet access into / out of the house or certain rooms and automatically feed pets, etc.

3 Disadvantages: How do you set it up to do all these things around the home (could be complicated/complex)? Do you need other expensive equipment to go with it – like an intelligent fridge or special lights and door locks? Could it be confusing for people to use? What if it breaks / runs out of power? There could be safety/security issues if it gets lost or stolen, or if someone hacks into it. Over-reliance on a gadget? Could argue it could affect literacy skills (people don't need to read or write). You could disturb other people in the house by constantly having to speak out loud the instructions.

Extra activity

Ask students to think of benefits, uses and disadvantages of the following devices: bluetooth headphones, night vision glasses, virtual reality headsets.

9

• Organize the class into new pairs. Ask students to compare ideas and discuss the questions.

• Monitor and help with ideas and vocabulary.

• Ask pairs to report back to the class on the ideas they discussed. You could conclude by discussing as a class which one feature would be the most useful.

UNIT 3 Review and memory booster

Memory Booster activities

Exercises 3, 5, 6 and 7 are Memory Booster activities. For more information about these activities and how they benefit students, see page 10 of this Teacher's Book.

I can ... check boxes

As an alternative to asking students to simply tick the *I can* ... boxes, you could ask them to give themselves a score from 1 to 4 (1 = not very confident; 4 = very confident) for each language area. If students score 1 or 2 for a language area, refer them to additional practice activities in the Workbook and Grammar summary exercises.

Grammar

1

- Ask students to work individually to choose the most appropriate verb forms to complete the article. Let students compare answers in pairs before eliciting answers from the class.

> ANSWERS
>
> 1 will face   6 might never happen
> 2 will have risen   7 is going to
> 3 'll tell   8 is about to boom
> 4 're having   9 will be celebrating
> 5 will be   10 will have solved

2

- Ask students to read the article again and discuss the question.

> ANSWER
>
> The author thinks that, if successful, a super battery would solve the problem of global warming. The energy from wind and solar power doesn't emit CO_2, but we have no control over when the energy is available. A super battery would store this energy and make it available to us at any time, meaning we could rely on environmentally safe energy.

3 >> MB

- Ask students to answer the questions about the future forms that are used in the text. Then tell them to write two similar questions to ask their partner.

> ANSWERS
>
> 1 *will be celebrating*
> 2 *I'll tell*
>
> Example questions:
> Can you find a future form that ...
> predicts something based on some evidence? (*is going to produce*)
> predicts something happening very soon? (*is about to boom*)
> is a prediction based on personal opinion? (*might never happen*)
> describes an arrangement? (*we're having a cold meal tonight*)
> describes an action completed before a certain time in the future? (*by the end of the century ... will have risen*)

Vocabulary

4

- Ask students to complete the missing words. Let students compare answers in pairs before checking with the class.

> ANSWERS
>
> 1 cutting; date; lasts
> 2 runs; economical; interest
> 3 labour
> 4 handy; weighs
> 5 neat; hold

5 >> MB

- Ask students to work individually to match the objects to the materials. They must rewrite each object next to the material each one is made of. Let students compare answers in pairs before checking with the class.

> ANSWERS
>
> 1 a cotton sheet   5 a brick (or concrete) wall
> 2 a leather wallet   6 rubber (or leather) boots
> 3 a concrete floor   7 a plastic (or glass) bottle
> 4 a glass window   8 a cardboard box

Real life

6 >> MB

- Ask students to work individually to put the words in the correct order for each sentence. Students then decide in which sentences the person has a problem (P).

> ANSWERS
>
> 1 I can't get the shower to work. (P)
> 2 Have you tried turning the thermostat up?
> 3 I can't seem to connect to the internet. (P)
> 4 Do you have any idea how I can turn off the heating? (P)
> 5 I'll give that a try, thanks. (P)
> 6 I don't know if it's just me, but the TV won't work. (P)
> 7 I'm afraid there's not much I can do about it.
> 8 There's a bad smell coming from the bathroom. (P)

7 >> MB

- Ask students to work in pairs to look at the problems in Exercise 6 and act out the conversations. You could then ask students to change partners and repeat the activity.

Unit 4 Art and creativity

Opener

1

- Ask students to look at the photo and the caption. Discuss the questions with your class. Elicit ideas from the students in feedback.

> ANSWERS
>
> Students' own ideas

2

- Organize the class into pairs to categorize the words and phrases. Start by eliciting a further example for each of the three categories. Monitor and support students as they do the task.

- Then ask students to write at least four sentences describing who does what and where. Alternatively, you could ask them to make the sentences verbally in their pairs.

- In feedback, elicit answers and check the meaning and pronunciation of any words students aren't sure of. Ask students to share some of the example sentences they thought of that use combinations of the words.

> ANSWERS
>
> Who: an actor, an artist, a band, a busker, a circus performer, a comedian, a dancer, an orchestra
>
> What: a classical concert, an exhibition, a gig, a musical, a performance, a play, a show
>
> Where: a concert hall, a gallery, a live music venue, a (night)club, the street, a theatre
>
> Example sentences:
>
> A busker puts on a show in the street.
>
> An artist has an exhibition in a gallery.
>
> A band plays a gig in a live music venue.
>
> An orchestra performs a classical concert in a concert hall.
>
> A comedian puts on a show in a theatre or a club.

Vocabulary notes

A *busker* is a street performer (especially a musician) who performs in the street for money from passers-by.

Performance and *show* are general words used to describe an event in which somebody performs (music, singing, dance, juggling). A *play* is only used for acting in the theatre.

The word *concert* is used to describe a classical music performance or a 'big' show by a singer or band. When a band plays a smaller venue, the performance is called a *gig*.

Venue is a general word for any place where a performance is held.

3 🎵 [31]

- Tell students they are going to listen to a conversation about two people who are creative in their free time. Play the recording. Students listen and note answers to the questions. Let students compare their answers in pairs before checking with the class.

- **Optional step** In feedback, find out what else students heard about each of the two people being described. For example: *1 She's shy, she was brought up in a circus, she does it for fun, not for money; 2 He's into football, writes on the train, and keeps his poems private, one of his poems is about his son.*

> ANSWERS
>
> 1 1 teacher   2 accountant
>
> 2 1 street performer/acrobat   2 writes poetry

Audioscript 🎵 [31]

A: People are full of surprises, aren't they? There's a teacher that I work with who's really quite a shy person, you know, never really stands out in a group. I worked with her for about two years and then I found out that on certain weekends she becomes a street performer.

B: What kind of street performer?

A: Well, she turns out to be some kind of acrobat. She was brought up in a circus and at weekends she still meets up with friends and puts on shows of circus skills in public places, like a busy shopping street on a Saturday afternoon. She doesn't do it for money – at least I don't think so – just for fun. The thing is it's just not at all what you imagine when you meet her, because she doesn't seem that outgoing …

B: That's interesting – reminds me a bit of my neighbour. He's an accountant and is really into football – in fact he watches a lot of sport, I think. But he also writes poetry. He does it on the train when he's commuting to work – 'cos it takes about an hour each way to and from work. I don't think many people have read it, because he's rather private, but he showed me a poem the other day. He'd written it when his little boy was sick – it was very touching, actually, and beautifully written.

Vocabulary notes

acrobat = a circus performer who does gymnastics

commuting = travelling to work and back home every day, e.g. by train, bus, etc.

touching = something that makes you feel emotional or sympathetic

4

- Organize the class into new pairs to discuss the questions. In feedback, ask anyone with an interesting personal story if they would like to share it with the class.

Extra activity

Ask students in their pairs to share 'first experiences'. Start by giving an example yourself – talk about the first time you went to a concert, gig or play, or about the first time you performed in a school play or on stage. Ask students to think of a 'first experience' of their own to share with their partner.

4a Reverse graffiti

Lesson at a glance

- reading: unusual street art
- vocabulary: art
- grammar: determiners
- speaking: art and music

Reading

1

- Start by asking students to explain what *graffiti* is (= a form of street art which ranges from illegally writing words on walls to painting enormous pictures on the sides of buildings, bridges or trains).

- Discuss the questions in Exercise 1 with the class. You could ask them to work in pairs or small groups first before eliciting ideas from them in feedback.

ANSWERS

Students' own answers

2 💿 [32]

- Ask students to predict what they can from the photo and the title (see Teacher development below). Elicit as many ideas as you can, but don't reveal the true answer.

- Ask students to read the article and check their ideas.

- **Optional step** The reading text is recorded. You could play the recording and ask students to read and listen.

ANSWERS

Reverse graffiti artists take a dirty wall and make images by removing the dirt. They aim to draw attention to the pollution in our cities.
Possible predictions:
Drawing designs or writing slogans that are the wrong way round.
Graffiti that is legal and paid for by the state.
Cleaning up graffiti from the walls.

Teacher development

Predicting

The more students speculate and predict about the content of a text, the better prepared they are to read, and the more interested they are to find out answers. Here are some ways of getting students to predict before reading or listening to a text:

1 Ask students to guess what a text is about from what is on the page – the title, a photo or diagram, the layout of the text, or a quote from the text that has been emphasized in larger letters.

2 Ask students to predict content from key words. Choose five or six key words or phrases from the text and write them on the board. Use the opportunity to check the meaning of the words (it's a good idea to include any words or phrases in the text that may be new to students). Ask students to say what the text is about based on possible relationships between the key words.

3 Ask students to predict content from topic sentences. Ask students to read the first sentence of the text, or the first sentence of each paragraph in the text. Ask them to predict the content from using only what these specific sentences say.

4 Ask students to predict from prior knowledge. If your students have some knowledge of the topic in the text, ask them to make guesses about the information they are likely to find in the text, or the points of view that may be expressed.

5 Ask students to predict language rather than content. Once students know what the topic of a text is, they should be able to predict what words, phrases or tenses might appear in the text.

3

- **Optional step** Ask students to read through the sentences and predict what the missing words might be, or what part of speech they might be (Countable or uncountable nouns? Singular or plural nouns?), before they read the article again.

- Ask students to read the article again and use the information in the article to complete the sentences. Point out that they only need one word for each space. Let students compare answers in pairs before checking with the class.

ANSWERS

1 permission   2 dirt   3 pollution   4 crime   5 tunnel

Background information

São Paulo (pronounced /ˌsaʊ ˈpaʊloʊ/ by English speakers) is Brazil's largest and most populous city. It is located in the southeast of the country.

4

- Ask students to work in pairs to retell the story from the two different points of view.

- **Optional step** Give students a few minutes of individual preparation for this task. Tell each pair to decide who is A and who B. Then ask individuals to think of what to say. Include question prompts to help students. For example: (If you are Alexandre) *Why are you a graffiti artist? How do you feel about pollution in cities? What do you want to achieve?* (If you are the city authority) *What did you do about reverse graffiti? Why did you do it? What kind of a city would you like? What would you say to Alexandre Orion?* Ask students to retell the stories once they have prepared.

Extra activity

Ask students to find words or phrases connected with graffiti and art in the text. In feedback, explain the words or get students to explain them: *a blank wall* (= a wall with nothing on it), *spray-paint* (= to paint something using paint that comes in aerosol cans), *images, artist, mural* (= a large painting on a wall), *an artwork*.

Vocabulary art

5

- **Optional step** With books closed, write *Art* on the board. Ask students to think of as many words or compound words they can think of using the word *art*.

- Ask students to work in pairs to complete the sentences using the words and phrases in the box. Let students compare their answers in pairs before checking answers as a class.

- Read out the information in the wordbuilding box.

Refer students to Workbook page 35 for further information and practice.

ANSWERS

1 art exhibition; art gallery; artists
2 street art; street art/artwork
3 Fine art; the arts
4 arty; artistic

Vocabulary and pronunciation notes

Other words connected with art: *art form* (= activity that creates art); *modern art, primitive arts graphic art*

arty = this word can be negative as well as positive – it can mean very interested in art, or it can mean pretending to know a lot about art and being superior

Note the word stress: *ar̲tists, artis̲tic*

Extra activity

Organize the class into pairs or small groups. Write the following words on the board: *music, sport, drama, fiction*. Tell each pair or group to choose a word. Then give them three minutes to think of as many words related to their chosen word as possible (or three minutes to find as many words as they can in a dictionary). In feedback, find out which team got the most answers, and which head word produced the most related words.

Here are example answers for *music*:

Music: *musician, musical, music hall, musical instrument, a piece of music, pop music, classical music, music stand, sheet music*

Grammar determiners

6

- Ask students to read the information and examples in the grammar box and underline the examples of determiners in the article. Go through the answers with the class in feedback (see Grammar notes below).

ANSWERS

Some graffiti artists use pictures, *some* use words, *some* both.

no permission to paint
most city authorities
certain places, such as
Each artist has their own style
all (artists) share a common aim
many car tunnels
Every motorist sits in the comfort of their car
any consideration to the cost
Both options seemed unsatisfactory
any graffiti was wrong
all parts of the tunnel
both sides of the tunnel
the whole tunnel
every other car tunnel in São Paulo

Singular countable nouns are used with the following determiners: *each, every, either, the whole*.

Plural or uncountable nouns are used with the following determiners: *some, most, all*.

Plural (but not uncountable nouns) are used with the following determiners: *certain, both*.

All types of nouns can be used with the following determiners: *no, any*.

Many is used with plural nouns and *much* is used with uncountable nouns.

Refer students to page 162 for further information and practice.

ANSWERS TO GRAMMAR SUMMARY EXERCISES

1

1 All the	5 Some
2 either	6 any
3 certain	7 no
4 Most	8 Neither

2

1 each	4 any
2 all	5 every
3 an	6 most of

3

1 any	5 both
2 The majority	6 Each
3 The whole	7 Either
4 certain	

Grammar notes

Each and *every* are both determiners used with singular nouns to indicate quantity. *Each* indicates two or more objects or people and *every* indicates three or more. We tend to use *each* if we are thinking about members of a group individually, and *every* if we are thinking of them in total. So, compare *Each artist has their own style* (individually) and *Every artist has their own style* (all in the group).

most = a majority of

the whole = all of one thing

certain = not all, just some specific ones

We use *both*, *either* and *neither* to refer to two people or things: *both* = that one and the other one / this one and that one; *neither* = not one and not the other; *either* = any one of the two / this one or the other one.

7

- Ask students to rewrite the sentences using the word in brackets. Let them compare their answers in pairs before checking with the class.

ANSWERS

1 Each motorist sits in the comfort of their car.
2 Neither option seemed satisfactory.
3 Orion had committed no crime(s).
4 They decided that all graffiti was wrong.
5 They chose to clean the whole tunnel.
6 In certain places, like some old industrial buildings, they tend to leave it.

8

- Ask students to work individually to choose the correct determiners to complete the text. Let students compare answers in pairs before eliciting answers from the class.
- This is an opportunity to get students to think about the subtle differences in use here, so be prepared to talk through and explain any confusion (see Grammar notes below).

ANSWERS

1 certain	5 no
2 both	6 all the
3 all	7 Most
4 any	

Grammar notes

Note the following:

1 *any* is not normally used in affirmative sentences
2 *either* is used with singular nouns
3 *each* is used with singular nouns
4 *some* is not used with singular nouns
5 you need to use *not* with *any* to make it negative
6 *the whole* is used with a singular noun
7 *every* is used with singular nouns

9 🔘 [33]

- Ask students to work in pairs to discuss which determiners could go in each space. Point out that there may be more than one possible answer.
- Tell students they are going to listen to an interview with an artist. Ask them to complete the statements as they listen. Play the recording. Let students compare answers in pairs before feedback.

ANSWERS

1 All (*Any* also possible)
2 some (*no* also possible)
3 certain (*some* also possible)
4 either
5 any
6 no

Audioscript 🔘 [33]

I = Interviewer; **W** = Will

I: OK, Will, I know as an artist yourself, you have strong feelings about what art is and isn't. So, I'm going to give you some statements about what various people say art should be and I want to know which you agree with. OK?

W: Err, OK.

I: So, here's the first one then, 'All art should contain something pleasing for the viewer.'

W: No, not necessarily – the artist's intention might be to make you feel uncomfortable, not to give you a warm feeling.

I: OK. What about this? 'Art should involve some hard work on the part of the artist.'

W: That's more interesting, but the answer's still 'not necessarily' – Monet did some paintings in five minutes.

I: Well, then that links to the next one, perhaps. 'To be an artist, you need to possess certain technical skills.'

W: Well, you often hear people say things like 'My three-year-old daughter could have done that,' meaning there's no technical skill involved. But an artwork doesn't have to be technically difficult; it could just be a clever idea.

I: OK. 'Art should make a social or a political point; without either message it's not true art.'

W: No, certainly not. Is the Mona Lisa political? I don't think so.

I: What about this one? 'The viewer shouldn't have to make any effort to understand a work of art.'

W: No, I disagree with that. The artist has made an effort to produce something, so the viewer should make an effort to understand it.

I: OK and lastly, 'There's no such thing as bad art.'

W: Yes, I agree. My role is to present an idea in a visual form. Your role is to give yourself time to look at it. Then you can say either, 'Yes, I really like that,' or 'No, that doesn't do anything for me.' But you can't say, 'that's not art,' or 'it's bad art'.

10

- Ask students to work in groups of four or five to discuss the statements in Exercise 9.

Speaking ⟨my life⟩

11

- Ask students to work individually to complete the sentences in their own words. Then organize students into pairs to discuss the sentences.

- Ask students to work with at least one new partner to discuss their sentences again. This will ensure that they get lots of practice at using language from the lesson.

- In feedback, ask students what they found out about classmates, and which students had similar ideas to them.

- **Optional step** As students speak, monitor and note down errors you hear. Concentrate on errors with the use of determiners. At the end of the activity, write up five or six short sentences containing some of the errors you heard. Ask students to work in pairs to correct the errors.

> EXAMPLE ANSWERS
>
> 1 I like certain *artists / styles of music*.
> 2 Some *modern art / classical music* is really difficult to understand.
> 3 I don't have any *favourite painters / artists / styles of art*.
> 4 Both *my parents/brothers* are musicians.
> 5 All *art galleries* should have free entrance.
> 6 At my school, we had no *art/music lessons*.
> 7 Some people say that all *pop music* is the same, but I think that each *country/artist has its own style of music*.

4b All about Melbourne

> **Lesson at a glance**
> - listening: what's on in Melbourne
> - grammar: expressions of quantity
> - pronunciation: weak form *of*
> - speaking: participation in the arts

Listening

1

- Ask students to work in pairs to ask and answer the questions. Alternatively, you could choose to just discuss one of these questions with the whole class as a lead-in.

- In feedback, ask students to share the information they discussed.

- **Optional step** If you feel your students may have little to say about Australia, write the following on the board and ask students to think of one or two examples of each (possible answers in brackets): *historical sites* (Sydney Harbour Bridge and Sydney Opera House, Port Arthur), *wildlife* (kangaroos, koalas, crocodiles), *natural wonders* (Uluru, rainforest, coral reefs, Kakadu national park, Bondi beach), *sports* (cricket, rugby, Formula 1 car racing), *cultural activities* (Australian bands, Australian films, opera).

> EXAMPLE ANSWERS
>
> 1/2 Students' own answers
> 3 Stereotypical possibilities would include going to a sports event (cricket, rugby, Aussie rules football), having a barbecue, watching an episode of the television programme *Neighbours*.

2 🎵 [34]

- Tell students they are going to listen to a radio programme about Melbourne. Ask them to read questions 1–3 carefully. Play the recording. Tell students to listen and make notes.

- Elicit answers in feedback.

> ANSWERS
>
> 1 Sydney is more naturally beautiful / has more natural attractions; Melbourne has more man-made attractions.
> 2 theatre, music, street culture, fashion, cafés, restaurants, pubs, museums, galleries
> 3 sports

Audioscript 🎵 [34]

A visitor to Australia once noted that 'Nature has done everything for Sydney, man nothing; man has done everything for Melbourne, nature nothing. This sums up the essential difference between Australia's two largest cities. Melbourne is Australia's second city, but it has plenty of first-class qualities, from a buzzing arts scene to its enormous range of restaurants. It may have a few grey days, and a muddy river instead of a beautiful harbour, but don't let that worry you. A lack of natural attractions has meant that Melbourne has had to create its own man-made pleasures … and in doing so it has become Australia's cultural capital. Theatre, music, street sculpture, fashion all thrive – in fact, there are hardly any forms of artistic expression which you can't find here – alongside a cosmopolitan mix of cafés, restaurants and pubs.

What's great about Melbourne for the visitor is how accessible all these arts are. As well as traditional museums and galleries like the National Gallery of Victoria and concert halls, like Hamer Hall, there are an enormous number of smaller art spaces and venues which cater for every kind of taste. Art is something which the majority of locals enjoy. In fact, for most inhabitants of Melbourne a visit to the cinema or an art exhibition is a routine event. Several festivals take place during the winter months including the International Film Festival in July and the Fringe Festival in September, which has loads of interesting comedy, dance and theatre acts.

If the locals appreciate their art, they absolutely love their sport. Lots of people around the world know the Australian Formula 1 Grand Prix and the Australian Open Tennis, which attracts over half a million spectators to Melbourne in a carnival atmosphere, but few people will be familiar with the sports Melburnians themselves follow. Cricket and Australian Rules football enjoy a huge amount of support and, if you have a little time to spare, a visit to see either is well worth it just for the atmosphere. If you're looking to participate rather than just watch, why not try a bit of surfing or swimming? Cycling, jogging or a visit to one of Melbourne's many gyms are other possibilities. All this information is on our website at thetravelshow.org, so do have a look if …

3 🎧 [34]
- Ask students to read sentences 1–6 carefully.
- Play the recording again. Students listen and work individually to choose whether the sentences are true (T) or false (F). Ask students to correct false sentences before comparing answers in pairs.

ANSWERS

1 F (Melbourne's weather is not always sunny and it doesn't have many places of natural beauty: *man has done everything for Melbourne, nature nothing*; *A lack of natural attractions has meant that Melbourne … ; It may have a few grey days*)

2 F (Melbourne isn't known as the architectural capital of Australia, it's known as the cultural capital: *it has become Australia's cultural capital*)

3 F (The arts are enjoyed by many local people: *Art is something which the majority of locals enjoy.*)

4 F (Festivals take place in Melbourne in the winter months: *Several festivals take place during the winter months …*)

5 T (*Lots of people around the world know the Australian Formula 1 Grand Prix and the Australian Open Tennis …*)

6 T (*few people will be familiar with the sports Melburnians themselves follow …*)

4
- Discuss the questions with your class. You could ask students to discuss the questions in pairs first. To conclude, ask different pairs to say what they would like to do there.

Extra activity 1

Ask students to do this task in pairs or small groups: *Compare your city or a city you know well to Melbourne. In what ways is it more or less attractive to visitors than Melbourne?*

Extra activity 2

If you have internet access in class, ask students to imagine they are in Melbourne today. Tell them to work in pairs and go online and find an event or place which they would like to go to in Melbourne today. For example, it could be a cultural event, a historical place, or an interesting place to eat in the city. Students then report back to the class what they are planning to do and why.

Grammar expressions of quantity
5
- Read the information in the grammar box to the class.
- Ask students to look at Exercise 5 and match a–c with the words or expressions of quantity. Let students compare answers in pairs.

ANSWERS

a many, a large number of, a large/huge amount of, a lot of, lots of, plenty of, loads of

b not many, (a) few, a small number of, several, not much, (a) little, a bit of, a small amount of, almost no, hardly any, some, enough

c a lack of, no, not any, the majority of

Refer students to page 162 for further information and practice.

ANSWERS TO GRAMMAR SUMMARY EXERCISES

4
1 plenty of, loads of
2 much, a lot of
3 a lack of, almost no
4 any, a huge amount of
5 a small number of, a few
6 hardly any, almost no

5
1 hardly any
2 too much
3 loads of
4 several
5 a little
6 no / not any

6
1 a 2 b 3 b 4 a

UNIT 4 Art and creativity

Grammar notes

We generally use *a lot of* (or the less formal *lots of*) in affirmative sentences, but *much* and *many* in questions and negative sentences, and we use *much* with uncountable nouns and *many* with countable nouns. Compare: *I have a lot of money/friends; I don't have much money; I don't have many friends.*

Note, however, that this 'rule' (often taught to students) isn't always true in natural usage. *I don't a have a lot of time* and *We have many things to talk about* are, for example, perfectly acceptable sentences.

We use *(a) little* with uncountable nouns and *(a) few* with countable nouns. Compare: *I have a little money; I have a few friends.* If we omit 'a', then *little* and *few* make the sentence negative rather than positive. Compare: *I have a little money. Let's go out!* and *I have little money. I can't pay my bills.*

Compare the use of *any* and *enough*. Both are often used with *not*:

There aren't any attractions. (= There are no attractions.)

There aren't enough attractions. (= There are some attractions, but there are insufficient in number.)

6

- Ask students to look at audioscript 34 on page 183 of the Student's Book and find and underline the expressions. In feedback, you could ask students to build up a list on the board.
- **Optional step** Once students have the list, ask them to rewrite the sentences with different words. Let students compare answers in pairs.

ANSWERS

1 plenty of, an enormous number of, the majority, loads of, lots of, a huge amount of, many, enormous range of
2 a lack of, hardly any, few
3 a few, several, a little, a bit of

7

- Ask students to work individually to choose a word to replace the underlined words in the sentences.
- Let students compare answers in pairs before checking with the class.

ANSWERS

a a lot of / lots of / plenty of / an enormous number of / loads of
b lots of / loads of / a huge amount of
c don't ... a lot of / lots of / loads of / a huge amount of
d aren't ... lots of / an enormous number of / loads of
e a few / a (small) number of / several
f a little / any

8

- You could choose to discuss these questions and sentences as a class or ask students to talk in pairs first. If you choose to get students to talk in pairs, monitor discretely and note where students are confident and accurate or unsure and inaccurate.
- In feedback, spend time on the areas where students had problems. Refer students to the Grammar summary on page 162.

ANSWERS

1 In 1a, *a few* is positive – only a few. In the context, the speaker is downplaying Melbourne's reputation for being wet. In 1b, *few* is negative. In the context, it is an admission and a criticism.
2 There is no real difference between the sentences in meaning and grammar.
3 In 3a, it isn't natural to use *much*. We tend to only use *much* in questions and negative statements. In contrast, we often use *many* in affirmative sentences. In 3b, it would be natural to use *a lot of* in this negative sentence.

9

- Ask students to work individually to choose the correct options to complete the sentences. Let students compare answers in pairs before checking with the class.

ANSWERS

1 a lot of (affirmative sentence)
2 number (plural noun)
3 no (correct expression is *almost no*)
4 a few (being positive and optimistic – you can get a ticket)
5 some (uncountable noun)
6 Hardly (correct expression is *Hardly anyone*)
7 little (being negative – Australian Rules football is dull)
8 many (plural noun)

Pronunciation weak form *of*

10a [35]

- Play the recording. Students listen and note how *of* is pronounced.

ANSWERS

In these phrases, *of* is not stressed. Consequently, it is reduced to a weak, barely pronounced /əv/ sound. In some varieties of fast speech, it is reduced further to /ə/: *a lot of people* /əlɒtə'piːpəl/.

Audioscript [35]

1 a bit of relaxation time
2 a lot of information
3 a huge amount of support
4 lots of people
5 a huge number of galleries
6 a lack of natural attractions

10b

- Ask students to practise saying the phrases in pairs. Monitor and correct the weak pronunciation of *of*.

Extra activity

Ask students to make true personal sentences using a maximum of five of the phrases. Then ask them to practise saying the sentences.

Speaking — my life

11

- Organize students into new pairs. Ask students to read the information in the infographic and decide which expression of quantity to use to complete each sentence. Point out that there is more than one possible answer in some cases.

ANSWERS

1 lot; number   4 Many; hardly
2 Lots; few   5 little; amount, enough/any/many
3 lack

12

- Ask students to work in groups of four or five to prepare and carry out research. Start by asking each group to choose an area to research and to prepare questions. Point out that examples of visual arts and crafts include painting, drawing, pottery, sculpture, clothes making, metalwork and jewellery making.
- When groups are ready, ask all students to stand up and use their questions to walk round and talk to three or four people. As students speak, walk round and listen to how well your students use expressions of quantity. Note down some errors as you monitor.
- After five minutes, ask students to sit back down and share information with their group. Groups then prepare a presentation based on their findings.
- Ask one student in each group to stand up and present a summary of findings to the class. Again, note any errors with expressions of quantity.
- **Optional step** You could ask students in groups to prepare an infographic or chart to visually show the information they found during their survey. Ask them to use this in their presentation.
- At the end of the activity, write errors on the board and ask students to work in pairs to correct them.

EXAMPLE ANSWERS

Here are possible questions students might ask:
Do you belong to … ?
Do you ever/regularly go to … ?
How often do you go to / attend / take part in … ?

Extra activity

Ask students to create an infographic or chart and write a summary of their findings for homework.

4c Why do we need music?

Lesson at a glance

- reading: how music helps us
- critical thinking: identifying opinions
- word focus: *spend*
- speaking: music playlists

Reading

1

- Tell students to work individually to write down their favourite songs or pieces of music. Then ask students to work in pairs to discuss the songs or pieces of music they have chosen by using questions 1–3. In feedback, elicit students' ideas.
- **Optional step** You could find and play examples of pop, traditional/folk, classical, rock, R&B/soul and/or hip-hop and ask students to say what type of music each one is, and which ones they like and why.

2 🎵 [36]

- Ask students to look at and discuss the title of the article.
- Ask students to read the article and find out whether the article's answer to the question in the title is similar to or different from students' ideas.
- **Optional step** The reading text is recorded. You could play the recording and ask students to read and listen.
- Let students compare answers in pairs before discussing as a class.

EXAMPLE ANSWERS

We need music because: it's enjoyable, relaxing, inspiring, soothing; it makes us feel good; it's the soundtrack of our lives; humans have always had music; it makes us feel part of a community; it allows us to express ourselves; it encourages movement and dance; it can create atmosphere in public places, such as restaurants.

3

- Ask students to cover the article and try to remember information from the text. Tell them to work in pairs to note down details for points 1–5. Then let students compare answers with another pair. In feedback, either check answers with the class, or let students check their notes against the text.

ANSWERS

1 a fifth of our waking lives
2 the musical way of speaking to babies
3 sad songs help us regulate our negative feelings and/or lift our mood
4 most hip-hop artists in America rap about fame and money, but those in other part of the world rap about the injustice that people in poor communities feel
5 its patterns are culturally specific and follow certain systems

4

- Ask students to work individually to choose the correct meanings. Elicit the first answer to get students started. Tell them to check their answers in pairs.

ANSWERS

1 a   2 b   3 c   4 a   5 a

Vocabulary notes

give (someone) goosebumps = this expression comes from the idea that when we are excited or nervous, the hairs on our neck or arms stand on end in little bumps like on a plucked goose

conquest = usually used to describe when an army or nation defeats another and claims its territory

Other phrases in the article that may be new to students:

waking lives = our lives excluding when we are asleep

deeply rooted in = over a period of time has become an important part of

a rousing theme = a tune or song that energizes people and makes them feel proud, motivated or excited

lift (people) = to raise their spirits

Extra activity

Ask students to find and collect words connected with *song* in the text: *a national anthem* (= the official national song played at important public occasions), a *lullaby* (= a song sung to a baby). Ask them to use dictionaries to find other words: *aria* (= in opera), *carol* (= at Christmas), *hymn* (= in church).

Background information

McGill University is an English language university in Montreal Canada. It was opened in 1821 and is one of the world's leading universities.

Hen Wlad Fy Nhadau (*Land of My Fathers* in English) is the national anthem of Wales. It was written as a hymn in the nineteenth century and is particularly rousing when sung by Welsh rugby fans before international matches. Rugby is the national sport of Wales.

Hip-hop music originated from parties in poor, largely African-American housing projects in the Bronx, New York, in the early 1970s.

Critical thinking identifying opinions

5

- Ask students to find the opinions in the article and match them with the person who expressed the opinion: the author (A), Valorie Salimpoor (S) or an unknown source (U). In feedback, ask students to justify their answers by referring to the text.

ANSWERS

1 A (*... unlike food or shelter, it is not something we actually need in order to survive.*)
2 S (*Valorie Salimpoor ... believes that the answer lies in music's ability to stimulate us both emotionally and intellectually.*)
3 U (*Why ... do we like listening to sad songs when we have experienced loss or are feeling down? ... Some people say the reason is ...*)
4 A (*Music's emotional power also comes from the fact that it can make a verbal message stronger.*)
5 S (*On an intellectual level, Salimpoor says that music challenges our brains to understand and recognize certain systems and patterns.*)
6 A (*Humans have various needs – physical, emotional and psychological – and while music may not fulfil the first, it clearly plays an important role in satisfying the others.*)

6

- Ask students to work in pairs to discuss the questions before presenting their views to the class.

EXAMPLE ANSWERS

a opinions supported by clear evidence: 2 (examples of rousing themes and calming lullabies), 4 (*rap and hip-hop began in America as songs with a social message*), 5 (Salimpoor's research)
b opinions that need more evidence: 3 (no-one really knows the answer)
c opinions that are convincing because they reflect our experience: 1, 2, 3, 4 and 6
d opinions that summarize the main argument: 2 and 6

Word focus *spend*

7

- Read the example sentence to the class. Point out that these are set phrases so they will have to guess what the missing word is.
- Ask students to complete the sentences with the words *money* or *time*. Let students compare answers in pairs.
- **Optional step** In feedback, ask students to write down the phrases in their vocabulary notebooks (perhaps in personalized sentences). This should help to stress the idea that they are set phrases that need to be learned.

ANSWERS

1 money	4 money; money
2 time	5 time
3 time	

8

- Ask students to complete the sentences with their own ideas. Elicit one or two ideas to get students started. Let students compare their ideas in small groups.

EXAMPLE ANSWERS

1 I spent hours trying to *get through to the gas company / find the restaurant / think of what present to buy you.*

2 I've spent a fortune on *my new car / holidays / decorating the house.*

3 Once I spent a night in *the rainforest / a cave / a five-star hotel.*

4 I don't spend a lot on *clothes / myself / eating out.*

Vocabulary notes

We *spend* time or money. So, *spend minutes/hours/days/ages,* etc. and *spend millions/loads/dollars,* etc.

Note the forms:

spend (time/money) *on* (somebody/something): *I spent £100 on a new handbag.*

spend (time/money) *doing* (something) *with* (somebody/something): *I spent hours rehearsing the play with Andy and Jed.*

Extra activity

Ask students to research the verb *spend* in the dictionary and find other useful phrases: *spend the day … , spend the rest of their lives … , spend ages doing something,* etc.

Ask students to write and share personalized sentences using the phrases.

Speaking ⌐my life⌐
9

• The success of this exercise will depend on how 'into' music your students are. It's a good idea to prepare a short playlist of your own, which you could use as a model and for inspiration. Show it to the class and explain why you choose individual songs.

• Ask students to work individually to prepare their playlist suggestions. Monitor and help, especially with the translation of song titles.

• When students are ready, ask them to work in groups to discuss their choice of songs. At the end of the activity, have a class vote on who had the most interesting playlist.

Extra activity

Extend the activity by asking students in groups to think of a playlist for another situation, e.g.:

to help you relax

to listen to before an exam

to listen to before playing a team sport

to play during a wedding reception party

Once they have completed their playlist, you could ask an individual from each group to read out the playlist. Other groups then try and guess for which situation the playlist was created.

4d Personal tastes

Lesson at a glance
• real life: describing likes and dislikes
• pronunciation: disappearing sounds

Real life describing likes and dislikes
1

• Ask students to discuss the questions in pairs. You could ask them to make a list of well-known musicals. You may have to translate the titles. In feedback, make sure you mention *The Lion King* and ask students what they know about it.

EXAMPLE ANSWERS

Classic musicals: *West Side Story, Singin' In The Rain, Cabaret, Bugsy Malone, Grease*

Currently popular musicals: *Phantom of the Opera, Wicked, Mamma Mia!, Les Misérables, Cats, Chicago*

2 🎧 [37]

• Tell students that they are going to listen to two people talking about the musical *The Lion King.* Ask students to read the table. Then play the recording. Students listen and put a tick or cross in the correct columns.

• Let students compare answers in pairs before checking with the class.

ANSWERS

musicals in general ✗
the visual effects ✓
Disney comic characters ✗
this production of *The Lion King* ✓
the music ✗
Elton John ✓
cost of tickets for musicals ✗

Audioscript 🎧 [37]

J = Jake; T = Tom

J: Hey, Tom, how was *The Lion King*?

T: I loved it, actually – and I'm not really a fan of musicals. Do you like them?

J: Not really, no. I can't get on with the music in them – with a few exceptions perhaps – *West Side Story* and *Grease.* They're both brilliant. So what was so good about it?

T: Well, it's absolutely stunning, the opening scene particularly. All the animals – giraffes, wildebeest, zebra, antelope – come onto the stage together to set the scene at the beginning, and the costumes are amazing. They're difficult to describe really – you can see the people in them, but they seem to move like real animals. Everyone in the audience was spellbound.

J: Wow. And is the story the same as in the Disney film? 'Cos in that there were some rather annoying characters, like that bird who was supposed to be there for comic effect – what was its name?

T: Zazu. Yeah, I know what you mean – that kind of Disney character can get on your nerves – but I didn't notice that with this production – it's more adult than the film. As I say, it was excellent.

J: And what about the music? Did you like it?

T: Well, not especially, but it wasn't bad and it's got an African feel to it, so it kind of works with the story. It was written by Elton John, interestingly, and I've got a lot of respect for him.

J: Oh, OK. Well, I might check it out then. Were the tickets reasonable?

T: They're not cheap. I can't bear the high prices they charge for musicals and theatre these days – it just seems wrong. But actually, I didn't mind for this one – I thought it was money well spent.

Background information

The Lion King was originally a 1994 Disney animated film. It was produced as a musical in 1997 with music by Elton John and lyrics by Tim Rice. It has been running in London's West End since 1999. It tells the story of Simba, a young lion who will grow up to be king. The London musical features actors in animal costumes as well as giant, hollow puppets.

Sir Elton John is an English singer-songwriter, musician and composer who has had numerous hits around the world.

West Side Story is an American musical with music by Leonard Bernstein and lyrics by Stephen Sondheim. It was first performed in 1957 and was inspired by William Shakespeare's play *Romeo and Juliet*.

Originally a 1971 musical, *Grease*, a story of a high school love affair, was made into a film starring John Travolta in 1978.

3 💿 [37]

- Ask students to look at the expressions for describing likes and dislikes and to work in pairs to discuss which were used in the recording. Then play the recording. Students listen and mark the phrases they hear.

ANSWERS

I loved it …

I'm not really a fan of … I can't get on …

They're both brilliant.

it's absolutely stunning

(the costumes) are amazing

… can get on your nerves

it was excellent.

not especially

it wasn't bad

I've got a lot of respect for …

I can't bear …

I didn't mind …

Pronunciation disappearing sounds
4a 💿 [38]

- Play the recording. Students listen and underline the disappearing sound, or the part of the word that is not pronounced (see Pronunciation notes below).
- You could play the recording again for students to listen and repeat.

Audioscript 💿 [38] (and answers)

diff<u>e</u>rent

ev<u>e</u>ryone

gen<u>e</u>rally

Pronunciation notes

Different /ˈdɪfrənt/ is pronounced with two syllables. *Everyone* /ˈɛvrɪwʌn/ and *generally* /ˈdʒɛnrəli/ are pronounced with three syllables.

4b 💿 [39]

- Organize the class into pairs. Ask students to work together to underline the disappearing sounds and practise saying the words.
- Play the recording. Students listen and check.

Audioscript 💿 [39] (and answers)

be<u>a</u>utifully

choc<u>o</u>late

comf<u>or</u>table

int<u>e</u>resting

med<u>i</u>cine

ordin<u>a</u>ry

secret<u>a</u>ry

Pronunciation notes

Note that not all varieties of English miss out these disappearing sounds. For example, British English *secretary* is pronounced /ˈsekrətri/ with three syllables, whereas in American English, *secretary* is generally pronounced /ˈsekrəˌteri/ with four.

5

- Ask students to work individually to cross out the option which does not fit in each sentence. Let students compare answers in pairs before checking with the class.

ANSWERS

1 a bit
2 very much
3 rather
4 very
5 so
6 especially

6

- Ask students to think of a musical, play, film, concert, TV programme or exhibition they have enjoyed. You could start them off by eliciting recent performances, or by giving an example of something you have enjoyed.

- Organize the class into groups of four or five. Ask students to describe their choices to the group and compare and discuss their likes and dislikes.

- **Optional step** Give pairs some language preparation time before they speak. Refer them back to the 'describing likes and dislikes' box and ask them to think of the phrases they want to use in their conversation.

- As students speak, listen for errors and prompt students to use expressions correctly.

Extra activity

Write the names of some classic musicals on the board: *West Side Story, Grease, Cabaret, Oklahoma, Mary Poppins, The Sound of Music*. Organize the class into groups and ask each group to choose a musical they don't know much about. Tell them to research it on the internet, and find out about the plot, the songs and the stars who have performed in it. Then ask them to present the musical to the class and say whether or not they would recommend it and why.

4e You've got to see this

Lesson at a glance
- writing: an online review
- writing skill: personalizing your writing

Writing an online review
1

- Ask students to read the review. Discuss the questions with the class and elicit their personal responses.

EXAMPLE ANSWER

I would follow their recommendation because the exhibition is a welcome break from museums and shopping, it makes you appreciate the park, and it's free.

Background information

Kensington Gardens are one of the Royal Parks of London, and lie immediately to the west of Hyde Park in western central London. They were once the private gardens of Kensington Palace.

Sir Anish Kapoor is a British-Indian sculptor who was born in Mumbai, India, but has lived and worked in London since the early 1970s. He represented Britain in the Venice Biennale in 1990, and received the Turner Prize for art in 1991. As well as *Sky Mirror*, he is well known for *ArcelorMittal Orbit*, the permanent artwork he designed for the 2012 London Olympics.

2

- Ask students to work individually to answer the questions about the review before comparing in pairs. Discuss the questions with the class and elicit answers.

ANSWERS

1 Order:
  1 an introduction
  2 the occasion of the visit
  3 the content of the exhibition
  4 the details of where and when it is on
  5 the author's recommendation
2 where it is, when it is on until, how much it costs (free), what you can see, why you should go
3 personal

Writing skill personalizing your writing
3

- Read the features of personal and impersonal writing to the class. Give some examples of active, rather than passive, verbs (*go, visit, look at*), contracted forms (*you'll, don't*), uncontracted forms (*do not, you will*), phrasal verbs (*get up, bring up, try out*) and formal verbs (*encounter, contemplate*).

- Ask students to work in pairs to find and underline examples of personal language in the review. Check answers with the class.

• **Optional step** Draw students' attention to the use of pronouns in the review. Point out that in more personal writing, we can use the pronoun 'I'.

ANSWERS

Active verbs: *checking out; visit; took a walk; we'd have missed; see*, etc.

Contracted forms: *it's; we'd; I'd; it's free*, etc.

Phrasal verbs: *checking out; worked with; work out*

Personal details: *my boyfriend and I took a walk; I was so glad we did; The one I liked best; It was so funny to … ; I'd definitely recommend …*

Conversational linking phrases: *as well as; otherwise; rather than; Another; so that; And by the way*

Share your feelings: *I find … ; I was so glad we did; The one I liked best; It makes you appreciate what is already a really delightful park even more; I'd definitely recommend …*

4

• **Optional step** Brainstorm ideas about what your students could write about. This will depend on the age and experiences of your class. A more mature group may wish to write about an exhibition or play, but a younger group may prefer to write about a film or concert.

• Ask students to write their personalized review. Tell them to plan it first (see Teacher development below). It's a good idea to ask students to note down any phrases they would like to try to use – these could be their own ideas, or they could be phrases from the model text (e.g. *It's worth checking out … ; The one / What I liked best was … ; It makes you appreciate what …*).

• It's important to allow an extended preparation stage. Move around the class helping with ideas and vocabulary.

5

• When students have completed their reviews, ask them to exchange them with a partner and to use the questions to check the reviews.

• **Optional step** Pass the reviews round the class, or, if your class is large, around groups of six in the class. Each student comments on the review by writing notes at the bottom of the page. At the end, ask the class or groups which reviews made them really want to go and see something.

Teacher development

Writing a personalized text

Asking students to write a personalized text means that you can't provide a model text that students can follow step by step as this takes away the 'personalized' aspect. As a result students will need supported preparation and planning. Allow at least 30 minutes, and ideally 45 minutes for this lesson. It's best done in class, but if you set it for homework ensure students have prepared plenty of notes and ideas in class beforehand. Here is a procedure to follow:

1 Invest time helping students decide what to write about and encouraging them to become fully involved in the task. Include a stage for brainstorming ideas or researching what to write about.

2 Ensure students plan the outline of their writing. Encourage them to refer to and adapt the order information was provided in the model review:
   • an introduction
   • the occasion of the visit
   • the content of the exhibition
   • the details of where and when it is on
   • the author's recommendation

Ask them to write each stage of the order as a heading and to make notes under each heading. The notes should include the basic content as well as any useful phrases or vocabulary items they could include.

3 Encourage students to revise their text. They should write their first drafts on their own. Then they should share what they have written and get feedback. They could exchange texts in pairs, or pass texts round the class. In smaller classes, create a supportive, whole-class sharing activity – write a text of your own, sit students in a circle and ask them to pass their text to the person sitting on their right. Everybody reads the text and writes a comment before passing the piece of work on. In this way your model and everyone's ideas are shared in a collaborative way.

4 Ask students to write a second draft based on the feedback they have received. You could have a second feedback stage before asking students to write a third draft (perhaps for homework).

4f Art for the people

Before you watch

1

- Ask students to read the background to the video and explain to their partner what GCHQ does. In feedback, ask students if they know of something similar in their own country.

Background information

GCHQ (Government Communications Headquarters) is a British government agency that checks communication on the internet and other electronic media in order to protect national security. It's based in a building known as the Doughnut (because of its round shape) in the suburbs of the small city of Cheltenham in rural southwest England. In 2013, the former National Security Agency contractor, Edward Snowden, revealed that GCHQ was in the process of collecting all online and telephone data in the UK. This has caused some members of the British public to worry about invasion of privacy.

Key vocabulary

2a

- Ask students to read sentences 1–6 and guess the meaning of the words in bold.

2b

- Tell students to match the words in bold in Exercise 2a with the definitions (a–f).

ANSWERS

1 b   2 f   3 e   4 a   5 d   6 c

Background information

In the UK, public phone booths are also called phone boxes.

While you watch

3 ■◀ [4.1]

- Ask students to watch the whole video and answer questions 1–4. Let students compare answers in pairs before discussing as a class.

ANSWERS

1 on a house (in Cheltenham); wooden boards and scaffolding
2 some men who look like spies
3 local residents who want to keep the mural in the town
4 a picture of a child working at a sewing machine (with a price of £750,000)

Videoscript ■◀ 4.1

0.00–0.34 Presenter   This art-lover in Cheltenham is willing to go to extreme lengths to expose a hidden art work. That's because beneath these wooden boards and scaffolding is a mural by one of the world's most famous and elusive artists, Banksy. Banksy's spy booth appeared in April, making fun of the issue of Government surveillance in the home of GCHQ, the intelligence and communications headquarters in Cheltenham. Now the owner of the property wants to sell the artwork and the wall it's on. It's caused protest from the local community.

0.35–0.49 Resident 1   It's about GCHQ. Of course, this is the best place for it. It's … it's something for the town. It's public art really. Umm … it's not meant to be in private hands and to be seen by just a few people in someone's house.

0.50–0.59 Presenter   When the scaffold went up, it was hoped it was just for building maintenance. But it's since been reported that a collector has bought the work and plans to take it out of the town.

1.00–1.14   What happens to the piece ultimately remains something of a mystery: whether it falls into the hands of a private collector or goes into a gallery for people to see. But one thing is for certain: the people here in Cheltenham are so keen to see it, they're willing to tear these boards off themselves.

1.15–1.22   Campaigners argue that because the spy booth relates directly to Cheltenham, it belongs here and to the community.

1.23–1.29 Resident 2   It's become such an important thing here. It's brought the people in from all over the world to see it.

1.30–1.33 Resident 3   This type of art is public property. It should be free to everybody.

1.34–1.43 Resident 4   I think the setting is ideal. It's set round the telephone box. Mmm, you know, … it epitomizes what Cheltenham should be.

1.44–2.08 Presenter   The sale of the mural has re-started the debate over what's *public* art and what can be bought by a private individual. The Slave Labour mural which appeared on the side of a discount store in North London was removed and sold at auction for around three quarters of a million. The one person missing from this campaign is the artist himself, who remains anonymous. Perhaps it's time for the real Banksy to stand up.

4 ■◀ [4.1]

- Ask students to read the statements. Revise the word *mural* (= a wall painting) which students may have forgotten from earlier in the unit.

- When students are ready, play the video again. Students choose the correct options to complete the statements. Let students compare their answers in pairs before discussing as a class.

ANSWERS

1 remove
2 funny
3 sell
4 wherever the collector decides
5 Cheltenham
6 shouldn't
7 London
8 isn't

Background information

Banksy is a graffiti artist, political activist and film director. He is anonymous and refuses to reveal his true identity. He started out in Bristol in the early 1990s, producing satirical street art. He uses a distinctive stencilling technique (he spray paints over a cut out shape) and dark, witty humour. His work is obviously controversial, raising such questions as: *Is it art? Is it vandalism? Is it owned by the public or should private investors be able to buy it? Should it stay where it is or be in a museum or art gallery?* You could raise any of these questions for debate with your students.

After you watch

Vocabulary in context

5a ■◀ [4.2]

- **Optional step** You may wish to ask students to look at the words in the glossary on the page and check that they understand the words.

- Explain that students are going to watch some clips from the video which contain some new words and phrases. They need to choose the correct meaning of the words.

- Play the clips. When each multiple-choice question appears, pause the clip so that students can choose the correct definition. You could let students compare answers in pairs before discussing as a class.

ANSWERS

1 c   2 a   3 c   4 c   5 a   6 b

Videoscript ■◀ 4.2

1 ... that's because **beneath** these wooden boards and scaffolding is a mural by one of the world's most famous and elusive artists.
   a on top of
   b behind
   c under

2 It's caused **protest** from the local community.
   a complaints
   b interest
   c worries

3 What happens to the piece **ultimately** remains something of a mystery.
   a immediately
   b in the short-term
   c in the end

4 I think the setting is **ideal**.
   a wrong
   b unusual
   c perfect

5 The Slave Labour **mural**, which appeared on the side of a discount store ...
   a wall painting
   b advertisement
   c notice

6 ... on the side of a **discount store** ...
   a book shop
   b shop selling cheap goods
   c shop selling luxury goods

5b

- Students work individually to complete the sentences. Elicit one or two ideas for the first sentence to get them started. Let students compare sentences in pairs.

EXAMPLE ANSWERS

1 There has been a lot of protest about *the new development in town / university fees*.
2 My ideal place to live would be *near the seaside / in a hot country / in a cosmopolitan city*.
3 My favourite discount store is not *far from my house / stocks all sorts of goods*.

6

- Organize the class into groups of three. Ask students to work together to act out the roleplay. You could ask students to prepare first. Ask presenters to think of questions to ask and ask residents to think of points they want to make.

- As students act out the roleplay, monitor and note interesting information or errors which you could comment on during feedback.

7

- Organize the class into small groups. Ask students to read the task carefully. Tell students that when choosing who they would like to make the artwork they could consider whether it should be a local artist or a famous artist, or perhaps local schoolchildren or members of the community.

8

- Once students have discussed and made decisions, put groups together to exchange and evaluate suggestions, or ask different groups to present their ideas. The rest of the class listen and then make comments.

Extra activity

Here are alternative discussion points:

1 If you were Banksy, what artwork would you put on the side of the building you are currently in?

2 In your opinion, who owns a piece of work by Banksy that's found on a building? What should happen to it?

UNIT 4 Review and memory booster

Memory Booster activities

Exercises 3, 5, 6 and 8 are Memory Booster activities. For more information about these activities and how they benefit students, see page 10 of this Teacher's Book.

I can ... check boxes

As an alternative to asking students to simply tick the *I can ...* boxes, you could ask them to give themselves a score from 1 to 4 (1 = not very confident; 4 = very confident) for each language area. If students score 1 or 2 for a language area, refer them to additional practice activities in the Workbook and Grammar summary exercises.

Grammar

1
- Ask students to complete the text using the words in the box. Elicit answers from the class.

ANSWERS

1	every	6	a lot
2	whole	7	Many *or* A few
3	lack	8	a few *or* many
4	number	9	no
5	much	10	Both

2
- Ask students to read the text again and decide whether the statements are true (T) or false (F).

ANSWERS

1 F 2 T

3 >> MB
- Tell students to work individually to write two sentences using at least one of the words in the box in each sentence. Then ask students to rewrite the sentences with the words from the box missing.
- Ask students to work in pairs and take it in turns to read out their sentence for their partner to guess the missing word.

ANSWERS

Students' own answers

Vocabulary

4
- Ask students to match each person or performance with a place to make six pairs of words. You could then ask students to work in pairs to put each combination into a sentence that demonstrates their meanings in context.

EXAMPLE ANSWERS

An artist exhibits their work in **a gallery**.

A busker plays musical instruments or sings in **the street**.

A gig is an informal concert that might take place in **a live music venue**.

I went to see **a musical** at **a theatre** in London last week.

I acted in **a play** in **a theatre** near my school when I was a child.

Have you ever heard **an orchestra** play in **a concert hall**?

5 >> MB
- Ask students to work in pairs to describe the type of art or artists they see in each photo. Encourage them to remember and use as many vocabulary items from the unit as possible.

ANSWERS

Students' own answers

6 >> MB
- Ask students to work in pairs to write as many words or phrases as they can from the root word *art*. At the feedback stage, write the words on the board around the word 'art'. You could then invite individual students to give an example sentence for each of the words or phrases.

EXAMPLE ANSWERS

arty, artful, artistic, artist, artistry, artwork, the arts, art club, art gallery, art exhibition, art director, art form, art therapy, fine art, clip art, pop art, street art, martial arts

Real life

7
- Ask students to work individually to complete the exchanges. Tell them to use one word in each gap. Let students compare answers in pairs.

ANSWERS

1	really	7	time *or* respect
2	anything	8	get
3	keen	9	of
4	kind	10	all
5	thing	11	nerves
6	fan		

8 >> MB
- Ask students to work in groups of three or four. Tell them to use the first four words of each exchange in Exercise 7 to begin a conversation about TV programmes that they like and dislike.

Unit 5 Development

Opener

1

- Ask students to look at the photo and the caption. Discuss the questions with your class. Elicit answers from the students in feedback, encouraging them to give reasons to support their ideas.

EXAMPLE ANSWERS

A hydroelectric dam may benefit local people by providing electricity and local jobs, and by controlling the flow of a river.

The construction of a dam may improve the landscape by controlling the flow of a river so that it doesn't flood and destroy surrounding countryside, and by creating a lake which may be attractive in itself.

However, it may damage the landscape by raising water levels so that it covers land or by taking water away from land further downriver.

It may improve the lives of local people, but it could mean that they have to move house or it may change the local way of life.

Background information

The Belo Monte Dam is a hydroelectric dam which is currently under construction on the Xingu River in the state of Para, Brazil. The first turbines there started working in 2016 and the project is due to be completed by 2019.

2 🎧 *[40]*

- Tell students they are going to listen to someone describing the dam development. Ask them to listen and compare what the speaker says with students' answers to Exercise 1. Play the recording.
- In feedback, invite students to comment on whether the answers were similar or not.

ANSWERS

The development may benefit people by generating huge amounts of electricity for people all over the country. It has also already created 19,000 new jobs and boosted the local economy.

400 square kilometres of rainforest have been cleared and the diversity of plants and animals may be lost. Eighteen different tribal communities will lose their land and many of their traditional jobs.

Audioscript 🎧 *[40]*

When it's complete, the Belo Monte dam in northern Brazil will be the fourth largest hydro-electric power project in the world. It will generate huge amounts of electricity that will benefit people all over the country. It will also enhance Brazil's reputation as a major producer of renewable energy. Renewable energy already accounts for nearly half of the energy Brazilians consume.

As with any such development, there are arguments for and against the dam. In its favour is the fact that the country needs electricity as its population expands and that this is the cheapest way to get it. Its construction has also created 19,000 new jobs, which has boosted the local economy. But environmentalists are concerned because 400 square kilometres of rainforest have been cleared to make way for the dam and its reservoir. They are worried that the huge diversity of plants and animals that thrives here will be lost. Also eighteen different tribal communities will lose their land and many of their traditional jobs, like hunting and fishing. Supporters of the project say that even though these people have had to move, in the long-term the dam will improve their lives.

Vocabulary notes

reservoir = an artificial or natural lake where water is stored, e.g. so that it can be supplied to the houses in an area

tribal = relating to a 'tribe' – a large group of related families who live together in the same area (usually rural) and share a common language, religion and customs

3

- Ask students to match the verbs in box A with expressions with a similar meaning from box B. Let students compare answers in pairs.

ANSWERS

<u>be</u>nefit = be good for

boost = help to increase

en<u>han</u>ce = add to and improve

ex<u>pand</u> = get bigger

im<u>prove</u> = make better

thrive = do well

Vocabulary notes

Enhance and *improve* have similar meanings and can sometimes be used interchangeably. *Enhance* is often used to say that something is made more attractive or more valuable. *Improve* is used more generally. It is used to say that something is made better. Compare *The treatment improved his health*, *He improved his English on the course* and *His living standards improved*, with *The artist's death enhanced the value of his work* and *The building's appearance was enhanced by the reconstruction*.

4 🎵 [40]

- Explain that students are going to listen to the speaker again and tick the verbs in box A from Exercise 3 that the speaker used. Play the recording. Let students compare their answers in pairs before discussing as a class.

ANSWERS

benefit

enhance

expand

boost

thrive

5

- Ask students to work individually. Tell them to prepare brief written notes about both their own personal development and the development of the place where they live. Set a five-minute time limit.

- **Optional step** You could support students in doing this activity by talking for about one minute about an example area from your own experience (see Teacher development below). This provides a teacher model.

- Organize the class into small groups to share descriptions. In feedback, ask anyone with an interesting experience to share it with the class.

EXAMPLE ANSWERS

Boosted your confidence: going on a public speaking course, giving talks at university, winning a sports award, getting positive feedback from a teacher, employer or sports coach, getting a new job or a promotion, selling something you have made, giving a successful public performance

Benefited the local economy: new factory opened, local cultural event or festival, new transport system or links (e.g. bus, train), new shopping centre, faster broadband access, new residential areas, new green energy supplies, community organizations

Enhanced the quality of life in your country: better healthcare, wider access to education, more trade, improved access to water/energy/broadband, better transport systems, more jobs available

Is thriving in your city or region: new business park, the shopping centre, the arts scene, tourism, youth projects, farming, manufacturing

Teacher development

The teacher model

If students have to describe an experience, or tell a story or anecdote, it is a good idea to model a version of what you want students to attempt to say first. Make this engaging by telling personal stories or revealing ideas or examples from your own experience. Giving a model achieves the following:

1 It avoids long instructions – you are showing students what to do, not telling them.

2 It provides a live listening. Students get to hear a good, accurate version and get to listen to somebody speaking English well and with a genuine purpose. It offers an excellent change to listening to recorded audio material.

3 It is fun and motivating. Students like listening to the teacher, and tend to like like finding out things about him or her.

4 It motivates students to try to produce a comparable piece of speaking and helps them to make what they say more interesting and more accurate.

5 Another advantage of providing a teacher model is that it allows you to model vocabulary you want students to use or revise, and it allows you to tailor what you want students to say to their interests, their cultural context and/or to current affairs.

5a From reality to fantasy

Lesson at a glance
- reading: urban development
- grammar: verb + infinitive or -ing
- vocabulary: urban features
- speaking: changes in your town

Vocabulary urban features

1
- Start by asking students to explain what *urban features* are (= things you find in a city). Elicit some examples (e.g. *bridges, flyovers, blocks of flats*).
- Ask students to work in pairs to make urban features by combining the words in boxes A and B. Elicit one or two examples to get students started. Ask students to check their answers on page 153 of the Student's Book.
- **Optional step** Make this activity competitive by setting a four-minute time limit. Once the four minutes has finished, stop the activity and find out which pair has the most correct combinations.

> **ANSWERS**
>
> apartment block, bus station, business centre / business park, car park, city centre / city hall, green space, high-rise building, leisure centre, luxury apartments, office block / office building, pedestrian area / pedestrian zone, railway station, residential building / residential area, shopping centre / shopping mall, town centre

2
- Discuss the questions with the class. You could put students in pairs or small groups to work together.

> **ANSWERS**
>
> Students' own answers

Reading

3
- Ask students to look at the photo and discuss questions 1–3 in pairs.
- **Optional step** Depending on your students' experiences and background, you could do one of the following to set the scene and create interest in the topic: 1 Ask if anyone has been to Dubai and ask them to describe it; 2 Ask students to write three facts and three opinions about Dubai (e.g. Facts: It's hot; It's in a desert; It has amazing tall buildings; Opinions: It's expensive to live there; Most people are in the oil industry; It's an artificial environment to live in); 3 Ask students who know little about Dubai to research the place on the Internet and find out where it is, why it is famous and what you can do there.

> **ANSWERS**
>
> 1 Perhaps from a plane or helicopter – but actually from the top of the world's highest tower the Burj Khalifa.
> 2 Downtown Dubai around the Dubai Mall: the shapes of buildings and roads and a lake can be seen.
> 3 Students' own ideas

Background information

Dubai /duːˈbaɪ/ is the capital of the Emirate of Dubai, one of the seven emirates that make up the UAE (United Arab Emirates). It is on the coast of the Persian Gulf. Oil was discovered in the emirate in 1966, and following that discovery the country's rulers began an enormous development programme. The emirate's western-style model of business drives its economy with the main revenues now coming, not from oil, but from tourism, aviation, real estate and financial services.

4 🞄 [41]
- Ask students to read questions 1–5. If you have a knowledgeable class, ask them to predict some of the answers.
- Ask students to work individually to read the article and answer the questions. Let students check their answers in pairs before discussing as a class.
- **Optional step** The reading text is recorded. You could play the recording and ask students to read and listen.

> **ANSWERS**
>
> 1 About sixty years ago, it was a sleepy village occupied by pearl divers, fishermen and traders. A small river ran through the village to the sea. Today, it is an 'air-conditioned fantasy world of nearly three million people', with many iconic buildings and amazing shopping malls.
> 2 the world's tallest high-rise building; the world's biggest shopping mall; the world's largest motorway intersection
> 3 tourists, investors (although less since the 2008 financial crisis), the rich and famous, and shoppers
> 4 The rest of the world watches with a mixture of wonder and suspicion.
> 5 Students' own ideas

Vocabulary notes

There once was a sheikh with big dreams = note the use of story-telling style here

sleepy village = quiet village where not much happens

pearl divers = people who swim deep under water to find the white stones in oyster shells that are valuable

landmark = a well-known building or place of interest that you can see or recognize easily

palm tree = a tropical tree without branches that is common in hot, dry countries

gateway = entry point

intersection = the place where a number of roads meet

ran through = went through

a model = a good example

Grammar verb + infinitive or -ing

5

- Ask students to look at the information in the grammar box and then underline examples of the language patterns in the article. Go through the answers with the class in feedback.

> ANSWERS
>
> 1 seemed to be, failed to sell, want to copy, chosen to reject
> 2 get people to invest
> 3 helped little Dubai become
> 4 carry on developing, risked losing

Refer students to page 164 for further information and practice.

> ANSWERS TO GRAMMAR SUMMARY EXERCISES
>
> **1**
> 1 to go   5 work
> 2 to help   6 watching
> 3 making   7 to come
> 4 building
>
> **2**
> 1 to drive   6 exercising
> 2 driving   7 working
> 3 drive   8 to work
> 4 to exercise   9 work
> 5 exercise
>
> **3**
> 1 to expand   5 queueing
> 2 to make   6 hiring
> 3 to take   7 write
> 4 fly

Grammar notes

Students need to practise and learn these verb patterns as they come across them. Point out that we use -ing after prepositions (carry on doing).

The pattern verb + object + infinitive (without to) is less common than the others so students could make a useful list of verbs that follow this pattern. For example: make/let/help (somebody) do (something); verbs of perception – hear, see, feel, notice and watch (somebody/something) do (something).

Verbs expressing hopes, intentions and decisions are often followed by infinitive with to: decide, hope, plan, prepare, want to do (something).

The verbs like, love and hate are generally used with -ing (I like shopping) but can be used with the infinitive with to (I like to have eggs with my breakfast). The difference is subtle (we use -ing with general activities and the infinitive to talk about something specific). It is safest to say that English speakers generally use the -ing form.

Note that some patterns can be varied with a change of meaning. For example, He asked us to leave (= we leave) and He asked to leave (= he leaves). And some can be changed without a change of meaning. For example, It helped Dubai become … and It helped Dubai to become …

6

- Ask students to work individually to complete the facts by writing the correct form of each verb. Elicit the first answer to get the class started. Let students compare their answers in pairs before discussing as a class.

> ANSWERS
>
> 1 growing – keep on + -ing because on is a preposition
> 2 to make – decide + infinitive with to
> 3 reducing – involve + -ing
> 4 Dubai to become – note that allow has a similar meaning to let, but a different structure: allow (somebody/something) to do (something)
> 5 shopping – like + -ing
> 6 to create – manage + infinitive with to
> 7 its police drive – let (somebody/something) do (something)
> 8 building – enjoy + -ing

7

- This is an opportunity to get students to personalize the language they have learned (see Teacher development below). Sentences 5 to 8 give students a chance to say something true and interesting about themselves. Start by sharing a few personal sentences of your own before asking students to write these sentences.

- Ask students to work individually to complete the sentences in their own words. Let students compare answers in pairs before eliciting examples from the class.

- **Optional step** You could also exploit the language here by asking students to share and discuss some of their more interesting sentences in small groups.

> EXAMPLE ANSWERS
>
> 1 don't mind/like or 'm not keen on
> 2 managed / decided / 'm hoping
> 3 offered/wanted
> 4 failed / didn't manage; carry on / keep on / continue
> 5 listening to music while I work; (to) concentrate or playing football / (to) keep fit
> 6 to study every evening; failing my exams or to stop running; damaging my knees
> 7 going to the gym; to pay for the membership
> 8 to stay out late / to go to parties; go out after 9pm / go out to parties until I was sixteen

Teacher development

Personalizing

Personalization is an important part of language learning. Any new piece of language can be made more relevant and memorable if students are encouraged to use it 'for real' by saying something about their lives, their experiences or their opinions. Here are some ideas:

1 Ask students to write true sentences from sentence starters (*I can't afford to ... because ...* ; *I can't stand ... because ...* ; *My company makes me ...* ; *I dislike people who make me ... / always ask me to ...*). This makes students think about how they can express themselves with the new language and it leads to interesting discussion.

2 At the end of a lesson, ask students to write four true and meaningful sentences using language from the lesson. They don't necessarily have to share the sentences with the class, but they should write something that is meaningful to them and would be useful in future.

8

- **Optional step** Tell students to read the text quickly for comprehension. Ask students to say whether the author is generally positive or negative about the redevelopment of a city centre (= generally negative and critical).

- Ask students to complete the description with the verbs in the box. Elicit the first answer to get them started. Let students compare answers in pairs before feedback.

ANSWERS

1 decided	2 involved	3 considered	4 seemed
5 needed	6 suggested	7 allowed	8 let
9 avoided	10 afford		

Speaking ⟨ my life ⟩

9

- Ask students to use the text in Exercise 8 to write a similar description of an area in their town or city. Set this up by eliciting places students could write about. If your students all live in the same city, brainstorm areas that have been redeveloped and the changes that have happened. Write up useful words and phrases on the board.

10

- Organize the class into new pairs. Ask pairs to share the information they wrote. You could tell students not to just read out the description they wrote, but to turn it over and try to remember and say the sentences they prepared.

- **Optional step** As students speak, monitor and note down errors you hear. Concentrate on errors with verb patterns. At the end, in feedback, write up five or six short sentences containing errors you heard. Ask students to work in pairs to correct the sentences.

EXAMPLE ANSWERS

A few years ago the council decided to redevelop the area around the canal. The redevelopment involved putting in new paths and bridges. Now, this area of the town is very attractive and there are new bars and cafes in the area, too.

or

In 2010, the council proposed building a leisure centre on the edge of town. However, they failed to ask local people what they wanted. They closed down the popular outdoor gym in the park and sold basketball courts to housing developers. In the end, the leisure centre wasn't successful. Nobody wanted to use a facility that was expensive and so far from the town centre.

5b The Kerala model

Lesson at a glance

- listening: social development in southern India
- grammar: verbs with -ing and to + infinitive
- vocabulary: urban features
- speaking: a happy society

Listening

1

- **Optional step** Pre-teach the vocabulary in the box by defining the words (see Vocabulary notes below) or let students guess the words as they do the task and feedback on definitions at the end.

- Ask students to look at the photos and choose adjectives to describe them. You could ask students to discuss the photos in pairs first before eliciting ideas.

- In feedback, ask students to share their ideas.

> EXAMPLE ANSWERS
>
> Photo 1: exotic, hectic, remarkable
> Photo 2: exotic, green, peaceful, remarkable
> Other adjectives: 1: lively, busy, urban, poor; 2: beautiful, tranquil, unspoilt, touristy

Vocabulary notes

exotic = unusual because it is in or from a place very different from our own

hectic = very busy and fast-paced

peaceful = quiet and calm

remarkable = unusual, amazing and different

wealthy = very rich

Extra activity

If your class is mature and worldly, ask students if they have been to India or a similar country. Ask: _In what ways are the photos typical of the country you visited? What did you find most exotic about the place you visited?_

Background information

Kerala (/ˈkɛrələ/ is a state in the far south-west of India. It has a long coastline with great beaches and tropical greenery and is popular with tourists as a result.

2 [42]

- Ask students to read the list of aspects carefully. Ask students to listen and tick the different aspects the journalist mentions. Play the recording.

- Let students compare answers in pairs. Elicit answers in feedback.

> ANSWERS
>
> income, education, health, politics, mix of people

Audioscript [42]

I = Interviewer; **J** = Journalist

I: I know you like exotic places – have you tried visiting anywhere in the Indian sub-continent?

J: Yes, I was just recently in India …

I: Were you?

J: Yes, in Kerala in the south-west. Actually, I was intending to go on to tour other parts of India, but Kerala was so fascinating I stayed on.

I: Were you on holiday?

J: No, well, it was meant to be a holiday, but actually it turned into a bit of a work trip.

I: Oh dear.

J: Oh, no. I don't regret changing my plans – I became so interested in the place that I started to write an article about it for the newspaper I work for.

I: Really? Is it a travel article?

J: Not really. It's more sociological, I guess. I'm trying to show what a remarkable place Kerala is in the developing world. You see, it's a small state with a big population. The average income is only about $300 a year and usually that would mean people having a fairly poor quality of life, but that's not the case. In fact, Kerala's a kind of model of social development. The population is **highly literate** and **well educated** and they seem **reasonably well off**, well, compared to other parts of India, anyway. They're healthy and they live almost as long as Americans or Europeans; infant mortality's also very low. And women, who've, umm, always traditionally been the head of the household, continue to be very active – and equal – participants in society.

I: That's interesting. I remember going there with my wife in the 1990s. But we were just tourists and my memories of it are just as a very tranquil and beautiful place, with lovely beaches and lagoons.

J: Well, of course those are the parts that tourists like to spend time visiting. But tranquil is not necessarily the adjective I would use. Trivandrum, the main city, where we stopped to visit an Indian journalist I know – who's very **well informed** about the country – is absolutely hectic. The people there are very **politically active**: they never stop debating; there are often strikes on the buses or parades of demonstrators – some medical students started protesting when we were there and went on protesting for four days.

I: Well, that doesn't sound great.

J: No, but it is. It's a sign of a successful society. The thing is that the whole system seems to work. That's because, first, Keralites are **naturally tolerant** people: you find Hindus, Muslims and Christians all living peacefully alongside each other and, actually, you could include foreigners in that – they're treated no differently to anyone else. And secondly, the government has invested a lot in health and education, and it goes on investing a lot. The land is incredibly fertile and well organized – small farmers cultivate every inch of it and none's wasted, which I regret to say isn't always the case in some developing countries.

I: Well, it sounds like it'll be an interesting article. Remember to send me a copy when it's published.

J: Of course I will.

3 [42]

• Ask students to read sentences 1–6 carefully.

• Play the recording again. Students listen and choose true or false. Ask students to work individually to correct false sentences before comparing answers in pairs.

ANSWERS

1 F (*it was meant to be a holiday*)
2 T (*it's a small state with a big population*)
3 T (*In fact, Kerala's a kind of model of social development. The population is highly literate and well educated*)
4 F (*And women … continue to be very active – and equal – participants in society*)
5 F (*The people there are very politically active …*)
6 T (*That's because, first, Keralites are naturally tolerant people: you find Hindus, Muslims and Christians all living peacefully alongside each other and, actually, you could include foreigners in that – they're treated no differently to anyone else.*)

4

• Discuss the questions with your class. You could ask students to discuss the questions in pairs first.

• **Optional step** Ask students to say whether they would like to go to Kerala, and, if so, why.

ANSWERS
Students' own ideas

Wordbuilding adverb + adjective
5

• Read the information in the box to the class.

• Ask students to look at audioscript 42 on page 183 and find and underline adverb + adjective combinations in bold. Ask students to match the combinations with the meanings. Let students compare answers in pairs.

Refer students to Workbook page 43 for further information and practice.

ANSWERS

1 well educated
2 naturally tolerant
3 politically active
4 highly literate
5 reasonably well off
6 well informed

6

• Ask students to work individually to complete the phrases. Elicit the first answer to get students started. Note that there is sometimes more than one possible answer. Let students compare answers in pairs.

ANSWERS

1 well (*badly* or *highly* are also possible)
2 badly
3 reasonably
4 well (*badly* is possible)
5 highly (*extremely* is possible)
6 extremely

Vocabulary notes

Note that these adverb + adjective combinations are about collocation. There is no grammatical reason why, for example, *an extremely damaged car* is wrong – it simply isn't a combination a native speaker of English would use.

When an adverb + adjective combination precedes a noun it's usually hyphenated (e.g. *a well-organized event*), but when it doesn't precede the noun it isn't hyphenated (e.g. *The event was very well organized*). However, we don't tend to hyphenate adverbs that end in -y or -ly, such as *very, really* or *extremely*, before adjectives (e.g. *She's an extremely talented singer*).

Extra activity

Ask students to provide personalized examples for each of the compounds. For example: *The Olympics are usually a well-organized event; I think Beyonce is an extremely talented singer.*

Pronunciation rhyming words
7a [35]

• Ask students to match the words from the listening (1–9) with the word that rhymes (a–i). Play the recording. Students listen and check their answers.

• Organize the class into pairs to practise saying the words to each other (see Pronunciation notes below). Student A says a word from the first column. Student B says the word from the second column that rhymes.

• **Optional step** Ask students to think of other words that rhyme with the words in the exercise.

ANSWERS
Examples of other words that rhyme have been added in brackets.
1 e (late, great)
2 h (four, door)
3 d (so, grow)
4 i (red, dead)
5 f (horse, Norse)
6 b (reign, stain)
7 c (shopped, dropped)
8 g (won, come)
9 a (paste, laced)

Audioscript 🔗 [35]

1 state – weight
2 poor – law
3 low – though
4 head – said
5 course – force
6 main – plane
7 stopped – opt
8 none – fun
9 waste – faced

Pronunciation notes

English (notoriously) does not follow sound/spelling rules in the way some other languages do, which means that two words with similar spelling can have different pronunciation (e.g. *low* and *now*) and two words with very different spelling can be pronounced the same (e.g. *way* and *weigh*).

You may wish to point out, in particular, the way 'g' or 'gh' is used in many words. Sometimes, they are silent (*weight*, *though*) and sometimes they are pronounced (*cough*, *tough*). They often have an effect on the vowel sound, changing its pronunciation (e.g. *sin – sign*).

Note that while these paired words rhyme in standard British Received Pronunciation, they don't necessarily rhyme in other varieties of English. *Law* and *poor* don't rhyme in American English, for example, and *none* and *fun* don't rhyme in northern Britain.

7b

- Ask students to think of words that rhyme. You could let students work in pairs to do this or check in pairs after thinking of their own examples.

- **Optional step** Make the activity competitive. Ask students to work in pairs to think of as many examples for each of the words as they can. After three minutes, say stop, and find out which pair has most examples.

> **EXAMPLE ANSWERS**
>
> break: make, take, wake, lake, sheikh, ache (also *brake*, which has the same sound as *break* but a different spelling)
> foot: put, nut
> height: light, site, white, night
> signed: mind, rind, wind, lined, dined
> walk: fork, pork, auk, hawk
> word: bird, stirred, herd, heard, purred

Extra activity

Try out this fun poem below with your students. You could photocopy it and hand it out then ask different pairs to prepare two lines each. Tell them to predict the pronunciation of each word, check in learner's dictionaries, and then practise saying their two lines. At the end, either get your class to take turns to read out their section of the poem or play the poem for students to hear (a recording can be easily found online):

I take it you already know
Of tough and bough and cough and dough?
Others may stumble, but not you
On hiccough, thorough, slough and through.
Well don't! And now you wish, perhaps,
To learn of less familiar traps.
Beware of heard, a dreadful word
That looks like beard but sounds like bird.
And dead: it's said like bed, not bead,
For goodness sake don't call it deed!
Watch out for meat and great and threat
(They rhyme with suite and straight and debt).
A moth is not a moth as in mother
Nor both as in bother, nor broth as in brother,
And here is not a match for there,
Nor dear and fear, for bear and pear.
And then there's dose and rose and lose –
Just look them up – and goose and choose
And cork and work and card and ward
And font and front and word and sword
And do and go, then thwart and cart,
Come, come! I've hardly made a start.
A dreadful Language? Why man alive!
I learned to talk it when I was five.
And yet to write it, the more I tried,
I hadn't learned it at fifty-five.

Grammar verbs with *-ing* and *to* + infinitive

8

- Read the information in the box to the class.
- Ask students to work in pairs to discuss the different meanings of the verbs in each pair of sentences.

> **ANSWERS**
>
> 1 *remember going* = I went somewhere in the past – now I have a memory of it.
>
>   *remember to send* = used to remind someone to do something they promised to do or have to do
>
> 2 When you *try doing* something, you do it with the intention of finding out what will happen when you do it.
>
>   When you *try to do* something, you make an effort. It may be difficult and you may expend energy in the attempt to do it. You may succeed, or you may fail.
>
> 3 *we went on to visit* = We were doing something (visiting Paris) and then we changed to do something else (visit Bordeaux).
>
>   *went on protesting* = They were doing something (protesting), and they continued to do that action (protest).

4 *It was meant to be* = it was intended to be ... or I wanted it to be ...

It means somebody having/doing = often used to explain what is involved in a situation

5 *I don't regret changing my plans* = I made plans, and now I am still happy with them. I don't feel sorry or bad about making those plans.

regret to say = (a fixed expression often used in formal or written situations) I am about to say something I feel sorry or bad about.

6 *stopped to visit* = I stopped (travelling). Why? Because we wanted to visit someone.

Keralites never stop debating = Keralites debate a lot and continue doing this. They don't stop.

Refer students to page 163 for further information and practice.

ANSWERS TO GRAMMAR SUMMARY EXERCISES

4

1 b   2 b   3 a   4 b   5 a   6 b

5

1 to calm down	2 to inform
3 drinking	4 living
5 to tell	6 coming

6

1 to organize	2 to talk
3 leaving	4 making
5 to eat	6 sightseeing
7 to join	

9

- Ask students to read the text briefly and say what it is about.

- Ask students to complete the comments with the correct form of the verbs in brackets. Let students compare answers in pairs. In feedback, elicit and discuss possible answers. Ask students to refer back to the grammar rules to justify the forms they chose to use.

ANSWERS

1 reading   2 to visit   3 to improve   4 allowing
5 giving   6 investing / to invest   7 to say
8 to work   9 living   10 to move

10

- Ask students to complete the sentences in their own words. Elicit two or three ideas to get students started and set a three-minute time limit so that students have some focused preparation time.

- Organize the class into new pairs or small groups of three or four to share their information. Monitor and note how accurately students use the verb patterns. Note down any errors to focus on in feedback.

EXAMPLE ANSWERS

1 Travel: The first place I remember going to on holiday was the north of France. We went there on the train.

2 Education: I regret not studying maths/harder when I was at school. I would like to work in business.

3 Plans: I've been meaning to change jobs for some time. My job is so dull and I'm ready for a new challenge.

4 Parents: After he left school, my father went on to set up his own company. It turned out to be a big success!

5 Free time: Recently I've started doing aerobics classes. I'm not sure I want to carry on with them, though!

6 Work: Before I start work each day I like to eat a big breakfast. It means I start the day well and can wait longer for my lunch.

7 Eating: I prefer eating in to eating out. It's cheaper and I find it more relaxing.

Speaking my life

11

- Ask students to work in pairs to take turns asking and answering the questions.

- When pairs have completed their interviews, put them with another pair to compare answers.

- Ask one student in each group to stand up and present findings to the class.

- **Optional step** You could ask students to work in groups to decide how to interpret their results, and to say how happy they think their society is.

- As students speak, walk round and listen to how well your students use verb patterns. Note down some errors as you monitor. Do the same during the presentations. At the end, write errors on the board and ask students to work in pairs to correct them.

5c The teenage mind

Lesson at a glance
- reading: the teenage mind
- critical thinking: ways of arguing
- word focus: *fall*
- speaking: stages of life

Reading

1
- Ask students to look at the stages of human development and answer the questions. In feedback, elicit students' ideas.
- **Optional step** Your students' views will naturally depend on their ages. If you have a mixed-age class, use the opportunity to have a fun debate about when teenagers become adult, and when middle age begins.

EXAMPLE ANSWERS

This depends on your point of view, but here are some rough estimates:
1 infancy: 0 to 2 or 3
childhood: 3 or 4 to 12
adolescence: 12 to 17 or 18
adulthood: from the age of 18
2 a teenager: 13 to 18
a baby: 0 to 12 or 18 months
a middle-aged man: from about 45 to 65 years
a young woman: from about 16 to 30 or 35
a toddler: 2 or 3 (a toddler is a baby or infant who can walk, but unsteadily)

2 🕮 [44]
- Ask students to work in pairs to think of three typical characteristics of teenage behaviour. Elicit one or two ideas to get students started.
- Ask students to read the first paragraph of the article and compare ideas.
- **Optional step** The reading text is recorded. You could play the recording and ask students to read and listen.

EXAMPLE ANSWERS

Here are ideas from the text: not wanting to communicate with parents or adults in general, doing silly or dangerous things like skateboarding down a stair rail, constantly chatting to friends on social media

Other possible characteristics: being lazy and untidy, being rude, constantly asking for money, being energetic or alternatively sleeping for long hours, being enthusiastic

3
- Ask students to read the rest of the article and answer the questions. Let students compare answers in pairs before checking as a class.

ANSWERS
1 sensation seeking (excitement, risk), preferring the company of people their own age
2 Positive: sensation seeking can lead to a wider circle of friends and a happier, more successful life and preferring the company of their peers is positive because it is vital to build relationships with them as they share a common future. We should celebrate these differences, because they make teenagers the most adaptable human beings around.

4
- Ask students to work individually to read the article again and choose the correct options. Elicit the first answer to get students started. Tell them to check their answers in pairs.

ANSWERS
1 decreases 5 the teenagers' own
2 young children 6 useful
3 are fully aware 7 appropriately
4 gain 8 characteristics

5
- Ask students to find and underline the words and expressions in the article. Then ask them to choose the correct definition. Tell them to check their answers in pairs.

ANSWERS
1 a 2 a 3 b 4 c 5 b

Vocabulary notes

on the spur of the moment = a 'spur' is a piece sticking out on the outer edge of something, so this fixed expression suggests that you are acting without thought or planning

ultimately = in the end or eventually – what happens after other things have happened

Note the other potentially new words in the text:

excluded = not allowed in a group or a place

peer = somebody in your group, e.g. somebody of the same age or in the same class or social group

a stair rail = the long metal or wooden thing you hold on to when walking down stairs

impulsive = acting in an uncontrolled way, in which you do things suddenly and without preparation

Extra activity

Ask students to find and write down adjectives used in the text to describe teenagers or children: *difficult, silly, dangerous, impulsive, sensation-seeking, risky, adaptable.*

Ask students to say how accurate these adjectives are, and to suggest adjectives of their own.

Critical thinking ways of arguing

6

- Ask students to look at the ways to argue a point in a gentler and less direct way. Then tell them to underline the words and phrases in 1–3 that have the same effect.

ANSWERS

1 probably
2 might seem; can also be
3 at least; quite possibly

Vocabulary notes

The language used in the examples in Exercise 6 is often called 'hedging'. It is common in academic language and is used to either distance the author from the point being made or lessen the strength of the point being made, either because the author is unsure of the point or aims to persuade the reader by not being too direct or forceful.

Ways of hedging include using modal adverbs (e.g. *perhaps*) or modal verbs (e.g. *could*) or set expressions (e.g. *for me at any rate*).

7

- Ask students to work in pairs to discuss the questions. You could choose to do this open class or in pairs or small groups.
- In feedback, encourage an open discussion.

EXAMPLE ANSWERS

1 Using less direct phrases is useful when faced with a sceptical reader. Basically, the author is asking readers to accept what they are saying as they develop their argument, even if the reader doesn't agree with it. When the author writes *it might seem dangerous* or *it can be a positive thing*, the reader is more likely to follow this argument, but if the author writes *This clearly isn't dangerous* or *This is undoubtedly a good thing*, the reader might be resistant, or even stop reading, because the argument may be too direct and too firmly against what the reader already thinks.

2 Using less direct language is common in academic writing, in which the writer must persuade knowledgeable peers of their argument. It's also common in newspaper opinion columns in which the columnist tries to make a case and in political speeches.
Using less direct language is also common in formal emails and business correspondence as a way of being polite.
Students' own answers

Word focus *fall*

8

- Organize the class into pairs to discuss the phrases with the word *fall*.

ANSWERS

1 *fall out with* (*somebody*) = to have an argument and stop being friendly
2 *fall behind* (*with work*) = to make less progress than necessary – here, it is necessary to do extra work to catch up
3 *fall apart* = to break easily into pieces because they are old or badly made
4 (*plans*) *fall through* = to fail to happen (often disappointingly)
5 *fall for* (*somebody*) = to fall in love with, or be quickly attracted to somebody

9

- Ask students to work individually to prepare their own ideas. Elicit one or two examples to get students started. You could let students just think of ideas before speaking, or you could ask them to write the sentences.
- Let students compare their ideas in pairs or in small groups. In feedback, ask a few students to share their sentences with the class.

EXAMPLE ANSWERS

I've never fallen out with my classmates.
I've missed two lessons and fallen behind with my studies.
My school book is falling apart – I've studied so much!
Jo lost her job and all her career plans fell through.
A friend once fell for my brother. It was so embarrassing!

Extra activity

Ask students to use learner dictionaries to find three further phrases with the word *fall*. Ask students to write a true, personalized sentence to help them remember each expression they find.

Examples: *fall in love with someone, fall down, fall back on* (her experience, her friends), *fall about* (laughing)

Speaking my life

10

- **Optional step** Ask students to work individually to prepare ideas first. Monitor and help with vocabulary. Set a time limit and encourage students to write brief notes. The more students prepare, the better the final performance will be.
- Depending on time and preferences, the discussion activity can be done as a whole class or in small groups. If students talk in groups, ask one person from each group to briefly summarize that group's discussion at the end for the class.
- Use the opportunity at the end of the activity to give feedback on some of the errors you heard students make.

EXAMPLE ANSWERS

1 Childhood – positive aspects: a time of play, discovery, adventure, family holidays, toys, presents, little responsibility

Childhood – negative aspects: school, having to do what you're told, being told off, having fewer choices

Adolescence – positive aspects: friends, boy/girlfriends, smartphones and other technology, discovering movies and music, concerts, growing independence, holidays, planning an exciting future

Adolescence – negative aspects: parents, arguments, rules, exams, school/college, falling out with friends, not having your own money, not having as much freedom as you would like

Young adulthood – positive aspects: friends, boy/girlfriends, freedom, adventure, being your own boss, earning your own money, being able to live independently

Young adulthood – negative aspects: money worries, exams, getting a job, relationship problems, responsibilities

Early middle age – positive aspects: family, responsibility, positive career moves, wide group of friends, holidays

Early middle age – negative aspects: working hard, too much responsibility, financial concerns

Late middle age – positive aspects: freedom, chance to do your own thing, wide group of friends, experience

Late middle age – negative aspects: health, family leaving home, identity may change with retirement

Old age – positive aspects: hopefully no work, no financial concerns, grandchildren, freedom to travel and do new things, wisdom

Old age – negative aspects: health, mobility, possibly money worries, friends becoming ill or dying

2 As people age they tend to have fewer friends and see less of them (but establish stronger friendships with closest friends). Young people have less money but worry about it less whereas older people get increasingly concerned with it. Health becomes a bigger issue as you age.

3 Students' own answers

Extra activity

A roleplay debate: Organize the class into groups of four or five and ask each group to choose a different stage of life. They have three minutes to prepare reasons why their stage of life is the best. Students then present and debate their arguments. At the end have a class vote on who made the best case for their stage of life. If you have a mix of ages in your class, ask students to argue for the stage of life nearest their own.

5d A controversial issue

Lesson at a glance
- real life: debating issues
- pronunciation: sentence stress

Real life debating issues

1 [45]
- Ask students to look at the photo and the caption. Ask: *What's the sport? What do skate parks look like?*
- Play the recording. Students listen and answer the question.

ANSWER
There have been a number of complaints about noise coming from the skate park.

Audioscript [45]

Part 1
c = Councillor

c: Hello, everybody. Thanks for coming today. We do appreciate it because we need to hear from as many residents as possible before we come to a decision on the future of the skate park. As you know, there have been a number of complaints about noise coming from the park and noise disturbance is something that we at the council take very seriously. So, we'd like to hear your views, and any suggestions you might have for a way forward.

2
- Ask students to work in pairs to make a list of benefits and disadvantages to having a skate park near their home.
- In feedback, elicit ideas from different pairs. You could build up a class list of pros and cons on the board.

EXAMPLE ANSWERS
Benefits: a place for children/teenagers to go, close to parents' homes so younger children could have parental supervision, healthy exercise, encourages children to learn new skills, keeps kids from skateboarding on roads and around public buildings

Disadvantages: some people wouldn't like groups of teenagers hanging out, could be noisy, kids could drink there / do drugs

3 [46]
- Tell students they are going to listen to people at the public meeting debating what should happen to the park. Ask students to read the table. Then play the recording. Students listen and make notes.
- Let students compare answers in pairs before discussing as a class.

ANSWERS

First woman: constant noise coming from the skateboard ramps all day – from ten in the morning to sometimes as late as ten at night in summer … it's spoiling our enjoyment of our own gardens; there could be drugs and crime in the future

First man: a bit of an exaggeration – people can all hear each other talking; (bad) impact if closed down – a lot of kids will be left with nothing to do – will find public spaces to skateboard that aren't safe

Second man: concerned that the park has become a centre for young people to gather in the evening – worries that it's not safe

Second woman: healthy exercise for kids – they're not at home watching TV or playing video games – doing something active

Audioscript 💿 [46]

C = Councillor; M = First man; M2 = Second man;
W = First woman; W2 = Second woman

Part 2

C: … So, we'd like to hear your views, and any suggestions you might have for a way forward. So, yes, – the woman in the blue top. Would you like to introduce yourself and start us off?

W: Well, yes. I live about fifty metres from the skate park – our garden backs onto it. I'm sure that no one, me included, wants to spoil other people's fun. But the thing is that the constant noise coming from these skateboard ramps all day – from ten in the morning to sometimes as late as ten at night in summer … it's spoiling *our* enjoyment of our own gardens. Sometimes, we can't even hear each other speak!

M: Sorry, but I think that's a bit of an exaggeration. We can all hear each other talking OK and we're right next to it.

M2: For me, the noise is just one factor. And actually, I'm not too bothered by the sound of people having fun. I'm more concerned that the park has become a centre for young people to gather in the evening and I worry that it's not safe for them.

W: No, that's a very good point. I think it's just a matter of time before we are here again talking about some more serious problem – like drugs or crime.

W2: I think we're forgetting that this is healthy exercise these kids are having. They're not at home watching TV or playing video games. They're outside doing something active. And quite honestly, if that involves making a bit of noise, then that's something I can live with.

M: Thanks for that – I agree completely. I don't think most of you have really thought about the impact if you close this down. A lot of kids will just be left with nothing to do, or we'll have to find public spaces where we can skateboard and that aren't safe. The whole thing just doesn't make any sense to me.

4 💿 [46]

• Ask students to read the expressions in the language box and to work in pairs to discuss what the missing words are. Then play the recording again. Students listen and write in the words they hear.

• **Optional step** Ask students to practise saying the phrases. Tell them to choose five and read them out then close their books and try to remember and say the phrases.

ANSWERS

1	thing	6	bothered
2	For	7	concerned
3	forgetting	8	but
4	completely	9	thought
5	good	10	sense

Pronunciation sentence stress

5a/b 💿 [47]

• Ask students to decide which words are stressed. Let students compare their answers in pairs.

• Play the recording. Students listen, note and underline the strongly stressed words.

• Play the recording again for students to listen and repeat.

Audioscript 💿 [47] (and answers)

1 The <u>fact is</u> that <u>no</u> one likes to be <u>disturbed</u>.

2 Quite <u>honestly</u>, that's a <u>good</u> thing.

3 For <u>me</u>, that's not the <u>point</u>.

4 <u>Sorry</u>, but I think that's an <u>exaggeration</u>.

5 The whole thing just <u>doesn't</u> make any <u>sense</u> to me.

Pronunciation notes

We tend to stress the key words – the words that carry most meaning in the sentence. Note that this can often be subjective and can depend on what the speaker is trying to convey, or what they are responding to.

6

• Ask students to read about the proposed development. In feedback, ask students whether they think it's a good idea to redevelop or not. Try to establish whether there is broad agreement or disagreement in the class.

• Ask students to work individually to make notes both for and against the development. Tell students to decide whether to support it or oppose it based on their notes.

• As students work, monitor and help with ideas and vocabulary. Note, also, which students are for the proposed development, and which are against. Before debating the proposal, give feedback on students' ideas for and against the proposed development, and make sure everybody has plenty of ideas.

EXAMPLE ANSWERS

For: Library and swimming pool aren't used very often, so money can be used elsewhere.

Shopping centre and gym/club might create more jobs and boost the local economy.

Against: There are plenty of shops and gyms already.

Important to fight for public services – better to enhance and encourage usage than just to close.

Public swimming pool is affordable for more people – private gym will be exclusive.

Education (library) is more important than shopping.

7

- Organize the class into groups (see Teacher development below). If there is a split in opinion in the class, try to mix students so that each group has students with different opinions.

- Ask students to debate the issue and remind them to use expressions from the 'debating issues' language box. As students speak, listen for errors of use with the expressions.

- **Optional step** At the end of the debate, ask each group to agree on whether they should support or oppose the proposal. Find out who made the best case, and which students were persuaded to change their minds as a result of the debate.

Extra activity

Here is a second topic that you might choose to debate with your students:

Proposed development: Redevelopment of a green area in a housing estate. Currently the area has some small vegetable gardens for local residents and a small animal farm that children can visit. These will be replaced by shops, cafes, a playground and some public works of art.

Teacher development

How to conduct a class debate

1 Debates start with a proposal or a question that one team will argue for and another will argue against. Choose a topic to which your students can relate – perhaps one with practical application. Make sure your students understand the issue and any specialized vocabulary associated with it.

2 Organize your students to carry out the debate. It's useful to group your students into teams to research and argue the issue. One idea is to split your class into four groups (with at least three students in each group). Two groups (A and B) prepare to argue for, and two groups (C and D) prepare to argue against. Then hold two short class debates. A argues for, and C against. During the debate, B and D are judges and decide who presents the best case. Now hold the second debate, with B and D. Groups A and C are judges.

3 Allow plenty of time for students to research and prepare the issue, and help with any vocabulary they need. The more preparation, the better the debate.

4 For a more formal debate, follow this procedure:

a) The group in support of the issue receives two minutes to present their case to the audience.

b) The group in opposition to the issue then receives two minutes to present their case.

c) After both sides have spoken, both teams receive two minutes to prepare a response and summary.

d) The order of speech is reversed now and the opposition group presents their rebuttal and summary for the two minutes.

e) The last to speak is the team in support of the issue, who then presents their rebuttal and summary for two minutes. That brings the debate to an end.

5 To determine the winner, have judges vote on which team they thought made the most convincing argument. Give your own opinion as to who communicated clearly and responded to their opponent's arguments most effectively. This combination will identify your winners.

5e Big cities, big problems

Lesson at a glance
- writing: an opinion essay
- writing skill: linking words

Writing an opinion essay

1
- Ask students to discuss the questions in pairs. In feedback, elicit their ideas and reasons.

> **EXAMPLE ANSWERS**
>
> People live in big cities because: there are good jobs, often with better pay and prospects than in small towns or the countryside; there are interesting things to do – restaurants, nightlife, etc.; there are educational opportunities – school, universities.
>
> Problems in big cities: overcrowding; pollution; health problems – contagious diseases; crime; high rents and daily travel and living costs

2
- Ask students to look at the title of the essay. You could ask students if they broadly agree or disagree with the statement.
- Ask students to read the essay and find out what the writer's opinion is. Let students compare answers before checking as a class.

> **ANSWER**
>
> As long as the population of cities does not grow more quickly than the services available, cities are a good thing. They stop the population spreading into areas of the countryside, they provide jobs and they give people a more interesting life.

3
- Ask students to say whether the essay follows the given structure.

> **ANSWER**
>
> Yes

4
- Read the different types of introduction to the class. Ask students to say which type the writer has chosen.
- **Optional step** Ask students to work in pairs to write an alternative opening to the essay based on one of the other forms. Another option is to read out the alternative openings in the extra activity below and ask students to say which form each matches.

> **ANSWER**
>
> giving some statistics that illustrate the seriousness of the problem

Extra activity

Ask students to match these alternative openings with the different listed forms:

1 'The city is not a concrete jungle,' said zoologist Desmond Morris. 'It is a human zoo.' In many ways, I believe this is true.

(quoting what someone famous has said about this problem)

2 On my way back to my hotel, I saw two lovers kiss, four smartly dressed women come out of a theatre, and a group of schoolchildren watch a street performer. Only in a city can such lively activity be found.

(telling a story about the problem from the writer's own experience)

3 As thousands of people head home on slow, overcrowded commuter trains, they pass the homeless and unemployed, forced to beg to survive.

(giving a dramatic example of the problem)

Writing skill linking words
5a
- Ask students to put the highlighted phrases from the essay in the correct place in the table. Let students compare answers in pairs before checking with the class.

> **ANSWERS**
>
> Adding an argument: Furthermore, As well as, In addition
>
> Introducing a contrasting fact: Then again, On the other hand
>
> Explaining the consequences: Consequently, As a result, Because of this

5b
- Ask students to work individually to choose an appropriate linking phrase to complete the sentences. Let students compare their answers in pairs before checking with the class.

> **ANSWERS**
>
> 1 Furthermore / In addition
> 2 Then again / On the other hand
> 3 As well as

Grammar notes

Most of the linking words introduced here link two sentences. They go at the start of the second sentence and are followed by a comma.

The exception is *as well as*, which joins two clauses. It can go at the start of either clause and is followed by the *-ing* form of the verb. When adding an argument using *as well as*, the subjects of both clauses must be the same:

Cities are convenient for the residents. Cities are also very convenient for business.

As well as being very convenient for the residents, cities are also very convenient for business.

6

- Ask students to read the statement. Then ask students for their opinions. Find out whether they agree or not and ask why.

- Brainstorm ideas and language students could use in their essay. You could do this open class, writing up ideas on the board in note form, or you could put students in pairs or small groups to brainstorm. Set a five-minute time limit for this.

- **Optional step** Ask students to look back at the format for the essay: Introduction → Arguments for → Arguments against → Conclusion. Tell them to use their ideas to make notes under each heading.

- Once students are happy with their notes and format, ask them to write the opinion essay. Remind them of the four different types of openings they could use.

7

- Ask students to exchange their essay with a partner. Students read the essays and give verbal feedback to their partner on the points. Ask students to revise their essays in the light of their partner's feedback.

- **Optional step** Alternatively, you could get students to write feedback at the bottom of their partner's essays before returning them, or you could pass the essays round the class or a group in the class so that three or four students can give feedback on each essay.

5f Scandinavian mega-bridge

Before you watch

1

- Ask students to work in pairs to discuss the questions.

> **EXAMPLE ANSWERS**
> 1 It's a long bridge over a large stretch of water. It's probably a road and/or rail bridge. In the middle it has two towers (and a suspension section) and a wider space underneath, probably to allow ships to pass.
> 2 by ferry, via a tunnel, by plane

Background information

The Øresund Bridge (which can also be written as Öresund or Oresund) is called the Øresundsbroen in Danish and the Öresundsbron in Swedish. It runs nearly 8 kilometres (5 miles) from the Swedish coast to the artificial island Peberholm in the middle of the strait, and the crossing is completed by the 4 km (2.5-mile) Drogden Tunnel from Peberholm to the Danish island of Amager. It was completed in August 1999 when Crown Prince Frederik of Denmark and Crown Princess Victoria of Sweden met midway across the bridge-tunnel in celebration.

Key vocabulary

2a

- Ask students to read the sentences and guess the meaning of the words from their context. Start students off by eliciting the meaning of the first word.

- Let students compare their answers in pairs before moving on to Exercise 2b.

2b

- Ask students to match the words in bold in Exercise 2a with the definitions in Exercise 2b. Let students compare their answers in pairs.

> **ANSWERS**
> 1 d   2 c   3 b   4 e   5 a

Vocabulary notes

Note the stress: _metropolis_

Other famous straits include the strait of Gibraltar that separates Europe from Africa and the strait of Hormuz that connects the Persian Gulf and Arabian Sea.

While you watch

3 ■◀ [5.1]

- Ask students to watch the video and answer the questions. Play the whole of the video. Let students compare answers in pairs before discussing as a class.

ANSWERS

1 the distance (the Ørseund Strait is ten miles wide); the weather is bad ('lousy'); a high bridge might obstruct air traffic, a low bridge might block the shipping traffic
2 They built it as part-bridge and part-tunnel.

Pronunciation note

Note that there is an unusual contraction at the start of the recording: *What's it take to build one of the world's mega bridges?* The speaker is contracting *does* (not *is* or *has*).

Videoscript ■◀ 5.1

Part 1

0.00–0.12 What's it take to build one of the world's mega bridges?

0.13–0.28 In northern Europe, the Baltic Sea converges with the North Sea at the Øresund Strait. It's ten miles wide with lousy weather. And it's done a great job of keeping Denmark separate from Sweden.

0.29–1.03 The Øresund Strait is a frustrating barrier because each shore has something the other needs. Copenhagen, Denmark, needs cheaper housing. Malmö, Sweden, needs more jobs. Connect the dots and you could unleash an economic powerhouse. A bridge would make them one big metropolis, but it's never been possible. Until now.

1.04–1.27 Enter the Øresund Bridge. The world's longest cable-stayed bridge that can carry cars plus the enormous weight of trains. 3,583 feet of road and rail dangling from 160 cables.

1.28–1.49 Two hundred feet above the sea, the support towers soar 670 feet, jabbing at clouds and making the Øresund Bridge one of the tallest cement structures in Sweden.

Part 2

1.50–2.39 Companies from both countries must form a consortium to build the bridge together. The consortium's first challenge: figuring out how to build a bridge ten miles long. Immediately, they face a dangerous setback. On the Denmark side, right at the shoreline, is the Copenhagen international airport, Kastrup. Computer simulations show that building a bridge with high towers would obstruct air traffic … or worse. A low bridge would be safer for air traffic, but it would block Denmark's ship traffic.

2.40–2.47 When engineers can't build over the water, they consider building under it, with a tunnel ten miles long.

2.48–3.13 Peter Lundhus That would be the beautiful solution, building a tunnel from one side to the other, but that would be the expensive solution. So the third solution that we decided was, of course, to build part-bridge and then a tunnel where we were getting close to the airport. A bridge would have been easier or cheaper, but would not have been a good idea for the aeroplanes.

3.14–3.28 Somewhere, they need dry land for the tunnel to emerge from under water. They need an island, so they'll have to build one, from scratch.

4 ■◀ [5.1]

• Ask students to look at the table and think carefully about what type of information is missing.

• When students are ready, play the first part of the video (to 1.49) again. Students complete the table with words and numbers.

ANSWERS

1 ten miles
2 lousy *or* bad (or another synonym)
3 cheaper housing
4 more jobs
5 cars and trains
6 200 feet
7 670 feet
8 one of the tallest cement structures

5 ■◀ [5.1]

• Ask students to read the questions carefully.

• Play the second part of the video (1.50 to the end) again. Students note answers. Let students compare their answers in pairs before checking with the class.

ANSWERS

1 computer simulation, which showed how the bridge would obstruct air traffic
2 because it would block Denmark's ship traffic
3 beautiful, expensive
4 They needed dry land for the tunnel to come out onto from under water.

6

• Ask students to complete the summary. Let students compare their answers in pairs before discussing as a class.

ANSWERS

1 Strait   2 metropolis   3 consortium   4 air
5 expensive   6 tunnel   7 bridge   8 longest

After you watch
Vocabulary in context
7a ■◀ [5.2]

• Explain that students are going to watch some clips from the video which contain some new words and phrases. They need to choose the correct meaning of the words.

• Play the clips. When each multiple-choice question appears, pause the clip so that students can choose the correct definition. You could let students compare answers in pairs before discussing as a class.

ANSWERS

1 b   2 c   3 b   4 c   5 b   6 a

Videoscript ■◀ 5.2

1 It's ten miles wide with **lousy** weather.
  a good
  b very bad
  c unusual

2 The Øresund Strait is a **frustrating** barrier ...

   a risky

   b growing

   c annoying

3 **Connect the dots** and you could unleash an economic powerhouse.

   a combine the ideas

   b join the different points

   c get the people working together

4 Immediately, they face a dangerous **setback**.

   a difficult task

   b opposition to a plan

   c problem which blocks progress

5 ... they need dry land for the tunnel to **emerge** from under water.

   a come back

   b come out

   c come over

6 ... they'll have to build one, **from scratch**.

   a from the beginning

   b from simple materials

   c without any experience of this

7b

- Students work individually to complete the sentences. Elicit one or two ideas for the first sentence to get them started. Let students compare sentences in pairs.

EXAMPLE ANSWERS

1 The weather in *the west of my country* is always lousy.

2 The most frustrating thing about my job / my studies *is the long hours*.

3 The project suffered a big setback when *one of the buildings fell down*.

8

- Organize the class into groups of four or five. Ask students to work together to choose a town and prepare a presentation.

- When groups are ready, ask each group to briefly present their idea to the class.

EXAMPLE ANSWERS

Ideas for a transport plan include: a new tram system, a park and ride bus service from out of town to the centre, pedestrianized central areas, a new one-way system to limit the access of cars to the centre, a system whereby cars are not allowed in the centre on certain days, increased parking fees or a pay zone which makes cars pay if they drive into the zone, tourist routes marked by more signs

---

UNIT 5 Review and memory booster

Memory Booster activities

Exercises 3, 5, 6 and 8 are Memory Booster activities. For more information about these activities and how they benefit students, see page 10 of this Teacher's Book.

I can ... check boxes

As an alternative to asking students to simply tick the *I can* ... boxes, you could ask them to give themselves a score from 1 to 4 (1 = not very confident; 4 = very confident) for each language area. If students score 1 or 2 for a language area, refer them to additional practice activities in the Workbook and Grammar summary exercises.

Grammar

1

- Ask students to work individually to complete the interview between an interviewer and an official. Tell them to use the correct form of the verb: *-ing, to +* infinitive or infinitive without *to*. Let students compare answers in pairs before eliciting answers from the class.

ANSWERS

  1 to see *or* seeing

  2 (to) be

  3 to have

  4 to develop *or* developing

  5 to invest

  6 moving

  7 affecting

  8 to minimize

  9 supporting

10 give

11 using

2

- Ask students to read the interview again and answer the question.

ANSWER

Benefits: It's helped to make Laos energy independent and the money they make from selling energy is being invested in health and social programmes.

Problems: People have been moved from their homes and there has been destruction of natural forests.

---

3 >> MB

- Ask students to work in pairs to discuss the phrases. Tell them to identify which of the phrases mean the same thing, and if they mean something different, they should explain the difference.

ANSWERS

1 The phrase *stop to talk* means that the person stopped doing something else in order to talk, and *stop talking* means that the person was talking and then they finished talking.

2 same meaning

3 same meaning

4 same meaning

5 The phrase *remember to post* means that the person is planning to post something in the future and doesn't want to forget to do it and *remember posting* means that the person posted something in the past and is recalling that action.

Vocabulary

4

- Ask students to work individually to choose the correct options to complete the text. Let students compare answers in pairs before checking with the class.

ANSWERS

1 hectic	4 reasonably
2 toddlers	5 through
3 thrive	6 out with

5 >> MB

- Students work individually to complete the urban features using a word that rhymes with the word in brackets. Let students compare answers in pairs before checking with the class.

ANSWERS

1 block	4 mall
2 centre	5 park
3 zone	6 space

6 >> MB

- Ask students to work in pairs to describe the features of a city they know. Tell them to say what they like or dislike about the city. Monitor as they speak and encourage them to use vocabulary from the unit.

Real life

7

- Ask students to work individually to use the words in the box to complete the responses to the question. Let students compare answers in pairs before checking with the class.

ANSWERS

1 depend	4 appreciate
2 accept	5 concerned
3 make	6 considered

8 >> MB

- Organize students into groups of three or four. Tell them to respond to the idea using phrases from Exercise 7. You could then encourage them to develop the conversation with their own ideas.

Unit 6 Alternative travel

Opener

1

- Ask students to look at the photo and the caption. Discuss the questions with your class. Elicit ideas from the students in feedback.

> **EXAMPLE ANSWERS**
>
> Possible activities include hiking and mountain climbing in summer and skiing or snowboarding in winter. Other possibilities include cable car rides, and eating and drinking in the hotel with wonderful views.

Background information

Switzerland is a country in central Europe which is surrounded by land on all sides. It has some of the highest mountains in the Alps and is a centre for hiking and winter sports. It also has many lakes.

The country is made up of 26 cantons, each of which has its own constitution and government. Appenzell is a small, mountainous canton in the east of the country near the Austrian border.

Berggasthaus Aescher (shown in the photo) is a 170-year-old guesthouse built on a cliff, which can only be accessed by cable car. It was originally a hut housing farmers, goats and cows, and today offers beds for hikers and climbers.

2 💿 [48]

- **Optional step** Ask students to read the questions and predict what the speaker might or might not like about a stay in a mountainous guesthouse.

- Play the recording. Students listen and note answers to the questions.

> **ANSWERS**
>
> Likes: beautiful setting, views are amazing, food is fantastic
> Dislikes: long journey, not cheap, out of the way, sometimes no water

Audioscript 💿 [48]

I only get three weeks' holiday a year so I always choose the places I go to carefully. I try to go to places with dramatic scenery – and unusual places. It can take time to get to these, but, personally, I think it's worth it. I saw this hotel on the cover of a travel magazine and thought 'Yes, I've got to go there'. It's called the Aescher Guesthouse and it's in the most beautiful setting, overlooking a Swiss Alpine valley. To get there from Zurich, you have to take two different trains, then a cable car and then it's a walk down through some caves to the hotel. But when you get there, you won't regret it. The views are amazing and the food is also fantastic. The only downsides are that it's not cheap and also because it's so out of the way, sometimes there's no water so you can't always have a shower when you want one. I spent two days there hiking in the mountains. Some of the other guests went paragliding, you know, off the mountainside, which looked incredible, but that wasn't for me – I'm not actually great with heights!

3

- Ask students to work in pairs to choose the correct options. Check answers with the class before asking students to take turns to ask and answer the questions.

- As students speak, take the opportunity to listen and note errors and interesting comments made by students. In feedback, ask students with interesting opinions or experiences to share them with the class.

> **ANSWERS**
>
> 1 holiday   2 self-catering   3 view   4 luggage
> 5 scenery   6 journey   7 airline   8 take

Vocabulary notes

1 *holiday* – (here, uncountable) has the same meaning as *days off*, but *days off* is wrong because it is countable and therefore needs *How many*

2 *self-catering holiday/accommodation/apartment* – used to say that there is a kitchen so you can cook yourself, unlike in a hotel; *self-service restaurant / petrol station* – used to say that customers have to go and get their own food or petrol because there isn't a waiter or attendant

3 *a room with a view* = a room from which you can see something interesting (e.g. the beach or the mountains, not the car park); *sight* is not used here – *see the sights* means go and see the interesting places when on holiday

4 *luggage* = (uncountable) all the bags you take with you on holiday; *suitcase* = a particular type of luggage which is large, and opens on a hinge – *suitcase* is wrong here because it is a singular, countable noun – *suitcases* would be correct. *To travel light* is to travel with little luggage (e.g. with just a backpack).

5 *scenery* = the natural view, or elements of that view, that you look at; *countryside* is used to describe rural areas, so farmland and villages, not mountains or deserts

6 *journey* is a countable noun used to describe going from one place to another; *travel* is an uncountable noun used to describe the activity of travelling

7 *airline* = a company that flies planes, e.g. Virgin, Easyjet, Qantas; an *aeroplane* or *plane* is an individual machine that flies (note: *airplane* in US English)

8 *How long did it take?* = How much time from one place to another – *the flight took four hours*; *How long did it last?* = How much time did the event go on for – *the match lasted an hour longer than we expected*

Extra activity

Ask students to write four personalized sentences using words from the sentences. Three should be true and one false. Examples: *I get twenty days off every year*; *I once stayed in a hotel with a view of the Himalayas*; *It took an hour for me to get home yesterday.*

Ask students to work in pairs or groups and read out their sentences to each other. Their partners or group members must guess which sentence is false.

6a Staycations

Lesson at a glance
- vocabulary: holiday activities
- reading: holidays at home
- grammar: negative forms
- speaking: planning a staycation

Vocabulary holiday activities

1
- **Optional step** Start by asking students to explain the derivation of *staycation*: *stay + vacation*. It is a portmanteau word – a word blending the sounds and combining the meanings of two other words. It means a holiday (or 'vacation', in US English) in which you stay at home but behave as if you are on holiday – a 'stay-at-home-vacation'. You could do the extra activity below as a lead-in at this point.
- Ask students to work in pairs to talk about each holiday activity and think of three more activities. Elicit the first as an example to get students started. Let students compare with another pair before checking with the class.

ANSWERS

Other possible activities:

At the seaside: waterskiing, swimming, playing beach volleyball

In the city: shopping, going to clubs, going to the theatre or cinema

In the country: cycling, fishing, horse riding

Vocabulary notes

segway = (or Segway Personal Transporter) a two-wheeled, self-balancing, battery-powered electric vehicle

snorkelling = diving just under the surface of the water and swimming while breathing through a tube (a snorkel) that sticks up above the surface of the water.

Pronunciation note

Note the strong stress on the first syllable: *sightseeing*, *snorkelling*, *sunbathing*

2
- Ask students to discuss the questions in pairs or small groups.

Extra activity

Ask students to tell you any portmanteau words they know. Then write the following common portmanteaus on the board: *brunch, motel, liger, Britpop, fanzine, rom-com, sitcom, bromance*

Ask students to work in pairs to guess which two words they are formed from, and to guess the meaning.

brunch = breakfast and lunch – a meal eaten at about 11 am

motel = motor car and hotel – a hotel near the main road / highway where you can park your car easily

liger = lion and tiger – a cross between the two animals

Britpop = British and pop music – a type of indy pop or rock particular to the UK

fanzine = fan and magazine – a magazine made by fans

rom-com = romantic and comedy – a type of movie in which boy meets girl

sitcom = situation and comedy – a type of TV comedy programme

bromance = brother and romance – used to describe a close friendship between two men

Reading

3
- Ask students to discuss the questions in pairs. Instead of asking students to talk about the capital, change this to other major cities if more appropriate for your students.
- **Optional step** You could set this up by describing a city you know well first. This provides a good model of what to say, a live listening comprehension and, if you are a different nationality to your students, it makes for an interesting talk.

ANSWERS

Students' own ideas

4 🔊 [49]
- Ask students to read sentences 1 to 4. Explain *staycation* and *staycationers* if you haven't already.
- Ask students to read the article and choose true (T) or false (F) for each sentence. Let students check their answers in pairs before checking with the class. In feedback, ask students to justify answers by referring to the text.
- **Optional step** The reading text is recorded. You could play the recording and ask students to read and listen.

ANSWERS

1 F (*You could even camp in your garden or at a local campsite.*)
2 T (*things that you might do on holiday – like sightseeing, eating out, going swimming, etc. – but instead, you do them in your local area.*)
3 F (*you get none of the problems associated with travel – no packing to do, no long drives or delays at the airport*)
4 T (*they help to create the feel of a traditional vacation.*)

5
- Ask students to work individually and use the information in the blog to complete the sentences. Let students check their answers in pairs before checking them with the class.

ANSWERS

1 they are a cheaper kind of holiday.
2 people spend their money in restaurants, museums, etc.
3 foreign travel.
4 weeklong Japanese vacation (in her own city).

Vocabulary notes

Check that students are familiar with the following vocabulary:

be put off = to have a negative experience and feel you don't want to do something any longer or again

take it a step further = to do more than usual or more than originally planned

bonsai plants = miniature Japanese trees

ramen = a form of noodle dish

Grammar negative forms

6

- Ask students to look at the information and examples in the grammar box and complete the sentences with one word in each space. Go through the answers with the class in feedback.

ANSWERS

1 think, would	6 Let's
2 must	7 all
3 mustn't	8 is
4 so	9 too
5 to go	

Refer students to page 166 for further information and practice.

ANSWERS TO GRAMMAR SUMMARY EXERCISES

1
1 not
2 not wait
3 doesn't think it's
4 not to be
5 Don't
6 don't have to
7 mustn't

2
1 Let's not
2 We don't believe (that)
3 don't have to book a table
4 Don't forget to lock
5 'm afraid not
6 not to spend

3
1 None of 2 neither 3 no 4 either 5 no 6 neither

Grammar note

Negative statements

With the verbs *think, believe, suppose* and *imagine*, the negative auxiliary *don't/doesn't* is used to make the statement negative: *I don't think/believe Peter has left.* This is not the case with all verbs. For example, by contrast, we say, *I hope Peter hasn't left* and *I'm afraid Peter hasn't left.*

Have to and must

Have to is a semi-modal and behaves like a regular verb when turning into a negative: *I don't have to … / He doesn't have to … Must* is a modal auxiliary verb and behaves like an auxiliary verb when forming a negative: *I/He mustn't …* Note that there is a change in meaning when forming negatives here. *You must / have to leave now* (= there is an obligation to do it), *You mustn't leave now* (= it is prohibited – there is an obligation not to do it), *You don't have to leave now* (= there is no obligation either way – stay if you want).

Short answers

I hope not, I suppose not, I'm afraid not, etc. are used as negative short answers. For example, in the exchange, 'Has Peter left?' 'I hope not', the answer is short for *I hope he has not left*. The affirmative equivalent uses *so* (*I hope so, I suppose so*, etc.). Note that it is unusual to say *I think not* or *I believe not* – *I don't think/believe so* are more common. The word *guess* is used with a comparable meaning to *suppose* or *expect* here – *I guess so* and *I guess not* are used much more commonly in American English than British English.

Negative imperative

The negative imperative is straightforward in English: put *Don't* in front of the affirmative imperative, which looks the same as the infinitive form.

neither, none, no

We use *neither* in short answers to agree with a negative statement: *'I don't like skiing.' 'Me neither.'*

None can be used as a pronoun followed by *of* + noun. Here it is the subject of the sentence or clause and refers to members of a group of people or things: *None of the books are mine.*

No can be used as a determiner. It's used before a noun or gerund: *No students are allowed in; No smoking is permitted.*

7

- **Optional step** Ask students to read the text quickly for gist first. Set a focus question: *What advice does the writer give?*

- Ask students to choose the correct options to complete the text. Elicit the first answer to get the class started. Let students compare their answers in pairs before checking with the class.

ANSWERS

1 not forget   2 guess not   3 not to   4 don't have to
5 no one wants   6 none   7 no

Grammar note

1 *Let's* + *not* + infinitive
2 *guess* is always followed by *not* in a negative short answer (note that in affirmative short answers, we can say *I guess so*, *I think so* and *I believe so*, but in negative short answers, while *I don't think so* and *I don't believe so* are possible, we can't say ~~*I don't guess so*~~).
3 *try* + *not* + *to* + verb
4 here, we're saying there is no obligation to do this
5 you can't use *everyone* with a negative verb
6 *none* + *of* + noun; you can't say *no of*
7 *no* + noun

8

• Ask students to work individually to rewrite the sentences so that they have the opposite meaning. Elicit the first answer to get students started. Let students compare answers in pairs before eliciting answers from the class.

EXAMPLE ANSWERS

1 Let's not spend a lot of money on a foreign holiday.
2 Not all of the hotels had rooms available. *or* None of the hotels had rooms available. (Both sentences are possible, but they have different meanings. The first is saying most but not all had rooms available. The second sentence is saying that there are no rooms available anywhere.)
3 I don't think staycations really replace foreign holidays.
4 I imagine not. *or* I don't imagine so.
5 I told them not to wait until the last moment before booking their holiday.
6 Don't take a swimming costume – there's no swimming pool at the hotel.
7 If you don't want to go swimming, then we don't have to.
8 I don't like foreign travel and neither/nor does Sarah.

9

• Ask students to work in pairs and complete the sentences with their own ideas. Elicit a possible first answer to get them started. Let students compare answers with another pair before feedback.

EXAMPLE ANSWERS

1 You don't have to *spend a lot of money / travel far / go abroad* to have a good holiday.
2 In remote places, there are often no *amenities / places to stay / tour guides*, so *take bottled water and toilet paper / take your own tent / buy a guide book*.
3 If you get lost in a new place, try not *to panic/worry*. Instead, *look at a map / use your phrase book to ask for directions*.
4 Don't be put off by *high prices / bad reviews / bad weather*.
5 I don't think using a travel guidebook *is the best way of finding out about a city*.

Speaking ⟨ my life ⟩

10

• Organize the class into groups of three or four students. Ask groups to decide on a theme and an itinerary for their staycation. The aim here is to get students to use negative forms when giving opinions, making suggestions and giving short answers. It's a good idea for students to do some preparation first to ensure they use the language (see Teacher development below).

• **Optional step** You could ask students to plan a staycation for a particular group of people rather than for themselves (e.g. a group of pensioners, a group of gardeners, a group of friends that's celebrating someone's significant birthday, etc.).

• As students speak, go round and note down errors you hear. Concentrate on errors with negatives. At the end, write up five or six short sentences containing errors you heard. Ask students to work in pairs to correct the errors. Alternatively, if you don't want to interrupt the flow from Exercise 10 to 11, you could choose to feedback on errors after Exercise 11.

11

• Ask groups to join with another group to compare ideas.

• Once the new, larger groups have shared ideas, ask each one to present their ideas to the class in feedback. Have a class vote on which idea sounds the most fun and is easiest to carry out.

Teacher development

Preparing to use new language

Students at this level can talk about most topics, but in free speaking activities they tend to revert back to the same, known language. The more structured preparation time you provide, the more confident and accurate students will be when using new language. Here are some ideas to prepare students for a speaking activity such as Exercise 11:

1 Ask students to note down five things they want to say and five phrases they want to use to express their ideas. As students prepare, monitor and prompt them to use language from the lesson.

2 Brainstorm things people might say when discussing a staycation. Write up any useful phrases suggested – not whole sentences, just the key part of the phrase. Students can refer to these useful phrases on the board during the discussion.

3 Before the lesson write six useful phrases on a piece of paper in a list, e.g. *I don't believe we should … ; Let's not try to … ; Me neither! None of us want to … ; I don't think we have to … ; I hope we don't …* Photocopy the sheet so there is one copy per group and cut up the phrases into six strips. Students in each group of three take two pieces of paper at random. During the discussion they have to try to use these two phrases.

4 Write between 6 and 10 phrases (similar to those in idea 3 above) on the board at random. As students speak, they should try to use as many phrases as they can from the board. In feedback, find out which students were able to accurately use most expressions.

6b Voluntourism

Lesson at a glance
- vocabulary: travel
- listening: volunteer vacations
- grammar: question forms
- pronunciation: intonation in question forms
- speaking: a volunteer trip

Vocabulary travel

1

- **Optional step** Before opening the books, write the word *voluntourism* on the board and ask students to guess what it means. Answer: it's an example of a portmanteau word, and comes from *volunteer* and *tourism*. It's a form of tourism in which people travel to a different location to work for free, usually for a charity.

- Open the books and ask students to complete the list in Exercise 1 with the words. Let students compare their answers in pairs before checking with the class.

ANSWERS

1	guidebook	5	vaccinations
2	boarding	6	money
3	lotion	7	insurance
4	valid	8	details

Other possible items: buy mobile phone SIM card for foreign country; get international credit card; get visa; pack suitcase

Vocabulary notes

mosquito repellent = a spray or cream that stops insects from biting you

valid = if a document is valid, it will be legally accepted by officials (valid passport, driving licence, etc.)

vaccinations = injections that protect you against disease

Extra activity

Ask students to work in pairs to decide which of the things on the list are essential preparations and which aren't. Ask if they would add anything to the essential list.

Listening

2 🎵 [50]
- Ask students to read the definition, look at the photo, and discuss the question.
- Play the recording for students to check their predictions.

ANSWERS

Students may suggest: looking after animals on a wildlife reserve; helping in elephant conservation

The audioscript says: Volunteers help local people to find ways of making a living that don't involve poaching or killing local wildlife. So ... they help them to plant crops or develop ideas for tourist businesses.

Audioscript 🎵 [50]

P = Presenter; **K** = Katie Samuel

P: Now, have you ever thought of doing a bit of building work during your holidays? Or helping to look after animals on a wildlife reserve? You probably thought that sort of trip was for eighteen-year-olds on their gap year. But it seems these days a lot more working adults are opting for volunteer vacations. With us today is Katie Samuel, author of *Good Travel*, a guide to volunteering holidays. Katie, I can see this might be attractive to some, but don't most people just want to head off to the beach and relax?

K: Well, I think that depends on how your volunteer vacation is organized. The good companies are certainly aware that this should be a rewarding travel experience, not just a work trip.

P: But it's not really a holiday as we know it, is it?

K: Again, that depends on your definition. For me, a good holiday is a cultural experience where each side, traveller and host, gives something and takes something. A good example is a programme near the Tsavo National Park in Kenya, where volunteers help local people to find ways of making a living that don't involve poaching or killing local wildlife. So, they help them to plant crops or develop ideas for tourist businesses. In return, the locals take them for bush walks – like mini-safaris – and teach them about local wildlife and the history of their community.

P: But the volunteers pay for the trip, don't they?

K: Yes, of course, they have to pay for their airfares and living expenses and something to cover the cost of organizing the trip.

P: OK. And can you tell us what qualifications or skills these organizations are looking for, usually? I mean, surely they don't want people without experience just turning up to teach or build or whatever?

K: Actually, for the most part, volunteers can be trained to do the work. There are a few projects for professional nurses or teachers, but mostly training is given ... At the Cultural Restoration Tourism Project (CRTP), which restores cultural heritage sites around the world, volunteers are placed with local architects and artists. At the moment, they're restoring a 300-year-old monastery in Nepal and the volunteers are being trained in wall painting by a world-famous painter.

P: Wow. So is it the case that people could come back with a skill they didn't have when they went on holiday?

K: Absolutely. Though it might not be a skill you'll ever use again: helping to bottle-feed a lion cub – that's a project in Zambia – is unlikely to be of direct use to you back in your London office; but we all benefit more widely from new experiences, don't we?

P: Of course. So do you know where listeners can find upcoming volunteer vacation possibilities? Some websites, perhaps?

3
- Discuss the statements with your class. Ask students to justify their choice.

ANSWERS

b (Katie says: A good holiday is a cultural experience where each side, traveller and host, gives something and takes something.)

4 🔊 [50]

- Ask students to read the sentences carefully.
- Play the recording again. Students listen and complete the sentences (see Teacher development below). Ask students to compare answers in pairs and discuss the meaning of the expressions.

ANSWERS

1 gap	4 bush
2 head	5 living
3 trip	6 heritage

Vocabulary notes 1

gap year = many students leave school and delay going to university for a year in order to take a gap year – a year in which they travel, do volunteer work or get work experience

head off (to) = to leave and go (in a particular direction)

a work trip = a journey you make for work – the implication here is that a work trip involves going somewhere, staying in a hotel, working, then coming back – it isn't culturally rewarding

bush walks = the 'bush' is a word used to describe unfarmed land in places like Africa, so a bush walk involves walking through such land, often trying to spot wildlife

living expenses = the daily costs of living, e.g. buying lunch

heritage site = a place of historical or cultural importance to a country or people

Vocabulary notes 2

The use of the words *holiday* and *vacation* can be confusing as they are often interchanged, and there is a difference between British and American usage. In British English, people usually use the word *holiday* to describe going away somewhere (*a beach holiday, we went to Spain on holiday, we're going on our holidays*). It also describes the period of time when you are not at school or work (*the school holidays*). In US English, the word *vacation* is used instead (*we're on vacation in Miami, the college vacation*). Both British and US English use the word *holiday* to describe a national day off – *a public holiday* – and US English uses *the holidays* or *the holiday season* to describe the Christmas and New Year period.

Teacher development

Listening intensively for words

In Exercise 4, students are asked to listen intensively for particular words. This develops students' abilities to hear particular words or chunks of sound within longer extracts. It also introduces students to words as part of meaningful chunks of language which they can learn and use. In order

to develop your students' ability to listen for chunks, do the following:

1 Give them time to predict what words might be missing, or what parts of speech the words might be, before they listen. 2   Allow them to listen two or three times to extracts from the listening so that they can really focus on hearing chunks of language.

3 Introduce your students to the way words link together when spoken naturally, the way pronouns and auxiliary verbs contract, and the way words such as *of* and *to* are reduced to weak forms.

5

- Organize the class into small groups to discuss the questions. In feedback, ask each group to briefly summarize their discussions.

EXAMPLE ANSWERS

1 Students may suggest that a change is as good as a rest, that learning new skills and opening your eyes to how others live improves you as a person, and can help you bring a new perspective on your job, or that they don't like the idea of rich people paying to 'educate' poor people.

2 Students may or may not have strong views here. You could argue that it is good for the local economy – a way of spreading wealth to poorer countries. Or you could argue that holiday companies or governments in poorer countries are exploiting people.

3 stay with a local family; study the history and geography of a place; learn the language or other skills such as local cuisine or handicraft skills

Grammar question forms

6

- Ask students to read the information in the grammar box. Then play the recording so students can hear the pronunciation and intonation of the questions. They will need to recognize the intonation patterns to answer questions 1–5 (see Grammar note below).
- Discuss the questions with the class. Alternatively, ask students to discuss the questions in pairs first before eliciting answers.

ANSWERS

1 Sentences 2, 5, 6

2 Sentences 1, 3, 4, 7

3 Could people come back with a new skill? Where can listeners find volunteer vacation possibilities? Do they want people without experience just turning up?

4 We use the auxiliary verb from the statement with a pronoun. If there is no auxiliary present, we use *do* or *does* for the present simple and *did* for the past simple. If the statement is positive, the tag is negative (*It's not … , is it?*), and if the statement is negative, the tag is positive (*The volunteers pay … , don't they?*).

5 *is it?* (6) has falling intonation and *don't they?* (7) has rising intonation.

UNIT 6 Alternative travel

Refer students to page 166 for further information and practice.

ANSWERS TO GRAMMAR SUMMARY EXERCISES

4
1 Didn't you like
2 Wasn't
3 Isn't he coming
4 Haven't you eaten
5 Don't you have to
6 Shouldn't

5
1 where the station is
2 what time the museum opens
3 what time you're leaving
4 where you were yesterday evening
5 they're not/they aren't going on holiday again (, are they)
6 who that man is

6
1 aren't you 2 is he 3 could they 4 didn't you
5 are we 6 did she 7 have you 8 hasn't he

Grammar notes

Negative questions

We use negative questions in three situations:

1 asking for confirmation of something you believe to be true: *Didn't you go to London once? What was it like?* (= I believe you went to London once.)

2 expressing opinions politely: *Wouldn't it be nice to go away for the weekend?*

3 asking for confirmation of a negative belief: *Haven't you finished yet?* (the speaker is surprised something has not happened or is not happening)

Indirect questions

We use indirect questions to be more polite or tentative. They are particularly used when asking for information from a stranger (*Could you tell me where the post office is, please?*) or in a formal situation, such as making an enquiry about something (*Is it the case that no money will be refunded if I pull out?*). To form indirect questions from direct questions, word order changes. Compare: *Where is it?* and *Do you know where it is?*

Tag questions

A tag question is a grammatical structure in which a declarative statement or an imperative is turned into a question by adding an interrogative fragment (the tag). So, *You're tired* becomes *You're tired, aren't you?* Auxiliary verbs and pronouns are used to form the tag. Students sometimes find it hard to know which tag to use when an auxiliary is not provided. For example, *You lost the race* has no auxiliary verb. Students need practise to be aware that they need to add *didn't you?*

7

• Ask students to rewrite the sentences. You could ask students to work individually before comparing and checking answers in pairs, or you could ask students to work in pairs to help and support each other.

ANSWERS

1 Volunteer holidays are (quite) an interesting idea, aren't they?
2 Surely he doesn't intend to give up his well-paid job in order to travel?
3 Can you remember which travel company you used?
4 Tokyo isn't a cheap city, is it?
5 Didn't it rain a lot when you were in England?
6 You've been to America, haven't you?
7 Do you know if/whether this bus goes to the town centre?
8 You didn't forget your passport, did you?

Pronunciation intonation in question forms

8a 🔊 [52]

• Ask students to work in pairs to practise saying the questions in Exercise 7. Tell them to think about whether the intonation in the questions, especially the tag questions, should be falling or rising (see Pronunciation note below).

• Play the recording. Students listen and check how the questions are delivered. In feedback, ask students whether the intonation in each question was falling or rising.

ANSWERS

Falling intonation: the tag questions 1 and 6
Rising intonation: 2, 3, 5, 7 (plus the tag questions 4 and 8)

Audioscript 🔊 [52]

1 Volunteer holidays are an interesting idea, aren't they?
2 Surely he doesn't intend to give up his well-paid job in order to travel?
3 Can you remember which travel company you used?
4 Tokyo isn't a cheap city, is it?
5 Didn't it rain a lot when you were in England?
6 You've been to America, haven't you?
7 Do you know if this bus goes to the town centre?
8 You didn't forget your passport, did you?

Pronunciation note

Generally speaking, direct and indirect questions have a rising intonation at the end.

Tag questions may rise or fall at the end depending on whether they are real questions or questions the listener is expected to agree with. Compare these examples:

You're from Tokyo, aren't you?
I know this is true – I'm just checking.

Susie will call soon, won't she?

I don't know if she will call – I'm asking to find the answer or to be reassured.

In Exercise 7, we (probably) use falling intonation on 1 and 6 (in 1 the speaker expects the listener to agree, and in 6 he/she is pretty sure). We (probably) use rising intonation on 4 and 8 (in 4 the speaker says 'I imagine' suggesting he/she is hoping the listener will clarify, and in 8 the speaker is perhaps surprised or incredulous and is hoping for the answer 'no').

8b 🔵 [53]

- Play the recording. Students listen and note whether the intonation rises or falls on the tag question. Let students compare their answers in pairs before checking with the class. If necessary, play and pause the recording to help students decide.

- **Optional step** Ask students to work in pairs and choose two of the tag questions and put them in a dialogue in which they would naturally rise or fall. Ask a few pairs to model their dialogue for the class.

ANSWERS	
1 = falling	3 = falling
2 = rising	4 = rising

9

- **Optional step** Ask students to read the telephone conversation without worrying about the gaps first, and answer a focus question: *How can Mike apply to volunteer?* (by filling out a form and sending it).

- Ask students to read the telephone conversation and complete the questions. Let students compare answers in pairs. Do not check answers at this stage.

10 🔵 [54]

- Ask students to work in pairs to act out conversations. Play the recording. Students listen and compare their answers.

- In feedback, ask whether the intonation was rising or falling on each question (it rises on all the questions except number 1).

ANSWERS

1 I can work for just a few days, can't I?
2 How much does it cost?
3 Surely I have to pay for my accommodation?
4 Can you tell me where I can get the form?
5 You don't have something in Colorado, do you?
6 And can you tell me how long the training is?
7 You don't have any experience of cooking, do you?

Audioscript 🔵 [54] (with answers)

M = Mike; J = Jeff

M: Hi, I'm interested in helping out on the Continental Divide Trail this summer. My friend did four days helping to repair trails last summer. I can work for <u>just a few days, can't I</u>?

J: Absolutely. You can do anything from two days to two months.

M: That's great. I have about a week in June. I heard that volunteers usually pay something to take part. How much <u>does it cost</u>?

J: It's free.

M: Sorry – free? Surely <u>I have to pay for my</u> accommodation?

J: No, it's completely free. You just have to register by filling out a form and sending it to us.

M: Can you tell me <u>where I can get the</u> form?

J: Sure. It's an online form – on our website.

M: Great. And where on the trail can I work?

J: New Mexico, Montana, Wyoming …

M: <u>You don't have something</u> in Colorado, do you?

J: Yes, we do. We have spaces in Winfield, Colorado and a few in Mount Elbert.

M: And <u>can you tell me</u> how long the training is?

J: There's no training beforehand. We just train you as you work. But we are looking for a chef at the moment. You don't have any experience <u>of cooking, do you</u>?

M: No, I'm afraid not. I really just want to do a few days helping to build trails.

Background information

The Continental Divide Trail or Continental Divide National Scenic Trail goes from Canada, through five US states (Montana, Idaho, Wyoming, Colorado and New Mexico), to Mexico. It's over 5,000 kilometres long and traverses some demanding terrain, including desert in New Mexico, high peaks in Colorado and the Yellowstone National Park in Wyoming. Only about 200 people a year attempt to hike the whole distance and it takes about six months.

Speaking ⟨ my life ⟩
11

- Ask students to work with a new partner to act out the roleplay. Ask students to choose a volunteer holiday from the list and to decide who is A (the student making the enquiry), and who is B (the student answering the questions). Then give them a few minutes of preparation time: Student A must think of questions to ask, B must read and become familiar with the information in the fact file on page 155 of the Student's Book.

- Students act out the roleplay. They could then either change roles to act out the roleplay again, or change roles and choose a different situation to act out.

- As students speak, walk round and listen to how well your students use questions. Note down errors as you monitor. At the end, write errors on the board and ask students to work in pairs to correct them.

6c Unusual places to stay

Lesson at a glance

- reading: historical hotels
- critical thinking: analysing tone
- word focus: *mind*
- speaking and writing: an unusual hotel

Reading

1

- Ask students to work in pairs to make a list of different types of accommodation and to think of advantages and disadvantages. Set a two-minute time limit.
- Ask pairs to join another pair and share their ideas. In feedback, elicit types of accommodation and write them on the board. Ask students to say which ones they would like to stay in and why.
- **Optional step** You could use the IWB or whatever classroom projectors you have to show visuals of different types of accommodation. Elicit and drill the words from the visuals.

> **EXAMPLE ANSWERS**
>
> hotel/motel – advantages: comfortable, reliable, room service, restaurant; disadvantages: expensive, chain hotels have no atmosphere, no self-catering facilities
>
> guesthouse / bed and breakfast – advantages: cheaper than hotels, friendly, a way to meet local people; disadvantages: less comfortable than hotel, feel you are in another person's house, fewer facilities
>
> tent – advantages: cheap, can go anywhere, adventurous and fun, good for families; disadvantages: uncomfortable, awful in the rain, time-consuming to put it up, hard work
>
> caravan/campervan – advantages: cheap, can take it anywhere, can take lots of things from home, good for families; disadvantages: restricted in where you can go and where you can park it, small and cramped space
>
> holiday (self-catering) apartment – advantages: home from home, can cook what you like, space to relax, good for families; disadvantages: expensive, no facilities like a hotel, harder to meet people
>
> beach hut – advantages: adventurous, cheap, by the beach, cool; disadvantages: small, few amenities
>
> youth hostel – advantages: cheap, you can meet people, great if you are young, gives advice for travellers; disadvantages: uncomfortable, noisy, out of centre of town, often need to share a room with strangers

2 🔊 [55]

- Ask students to read the extract and answer the questions.
- **Optional step** The reading text is recorded. You could play the recording and ask students to read and listen.
- Let students compare answers in pairs before checking with the class. Students will have their own ideas, so be prepared to listen to arguments for different answers.

> **EXAMPLE ANSWERS**
>
> comfortable places to stay: period hotels (inside they have large double beds and private bathrooms); cave hotels (the rooms are comfortably furnished with antique furniture)
>
> the most disadvantages: prison hotels (sound unpleasant: 'unfriendly, unheated and uncomfortable'); cave hotels (must do without television or fridges); art hotels (rooms can be small and claustrophobic)

3

- Ask students to read the guide again and choose the correct options. You could play the recording for students to listen to as they read for the second time.
- Let students compare answers in pairs before checking with the class.

> **ANSWERS**
>
> 1 a   2 b   3 a   4 b   5 b   6 b   7 b   8 a

4

- Ask students to work in pairs or small groups to discuss the words. Encourage students to share what they know, and guess meanings if they can. In feedback, elicit ideas and check any words students are not sure of.

> **ANSWERS**
>
> Parts of a building: balcony, corridor, porch, saloon, shutters, vaulted ceiling
>
> Pieces of furniture: bench, chest of drawers, fridge

Vocabulary notes 1

corridor = a long hallway with rooms off it in a public building

bench = a wooden bench is a long, flat piece of wood with no arms or back on which you can sit or sleep

porch = a small, open area with a roof in front of the door of a house – typical of old American houses

saloon = here, a bar room – a period 'Wild West saloon' has a bar, dancing girls and cowboys playing cards to recreate an experience from the past

shutters = wooden coverings for windows that you can open and close

vaulted ceiling = a high ceiling with curved structures

Vocabulary notes 2

Check that students are also familiar with the following vocabulary:

reception = the place in a hotel where you arrive and sign in

primitive = simple and basic

renovated = changed and redecorated

oak = a type of wood/tree

peasant = a person who lives off the land

5

- Ask students to discuss which of the places in the guide they would prefer to stay in. You could organize the class into new pairs or small groups to do this.

Extra activity

Organize the class into groups of three. Ask students to imagine they have just moved into a new three bedroom flat. There are three beds in the flat but no other furniture. They have enough money to buy eight pieces of furniture but no more. Tell groups to talk together and decide which eight pieces of furniture to buy.

Critical thinking analysing tone

6

- **Optional step** Start by eliciting what *tone* is – here, the general attitude or feel of a piece of writing. Elicit examples: an amusing tone, a serious tone, a formal tone.
- Ask students to say which description – a, b or c – best describes the tone of the article they have just read, and why.

> ANSWERS
>
> b (because it has lots of 'light', amusing, personal comments which you might use in a conversation)

7

- Ask students to work in pairs to find examples of a light and conversational tone in the article, and note them down or underline them. Elicit one or two ideas first to get students started.
- In feedback, check answers and ask students how the tone makes them react to the article.

> ANSWERS
>
> PRISON HOTELS: *They are not lying; Sound unpleasant? It is. Mind you, for $12 per night, what do you expect?*
> PERIOD HOTELS: *Do you fancy stepping back in time to … ?; Bear in mind that …*
> CAVE HOTELS: *If you have even more primitive accommodation in mind, why not try … ? Cold, damp, dark? It doesn't have to be; … mine had a beautiful oak chest of drawers; a less peasant-friendly $300 per night.*
> ART HOTELS: *Not in Propeller Island. The decoration is so extreme that you are forced to get into the spirit of it; But if you don't mind that, it's the next best thing to …*
> Generally speaking, the light and conversational tone encourages people to 'hear' what the writer is saying – it is as if a friend is giving advice. Consequently, the reader is more likely to respond positively to positive recommendations by the writer.

Vocabulary notes

The examples of light and conversational tone listed above can be categorized as: speaking directly to the reader as if it were a conversation (*Do you fancy stepping back in time to … ?*); making personal comments and asides (*… mine had a beautiful oak chest of drawers*); and being ironic or amusing, or making jokes (*a non-peasant budget of … *).

Extra activity

Show the following sentences on the board or IWB:

1 *Built in the nineteenth century, the Royal Hotel is in a bad state of repair.*
2 *I found myself staying in a room in a really old Royal Hotel that was run-down and awful. How did I get here?*
3 *If you like old places, try the nineteenth-century Royal hotel. Mind you, be prepared for rooms that aren't all in great condition.*

Ask students to match the extracts with the types of tone in Exercise 6 (key: 1 a, 2 c, 3 b).

Ask students to choose a sentence or two from the article and rewrite it in a tone that is serious and factual or subjective and negative.

Word focus mind

8

- Organize the class into pairs to find and discuss the expressions with the word *mind*.
- Then ask students to work individually to guess the meaning of the expressions with *mind* 1 to 5. Let students compare ideas in pairs before checking with the class.

> ANSWERS
>
> Paragraph 1: *Mind you, … (verb)* = used for making something you have just said less strong or less general
> Paragraph 2: *Bear in mind (that) … (noun)* = remember or be aware that
> Paragraph 3: *If you have … in mind (noun)* = If you were thinking about … or If you wanted …
> Paragraph 4: *if you don't mind that … (verb)* = if it's not inconvenient or a problem for you that …
> 1 *in two minds* = undecided
> 2 *change your mind* = decide to do something different / change your opinion of something
> 3 *put your mind to it* = think hard about something or work hard to achieve something
> 4 *have a lot on my mind* = have a lot of concerns or worries to think about
> 5 *(my) mind's gone blank* = I suddenly can't think or remember

9

- Ask students to work in pairs to prepare and act out conversations using the phrases with *mind* from Exercise 8. You could choose to let your students prepare and script conversations first or let them improvise conversations.

EXAMPLE ANSWERS

2 'If you *change your mind* about coming with me, let me know before Friday.' 'No problem. I'll send you a text if I do change my mind.'

3 'I'm sure you can think of a solution if you *put your mind to it*.' 'OK. Thanks. I'll do my best.'

4 'Sorry I haven't got back to you about the weekend. I've *had a lot on my mind* lately.' 'That's OK. We'll probably just stay at home anyway.'

5 'Sorry, I know I've heard his name before, but *my mind's gone blank*.' 'Don't worry. Tell me the next time we meet.'

Extra activity

Ask students to use learner dictionaries to find other uses of *mind*. For example: *Mind the step/gap* = be careful; *mind the children* = look after them; *never mind* = it's not important – don't worry about it; *Would you mind … -ing?* = used to ask someone to do something politely, e.g. *Would you mind opening the window?*

Speaking and writing ◁ my life

10

- Organize the class into groups of three or four students to prepare ideas. Ask one person in each group to note ideas while everybody contributes. Set a five-minute time limit. At the end, students should have useful notes under the four headings provided.

- Before moving on to the writing stage in Exercise 11, ask students to briefly share their ideas with the class. Use the opportunity to make suggestions or suggest key vocabulary groups could use.

11

- Ask students to write a review of their unusual place to stay. You could ask groups to work together to produce one collective review, or ask students to write individually and to share their first draft with other people in their group before rewriting and completing their piece of work.

- Once groups or individuals have completed their reviews, ask them to read them out. The class can vote for the review that sounds most interesting.

- **Optional step** Instead of asking students to read out their reviews, collect them and pin them to the walls of the classroom. Students then walk round and read the reviews on the walls before voting for the best. An alternative idea is to ask students to sit in a circle and pass the reviews round in a clockwise direction.

6d Couch surfing

Lesson at a glance
- real life: getting around
- pronunciation: intonation in sentences with two clauses

Real life getting around

1

- Ask students to work in pairs to read the description and discuss couch surfing. Before they read the text, ask: *What is a couch?* Elicit that it's another word for *sofa*. US English tends to use *couch*. In feedback, elicit students' ideas, opinions and experiences.

EXAMPLE ANSWERS

Reasons to do couch surfing: free, great way to meet people, a way to find a place to stay in remote places, a way to have an adventure and experience a place 'for real'

Reasons not to do couch surfing: could be unsafe, you will have negative experiences – unfriendly or strange hosts, uncomfortable or noisy night

Background information

Couchsurfing.com runs a database through which people can contact people prepared to offer a bed or couch/sofa for the night for free. It's particularly popular with young travellers with little money and a taste for adventure.

New Hampshire is a state in the north-east of the United States. Casey Fenton, the student mentioned in the text who had the idea for a couch surfing website, came from this state.

2

- Ask students to read the phrases in the language box and decide who says each expression – the couch surfer or the host. You could ask students to work in pairs and compare ideas at this stage.

3 🎧 [56]

- Play the recording. Students listen and check their answers from Exercise 2.

ANSWERS

Couch surfer: expressions 1, 3, 4 and 11
Host: expressions 2, 5, 6, 7, 8, 9 and 10

Audioscript 🎧 [56]

M = Malcolm; P = Paul

M: Hi Paul, this is Malcolm, your host. You emailed me about staying next Thursday for a couple of nights.

P: Oh hi, Malcolm. Thanks for getting back to me. Is that still OK?

M: No, that's all fine. I just thought I'd give you a call to explain how to get here, because it's a bit complicated. How are you getting to Hamilton, first of all?

P: I'm coming in by train sometime in the afternoon.

M: OK. I wanted to pick you up, but my car's at the garage that day.

P: Hey, that's kind of you, but I can make my own way.

M: OK. Well, I'm at work 'til about five thirty, so feel free to come over any time after six.

P: That sounds perfect. And how do I get to you from the town centre?

M: Well, you could just get a taxi, but it's about eleven kilometres from the centre, so it won't be cheap. Alternatively, you can hop on a bus to Stoney Creek. Look out for the sports arena on your right and get off there. It's only a twenty-minute ride. From there, Cherry Heights is another fifteen minutes on foot, straight up King St. Once you reach the crossroads at Gray Road, the easiest thing is to give me a call and I'll come out and meet you.

P: So, bus to Stoney Creek, walk up King St to Cherry Heights and call you from there?

M: Yup. Call when you get to the crossroads at Gray Road.

P: OK, got it. That sounds great. If I get held up in any way, I'll let you know. But otherwise, expect a call around six thirty.

M: Great. See you next Thursday then. Bye.

P: Bye.

4 🔊 [56]

- Play the recording again. Students listen and complete the sentences. Let students compare answers in pairs before checking with the class.

- **Optional step** If students have problems catching the missing words, play the recording a third time, and pause the recording when the key information is provided to allow students to write.

ANSWERS

1 train
2 my car's at the garage that day
3 kind of you
4 you from the town centre
5 a taxi
6 a bus to Stoney Creek
7 sports arena
8 ride
9 give me a call
10 meet you
11 let you know

Vocabulary notes

get back to (someone) = to call or contact somebody by text or email (after they have already contacted you)

pick (someone) up = to meet a person (at their home or at a hotel or airport, for example) and give them a ride in your car to a place

make (my/your) own way = to go to your destination without any help

hop on (a bus) = to get on a bus without any planning, e.g. the next bus that arrives, rather than one that leaves at a specific time

get held up = to become delayed (by traffic, the weather, etc.)

Pronunciation intonation in sentences with two clauses

5a 🔊 [57]

- Play the recording. Students listen and note the intonation pattern. You could ask them to mark it, as in the examples in the Pronunciation note below.

- **Optional step** Play the recording again for students to listen and repeat.

Pronunciation note

Note the rise in the first clause and fall in the second:

I wanted to pick you up, ...

but my car's at the garage that day.

You could just get a taxi, ...

but it's about eleven kilometres from the centre.

5b

- Ask students to practise saying the sentences. Encourage your students to go up in terms of tone before the comma, then pause, then go down in tone from the word *but* (also see Teacher development below). Listen and correct their intonation where necessary. You could ask students to work in pairs, taking it in turns to read out the sentences.

Teacher development

Practising intonation

Practising intonation can be demanding for students because the intonation of sentences in English may differ from those in the students' L1. Some students also find it harder than others to hear and imitate the intonation patterns. Here are three ideas for practising intonation patterns:

1 Encourage students to experiment and to try to exaggerate the range of their intonation. English has a wide intonation range, which may not always seem natural to speakers of other languages.

2 Ask your students to hum the intonation pattern of a sentence. Instead of saying, *I'll try to get home by six, but I can't promise I will,* tell them to hum it or say *da-da-da-dee*. This is fun, but it also gets students to think of intonation as the music of a language. Start by humming example sentences yourself – this will give students a good idea of how they should sound.

3 Use hand signals to show whether the intonation of a sentence is rising or falling. You could ask students to repeat some sentences after you – as you raise the intonation, raise your palm, as the intonation falls, drop your palm. When students are practising in pairs, raise or drop the palm of your hand to demonstrate the intonation pattern they should be following.

6

- Ask students to work in pairs to roleplay a conversation between a couch surfer and host.

- **Optional step** It's a good idea to give students some preparation time first before expecting them to improvise a roleplay. Organize the class into new pairs, so they work with a less familiar student, and ask them to decide together which role they want to play and what city they want to set the roleplay in. Once they have made these decisions, tell them to take one minute to prepare what to say, using phrases from the language box. When students are ready, they act out roleplays.

- Once students have practised one conversation, tell them to change roles and have another similar conversation.

- As students speak, monitor and note errors and examples of good language use. At the end, give feedback on language students have used.

6e A disappointed customer

Lesson at a glance
- writing: a letter/email of complaint
- writing skill: formal language

Writing a letter/email of complaint

1

- Ask students to discuss the questions. You could do this open class or in pairs. It's a good idea to model the activity by sharing an experience of your own.

- **Optional step** Check students understand the verb *complain* and its noun *complaint*, and ask students if they have ever written a letter or email of complaint.

2

- Ask students to read the letter and answer the questions. Let students compare answers before checking with the class.

ANSWERS

1 There was no table available in the restaurant at the hotel, and they did not receive the same level of hospitality as regular, full-paying guests.
2 Investigate the matter and ensure that this situation does not arise in future with other guests.
3 Students' own ideas. It seems justified – they had to dine late, no one apologized, and the complainant is not seeking money, but trying to give the hotel useful feedback.

3

- Ask students to work in pairs to discuss and answer the questions.

ANSWERS

1 In formal letters, the writer's address is top right, and the receiver's address is on the left, below the writer's address, just above *Dear Sir/Madam*.
2 In formal letters, the writer signs off *Yours faithfully* when starting the letter *Dear Sir/Madam*. If the writer uses the receiver's name (e.g. *Dear Ms Hughes*), the writer signs off *Yours sincerely*.
3 in the opening sentence and paragraph
4 in the closing paragraph
5 In a formal email, the address of both writer and recipient would not be included, and the sender would type their name at the end rather than sign it. The sender would complete the *Subject* section of the email (or the *Re:* section of the email if it is a reply) with a very brief explanation of the purpose of the email, and would also consider whether the email should be *cc'ed*, or copied, perhaps to head office or someone more senior to the recipient.

Writing notes

In typed letters and emails, all text is aligned to the left with the exception of the sender's address in a letter, which is aligned to the right.

Note that the sender's address only is written, but the recipient's name (or company name) as well as the address (if present) is written.

In British addresses, a postcode composed of letters and numbers is included.

Writing skill formal language

4a

• Ask students to find and underline the formal words or phrases in the letter. Let students compare answers in pairs before checking with the class.

ANSWERS

1 express my dissatisfaction with	6 opted to dine
2 we were informed	7 wished
3 a discounted offer	8 my principal concern
4 receive	9 investigate
5 After some discussion with	10 ensure

Vocabulary notes

Other features of formal language you may wish to focus on include:

1 no short forms: *I am writing* ... not *I'm writing*

2 use of polite phrases involving modals such as *would, could* and *should*: *I would just like you to* ...

3 expressing times formally: *5.30 p.m.* not *half past five*

4 Other formal words: *available, situation, arise*

4b

• Ask students to work individually to rewrite the sentences replacing the expressions in bold with more formal language. Let students compare their answers in pairs before checking with the class.

ANSWERS

2 I **informed** the receptionist that I **had reserved the room** for two nights, not one.

3 After **some discussion with** the manager, she **apologized** and promised to **investigate** the problem with the shower. **However**, no action was taken.

4 I would have expected that the safety of the guests **was / would be the principal concern of the staff**.

5 Given the **inconvenience** this caused us, we expected **some compensation**.

6 The manager said no other rooms were **vacant**, but if the opportunity **arose**, she would move us.

5

• Ask students to read the situation. Then have a brief class discussion about how they will go about writing the letter or email of complaint. Establish what students are likely to mention in the first paragraph: *no staff were on duty during the night*. Elicit ideas for what to include as suggestions for action in the closing paragraph: *an investigation of the matter, a change of hotel policy, a refund for guests*.

• Ask students to work individually to write their letters or emails.

6

• Organize students into pairs and ask them to exchange their written work. Ask them to use the two questions to check their partner's letter or email and suggest how to improve it.

• **Optional step** Ask students to revise and rewrite their letter based on their partner's suggestions. You could also ask students to imagine they work at the Oxford Hotel and to write replies to their partners' letters.

6f The unexpected beauty of travelling solo

Before you watch

1

- Ask students to work in pairs to list the benefits (advantages) of travelling alone (solo) or with someone else.

- **Optional step** Ask students if anybody has travelled alone. Ask the rest of the class to think of questions to ask that student. Example questions: *Why did you decide to travel alone? Where did you go and why? What was the best part of the trip? What did you miss about having nobody to travel with?*

EXAMPLE ANSWERS

Benefits of travelling alone: you can go where you like, stay where you like, spend what you like; you can meet other travellers or locals easily; you can spend time taking photos, writing your blog, etc.; you don't have the arguments you have when you are with somebody else

Benefits of travelling with someone else: you can share your experiences; you can have fun – going out, making jokes, etc. you have someone to talk to – especially when eating out; it is cheaper to stay somewhere when you can share a room

---

2

- Ask students to discuss their lists with another pair. Then elicit ideas from the class and find out which students think travelling solo is best.

While you watch

3 ■◀ [6.1]

- Ask students to watch the whole video and answer the questions. Let students compare answers in pairs before checking with the class.

ANSWERS

1 cities, beaches, a festival
2 It seems that he planned the trip with his girlfriend, but for some reason she couldn't come.

Videoscript ■◀ 6.1

0.00–0.12 Answerphone Your call cannot be taken at the moment, so please leave your message after the tone.

0.13–0.45 Woman Hey … thought I'd try to catch you before you got on the plane. But I guess it's too late. I know I've said it before, but I am really sorry that I couldn't come with you. I was really excited and I know that we spent a lot of time planning it, but you know that I couldn't come. I had to stay. I'm really, really happy that you decided to go anyway though, even though you were really nervous about going by yourself. Anyway, give me a ring when you can or send me a message or something.

1.04–1.47 It's me again. I've been sending you messages and trying to ring on Skype, but no luck so far. I guess you're really busy, but it would be good to hear from you are. I just want to know you're OK. I'm trying to figure out where you are. I guess in Poland if you're sticking to the plan, but maybe you've decided to change things. I know what happened was really tough and I know that you blame me, but I hope that you're still having a good time and doing everything you wanted to do. OK – speak to you soon.

2.02–3.01 It's really weird to keep talking to your answering machine, but I don't know what else to do. You still haven't got in touch with me. It's been such a long time. I guess you're still angry or maybe you just don't want to talk to anyone right now. I always think when you're somewhere by yourself you experience it so much more. Like you're more aware of what's going on around you. And I bet you've taken some great shots with your camera. I know you never go anywhere without it. Maybe we can watch them together when you get back. Just stay safe and hope you're having a great time.

3.02–3.03 Hello.

3.04–3.05 Man Hi.

4 ■◀ [6.1]

- Ask students to read the statements. Ensure students understand the meaning of *blame* (= say it was another person's fault).

- When students are ready, play the video again. Students choose true (T) or false (F). Let students compare their answers in pairs before checking with the class. Note that students have to interpret, or 'listen between the lines', to get the answer – and that sometimes the answer is open to interpretation.

ANSWERS

1 T (*I was really excited*) but it could be argued F (*you know that I couldn't come. I had to stay.*)
2 F (*you were really nervous about going by yourself*)
3 F (*I just want to know you're OK*)
4 F (*I know what happened was really tough and I know that you blame me*)
5 T (*I guess you're still angry or maybe you just don't want to talk to anyone right now.*)
6 T (*I bet you've taken some great shots with your camera. I know you never go anywhere without it.*)
7 F (*Just stay safe and hope you're having a great time.*)
8 F (he calls her)

5

- Ask students to discuss the question. You do this as a class or ask students to discuss in pairs first.

EXAMPLE ANSWER

It seems likely that the man and woman were in a relationship and there was a problem: she had to stay. Perhaps because they had an argument, or a disagreement about where their relationship was going.

6

- Ask students to complete the table by writing as many things as they can remember seeing in the video. Let students compare their answers in pairs.

7 🎥 6.1

- Play the video again. Tell students to add anything more they see to their lists.
- Ask students whether they think the video makes a good case for travelling alone. You could ask them to discuss this with a new partner, in small groups, or in open class.

ANSWERS

Types of transport	Types of weather	Activities
train	sun	driving
tram	blue sky	walking
skateboarding	snow	walking a dog
bus	rain	walking in a park
boat		playing the saxophone
walking		fire-dancing
bicycle		biking
metro		performing stunts on a bike
		high-wire
		playing the drums
		nightclub/dancing
		beach volleyball
		taking photographs
		clearing leaves

After you watch

Vocabulary in context

8 🎥 6.2

- Explain that students are going to watch some clips from the video which contain some new words and phrases. They need to choose the correct meaning of the words and phrases.
- Play the clips. When each multiple-choice question appears, pause the clip so that students can choose the correct definition. You could let students compare answers in pairs before discussing as a class.

ANSWERS

1 b   2 c   3 a   4 a   5 c

Videoscript 🎥 6.2

1   … thought I'd try to **catch** you before you got on the plane.

  a listen to

  b speak to

  c see

2 I'm trying to **figure out** where you are.

  a remember

  b imagine

  c understand

3 I guess in Poland if you're **sticking to** the plan …

  a following closely

  b changing often

  c thinking hard about

4 I know what happened was really **tough** …

  a difficult

  b unexpected

  c sad

5 It's really **weird** to keep talking to your answering machine …

  a difficult

  b unpleasant

  c strange

8b

- Students work individually to complete the sentences. Elicit one or two ideas for the first sentence to get them started. Let students compare sentences in pairs.

EXAMPLE ANSWERS

1 The thing I find most weird about people and their phones is when they *look at them even when they are with friends.*

2 It's very tough to *lose your job / get over a failed relationship.*

3 I can't figure out why *bad things happen.*

9

- Tell students that they are going to leave phone messages for a friend while they are on their travels. First ask students to work individually to plan a solo trip. Give students two minutes to think of places to visit and prepare things to say. Monitor and help with ideas and vocabulary.

- Organize the class into pairs. Ask students to sit back-to-back and take turns to leave voice messages for each other. You could make it more interesting by encouraging students to also give the pre-recorded message that invites the caller to leave voicemail.

- When students have finished, tell them to change partners and tell the new partner about the message received from the first partner.

UNIT 6 Review and memory booster

Memory Booster activities

Exercises 1 and 4 are Memory Booster activities. For more information about these activities and how they benefit students, see page 10 of this Teacher's Book.

I can ... check boxes

As an alternative to asking students to simply tick the *I can ...* boxes, you could ask them to give themselves a score from 1 to 4 (1 = not very confident; 4 = very confident) for each language area. If students score 1 or 2 for a language area, refer them to additional practice activities in the Workbook and Grammar summary exercises.

Grammar

1 >> MB

- Ask students to look at the photo and write questions to ask their partner about it by completing the sentences below the photo. When students have completed the questions, ask them to work in pairs to ask and answer their questions.

> **EXAMPLE ANSWERS**
> 1 Do you know where *this place is / this photo was taken*?
> 2 It looks *really attractive, doesn't it*?
> 3 Have you ever *visited a place similar to this*?

2

- Ask students to work individually to complete the conversation between Marianna and Paulina. Tell them to use the words in brackets or a tag question. Let students compare answers in pairs before checking with the class.

> **ANSWERS**
> 1 aren't you
> 2 not to go
> 3 don't I find
> 4 isn't it
> 5 don't you think
> 6 don't want to stay
> 7 hope it doesn't rain
> 8 hope not
> 9 you'll stay *or* you are going to stay
> 10 haven't you decided
> 11 don't think I'll use *or* 'm not thinking of using
> 12 won't have to worry

3

- Ask students to read the conversation again if necessary and answer the question.

> **ANSWER**
> She's from Poland. She's going to travel around the north of Poland. She's going to do this because she wants to find out more about her own country and see some places she's always wanted to go to.

Vocabulary

4 >> MB

- Ask students to work in pairs to describe and discuss what they remember about the places to stay in the photos. They should say which of the things in the box you can do in each one, and which you can definitely not do in any of them. Encourage them to use as many vocabulary items from the unit as possible as they discuss the questions.

> **ANSWERS**
> Students' own answers

5

- Ask students to work individually to complete the questions with one word in each space. Then ask them to work in pairs to compare their answers and practise asking and answering the questions.

> **ANSWERS**
> 1 off   2 have   3 taken   4 valid
> 5 vaccinations *or* vaccinated   6 bear

Real life

6

- Ask students to work individually to match sentence beginnings with the endings. Let students compare answers in pairs before checking with the class.

> **ANSWERS**
> 1 h 2 f 3 e 4 a 5 g 6 b 7 c 8 d

7

- Ask students to work individually first to choose a location and think about what language they can use to explain to someone how to get to that place by public transport.
- Tell students to work in pairs and take it in turns to give the information. You could tell the student giving directions not to disclose what the final location is. Can their partner guess from the information they are given?

Unit 7 Customs and behaviour

Opener

1

- Ask students to look at the photo and the caption. Organize the class into pairs to discuss the question and make two separate lists of behaviour (polite/thoughtful and rude/inconsiderate). In feedback, elicit and discuss students' ideas.

- **Optional step** Open up the discussion during feedback to how people behave on public transport in your students' country or countries.

EXAMPLE ANSWERS

Polite/thoughtful behaviour: helping people with heavy bags; giving up a seat for an old person or a pregnant woman; offering help to tourists who don't know where to get off; allowing someone to get on or off the train before you

Rude/inconsiderate behaviour: pushing; talking loudly (especially on a phone); having a big bag (especially on your back) and not looking where you are going; eating hot or smelly food; standing near the door and blocking people; staying in a seat when older people don't have one; playing loud music that people can hear through your headphones

---

Background information

The photo shows the Tokyo subway in Japan. Tokyo's subway networks carry over eight million passengers daily.

Note that *subway* is the American term for an underground train network (compare the underground or tube in London; the metro in Paris).

2 [58]

- Tell students that they are going to listen to someone who has lived in Tokyo describing customs on the Tokyo subway. Play the recording. Students listen and note answers to the questions.

- Let students compare answers in pairs before checking with the class.

ANSWERS

1 Students' own answers
2 Possible answer: The 'Oshiya' – people employed to push commuters into the crowded car – is perhaps the most surprising behaviour.

Audioscript [58]

I'm from New York, so I'm used to the subway, but there were some things in Tokyo that were definitely new to me. First off, don't use your phone. If someone calls, it's OK to answer quickly – you know, say 'I'm sorry, I'm on the train,' and then hang up. But in general, people are really quiet and private, so don't ever talk loudly. Some things are the same as New York – probably in a lot of places, I guess – like giving up your seat to an old person or not eating hot food and if you have a large backpack, you put it on a shelf so it's not in people's way. But some other things seem pretty odd. The one that got me the first time was someone next to me who fell asleep and put their head on my shoulder. Seems there's nothing wrong with that – I've seen it happen to a few people now. You'll also often see people wearing face masks when they have a cold – that's because coughing or sneezing or using a tissue in public is rude. What else? Oh yeah, when you get on the train during rush hour, you'll find there are people – they're called Oshiya – who are employed to push you, like, physically, into the crowded car.

3

- **Optional step** Start by asking students what rules there might be for students attending university lectures or seminars. Elicit a list of ideas.

- Ask students to work individually to look at the rules of behaviour and complete the sentences with the words. Let students compare their answers in pairs before checking with the class.

ANSWERS

1 switch   2 interrupt; Raise   3 stare   4 chew   5 show

4

- Organize the class into groups of four or five to discuss the rules from Exercise 3. In feedback, ask a few students to share their opinions or experiences with the class.

- **Optional step** Ask students these follow-up questions: *What rules do you have to follow in your college or workplace? Are there any rules you regularly break? If so, why?*

Extra activity

Ask students to work in groups to make a student's charter for your classroom. Tell them to prepare five golden rules that they think the class should follow. Depending on the age and familiarity of your students, they might want to do this seriously (*Switch off your mobile phones; Only talk in English in class*) or light-heartedly (*Don't interrupt Mario when he's telling one of his long stories!*).

7a Cruel to be kind

Lesson at a glance
- reading: tiger mothers
- vocabulary: raising children – verbs
- grammar: zero and first conditionals; time linkers
- speaking: traditional rules of behaviour

Reading

1

- Ask students to look at the photo and discuss the question in pairs. In feedback, encourage detailed descriptions and suggestions from the class.

EXAMPLE ANSWER

This is probably a picture of a mother and her daughter. The girl's playing/practising her cello. The mother may be saying something to her daughter about doing her cello practice. Perhaps the girl is making too many mistakes. The girl's paying attention to what her mother is saying.

2

- Ask students to discuss and categorize the ideas in the list. You could choose to do this in open class or organize students into small groups first to talk and express their views. Encourage them to give reasons for their decisions.

EXAMPLE ANSWERS

There are many possible points of view, but as an example, students could argue that practising a musical instrument should be left to the child (otherwise they will hate it and become resentful), but that doing homework should be controlled strongly (otherwise they will fall behind at school).

3 🎧 [59]

- Ask students to read the article and answer the questions. Let students compare their answers in pairs before checking with the class.
- **Optional step** The reading text is recorded. You could play the recording and ask students to read and listen.

EXAMPLE ANSWERS

1 A 'tiger mother' is a strict and ambitious mother, who takes an honest and direct approach to parenting.
2 They are strict and control these things a lot. For example, children have to do homework and music practice before they can watch TV, play computer games or go out with friends; top grades at school are expected.
3 Tiger mothers are more strict; western parents are softer (less strict) and give their children praise, even if they don't do things to a high standard.
4 Her children get top grades at school and are proficient at violin and piano.

Vocabulary notes

Check that students are familiar with the following vocabulary (note that *bring up children* and *nag* are featured in Exercise 4):

bring up children = to look after (and be responsible for) children until they become adult

instinct = natural feelings

soft on children = if you are soft, it means you are not strict enough

shaming = making people feel bad or embarrassed

nagging = frequently talking to someone in a critical way, often trying to get them to do something they don't want to do

push children = to encourage children to try harder, often in a way that is very demanding

Background information

Battle Hymn of the Tiger Mother is a book by American author and lawyer Amy Chua and was published in 2011.

Vocabulary raising children: verbs

4

- Ask students to work in pairs to discuss the difference in meaning between the pairs of verbs. Explain that the first verb in each pair appeared in the article. Elicit the first answer to get students started.

- In feedback, elicit answers and explain and define the words (see Answers below).

- **Optional step** You could make the feedback a dictionary task. Ask students to look up words they aren't sure of in order to confirm what they discussed with their partner.

ANSWERS

1 *bring up* = to look after (and be responsible for) children until they become adult;
   educate = to teach, often at school, college or university
2 *praise good behaviour* = to say nice things about something someone has done;
   reward good behaviour = to give a person something because they have done something well
3 *rebel against* = to oppose someone in authority – in this case, parents;
   disobey = to deliberately do the opposite of what someone asks you to do, or to deliberately not follow a rule
4 *encourage* = to suggest in a positive way or try to persuade your children that it would be good to do something, or try to give them confidence to do something;
   force = to make your children do something (that they don't want to do)
5 *give in to* = to finally agree with someone (when previously you have been arguing about something) or finally agree to do something;
   spoil = to always let children have everything they want, so that they learn only to think of themselves

6 *nag* = to frequently talk to someone in a critical way, often trying to get them to do something they don't want to do;
tell someone off = to tell someone they have done something wrong, usually in an angry or critical way

7 *shame* = to say things (about someone) which makes that person feel embarrassed or bad about a particular situation;
punish = to give someone a punishment (something unpleasant) or make them suffer because they have broken the rules (or the law)

Extra activity

Ask students to write personalized sentences to show the meaning of any verbs they were not familiar with.

Grammar zero and first conditionals

5

• Ask students to look at the information and examples in the grammar box. Tell them to discuss and answer questions 1–4. You could do this open class or in pairs. Go through the answers with the class in feedback.

> ANSWERS
>
> 1 zero = *if* + present simple, present simple
> first = *if* + present tense, *will* + infinitive
> 2a zero conditional
> 2b first conditional
> 3 the zero conditional sentences
> 4 *unless* = if not
> *as long as* = (only) on the condition that

Refer students to page 168 for further information and practice.

> ANSWERS TO GRAMMAR SUMMARY EXERCISES
>
> **1**
> 1 If you ~~won't~~ **don't** book a ticket before you go, you won't get a seat at the concert.
> 2 If I ~~was~~ **am** late to my lesson, the teacher gets angry.
> 3 It's dangerous to drive when it ~~will snow~~ **snows** hard.
> 4 When I finish working, I'll call you.
> 5 You ~~did~~ **'ll do** better in your exams~~,~~ if you study hard now.
> 6 The football match will be cancelled~~,~~ if the weather is bad.
>
> **2**
> 1 You won't get the job unless you practise for your interview.
> 2 You can borrow my car as long as you promise to be careful.
> 3 You can go out as long as you finish all your homework.
> 4 Unless she works hard, she'll never be successful.
> 5 You can borrow my umbrella as long as you remember to give it back.
> 6 Unless you practise every day, you won't get better at playing the piano.
> 7 We can go out for a picnic as long as it doesn't rain.

> **3**
> 1 g – Please call me as soon as you **get** this message.
> 2 a – Before they go out for a walk this morning, **they'll have** something to eat.
> 3 b – I'll wait with you at the station until your train **arrives**.
> 4 d – While you're cleaning the house, I**'ll take** the dog out for a walk.
> 5 e – You'll never be able to run the marathon unless you **start** training.
> 6 f – After he finishes work, he'**ll join** his friends at the gym.
> 7 c – I always get a headache when I **don't drink** enough water.

Grammar notes

unless

Unless can mean 'except if' as well as 'if not'. So, *They'll fail if they don't work hard* and *They'll fail unless they work hard* are synonymous. However, in the sentence, *I won't go unless you come*, *unless* can't be replaced with 'if not'.

as long as

As long as means 'on condition that' and is a synonym of *if* when the speaker is setting a specific condition that must be followed: *As long as you are under 16, you can take part.* In other uses of *if*, where there is no specific condition, it can't be used: *If it rains, we'll get wet.*

even if

Note that there is an example of *even if* in the text which students may notice: *They praise them for every effort, even if the result is coming last.* It means 'it doesn't matter whether'.

6

• Ask students to work individually to choose the correct options to complete the zero and first conditional sentences. Let students compare their answers in pairs before checking with the class.

> ANSWERS
>
> 1 carries on; will ruin
> 2 become; don't have
> 3 We'll go; you've finished
> 4 is misbehaving; is
> 5 are; is
> 6 is; tells
> 7 have; will try
> 8 always feel; see

Grammar note

1, 3, 7 are first conditional sentences: *If* + present, *will* + infinitive.

2, 4, 5, 6, 8 are zero conditional sentences: *If* + present, present.

7

- Ask students to look at the information and examples in the grammar box. Tell them to choose the correct option to complete the rule.

> **ANSWER**
>
> present

8

- Ask students to look at the prompts and write complete sentences about the future using appropriate verb forms. Elicit the first sentence to get students started. Ask students to work individually before comparing their answers in pairs. Then check answers with the class.

> **ANSWERS**
>
> 1 I'll go and get some milk before the shop closes.
> 2 She's going to stay in her job until she finds / has found a better one.
> 3 I won't be able to call you while I'm driving.
> 4 She's going to / She'll meet us after she finishes / after she's finished work.
> 5 As soon as everyone has boarded / boards the plane, we'll be able to leave.
> 6 I won't make a decision until I've spoken to Emma about it.
> 7 I'll have to take the bus to work while the car is being repaired.
> 8 Dinner will be ready for you when you get home.

Teacher development

Assessing accuracy practice exercises

Life Second Edition provides plenty of accuracy practice exercises, both in the Student's Book and Workbook. These range from very controlled activities which test form, to more creative activities where students produce personalized sentences from prompts or situations. As a teacher, your role is to assess what your students need and then choose appropriate practice activities that address those needs. Here are factors to consider:

1 If your students are making basic form errors, or are not clear about meaning and use from the presentation and grammar explanation, lots of repetitive practice is useful. If they are clear about form and meaning, it may be better to avoid repetitive practice in favour of fluency work using the grammar forms. For example, Exercise 8 in the grammar section in this unit tests verb forms after time linkers. If your students are clear about the rules, make this a quick check – elicit the answers open class, or get students in pairs to take turns forming sentences orally. If students are unclear or make errors, take more time here – ask students to write sentences, check with a partner, and tell you the rule in feedback.

2 If your students are due to take English exams, accuracy is an important aim. In an exam class, take time to focus on exercises that practise accuracy and set accuracy-based exercises from the Workbook for homework. Other students may be more interested in fluency and communication. In a communicative classroom, use lesson time to practise using new language in personalized speaking activities. For example, Exercises 10 and 11 in the grammar section in this unit encourage students to speak and to be creative with new language. Devote more time to these exercises, and deal with accuracy by providing feedback on their use of spoken language.

3 Use your available time effectively. If you have lots of time, doing plenty of accuracy work before asking students to personalize and speak is very valuable. It means they will be more accurate and confident at the fluency stage. If you are short of time, reduce accuracy work to make sure you give your students time for fluency practice. Further accuracy exercises can be set for homework.

9

- Ask students to work individually to choose the best options to complete the sentences. Elicit the first sentence to get students started. Let students compare their answers in pairs before checking with the class.

> **ANSWERS**
>
> 1 until   2 as long as   3 after   4 Unless   5 if   6 while

10

- Ask students to complete the sentences in their own words. Elicit possibilities for the first sentence to get students started. Let students compare their answers in pairs before checking with the class.

> **EXAMPLE ANSWERS**
>
> 1 you won't be able to go out and play with your friends. / you'll be hungry later. / you'll have to eat it cold for breakfast.
> 2 they have children themselves. / they become parents themselves. / they grow up.
> 3 you'll get good grades. / you'll be able to go to university. / you'll find school more rewarding.
> 4 you'll have a better relationship with them. / you won't be able to discipline them. / you'll end up spoiling them.
> 5 they have found a job. / they feel they are ready to leave. / they have found their own place.
> 6 I don't mind what (job) they do. / I'm happy.

Speaking my life
11

- Start by eliciting two or three rules from students to get them started. Then ask them to make their own list of five. Monitor as students work and check that each student has five rules.

- Organize the class into groups of four or five. Ask students to compare and discuss the rules they thought of.

- **Optional step** As students speak, note down errors you hear. Concentrate on errors with conditionals. At the end, in feedback, write up five or six short sentences containing errors you heard. Ask students to work in pairs to correct the errors.

EXAMPLE ANSWERS

'Don't eat with your mouth open.' – *This is a good rule – it's important to have good table manners.*

'Always say please and thank you.' – *This is good – you should be polite and think of others.*

'Sit still.' – *This is too restrictive for young children – they should feel free to express themselves.*

'Hold Mummy or Daddy's hand when you cross the road.' – *I think this is a sensible road safety rule.*

7b A matter of taste

Lesson at a glance

- listening: a matter of taste
- grammar: *usually, used to, would, be used to* and *get used to*
- pronunciation: /juː/ and /uː/
- vocabulary and speaking: food and eating habits

Listening

1

- **Optional step** First elicit a list of strange (but possible) things to eat, e.g. *insects, worms, snakes, fish eggs, ears, crocodile, ostrich*. You could elicit key words from the text here (animals: *reindeer, walrus, seal, whale* and food groups: *protein, fat, carbohydrate, vitamins, dairy products*). You will need pictures to teach the first group of words and examples to teach the second (e.g. *eggs and meat have protein*).

- Discuss the questions with the whole class. It's a good idea to provide a teacher model first – tell students a short story about something strange or horrible you have eaten.

EXAMPLE ANSWERS

I've eaten crocodile. I ate it because I was on holiday in Africa and it seemed like an adventurous thing to do. It tasted like chicken – it was quite nice, actually.

---

2 💿 [60]

- Tell students they are going to listen to an extract from a radio programme about the diet of the indigenous people of northern Alaska. Ask students to read the questions.

- Play the recording. Students listen and note answers to the questions. Let students compare answers in pairs before checking with the class.

ANSWERS

1 meat and fat (seal, walrus, reindeer, whale skin and blubber, frozen fish)
2 The speaker is surprised that a diet of just meat and fat can be 'enough'.

Background information

In **Alaska** (the northern state of the USA to the west of Canada) there are two main groups of indigenous peoples: the Inupiat and Yupik people. The Inupiat are closely related to the Inuit. Note that the term Eskimo is considered derogatory in Canada, where Inuit is preferred. However, in the USA, the word Eskimo is sometimes used, but is used as an umbrella term for all these northern peoples, and is not considered derogatory.

Audioscript 💿 [60]

On the whole, most of us eat a pretty balanced diet – a mixture of fruits, vegetables, grains, meat and fish, eggs and dairy foods. Diet fashions come and go – the protein diet, the grapefruit diet, the starving-two-days-a-week diet, and so on … but, for the most part, we are used to eating a range of foods. It's true that in poorer regions of the world, people eat less meat and more grains and vegetables, and in richer parts more meat and sugary foods … and more fatty food. But everyone at least aims to have some kind of balance. And that's why I was so intrigued to read recently about the traditional diet of the indigenous people of northern Alaska, who are sometimes collectively known as the Eskimo.

Historically, the Eskimo didn't use to have a so-called balanced diet at all. Because of sub-zero temperatures and a lack of plant life, these Alaska natives had to survive on what they could hunt and fish close to home. They would hunt seal and walrus and reindeer and then they'd cook their meat in seal oil. Sometimes they'd eat frozen fish, and when times were really hard in winter, they used to eat whale skin and blubber, which, by the way, I'm told is like chewing car tyres.

But how could a diet of just meat and fat possibly be healthy? Well, according to Harold Draper, an expert in nutrition, there's no such thing as essential foods; only essential nutrients. And there's not only one way to get those nutrients. In the West, we have got used to eating certain foods in order to get each nutrient: for example, we usually eat fruit to get more vitamin C and dairy products for calcium and vitamin D. But during the long winters, the Eskimo found the nutrients and vitamins they needed from their diet of fish and wild animal meat. As to the large amount of fat they consumed, it was a healthier kind of fat, not the saturated fats that cause people in the West so many health problems these days. In fact, heart conditions among people on a traditional Eskimo diet used to be about half the number in the wider population of North America.

I say 'used to' because nowadays, a lot of the indigenous population live close to towns and eat more processed food – pizza, fries and fizzy drinks – and unfortunately with this has come a rise in obesity, diabetes and heart conditions.

3 💿 [60]

- Play the recording again. Students listen and choose the correct options to complete the sentences. Let students compare answers in pairs before checking with the class.

> **ANSWERS**
> 1 a   2 c   3 c   4 a   5 b   6 a

Vocabulary notes

Check that students are familiar with the following vocabulary:

well-off = rich (not poor)

tough = hard to eat

nutritious = good for you because the food is full of proteins, minerals, etc. (which are collectively called *nutrients*)

oily = full of oil – so with a thick, wet feel in the mouth

4

- Discuss the questions in open class or organize students into small groups to discuss. At the end, ask one person from each group to volunteer to summarize their discussion for the class.

> **ANSWERS**
> Students' own answers
> Students may say that processed food should be avoided because they contain cheap, unhealthy fats and lots of salt and sugar.
> Processed foods students may miss include sweets, biscuits, crisps and soft drinks but also bacon, breakfast cereals and tinned vegetables.

Grammar *usually, used to, would, be used to* and *get used to*

5

- Tell students to read the information and sentences in the grammar box. Then ask students to match the phrases in bold with the descriptions (a–e). Let them compare with a partner before confirming answers with the class.

> **ANSWERS**
> a 2, 3, 4   b 4   c 1   d 5   e 6

Refer students to page 168 for further information and practice.

> **ANSWERS TO GRAMMAR SUMMARY EXERCISES**
> **4**
> 1 I would cook with my mother a lot when I was young.
> 2 We used to live in the town centre until two years ago.
> 3 He didn't use to like drinking coffee before a long run.
> 4 When they were little, their grandma would take them to the cinema once a month.
> 5 Did you use to have a best friend at school?
> 6 For years, I would visit my aunt in Lima every summer.
> 7 Our football coach would make us run for twenty minutes before each session.
> **5**
> 1 I'm used to making speeches
> 2 I'm getting used to commuting
> 3 wasn't used to eating
> 4 Are you used to wearing
> 5 got used to living
> 6 's not used to cooking

6

1 used to dream
2 wasn't used to seeing
3 get used to living
4 got used to taking
5 I'm not used to waking up *or* I haven't got used to waking up
6 I'm used to trying or I've got used to trying
7 get used to doing

Grammar note

Form

Remind students that *usually* (= most of the time) tends to go between the subject and main verb.

Ask students to notice the difference in form between *used to* + infinitive and *be/get used to* + *-ing*. The former is a modal verb (*used to*) while the latter is an adjective followed by a preposition. Because *to* is a preposition in this form it's followed by *-ing* (the gerund: an *-ing* form functioning as a noun).

In everyday use, people tend to use *didn't* to make *used to* negative: *We didn't use to have a so-called balanced diet.* However, it's possible to use *not* after *used* (like other modal verbs): *We used not to have a so-called balanced diet.* This sounds formal and archaic to some native speakers, and correct to others.

Meaning

We use *used to* + infinitive as an alternative to the simple past when we want to talk about something that was true or happened regularly but is no longer true or happening.

We use *would* + infinitive when we want to talk about something that happened regularly but is no longer happening. We cannot use *would* with stative verbs in this sense.

Compare *I'm used to these foods* (I'm familiar with eating them) to *I'm getting used to these foods* (I'm not familiar but the situation is changing).

6

- **Optional step** Ask students to read the texts quickly first to get a sense of what the texts are about, and without worrying about the correct forms. Set a focus task: *What countries are mentioned?* (China, the USA, the UK).
- Ask students to choose the correct options to complete the paragraphs. You could ask students to work individually before comparing and checking answers in pairs, or you ask students to work in pairs to help and support each other.

ANSWERS

1 do not usually finish	7 get used to dining
2 get used to	8 used to be
3 are used to eating	9 didn't use to eat
4 usually assumes	10 usually have
5 used to sit	11 used to eat
6 usually eat	12 would go

7

- Ask students to work individually to complete the sentences. Elicit the first answer to get students started. Let students compare their answers in pairs before checking with the class.

ANSWERS

1 used to eat
2 usually have
3 used to take; get used to
4 would hide *or* used to hide
5 used to have; was used to eating (*or* 'm used to eating *or* usually eat)

8

- Ask students if any of the statements in Exercise 7 are true for them. Encourage class discussion.

ANSWERS

Students' own answers

Pronunciation /juː/ and /uː/

9a 🔊 [61]

- Focus students' attention on the words in bold. Play the recording. Students listen and repeat, paying attention to the pronunciation of *u* in the words.

Pronunciation notes

Usually /ˈjuːʒʊəli/ can be difficult for students to say, because of the /ʒ/ sound and the /ju/ sound.

Note the unvoiced /s/ and /t/ sounds in *use* and *used* in these examples.

9b

- Organize the class into pairs to practise saying the words. Elicit or model the first pronunciation to get students started. In feedback, invite individual students to say one or two of the words in front of the class.

Pronunciation notes

The consonant sound runs into the /juː/ sound in each of these examples: note the /sjuː/ in the second syllable of *consume*, and the /kjuː/ in the first syllable of *cucumber*.

Note that in some varieties of English, *tuna* can be pronounced /ˈtʃuːnə/ (a 'ch' sound) as well as /ˈtjuːnə/.

In American English, the /j/ sound tends to be omitted, so, *produce* = /prəˈdus/ and *tuna* = /ˈtuːnə/.

9c 🔊 [62]

- Ask students to practise saying the words. You could put students in pairs to practise this.
- Play the recording. Students listen and check. Point out the rule: after /r/ and /dʒ/ we don't say /j/.

Audioscript 💿 [62] (and answers)

fruit   /r/

juice   /dʒ/

June   /dʒ/

junior   /dʒ/

rule   /r/

true   /r/

Vocabulary and speaking food and eating habits ⟨ my life ⟩

10 💿 [63]

- Ask students to work in pairs to try to pronounce the words and categorize the words into the table.
- Play the recording and tell students to listen to check their answers.
- Tell students to work in their pairs to think of two more items for each category (see examples in brackets in Answers). Then ask them to compare with another pair.

	ANSWERS	
1	Snacks and sweets	almonds, a chocolate bar, crisps, (boiled sweets, popcorn)
2	Fruit and vegetables	cucumber, lettuce, raspberries, (strawberries, carrots)
3	Dairy products	yoghurt, (milk, cheese)
4	Breakfast cereals	muesli, (cornflakes, puffed rice)
5	Sauces	ketchup, (mayonnaise, brown sauce)
6	Soft drinks	fruit juice, fizzy water, (cordial, lemonade)
7	Protein-rich foods	almonds, eggs, lamb, tuna, yoghurt, (cheese, lentils)

Audioscript 💿 [63]

almonds   a chocolate bar   crisps   cucumber
eggs   lettuce   fizzy water   fruit juice   ketchup
lamb   muesli   yoghurt   raspberries   tuna

Pronunciation notes

Note the following:

Silent letters: the silent /l/ in *almonds*, /o/ in *chocolate*, /b/ in *lamb* and /h/ in *yoghurt*

The hard to say consonant clusters: *sps* in *crisps* and *pb* in *raspberries*

muesli = /'mjuːzlɪ/

11

- Start by asking students to read through the five listed areas.
- Ask students to prepare questions individually or in pairs. Set a short time limit and monitor to help with ideas.
- When students are ready, ask them to stand up, walk round, and interview three classmates in five minutes.

12

- Ask students to sit with a partner (if students prepared in pairs, put them with their original partner). Tell them to prepare conclusions using language from the lesson and to present their findings to the class.
- **Optional step** As students speak, when asking questions, and when making presentations, note down errors you hear to focus on in feedback at the end of the activity. Note that this activity revises a range of previously taught material: quantifiers, countable and uncountable nouns and question forms, for example.

Teacher development

A class survey

Surveys provide useful opportunities for students to interact and to collect and analyse real information. They involve a genuine information gap, enable students to find out about each other, and can be very motivating. Some recommendations:

1 Set a clear goal. You could ask students to decide what they want to find out from their survey (e.g. they could prepare questions about snacks and sweets in order to find out whether classmates are eating too many or not). You could give them a role (e.g. they are a sweet manufacturing company or a health watchdog). Tell them that they will have to analyse the information they find for a report or presentation.

2 Provide preparation time. Give students enough time to work in pairs or groups to prepare and write their survey questions. The more thorough the preparation, the better the survey.

3 Manage the activity efficiently. Make space in the classroom for students to circulate and ask questions. Put groups or pairs together in a circle or round a table to prepare and to collate findings. Set clear limits – tell students how much time they have to ask questions and how many people they need to speak to.

4 Bring the survey to a satisfying conclusion. Provide enough time and a genuine motivation to collate and share findings. An individual from each pair or group could stand up and read a summary and conclusion the group has prepared. The group or individual students could write a report on their findings. Or students could engage in a debate based on the results of their findings.

5 Consider extension activities. Doing a survey need not be confined to the classroom. You could get your class to carry out a survey on another class, or ask individuals to interview people outside the classroom, possibly for homework.

7c Cultural conventions

Lesson at a glance

- reading: personal space and turn-taking
- critical thinking: questions and answers
- word focus: *same* and *different*
- speaking: turn-taking in conversations

Reading

1

- **Optional step** With books closed, write *cultural conventions* on the board. Ask students what the phrase means and ask if they can give an example. (It refers to specific things we do as part of our culture, e.g. shaking hands, kissing cheeks or bowing when you first meet someone.)
- Ask students to work in pairs to discuss what they would do if they were having a job interview. Pre-teach *posture* (= the way we hold our bodies when sitting or standing). In feedback, elicit ideas.

ANSWERS

Students' own answers

2

- Ask students to read the first paragraph of the blog and explain *personal space* and *turn-taking*. You could ask students to discuss the phrases in pairs first before checking answers with the class.

ANSWERS

personal space = how close we are used to standing or sitting next to other people

turn-taking = the 'rules' of conversation – how long you speak for and how long the other person waits before responding

3 💿 [64]

- Start by asking students to read the three statements, a–c. Check the meaning of the following words with the class: *proven* (= there is evidence for this); *anthropologist* (= a person who studies the origin, behaviour, and physical, social and cultural development of humans).
- Ask students to read the rest of the blog and say which statement best summarizes the author's findings about personal space and turn-taking. Let students compare answers in pairs before checking with the class.
- **Optional step** The reading text is recorded. You could play the recording and ask students to read and listen.

ANSWER

b

Background information

Edward Twitchell Hall, Jr. (1914–2009) was an American anthropologist who is remembered for developing the concept of proxemics (the study of human use of space and the effects that population density has on human behaviour, communication and social interaction).

4

- Ask students to read the blog again and find and note answers to the questions.
- Let students compare answers in pairs before checking with the class. In feedback, ask students to justify their answers with reference to information in the blog.

ANSWERS

1 misunderstanding or offence (e.g. the American man at the airport who felt uncomfortable because someone sat right next to him)
2 'contact' culture = a cultural group who are more likely to touch each other or stand close to each other; 'non-contact' cultures = the opposite
3 There is very little scientific evidence.
4 Nordic countries are on the extreme of turn-taking – they allow the longest gaps between speaking.
5 0.2 seconds
6 As human beings, we find contrasts entertaining.

5

- Ask students to match the definitions to words in the blog. Elicit the first answer to get students started. Let students compare answers in pairs before checking with the class.

ANSWERS

1 exaggerated (line 3)
2 offence (line 23)
3 anecdotal (line 28)
4 scale (line 47)
5 minimal (line 58)
6 the norm (line 62)

Vocabulary notes

Note the subtle difference between these phrases in the blog:

cause an offence = to do something to make somebody feel angry or upset (e.g. pushing someone or saying something rude)

lead to a misunderstanding = to do something that makes somebody a little annoyed because they are not sure why you are doing it (e.g. pushing against someone on a train – perhaps you mean nothing – it's just crowded – or perhaps you are doing it for another reason)

feel uncomfortable = to feel that something is wrong – that you are not happy with the situation

Critical thinking questions and answers

6

- Ask students to discuss the questions in small groups before eliciting answers in feedback.

> **EXAMPLE ANSWERS**
>
> The question: Are cultural differences in communication real or something imagined or exaggerated?
>
> Yes, he does answer the question – he thinks these differences are exaggerated: *How do these stories with exaggerated differences come about?* and that *we must be cautious when we make comparisons and bear in mind that our similarities are, in fact, much greater than our differences.*

7

- Ask students to discuss the questions in pairs.

> **EXAMPLE ANSWERS**
>
> 1 One reason could be that when it comes to personal space and waiting for a response we are very sensitive to any variation from the norm. But [the writer suspects] that the main reason is, as human beings, we find contrasts entertaining.
>
> 2 We should bear in mind that our similarities are, in fact, much greater than our differences. Scientific data, for example, shows that there is very little cultural difference in the actual time delays in turn-taking.

Word focus *same* and *different*

8

- Ask students to look at the expressions with *difference*, and then to work individually to complete the idioms. Let students compare answers in pairs before checking with the class.
- Ask students which two idioms mean the same and which two are complete opposites.

> **ANSWERS**
>
> | | |
> |---|---|
> | 1 difference | 4 different |
> | 2 same | 5 difference |
> | 3 different | 6 same |
>
> Idioms that mean the same: *all the same to me*, *makes no difference to me*
>
> Idioms that are opposites: *a completely different matter*, *one and the same thing*

Vocabulary notes

have a difference of opinion = to disagree

all the same to me = it's not important; I don't mind

a completely different matter = very different to or opposite to the thing mentioned before

singing a different tune = saying/thinking something very different

makes no difference to me = it's not important; I don't mind

one and the same thing = exactly the same

Extra activity

Ask students to work in pairs to prepare and act out a dialogue containing two of the idioms from this lesson.

Speaking ⟨ my life ⟩

9

- Ask students to work in pairs to discuss personal space and turn-taking in their culture. Then ask each pair to work with another pair to share and contrast answers.
- **Optional step** If your students are from different cultures, you could ask them to make a list of similarities and differences between their cultures.
- As students speak, monitor and note down useful pieces of language they use, or errors they make, which you could focus on in feedback.

10

- Tell students to look at the list of most common first words used in turn-taking. Then ask students to work in pairs to discuss the questions.
- In feedback, elicit ideas and write up any further useful words and expressions on the board.

> **ANSWERS**
>
> Students' own answers

11

- Tell students they are going to have short conversations using the opening questions and statements (a–d). Give students two or three minutes preparation time to form their opinions and think how to use the turn-taking words from Exercise 10.
- When students are ready, organize the class into new pairs and ask them to have conversations. In feedback, invite students to share a brief summary of what they said with the class.
- **Optional step** You could make this a mingling activity. Ask students to walk round the class and discuss each topic with a different student.
- As students speak, monitor and note down useful pieces of language they use, or errors they make, which you could focus on in feedback.

> **ANSWERS**
>
> Students' own answers

Background information

You could ask students to consider the following:
Recent research has shown that people in countries such as Canada, the US, Zimbabwe and Australia smile a lot, while those in China, Indonesia, Bangladesh, Russia and Switzerland smile a lot less. In Japan, people tend to smile with the eyes, not the mouth.

North Europeans generally use few if any hand gestures, whereas people from Mediterranean or North African countries use gestures a lot.

Extra activity

Ask students to contrast the picture of a London underground station on this Student's Book page with the picture of the Japanese subway carriage on the opening page of the unit (page 81). Ask students to comment on the attitude towards personal space of the people in each picture.

7d Wedding customs

Lesson at a glance
- vocabulary: weddings
- real life: describing traditions
- pronunciation: the letter s

Vocabulary weddings

1

- **Optional step** With books closed, write *weddings* on the board. Ask students what words they know connected to this word/topic and write as many words as possible on the board.

- Tell students to read the information in the wordbuilding box. Ask them to work in pairs to match the words with their definitions. In feedback, elicit and check answers.

ANSWERS

1	stag do	5	groom
2	hen do	6	veil
3	reception	7	engagement
4	bride	8	fiancé(e)

Vocabulary notes

stag/hen do – a 'do' is a party (we can also say a 'hen party' or 'stag party'). In many western cultures, stag and hen dos range from a simple get-together for a meal or a drink to a weekend away in a foreign city or doing adventure sports.

reception – in the UK, a wedding reception usually involves a big meal, people making speeches and music and dancing

fiancé (a man) and *fiancée* (a woman) are words borrowed from French and are both pronounced /fɪˈɒnseɪ/.

2

- Discuss the question with your class. If you have a range of cultures in class, use the opportunity to get students to share their knowledge.

- **Optional step** Elicit common examples from your class of word pairs connected with family: *husband and wife, brother and sister, aunt and uncle, parent and child.* Then ask students in pairs to think of other word pairs under different topic headings (e.g. *food: salt and pepper, fish and chips, knife and fork*).

Refer students to Workbook page 59 for further information and practice.

EXAMPLE ANSWERS

Pre-wedding customs in the UK: hen do, booking the venue, inviting friends or relatives to be bridesmaids, setting up a wedding list, fitting the dress, sending out the invitations, getting your hair done

Real life describing traditions

3 💿 [65]

- Ask students what they think a 'henna night' is. Explain that henna is a reddish-brown plant extract used in South and Southwest Asia, the Middle East and North Africa to decorate the skin.
- Play the recording. Students listen and answer the question. Let students compare their answer in pairs before checking with the class.

> **ANSWER**
>
> The bride and female family members and friends attend the event, and the women celebrate with music, song and dance.

Audioscript 💿 [65]

M = Marie; E = Esther

M: I know of henna painting as a custom from Indian weddings, but you came across it in Turkey, didn't you?

E: Yes, in eastern Turkey when I was travelling there. It takes place a few nights before the wedding.

M: Was it a bit like a hen night?

E: Well, in the sense that it marks the last evening that a bride spends as a single woman – with her female family and friends, I suppose it is a bit like that. What happens is typically, the women from both families get together, with the bride, to celebrate with music, song and dance. But it's not just a party. It's an occasion for sadness too, because it symbolizes the end of life as a single person and the start of another stage.

4

- Ask students to work individually to read the information in the language box and complete the first four expressions.
- **Optional step** Play the recording a second time if necessary.
- Let students compare answers in pairs before checking with the class.

> **ANSWERS**
>
> 1 a few nights
> 2 last evening
> 3 sadness (too)
> 4 end of life

Vocabulary notes

mark an occasion = to do something to show that an event is important and to be celebrated

as a rule = generally; this is what usually happens

5 💿 [66]

- Ask students to read the stages carefully. Then play the recording of the second part of the description. Students listen and order the stages of the ceremony.

- Let students compare answers in pairs before checking with the class.

> **ANSWERS**
>
> The order is: f, b, d, e, c, a
>
> (Note that when the singing starts in relation to the other actions is not made 100% clear in the audioscript.)

Audioscript 💿 [66]

M = Marie; E = Esther

M: So what happens exactly?

E: Well, the ceremony begins with preparation of the henna. It's traditional for this to be done by the daughter of a couple who have had a successful marriage themselves. Then, after the bride's head has been covered in a red veil, her hands and feet are decorated with henna. After that, a gold coin is put into the remaining henna. While this is happening, the guests start to sing, umm, separation songs – these are rather sad, as you can imagine. The party continues well into the night. Then, on the morning of the wedding, a child presents the hennaed coin to the groom as a symbol of future prosperity and good fortune.

6 💿 [67]

- Ask students to work in pairs or small groups to retell the events described in the recording.
- Then play the whole recording – both the first and second part. Students listen and compare their version. Let students compare answers with their partner or group. Elicit, in feedback, any parts of the story they didn't remember.
- **Optional step** Before asking students to recall the stories, write a few prompts on the board to help them: *eastern Turkey / celebrate / sadness / veil / henna / gold coin / good fortune.*

Extra activity

Ask students to describe weddings that they have attended (in their culture or in another culture), using some of the words and phrases from the recording. If you have a multicultural class, use this opportunity to get students to share experiences.

Audioscript 💿 [67]

Note that audioscript 67 consists of audioscript 65 and 66 combined.

Pronunciation the letter s

7a 💿 [68]

- Ask students to read the words from the description. Play the recording. Students listen and note how each underlined *s* is pronounced.
- **Optional step** Play the recording again so students can listen and repeat, or ask students to practise saying the words in pairs.

Audioscript 🔊 [68] (with answers)

custom /s/	pleasure /ʒ/
dress /s/	spends /z/
friends /z/	suppose /z/
music /z/	weddings /z/
occasion /ʒ/	

Pronunciation notes

s is pronounced /s/ after unvoiced consonants (*pots, books*) and pronounced /z/ after voiced consonants (*pods, bugs*).

After vowel sounds, there are no clear rules. Note that pronouncing /s/ or /z/ can change the meaning here. Compare: *pace* /peɪs/ and *pays* /peɪz/, or *close* with a /s/ (= near) and *close* with a /z/ (= opposite of *to open*).

The /ʒ/ sound is often (but not always) used when s is followed by the suffixes *-ion, -ual* or *-ure* (e.g. *measure, exposure, visual, television, division, conclusion, confusion*).

7b 🔊 [69]

- Tell students to work in pairs to decide how s will be pronounced in the words. Then ask students to listen and check.
- Ask students to work in their pairs to think of two more words or each sound. Let students compare their answers in pairs before checking with the class.
- **Optional step** Ask students to practise saying the words. Monitor and comment on whether students are right or not.

> ANSWERS
> decision /ʒ/ eastern /s/ lose /z/ plans /z/ rings /z/
> single /s/ surprise /s/, /z/ usual /ʒ/
> Other possibilities:
> /ʒ/: casual, vision
> /s/: loose, parks
> /z/: rose, hands

8

- Ask students to think about what special events or customs take place after a wedding in their country. If your students are from the same culture, you could make a list of four or five events for them to consider. If you have a multicultural class, just elicit ideas at this stage and create interest.
- Ask students to work individually to prepare notes. Set a five-minute time limit and tell students to use the list of headings to guide them. Circulate and help with ideas and vocabulary.

9

- Organize the class into groups of three or four to describe the customs. As students speak, monitor and note errors and examples of good language use.
- In feedback, invite students to share with the class what they can remember of their partners' descriptions. At the end, provide some feedback on language students have used.

Extra activity

Ask students to go online and find five key events in a marriage ceremony in a culture they don't know about. This could be done for homework. In the next lesson, ask students to make a class presentation in which they tell the class what they found.

Teacher development

A class presentation

At this level, asking students to prepare and give a class presentation can be interesting and motivating. Here's a suggested procedure:

1 Set the topic. In class time, establish the topic for the presentation (e.g. a description of a marriage ceremony students are familiar with). Brainstorm ideas and useful language students might need. Introduce some key phrases: *I'd like to talk about … ; One of the most interesting aspects of … is … ; What surprised me most was …*

2 Preparation at home. For homework, ask students to prepare their presentation. This may involve internet research or asking people they know for information. Tell students to make detailed notes for their presentation rather than a script.

3 Giving the presentation. In a large class, you could split students into groups of four or five. Each person in turn makes a presentation to the group. Alternatively, in a small class, you could start each lesson for a week or more with one presentation from a different student. Students get used to the idea that someone will talk at length at the start of each lesson.

4 Provide a reason to listen. Set a task to make sure the rest of the class listen and engage with the presentation, e.g. tell students to think of two questions to ask at the end as they listen or ask students to make notes.

5 Provide meaningful feedback. Comment on the content and also (some) errors you hear. When one student speaks at length, it's a good opportunity to listen, note performance and provide a useful written copy of the common errors for that student.

7e Firework festival

Lesson at a glance
- writing: a description
- writing skill: adding detail

Writing a description

1
- Ask students to work in pairs and describe what they can see in the photo. In feedback, elicit ideas, but do not comment on answers at this stage (they will find out more in the text).
- **Optional step** Ask: *Where do you think this festival is? What is it celebrating? What is the text about?* Then ask students to read the text quickly to check their predictions. Use the opportunity to check any key vocabulary: *fireworks* (= they explode and burn and produce coloured light), *burn* (= verb meaning to be on fire), *cardboard* (= a hard, thick form of paper used for boxes), *plaster* (= the material people put on walls and ceilings which goes hard to make a flat, smooth surface), *statues* (= large, stone monuments that usually represent people).

EXAMPLE ANSWERS
The photo shows unusual, large statues or figures in the streets of a city. It appears that these huge characters are burned in the streets, possibly as part of a festival or parade.

2
- Ask students to work individually to read the description of a festival and answer the questions. Let students compare answers in pairs before checking with the class.

ANSWERS
a *Las Fallas* or the Festival of fire
b 15th–19th March
c marks the beginning of spring / welcomes in the new season (spring)
d the *ninots* or statues
e parades, music, food and drink, fireworks
f burning of the statues at midnight on the last night of the festival

Background information

Las Fallas (or *Les Falles* in Valencian) is a traditional celebration held to commemorate Saint Joseph in the city of Valencia, on Spain's east coast. Each neighbourhood of the city has an organized group of people, called a *casal faller*, which works all year to raise money to produce a construction for the event. Each giant puppet is called a *ninot*, and the whole construction on which they appear is a *falla*. Everything is eventually burned.

3
- Ask students to read the description of the festival again and underline all the adjectives. Let students compare answers and discuss the follow-up question in pairs before checking with the class.

ANSWERS
1 unusual, exciting, joyful, extraordinary, creative, spectacular, unique, noisy
2 the impression of an exciting and spectacular festival

Writing skill adding detail

4a
- Ask students to work individually to answer the questions. Let students compare answers in pairs before checking with the class.

ANSWERS
1
the festival in general: location (Valencia, Spain), what it consists of (statues, parades, music, food, fireworks) and when it takes place (beginning of spring)
the beginning of spring: a description of what the beginning of spring represents (everything bad is burned to welcome the new season)
the *ninot* statues: size (as tall as houses) and what they are made of (cardboard, wood and plaster), and examples of what they might be of (characters from real life)
the characters from real life: politicians, celebrities
the celebrations: how long these go on (two days), what people do (drink, eat paella, watch fireworks, have fun)
the final display: when (at midnight), what happens (the statues are set on fire) and a description (unique and noisy)
2
one of the most unusual and exciting festivals in the world; a joyful mixture; extraordinary statues called ninots *... as tall as houses; unique and very noisy* – adjectives
marks the beginning of spring; they have taken months to build and costs thousands of Euros; the traditional local dish – an explanation
parades, music, food and fireworks; made of cardboard, wood and plaster; drinking, eating paella ... watching fireworks and ... having fun – a list
like politicians and celebrities – an example

4b
- Ask students to work in pairs to add detail to the description of a music festival (sentences 1–4). Elicit possible answers to complete the first sentence. Ask students to write the sentences.

EXAMPLE ANSWERS
1 main, large, huge, colourful
2 chatting, singing, dancing, looking at the sights (as they go)
3 tacos, Chinese food, speciality foods, local dishes
4 the weather is warmer, children are on holiday, the sea is a pleasant temperature

5

- **Optional step** Start with a class discussion. Brainstorm festivals students might describe and write up useful words or phrases on the board.

- Ask students to work individually for one minute making notes about what they plan to include in their description. Monitor at this stage and help with ideas and vocabulary. You could let students compare their ideas in pairs and ask for help.

- Ask students to work individually to write their description. You could set a time limit here (depending on how much time you have in your lesson) to keep students on schedule and focused on the task. Alternatively, set this writing stage for homework and do the checking and revising stage in the next lesson.

6

- Organize the class into pairs and ask students to exchange their written work with their partner. Tell students to check their partner's work using the questions and suggest how to improve it.

- **Optional step** Ask students to revise and rewrite their description based on their partner's suggestions.

Extra activity

Pin the descriptions on classroom walls or noticeboards. Ask students to walk round, read the descriptions and express their opinion. One possibility is to ask students to omit or blank out the name of the festival. Students must then guess the festival from the description.

7f Eating insects

Before you watch

1

- **Optional step 1** Ask students to look at the photo and the caption, and say what they think the video will be about. Ask: *What do you think a candy man is? How does the photo make you feel? What might be Larry's mission?*

- Ask students to match the names of the insects with the photos, and say what they know about each one.

- **Optional step 2** Drill the words for pronunciation. Notice the strong stress marks on the words in the answers below.

ANSWERS

Optional step 1 example answer:

The photo shows a stick with candy on the end (perhaps toffee or chocolate). On the candy are some sort of insect larvae or worms. A candy man is a person who makes or sells candy – the mission might be to make and sell this unusual type of insect-candy.

1 and 2

A <u>mea</u>lworm (long, fat larvae that fishermen use to catch fish)

B fly (or housefly – they are usually black and are annoying and buzz at windows or around the room)

C mos<u>qu</u>ito (small, buzzing creatures that bite you in the night and can carry malaria – one of the world's biggest killers)

D <u>ca</u>terpillar (the larvae of butterflies or moths; they are hairy and crawl slowly along leaves on little legs)

E <u>cri</u>cket (green insects that often swarm in large numbers; they make a clicking noise; they have long back legs and can jump huge distances)

F <u>cock</u>roach (big, black beetle with a very strong body; they often infest kitchens; they have high resistance to radiation)

Key vocabulary

2a

- Ask students to work individually to read the sentences and guess the meaning of the words in bold. Start students off by eliciting the meaning of the first word.

- Let students compare their answers in pairs. Do not check answers at this stage (students will match definitions in the next exercise).

2b

- Ask students to match the words in bold in Exercise 2a with the definitions. During feedback, check that students fully understand the meaning of the words in bold.

ANSWERS

1 b   2 e   3 a   4 c   5 d

Vocabulary notes

1 *advocate* (*of something*) = somebody who (publicly) argues or campaigns for something

2 *garnish* = a cookery word meaning the small amount of herbs, vegetables or fruit chefs arrange on a plate to make a dish look good – it's something you are not necessarily supposed to eat

3 *niche market* (*for something*) = a market (a product or service) that is very specialized and is for the small number of people who want it

4 *revolting* = horrible, disgusting (food)

5 *have snob appeal* = if something 'has snob appeal' people want to buy it because they feel superior to other people when they have the item (because it's designer, expensive, exclusive or worn by a celebrity)

3

- Tell students that they are going to watch a video about eating insects. Discuss questions 1–4 with your class before playing the video. You could organize the class into small groups to discuss the questions. In feedback, find out what students know. Do not comment at this stage as the answers are in the video.

Background information

If you have a multicultural class, or if you are in a country where people eat insects regularly, be aware that you may need to handle the topic sensitively. Concentrate on finding out what insects students eat and why rather than focusing on how unusual it may seem to some cultures.

While you watch

4 ■ [7.1]

- Ask students to watch the whole video and check their answers to the questions in Exercise 3. Let students compare answers in pairs before checking with the class.

ANSWERS

1 Asia, Africa, Australia and Latin America

2 No, it dates back to the earliest humans.

3 Because producing a pound of insects (e.g. caterpillar) takes fewer resources than producing a pound of beef, for example.

4 Yes – they are full of (*brim with*) vitamins and minerals.

Videoscript ■◀ 7.1

0.00–0.40 Presenter   Every resort town in the US has a candy store, but one store in Pismo Beach, California, goes beyond the usual toffee and caramel apples. If Hotlix has its way, Americans will be snacking on everything from caterpillars and cockroaches to mealworm-covered apples.

Larry Peterman is a candyman on a mission. For more than a decade, he's been promoting a valuable food source that most Americans find revolting. In a land of plenty, people resist. Larry knows why. From an early age, parents teach children to avoid insects.

0.41–0.49 Larry Peterman   In our culture, from the time that we're really small, we're taught to avoid insects – they might bite you like a mosquito – or just swat them.

This has got a good cricket in it!

0.50–1.37 Presenter   But kids aren't the only ones munching on bugs. Around the world, more than 1,400 insect species show up on menus. Insect eating, or entomophagy, is part of healthy diets in Asia, Africa, Australia and Latin America. This trend is anything but new. Archaeologists have found evidence of it dating to the earliest humans.

Advocates of insect-eating like to note that it's environmentally sound. Producing a pound of caterpillar takes a tenth of the resources needed to produce a pound of beef. And insects brim with vitamins and minerals. But despite all the benefits, most Americans can't stomach bugs.

1.38–1.39 Waiter   Welcome, welcome, welcome! Have a seat!

1.40–1.50 Presenter   Unlike Larry Peterman, who celebrates them at his dinner parties. The evening begins with Larry's version of the classic shrimp cocktail.

1.51–2.18 Larry Peterman   We've just finished preparing a cricket cocktail. It's a lot like a shrimp cocktail, only instead of shrimp, we use crickets.

OK, folks, here's the first course! Now, enjoy!

Dinner guest   I just ate a cricket!

Larry Peterman   While you're enjoying this, I'm going down and I'll get your next course.

2.19–2.23 Presenter   The main course is a stir-fry, with a special garnish.

2.24–2.27 Larry Peterman   Here we go! Dinner is served!

2.28–2.37 Dinner guests   Get ready … OK … uno, dos … three … go!

2.38–2.45 Presenter   Several courses later, Larry presents his pièce de résistance.

2.46–2.49 Larry Peterman   OK! Here it is, folks! What you've been waiting for!

2.50–2.51 Dinner guest   Oh no!

2.52–3.05 Larry Peterman   Now, don't let anybody dive in until everyone's been served, please!

We call it a Pismo Surfer. What it is is a banana with whipped cream, and a really good cockroach on it. You don't have to eat the wings, you don't have to eat the head, unless you want to.

3.06–3.09 Dinner guest   Do you know where this cockroach has been?

3.10–3.11 Dinner guest   How does it taste?

3.11–3.12 Larry Peterman   We can do another one next week if you like!

3.13–3.17 Presenter   Larry predicts he'll eventually win people over.

3.17–3.34 Larry Peterman   As we become more and more insect food-oriented, our tastes are going to change, and so I see a niche for somebody that does gourmet insects. Could have some snob appeal, like people taste flies and, 'Mmm, this is good. Hey, this bug is good!'

5

- Ask students to work in pairs to write the names of the missing insects.

- **Optional step** If necessary, play the video again so that students can complete their answers.

ANSWERS

1 mealworms
2 (good) cricket
3 crickets
4 mealworms (and a scorpion garnish)
5 cockroach

6 🎥 [7.1]

- Ask students to read the questions and note any answers they already know.
- Play the video again. Students watch and note answers. Let students compare their answers in pairs.
- **Optional step** If some students already know most of the answers before watching a second time, ask them to watch/listen for additional things during the second viewing – this could be visual information, spoken information, or words or specific phrases in natural speech.

ANSWERS

1 California (Pismo Beach)
2 for more than a decade
3 Because from an early age, parents teach children to avoid insects.
4 more than 1,400 insect species
5 where the cockroach has been

After you watch

Vocabulary in context

7a 🎥 [7.2]

- Explain that students are going to watch some clips from the video which contain some new words and phrases. They need to choose the correct meaning of the words.
- Play the clips. When each multiple-choice question appears, pause the clip so that students can choose the correct definition. You could let students compare answers in pairs before discussing with the class.

ANSWERS

1 b 2 c 3 a 4 a 5 c

Videoscript 🎥 7.2

1 ... we're taught to avoid ... or just **swat** them.
   a ignore or leave alone
   b hit or crush
   c spray
2 This trend is **anything but new**.
   a very new
   b quite new
   c not new

3 But despite all the benefits, most Americans **can't stomach** bugs.
   a hate the idea of eating
   b can't digest
   c are afraid of
4 ... don't let anybody **dive in** until everyone's been served ...
   a start eating
   b finish their food
   c test their food
5 Larry predicts he'll eventually **win people over**.
   a make people pay for his food
   b employ more people
   c convince people of his view

Vocabulary notes

swat (a fly) = to hit (a fly) using a fly swatter (bamboo or plastic stick with a flat end to hit the fly with)

anything but new = an emphatic way to say something is not new – it's saying that it's the opposite of new (compare *My husband is anything but generous – he's the meanest man I know!*)

can't stomach = if you *can't stomach* something, the very idea of it is horrible (e.g. *I can't stomach politicians who lie.*)

dive in = if you *dive in*, you grab and eat food quickly and hungrily, however, it is used jokingly, at a family dinner for example, to just say 'you can start now'

win (somebody) over = a phrasal verb meaning to convince or persuade, but in a positive way, by making a positive case

Here are other phrases to check:

a tenth of resources = 10% (of what you need to create something, e.g. food, energy, time, money)

pièce de résistance = a French term, used in English to describe the best thing that somebody has done or can do

a niche = here, a small opportunity

a gourmet = somebody who knows a lot about food and wine (so, *gourmet food* is food of a very high quality)

a snob = somebody who thinks they are better than other people (so, *snob appeal* is used in a disparaging way to describe something that people want because it makes them feel superior or sophisticated)

7b

- Students work individually to complete the sentences. Elicit one or two ideas for the first sentence to get them started. Let students compare sentences in pairs.

EXAMPLE ANSWERS

Students' own ideas, but some possibilities include:

1 The fashion for *criticizing celebrities* is anything but new.
2 I can't stomach *violent films. Please don't make me watch one!*
3 My friend disagreed with me about *living abroad*, but I was able to win her over by saying *how exciting it is to learn about new people and cultures.*

8

- Ask students to prepare to describe sweets or candy they ate as a child. Point out that *sweets* is British English and *candy* is American English (but they mean the same thing).

- When students are ready, ask them to describe the sweets to their partner, or put students in small groups to take turns to describe sweets.

- **Optional step** This is a good opportunity for providing a teacher model. Talk about the sweets you ate as a child – describe their appearance, taste and popularity, when and how you got them and ate them, and which ones were your favourites and why.

Extra activity 1

Ask students in small groups to think of three more dishes they could make with insects in, but where people wouldn't know they were eating insects. Students present their ideas to the rest of the class, and decide which idea is best.

Extra activity 2

Students talk about their favourite food, what foods they don't like, and why, and what they (can) do to make food they don't like more palatable.

UNIT 7 Review and memory booster

Memory Booster activities

Exercises 4, 6 and 8 are Memory Booster activities. For more information about these activities and how they benefit students, see page 10 of this Teacher's Book.

I can … check boxes

As an alternative to asking students to simply tick the *I can … * boxes, you could ask them to give themselves a score from 1 to 4 (1 = not very confident; 4 = very confident) for each language area. If students score 1 or 2 for a language area, refer them to additional practice activities in the Workbook and Grammar summary exercises.

Grammar

1

- Ask students to work individually to choose the correct options to complete the description about eating in Argentina.

ANSWERS

1 are used to eating	6 would
2 will get	7 get used to
3 usually takes	8 feel
4 start	9 used to be
5 used to eat	

2

- Ask students to read the description again and find four things that the writer finds strange about eating habits in Argentina.

ANSWERS

eating dinner late; eating a small breakfast; eating a big lunch; eating a lot of meat

3

- Tell students to work individually to complete the sentence with one of the grammatical forms in the text. Elicit the difference in use between the three possible ways of completing the sentence.

ANSWERS

ate (= present simple for single or repeated events in the past)

or *used to eat* (= 'use to' for a repeated past action, habit or situation)

or *would eat* (= a repeated action or habit, but not a situation, in the past)

4 >> MB

- Ask students to work individually to write two similar sentences to the sentence in Exercise 3, including spaces. They should write about their own past or present eating habits.
- Then ask students to work in pairs to read out their sentences. Can their partner guess the missing word(s)?

Vocabulary

5

- Ask students to work individually to complete the rules of good behaviour. Tell them to put the letters of the words in brackets in the correct order. Let students compare answers in pairs before checking with the class. You could ask students to discuss the rules and compare them to what is considered good behaviour in their own culture(s).

ANSWERS

1 interrupt	4 Switch off
2 stare	5 consideration
3 chewing	6 personal

6 >> MB

- Ask students to work in pairs to discuss which word is the odd one out in each case. Monitor and encourage them to give reasons for their decisions.

ANSWERS

1 spoil (the others are ways of telling someone you don't like their behaviour)
2 educate (the others are what parents or guardians do at home and primarily involve caring, *educate* usually happens at school and refers to learning)
3 shame (it's a negative word, the others are positive ways to respond to someone's behaviour)
4 cheese (is a type of protein, the others are carbohydrate)
5 engagement (it's the act of agreeing to get married, all the others are party-like events)
6 cucumber (EITHER because all the others are things you might have for breakfast OR because it contains a /juː/ sound <u>cu</u>cumber, while all the others are just /uː/)
7 veil (it's something the bride wears at a wedding, the others are people)
8 posture (it's the only noun, the others are verbs)

Real life

7

- Ask students to work individually to match the sentence beginnings with the endings to make sentences about a coming-of-age tradition. Let students compare answers in pairs before checking with the class.

ANSWERS

1 b 2 f 3 g 4 h 5 a 6 d 7 c 8 e

8 >> MB

- Ask students to work in pairs to take turns to describe a special celebration in their country. Tell them to use the phrases 1–8 in Exercise 7.

Unit 8 Hopes and ambitions

Opener

1

- Ask students to look at the photo and the caption. Ask students to say what a *bucket list* is (see Background information below). Pre-teach the word *mural* (= a painting or design on a wall).
- Ask students to find two wishes on the wall that they like. Elicit ideas from students in feedback.

Background information

A list of activities somebody wants to do before he or she dies is often called a 'bucket list'. This is because it's a list of things a person wants to do before he or she 'kicks the bucket'.

Kick the bucket is an informal idiom meaning *to die*. It comes from the idea that a condemned man, about to be hanged, stands on a bucket. When the hangman kicks the bucket, the condemned man is hanged.

2 [70]

- Play the recording. Students listen and note the examples of things that people write that they hear.
- Let students compare answers in pairs before checking with the class.

ANSWERS

I want to … plant a tree, fix my kitchen tap, live up to others' expectations, be a good parent. A lot of people have an ambition to travel and to learn another language.

Audioscript [70]

This mural's been on the side of a local shop in my neighbourhood for years. Anyone can write on it. You just have to pick up a piece of chalk and complete the sentence 'Before I die, I want to …' It's not the only one of its kind: there are quite a few other walls like it in other cities in the world. The idea was started by a woman in New Orleans and then it spread.

Sometimes I sit and watch people as they're thinking what to write on it, thinking about the dreams they'd like to come true. Some are goals that are easy to achieve, like 'I want to plant a tree'; some just make you laugh, like 'I want to fix my kitchen tap'. But others are more personal – people wanting to live up to others' expectations of them – 'I want to be a good parent' was one I found touching. The same things keep coming up too: like a lot of people have an ambition to travel and to learn another language. But overall you get this amazing variety of wishes. I guess some will fulfil their ambitions and some won't, but it shows that everyone – doesn't matter who they are – is trying to make sense of their direction in life.

3

- Ask students to work individually to complete the sentences. Then ask them to work in pairs and explain the differences in meaning between the words to their partner.
- During feedback confirm answers and check that students understand the differences between the words.

ANSWERS

1 goal (note that *hope* could also be used)
2 ambition (note that *goal* could also be used)
3 hope

Vocabulary notes

aim/goal/target = general words meaning that you have something specific you intend to achieve

ambition = often used in the context of careers or life choices, your ambition may be what you want to achieve for yourself in life

wish/hope/dream = something you want to achieve (that is more tentative and may be unrealistic)

expectation = something you think will happen for certain

4 [70]

- Ask students if they can remember and complete any of the missing words. Play the recording. Students listen and check/complete the phrases.
- Let students compare answers in pairs before checking with the class.

ANSWERS

1 come   2 achieve   3 live   4 have   5 fulfil

Vocabulary notes

dreams come true = a fixed expression meaning that your dreams or hopes become reality

live up to expectations = to achieve what people believe you are capable of

fulfil your ambitions = to achieve what you want to be or do

5

- Organize the class into pairs to discuss the questions. You could ask: *What would you write on the wall?*
- **Optional step** If you think your students may find it difficult to come up with ideas for what they would write on the wall, give prompts on the board to help them. For example:
  I'd really like to …
  be / have / experience / see / travel to / work as a / live in / learn
- As students speak, monitor and note errors and any interesting comments you hear. In feedback, invite students with interesting ideas or ambitions to share them with the class.

Extra activity

Make 'a bucket list wall' in the classroom. You could do this by using the whiteboard (if it's large) or the classroom wall or noticeboard – pin up a large sheet of A3 paper. Ask students to write their own wishes on the wall while others are not looking. Then ask students to read what everybody wrote and guess who wrote what.

Alternatively, to avoid having everybody up at the board at once, hand out slips of paper and ask students to write their list on the paper and then stick it to the board or classroom wall.

8a Rise of the 'rocket girls'

Lesson at a glance
- reading: the first human computers
- word focus: *make* and *do*
- grammar: second, third and mixed conditionals
- pronunciation: contracted or weak forms
- speaking: ambitions

Reading

1 🎧 [71]

- Tell students to look at the title of the article and the photos. Ask them to work in pairs to discuss the questions. In feedback, elicit ideas, but do not comment on them at this stage.
- Ask students to read the text and check their ideas.
- **Optional step** The reading text is recorded. You could play the recording and ask students to read and listen.
- **Optional step** Before students read, use the opportunity to brainstorm words students may expect to see in the text. A useful list might be: *rocket, space, astronaut, computer, engineer, lab/laboratory.*

> ANSWERS
>
> 1 They were female mathematicians who worked on the lunar project at NASA's Jet Propulsion Lab (JPL) in California in the 1960s.
> 2 They wanted to be engineers, but didn't have the necessary qualifications.

2

- Ask students to read the article again and correct the underlined words to make the sentences true. Let students check their answers in pairs before checking with the class.

> ANSWERS
>
> | | |
> |---|---|
> | 1 famous *or* well-known | 4 computers |
> | 2 humans | 5 well *or* closely |
> | 3 miss | 6 engineers |

Vocabulary notes

Check that students are familiar with the following vocabulary from the article:

NASA = North American Space Agency

determined = hard-working and ambitious; not willing to stop trying

bound for = on the way to

flexible hours = not fixed hours

lunar project = the project to go to the moon

Background information

Edwin 'Buzz' Aldrin (born 1930) was the Lunar Module Pilot on Apollo 11, and one of the first two humans to land on the Moon, and the second person to walk on it, on July 21st, 1969.

Eleanor Francis Helin (1932–2009) was an American astronomer and principal investigator of the Near-Earth Asteroid Tracking (or NEAT) program of NASA's Jet Propulsion Laboratory. She discovered numerous minor planets and comets.

Extra activity

Ask students to look at the statistic below, which come from later in the same article. Tell them to speculate about reasons for this.

In 1984 in the USA, 37% of university graduates in computer science were women. Today, that number is only 18%.

Possible answers: greater interest among men who are now filling most college places; sexual discrimination is limiting places for women; fewer opportunities for women in the workplace which is discouraging women from applying for university places

Word focus *make* and *do*
3

- Ask students to work individually to find five expressions with *make* and *do* in the article. Elicit the first as an example to get students started.

- Then tell students to choose the correct option to complete the sentences about *make* and *do,* and to match the expressions from the article with each rule.

- Let students compare answers in pairs before checking with the class.

- **Optional step** Brainstorm other expressions with *make* or *do* that students already know, or do a dictionary task and ask students to work in pairs to find three useful phrases to share with the class.

> ANSWERS
>
> *do mathematical calculations* (1 – performing work or a task)
> *made the smallest mistake* (4 – fixed expressions)
> *made the decision* (4 – fixed expressions)
> *made a special work environment* (2 – creating something)
> *doing something really valuable* (3 – *do* + an object pronoun, e.g. *something, it, that*)
>
> 1 do
> 2 make
> 3 do
> 4 make

Vocabulary notes

Do and *make* can be difficult for students – in their L1 they may use the same verb for both meanings, or may have two verbs, as in English, but use them differently. Explain that *do* is often linked to the idea of work, and *make* to creativity, but that many uses are idiomatic and simply have to be learned. A list of common phrases with *do* or *make* follows.

List of household chores (*do*):
do the housework
do the cleaning
do the washing up
do the washing (i.e. clothes)
do the hoovering / vacuum cleaning
Note this exception: make the bed

Jobs/Work/Study (*do*):
do some research
do your homework
do some revision
do a job
do some admin / do the paperwork
do the filing
do business

Indefinite (*do*):
I've done nothing today.
(We need to) do something about it.
do this / do that

Creating something (*make*):
make a cake
make breakfast
make a plan
make a list
make a treehouse (i.e. build)
make some decorations

Fixed expressions (*make*):
make progress
make a mess
make a complaint
make an excuse
make a speech
Note these exceptions: do your best, do someone a favour

4

- Ask students to work individually to choose the correct verb to complete the sentences. Let students compare answers in pairs before checking with the class. In feedback, you could ask students to match each use with a rule from Exercise 3.

> ANSWERS
>
> 1 make; do
> 2 doing; made
> 3 do; make
> 4 made; do
> 5 doing; making

Vocabulary notes

1 make a suggestion (rule 4); do the housework (rule 1)

2 do a class (rule 1); make friends (rule 4)

3 do something to help (someone) (rule 3); make a difference (rule 4)

4 make a note (of something) (rule 2); do the shopping (rule 1)

5 do everything you can (rule 3); make a profit (rule 2)

Grammar second, third and mixed conditionals

5

- Ask students to look at the information and examples in the grammar box. Then tell them to choose the correct option to complete the explanations. Check answers with the class.

> ANSWERS
>
> 1 present or future; imagined situation
> 2 past; past
> 3 present; past
> 4 past; present

Refer students to page 170 for further information and practice.

> ANSWERS TO GRAMMAR SUMMARY EXERCISES
>
> **1**
> 1 had; 'd/would take
> 2 'd/would have worn; 'd/had known
> 3 'd/would go; had
> 4 wouldn't have chosen; hadn't encouraged
> 5 spent; wouldn't be
> 6 'd/would have done; 'd/had practised
>
> **2**
> 1 d (ii)   2 a (i)   3 b (ii)   4 f (i)   5 c (i)   6 e (ii)
>
> **3**
> 1 hadn't left; wouldn't be
> 2 spoke; 'd/would have understood
> 3 'd/would come; hadn't; seen
> 4 lived; 'd/would have gone
> 5 would be; hadn't met
> 6 weren't/wasn't; 'd/would have been able

Grammar notes

Form

Remind students of the conditional forms. You could ask them to label the examples in the box:

Second conditional = *If* + past simple, *would(n't)* + infinitive without 'to'

Third conditional = *If* + *had(n't)* + past participle, *wouldn't* + *have* + past participle

Use

We use the second conditional to talk about unlikely or impossible situations in the present and/or future, in contrast to the first conditional, which is used for likely situations in the present and/or future. Point out that the past form is used to make the hypothesis less likely (not to indicate a past time). The third conditional is used to talk about imaginary situations in the past.

You could use concept check questions to make sure students understand the use of the three conditional forms, for example:

Example sentence: *If there were more women engineers today, she probably wouldn't have written the book.*

Ask: *In the if-clause, are we talking about the present or past?* (the present – today)

Ask: *Are there more women engineers today?* (No)

Ask: *In the 'result' clause, are we talking about the present or past?* (the past)

Ask: *Did she write the book?* (Yes)

6

- Ask students to work individually to decide what type of conditional sentence each sentence is, and to describe the actual situation and the result.

> ANSWERS
>
> 2 Third conditional sentence
>   Situation = *None of the engineers were men,*
>   Result = *so it was a special working environment.*
> 3 Mixed second and third conditional sentence
>   Situation = *I am bad / I am not good at maths,*
>   Result = *so I didn't study physics at university.*
> 4 Mixed third and second conditional sentence
>   Situation = *I haven't read Nathalia Holt's book,*
>   Result = *so I don't know all the facts about the rocket girls.*

7

- Ask students to work individually to write the conditional sentences. Point out that other words in the sentences may need to change. Elicit the first answer to get students started.

- Let students compare answers in pairs before eliciting answers from the class.

> ANSWERS
>
> 1 If they had given me a work visa, I would be able to (*or* could) work here legally.
> 2 If we lived closer to the city, we would see our friends more often. *or* If we didn't live a long way from the city, we would/could see our friends more often.
> 3 If I had understood the film, I wouldn't have walked out before the end *or* I would have stayed until the end.
> 4 If I was/were (more) used to the cold weather, I wouldn't have had to put on an extra jumper.
> 5 Going on holiday wouldn't be so expensive if we didn't have three children *or* if we had fewer children.

6 If she hadn't done (so) well in her law exams, she wouldn't (now) be working for a top legal firm (now).

7 I would have phoned you if I hadn't been waiting for another call.

8 If I was/were angry about what you did, I would have said something.

Note that it is possible for students to switch the clauses in these sentences (e.g. *I would be able to work here legally if they had given me a work visa; If we didn't have three children, going on holiday wouldn't be so expensive*).

Grammar note

Note that other modal verbs, such as *might* or *could*, can be used instead of *would* when expressing a lack of certainty or an ability.

Note that the subjunctive form *If I were* or *If he/she were* is the more grammatically correct form here. The subjunctive in English is identical to the past form, except for these examples. In common usage, however, native speakers regularly say *If I was* or *If he was*, so it has become acceptable to use both forms.

Pronunciation contracted or weak forms

8a 🎧 [72]

- Ask students to work individually to complete the sentences. Let students compare answers in pairs.
- Play the recording. Students listen and note the pronunciation. Check answers with the class.

ANSWERS

Possible ways of completing the sentences:

1 was/were; 'd/would
2 have; 'd been / had been
3 'd/had; would have / would've / 'd have
4 'd/had; 'd/would

What is heard in the recording:

1 *were* (weak form); *'d* (contraction of *would*)
2 *have* (weak form); *'d been* (contraction of *had*; weak form of *been*)
3 *'d* (contraction of *had*); *'d've* (contraction of *would*; contraction of *have*)
4 *'d* (contraction of *had*); *'d* (contraction of *would*)

Audioscript 🎧 [72]

1 If the rent were cheaper, I'd take the flat.

2 What would you have done if you'd been me?

3 So sorry! If I'd known you were waiting, I'd've asked Jo to get you a coffee.

4 If she had stayed at college, she'd now be a fully qualified journalist.

8b

- Organize the class into pairs to practise saying the sentences from Exercise 8a.
- **Optional step** Drill some of the sentences (see Teacher development below).

Teacher development

Drills and prompt drills

It's a good idea to drill conditional sentences in order to practise contracted or weak forms and to help students assimilate form and meaning. Here are suggestions:

1 Students listen and repeat full sentences. With books closed, read out the first sentence in a natural way (*If the rent were cheaper, I'd take the flat*). Ask students to listen carefully, then repeat after you. Next, ask students to repeat individually. If necessary, repeat parts of the phrase so students can listen and repeat specific segments. Repeat the process with other sentences on the page – you could shorten them to help students. For example, say: *If she'd stayed at college, she'd be a journalist.*

2 Students produce sentences from prompts. Elicit other possible result clauses for one of the *if*-clauses on the page. For example, for the clause *If she'd stayed at college*, you could elicit and write on the board: *be an architect, have a good job, feel happier and richer, know more stuff*. Then ask students to make sentences using the prompts. You could do this by saying sentences first, and asking students to repeat, by saying the *if*-clause and asking students to say the result clause, or by asking students to improvise their own sentences from the prompts.

9

- Ask students to work individually to complete the sentences in their own words. Elicit a possible answer to the first sentence to get them started. Let students compare their sentences in pairs before feedback.

EXAMPLE ANSWERS

1 If I hadn't had such a good English teacher, perhaps I wouldn't be here now / wouldn't have passed my exams.

2 If I were more ambitious, perhaps I would go for that job in New York / would have become an architect.

3 I wouldn't be doing what I do today, if my parents hadn't supported me.

4 If I had studied economics instead of English, I'd be better off now.

5 If I hadn't met Jane, I wouldn't have got married.

6 I'd recommend anyone to watch/read *War and Peace*. If I hadn't watched/read it, I wouldn't be the person I am today.

Speaking my life

10

- Ask students to think of a friend or family member who has achieved their ambition and one who has changed their ambition. Tell them to work individually to prepare sentences. Monitor and help with ideas. Ensure that students are using conditional forms.
- Organize the class into groups of three or four students to share stories about friends and family members.

- **Optional step** As students speak, note down errors you hear. Concentrate on errors with conditionals. At the end, during feedback, write up five or six short sentences containing anonymous errors you heard. Ask students in pairs to correct the errors.

Extra activity

Play the chain game. The idea is that students make a 'chain' of conditional sentences by turning result clauses into *if*-clauses. Here is an example: *If we'd worked harder, we would have got the contract* → *If we'd got the contract, we would have got a bonus* → *If I'd got a bonus, I would have paid my debts* → *If I'd paid my debts, I wouldn't be living on the street now.*

Read out the example above, then write one or more of the following on the board:

If we'd won the match, …

If I'd bought a lottery ticket, …

If I hadn't eaten the chocolate cake, …

Organize the class into groups of three or four. In their groups, students take turns to say the next conditional sentence in the chain. The aim is for each group to keep the chain going for as long as possible.

8b I wish I could …

Lesson at a glance
- listening: superpowers
- wordbuilding: noun suffixes
- grammar: *wish* and *if only*
- pronunciation: /ʃ/ and /tʃ/
- speaking: wishes

Listening

1
- Tell students to look at the photos and the captions. Open up the discussion to the class.
- **Optional step** Ask students what they think the positives and negatives of each job might be.

> EXAMPLE ANSWERS
>
> A *telecommunications engineer* is responsible for designing and overseeing the installation of telecommunications equipment and facilities, such as complex electronic switching systems, IP data systems and radio systems.
>
> A *conservationist* is someone who works to protects the environment and wildlife (there are five big cats: lions, leopards, tigers, jaguars and snow leopards).
>
> A *geologist* is a scientist who studies the matter that makes up the Earth as well as the processes and history that have shaped it.
>
> A *geographer* studies Earth's natural environment and human society.
>
> A *biologist* studies living things such as humans, animals and bacteria, to gain a better understanding of how living things work and how external factors influence each organism.
>
> An *astrophysicist* uses science to investigate the nature of stars, planets and solar systems, rather than their positions or motions in space.
>
> A *filmmaker* makes films (the term is often used to describe people who make documentaries or short films – *director* is usually used with someone who makes feature films).

2
- Ask students to read the information in the wordbuilding box. Elicit further examples of jobs that use these suffixes (e.g. *teacher, lawyer, actor, director, physician, musician, pianist, pharmacist, shop assistant, flight attendant*).
- Ask students to look at the verbs and nouns and say what the jobs are. You could ask students to work in pairs to do this before checking answers with the class.
- **Optional step** Drill the words for pronunciation (see word stress in Answers below) during feedback.

> ANSWERS
>
> | | |
> |---|---|
> | 1 electrician | 6 translator |
> | 2 economist | 7 historian |
> | 3 baker | 8 receptionist |
> | 4 firefighter | 9 librarian |
> | 5 lawyer | 10 business consultant |

Refer students to Workbook page 67 for further practice.

3 🔊 [73]

- **Optional step** Explain that a 'superpower' is a special ability that humans don't usually have. Elicit a list of possible 'superpowers' from your class: being able to fly; X-ray vision; the ability to teleport (= go from one place to another by disappearing and reappearing); invisibility; mind-reading; great strength; immortality; the ability to change shape, fight off bullets or turn into an animal.
- Play the recording. Students listen and note what superpower each explorer wanted. Let students compare answers in pairs before checking with the class.

> ### ANSWERS
> 1 invisibility / to be invisible
> 2 to be able to fly
> 3 the ability to make people (magically) understand (what you're trying to say)
> 4 to be invisible
> 5 teleporting or to be able to travel any place I wanted to
> 6 to be invisible
> 7 to read other people's minds
> 8 to turn anything into any kind of food I wanted

Audioscript 🔊 [73]

Note that the *National Geographic* Explorers' words are spoken by actors.

Speaker 1: Albert Lin

It's got to be invisibility, right? Like, because if you could be invisible you could see the entire world in the craziest way.

Speaker 2: Laly Lichtenfeld

I'd like to be able to fly. It'd help me see the bigger picture.

Speaker 3: Andrés Ruzo

I wish I had the ability to make people magically understand. You know how frustrating it is, when you wish other people would get what you're trying to say and they just don't. You think 'Goodness, I wish they'd stop looking at me in that confused way!'

Speaker 4: Alizé Carrère

If I had a superpower, it would be to be invisible, so people couldn't see me.

Speaker 5: Andrew Thompson

Teleporting would be pretty cool. I could travel any place I wanted to. I wish I'd had that power earlier in my career. It would have saved me a lot of air miles. I could also use it to transport things I'd forgotten to take with me on my travels.

Speaker 6: Catherine Workman

I would definitely be invisible. I'd go to the White House and listen in on all their conversations.

Speaker 7: Neil deGrasse Tyson

I wish I could read other people's minds. But I would like to be able to turn that power on and off – sometimes you just don't want to know what people are thinking! Also I'd want to read not just people's minds but the minds of animals too, like dogs. I've always wondered what they're thinking.

Speaker 8: Ricky Qi

Sometimes I think 'If only I could turn anything into any kind of food that I wanted' – that would be the most awesome superpower.

4 🔊 [73]

- Ask students to read the sentences carefully. Ask students what sort of words are missing (nouns, verbs, adjectives or prepositions?). Point out that, in the recording, the speaker may use a slightly different form of the word than is required to complete the sentences.
- Play the recording again. Students listen and complete the sentences. Ask students to compare answers in pairs.
- **Optional step** Discuss the meaning of the expression *see the bigger picture* (see Vocabulary notes below).

> ### ANSWERS
> 1 craziest
> 2 picture
> 3 frustrated
> 4 see
> 5 air miles
> 6 White House
> 7 turn it off
> 8 awesome

Vocabulary notes

see the bigger picture = an idiom meaning that you see and understand all the most important facts about a situation and the effects that it has on other things

the White House = where the US president lives

awesome = amazing (an Americanism)

5

- Organize the class into pairs or small groups to discuss the questions. In feedback, ask each group to briefly say what they discussed.

> ### ANSWERS
> Students' own ideas

Extra activity

Write the following X-Men on the board: *Professor X* (telepathic); *Magneto* (controls metal); *Phoenix* (telepathic); *Angel* (can fly – has wings); *Beast* (strong and agile); *Wolverine* (can regenerate); *Changeling* (changes shape); *Havok* (absorbs cosmic energy and makes explosions); *Storm* (controls the weather); *Rogue* (takes on other people's personalities).

Ask students to choose a character and prepare a short paragraph describing their superpowers for homework. In the next lesson, students could share their information in groups.

Grammar *wish* and *if only*
6

- Tell students to read the information in the grammar box. Then ask them to say whether the sentences are true (T) or false (F), and to correct the false sentences.

- **Optional step** You could ask students to work in pairs to discuss the sentences before checking with the class. Monitor as students speak and see how well students understand this language area and what problems they have.

ANSWERS

1 F (The speakers are talking about a wish for the present; they are referring to a situation that is unreal or unlikely.)
2 F (*If only* is used to express a strong wish that things could be different – it means the same as *I wish*, but is stronger.)
3 F (the speaker is expressing a wish about a past situation.)
4 T
5 T

Refer students to page 170 for further information and practice.

ANSWERS TO GRAMMAR SUMMARY EXERCISES

4
1 were/was
2 didn't have to
3 lived
4 could
5 weren't
6 saw / could see

5
1 I'd had
2 didn't have to
3 had taken
4 there were
5 wouldn't make

6
1 wouldn't keep
2 'd/had learned
3 wouldn't shout
4 'd/would clean
5 hadn't left
6 'd/had bought

Grammar notes

When hypothesizing, we go one tense back, so;
I wish I had the ability = I don't have the ability, but I want the situation to be different.
If I only I could turn it into food = I can't turn it into food, but I want the situation to be different.
I wish I had had that power = I didn't have the power and regret this.
I wish you/they/people would stop doing that = People won't stop and I want the situation to change (I hope someone or something else can act to change the situation; often, the speaker is angry, irritated or complaining).
We use *if only* to express a strong wish that things could be different. It means the same as *I wish,* but is stronger.

7
- Ask students to choose the correct verb forms to complete the text. You could ask students to work individually before comparing and checking answers in pairs, or you could ask students to work in pairs to help and support each other.

ANSWERS

1 had
2 hadn't done
3 you'd taken
4 remembered
5 could remember

Grammar notes

1 *wish* + past (NOT *wish* + *would* + *have*)
2 *hadn't done* – using past perfect to show past regrets
3 *had taken* – using past perfect to show past regrets
4 *wish* + past
5 We cannot say *I wish I would remember*. It would mean 'I wish I was willing to remember'. We can say *I wish you would remember …* ; *I wish I could remember* = I wish I was able to remember.

8
- Ask students to work individually to complete the sentences. Let students compare their answers in pairs before checking with the class.

ANSWERS

1 'd/had learned
2 was/were
3 wasn't/weren't
4 hadn't/had not gone
5 would hurry up
6 knew
7 wasn't/weren't
8 would stop
9 could sing
10 had baked

Grammar notes

1, 4, 10: regrets or wishes about the past
2, 3, 6, 7, 9: wishes about the present (speaker wants these situations to be different now)
5, 8: wishes about the present (speaker is annoyed and wants someone or something to change the situation)

9
- Tell students to read the information in the box. Ask students to complete the sentences.

ANSWERS

1 wasn't/weren't so far away
2 was/were warmer
3 was/were cheaper
4 were/would be quieter

Pronunciation /ʃ/ and /tʃ/
10a [74]
- **Optional step** Start by modelling the two sounds and asking students to repeat. Show students how to make the sounds (see Pronunciation notes below).
- Play the recording. Students listen and underline the word that they hear in each pair.

Audioscript 🎧 [74] (and answers)

1	wish	4	chin
2	chop	5	wash
3	catch	6	choose

Pronunciation notes

Some nationalities find it harder than others to hear and produce these sounds. To both Spanish and Thai speakers, for example, the sounds may seem identical.

To produce the 'sh' /ʃ/ and 'ch' /tʃ/ sounds, round your lips, and keep your top and bottom teeth close to each other. Try saying *she's* then *cheese*. /ʃ/ requires a flow of air through your teeth, which allows you to hold the sound for a long time. /tʃ/ is produced with one puff of air through the teeth which is then stopped. Get your students to make and hold the /ʃ/ sound for a few seconds, and point out that you can't do that with the /tʃ/ sound.

10b

- Organize the class into pairs. Ask students to take turns to read out one word from each pair. Their partner must listen carefully to the pronunciation and guess which word their partner has said.

Extra activity 1

Use one of the minimal pairs activities mentioned in Teacher development below to practise these sounds.

Extra activity 2

Ask students in pairs or groups to think of other consonant sounds that they often confuse. Tell them to devise a minimal pairs exercise to practise one problem pair (or, once they have selected a problem area, write on the board one of the minimal pairs exercises provided below). Examples they might choose: /v/ and /w/ (German speakers); /b/ and /v/ (Spanish speakers); /p/ and /b/ (Arabic speakers); /l/ and /r/ (Japanese speakers).

Possible minimal pairs to use:

/v/ and /w/: vest/west, vain/wane, vile/while
/b/ and /v/: ban/van; bowl/vole; best/vest
/p/ and /b/: pan/ban, pen/Ben, pin/bin
/l/ and /r/: lice/rice; lent/rent; lip/rip
/f/ and /v/: fan/van; file/vile; fine/vine
/t/ and /θ/: tree/three; tin/thin; taught/thought
/e/ and /ɪ/: ten/tin; when/win; bet/bit
/i:/ and /ɪ/: sheep/ship; beat/bit; leak/lick

Teacher development

Minimal pairs

A minimal pair is a pair of words that vary by only a single sound: /f/ and /v/ in *fan* and *van*, or /e/ and /ɪ/ in *desk* and *disk*, for example. Minimal pairs exercises test students' ability to first recognize then produce sounds that are similar and hard to discern.

Here are some typical exercises:

1 Students listen to a pair (e.g. *fan – van*) and say which one they hear; students listen to three words (e.g. *fan – van – fan*) and say which word they hear twice.

2 Students listen to the word in a sentence and say which word they hear: *That's a very nice van.* Fan or van?

3 Students play a game in which they have to recognize sounds in minimal pairs. A popular example is 'phonemic battleships' (look this up in your search engine). Another game is to devise a simple street plan and label the streets: *First Street / Vurst Street, Ferry Street / Verry Street,* etc. Students have to say where they are on the map – their partner points to the map: 'I'm in Ferry Street.' 'OK. You're here!'

Speaking my life

11

- Ask students to work in pairs to choose a situation and follow step 1. Set a time limit of five minutes to choose a situation and brainstorm problems.

- Once pairs have completed the list of problems, tell them to follow step 2 and prepare wishes. You could ask students to write whole sentences or to think and note problems in preparation for improvising sentences when they share their ideas later.

EXAMPLE ANSWERS

A new job:
I don't feel confident. ➜ If only I felt more confident.
Nobody speaks to me. ➜ I wish people would speak to me.
It's hard work. ➜ I wish it wasn't such hard work.
A new course:
I don't understand the teacher. ➜ I wish I understood the teacher.
Some of the topics are boring. ➜ If only the topics were more interesting.

12

- Ask students to work with a new partner. Allow plenty of time for students to share and compare ideas.

- As students speak, monitor and note down any errors they make, especially with conditional forms. In feedback, write five or six errors on the board in short sentences and ask students to correct them in pairs.

8c Saving Madagascar

Lesson at a glance
- reading: Madagascar's unique environment
- critical thinking: emotive language
- vocabulary and speaking: strong feelings

Reading

1

- Tell students to look at the facts on page 99 about the island of Madagascar. Ask students to work individually to write three questions about the facts. Check *flora* (= plant life) and *fauna* (= animal life).

- Ask students to work in pairs. Students cover the page and take turns to ask and answer the questions.

> **EXAMPLE ANSWERS**
>
> How big is Madagascar?
>
> How much of its flora and fauna is found nowhere else on Earth?
>
> What is produced on Madagascar?
>
> How many people live on Madagascar?
>
> How many different species of lemur live only on Madagascar?
>
> How many different ethnic groups live on Madagascar?
>
> How long does it take a rosewood tree to reach maturity?
>
> How many tonnes of ebony and rosewood were exported in 2009?

Background information

Vanilla is a flavouring derived from the fruit of certain orchids.

Lemurs are monkey-like animals that live in trees.

Ebony is a dense black hardwood; *Rosewood* is brownish and has a strong sweet smell.

2 🔊 [75]

- Ask students to read the article and work individually to answer the questions.

- **Optional step** The reading text is recorded. You could play the recording and ask students to read and listen.

- Let students compare answers in pairs before checking with the class.

> **ANSWERS**
>
> 1 the forests / the (rosewood and ebony) trees / wood
>
> 2 The trees are cut down (with hand axes) and are transported away by river to be shipped to China, Europe and America.
>
> 3 the collection of medicinal plants which are then sold to foreign companies like Chanel; guiding tourists to see/ photograph the lemurs; the setting up of a wild orchid conservatory that tourists pay to visit

Background information

Madagascar is an island in the Indian Ocean, off the coast of Southeast Africa. The island split from larger continents 88 million years ago and its flora and fauna have therefore been able to survive and diversify in isolation.

There are nine species of **baobab tree**, and six species only live in the drier parts of Madagascar. It's the national tree of Madagascar, and is sometimes called 'the tree of life'. The trees reach heights of 5 to 30 metres.

3

- Ask students to read the text again and choose the correct options to complete the sentences.

- Let students compare answers in pairs before checking with the class.

> **ANSWERS**
>
> 1 c   2 a   3 b   4 b   5 c   6 c   7 c   8 b

Extra activity

Ask students to find words in the text that are connected in some way to 'wood' or 'trees'. Ask students in pairs to explain why they chose the words. A possible list: *baobab trees, forest, cut down, timber, burned/burning, hardwood, fallen, loggers, rosewood, ebony, furniture, musical instruments, hand axes, logs, rafts.*

Critical thinking emotive language

4

- **Optional step** Start by introducing the idea of *emotive* language (= language that makes you have a strong feeling). Write *a novel* on the board. Then write up the following adjectives that go with *novel*: *heart-breaking, long, incredible, exciting, well-written, nightmarish.* Ask students to say which words are emotive (all except *long* and *well-written*). Ask students to give you other emotive adjectives that go with the word 'novel'.

- Ask students to read the article again and find the emotive words or phrases. Let students compare answers in pairs before checking with the class.

> **ANSWERS**
>
> 1 *nature has given Madagascar **incredible riches** (lines 3–4), visitors … **wide-eyed with amazement and delight** (lines 11–12)*
>
> 2 *the island's **desperate situation** (line 13), In this **bleak landscape** (line 54), the **darkness** (line 55)*
>
> 3 ***Alarmed** ecologists … (line 21)*
>
> 4 *the loggers who **continued to rob the forests** … (line 30)*
>
> 5 *The wood from these **majestic** trees (line 33)*
>
> 6 *It is **dangerous** and **back-breaking** work (line 40)*
>
> 7 *bring down a tree that has **stood tall for many centuries** … drag … (lines 41–42) not the only **victims** (line 47)*
>
> 8 *the **greed** of Madagascar's rosewood industry (line 66)*

5

• Discuss the questions with your students. There is no definitive answer. It could be argued that being emotive persuades the reader, or that being balanced and objective is safer because it does not antagonize the reader.

EXAMPLE ANSWERS

A possible rewrite of the first paragraph:

Madagascar is the world's fourth largest island at over 225,000 square miles. Although all islands have their own unique ecosystems, Madagascar's ecosystem is unique. Roughly ninety per cent of its animal and plant life is not found anywhere else. Its baobab trees and lemurs look particularly unusual.

Vocabulary and speaking strong feelings my life

6

• Ask students to work individually to replace the words in bold with the emotive words from the article. Let students compare answers in pairs before checking with the class.

ANSWERS

1 unique   2 delight   3 alarmed   4 majestic
5 back-breaking   6 bleak

7

• Ask students to work in pairs to prepare and write a description of a special place. Monitor and help with ideas and vocabulary and encourage students to use emotive language.

• When students have finished, pass the descriptions round the class, or pin them on classroom walls or the noticeboard, and encourage students read and comment on each other's work.

EXAMPLE ANSWERS

Port Meadow is a **beautiful** area of 'common land', which means it belongs to the community, right in the heart of Oxford. It is a place where locals can **celebrate** nature and **escape** the pollution and **chaos** of the city. Yet in recent years, the council has allowed **greedy** developers to build closer and closer to the edge of it. The developers have **failed to show any sympathy** to how these buildings affect their surroundings. They are only interested in how they can get the **maximum profit** from each development. The result is a number of **giant, ugly** tower blocks that have **destroyed** the **unspoilt** views across the meadow. It is an environmental **crime** and should be stopped before further **damage** is done.

8d Choices

Lesson at a glance
• real life: discussing preferences
• pronunciation: *do you, would you, shall we*

Real life discussing preferences

1

• **Optional step** Start by explaining the adjectives *choosy* and *picky*. They come from the verbs *choose* and *pick* and describe a situation where you don't just buy the first thing you see, but take time to decide what to buy, wear or do. Examples: *I'm choosy about what I wear; I'm picky about where I stay on holiday.*

• Ask students to discuss what they are choosy about. You could ask students to work in pairs first. In feedback, elicit students' ideas, opinions and experiences.

Extra activity

Ask students to make a list of other things they are choosy about. Possibilities: shoes and socks; whether sweaters are loose or tight; where you stay on holiday; the size and comfort of a bed; the colour of curtains.

2 🎵 [76]

• Tell students they are going to listen to five short conversations. Ask students to read the table carefully, and predict what question each person has been asked.

• Play the recording. Students listen and complete the table. Let students compare their answers in pairs before discussing with the class.

ANSWERS

Choice	Preference	Reason
1 drive 2 be driven (by his friend)	2	feels tired
1 pasta 2 *Indian food (from takeaway)*	1	*prefers simple food to spicy food / likes simple food more than spicy food*
1 a walk in old town 2 *go to a museum*	1	*the weather's going to be sunny / it's going to be sunny*
1 see a film 2 *go to a music festival (in the park)*	2	more fun
1 *only be able to shout* 2 only whisper	can't say	*either would be really annoying (for other people)*

Audioscript 🔊 [76]

Conversation 1

A: Would you like to drive or shall I?

B: I'd rather you drove, if you don't mind. I'm feeling a bit tired.

A: No, that's fine. Actually, I prefer driving to being a passenger.

Conversation 2

A: What would you like for supper? I could cook some pasta or we could get some Indian food from the local takeaway.

B: Well, if you don't mind cooking, pasta sounds great. I like simple food more than spicy food.

Conversation 3

A: So what would you like to do tomorrow? We could just have a walk around the old town. Or, if you prefer, we could go to a museum.

B: To be honest, I'd rather not go to a museum. I think the weather's going to be sunny and it seems a pity to be inside on a nice day.

A: OK. Great. Shall we have a walk then?

Conversation 4

A: What do you feel like doing this weekend? We're thinking either we could go and see the new Matt Damon film or there's a free music festival in the park, but I'm not sure who's playing. Umm, what do you think?

B: Well, if it were up to me, I'd say let's go to the festival in the park. It doesn't matter if the music isn't very good. I think that would probably be more fun.

A: OK. I'd prefer to do that too.

Conversation 5

A: OK. Here's a question. You have to answer one or the other, OK?

B: Umm, OK.

A: If you had to choose, would you rather only be able to shout or only be able to whisper?

B: What? That's impossible – either of them would be really annoying for other people.

3 🔊 [76]

- Ask students to work in pairs to complete the expressions in the language box.
- Play the recording again. Students listen and check their answers.
- **Optional step** If students have problems hearing the missing words, play the recording a third time, and pause the recording when the key information is provided to allow students to write.

> **ANSWERS**
> 1 to 2 more than 3 had 4 only be able 5 not go
> 6 drove 7 were 8 'd 9 would 10 to

Extra activity

Write *I prefer*, *I'd prefer* and *I'd rather* on the board and ask students to say how the patterns after each phrase differ. In feedback, go through the different forms used when expressing a general or specific preference (see Grammar note below).

Grammar note

In general:

I prefer + noun/gerund + *to* + noun/gerund

On a specific occasion:

I'd rather + verb without *to*

I'd prefer + verb with *to*

Note that the use of *would* and conditional forms when expressing preferences makes them more tentative and polite.

Pronunciation *do you, would you, shall we*

4 🔊 [77]

- Play the recording. Students listen and notice how the underlined words become merged (see Pronunciation note below). Ask students to practise saying the sentences in pairs.
- **Optional step** Play the recording again for students to listen and repeat.

Audioscript 🔊 [77]

1 <u>Do you</u> prefer tea to coffee? /dʒuː/

2 <u>Would you</u> like to come with us? /wʊdʒuː/

3 <u>Shall we</u> find another restaurant? /ʃwiː/

4 <u>Would you</u> rather eat out tonight? /wʊdʒuː/

Pronunciation note

In natural speech, the auxiliaries and pronouns tend to merge together so that they sound like one word: *Do you* becomes /dʒuː/; *Would you* becomes /wʊdʒuː/; *Shall we* becomes /ʃwiː/.

Note that *you* could be further reduced to a very weak /jə/ sound in fast natural speech.

Teacher development

Using phonemes

Think about using phonemic script to raise your students' awareness of sounds in natural speech in English. Here are some ideas you could use when doing the pronunciation exercise in Exercise 4:

1 Write /dʒuː/, /wʊdʒuː/ and /ʃwiː/ on the board and ask students to match them to the underlined phrases in Exercise 4.

2 Write /dʒuː/, /wʊdʒuː/ and /ʃwiː/ on the board and ask students to practise saying the merged sounds by reading the phonemes (not the regular spelling).

3 Ask students to use a phonemic chart to find the symbols for the underlined words they hear when listening to the audio.

5

- Ask students to work individually to complete the questions with the correct form of the verbs. Let students compare their answers in pairs before checking with the class.

> ANSWERS
>
> 1 never eat; never eat
> 2 to have
> 3 gave; said
> 4 giving; receiving (*to give* or *to receive* is also possible here)
> 5 be; not be; have
> 6 gave; to earn

6

- Ask students to work in pairs to ask and answer the questions in Exercise 5. Monitor and note how well students manipulate the patterns when expressing preferences, and correct when necessary.
- In feedback, ask students to tell the class what they found out about their partner.

> ANSWERS
>
> Students' own answers

7

- **Optional step** It's a good idea to give students some preparation time first before expecting them to improvise a roleplay. Tell them to work individually for one minute to prepare what to say, using phrases from the language box.
- Ask students to work in pairs to roleplay conversations. Once students have practised two or three conversations, ask them to work with a new partner to practise again.
- As students speak, monitor and note errors and examples of good language use. At the end, provide some feedback on language students have used.

8e A wish for change

> ## Lesson at a glance
>
> - writing: an online comment
> - word focus: *better*
> - writing skill: giving vivid examples

Writing an online comment

1

- Ask students to discuss the questions. You could do this open class or in pairs.
- **Optional step** Check the key vocabulary here: *a blog / to blog* (= write a blog – an ongoing series of articles or diary entries online); *a comment / to comment* (= to add a personal opinion about something you read online).

> EXAMPLE ANSWERS
>
> People may read comments to find out what range of views there are, or out of interest or curiosity, or to see how their user group feels.
>
> People may ignore comments as they are often ill-informed, irrelevant or annoying.

2

- Ask students to work individually to read the comment and find answers to the questions. Let students compare answers before checking with the class.

> ANSWERS
>
> 1 Valerie Dupeyrat, an energy services advisor; a blog about the waste in hotels
> 2 She wanted to highlight energy waste in other areas of modern life.
> 3 Students' own answers

3

- Ask students to work in pairs to discuss and answer the questions.

> ANSWERS
>
> a paragraph 2
> b paragraph 3
> c paragraph 1
> d paragraph 1
> How the comment is organized:
> 1) a reference to the article it's commenting on and a summary of the problem
> 2) examples that illustrate the problem
> 3) a recommendation or request for action

Word focus *better*

4

- Ask students to read the comment again and underline phrases with the word *better*. Let students compare answers in pairs.

- Ask students to match the phrases with the definitions and then check answers in pairs. In feedback, ask students to say how the meaning and use of *better* changes (see Vocabulary notes below).

ANSWERS

(*It would*) *be better to* (*mention*) = c
(*try to*) *go one better* (*than*) = d
they should know better = a
We would be better off = b

Vocabulary notes

it would be better to = often used to make a suggestion or offer advice

(*try to*) *go one better* (*than*) = (try to) improve on something – the idea here is that you work one more hour, or do one more thing than someone else

they should know better = a phrase used to criticize somebody's actions, saying that what they have done is disappointing because it's immature or not thought through properly

we would be better off = we would be in an improved position – this is often followed by an *if* clause (*we'd be better off if we …*)

Writing skill giving vivid examples

5a

- Ask students to work in pairs to discuss the question and find the examples.

ANSWER

She says that lights are left on all night, and towels are used once and then sent to the laundry.

5b

- Ask students to work individually to find five more examples of energy waste. Let students compare answers in pairs before checking with the class.

ANSWERS

the doors of shops are left open (so hot air escapes); lights in office buildings are left on at night; there are enormous flashing advertising screens (in town); cooling cabinets in supermarkets are completely open; her children leave their computers on when they go out and their phone chargers plugged in with no phone on the other end

6

- Ask students to work individually to complete the phrases. Let students compare their answers in pairs before opening up the discussion to the class.

EXAMPLE ANSWERS

Trains which never run on time / are cancelled/ overcrowded/dirty/expensive

Mobile phones that lose battery charge too quickly / have loud ringtones / run out of memory

TV shows about pointless/unimportant/irritating things

Supermarket food that has got too much packaging / is full of additives / has been imported from distant countries

Computer programs which crash all the time or don't work / are confusing to use / frequently need updating

7

- **Optional step** Start with a class discussion about which annoying things from Exercise 6 students might write about. Try to ensure that students choose to write a comment about something they are interested in and have an opinion about.

- Ask students to work individually and spend one minute making notes about what to include in their comment. Monitor at this stage and help with ideas and vocabulary. You could let students compare their ideas in pairs and help each other.

- Tell students to use their notes to write the comment.

EXAMPLE ANSWER

I found your article about trains which do not run on time very interesting, but I think this is only one part of a wider problem: that trains nowadays do not offer a good service.

I think there are a number of key issues: tickets are often overpriced; the trains themselves are often full of litter – there are not enough litter bins, and these are not emptied frequently enough; the onboard toilets are often dirty or out of order; and finally, on busy services, you can often not even get a seat. The train companies should know better.

What can the train companies do about it? Just increasing the price of tickets is not satisfactory. The train companies need to improve the services that go with train travel, and they should pay a fine if the services that they promise are not provided. (144 words)

8

- Organize the class into pairs and ask students to exchange their written work. Ask them to check their partner's comment and suggest how to improve it.

- **Optional step** Ask students to revise and rewrite their letter based on their partner's suggestions.

Extra activity

Pin half the comments on classroom walls or noticeboards. Ask students who made the comments to stand by them. The other half of the class walk round, read the comments and express their opinion.

8f What would you do if money didn't matter?

Before you watch

1

- Ask students to read the title of the video and write their answer to the question on a piece of paper. You could ask this question with books closed. Tell students to keep the answer secret as they will discuss it at the end of the lesson.

> ANSWERS
>
> Students' own ideas

Key vocabulary

2a

- Ask students to read the sentences and guess the meaning of the words in bold. Start students off by asking them to guess the meaning of the first word – point out how the context of the sentence will help them make guesses.
- Let students compare their answers in pairs but do not check answers at this stage.

2b

- Ask students to work individually to match the words in bold in Exercise 2a with the definitions.
- Let students compare their answers in pairs before checking with the class.

> ANSWERS
>
> 1 b   2 d   3 a   4 e   5 c

While you watch

3 🎥 [8.1]

- Ask students to watch the video and answer the questions. Play the whole video. Let students compare answers in pairs before checking with the class.

> ANSWERS
>
> 1 What do you desire? / What do I desire?
> 2 He says you will spend your life completely wasting your time: you'll be doing things you don't like doing in order to go on living, that is to go on doing things you don't like doing …

Videoscript 🎥 8.1

Part 1

0.00–1.30 What do you desire? What makes you itch? What sort of a situation would you like? Let's suppose … I do this often in the vocational guidance of students. They come to me and say, 'Well, we're getting out of college and we haven't the faintest idea what we want to do.' So I always ask the question: 'What would you like to do if money were no object? How would you really enjoy spending your life?' Well, it's so amazing – as a result of our kind of educational system, crowds of students say, 'Well, we'd like to be painters, we'd like to be poets, we'd like to be writers, but as everybody knows you can't earn any money that way.' Or another person says, 'Well, I'd like to live an out-of-doors life and ride horses.' I say, 'Do you want to teach in a riding school? Let's go through with it – what do you want to do?' When we've finally got down to something which the individual says he really wants to do, I will say to him, 'You do that and forget the money.' Because if you say that getting the money is the most important thing, you will spend your life completely wasting your time: you'll be doing things you don't like doing in order to go on living, that is to go on doing things you don't like doing … which is stupid.

Part 2

1.30–3.00 Better to have a short life that is full of what you like doing than a long life spent in a miserable way. And after all, if you do really like what you're doing – it doesn't matter what it is – you can eventually turn it, you can eventually become a master of it. It's the only way to become a master of something, to be really with it … and then you'll be able to get a good fee for whatever it is. So don't worry too much … that's … everybody … somebody's interested in everything. And anything you can be interested in, you'll find others who are. But it's absolutely stupid to spend your time doing things you don't like in order to go on spending your time doing things you don't like and to teach your children to follow in the same track. You see, what we're doing is we're bringing up children and educating them to live the same sort of lives we're living … in order that they may justify themselves and find satisfaction in life by bringing up their children to bring up their children to do the same thing. So it's all retch and no vomit: it never gets there. And so, therefore, it's so important to consider this question, 'What do I desire?'

4 🎥 [8.1]

- Ask students to read the summary.
- When students are ready, play the first part of the video (0.00–1.28) again. Students choose the correct options to complete the summary. Let students compare their answers in pairs before checking with the class.

> ANSWERS
>
> 1 college students
> 2 painters, writers
> 3 satisfaction, happiness
> 4 really want to do
> 5 stupid, a waste of time

5 🎥 [8.1]

- Ask students to read the notes headings 1–4.
- When students are ready, play the second part of the video (1.28 to the end) again. Students make notes as they watch. Let students compare their answers in pairs before checking with the class.

ANSWERS

1 It's better to have a short life that is full of what you like doing than a long life spent in a miserable way.
2 You can eventually become a master of it (and then you'll be able to get a good fee for whatever it is).
3 There will always be someone who is interested in the same things as you.
4 We're teaching our children to live the same sort of lives we're living.

Extra activity

Ask students to watch the video again, only this time play the video without sound. Stop at key points (e.g. when we see the horse riding) and ask students to say what the narrator was saying at each point where you stop.

After you watch

Vocabulary in context

6a

- Explain that students are going to watch some clips from the video which contain some new words and phrases. They need to choose the correct meaning of the words.
- Play the clips. When each multiple-choice question appears, pause the clip so that students can choose the correct definition. You could let students compare answers in pairs before discussing with the class.

ANSWERS

1 c   2 a   3 a   4 b   5 a

Videoscript ◼️ 8.2

1 '... we **haven't the faintest idea** what we want to do.'
   a haven't a clear idea about
   b haven't a good idea about
   c have no idea about
2 'What would you like to do if money were **no object**?'
   a not a problem
   b not of any value
   c not a goal
3 '... you'll be doing things you don't like doing in order to **go on living** ... '
   a continue living
   b be able to live
   c earn money to live
4 '... you can **eventually** become a master of it.'
   a easily
   b in the end
   c probably

5 '... and to teach your children to follow **in the same track**.'
   a do the same things
   b be in the same boring job
   c have similar hopes and ambitions

Vocabulary notes

we haven't the faintest idea = the word *faintest* here is used to used to add emphasis, e.g. *He hasn't the faintest idea what he is doing* is a very critical way of saying somebody is incompetent

If something is *no object*, then it provides no barrier or limit. So, *money is no object* means you have all the money you need.

Note that *go on* is followed by an *-ing* form.

6b

- Students work individually to complete the sentences. Elicit one or two ideas for the first sentence to get them started. Then let students compare sentences in pairs.

EXAMPLE ANSWERS

1 I haven't the faintest idea where *to start looking for jobs / I put my glasses.*
2 If you keep trying out different jobs, eventually *you will find the one you like the most / get bored of changing jobs / know what you want to do.*
3 I don't know how long I will go on *looking for a job / working for this company / living with my parents.*

7

- Ask students to read and discuss the comments about the video in groups of three or four. Set a time limit of five minutes.
- Once groups have discussed the comments, ask students to work individually to write their own comment.

8

- Organize the class into pairs. Ask students to share with their partner what they wrote in answer to the question at the beginning of the lesson in Exercise 1. Tell them to say whether their view has changed after watching the video.
- **Optional step** You could develop this into a wider class discussion of how important enjoyment of your job is and how important work/life balance is.

UNIT 8 Review and memory booster

Memory Booster activities

Exercises 3, 5 and 7 are Memory Booster activities. For more information about these activities and how they benefit students, see page 10 of this Teacher's Book.

I can ... check boxes

As an alternative to asking students to simply tick the *I can* ... boxes, you could ask them to give themselves a score from 1 to 4 (1 = not very confident; 4 = very confident) for each language area. If students score 1 or 2 for a language area, refer them to additional practice activities in the Workbook and Grammar summary exercises.

Grammar

1

- Ask students to read the post on a travel forum and answer the question. Elicit the answer from the class.

ANSWER

waterproof and windproof clothing; a power cable with lots of sockets; seasickness tablets

2

- Ask students to work individually to write conditional or *wish* sentences to express the same idea as the underlined sentences in the text. Monitor and make sure students have understood the instructions and are using the correct forms. You may wish to do the first one with the class as an example.

ANSWERS

1 I wish I could express in words how incredible it was.
2 It would be better if they made this a hiking tour.
3 I wish I had looked at this forum (myself) before I left.
4 I would have got cold and wet if I hadn't taken a lot of waterproof and windproof clothing.
5 If they had had more power points, that wouldn't have been (so) important.
6 If I had known they had a good laundry service on the boat, I would have taken fewer clothes / I wouldn't have taken so many clothes.

3 >> MB

- Ask students to work in pairs to explain why the different forms are used in each pair of sentences.

ANSWERS

1 a describes a state you don't like (but can't change)
  b describes an action that you want to happen to change something (but isn't always possible)
2 a refers to the past consequence of an earlier event
  b refers to a present consequence of a past event

Vocabulary

4

- Ask students to work individually to choose the correct options to complete the sentences. Then tell them to work in pairs to decide which of the sentences about the 'rocket girls' are true.

ANSWERS

1 did (true)
2 did (true)
3 made (false – the calculations had to be extremely accurate)
4 did; did (not stated in the reading text)
5 make (false – the women formed close working relationships and helped each other)
6 made (false – it was Macie Roberts, one of the group's early leaders)
7 made (true)

5 >> MB

- Ask students to work individually to complete the phrases using the emotive words in the box. Check answers and then tell students to write a sentence using each phrase.
- Ask students to work in pairs and take turns to read out their sentence, leaving out the phrase. Can their partner say what the missing phrase is?

ANSWERS

1 a **bleak** desert landscape
2 **back-breaking** work
3 a **unique** experience
4 the **delight** on her face
5 he was **alarmed** by the news
6 a **majestic** animal

Real life

6

- Ask students to work individually to complete the exchanges with one word in each space. Let students compare answers in pairs before checking with the class.

ANSWERS

1 rather   5 to
2 prefer   6 off
3 mind   7 rather
4 would   8 didn't

7 >> MB

- Ask students to work in pairs to talk about their own preferences. Tell them to make sentences with *I'd rather* + verb + *than*. Monitor and give support, making sure students are using the forms correctly.

Unit 9 The news

Opener

1

- Ask students to look at the photo and the caption. Discuss the questions with your class. Elicit ideas from students in feedback but do not comment at this stage as they will find out more from the recording.

Background information

The photo shows parents of freshmen (new first-year university students) asleep on mats laid out on the floor of a gymnasium inside a university campus in Wuhan, in central China's Hubei province. The university set out about 500 mats for parents accompanying freshmen students on their first days of university.

2 🎵 [78]

- Play the recording. Students listen to the news radio report and note answers to the questions.
- Let students compare answers in pairs before checking with the class.

ANSWERS

1 so that they can be near their children in their first few days at college (when they may be anxious)
2 Many Chinese families are not particularly well-off so the parents couldn't afford to stay in a hotel.
3 Students' own answers. The speaker thinks the behaviour of the parents is 'impressive'.

Audioscript 🎵 [78]

N = Newsreader; M = Martha Cash

N: And in China, hundreds of parents of first-year students at the University of Wuhan have been sleeping on the floor of the university's gym so that they can be near their children in their first anxious days at college. As Martha Cash, our Far East correspondent, reports.

M: For China's many middle class parents, getting their children – and often it's an only child – into university is an extremely important step in building a better future for their families and many parents put all their savings into achieving this goal. But winning a place

at university is not the end of the story. The parents are keen to settle them into their new college life and to follow their child's progress through university. The University of Wuhan recognizes this and it also recognizes that many Chinese families are not particularly well-off: staying in a local hotel during their children's first days at college is not an option for them. So the university offers free accommodation to parents – up to five hundred at a time – in the form of mats in the university gym. As an expression of parental concern, it's certainly impressive.

Extra activity

Ask students to say what adjectives they would use to describe the parents mentioned in this news story. Possibilities: *incredible*, *committed*, *interfering*, *protective*, *unnecessary*

3

- Elicit ways of gathering news from students and build up a list on the board.

EXAMPLE ANSWERS

national or local newspapers (online or in print), TV, radio, magazines, social media, websites, word of mouth, blogs, local noticeboards

4

- Organize the class into groups of four or five to look at the pie chart and discuss the questions. In feedback, invite individual students to share interesting opinions or experiences with the class.

- **Optional step** Ask students this follow-up question: *How do you think other generations usually get their news?* (e.g. TV or radio bulletins and national or local newspapers).

ANSWERS

1 via Facebook and Twitter
2 Students' own answers
3 Students' own answers

9a A life revealed

Lesson at a glance
- vocabulary: reporting verbs
- reading: an iconic image
- grammar: verb patterns with reporting verbs
- speaking and writing: news stories

Vocabulary reporting verbs

1

- Ask students to work individually to cross out the word that doesn't fit in each sentence. Elicit the first answer to get students started. Then organize the class into pairs to discuss the difference in meaning between the other two words in each sentence.

- In feedback, elicit answers and explain and define the words (see Vocabulary notes below).

- **Optional step** You could make the checking phase a dictionary task. Ask students to look up words they aren't sure of in order to confirm what they discussed in pairs.

ANSWERS

The words which do not fit:
1 denied   2 thank   3 offered   4 persuaded
5 complain   6 criticized   7 convinced   8 threatened

Vocabulary notes

1 *admit* = to say you are to blame;
agree = to say you have the same opinion as someone else;
(*deny* = to say you are not to blame)

2 *blame* = to say it was somebody's fault;
accuse = to say it was someone's fault in a stronger, or more official, way, e.g. saying they are guilty of a crime;
(*thank* = to say thank you to someone for doing something helpful)

3 *advise* = to give advice;
warn = to give strong advice because something is dangerous or there will be negative consequences;
(*offer* = to say you will give someone something if they want it – note that you need an object with this verb: *offer somebody something*)

4 *ask* = to question in a simple, neutral way;
beg = to ask in a strong, desperate way because you have a serious problem or really need something;
(*persuade* = to make somebody change their opinion or decision – note that you need an object with this verb: *persuade somebody to do something*)

5 *claim* = to state or assert that something is the case, typically without providing evidence or proof;
explain = to say what the situation is with reasons;
(*complain* = to say you are not happy or satisfied with a situation)

6 *congratulate* = to say well done to someone;
praise = to express strong approval or admiration for someone or something, usually in public;
(*criticize* = to make negative comments about something)

7 *recommend* = to say something is good and that someone else should do it or try it;
urge = to recommend in a very strong way, e.g. you really must do it!;
(*convince* = to make somebody see your point of view – note that you need an object with this verb: *convince somebody to do something*)

8 *promise* = to tell someone that you will do something;
swear (*swore*) = to make a very strong commitment to do something, e.g. a serious promise;
(*threaten* = to tell somebody you will do something bad to them if they don't do what you want)

Reading

2 🔊 [79]

- Ask students to look at the photo and discuss the questions in pairs. Briefly elicit ideas, but don't comment on what students say.

- Ask students to read the text and check their answers.

- **Optional step** The reading text is recorded. You could play the recording and ask students to read and listen.

ANSWERS

1 Students' own answers

2 Afghanistan; the girl in the first picture is around twelve years old; the woman in the second picture is around 29 years old

3 They are the same person and the photos were taken at different times.

3

- Ask students to read the article again and answer the question.

- **Optional step** The reading text is recorded. You could play the recording and ask students to read and listen.

ANSWER

Steve McCurry was reporting on the lives of Afghan refugees in a camp in Pakistan in 1984 when he took the first photo. He returned in 2002 to follow up on the story.

4

- Tell students to read the article again. Ask students to work individually to find the contrasting facts and complete the sentences. Point out that we use *even though* when the second clause of the sentence is a surprising contrast.
- Let students compare their answers in pairs before checking with the class.

ANSWERS

1 he was a stranger. (*or* she'd never had her photo/picture taken before.)
2 Steve McCurry admits thinking at the time that his picture was nothing special.
3 time and hardship had erased her youth and her skin was weathered.
4 it is (very) hard. (*or* it has been (very) hard.)

Vocabulary notes

Check that students are familiar with the following vocabulary:

refugee = a person who has lost their home and left their country, especially during times of war

ignore = to not notice or recognize

not aware of = doesn't know about

Background information

National Geographic photographer **Steve McCurry** (born 1950) has won numerous awards, including Magazine Photographer of the Year, awarded by the National Press Photographers Association, and the Royal Photographic Society's Centenary Medal. His most famous photo, 'Afghan Girl', originally appeared in *National Geographic* magazine.

Tora Bora is a remote, mountainous area of Afghanistan where a lot of fighting has taken place in recent conflicts.

Grammar verb patterns with reporting verbs

5

- Ask students to work individually to find and underline the verbs and the forms that follow them in the article. Let students compare answers in pairs before checking answers with the class.

ANSWERS

she <u>agreed to let</u> him. (*agree + to + infinitive*)
he <u>admits thinking</u> at the time that his picture was nothing special. (*admit + -ing*)
Her intense expression <u>warned us not to ignore</u> the victims of war ... (*warn somebody + to + infinitive*)
In 2002, National Geographic <u>persuaded McCurry to return</u> to Pakistan ... (*persuade somebody + to + infinitive*)
He <u>offered to fetch</u> her from her home in the Tora Bora mountains. (*offer + to + infinitive*)

He <u>blamed the war for forcing</u> them ... out of their homeland. (*blame something/somebody + for + -ing*)
and <u>begged people to give</u> her food and blankets. (*beg somebody + to + infinitive*)
she does not <u>complain about having</u> had a hard life. (*complain about + -ing*)
There are three basic verbs patterns:
1 verb (+ someone) + *to* + infinitive
2 verb + *-ing*
3 verb (+ someone) + preposition + *-ing*

6

- Tell students to look at the information in the grammar box. Ask the students to work in pairs to explain to each other where in the grammar box they would place each verb from Exercise 5.

ANSWERS

verb + *to* + infinitive: *agree, offer*
verb + someone + *to* + infinitive: *warn, persuade, beg*
verb + *-ing*: *admit*
verb + preposition + *-ing*: *complain*
verb + someone/something + preposition + *-ing*: *blame*

Refer students to page 172 for further information and practice.

ANSWERS TO GRAMMAR SUMMARY EXERCISES
1
1 b   2 f   3 a   4 d   5 c   6 e
2
1 recommended visiting
2 threatened to leave
3 apologized for being
4 invited me/us
5 advised her to go
6 encouraged me to learn
3
1 eliminating
2 to watch
3 to stop
4 to recycle
5 to do
6 to introduce
7 starting

Grammar notes

Point out the way that a negative is reported with *not* (e.g. *warn someone not to do* or *complain about not doing*).

Verb patterns involving reporting verbs need to be practised, learned and memorized.

7

- Ask students to work in pairs to discuss what the person actually said (or thought) in each sentence that they underlined in Exercise 5.
- Ask students to compare answers with another pair before checking answers with the class.

ANSWERS

Yes, you can.

I thought at the time that my picture was nothing special.

Don't ignore the victims of war.

Please return to Pakistan.

Shall I fetch her? / I can fetch her. / I'll fetch her.

The war forced us out of our homeland.

Please give me food and blankets. (*or* I beg you to give me food and blankets.)

I haven't had such a hard life. / I've had a hard life, but I'm not angry/upset about it.

8

- **Optional step** Ask students to read the article quickly first. Set a focus question: *What is the writer's point of view?* (photographers should talk to their subjects first to get to know their subjects' story, because then their photographs will have more meaning).
- Ask students to work individually to complete the article with the correct forms. Remind them to add an appropriate preposition where necessary. Let students compare their answers in pairs before checking with the class.

ANSWERS

1 of being   2 acting   3 for doing   4 to take
5 to pose   6 to let   7 on being   8 to asking
9 to talk   10 getting

Grammar notes

Note that sometimes other forms may be possible after these verbs. For example, you could say *deny that they acted unethically* in 2, or *recommend that they should get to know* in 10. If this is queried by students, point out that these 'that' clauses are an alternative way of reporting.

9

- Ask students to work individually to report the statements. Elicit the first answer to get students started and point out that sometimes they will need to change the tense of verbs given in brackets. Let students compare answers in pairs before eliciting answers from the class.

ANSWERS

2 She encouraged me to consider a career in journalism.

3 She accused him of always putting his own interests first.

4 She suggested waiting to see what he said first.

5 She promised to look at my article when it was finished.

6 She apologized for not introducing me to her boss.

7 She urged people to make up their own minds.

8 She offered to lend me her camera.

Speaking and writing ⟨ my life ⟩

10

- To begin with, ask students to work individually to choose a reporting verb from the box and use it to write about something true that happened to them. Go through the example so students can see what is required.
- Once students have prepared their stories, ask them to work with a partner so that they can share their stories. Encourage students to comment on and correct each other's work.
- **Optional step** As students tell their stories, note down errors you hear. Concentrate on errors with reporting verb patterns. At the end, in feedback, write up five or six short sentences containing anonymous errors you heard. Ask students in pairs to correct the errors.

ANSWERS

Students' own answers

9b And finally ...

Lesson at a glance
- vocabulary: positive adjectives
- listening: good-news stories
- grammar: passive reporting verbs
- speaking: good-news stories

Vocabulary positive adjectives

1
- **Optional step** With books closed, write *good-news story* on the board. Ask students: *Do you prefer funny, happy news stories to serious news stories? Why? Why not? What news sites or news feeds do you access? Why?*
- Refer students to the wordbuilding box and point out that we often add *-ing* to verbs to make adjectives that describe feelings.
- Ask students to complete the definitions by forming adjectives from the verbs in the box. Let students compare answers in pairs before checking with the class.
- **Optional step** Drill the adjectives to show the main stress (see Vocabulary notes below).

ANSWERS
1 encouraging (*inspiring* is also possible here, but is usually used to describe a story that makes you feel you can achieve good things)
2 amusing
3 inspiring
4 astonishing
5 charming; engaging

Refer students to Workbook page 75 for further practice.

Vocabulary notes

Students often confuse *-ed* and *-ing* adjectives. Adjectives that end with *-ed* describe emotions – they tell us how people feel about something (e.g. *I was very bored in the maths lesson. I almost fell asleep.*) Adjectives that end with *-ing* describe the thing that causes the emotion (e.g. *It was a boring lesson*).

encouraging = makes you feel positive and hopeful about what you are doing or what is happening

amusing = (mildly) funny

inspiring = makes you want to be better or do better

astonishing = very surprising

charming = makes you smile because it's really nice

engaging = keeps you interested in a positive way

2
- Organize the class into pairs to think of and tell good-news stories. As students speak, prompt them with ideas and vocabulary, and monitor their language use. Note any good ideas from students which you could refer to in whole-class feedback at the end.

EXAMPLE ANSWERS

encouraging: medical/scientific/technological progress
amusing: animals or young people doing crazy things
inspiring: stories about people raising money for charities
astonishing: unusual weather stories, scientific discoveries
charming: stories about unusual family events
engaging: interesting mysteries

Teacher development

Monitoring students effectively

In class, we often ask students to speak freely in pairs or groups in order to practise recently learned language. Some students may speak in a more relaxed and fluid way without the presence of the teacher; they are able to use the language for real without pressure or comment. Other students may feel that the activity is frustrating unless the teacher listens and comments on performance. Here are some techniques for monitoring and giving feedback:

1 When students first start talking, circulate around the class fairly quickly, making sure everybody is engaged and is clear about the task.

2 Then go round the class again. This time, spend more time systematically listening and engaging in what each pair of students is saying. Make supportive comments on what you hear. This could be praise or prompts to help them speak more effectively.

3 When monitoring, spend only a short time listening to each pair, but make sure it's long enough to hear a few things they say, and to show your interest. You may need to bend down to hear students more easily.

4 As you monitor, write down anything useful that you could comment on at the end of the activity. This could be errors, good pieces of language use or interesting stories or ideas that students come up with. Be ready to show that you listened carefully and have useful feedback for the class following the speaking activity.

Extra activity

Write the following story titles on the board and see if students can create good-news stories from them. This could be done for homework.

Dog to the rescue

Lucky old lady

At the bottom of the bin

Listening

3 🔵 [80]

- **Optional step** Pre-teach key words and create a prediction task by writing two or three words from each story on the board and asking students to say how they might fit each story. A possible list: *refugee, wardrobe, reward; riot shield, sledge, disciplined; scientist, ageing process, trials.*

- Ask students to look at the photo and guess what the stories might be. You could do this open class or you could ask students to work in pairs first. Pre-teach key words: *wallet, wardrobe, sledge, riot shield* (= the clear piece of protective plastic that police stand behind during a riot – when people are protesting or fighting).

- Play the recording. Students listen and make notes individually (see Teacher development below). Once students have completed their notes, organize the class into groups of three and ask students to compare their notes and add details.

> **EXAMPLE ANSWERS**
>
> Here is a sample of key words and phrases you could expect students to note:
>
> Story 1: refugee ... Germany ... called hero – €150,000 to police ... in wardrobe ... right thing ... police look for true owner ... financial reward (three per cent of money found – €4,500).
>
> Story 2: police ... riot shield ... sledge down hill ... Oxford ... Christmas ... heavy snow ... actions filmed ... posted on YouTube ... liked by public ... commanding officer not amused ... criticized ... to be disciplined.
>
> Story 3: Latvian scientist in UK ... drugs ... live to be a hundred ... US drugs company The Life Extension Foundation ... slow down ageing process ... Dr Zhavoronkov tests drugs on himself ... 37 ... feels younger.

Audioscript 🔵 [80]

1

And finally ... A refugee in Germany has been called a hero after he handed in to the police €150,000 in cash that he found hidden in a wardrobe. In spite of having little money himself, the 25-year-old Syrian, who is believed to have been in Germany for less than a year, decided the right thing to do was to give the money back. The wardrobe was a gift from a charity to help the man furnish his apartment. Local police are now said to be looking for the money's true owner, but praised the man for his honesty. As well as getting the respect of the nation, the man will receive a financial reward, since, under German law, he is entitled to three per cent of the money found – in this case around €4,500.

2

And finally ... A group of police officers have been criticized by their police chief after one of them used his riot shield to sledge down a hill near Oxford. The incident happened over the Christmas period when heavy snow had fallen. The officers helped their colleague to sit on his riot shield and then pushed him down the hill. However, unknown to them, their actions were filmed by a local

man who then posted the video on Youtube. Although the video was liked by the general public, their commanding officer was not amused. 'We all enjoy the snow,' he said, 'but this was not appropriate use of police time and equipment.' It is thought that the officers involved will be disciplined in the coming days.

3

And finally ... A Latvian scientist based in the UK is reported to be close to finding drugs that will help people live to ages of a hundred and beyond. What is more, he is confident that he himself will live to at least 150. Dr Zhavoronkov is working with US drugs company The Life Extension Foundation which hopes soon to be selling a range of products that will slow down the ageing process and improve people's health. To reduce the high cost of new medicine trials, Dr Zhavoronkov has been testing the drugs on himself. Now aged 37, he claims to feel much younger than he did a few years ago.

> **Teacher development**
>
> **Note-taking**
>
> Listening and taking notes can be quite difficult for language students. Here are some tips:
>
> 1 Let students listen once first with a simpler gist or focus task before asking them to take notes. For example, in Exercise 3, above, you could just ask students if they predicted the stories correctly.
>
> 2 Ask students to listen and note just key words. These are the words that are both most clearly and strongly stressed and the words that carry most meaning.
>
> 3 Give students time to add to their notes after they have listened, remembering details they didn't have time to write. Encourage them to share notes in pairs or groups and to build up a good understanding as a group.
>
> 4 Play the recording a further time so that students can confirm their notes.

4 🔵 [80]

- Play the recording again. Students listen and answer the questions. Let students compare answers in pairs before checking with the class.

> **ANSWERS**
>
> 1 He was entitled to three per cent of the money he found (approx. €4,500).
>
> 2 The public were full of respect for the police officer; the commanding officer was angry ('not amused') as he thought it wasn't a good use of police time and equipment.
>
> 3 He has been testing the drugs on himself; he claims to feel much younger than his 37 years.

5

- Organize the class into pairs to remember and retell the stories. Alternatively, you could ask students to retell the stories from the notes they have made. In feedback, ask each pair to briefly say why they thought stories were encouraging, inspiring, etc.

ANSWERS

Students' own ideas

The honest refugee story is encouraging and inspiring.

The sledging police officer is charming, perhaps astonishing.

The drugs trial is astonishing and encouraging.

Grammar passive reporting verbs

6

- Tell students to read the information and examples in the grammar box on Student's Book page 108. Then ask them to answer the question.

ANSWER

No. We don't know who is doing the thinking, believing, saying and reporting in each sentence.

Refer students to page 172 for further information and practice.

ANSWERS TO GRAMMAR SUMMARY EXERCISES

4

1 It is believe**d** that two prisoners have escaped.
2 It is known that the journalist **is** to be arrested.
3 The director is expected **to** resign.
4 The photos are thought to **have** been taken in 1990.
5 She is said to **be writing** a book at the moment.

5

1 to arrive, to be arriving
2 to have found
3 to be living
4 to be
5 to cause, to be causing, to have caused
6 to have been caused

6

1 is understood (that) the high street is being closed.
2 is believed to have spent a lot of money on it.
3 is reported that there will be live music, a fairground and food stalls.
4 is said to have been really crowded and badly organized.
5 is thought that the organizers have made some improvements.
6 are expected to be offering free food on the first day.

7

- Ask students to discuss the questions with the class or in pairs. In feedback, you could write up and label the different forms (see Grammar note below).

ANSWERS

a 4 (*is reported to be …*)
b 3 (*are … said to be looking for …*)
c 2 (*is believed to have been in Germany …*)

Grammar note

Using the passive with reporting verbs in English distances and impersonalizes. Compare *I believe he is in Germany* (personal – my opinion) to *He is believed to be in Germany* (impersonal – the speaker/writer is distancing himself from the accuracy of this statement).

Note the forms:

passive reporting verb + infinitive

He *is believed* to have been in Germany …

They *are said* to be looking for …

He *is reported* to be …

8

- Ask students to rewrite the sentences. You could ask students to work individually before comparing and checking answers in pairs, or you could ask students to work in pairs to help and support each other.

ANSWERS

2 It is believed that the 25-year-old Syrian has been in Germany for less than a year.
3 It is said that the local police are looking for the money's true owner.
4 It is reported that a Latvian scientist based in the UK is close to finding …

9

- Ask students to work individually to rewrite the sentences. Let students compare their answers in pairs before checking with the class.

ANSWERS

1 The man is said to be from the Homs area of Syria.
2 It was confirmed that the man will receive a financial reward.
3 The same police officers are said to have done similar things before.
4 We all enjoy the snow, but this was not thought to have been an appropriate use of police time.
5 A lot of rich customers are known to be waiting to buy these new medicines.
6 It is not generally believed that drugs can prevent ageing.

10

- Ask students to work individually to read and rewrite the sentences. Let students compare their answers in pairs before checking with the class.

ANSWERS

1 It is said that Costa Rica is the happiest country in the world.
2 It is believed that the family are celebrating their $10 million lottery win in private.
3 It was known that Frank was / had been a gifted musician at school.
4 Laughing regularly is known to increase life expectancy.
5 He was thought to have given up hope of ever seeing his family again.
6 Scientists are reported to be getting very close to finding a cure for the disease.

11

- Organize the class into pairs to complete the good-news story. Elicit the first answer to get students started. In feedback, ask students to refer back to the rules and patterns in the grammar box when explaining their answer.

ANSWERS

1 it is now thought
2 is known
3 it was demonstrated
4 to be
5 to have stopped
6 to be getting

Speaking my life

12

- Organize the class into groups of three to prepare a good-news story. Give them five minutes to choose a headline and brainstorm what it might be about and what information to include. Monitor and help with ideas and vocabulary.

- Once they have ideas, tell students to work together in their groups to write the stories. Make sure, however, that all students write their own version of the story they have agreed on. It's a good idea to set a word limit to focus students on the task – ask them to write a maximum of 100 words (or, if you want students to be very concise, give a 50-word limit).

- Once they have completed stories, ask students to take turns to practise reading them out in their groups. Students could suggest improvements and alterations. Tell them to check whether students have used passive forms correctly and appropriately.

- Mix groups or put students in pairs with someone who worked in a different group to share their story. Students take turns to read their texts.

EXAMPLE ANSWER

And finally, a woman escaped from her burning house yesterday after her pet cat raised the alarm. Although the house is known to have smoke alarms fitted to it, the woman slept deeply as her cat tried to wake her. It is believed that she only woke up when the cat bit her ear – just in time for her to escape from the building.

Extra activity

Play 'newsroom'. Ask groups of three students to prepare a different story each. Then mix the students to form groups in which each student has prepared a different story. Students briefly tell their story and the group decide on a newsroom running order for the stories. Each group then presents the news, telling each of their stories in the agreed order.

9c From hero to zero

Lesson at a glance

- reading: the power of the press
- critical thinking: different perspectives
- word focus: *word*
- speaking: the media

Reading

1

- **Optional step** With books closed, write *From hero to zero* on the board. Ask students what it means and ask if they can give an example. (It refers to someone who has gone from being a hero to people to being the opposite – a failure – a 'zero': a famous example is Canadian sprinter Ben Johnson, who, in 1988, won Olympic Gold in the 100 metres, only to be disqualified for doping the next day.)

- Ask students to read the headlines. You may need to check *fallen hero* (= a person who was a hero, but is now seen in a negative way) and *ice fault* (= a problem caused by ice).

- Organize the class into pairs to discuss what they think happened in the story. In feedback, elicit ideas but do not comment on them at this stage.

Background information

Heathrow = London's largest airport

BA = British Airways, a global airline company

2 [81]

- Ask students to read the story and check what happened with their partner. In feedback, find out how students' stories differed from the story in the Student's Book.

- **Optional step** The reading text is recorded. You could play the recording and ask students to read and listen.

3

- Ask students to work individually to read the story again and decide whether each statement is true (T) or false (F).

- Let students compare answers in pairs before checking with the class. In feedback, ask students to justify their answers with reference to the story.

ANSWERS

1 F (*With the plane losing height fast, Burkill asked his co-pilot, John Coward, to take the controls*)
2 F (*passengers escaped without serious injury*)
3 F (*he had ... a loving wife*)
4 F (*it was only read by senior management ... No word of it reached his colleagues*)
5 T (*it praised Captain Burkill's decision*)
6 F (*He began applying for jobs with other airlines*)

4

• Ask students to work individually to complete the sentences with words from the article. Elicit the first answer to get students started and point out that the words in brackets provide a synonym or definition. Let students compare answers in pairs before checking with the class.

ANSWERS

1 villain (line 4)	4 let down (line 27)
2 miraculously (line 14)	5 betrayed (line 36)
3 competent (line 21)	6 awarded (line 55)

Vocabulary notes

Check that students are familiar with the following vocabulary:

freeze at the controls = to suddenly not be able to act (because of fear) when at the plane's controls

panic = to lose control because of fear or stress

a playboy = a man who lives a luxurious, often immoral lifestyle

wrongdoing = something wrong or illegal

a rumour = a story that has no basis in fact

wing flaps = parts of the wing of a plane that can be moved up or down

Critical thinking different perspectives

5

• **Optional step** Start by explaining *perspective* (= your point of view; how you see things) and *motivation* (= the reason why you do something).

• Ask students to read the story again and complete the notes. Let students compare answers in pairs before checking with the class.

ANSWERS

People involved	Their view on the accident and Burkill's role in it	Motivation for taking this view
Peter Burkill	He took a risk but it worked and the rest was luck.	He did what any pilot would have done.
BA staff	They thought he had panicked and frozen.	not clear – as a result of rumours
BA management	They decided Burkill was not to blame, but they waited for the official report.	They were afraid of bad publicity.
AAIB	The actions of Burkill and the crew had saved the lives of the passengers on board.	It was their job to investigate and report their findings independently.
the press	They said Burkill had frozen and they claimed that John Coward was the real hero.	They wanted to sell more papers.

6

• Discuss the questions with your students.

EXAMPLE ANSWERS

There is no definitive answer. The story suggests that Burkill should be believed – the investigation was objective and showed he had done nothing wrong. The newspaper's readers probably believed he had panicked.

Word focus *word*

7

• Ask students to find and underline four expressions with *word* in the article. Then ask them to match the expressions with the definitions.

• Let students compare answers in pairs before checking with the class.

ANSWERS

1 had the last word (line 61)
2 Word went around (line 19)
2 it wasn't even his word against the press (line 28)
3 No word of it (line 44)

8

• Ask students to work in pairs to discuss and decide on the meaning of the expressions in each sentence. Encourage students to use the context of each sentence to help them guess meanings.

• **Optional step** Ask students to use dictionaries to find and categorize the different meanings of *word* in each expression (see Vocabulary notes below).

ANSWERS

1 don't just believe what I say
2 didn't know what to say
3 personal recommendations
4 promised

Vocabulary notes

Note the meanings of *word*:

1 a unit of language (*your first words as a baby*; *the words on a page*)

2 things you say (*in my own words*, *his last words*)

3 a short conversation (*Can I have a word with you?*)

4 news or information (*we've had no word*; *send word to*)

5 a 'piece of' (*a word of advice/warning*)

6 a promise (*keep/give/break your word*)

Extra activity

Write the following questions on the board (or dictate them):

When was the last time you gave your word?

When newspapers tell us things, should we have to take their word for it?

When was the last time you were lost for words?

Organize the class into pairs or small groups to ask each other the questions. In feedback, ask students to say what they found out about their classmates.

Speaking my life

9

• Ask students to work in groups of three or four to discuss the questions about the media in their own country.

• **Optional step** Pre-teach some key words here: *balanced* (= objective, fair, showing both sides of an argument), *scandal* (= something in public life that shocks people). You could also introduce some synonyms of *balanced* (objective, fair-minded, neutral, impartial) and some antonyms (biased, unfair, unbalanced, one-sided).

• As students speak, monitor and write down useful pieces of language they use, or errors they make, which you could focus on in feedback.

ANSWERS

Students' own answers

9d Spreading the news

Lesson at a glance
• real life: reporting what you have heard
• pronunciation: the schwa

Real life reporting what you have heard

1

• **Optional step** With books closed, start by writing *gossip* on the board. Ask students what it means (= conversation about unimportant subjects, usually involving people's private lives). Point out that it can be a verb (*to gossip*), a person (*a gossip*) or a noun (*some great gossip*). Introduce some collocations: *office gossip, gossip columnist, a piece of gossip, spread gossip* (= when lots of people tell gossip and soon everybody knows). Ask students: *What gossip have you heard this week?*

• Tell students to look at four of the most common topics that people gossip about. Ask them to share examples of gossip about each topic with the class.

EXAMPLE ANSWERS

a a businessperson has given a politician money to help a deal go through; a banker has been caught taking money for himself

b a colleague is having a relationship with another woman who is not his wife; a neighbour has been seen with a new boyfriend or girlfriend

c two film stars are getting divorced; someone famous looks like they may be pregnant

d a well-known politician has a criminal record or a love child; someone has reacted in a negative and dramatic way to an event

2 [82]

• Ask students to look at the four categories in Exercise 1. Tell them they are going to listen to two conversations and they need to decide which category of gossip each conversation falls into.

• Play the recording. Students listen and answer the question. Let students compare their answers in pairs before checking with the class.

ANSWERS

Conversation 1: money and status
Conversation 2: people's character and reputation

Audioscript 🔊 [82]

Conversation 1
J = Jess; **P** = Phil

J: Hi, Phil. How are things?

P: Not bad. But I'm a bit fed up with working so hard and never getting any reward for it.

J: Yeah, I know what you mean. By the way, did you hear about Liam? Apparently, he's been promoted.

P: Liam? But he's only been here a year!

J: I know. But according to Sarah, he's been given the job of area manager.

P: Area manager? I don't believe it. He's not even that good at his current job.

J: Well, she also reckons that he's going to get a massive pay rise – something like double his current salary.

P: Yeah, well, I'd take that with a pinch of salt. I don't think the company has money to throw around at the moment. But all the same, I don't know. If it's true, where's the justice? Here we are working our socks off …

Conversation 2
F = Freddie; **C** = Caitlin

F: Hi, Caitlin. Hey, you know Dr Harris at the local surgery?

C: Yes.

F: Well, someone told me he was fired from his job yesterday. It seems he's not even a proper doctor.

C: What? Who told you that?

F: Tara.

C: Hmm, I wouldn't take too much notice of what Tara says. She tends to exaggerate things.

F: No, no, I'm pretty sure it's true. I asked Samara too and she told me about someone at the hospital she used to work at who had gone from one hospital to another across the country using a fake CV.

C: Oh my goodness, that's terrible.

F: I know. But actually, that doesn't surprise me. You do hear of things like that happening.

C: Maybe, but I *would* be very surprised. Dr Harris seemed like a nice genuine guy to me.

3
- Ask students to work in pairs to discuss the questions.
- **Optional step** If students are unsure, play the recording a second time.

> ANSWERS
> 1 He's (apparently) been promoted / been given the job of area manager and is going to get a big pay rise.
> 2 Because Liam's only been working at the company for a year.
> 3 He's been fired from his job because he's not a proper doctor.
> 4 No.

4 🔊 [82]
- Ask students to read the information in the language box and use the expressions to complete the sentences. Elicit the first missing expression to get students started. Let students compare their answers in pairs.
- Play the recording again. Students listen and check their answers.
- **Optional step** If students have difficulty catching the missing words, play the recording again, and pause the recording when the key information is provided to allow students time to write.

> ANSWERS
> 1 did you hear about; Apparently; But according to; don't believe it
> 2 reckons; 'd take that with a pinch of salt
> 3 someone told me; It seems; tends to exaggerate
> 4 doesn't surprise me

Grammar and vocabulary notes

These 'reporting what you have heard' phrases distance the speaker – they are not the speaker's views, only what they have been told.

reckon = to think, believe

according to = in the opinion/belief of

apparently/supposedly = the speaker uses these phrases as distancing devices – this is what appears true, but it isn't verified

I wouldn't take his/her word for it. / I wouldn't take too much notice of what he/she says. = I wouldn't believe him/her (suggesting that he tends to lie or be untrustworthy)

exaggerate = to make things sound bigger/better/worse than they are

I'd take that with a pinch of salt = an expression meaning it is unlikely to be true

Extra activity

Ask students to practise the conversations in Exercise 4 in pairs. Then tell students to create their own conversations using some of the expressions.

Pronunciation the schwa
5a 🔊 [83]
- Read the introduction to the class. Play the recording. Students listen and repeat the words using weak pronunciation on the unstressed syllables. Ask students to practise saying the words in pairs.

Pronunciation note

In natural speech, unstressed vowel sounds are generally reduced to the schwa sound /ə/. This is a very weak sound – get students to notice that it's merely a soft sound in the throat and barely audible.

The word schwa (/ʃwɑː/) refers to this weak, unstressed mid-central vowel sound /ə/. It derives from the Hebrew word *shva*.

5b 🎵 [84]

- Ask students to listen, underline the stressed syllable, and circle the schwa in each word. Let students compare their answers in pairs before checking with the class.

ANSWERS

according   generally   happened   information

proportion   reckon   surprisingly

Pronunciation note

Note that a range of vowels (*a, e, o, u* but rarely *i*) can be reduced to /ə/. Sometimes a sound is lost altogether, e.g. note that the second 'e' in *generally* /ˈdʒɛnrəliː/ is not pronounced, nor is the second 'e' in *happened* /ˈhæpənd/. In the words *information* and *surprisingly*, 'for' and 'sur' are reduced to /fə/ and /sə/.

5c

- Ask students to work in pairs to practise saying the words in Exercise 5b. Encourage students to exaggerate the stressed syllable and reduce the unstressed vowel to a minimal sound. This will raise awareness of how English – a stress-timed language – differentiates between stressed and unstressed vowel sounds.

6

- Decide with (or for) your students whether to prepare facts about themselves or about celebrities. This may depend on your students' interest in celebrity gossip or willingness to talk about themselves. Give students a minute or two to prepare ideas individually. Monitor and help with vocabulary.

- Ask students to work in pairs and share their facts (two true, one false). Then ask students to stand up, walk round, and share with other members of the class the 'gossip' they have just heard. Set a five-minute time limit and tell students to speak to three different people in the class.

- Ask students to work in their original pairs to share the 'facts' that each person heard.

- Ask pairs to discuss which of the 'facts' are true and which are false. In feedback, find out which pairs successfully separated true stories from false ones.

- As students speak, monitor and note errors and examples of good language use. At the end, provide some feedback on language students have used.

Extra activity

Ask students to work in pairs to go online and research a true, current piece of gossip about a celebrity. Tell them to make notes on it. Then tell them to invent a second, false story. Pairs then read out their two 'gossip stories' and the rest of the class must guess which story is true.

9e News story

Lesson at a glance
- writing: a news article
- writing skill: using quotations

Writing a news article

1

- **Optional step** Ask students to look at the photo. Ask: *Where is it? What can you see? What do you think the text is about?* Then ask students to read the text to check their predictions.

- Ask students to read the article and answer the questions.

- **Optional step** Check the key vocabulary: *screeching tyres* (= the noise the tyres on cars make on the road at high speed), *inconsiderate* (= not thinking of other people), *posh* (= very expensive and upper class).

ANSWERS

1 fast cars in city streets that are noisy and dangerous
2 a ban or confiscation of the cars
3 fans of super cars, but also perhaps the hotels and restaurants

2

- Ask students to complete the notes (1–5) about structuring a newspaper article using functions a–e. Let students compare answers before checking with the class.

ANSWERS

1 c   2 d   3 a   4 e   5 b

Extra activity

To conclude, ask these questions:

Which elements of the story mentioned in the first paragraph did the writer expand on in the next paragraph? (the writer gave us more information on people visiting London, London's richest central areas, types of supercars, and who warned that the rich and their cars will be banned)

What information did the quotation add to the story? (the quotation says why supercars are a danger and why action must be taken)

Writing skill quotations

3a

- Ask students to work individually to look at the sentences and choose the correct options to complete the rules. Let students compare answers in pairs before checking with the class.

> **ANSWERS**
>
> a capital   b inside   c before   d before

Punctuation note

Note that American English differs from British English here. US English uses double quotation marks, e.g. *"Hello," he said* rather than single quotation marks, e.g. *'Hello,' he said.*

3b

- Ask students to add the correct punctuation. Provide or elicit the first piece of punctuation to get students started. Let students compare their answers in pairs before checking with the class.

> **ANSWERS**
>
> 1 'Shall we eat, Grandma?' he asked.
> 2 'I know exactly what he said,' she said.
> 3 'That's very kind,' she said, 'but I can manage.'
> 4 General Sedgewick turned to his men and said, 'Don't worry, boys, they couldn't hit an elephant at this distance …'

Punctuation note

Note the amusing difference in meaning between *'Shall we eat, Grandma?' he asked* (= asking Grandma if it is time to eat) and *'Shall we eat Grandma?' he asked* (= making a suggestion to eat Grandma as food).

Extra activity

Ask fast-finishing students to punctuate the following sentences:

i am tired the boy said and then went to sleep
('I am tired,' the boy said and then went to sleep.)
we really should be going now she said
('We really should be going now,' she said.)
are we there yet she asked
('Are we there yet?' she asked.)

Alternatively, ask students to write other sentences with no punctuation, and pass them to other pairs in the class to punctuate.

4

- **Optional step** Start with a class or group discussion. Ask students to choose a headline and brainstorm words, expressions and information they could include in the story.
- Ask students to work individually and spend one or two minutes making notes about what they want to include in their article. Monitor at this stage and help with ideas and vocabulary. You could let students compare their ideas in pairs and ask for help.
- Ask students to write their story. This could be done for homework.

5

- Organize the class into pairs and ask students to exchange stories with their partner. Tell students to check their partner's work and suggest how to improve it.
- **Optional step** Ask students to revise and rewrite their letter based on their partner's suggestions.

Extra activity

Pin the stories on the classroom walls or noticeboard. Ask students to walk round, read the stories and express their opinion.

9f **News: the weird and the wonderful**

Before you watch

1

- Explain that students are going to watch two 'good-news' stories. Ask them to look at the photo and the caption, and answer the question.

> ANSWER
>
> Students' own answers

Key vocabulary

2a

- Ask students to read the sentences and guess the meaning of the words from their context.
- Let students compare their answers in pairs before moving on to Exercise 2b.

2b

- Ask students to match the words in bold in Exercise 2a with the definitions in Exercise 2b. Let students compare their answers in pairs.

> ANSWERS
>
> a 5 b 2 c 6 d 4 e 3 f 1

3

- Ask the class which group of words (1–3 or 4–6) goes with each story. Elicit ideas and reasons, but don't confirm answers – students will find out more when they watch the video.

While you watch

4 ▄◀ **[9.1]**

- Ask students to watch the whole video. Tell them to answer the questions as they watch. Let students compare answers in pairs before discussing as a class.

> EXAMPLE ANSWERS
>
> 1 Students' own opinions
>
> 2 Story 1: Hero Humpbacks / Heroes of the seas / Protectors of the seas
>
>   Story 2: No ordinary fried chicken seller / Mr Teflon

Videoscript ▄◀ 9.1

Story 1: Humpbacks to the rescue

0.00–0.37 An amazing fact about one of nature's larger – and gentler – animals, the humpback whale, has recently come to light. Humpbacks are already known to use their superior size and weight to fight off killer whales or orcas when their young are under attack. But now, researchers have found that they also protect other species from attacks by orcas. A study for the Journal of Marine Science found that in over 80% of cases where humpback whales fight off orca attacks, the humpbacks are

defending other animals, such as seals, sealions, sunfish and grey whales.

0.38–0.46 Orcas are much smaller whales, weighing on average around four or five tons. But they are ruthless hunters, hunting in large packs and coordinating their attacks to overwhelm their prey.

0.47–0.57 Once they have made sure there is no escape, the orcas' sharp teeth make quick work of any victim, … such as this unfortunate sealion.

0.58–1.29 But the researchers have observed several instances of single humpbacks trying to prevent the orcas getting to their prey, using their huge bodies to get in the way and swiping at the orcas with their long flippers. The fights can last up to six or seven hours, with, it seems, no particular advantage to the humpbacks – at least none that the researchers have found. Could it be that they are just kind neighbours to other more vulnerable sea creatures?

Story 2: Mr Superhands

1.30–1.45 Narrator An ordinary-looking fried chicken stall in Chiang Mai, Thailand. But this is no ordinary fried chicken seller. Seven years ago, Khan, the owner of the stall, discovered that he was immune to burns from hot oil.

1.46–2.28 Khan Subtitles: *I found out about seven years ago. A squirrel was eating a mango on the tree and it fell into my fried chicken wok. The oil splashed all over me. On my head and on my body. Then the taxi took me home and the next day after I woke up I was going to go to see the doctor. I looked in the mirror and found my skin had no burns or anything. So the next day I just came back to work to fry chicken again.*

2.30–3.13 Tourist 'This guy's crazy. It's just unbelievable. It does nothing to his skin. He just dips it in water. Dripped a tiny bit of oil – tiny bit – burning like crazy. Someone told me the story about how he burned himself. He wasn't even burned then. Covered in oil and wasn't even burned then either. I've no idea how he does it … no idea.'

3.14–3.28 Narrator Some might be put off by Khan's strange ability, but it's proved to be great business for his stall because many tourists, like these young men, come to see for themselves.

5 ▄◀ **[9.1]**

- Ask students to read questions 1 to 5 and complete any answers that they remember.
- When students are ready, play the first news story (0.00–1.29) again. Let students discuss their answers in pairs before checking as a class.

> ANSWERS
>
> 1 larger, gentler, huge, kind
>
> 2 seals, sealions, sunfish and grey whales
>
> 3 smaller, ruthless, sharp (teeth)
>
> 4 They use their huge bodies to get in the way and they swipe at the orcas with their long flippers.
>
> 5 Researchers have found no particular advantage to the humpbacks.

6 ▄◀ **[9.1]**

- Play the second news story (1.30 to the end) again. Ask students to complete the summary of the story by putting one word in each space.
- Let students compare their answers in pairs before checking as a class.

ANSWERS

1 stall 2 ordinary 3 Seven 4 squirrel 5 mango
6 splashed 7 body 8 taxi 9 doctor 10 mirror
11 burns

7 ◼◀ [9.1]

- Play the last part of the second news story (2.30 to the end) again. Ask students to complete the statements by choosing the correct options. Let students compare their answers in pairs before checking as a class.

ANSWERS

1 incredible
2 any
3 sales

After you watch

Vocabulary in context

8a ◼◀ [9.2]

- Explain that students are going to watch some clips from the video which contain some new words and phrases. They need to choose the correct meaning of the words.

- Play the clips. When each multiple-choice question appears, pause the clip so that students can choose the correct definition. You could let students compare answers in pairs before discussing as a class.

ANSWERS

1 b 2 c 3 a 4 c 5 a

Videoscript ◼◀ 9.2

1 An amazing fact about one of nature's larger – and gentler – animals, the humpback whale, has recently **come to light**.

  a become famous
  b become known
  c been discovered again

2 … hunting in large packs and coordinating their attacks to **overwhelm** their prey.

  a surround in large numbers
  b frighten with their size
  c defeat with superior force

3 … the orcas' sharp teeth **make quick work of** any victim …

  a deal with quickly and easily
  b tear into many pieces
  c make a light meal from

4 … just good neighbours to other **more vulnerable** sea creatures?

  a of smaller size
  b non-violent
  c in a weaker position

5 Some might be **put off** by Khan's strange ability …

  a find rather disgusting
  b find rather confusing
  c find rather worrying

8b

- Students work individually to complete the sentences in their own words. Let students compare sentences in pairs.

EXAMPLE ANSWERS

1 You made quick work of *eating all that cake*!
2 I am really put off when I see *that the toilets in a restaurant aren't very clean.*
3 *My brother* is in a vulnerable situation because *he's just been made redundant from his job.*

9

- Organize students into groups of three or four. Tell them to discuss which news story interested them most and why. What more would they like to know about each one?

10

- Tell students they are going to watch the first news story again, but with the sound off. They are going to provide the narration for it. Ask students to work in pairs and follow the procedure in the Student's Book.

- To conclude, play the video several times, inviting different pairs to share their narration with the class.

Extra activity

As an alternative, you could ask them to write a newspaper report based on the content of the video. Explain that the style may need to be different, and the language possibly more formal. This could be done for homework.

11

- Organize the class into new groups. Tell them they are going to act out the second news story. Ask them to follow the procedure in the Student's Book.

- While students are working, monitor and help with vocabulary and note any errors to give feedback on later.

UNIT 9 Review and memory booster

Memory Booster activities

Exercises 4, 6 and 8 are Memory Booster activities. For more information about these activities and how they benefit students, see page 10 of this Teacher's Book.

I can ... check boxes

As an alternative to asking students to simply tick the I can ... boxes, you could ask them to give themselves a score from 1 to 4 (1 = not very confident; 4 = very confident) for each language area. If students score 1 or 2 for a language area, refer them to additional practice activities in the Workbook and Grammar summary exercises.

Grammar

1

- Ask students to work individually to complete the good-news story with the correct verb patterns. Elicit answers from the class in feedback.

> **ANSWERS**
> 1 to have gone
> 2 for keeping
> 3 not panicking
> 4 is believed
> 5 to get
> 6 to reacting *or* to having reacted
> 7 for causing
> 8 are known
> 9 to be
> 10 to have had
> 11 to find
> 12 (to) stay

2

- Ask students to read the story again and decide which statements are true (T) and which are possibly true (PT). Let students compare answers in pairs before checking with the class.

> **ANSWERS**
> 1 PT 2 T 3 T 4 PT

3

- Tell students to work individually to rewrite sentences 4 and 6 from the article using the words given. Then ask students to work in pairs to compare their sentences.

> **ANSWERS**
> 4 Yamato is believed to have been misbehaving.
> 6 Mr Tanooka blames himself for reacting / having reacted too harshly.

4 » MB

- Ask students to work individually to use a reporting verb or passive reporting verb to make two more sentences about what they think Yamato did after he was found. Monitor and check that students are using the forms correctly.

- You could ask students to work in pairs and take turns to read out their sentences. Their partner should respond, ideally using some of the phrases for expressing belief and disbelief from Student's Book page 112.

> **EXAMPLE ANSWERS**
> According to news reports, the boy immediately asked to be taken to a fast food restaurant.
> It is said that the boy was taken to a hospital to be checked by doctors.
> It seems that Yamato made an excellent recovery in the days after his frightening experience.
> I heard that he is now interested in survival techniques and has read some books on the subject.

Vocabulary

5

- Ask students to work individually to choose the correct options to complete the sentences. Let students compare answers in pairs before checking with the class.

> **ANSWERS**
> 1 take; suggest
> 2 of; denies; against
> 3 for; urge; convince

6 » MB

- Students work individually to write answers to the questions about the people in the news stories in Unit 9. Alternatively, you could put students in pairs to share what they can remember verbally.

> **ANSWERS**
> 1 Chinese parents usually insist on accompanying their children when they first go to university in order to settle them in.
> 2 She agreed to let him take a photograph of her.
> 3 He was accused of freezing at the controls of a passenger plane when the engines failed.

Real life

7

- Ask students to work individually to decide if each speaker is reporting (R), expressing belief (B) or expressing disbelief (D). Elicit answers from the class.

> **ANSWERS**
> 1 R 2 D 3 R 4 D 5 R 6 B 7 B 8 D

8 » MB

- Organize the class into groups of three or four. Ask each student to write down one or more recent claims someone has made in the news. In their groups, students take turns to read out and respond to these claims using expressions of belief or disbelief.

Unit 10 Talented people

Opener

1

- Ask students to work in pairs to match words with definitions. Elicit the first match to get students started. Check answers with the class.

Vocabulary notes

Use examples to check students understand these words. For example, say the following and elicit the words that describe them:

1 *I have a degree in Chemistry.* (qualification)

2 *I am easy-going and reliable.* (quality)

3 *I'm an expert in astrophysics.* (knowledge)

4 *I can fix electrical problems.* (skill)

5 *I can sing most tunes well.* (talent)

6 *I've been a teacher for years.* (experience)

7 *My parents were also teachers.* (background)

2

- Ask students to look at the photo and the caption. Discuss the questions with your class. Elicit ideas from students in feedback but do not comment on answers at this stage (students will find out when they listen).

EXAMPLE ANSWERS

physically strong, patient, understanding, enjoys working with animals, flexible but consistent, knowledge of elephants, learning from experience or from other people, working as an apprentice with a more experienced mahout

Background information

The word *mahout* derives from a Hindi word. A mahout is an elephant rider, trainer or keeper. An elephant is matched with a mahout very early in its life and the elephant and its mahout usually remain bonded to each other throughout their lives.

3 🎧 [85]

- Play the recording. Students listen to the description of a mahout's job and compare it with their answers from Exercise 2.

- Let students compare answers in pairs before checking with the class.

EXAMPLE ANSWERS

Here are the key points: knowledge of how to care for an elephant passed down from one generation to the next; no formal qualifications for the job; must be extremely patient; have to teach elephant commands; must develop an understanding of the elephant; a very physical job

Audioscript 🎧 [85]

Both the mahout and the elephant start their training at a young age. A mahout generally begins to learn his trade when he's about ten years old. At this age he is given a baby elephant to look after and he will probably stay with this one animal for the rest of his life. It's traditionally a family trade, with knowledge of how to care for an elephant passed down from one generation to the next. There are no formal qualifications for the job, but you need to be extremely patient. An elephant will learn as many as 65 commands in its life, depending on what work it's expected to do – some carry logs and other heavy objects, others are trained to carry people. The mahout has to teach his elephant all these commands. He must also develop an understanding of his elephant, so that he knows when it's sick or tired or unhappy. This is something that only comes with time and experience. It's a very physical job and extremely hard work. The elephant must be fed and bathed daily and watched carefully in case it tries to run away.

4

- Ask students to prepare questions individually first. Then organize the class into pairs or small groups to ask their questions. In feedback, invite students with interesting skills, talents or experience to share with the class.

Extra activity

Ask students to interview their partner to complete a simple CV using the following headings:

Name:

Age:

Nationality:

Background:

Qualifications:

Experience:

Personal qualities:

Special skills or talents:

10a An ordinary man

Lesson at a glance
- reading: an extraordinary career
- vocabulary: careers
- grammar: articles: *a/an*, *the* or zero article
- pronunciation: linking vowels
- speaking: a career path

Listening and reading

1 🎵 [86]
- Ask students to look at the photo and discuss the questions in pairs. In feedback, elicit ideas, but do not comment on answers at this stage (students will find out more when they listen).
- Ask students to listen and check their answers.
- **Optional step** Before moving on to the reading text, ask students what they know about the subject and elicit and check key words: *astronaut, spacecraft, pilot, Apollo*. See the Background information below.

ANSWERS
1 Buzz Aldrin
2 in 1969 (the Moon landing)
3 'That's one small step for man, one giant leap for mankind.' (*or* 'That's one small step for a man, one giant leap for mankind.')

Audioscript 🎵 [86]

This is a photo of the astronaut Buzz Aldrin, taken by the first man on the moon, Neil Armstrong, in 1969. You can see Armstrong taking the photo in the reflection on Aldrin's helmet. It was Armstrong who famously said 'That's one small step for man, one giant leap for mankind' when he put his foot on the moon. Actually, what he really said was 'That's one small step for a man, one giant leap for mankind', but no one heard the 'a' because of radio interference.

Background information

Armstrong's famous quote shows the importance of the indefinite article in English.

That's one small step for man, one giant leap for mankind doesn't really make sense as man and mankind mean the same – he has just contradicted himself.

That's one small step for a man, one giant leap for mankind is what Armstrong wanted to say (and claims to have said). Here, 'a man' refers to Armstrong himself.

2
- Ask students to work individually to read the article and answer the question. Let students compare their answers in pairs before checking with the class.

ANSWER
a professional, passionate about flying, determined, modest

3
- Ask students to read the article again carefully to find answers to the questions.
- Let students compare their answers in pairs before checking with the class.

ANSWERS
1 Because *he was hired to do a job. He did the job and then he went home and kept quiet about it.* The implication is that he did his job perfectly and without any arrogance or self-promotion.
2 He learned to fly before he left school and then he did a course in aerospace engineering at university. He then served in the US Navy as a pilot for three years.
3 He had a passion for flying and his aim was to push the limits of flight.
4 We don't need any more explanation as the story is well known.
5 He became a teacher and also worked for an avionics firm. At weekends he went flying to get away from all the attention.
6 Everyone who had worked on the Apollo space programme.

Background information

Apollo 11 was the first spaceflight to land humans on the Moon. Mission commander Neil Armstrong and pilot Buzz Aldrin landed the lunar module Eagle on July 20, 1969, and Armstrong became the first person to step onto the lunar surface six hours later on July 21. Aldrin joined him twenty minutes later. There was a third astronaut, Michael Collins, who piloted the command module Columbia in lunar orbit. The astronauts spent just under a day on the lunar surface.

The Korean War (1950 to 1953) began when the communist north of the country invaded the US-backed south. It ended in military stalemate, and the setting up of a divided country: communist North Korea and capitalist South Korea.

Vocabulary careers

4
- Ask students to work in pairs to find verbs in the article that collocate with the nouns. Elicit the first answer to get students started.
- In feedback, elicit answers and check that students understand all the vocabulary. Then ask students to give examples from Armstrong's career to illustrate the meaning of each verb + noun collocation.
- Read the wordbuilding box with your students.

ANSWERS

1 follow (*followed a career that came from a passion for flying*)

2 graduate from (*graduated from high school*)

3 do (*did a course in aerospace engineering at Purdue University*)

4 serve in / leave (*served in the US Navy as a pilot for three years; He left the navy …*)

5 become (*become an astronaut; he became a teacher*)

6 work for (*worked for an avionics firm*)

7 do; get; apply for (*hired to do a job; got a job with the Lewis Flight Propulsion Laboratory; applied for the job*)

Refer students to Workbook page 83 for further practice.

Vocabulary notes

follow a career = to stay in the same profession, getting promoted and becoming more experienced

graduate = to leave school or college with a qualification

serve in the navy = to spend a period of time working for the navy – the word 'serve' is used with jobs in the military or police

apply for a job = to write, call or send in your CV to try to get a job

Extra activity

Ask students to make true sentences about people in their family, using some of the collocations in this section.

Grammar articles: *a/an, the* or zero article?

5

- Ask students to look at the grammar box and complete the statements with the correct type of article. Let students compare answers in pairs. Check answers with the class.

ANSWERS

1 *a/an* (indefinite article)

2 zero article

3 *the* (definite article)

Refer students to page 174 for further information and practice.

ANSWERS TO GRAMMAR SUMMARY EXERCISES

1

1 ✓

2 ✗ She hasn't found **a** job yet.

3 ✗ I'd like to live in ~~the~~ Paris.

4 ✓

5 ✗ They're going to the museum in **the** morning.

6 ✓

7 ✗ That's probably **the** best film I've ever seen.

2

1 I had a long chat about gardening with **a** man …

2 Oh, it's **the** man over there.

3 That's Thomas – he's **a** lovely neighbour.

4 Yes, he showed me **a** picture of it on his phone.

5 Well, he seems very ordinary, but he's actually **a** famous mountaineer!

6 And he takes tour groups up mountains three or four times **a** year.

7 He also gives talks about it all around **the** world.

8 We only talked about **the** best flowers to plant in spring.

3

1 *the*   2 zero article   3 *the*   4 *The*   5 *the*   6 *the*

7 *a*   8 *a*   9 zero article   10 *a*

Grammar note

Point out the difference between these two sentences:

*She went to **school** on Saturdays when she was young.*

*She went to **the school** on Saturday to take her son to play football.*

With *school, university, hospital, church, prison* and other similar words we do not usually use the definite article after *go* to talk about normal attendance. However, we do use the definite article in other contexts, e.g. to talk about the building or place rather than the whole institution.

Article use can vary greatly between languages. Many languages don't use them (Russian and Japanese, for example) and others tend to use the definite article a lot more often than English (French and Spanish, for example). This can make it difficult for students to use articles correctly. Practice makes perfect. Concentrate on written and spoken practice rather than analysing the rules, which students are likely to have come across before.

6

- Ask students to work individually to read the first paragraph and match the articles and nouns in bold with the uses in Exercise 5. Let students compare their answers in pairs before checking with the class.

ANSWERS

1 3 (before a superlative adjective)

2 3 (a specific group of people)

3 1 (first time 'job' has been mentioned)

4 3 (referring back to something already mentioned)

5 2 (a generally familiar place)

6 3 (a specific person)

7 3 (a specific thing)

8 2 (people in general)

9 1 (one of many)

7

- Ask students to read the article again and find examples of the specific uses of the zero and definite articles. Let students compare answers in pairs before eliciting answers from the class.

ANSWERS

1 a Korea
 b aerospace engineering
 c July
2 a the USA
 b the US Navy / the Lewis Flight Propulsion Laboratory
 c the weekend *or* in the 1930s

ANSWERS

1 *a; a*
2 *a; the; a*
3 zero article; *the; the*
4 *The; the; the;* zero article; zero article
5 *a; the; the*
6 *the;* zero article; zero article

8

- Ask students to work individually to complete the sentences. Elicit the first answer to get students started. Check answers with the class.

- **Optional step** Ask students to say which rule they applied in choosing each answer.

ANSWERS

1 zero; *the;* zero article
2 *the;* zero article
3 *the;* zero article; *the;* zero article
4 *the;* zero article; zero article; *the*
5 *the;* zero article; zero article; *the;* zero article; *the*
6 *the;* zero article

Grammar notes

1 *New Zealand* (a country); *the weather* (specific to New Zealand); *in (the) summer* (both *in summer* and *in the summer* are possible, although we tend to omit the articles with seasons)

2 *the police* (specific and unique – only one police force); *university* (we say *go to / leave university* when we are more interested in the fact of having done higher education than in the place – so, you say, *I left university in 2011* but *I left the university through the back entrance and walked across the park*)

3 *at the weekend, in the morning* (a period of time); *play tennis* (*play* + sport but *play* + *the* + musical instrument); *have breakfast/lunch/dinner* (no *the* with meal times)

4 *the countryside* (specific and unique); *last week* (we don't use *the* before phrases beginning with *last* or *next*); *Lake Windermere* (no *the* before lakes); *the north of England* (specific place; *in the north/south/east/west of …*)

5 *the UK* (abbreviated countries have *the: the USA, the UAE*); *most people* (people in general, no *the*); *go to bed* (set phrase like *go to school, go home*); *in the evening/morning* (period of time); *at 7.30* (no *the* in front of times)

6 *the shops* (specific – we know which shops); *go home* (set phrase)

9

- Ask students to work in pairs. Tell them to take turns to read a sentence and put in the article where needed. You could make it a competitive game by asking students to award points for correct answers.

- As students speak, monitor and note how accurately students notice and correct errors. In feedback, summarize any areas where you think students are still making errors with articles.

Grammar notes

1 *a plane, a car* (we use *a* to talk about one person or thing in general)

2 *a boy* (in general – one of many); *play the horn* (*play* + *the* + musical instrument); *a musician* (in general – one of many)

3 *Korea* (a country); *the wings, the sea* (specific things)

4 *the first meal, the astronauts* (specific); *the Moon* (unique – only one); *bacon, peaches* (uncountable and countable plurals mentioned for the first time)

5 *a member* (mentioned for first time); *the team* (specific group); *the disaster* (specific)

6 *In the 1990s* (set phrase – specific period); *autographs, people* (plural nouns mentioned for the first time; people in general)

Pronunciation linking vowels

10 💿 [88]

- **Optional step** Write the following on the board: *I want to be an astronaut.* Tell students that, when saying this sentence in natural speech, there's a hidden consonant that's not shown in the spelling. Ask students to speculate what the consonant is. Then drill the sentence showing that the missing consonant is a /j/ sound which links the vowel sounds at the end of *be* and the start of *an*.

- Read the explanation of hidden consonants with your class. Ask them to read the phrases to themselves and decide which sound links the marked words. Then play the recording for them to listen and check.

- Play the recording again, pausing after each phrase for the class to repeat chorally and individually.

- Ask students to practise saying the phrases in pairs.

ANSWERS

1 /j/   2 /w/   3 /r/   4 /r/   5 /j/   6 /w/

Pronunciation notes

When two vowel sounds meet, we tend to insert an extra sound, a /j/, /w/ or /r/, to make the words that end and begin with vowels easier to say. This is a device called intrusion.

We use intrusive /r/ after words ending with the vowel sounds /ə/, /ɔː/ or /ɑː/. Note that this is regardless of spelling. The word *saw* may end with *w*, but, phonemically, it ends with /ɔː/, so it is linked using an intruding /r/.

We use intrusive /w/ after words ending with the vowel sounds /uː/, /aʊ/ or /əʊ/.

We use intrusive /j/ after words ending with the vowel sounds /iː/, /aɪ/, /eɪ/ or /ɔɪ/.

Extra activity

Write up these simple instructions and ask students to practise saying them with the correct intrusion: *Draw a picture, See a play, Play a CD, Go away, Do a favour, Tie a knot, Be a good friend*

Speaking ⟨my life⟩

11

- **Optional step** Start by drawing and explaining your own career path, or that of an imaginary person. If you have time to prepare before class, you could draw and project an interestingly detailed path. If not, you could draw it on the board as you explain it. Providing a teacher model of an activity can be useful (see Teacher development below).

- Ask students to draw their own (or a relative's) career path, using the stages suggested as a guide. One way of doing this is to get students to write the stages in a list with arrows joining each one on a large piece of paper. Then ask them to make notes around each heading in a different colour. Monitor and help with ideas and vocabulary.

- Organize the class into pairs. Ask students to take turns to explain their paths. In feedback, ask students to tell the class what they found out about their partner.

- As students speak, ask partners to listen out for the correct use of articles. Monitor and listen for errors yourself, noting down any errors you hear with the use of articles. During feedback, write on the board five or six short sentences containing anonymous errors you heard. Ask students to work in pairs to correct the errors.

Teacher development

The teacher model

Taking time to prepare and provide a teacher model is useful for a variety of reasons.

1 It shows students exactly what you want them to say or do, without the need to give complex instructions. It also encourages students to attempt something as ambitious as the model when they speak.

2 Listening to the teacher talk about his/her life and life experiences can be an interesting whole-class activity. Students are naturally curious, have questions and become interested in you. This is good for morale and bonding.

3 A live listening is a real listening. Set simple listening tasks and speak at length – it builds your students' confidence in being able to listen to and understand a native or near-native speaker talking at length and naturally.

10b The real-life Batman?

Lesson at a glance
- listening: an unusual talent
- vocabulary: the senses
- grammar: relative clauses
- writing and speaking: definitions

Listening

1

- Ask students to look at the photo and the caption. Tell them to work in pairs to discuss the questions. Batman is a fictional superhero that has appeared in comics and films.

- **Optional step** Ask students what the title could refer to. A 'real-life Batman' could be someone with superpowers, someone who inspired the creation of the character Batman, someone who dresses like Batman, someone who likes or knows about bats, or someone with abilities similar to those of bats.

ANSWERS

1 A bat is a small mammal that looks a little like a mouse, with large wings. They usually fly at night. Some bats use echolocation to locate and identify objects. Batman is a fictional superhero that has appeared in comics and films.

2 He's riding a bike in a park or in the countryside. It doesn't seem particularly unusual.

2 💿 [89]

- Play the recording. Students listen and answer the questions. Let students compare answers in pairs before checking with the class.

ANSWERS

Daniel is blind. He got his nickname because he uses the technique of echolocation, which is also used by bats.

Audioscript 💿 [89]

Daniel Kish, **who** was born blind, taught himself to 'see' using the technique of echolocation when he was a small child. As he moves around, Kish clicks his tongue and then listens for the echo **which** comes back. If the echo is loud, then he knows that an object is near; if the echo is not so loud, he knows the object is further away. He has become so skilled at using this technique **that** he can do many things that blind people cannot ordinarily do. By clicking his tongue two or three times a second, he can ride a bicycle, go hiking in the countryside and play ball games.

Echolocation is a skill **which** is also used in the animal world, **where** it is often key to survival. The best-known example is bats. This has led to Kish being called 'the real real-life Batman', a description he welcomes. Just like bats, Kish can tell from the quality of the echo not only how far away an object is, but also its size and its density. A wooden fence, for example, **whose** surface is softer than brick or metal, gives a 'warmer' echo than a brick wall. So what can he actually 'see'? Up close, at about five metres, he can recognize cars and bushes. Houses come into focus at about fifty metres.

Kish now spends a lot of his time training other blind people in his technique, **which** he calls FlashSonar. He says that many blind people already use echolocation in a passive way, but **what** they don't know is how to use it actively. The average person can develop good echolocation skills in about a month if he or she trains for a couple of hours a day, **which** is pretty fast. Kish is also looking at the possibility of training fully-sighted people, like firefighters, to use this skill in situations **in which** their vision is limited, like in a smoke-filled building. He is amused by the nickname **for which** he is now famous, but, mostly, he just loves **what** he is doing and sees great potential for it.

3 🎵 [89]

- Ask students to work individually to choose the correct options to complete the summary. Elicit the first answer to get students started.

- Play the recording again. Students listen and check their answers. Let students compare answers in pairs before checking with the class.

ANSWERS	
1 birth	5 fifty
2 tongue	6 passively
3 ball games	7 a month
4 how solid it is	8 fully sighted

Vocabulary notes

click your tongue = to press your tongue against the top of your mouth to make a short noise

echo = the repeated sound that is made when you shout in a cave or tunnel

density = how thick and heavy something is

nickname = a informal name that your friends usually give you

4

- Organize the class into pairs to discuss the questions. Elicit answers and ideas in feedback.

ANSWERS
Fully-sighted people, like firefighters, could use this skill in situations in which their vision is limited, like in a smoke-filled building.
Other possible situations: when doing hobbies like caving or pot-holing; perhaps when exploring extreme places; when walking home late at night

5

- Ask students to work individually to complete the descriptions with the five senses in the box. Let students compare answers before checking with the class.

ANSWERS	
1 eyesight	3 sense of smell; hearing
2 sense of taste	4 feeling

6

- Ask students to work individually to underline the adjectives used to describe each sense in Exercise 5. Then tell them to find the three additional adjectives.

ANSWERS
Adjectives used to describe each sense: <u>amazing</u> eyesight, <u>poor</u> sense of taste, <u>keen</u> sense of smell, <u>hard</u> of hearing
a short-sighted
b deaf
c numb

7

- Ask students to work in pairs or small groups to discuss the questions.

ANSWERS
Students' own answers

Grammar relative clauses

8

- Tell students to read the information in the grammar box. Then ask them to answer questions 1–5.

ANSWERS
1 essential information = defining relative clause; extra information = non-defining relative clause
2 *The 'real-life Batman' is a description **which/that** he welcomes.*
3 You can't leave the relative pronoun out in sentence 1 because it refers to the subject of the sentence. You can leave it out in sentence 2 because it is the object.
4 *what*
5 *… the nickname he is now famous for* is more informal.
6 *whose*

Refer students to page 174 for further information and practice.

ANSWERS TO GRAMMAR SUMMARY EXERCISES
4a
1 c – that/which
2 a – where
3 f – who/that
4 b – what
5 d – that/when
6 e – whose
4b
1 and 5

5

1 That's the woman (who) I played tennis with last week.

2 Is this the shop where you bought your new coat?

3 This isn't the same airport that/which we flew to last year.

4 Are you the person (that/who) I spoke to when I called earlier?

5 Please show me the credit card (that/which) you paid with.

6 This is the kind of music (that/which) I always listen to when I'm driving.

6

1 We live in Salto, which is in the north west of Uruguay.

2 I went to the cinema with Igor last night, which was fun.

3 My friend Louis, who is a doctor, has just started a new job.

4 The museum was closed when we went there, which was disappointing.

5 You should speak about this to my sister Lena, who knows a lot about this kind of thing.

6 DDT bank, which employs over 20,000 people, has serious financial problems. *or* DDT bank, which has serious financial problems, employs over 20,000 people.

Grammar note

The rules for the use of relative clauses can feel complicated to both teachers and students. One way of demystifying the subject is to get students to look at the examples of sentences in the grammar box, think about how they would say them in L1, and to make a list of similarities and differences between English and their L1. If your students are European, there is a good chance that similarities outweigh differences. Get students to note the key rules that are different.

9

• Ask students to work in pairs. Tell them to look at audioscript 89 on page 188 of the Student's Book and find the relative pronouns in bold. Ask students to discuss in pairs what these relative pronouns refer to before checking with the class.

> ANSWERS
>
> 1 *who* = Daniel Kish
>
> 2 *which* = the echo
>
> 3 *that* = many things
>
> 4 *which* = a skill
>
> 5 *where* = in the animal world
>
> 6 *whose* = a wooden fence
>
> 7 *which* = his technique
>
> 8 *what* = the thing that/which
>
> 9 *which* = developing echolocation skills in a couple of hours a day
>
> 10 *in which* = situations
>
> 11 *for which* = the nickname
>
> 12 *what* = the thing that/which

10

• Start by eliciting other possible sentences based on the first prompt (e.g. *Batman is a character everybody has heard of*; *Batman is a character whose mission is to save mankind*).

• Ask students to write definitions of the people and things using defining relative clauses. Let students compare their answers in pairs before checking with the class.

> EXAMPLE ANSWERS
>
> 2 Daniel Kish is a man who was blind from birth.
>
> 3 A blind person is someone who can't see.
>
> 4 Echolocation is a technique which/that is used by bats to find their way.
>
> 5 A click is a sound (which/that) you can make with your fingers or tongue.
>
> 6 Bats are animals which/that fly at night.

11

• **Optional step** Note that Exercises 11 and 12 offer further controlled written accuracy work on these complex forms. Decide how much practice your students need, and whether you wish to miss out (or set for homework) one or both of these exercises and move on to speaking practice.

• Ask students to choose the correct relative pronoun to complete the sentences. Elicit the first answer to get students started. In feedback, ask students to refer back to rules when explaining their answer.

> ANSWERS
>
> | | | | |
> |---|---|---|---|
> | 1 | that | 5 | which |
> | 2 | who | 6 | which |
> | 3 | to whom | 7 | What |
> | 4 | what | 8 | whose |

Grammar notes

1 This is a defining relative clause with an object relative pronoun, so we can use *which* or *that* or omit the pronoun.

2 This is a non-defining relative clause, so we cannot use *that*. We use *who* because it refers to a person.

3 This is a defining relative clause and is formally expressed – the preposition is followed by the object pronoun *whom*. It is possible to rewrite it less formally as: *... the person (who/that) it's addressed to.*

4 *what* = the thing that

5 This is a defining relative clause with an object relative pronoun, so we can use *which* or *that* or omit the pronoun.

6 This is a non-defining relative clause used to comment on the previous phrase. We can't use *that* because it is non-defining, and we can't use *who* because the pronoun refers to a situation (sharing a flat).

7 *what* = the thing that

8 *whose* is replacing a possessive – 'his support'

12

- Ask students to combine the sentences to make relative clauses. Elicit the first answer to get students started. You could ask students to work in pairs to help and guide each other.

ANSWERS

1 That's the man (who/that) Maya was talking about the other day.
2 Only two per cent of blind people use a white stick, which is surprising. (Note: relative clause used to comment on the previous phrase)
3 I think they achieved what they wanted (to). *or* I think they achieved what they wanted to achieve.
4 The study, which looked at how well people can use maps, had very interesting results. *or* The study, which had very interesting results, looked at how well people can use maps.
5 Frank, whose first job was as a cashier, is now the managing director of Tetbury Supermarkets.
6 The homeless people, who the money was really intended for, never received a penny. *or* The homeless people, for whom the money was really intended, never received a penny.
7 It's a small country which has had a big influence on the history of the region.
8 His brother, who is six years younger than him, is also a basketball player. *or* His brother, who is also a basketball player, is six years younger than him.

Speaking ⌐ my life

13

- Organize the class into pairs. Tell half the pairs they are A and the other half that they are B. Give them five minutes to prepare clues for the answers they find on the relevant pages of the Student's Book. Monitor and help with ideas and vocabulary.
- Once they have written the clues, tell each A pair to sit down with a B pair. Ask students to take turns to read out clues so that each pair can complete the crossword.
- In feedback, point out any errors with relative clauses that you notice during this exercise while monitoring.

ANSWERS

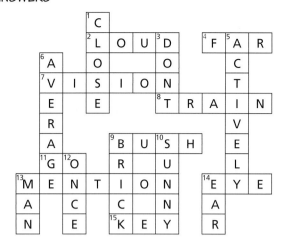

Example clues down:
1 a word that means the same as *near*; a word that's the opposite of *open*
3 a word we use to say the opposite of *do*
5 a word that is the opposite of *passively*; a word which means in a positive, lively way
6 an adjective which means *in the middle*
9 this is something you use to build houses
10 an adjective that describes a day when the sky is blue and the weather is good
12 a word that means *on one occasion*
13 a person who's not a woman
14 something on our head that we hear with

Example clues across:
2 a word which is the opposite of *quiet*
4 a word which is the opposite of *near*
7 a word that describes being able to see
8 a word which might mean *practise*, but might also describe a machine you travel on
9 a word that describes a type of plant (or the name of a president)
11 a verb that is the opposite of *come*
13 a verb that describes when you say something in passing
14 a part of the body whose function is to see things
15 a small metal thing we use to open doors

10c The king herself

Lesson at a glance
- reading: a woman who was king
- critical thinking: examining the evidence
- word focus: *self*
- speaking: job characteristics

Reading

1

- **Optional step** With books closed, write *The king herself* on the board. Ask students to think about what it means, why it's unusual and what the reading text in the lesson could be about.
- Organize the class into pairs to look at the title of the article and discuss what's strange about putting the words *king* and *herself* together. In feedback, elicit ideas, but do not comment at this stage (students will find out more when they read the article).
- **Optional step** Brainstorm and check key words from this topic: *pharaoh* /ˈfɛərəʊ/, *mummy, tomb* /tuːm/, *heir* /ɛə/, *rule, Egypt.*

> **EXAMPLE ANSWERS**
>
> *King* is a masculine noun (the feminine is *Queen*) so *herself* should not technically be used with *king*.

Background information

Hatshepsut /hætˈʃɛpsʊt/ was the fifth pharaoh of the Eighteenth Dynasty of Egypt. Her name means 'most noble of ladies'. Her reign was successful and peaceful – she established trade routes and was responsible for many building projects.

Howard Carter was a famous British archaeologist of the early twentieth century – most famous for discovering the intact tomb of pharaoh Tutankhamun.

The Karnak /ˈkɑːnæk/ **Temple Complex** in Egypt is a huge open-air museum of ruined temples and monuments from ancient Egypt.

2 💿 [90]

- **Optional step** Give students time to read the events in Hatshepsut's life first. Pre-teach any key words if you haven't already done so (see Vocabulary notes below). Note that some key words are in the glossary below the text.
- Ask students to read the article and order the events chronologically. Let students compare answers in pairs before checking with the class.
- **Optional step** The reading text is recorded. You could play the recording and ask students to read and listen.

> **ANSWERS**
>
> Correct order: g, f, c, d, b, a, e

Vocabulary notes

numerous = many
smashed = destroyed
the custom = what usually happens
erase = remove completely

3

- Ask students to work individually to read the article again and choose the correct options to complete the sentences.
- Let students compare answers in pairs before checking with the class. In feedback, ask students to justify their answers with reference to the article.

> **ANSWERS**
>
> 1 c (*identified a mummy called KV60a from a less important tomb, as that of Hatshepsut*)
> 2 c (*her hopes as to how she will be remembered … 'as I think what the people will say … who shall speak of what I have done'*)
> 3 a (*ordering all images of her as the king to be removed from monuments and temples … Yet the images of her as queen were left undamaged.*)
> 4 a (*Hatshepsut … produced one daughter. Another, less important wife, Isis, gave Thutmose II the male heir*)
> 5 b (*At first, Hatshepsut respected convention and just handled political affairs while the young king was growing up.*)
> 6 b (*… depicted as a male king, with headdress and beard, standing in a self-confident manner with legs apart.*)

Critical thinking examining the evidence

4

- **Optional step** Before students look at sentences 1–5, ask them whether they can come to any conclusions about Hatshepsut from the evidence they read in the article. Elicit ideas, e.g. students may suggest that she was brave or wise. Whatever they say, ask: *What evidence did you find in the text to support that idea?*
- Ask students to work individually to read the article again to find evidence (or not) for the five statements.

5

- Ask students to work in pairs to compare their scores and the evidence they found before checking with the class. In feedback, ask students to refer to the article to explain their percentages.
- Ask students whether they think the story had a happy or sad ending.

EXAMPLE ANSWERS

1 100% – *one of the greatest builders of ancient Egypt, who built numerous monuments and temples; her hopes as to how she will be remembered; she began peforming kingly duties; after a few years she … fully assumed the role of 'king'*

2 0% – *there is no evidence or mention of her feelings*

3 80% – *Her stepson, Thutmose III, … grew increasingly frustrated. After Hatshepsut's death, he took his revenge, doing his best to erase her memory as pharaoh from history.*

4 70% – *Many inscriptions still exist which have references to 'my people'. These suggest that she knew she had broken the rules and wanted her subjects' approval.*

5 100% – *in the long term it is Hatshepsut, the King Herself, who has achieved greater fame.*

There is no definitive answer as to whether the story has a happy or sad ending. The fact that Thutmose III did not erase Hatshepsut from history, and that many of her images and monuments survive, as does her fame, suggests a happy ending.

Word focus *self*

6

- **Optional step** Write *self* on the board. Ask students to work in pairs to think of as many words beginning with the prefix *self* as they can in one minute.

- Ask students to explain the expressions in bold. Tell them to use the context of each sentence to work out the meaning.

ANSWERS

self-confident = when you feel you can do things well and people respect you

self-help (*books*) = books that advise people on how to solve their own problems (e.g. self-help group; self-help websites)

self-made (*man/woman*) = a person who has earned all their wealth themselves without inheriting or being given money

self-conscious = worried about how you appear to others

self-control = the ability to hide and not show your feelings even when you are angry or under pressure

self-interest = if you do things for reasons of self-interest, you do them because it helps you in some way

7

- Ask students to work individually to write two sentences using expressions from Exercise 6. You could provide a model to get them started.

- When students are ready, ask them to work in pairs to share their sentences. Tell them to read each sentence without the key phrase (tell them to say 'beep' instead of the phrase with *self*). Their partner must guess the missing word or phrase.

EXAMPLE ANSWERS

Ronaldo is a great footballer, and appears very <u>self-confident</u>, probably because he believes in his ability.

Donald Trump may have become US president – but he isn't a <u>self-made man</u> – he inherited a lot of money from his father.

A lot of people criticize celebrities in the press – you need a lot of <u>self-control</u> not to get angry or to respond to criticism.

Extra activity

Ask students to use dictionaries to find other useful words with the prefix *self*. Ask each pair to choose one word they think is useful and to write a sentence to show its use.

Possible words: *self-belief, self-defence, self-discipline, self-portrait, self-taught*

Speaking   my life

8

- Tell students to work in pairs to read the job characteristics. Ask them to discuss which options they think describe the job of a leader or a manager. Elicit ideas in feedback.

EXAMPLE ANSWERS

Leaders or managers tend to work in companies with a team, so a possible list of options would be: working 9–5 (but with overtime); being employed; working with people; using your brain; taking decisions; being full-time; being part of a team

9

- Put pairs together to form groups of four, or ask students to mingle and speak to two other people. Tell them to choose some questions from the options to ask. Prompt them to use *Do/Would you prefer …* or *Do/Would you rather …* to ask the questions.

- As students speak, monitor and note down useful pieces of language they use, or errors they make, which you could focus on in feedback.

- In feedback, find out what answers students were given and what dream job they suggested.

Extra activity

You could extend this activity. Ask pairs to prepare a career questionnaire by using the options from Exercise 8, but also by preparing questions about salaries, conditions, work/life balance, etc. Once students have prepared a detailed set of questions to ask, they can interview one or two people in detail and suggest career options.

UNIT 10 Talented people

10d The right job

Lesson at a glance
- real life: describing skills, talents and experience
- pronunciation: difficult words

Real life describing skills, talents and experience

1

- **Optional step** With books closed, start by writing *Shelterbox* on the board. Tell students that it's the name of a charity. Ask what the charity could be for and elicit ideas in a prediction exercise. Explain that *a shelter* is a place where people are protected from bad weather or from danger.

- Ask students to read the description and answer the question. You could ask students to discuss the question in pairs before eliciting answers from the class. Do not comment on answers at this stage (students will find out more when they listen to the recording).

> ANSWERS
> *Shelterbox* is a charity which sends boxes of essential items to places where disasters have struck.

Vocabulary notes

essential = absolutely necessary

cooking utensils = something that you use for cooking with, e.g. knives, spoons, pots, pans

kit = a set of equipment for a specific purpose

2 🎵 [91]

- Tell students they are going to listen to someone being interviewed for a job at Shelterbox. Play the recording. Students listen and answer the questions. Let them compare their answers in pairs before checking with the class.

- **Optional step** You could check the meaning and pronunciation of some of the words in the Vocabulary notes below before playing the recording a second time.

> ANSWERS
> 1 working abroad
> 2 the candidate may soon leave for a better-paid job

Audioscript 🎵 [91]

S = Sarah; P = Phil

S: So, you're 24 years old, you graduated a year ago and you're looking for work with a charity. What attracted you to Shelterbox?

P: Well, I'm familiar with your work because I have a friend who volunteered for you last year – packing boxes – and I think it's a fantastic concept. But, umm,

mainly I'm very keen on the idea of working abroad – in different countries.

S: I see, and what makes you think you'd be suited to that? I see you studied economics at Cambridge. Don't you think that's a rather different world?

P: Yes, it's true that I specialized in economics but actually, I'm good at coping with difficult environments. I spent three months helping to build a school in Chennai in India last summer. And the year before that I trekked across the Mojave Desert. So I think I'd be suited to the work.

S: OK – well, they're certainly not easy places to adapt to, although in fact you'd also be spending a good part of the time here in the office doing paperwork.

P: Yeah, that's also fine. I was expecting that. I have quite a lot of experience of sitting at a desk for my studies. What sort of paperwork is it?

S: Well, each trip involves a lot of preparation and a certain amount of follow-up too. Keeping spreadsheets, writing reports. Are you OK doing that sort of thing?

P: Yeah, I'm quite good with computers. I'm comfortable with all the usual programs – Excel, Word, some financial software.

S: OK. There's just one thing that's worrying me though. You're clearly a bright person and you have a good degree. How do we know that you won't just do this job for a few months and then go and get a better paid job with a bank or consultancy business?

P: That's a good question. It's actually what a lot of my friends from university have done but I'll tell you why that's not for me. Firstly, I'm really serious about wanting to help people in need. Secondly, I think I need to become more knowledgeable about the world, before I use my economics degree to do something else. If you put your faith in me, I will be absolutely committed to doing the best job that I can, for two or three years at least.

Vocabulary notes

volunteer = to offer to do a job for no money

suited = if you are suited to job, you have the right skills and personality for it

specialized in = if you specialize in a subject, then you concentrate on or study that topic in detail

put faith in = to trust

committed = determined to work hard to do something

3 🎵 [91]

- Ask students to read the expressions in the language box and note the use of prepositions in each expression.

- Play the recording again. Students listen and complete the expressions. Let students compare answers in pairs before checking with the class.

- In feedback, go through the phrases checking meaning and use (see Vocabulary notes below).

- **Optional step** Ask students to check answers by looking at audioscript 91 on page 188 of the Student's Book.

ANSWERS

1 volunteered for you last year
2 working abroad
3 economics
4 difficult environments
5 the work
6 sitting at a desk
7 computers
8 the usual programs
9 help people in need
10 the world

Vocabulary notes

Note the fixed adjective + preposition collocations: *familiar with, keen on, specialized in, good at, suited to, good with, comfortable with, serious/knowledgeable about.* Point out that they are followed by a noun or an -*ing* form (prepositions are always followed by -*ing*).

Note the difference between being *good at* and *good with*. If you are *good at something* (a sport, a skill, etc.), then you do it well. If are *good with something* (your hands, computers, etc.), then you use them well.

familiar/comfortable with the latest programs = we use *familiar* to say that we know about something, and *comfortable* to say that we have used something and have no problems with it

4

• Ask students to work in pairs to discuss whether the candidate did a good job of selling himself to the interviewer. In feedback, elicit ideas and ask students to justify answers by referring to what they heard.

EXAMPLE ANSWERS

He probably made a positive impression. The candidate seems prepared, answers questions confidently, says a lot of positive things about his skills and describes lots of interesting experiences. He's enthusiastic and promises to be committed.

Pronunciation difficult words
5a 🅖 [92]

• Read the introduction to the class. Ask students to grade their confidence in saying the words (you could ask them to grade their confidence from 1 to 10).

• Play the recording. Students listen and compare the pronunciation with how they expected each word to sound. Ask students to practise saying the words in pairs.

Pronunciation notes

although /ɔːl'ðəʊ/
business /'bɪznɪs/
comfortable /'kʌmftəbəl/
environment /ɪn'vaɪrənmənt/
foreign /'fɒrɪn/
knowledgeable /'nɒlɪdʒəbəl/
months /mʌnθs/
specialized /'spɛʃəlaɪzd/
suited /'suːtɪd/
world /wɜːld/

5b 🅖 [93]

• Play the recording. Students listen and write the words. Let students compare answers in pairs. Check the spelling of the words with the class and then ask students to practise saying the words in their pairs.

Audioscript 🅖 [93]

clothes February folk island lengths receipt surface thorough

Teacher development

Pronunciation of difficult words

A feature of English is the fact that the spelling of words is often not phonetic. As a result, it can be hard for students to know how to say new words. Here are some ways to help:

1 Introduce words aurally rather than letting students see them first on a page. So, if you are pre-teaching a set of words, say them and ask students to repeat them first. Then write the word on the board for students to copy, or ask students to look at the written form of the words in their Student's Book.

2 Introduce or check words with reference to the phonemic chart, e.g. ask students to note *world* with /wɜː(r)ld/ next to it. That way they have a reference to remind them of pronunciation. Similarly, if students use dictionaries, make sure they note the pronunciation in the entry and not just the meaning.

3 Introduce and point out some of the typically challenging pronunciation patterns of English:

a some letters can be silent – the *n* in *environment*, the *or* in *comfortable*, the *p* in *receipt*; *w, g* or *k* at the start of some words (*write, gnat, know*, etc.)

b the letters *g* and *gh* are often silent in words but may affect the pronunciation of other letters (*right, cough, thorough, though, through*, etc.)

c some specific sounds are difficult to pronounce, e.g. /ʃ/ in *wish* and /tʃ/ in *church* (though note that this may depend on the students' L1)

d consonant clusters can also be difficult – *lengths*, for example, has three consonants in a row: /lɛŋkθs/.

6

- Organize the class into new pairs. Ask students to decide which role (A or B) to take. Give a time limit of five minutes for preparation. Ask each Student A to choose one of the jobs and to plan what to say in the interview. Encourage them to look back at the language box and use the expressions to organize their ideas. Tell each Student B to prepare general questions to ask.

- **Optional step** Instead of preparing individually, ask students to prepare in pairs of As and pairs of Bs. When they are ready, split the pairs so that an A is now with a B.

- Ask students to roleplay the interviews. Tell fast-finishing students to swap roles and act out a second interview.

- As students speak, monitor and note errors and examples of good language use. At the end, provide some feedback on language students have used.

EXAMPLE ANSWERS

A travel guide for a tour operator taking groups on walking holidays: good at coping with demanding holidaymakers; familiar with public paths and nature; specialized in first aid, survival techniques and medical emergencies

A sales assistant in a children's bookshop: knowledgeable about children's literature; good with customers; experience with children

A tester of new video games: comfortable with computer technology; good with their hands; knowledgeable about games

A fund-raiser for your old school or university: good with people; good at persuading people to give money; comfortable with asking people for money; enthusiastic; imaginative

A volunteer firefighter (part-time): serious about wanting to do a dangerous job; familiar with safety procedures; good with their hands; physically fit; has previous volunteering experience

A trainee chocolate maker: good with their hands; suited to working creatively; knowledgeable about chocolate; quick learner; good team worker

10e First impressions

Lesson at a glance
- writing: a personal profile
- vocabulary: personal qualities
- writing skill: using *with*

Writing a personal profile
1

- Ask students to discuss the questions. You could ask students to discuss the questions in pairs first, before opening up the discussion to the class.

EXAMPLE ANSWERS

a job application: educational background, qualifications, job experience, personal description, references, contact details

a social networking site: name, age, sex, nationality, interests, likes and dislikes, relationship status

a university application: name, age, sex, nationality, educational background, qualifications, hobbies and interests, personal achievements, experience of voluntary work, references

a holiday rental website: name, nationality, references, what you are looking for, holiday dates, bank details

a voluntary organization: name, age, sex, nationality, educational background, qualifications, job experience, personal description, interests, references

2

- Ask students to work individually to read the profiles and match them with a purpose (a–e) from Exercise 1. Let students compare answers in pairs.

- **Optional step** In feedback, ask students what kind of information is in each profile.

ANSWERS

1 d This is an Airbnb guest profile.
2 b This is a LinkedIn profile; LinkedIn is a social networking site for business people.
3 c This is a university student's personal statement.

3

- Ask students to work individually to look at the profiles and answer the questions. Let students compare answers in pairs before checking with the class.

ANSWERS

1 1 and 3 are in the first person; 2 is in the third person.
2 1 is less formal: it uses abbreviations (*I'm, We've*); it uses 'chatty', friendly language (*just moved; When I'm not working*).
3 Students' own ideas. All are well-written for their purpose and can therefore be said to be persuasive; perhaps 3 is the most persuasive because the writer is really selling him/herself.

Vocabulary personal qualities

4a

- Ask students to work individually to find adjectives and match them with the definitions. Let students compare answers in pairs before checking with the class.

ANSWERS

1 bright
2 curious
3 passionate
4 creative
5 experienced
6 independent-minded
7 easy-going
8 adaptable

4b

- Ask students to decide and say which of the adjectives describe themselves. You could put students in small groups to do this task.
- **Optional step** It's a good idea to introduce phrases connected with gradability here. Write on the board: *very/really, quite/fairly, not very / not particularly / not all that*. Ask students to use these phrases when describing their personalities.

ANSWERS

Students' own ideas

Writing skill using *with*

5a

- Ask students to rewrite the phrase using a relative clause. Let students compare answers in pairs before checking with the class.
- In feedback, point out how we can use *with* instead of a relative clause (see Vocabulary notes below).

ANSWERS

A retail manager who has a background in men's and ladies' fashion.

Vocabulary notes

We can use the preposition *with* to state what possessions, qualities or features someone or something has. In this use, it has a comparable meaning to a defining relative clause. Examples include: *a boy with red hair; a room with a high ceiling; an animal with stripes on its back.*

Note that *with* is followed by a noun or noun phrase.

5b

- Ask students to work individually to rewrite the phrases using *with*. Let students compare answers in pairs before checking with the class.

- **Optional step** Elicit the second sentence as an example (*... with a passion for languages*) to start students off. It is best to elicit this one (rather than the first sentence) as it shows how the preposition after the noun is sometimes different from the preposition used after a verb or adjective.

ANSWERS

1 an IT expert with experience of software design
2 a recent graduate with a passion for languages
3 a young couple with a love of travel
4 a creative individual with an interest in fashion
5 a bright manager with an ambition to succeed
6 an easy-going musician with a talent for cooking

6

- **Optional step** Start by brainstorming ideas in open class. Elicit words, expressions and information students could include in their profile. Encourage students in the class to choose a profile type to write that they are familiar with and likely to want to use.
- Ask students to spend one or two minutes making notes about what they want to include in their profile. Monitor at this stage and help with ideas and vocabulary. You could let students compare their ideas in pairs and ask for help.
- Ask students to write their profile. You could set this as homework.

7

- Organize the class into pairs. Ask students to exchange their written work with their partner. Tell them to check their partner's work using the questions and suggest how to improve it.
- **Optional step** Ask students to revise and rewrite their profile based on their partner's suggestions.

Homework

If you have the technology, ask students to write and post their profiles online – perhaps on your class website or forum. Then other students can add comments to the profiles.

10f Queen of Egypt

Before you watch

1

- Ask students to look at the photo and the caption, and answer the questions in pairs. In feedback, you could build up a list of what students know about Cleopatra on the board.

> **ANSWERS**
>
> Here is some basic information your students might know:
>
> Who she was: Queen of Egypt
>
> When and where she ruled: in ancient Egypt at the time of the pharaohs and pyramids (or so many think); actually, she ruled just over 2,000 years ago (born 69BC) during a time when Egypt was subject to the Roman Empire
>
> Important events in her life: students may know of her meetings with Roman generals Julius Caesar and Mark Antony, and of her death, when she was bitten by a snake

Background information

Cleopatra (69–30BC) was the last but one of the Ptolemaic pharaohs, a line of Greek-speaking pharaohs who ruled Egypt between 305BC and 30BC. The male pharaohs were all called Ptolemy and the females were all called Cleopatra – the famous Cleopatra that we all think of was Cleopatra the Seventh.

After her failed attempt to secure her succession through relationships and alliances with Julius Caesar and Mark Antony, the Ptolemaic dynasty ended (Cleopatra's son by Caesar – Caesarion – was killed on the orders of Octavian). Octavian became Emperor Augustus and Egypt became a province of Rome.

Key vocabulary

2a

- Ask students to read the sentences and guess the meaning of the words from context.
- Let students compare their answers in pairs before moving on to Exercise 2b.

2b

- Ask students to match the words in bold in Exercise 2a with the definitions. Let students compare their answers in pairs.

> **ANSWERS**
>
> a civil war (sentence 3)
> b the throne (sentence 1)
> c successor (sentence 1)
> d infuriated (sentence 2)
> e controversy (sentence 2)
> f rivals (sentence 3)

Teacher development

Using knowledge and context to guess words

Guessing the meaning of words is a useful skill. It improves reading and listening skills, and enables students to increase their range of passive vocabulary quickly and easily without the labour of checking words in dictionaries or with the teacher.

Here is a way of focusing on how students' knowledge of a word and its context can help students develop this skill:

To show students how important existing knowledge and context can be, focus on one word your students don't know, e.g. *infuriated* in sentence 2.

1 Ask: *What part of speech is 'infuriated'? How is it used?* (It's a past participle (-ed ending) used in the present perfect.)

2 Ask: *What is the subject of the sentence with 'infuriated' in it?* (His comments) *And the object?* (young people)

3 Ask: *How might young people might feel about the comments?* (Suggestions might include *upset, disgusted, angry, shocked, saddened*.)

4 Ask: *Is the word similar to a word in your language? Or does a part of the verb, or the look or sound of the word, suggest a meaning?* (Students may suggest that *fury, furious* or the latinate word *furioso* may be roots of the word.)

5 Tell students to guess meaning from their investigations and thoughts from the process above. This should show how useful it is to investigate words in context in this way.

While you watch

3 ◼️ [10.1]

- **Optional step** You may wish to read out the listed names and focus on their pronunciation before playing the video (see Pronunciation notes below). Ask students what they already know about any of the characters.

- Tell students to watch the video and match the characters in the story (1–6) with their descriptions (a–f). Play the whole video. Let students compare answers in pairs before checking with the class.

> **ANSWERS**
>
> 1 e   2 a   3 d   4 c   5 f   6 b

Pronunciation notes

Cleopatra

Ptolemy = /ˈtɒləmi/ (a silent *p*)

Julius Caesar = /ˈsiːzər/

Caesarion = /sɫˈzæriən/

Mark Antony

Octavian

Videoscript ■◀ 10.1

0.01–1.19 She has a reputation for beauty, power, controversy and, ultimately, tragedy.

In 69 BC, Cleopatra was born into Egypt's Ptolemaic dynasty; a dynasty in decline and under the protection of Rome.

At the age of eighteen, she became queen, and ruled Egypt with her younger brother, Ptolemy the Thirteenth. But the royal couple did not have a good relationship and Cleopatra was soon forced from power. But losing did not suit Cleopatra and she waited for a chance to prove her capabilities.

That opportunity came when Julius Caesar, the winner in Rome's recent civil war, arrived in Alexandria, Egypt, in pursuit of a rival Roman general.

According to legend, Cleopatra managed to get herself into Caesar's court rolled up inside a rug.

Caesar was completely charmed. He defeated Cleopatra's rivals and helped her seize the throne.

Shortly after, she gave birth to a boy, Caesarion, whom she claimed was Caesar's son.

1.20–1.37 Egypt was a very rich country and Cleopatra was fiercely determined to keep it independent of Rome. Her relationship with Caesar kept the Romans from taking direct control of Egypt. But after Caesar's murder, her position, and the future of her country, became uncertain.

1.38–2.02 Searching for people who could help her among Rome's new leaders, she was overjoyed when Mark Antony, one of Caesar's potential successors, sent for her.

Like Caesar before him, Mark Antony was charmed by the elegant Egyptian queen ... and her riches.

Together they ruled Alexandria, an arrangement that made Cleopatra a fully independent ruler.

2.05–2.37 Cleopatra and Antony shared a hunger for power.

They eventually married and became the power couple of the eastern Mediterranean.

Antony tried to help her acquire some Roman lands. And he declared Cleopatra's son, Caesarion, to be the son and true successor to Julius Caesar.

2.40–3.13 That insulted and infuriated Mark Antony's Roman rival, Octavian, who went to war against them.

Antony and Cleopatra were quickly beaten at the Battle of Actium in 31 BC.

Legend tells us that Cleopatra spread numerous false rumours of her death.

His mind distorted by grief, Antony killed himself. But word came she was still alive and Antony's followers carried him to Cleopatra, where he died in her arms.

3.15–3.29 After twenty-two years as queen, Cleopatra was fighting a losing battle. She tried unsuccessfully to make peace with Octavian. Utterly unable to bear the pain of losing to the Romans, she took hold of a poisonous snake and let it kill her with its bite.

3.30–3.48 With her death, the Ptolemaic dynasty was finished and Egypt fell firmly into Roman hands.

Although her ambitions were never realized, Cleopatra lives on in history through her personal story of love and tragedy.

4 ■◀ [10.1]

- Ask students to read sentences 1–12 carefully and note what sort of information is missing in each.

- When students are ready, play the video again. Students work individually to complete the sentences. Let students compare their answers in pairs before checking with the class.

ANSWERS

1 69   2 18   3 bad   4 rug   5 throne
6 Caesar's   7 power   8 married
9 Caesarion   10 31   11 dead   12 snake

After you watch

Vocabulary in context

5a ■◀ [10.2]

- Explain that students are going to watch some clips from the video which contain some new words and phrases. They need to choose the correct meaning of the words.

- Play the clips. When each multiple-choice question appears, pause the clip so that students can choose the correct definition. You could let students compare answers in pairs before discussing with the class.

ANSWERS

1 b   2 a   3 c   4 c   5 a   6 c

Videoscript ■◀ 10.2

1 ... a dynasty **in decline** and under the protection of Rome.

  a not in fashion

  b decreasing in importance

  c in great difficulty

2 Julius Caesar ... arrived in Alexandria, Egypt, **in pursuit of** a rival Roman general.

  a trying to catch

  b trying to appear like

  c hoping to make peace with

3 He defeated Cleopatra's rivals and helped her **seize** the throne.

  a destroy

  b return to

  c take by force

4 She was **overjoyed** when Mark Antony ... sent for her.

  a very suspicious

  b very anxious

  c very happy

5 His mind distorted by **grief**, Antony killed himself.

  a deep sadness

  b great ambition

  c deep regret

6 Cleopatra **lives on** in history ...

  a is famous

  b continues to live

  c is remembered

5b

- Students work individually to complete the sentences. Elicit one or two ideas for the first sentence to get them started. Let students compare sentences in pairs.

EXAMPLE ANSWERS

1 my friend got her dream job. / my friends were getting married. / I had passed my exam.
2 industry in my country / sales of CDs / communication by letter
3 music / work / legacy / contribution to music

6

- Ask students to describe Cleopatra. You could put students in pairs first to prepare ideas.

EXAMPLE ANSWERS

brave – she fought to keep her throne
resourceful – she used alliances and her attractiveness to keep power and influence
untrustworthy – she spread rumours and would do anything to keep power

7

- Organize the class into groups of four or five. Ask students to discuss the questions. In feedback, ask different groups to tell the class about the characters they thought of.

ANSWERS

Students' own answers

Extra activity

Ask students to prepare and give a presentation on a famous person in history. You could set this as a homework task, or, if your students have internet access in class, they could research and prepare in class time.

Set some headings to guide students in their preparation: *Who? When? Where? What achievements? What personal qualities? What legacy?*

UNIT 10 Review and memory booster

Memory Booster activities

Exercises 5 and 7 are Memory Booster activities. For more information about these activities and how they benefit students, see page 10 of this Teacher's Book.

I can ... check boxes

As an alternative to asking students to simply tick the *I can* ... boxes, you could ask them to give themselves a score from 1 to 4 (1 = not very confident; 4 = very confident) for each language area. If students score 1 or 2 for a language area, refer them to additional practice activities in the Workbook and Grammar summary exercises.

Grammar

1

- Ask students to work individually to complete the first part of the article (1–10). Explain that they must use *a*, *an*, *the* or leave a space for no article.
- Then ask students to complete the second part (11–16) using relative pronouns. Let students compare answers in pairs before checking with the class.

ANSWERS

Part 1:

1 *an*	6 *the*
2 zero article	7 *the*
3 zero article	8 *The*
4 *an*	9 zero article
5 zero article	10 zero article

Part 2:

11 whose	14 that/which
12 that/which	15 where
13 who/that	16 when

2

- Ask students to work individually to answer the question about the article in Exercise 1.

ANSWERS

It's small enough to be launched but big enough (when inflated) to accommodate six astronauts.

3

- Ask students to work individually to write sentences defining two of the things from Unit 10 in the box. Monitor as students work, making sure that they use at least one article and one relative pronoun in each definition.
- Tell students to rewrite the sentences leaving spaces for the articles and pronouns. Students give their sentences to a partner for them to complete the gaps.

EXAMPLE ANSWERS

A **blind** person is a person who cannot see.

An **echo** is the repeated noise that you hear when a sound hits a surface and returns.

If there is a **flood**, then there is a place which has become covered in water that shouldn't be there.

The **heir** in a family is the person who will receive money, property or a title when another person in that family dies.

The initials '**BC**', which are used after the number of a year, mean 'before Christ' and refer to a time before the birth of Jesus Christ.

Vocabulary

4

• Ask students to work individually to complete the words to make sentences about jobs and careers. Let students compare answers in pairs before checking with the class.

ANSWERS

1 degree; graduated	4 applied; follow
2 served	5 become
3 adaptable; easy-going	

5 ≫ MB

• Ask students to work in pairs to discuss which of the areas listed in the box is being described in each sentence in Exercise 4.

• Then ask students to make similar sentences to describe themselves in each area. Elicit some of the sentences from individuals in the class.

EXAMPLE ANSWERS

1 qualifications
2 background, experience, knowledge
3 qualities
4 skills, talents
5 background

Real life

6

• Ask students to work individually to complete the sentences with the correct preposition. Let students compare answers in pairs before checking as a class.

ANSWERS

1 with	5 about; in
2 in	6 on
3 to	7 of; about
4 at; with	

7 ≫ MB

• Tell students to work individually to rewrite the sentences in Exercise 6 so that four sentences are true for them and two are false. Make sure that students do not show their sentences to each other while they are writing.

• Ask students to work in pairs and take turns to read all seven sentences out. Their partner must try to guess which two sentences are false.

Unit 11 Knowledge and learning

Opener

1

- Ask students to look at the photo and the caption. Discuss the questions with your class. Elicit ideas from students in feedback, but do not comment on ideas at this stage (students will find out more when they listen to the recording).

> EXAMPLE ANSWERS
>
> 1 Students' own answers
> Some possibilities: It's specifically aimed at children, so interactive, hands-on displays, activities and play areas for children, and life-sized models of dinosaurs.
>
> 2 Students' own answers

Background information

The Children's Museum of Indianapolis is the world's largest children's museum. It has five floors of exhibitions and has more than one million visitors annually.

Indianapolis /ˌɪndiəˈnæpəlɪs/ is the capital of the US state of Indiana in the American Midwest.

2

- Ask students to work individually to match the verbs to do with learning (1–5) with the verbs with a similar meaning (a–e). Elicit the first match to get them started. Let students compare their answers in pairs before checking with the class.

> ANSWERS
>
> 1 d   2 c   3 a   4 e   5 b   6 f

Vocabulary notes

Help students understand these words by adding some context:

*Over many years of travelling, I have **acquired** an understanding of many languages.*

*I'm **unaware of** any reason why I shouldn't get the job.*

*The students **engaged with** the subject because it was so interesting.*

*I didn't really **get** what you were saying – can you explain again?*

*Professor Smith **inspired** me to become a biochemist.*

*I had a month to study American law – it was hard to **take in** so much!*

3 🎵 [94]

- Tell students to look at the questions and note the use of the verbs to do with learning. Play the recording. Students listen and note answers to the questions.

- Let students compare answers in pairs before checking with the class.

> ANSWERS
>
> 1 the interactive displays – the dinosaurs and dressing up
> 2 things about China – like herbal medicine
> 3 the stories of children who had difficult childhoods
> 4 because the museum is too big

Audioscript 🎵 [94]

I love this museum. We went to Indianapolis specially to visit it, because we'd heard such great things about it. There are a lot of interactive displays that younger kids can **engage with**. My kids, who are seven and nine, loved the dinosaurs and also dressing up as a prince and princess. My partner and I learned a lot too. They had a whole section on China – part of the 'Take me there' section on foreign cultures. It had so many things I **was** completely **unaware of** – like Chinese herbal medicine. The other thing I really liked was the 'Children making a difference' section. It had stories of children who had difficult childhoods, but have succeeded – like kids who faced prejudice or discrimination. Their stories really **inspired** me … I'm definitely going to take the kids back when they're old enough to really **get** these stories. I just think the mixture of visual displays and hands-on stuff and real life stories … it's such a great way to **acquire** knowledge. I guess if I have any criticism of the museum, it's that it's too big – there's probably too much to **take in**.

Vocabulary notes

prejudice = an unreasonable feeling or opinion about someone, often based on imagined information rather than fact or experience

discrimination = unfair treatment of someone based on their race or gender, rather than individual merit

4

- Organize the class into pairs or small groups to discuss the questions. In feedback, invite students with interesting answers to the questions to share with the class.

> ANSWERS
>
> Students' own answers

Extra activity

Ask students to find the vocabulary from Exercise 2 in the audioscript (see emboldened words in audioscript 94) and to note how the language is used. Tell them to write personalized sentences using the vocabulary.

11a Innovation in learning

Lesson at a glance
- vocabulary: education
- reading: an innovative school
- grammar: *could, was able to, managed to* and *succeeded in*
- speaking: learning experiences

Vocabulary education

1
- Ask students to work individually to choose the correct options to complete the sentences. Elicit the first answer to get students started.
- In feedback, elicit answers and check students understand all the vocabulary.

> ANSWERS
> 1 take
> 2 by heart
> 3 Cramming
> 4 dropped out of
> 5 academic knowledge
> 6 marks

Vocabulary notes

1 *take an exam* = to do it; *pass an exam* = to get the right grade

2 If you *learn by heart*, you memorize something. A multiplication table is a list that shows the results of multiplying all the combinations of two numbers between 1 and 12, e.g. 7 x 8, 3 x 9.

3 *revising* = reading and studying your notes in preparation for an exam; *cramming* = revising at the last minute and very intensively

4 *drop out of college* = to leave before getting a qualification; *turn up* = to arrive

5 *academic knowledge* = facts (e.g. 1789 French Revolution); *practical experience* = learning by doing things

6 *notes* = what you write in lessons and lectures; *marks* = the number you get in tests and exams (e.g. 76%, or 8 out of 10)

2
- Ask students to work in pairs to discuss the questions about education. In feedback, ask a few pairs of students to briefly summarize their discussion. Note that the main aim here is to enable students to use the new vocabulary.

> ANSWERS
> Students' own answers

Reading
3 [95]
- Start by asking students what they think the title *Innovation in learning* might mean (= doing something new and different when teaching people).
- Ask students to read the article about the Lumiar School in Brazil and find answers to the question. Let students compare their answers in pairs before checking with the class.
- **Optional step** The reading text is recorded. You could play the recording and ask students to read and listen.

> ANSWERS
> They don't have (conventional) classrooms. (*Pupils occupy 'spaces' rather than rooms and learning takes place 'everywhere': in play areas, the hall, the dining room.*)
> Students can move between different lessons when they want. (*If a pupil does not feel engaged in a lesson, they can go to another one or to the library to read.*)
> Students learn through projects which they have created, rather than teachers just telling students about things. (*Most learning is done through projects which pupils design with their fellow students and teachers.*)

4
- Ask students to work individually to complete the sentences using words from the article. Elicit the first word to get students started.
- Let students compare their answers in pairs before checking with the class.

> ANSWERS
> 1 company   2 projects   3 life skills   4 money

Grammar *could, was able to, managed to and succeeded*

5
- Ask students to look at the grammar box and complete the rules using the correct forms. Let students compare answers in pairs before checking answers with the class.

> ANSWERS
> 1 could; was/were able to
> 2 could; was/were able to
> 3 succeeded in; managed to; was/were able to

Refer students to page 176 for further information and practice.

ANSWERS TO GRAMMAR SUMMARY EXERCISES

1

Sentences 2 (*couldn't*) 3 (*could*) 5 (*couldn't*)

2

Correct forms:

1 was able to, managed to

2 couldn't

3 succeeded in

4 managed to, was able to

5 couldn't, weren't able to

6 was able to, could

3

1 f – to run

2 a – use

3 e – increasing

4 c – to paint

5 b – to visit

6 d – make

Grammar notes

Form

could + infinitive without *to* (*could* = a modal verb)

was/were able to / *managed to* + infinitive

succeeded in + *-ing* (*in* is a preposition so it's followed by *-ing*)

Meaning

Could is used to ask for permission, express possibility or to make a request, as well as to express ability when referring to the past. *Was/were able to* is used as an alternative to *could* when we are discussing ability.

We tend to use *could* when we are talking about ability generally.

We tend to use *was able to* or *managed to* if we are talking about what happened in a particular situation or when we are referring to a specific achievement.

We often use *managed to* and *succeeded in* when there is an idea that the specific achievement was difficult or challenging (e.g. *Blake managed to hang onto the edge of the cliff*).

Succeeded in is used in more formal contexts. Compare: *I managed to climb through the window; The research team succeeded in solving the problem.*

With verbs that refer to the five senses (e.g. *see, hear, touch, smell*), and with verbs that refer to thought processes (e.g. *understand, believe*), we normally use *could*, even when we are talking about specific occasions: *I could see that he'd been running.*

6

• Discuss the sentences with your class. Ask them to look back at the forms in the grammar box to decide which ones to use.

ANSWERS

1 could practise

2 succeeded in coming up with / was able to come up with

7

• Ask students to work individually to choose the correct option to complete the sentences. Let students compare their answers in pairs before checking with the class.

ANSWERS

1 couldn't *or* wasn't able to

2 was able to take

3 could

4 Did she manage

5 could

6 was able to

7 succeeded in getting

8 didn't manage *or* wasn't able

8

• **Optional step** Ask students to read the article for understanding first. Ask: *What's important for Semler?* (To have people around him who can think for themselves.)

• Ask students to work individually to complete the article with appropriate verb forms. Elicit the first answer to get them started. Let students compare answers in pairs before eliciting answers from the class.

ANSWERS

1 managed to reach / succeeded in reaching / was able to reach

2 could get / was able to get

3 managed to arrive / were able to arrive

4 could have / were able to have

5 could think / were able to think

6 managed to do / was able to do / succeeded in doing

Speaking ⟨ my life ⟩

9

• **Optional step** This is a good opportunity for a teacher model and live listening. Describe one of your own personal learning experiences to the class, and ask them to listen and then ask questions. This neatly sets up the task students have to do.

• Ask students to read the learning experiences and choose two. Then ask them to make notes in preparation for describing the experiences. Monitor and help with ideas and vocabulary.

• Organize the class into small groups. Ask students to take turns to explain their experiences. In feedback, ask students to tell the class what they found out about another member of their group.

• As students speak, monitor and listen for errors, noting down any errors you hear which you can write up and focus on in feedback. Write up five or six short sentences containing anonymous errors you heard. Ask students in pairs to correct the errors.

11b Memory

Lesson at a glance
- speaking: memory tests
- listening: memory
- wordbuilding: homonyms
- grammar: future in the past
- pronunciation: contrastive sentence stress
- speaking: making excuses

Speaking

1
- Tell students to look at the photo. Explain that a *junk shop* sells antique or second hand objects, usually for the home.
- Ask students to work in pairs to make a list of objects they see in the photo. Set a two-minute time limit and find out which pair has made the longest list.

EXAMPLE ANSWERS
children's buckets and spades, a stool, a hat stand, lamps, chairs, a rocking horse, a coal scuttle, a frying pan, toys, a fire surround and fire companion sets, a wicker basket, a sledge, tables, jars, telephones, a weighing scales, ornaments, a kettle, a cupboard, a rug, a drum

2
- Ask students to cover or close their books and their notes. Then ask them to write down all the words they can remember (see Teacher development below).
- Ask students to share their lists. Find out which students remembered most and elicit any techniques they used to memorize the words.

Extra activity
Ask students to imagine they have their own junk shop. Tell students to describe the shop as if they were showing someone around, pointing out all the objects.

Background information
Portobello Road Market is an historical market in Notting Hill, London. Along the long and winding road are many antique or retro shops as well as lots of cafés. Saturday is market day – lots of stalls are set up along the road to complement the permanent shops.

Teacher development

Memory techniques
A significant part of learning a language is memorizing large quantities of words and phrases. Consequently, it can be helpful to focus on the use of memory techniques with your students. Here are some tips:
1 People tend to remember words that go together in some way. Consider introducing words in lexical sets based on topic, part of speech or similarity of form.

2 Visualizing words can be an effective way to remember them. Get students to draw pictures to note, revise and recall words. When memorizing, get them to think of the set of words all together in a picture that they can mentally recall and look over.
3 Contextualizing words in a story can be helpful. As students recall the story in their head, the words they want to remember will come to mind.
4 Finding connections between words is a good way of remembering them: synonyms and antonyms, words that begin with the same letter or sound, etc. Encourage students to find and note these connections.

Listening

3
- Discuss the questions with your class and build up a list of things people forget on the board. You could ask students to brainstorm a list in pairs or groups first before eliciting answers from the class.

EXAMPLE ANSWERS
telephone numbers, credit card numbers, internet passwords, birthdays, car insurance renewal dates, people's names, where you put your keys or glasses, what you were about to look up on the internet, the name of a film or book

4 [96]
- Explain to students that they are going to listen to the first part of a talk on memory. Ask students to note down the failures of memory that the psychologist mentions.
- Play the recording. Let students compare their answers in pairs before checking with the class.

ANSWERS
your mind goes blank when you want to say something (i.e. you forgot what you wanted to say); you forgot to send a card for a friend's birthday; you couldn't remember someone's name; you forgot to post a letter; you forgot a (great) idea you wanted to write down

Audioscript [96]

Do these situations sound familiar to you? Have any of these things happened to you? You were about to make a comment in a discussion or meeting, and then your mind went blank. You were supposed to send a friend a card for their birthday, but then you forgot. You recognized someone in the street and would have spoken to them, but you didn't because you couldn't remember their name. You promised you would post a letter for someone and two days later you found it in your pocket. You were going to write down a great idea you had, but when you found a pen and paper, the idea had gone. I could go on, … but I won't because I'm sure everyone recognizes these common failures of memory.

5 🔊 [97]

- Play the second part of the recording. Students listen to the rest of the talk and answer the questions. Let students compare their answers in pairs before checking with the class.

ANSWERS
1 almost every day of her life – by date and time
2 It can be distressing and a burden.
3 Because of the growth of technology or Because we store things on computers and phones so we don't need to remember things ourselves.

Audioscript 🔊 [97]

Everyone thinks they would like to remember more, but, actually, would it make us any happier?

I want to tell you the story of a 41-year-old woman from California known in medical literature as 'AJ', who remembers almost every day of her life since the age of eleven. She remembers that at 12.34 p.m. on Sunday, the 3rd of August 1986, a young man she was attracted to called her on the telephone. She remembers that on the 28th of March 1992, she had lunch with her father at the Beverly Hills Hotel. It's a bit like it is for the rest of us when certain smells bring back strong memories … AJ's memory is stimulated in the most intense way by dates.

You'd think that being able to retrieve facts and knowledge in this way would make us more confident and wiser. But in fact, for AJ, an incredible memory can be distressing too. It is as much a burden as it is a benefit. That's because most people's memories are selective: we remember mostly important things and mostly good things too. AJ remembers every detail, good or bad, important or not.

So when we blame our poor memories for forgetting to send a birthday card, actually we should be grateful also for all the things that our memories hide because they don't need to be remembered or thought about.

Technology of course helps us with this. We don't need to remember the precise content of an email or the exact time of a meeting anymore, because it's stored on our computer or our mobile phone.

But interestingly, the growth of this technology, which psychologists call our external memory, is having an effect on what and how much we remember. Even our memories of happy events – like parties or holidays – get stored in photograph albums on our computers. So our internal memories are probably worse than those of people a hundred years ago. Medical science is trying to address the problem of poor memory and this is what I want to talk about next.

6 🔊 [98]

- Ask students to work individually to choose the correct options to complete the statements. Play the recording. Students listen and check their answers.
- Let students compare their answers in pairs before checking with the class.

ANSWERS
1 dates; smells   4 grateful for
2 more confident   5 external
3 important; good   6 poor

Vocabulary notes

medical literature = medical articles and reports in professional journals and books
evoke = to make you remember and think about
stimulate = to cause something to react in some way
retrieve = to get back, to find again
wise = having a great deal of useful knowledge about life
a burden = something which is physically or figuratively 'heavy', and becomes a problem
a benefit = something which helps us
a selective memory = a memory that doesn't remember everything but 'chooses what it wants to remember'
curse something = to regret or be annoyed by something, to wish a situation was different from what it is
grateful for = a feeling that you really want to show your thanks for something, e.g. *I'm grateful for your support.*

Extra activity

Ask students to work in pairs or small groups to make a list of aids they use to remind themselves of things. Here's a possible list: 'sticky notes' on fridges, keeping and carrying a diary or notebook, smartphone apps, checking your social networking site, 'sticky notes' apps on your computer or laptop. Brainstorm a list onto the board in feedback. Then ask students in pairs to talk about when and how they use the different memory aids.

Audioscript 🔊 [98]

Note that audioscript 98 consists of audioscript 96 and 97 combined.

Wordbuilding homonyms

7

- Read the information in the language box to the class. Elicit any common homonyms students can think of, e.g. *play* (v) (= e.g. to play tennis), *play* (n) (= what you see at the theatre), *flat* (n) (= a set of rooms for living in; an apartment), *flat* (adj) (= having a level, consistent surface), *bank* (n) (= the land alongside a river), *bank* (n) (= a financial establishment that lends people money).
- Ask students to look at the words in bold and choose the correct meanings (a or b). Let students compare answers in pairs before checking with the class.

ANSWERS
1 b   2 b   3 b   4 a   5 b

Refer students to Workbook page 99 for further practice.

UNIT 11 Knowledge and learning

Vocabulary notes

dates = palm tree fruits (commonly, from the Middle East)

a date = a specific day of the month or year, e.g. 6th May

go on a date = two people meet and go out to see if they want to have a relationship

found = the past of *find* and the opposite of *look for*

to found a company = to start a new company – here, *found* is the infinitive

a common space = a place where everybody can go

a common activity = an activity which a lot of people typically do

the rest of (something) = what's left (*He ate the rest of the cake.*)

have a rest = to stop working and relax

address a problem = to deal with or face a problem

an address = the name of the place where you live or work, e.g. *11 North Street*

Extra activity

Ask students to work in pairs to think of three homonyms. Tell them to write three pairs of sentences to show the meanings of the homonyms. Then ask them to read out their sentences to another pair of students. Tell them to say 'beep' instead of the homonym. Can their classmates guess the homonyms?

Grammar future in the past

8 [96]

- Tell students to read the information in the grammar box. Then ask them to try to remember the missing words to complete each sentence.
- Play the recording. Students listen and check or complete the sentences.

ANSWERS
1 the idea had gone.
2 your mind went blank.
3 you couldn't remember their name.
4 you forgot.

Refer students to page 176 for further information and practice.

ANSWERS TO GRAMMAR SUMMARY EXERCISES
4
1 was about to go
2 would have called
3 weren't going to be, wouldn't be
4 would definitely be
5 would improve
6 was supposed to use

5
1 were going to   4 was supposed to
2 was about to   5 would have
3 wouldn't
6
1 was about to go
2 was going to go
3 was supposed to be
4 you'd/you would never borrow
5 'd/would have bought

Grammar note

Future in the past forms are used to express the idea that in the past you thought something would happen in the future.

Compare the use of *be going to*, *be about to*, *be supposed to* and *will* (+ infinitive) to talk about the future with the use of *was/were going to*, *was/were about to*, *was/were supposed to* and *would* (+ infinitive). Effectively the uses are the same – just one tense back:

Jane was going to come, but she changed her mind. (a plan)

I had a feeling that the holiday was going to be a disaster. (a prediction)

He promised he would call. (a promise)

I'm about to go. (= on the point – it's happening in a moment); *I was about to go.* (= I was on the point ...) Note that *I was on the point of ...* ; *I was on the verge of ...* are more idiomatic synonyms of this use.

You were supposed to ... = people expected you to ...

Vocabulary notes

Note the use of *them* in this phrase: *You recognized someone in the street and would have spoken to them, but you didn't because ...*

Point out that in English, *them* can be used to refer to a single, unknown 'someone' to avoid using *him* or *her*, which are gender specific.

9

- Discuss the question with your class.

ANSWER
no

Grammar note

Use concept check questions to narrow down meaning. For each example sentence in the grammar box, ask:

Did you intend to do (the action)?

Did you actually do it?

Note that while the future in the past is mostly used with actions that weren't completed (*You were going to write a letter, but you didn't.*), it's possible to use the form with actions that actually are completed (*You promised you'd post the letter – and you did. Thank you!*).

11b Memory **203**

10

- **Optional step** Ask students to read the text quickly for understanding first. Set a focus task: *What is the memory patient's problem?* (He could only remember events before 1960 and only lived in the present.)
- Ask students to work individually to choose the correct verb forms to complete the description of another memory patient. Elicit the first answer to get students started. Let students compare answers in pairs before checking with the class.

> ANSWERS
>
> 1 was going to ask
> 2 was supposed to be
> 3 would have told
> 4 it would have meant
> 5 was about to ask
> 6 would be

11 💿 [99]

- Start by asking students to look at the first transformation and say how the sentence has changed (*am* becomes *was* – one tense change).
- Ask students to work individually to rewrite the original plans using future in the past forms.
- Play the recording for students to check their answers. Check answers with the class.

> EXAMPLE ANSWERS
>
> 1 was going to ask
> 2 was supposed to be (*was going to be* or *was planning to be* could be used here, but they are not in the recording; students may suggest *should have been*, which is also possible)
> 3 would have sent (*was going to send* is also possible, but is not in the recording)
> 4 were supposed to arrive
> 5 was about to announce
> 6 was going to build

Audioscript 💿 [99]

1 I was going to ask Sarah to come, but I asked Kate instead.

2 She was supposed to be in Cairo this week for a meeting, but she's ill so she couldn't go.

3 He would have sent me the original, but he couldn't find it so he sent me a copy.

4 We were supposed to arrive there by ten o'clock, but the train didn't get in until eleven.

5 He was about to announce his retirement, but now he thinks he'll stay until next year.

6 The council was going to build a new shopping mall, but residents opposed the idea.

Pronunciation contrastive sentence stress

12a 💿 [99]

- Ask students to work in pairs to underline the contrasting facts.
- Play the recording again and ask students to note the words that are stressed in order to exaggerate the contrast (see Pronunciation note below).
- Ask students to work in pairs to practise saying the sentences.

> ANSWERS
>
> 1 I was going to ask Sarah to come, <u>but I asked **Kate** instead</u>.
> 2 She was supposed to be in Cairo this week, <u>but she's **ill** so she couldn't go</u>.
> 3 He would have sent me the original, <u>but he couldn't find it so he sent me a **copy**</u>.
> 4 We were supposed to arrive there by ten o'clock, <u>but the train didn't get in until **eleven**</u>.
> 5 He was about to announce his retirement, <u>but now he thinks he'll **stay** until **next year**</u>.
> 6 The council was going to build a new shopping mall, <u>but residents **opposed** the idea</u>.

Pronunciation note

English is a stress-timed language so strong stresses are exaggerated in comparison to many other languages. In these examples the contrasting information is strongly stressed. Get students to notice how *Kate* is very strongly stressed in the first sentence. Get them to notice how all the key words are given a heavy stress in the other sentences (see the words in bold in the answer key).

12b

- Ask students to work individually to complete the sentences with a contrasting idea. Elicit one or two ideas to get students started.
- Once students have prepared sentences, tell them to underline the key words to stress.
- Ask students to work in pairs to read out their sentences. Their partner identifies which words were stressed and why.

> EXAMPLE ANSWERS
>
> 1 He was going to take the day <u>off</u>, but they needed him at <u>work</u> after all.
> 2 We were <u>supposed</u> to be going to Italy, but Jack fell ill, so they <u>couldn't</u> go.
> 3 I would have <u>driven</u>, but the <u>train</u> is <u>quicker</u> in fact.
> 4 They were about to buy a new <u>TV</u>, but then decided to get a new <u>tablet</u> instead.
> 5 I was going to order the <u>fish</u>, but the waiter said they'd run <u>out</u>.

Speaking my life
13

- Organize the class into pairs. Give students a few minutes to choose one of the three situations and prepare things to say. Encourage them to use future in the past forms as part of their excuses.

- Once they are ready, ask pairs to act out their conversation.

- Then organize the class into new pairs. Ask students to improvise other conversations using the suggested situations.

- In feedback, point out any errors with future in the past forms that you notice during this exercise.

Extra activity

Depending on the age of your class, vary the scenarios here, e.g. you lost somebody's watch; you didn't do your homework; you forgot to go to a party.

11c Who's a clever bird, then?

Lesson at a glance
- reading: how animals think
- critical thinking: explaining ideas
- word focus: *learn*
- speaking: types of learner

Reading
1

- **Optional step** Ask students to look at the picture and heading, and explain the use of the expression *Who's a clever bird, then?* (often expressed as *Who's a clever boy, then?* It's an amusing expression commonly taught to parrots – and a patronizing way to congratulate somebody or say well done).

- Organize the class into pairs to discuss the questions. In feedback, elicit ideas, but do not comment on them. You could build up a list on the board.

- **Optional step** Ask students the following questions as a way of pre-teaching key vocabulary and predicting the text: *Can parrots speak? Can they count? Can they see colours? Can they communicate with us?*

EXAMPLE ANSWERS

Dogs can learn tricks, and can develop skills such as herding sheep, rescuing climbers, guiding and helping blind and disabled people or sniffing out drugs.

Horses can be trained to jump fences or perform dressage moves.

Other animals such as elephants, camels, buffalo and oxen can be trained to carry or pull heavy things.

Primates such as chimpanzees and gorillas have been trained to do human-like things: using tools, lighting fires, spelling out words, using sign language, etc.

Background information

An online search shows that primates, ranging from bonobos and chimpanzees to monkeys and lemurs, are the brightest (they can count, communicate and use tools). Dolphins and whales are intelligent, as are elephants. Dogs, rats and pigs rate highly. Among birds, parrots, crows and pigeons are reported to be the most intelligent.

2 💿 [100]

- Ask students to read the article and answer the question. Let students compare answers in pairs before checking with the class.

- **Optional step** The reading text is recorded. You could play the recording and ask students to read and listen.

ANSWERS

He showed that he understood the concept of colour, shape and numbers. He also learned some language and was also able to express his feelings using it.

Vocabulary notes

acquire (information) = to get and keep (information)

adapt = to change in order to deal with a new situation

distinguish = to see the difference between

edible = you can eat it

predator = an animal that hunts and kills other animals (opposite = *prey*)

keep track of (your flock) = to watch or listen to know where your flock is and what it is doing

frustrated = the angry feeling you get when you can't do something

moody = changing from a good to bad stage of mind regularly, for no particular reason

Note the words connected with birds: *beak, perch, flock* (see the glossary); extend this area by asking students to think of other words, e.g. *wing, feather, claw, fly, flap.*

Background information

Irene Maxine Pepperberg (born 1949 in New York) is a scientist noted for her studies in animal cognition. She is a professor of psychology at Brandeis University and a lecturer at Harvard University. She was one of the first scientists to work on language learning in animals other than humans and is active in wildlife conservation, especially in relation to parrots.

3

- Ask students to read the article again and choose true (T), false (F) or not given (NG).

- Let students compare answers in pairs before checking with the class. In feedback, ask students to justify their answers with reference to the article.

ANSWERS

1 T (*I thought if he learned to communicate, I could ask him questions about how he sees the world.*)

2 T (*She let the store assistant choose him because she didn't want other scientists to say that she had deliberately chosen a clever bird.*)

3 F (he could distinguish some numbers – *He could count to six*)

4 T (*you can't do all of this with instinct; thinking must be involved.* Note that the text doesn't mention 'the wild', but it does mention 'predators'.)

5 NG (the text doesn't say how Alex felt about this)

6 T (*Alex also expressed feelings and awareness of others' feelings.*)

4

- Ask students to work in pairs to discuss the question. This is an opportunity for students to reflect on and give a personal response to the text.

ANSWERS

Students' own ideas

Critical thinking explaining ideas

5

- **Optional step** Ask: *How do writers explain complicated ideas to the reader?* Try to elicit ways of explaining ideas from your class.

- Ask students to read the article again and underline the sentences or phrases used to explain the points in the list (1–6).

- **Optional step** At the end, you could ask students which method of explaining ideas they found the most effective.

ANSWERS

1 *acquiring information about the world around it and interpreting it* (paragraph 1)

2 *I thought if he learned to communicate, I could ask him questions about how he sees the world.* (paragraph 2)

3 *most researchers thought Pepperberg was certain to fail. 'Some people actually called me crazy for trying this,' she said.* (paragraph 3)

4 *He also made up words for new things: he called an apple a 'banerry' (a combination of banana and cherry, his favourite fruits).* (paragraph 5)

5 *And like humans, these birds must adapt to changing relationships and environments.* (paragraph 5)

   (Also followed up in paragraph 6 with several examples: *distinguish colours / categorize things / know the shapes of predators / have a concept of numbers*)

6 *Alex also expressed feelings and awareness of others' feelings. If Pepperberg grew frustrated, Alex could notice this and offer an 'I'm sorry' to her; 'He's moody ... he interrupts the others, or he gives the wrong answer just to be difficult.'* (paragraph 7)

6

- Ask students to work in pairs to read the ways of explaining (a–c) and decide which of them are used to explain the ideas in Exercise 5.

- **Optional step** At the end, you could ask students which method of explaining ideas they found the most effective.

ANSWERS

1 a 2 a 3 c 4 b 5 b 6 b

Word focus *learn*

7

- **Optional step** Write *learn* on the board. Ask students in pairs to brainstorm any words connected with *learn*. For example: *study, teach, learn a language, learn a trade, learn how to do something, learning, learners.*

- Ask students to work in pairs to find and explain the two expressions with *learn*.

ANSWERS

1 to learn something so that you remember it without having to look at notes or have help in some way
2 to learn something through having a difficult experience or by making lots of mistakes

8

- Ask students to explain the expressions with *learn* to their partner. Tell them to use the context of each sentence to work out meaning.

ANSWERS

1 learning some things specific to a particular job which will make it easier
2 learn the basic things before you try to learn more complicated or difficult things
3 you can always learn new things, however old you are
4 have an experience (usually negative) whilst doing something which is memorable and therefore means you won't make the same mistake in the future
5 accept it (even if you don't like it)
6 understand when you have done things wrong (and therefore not make those mistakes in the future)

9

- Ask students to work individually. Tell them to choose two expressions from Exercise 8 and use them to write sentences about their own learning experiences. You could provide a model answer yourself to get them started.
- When students are ready, ask them to work in pairs to share sentences. Ask them to read each sentence and say 'beep' instead of the *learn* phrase. Students must guess the missing phrase.

EXAMPLE ANSWERS

I'm an electrician – I've **learned some tricks of the trade**, like how to use glue to fix a switch.

When I started my job in the office, I tried to deal with clients without any help, but things went wrong. I realized I needed training. **I've learned my lesson.** I now know you have to **learn to walk before you can run**.

I've finally learned how use Twitter. **It's never too late to learn.**

Extra activity

Ask students to share the following in groups:
– something they learned by heart at primary school
– something they have learned to live with
– a trick of their trade, or someone else's
– a mistake that taught them a lesson

Speaking my life

10

- Ask students to work in pairs to do the quiz on page 154 of the Student's Book.
- Tell students to check their answers on page 155 of the Student's Book. In feedback, find out what sort of learners your students are.

11

- Organize the pairs into small groups. Tell them to discuss the questions and add more ideas to the list.
- In feedback, find out what ideas students have, and draw some conclusions about how they can learn more effectively.

EXAMPLE ANSWERS

Auditory: read stories (in English newspapers, books, magazines) and retell them; listen to audio recordings – and repeat what you hear; talk to yourself in a foreign language – have an internal monologue; have speaking partners – people to practise with in real life or on Skype; listen to songs in English

Visual: use pictures to learn words; watch English language films with the subtitles on; keep a vocabulary book and draw illustrations of each new word

Kinaesthetic: use roleplay and drama – act out situations; use mime to learn words; do 'physical' things with language, e.g. physically categorize words and phrases on strips of paper

Teacher development

Visual, auditory and kinaesthetic learners

Learners receive and learn new information in a combination of visual, auditory and kinaesthetic learning styles. However, for each learner, one or two of these receiving styles tends to be dominant and therefore the most effective. The dominant receiving style may also vary depending on the type of task. Note that, in life, the way we receive information is often forced upon us. At nursery school, we learn kinaesthetically, through school it is often visually presented, and in college and on into the business environment, information tends to be presented through auditory means, such as lectures or presentations. In the language classroom, when possible, present information using all three styles. This will ensure that all learning types are catered for. Here are some ideas.

1 For auditory learners: Begin lessons with a brief explanation of what is coming; summarize what students have learned at the end; question learners to draw as much information from them as possible; include auditory activities, such as brainstorming in pairs and buzz groups.

2 For visual learners: Use graphs, charts, illustrations or other visual aids; have students draw pictures in the margins.

3 For kinaesthetic learners: Use activities that get the learners up and moving; play music, when appropriate, during activities; use roleplays and drama; give frequent stretch breaks (brain breaks).

11d Keep learning

Lesson at a glance
- real life: getting clarification
- pronunciation: linking in question forms

Real life getting clarification

1

- **Optional step** With books closed, start by writing *adult education* on the board. Brainstorm courses typically offered in adult education and write them on the board. Alternatively, download and show a real webpage, and ask students to find and make a list of courses.

- Ask students to look at the list of courses and use dictionaries to check meanings if necessary. You could ask students to discuss the question in pairs before eliciting answers from the class.

OPTIONAL STEP EXAMPLE ANSWERS

Adult education courses often focus on practical skills, so students may suggest the following when brainstorming courses: woodwork and carpentry, plumbing, electronics, bricklaying, gardening skills, computer skills, life drawing, local history, local architecture, archaeology, film appreciation, foreign languages, etc.

Vocabulary notes

basic = simple and at a beginner level

car mechanics = learning how a car works and how to repair problems

vlogging = a form of blogging for which the medium is video (it is also known as video blogging) – vlog entries often combine embedded videos with text

flower arranging = learning how to select and combine flowers to make beautiful displays

art appreciation = understanding art and how and why artists do what they do

screenwriting = writing for film or TV

web design = learning how to set up your own website with graphics

2 [101]

- Tell students they are going to listen to a telephone conversation between two people. Play the recording. Students listen and answer the questions.

- Let students compare their answers in pairs.

ANSWERS

1 a history of art course – for interest, but not an exam course

2 a one-year art appreciation course – the history of art course is an A-level exam course so isn't appropriate for Ahmad

3 He decides to have a think about it, i.e. he will consider the course, but he doesn't sign up for the course while on the telephone.

Audioscript [101]

A = Ahmad; L = Liz

A: Hi there, I'm interested in taking a class at your college – umm, the history of art course.

L: Is that the two-year A-level course?

A: Sorry, what do you mean by 'A-level'?

L: The A-level art history course is a two-year pre-university course with examinations at the end of each year.

A: Oh, no, no, no, I don't want to take any exams. It's just for interest.

L: OK. In that case, we have a one-year art appreciation course.

A: Sorry. Can you speak up a little? I can't hear you very well.

L: Yes, we have a one-year art appreciation course.

A: Umm, can you explain what the course involves?

L: Yeah, it's a two-hour class once a week and, basically, it teaches you how to look at art, so that you can appreciate it better.

A: No, sorry, I'm not really with you. Are you saying that it doesn't really deal with the history of art?

L: Umm, there's some history of art in it, but it's mainly learning about the techniques that artists use and what paintings mean.

A: Could you give me an example of the kind of thing students do in the class?

L: Typically, students look at works of art and comment on them. Then they're told more about the artist, what he or she was trying to achieve and then they look at their work again, to see if they see it differently.

A: OK. It sounds quite interesting. What was the course called again?

L: Art appreciation.

A: And when is it?

L: Every Tuesday – in term time, that is – from 7 p.m. till 9 p.m., starting on … one minute … yeah, starting on the 29th of September. The cost is £298 for the year, unless you're a registered student.

A: Hang on a second. That's too much to take in all at once. I'm trying to write it down. I didn't catch the start date. Did you say the 29th of November?

L: No, the 29th of September.

A: OK. Well, thanks. I'll have a think about it, but it sounds good.

L: No worries. Bye.

Vocabulary note

No worries = *Don't worry, That's fine* or *Don't mention it* depending on the context. It's an Australian expression that has become commonly used in British English.

Background information

In the **British education system**, students take GCSE (General Certificate of Secondary Education) external examinations at the age of 16 and A-level (General Certificate of Education – Advanced Level) exams at the age of 18. A-levels are seen as exams taken to get into college or university. In the two years at school before taking A-levels, students specialize in three or four A-level subjects (e.g. English, History and Art).

3

• Ask students to read the expressions and decide which ones Ahmed uses to ask for repetition (R) and which he uses to ask for explanation (E). Let students compare answers in pairs before checking with the class.

• In feedback, go through the phrases, checking meaning and use (see Vocabulary notes below).

ANSWERS

What do you mean by … ? E
Can you speak up a little? R
Can you explain what … ? E
I'm not really with you. E
Are you saying that … ? E
Could you give me an example of … ? E
What was … again? R
Hang on a second. That's too much to take in all at once. R
I didn't catch … R
Did you say … ? R

Vocabulary notes

speak up = to talk louder
I'm not with you = I don't understand what you want to say
Hang on = to wait (informal)
take in = to understand
catch = here, it means to hear

4 💿 [101]

• Ask students to listen to the conversation again and complete the expressions. Let students compare answers in pairs before checking with the class.

ANSWERS

What do you mean by A-level?
Can you explain what the course involves?
Are you saying that it doesn't really deal with the history of art?
Could you give me an example of the kind of thing students do in the class?
What was the course called again?
I didn't catch the start date.
Did you say the 29th of November?

Pronunciation linking in question forms
5a 💿 [102]

• Read the introduction to the class.

• Play the recording. Students listen and note the linking (see Pronunciation notes below).

• **Optional step** Ask students to practise saying the sentences. You could read them out and ask students to repeat, or play the recording again, and ask them to repeat.

Audioscript 💿 [102]

Are you saying the course is full?
Did you say Tuesday?
Can you speak up a little?
What do you mean?
Could you give me an example?

Pronunciation notes

Note the use of the weakly stressed /ə/ sound when saying these combinations in fast speech: *do you* /d(ə)jə/; *did you* /dɪdjə/; *could you* /kʊdjə/.

5b

• Organize the class into pairs to practise saying the sentences.

• **Optional step** Ask pairs to underline parts of each sentence where there is linking, and use phonemic script to show how to pronounce the linked sounds before practising the sentences.

Pronunciation notes

Note the linking between the auxiliary verb and pronoun (shown by a line) and the phonemic pronunciation of these sounds:

Can you /kənjə/ *explain what you mean?*
What are you /əjə/ *trying to say?*
Could you /kʊdjə/ *repeat that?*
Did you /dɪdjə/ *mean September?*
What do you /d(ə)jə/ *think?*

6

• Organize the class into new pairs. Ask students to decide which role to take (A or B). Give students two minutes to prepare what to say. Encourage them to look back at the getting clarification language box and use the expressions to organize their ideas.

• **Optional step** Instead of preparing individually, ask students to prepare in pairs of As and pairs of Bs. When they are ready, split the pairs so that an A student is with a B student.

• Ask students to roleplay the conversations. Tell fast-finishing students to swap roles and act out a second conversation.

• As students speak, monitor and note errors and examples of good language use. At the end, provide some feedback on language students have used.

11e The wrong course

Lesson at a glance
- writing: an email about a misunderstanding
- writing skill: linking contrasting ideas

Writing an email about a misunderstanding

1
- **Optional step** Start by asking students to look at the look and layout of the email, without reading it. Ask students who the email is for (we don't know the name), who it's from (Karen Redman) and what else they notice: fixed language (*Dear Sir/Madam; Yours faithfully*), three main paragraphs. Establish that it's a formal email.
- Ask students to work in pairs to read the email and discuss the questions. In feedback, ask students to justify answers with reference to language used in the email (see Teacher development below).

> **ANSWERS**
> 1 b   2 c   3 b

Teacher development

Recognizing tone and the writer's feelings

Recognizing tone and the writer's feelings in a text can be important for understanding meaning. Here are some suggestions to help students to read between the lines, where texts demand this.

1 Ask students to establish the relationship between writer and reader. So, in the text above, ask: *Who is writing?* (Karen – a student) *Who is she writing to?* (a person in charge of courses, but she doesn't know them) *What does Karen want?* (her money back).

2 Ask students to recognize formality (or lack of it). Ask: *Is the situation formal?* (Yes) *What formal conventions are used?* (no contractions, fixed expressions like *Dear Sir/Madam* and formal vocabulary – *enrolled, suitable for, unsatisfactory*). Karen's email is a mix of the very formal (*When I originally enquired ...* ; *I look forward to hearing from you*) and the personal (*I don't blame ... he does his best ... I am just holding everyone else back*).

3 Ask students to find any phrases that show emotion. In the email, there are only 'frustration' phrases (*I am just holding everyone else back*; *I hope you will understand how unsatisfactory the situation is for me*).

4 Ask students to find any phrases that complain or apologize. There are phrases that complain (*I was told that it was suitable for people with no previous knowledge ... ; everyone else on the course seems to know a lot already ... they move very quickly on to more complicated ideas*). There are no apologies. However, the complaints are balanced by expressions saying it is her fault or no one is to blame. The tone is balanced, fair and reasonable.

5 Get students to say what the tone is in their own words. Ask: *How would you feel about or respond to this email?*

2
- Ask students to discuss the questions and give reasons for their answers.
- **Optional step** Ask students to imagine they are administrators at the college and to work in small groups to decide on a response.

> **EXAMPLE ANSWERS**
>
> They may decide to give a refund because the course was misrepresented, because they don't want to have frustrated students, because the reasonable tone of the email persuaded them, or because they don't want an angry student or to get any negative publicity.
>
> They may decide not to give a refund because people can't just change their mind about a course halfway through, because the woman has no grounds for complaint – she is getting the course she paid for, or because the email was unpersuasive – the woman admits it is her fault – the tutor and course are good.
>
> Other possibilities include offering the woman a different course, offering a meeting to talk through the problem with administrators, offering a 1:1 session with the tutor, or suggesting ways she can keep up with the course.

Writing skill linking contrasting ideas

3a
- Ask students to work individually to find the sentences in the email that express the ideas, and say what words or phrases are used to link them. Elicit the first answer to get students started. Let students compare answers in pairs before checking with the class.
- In feedback, point out how the linking phrases are used in a sentence (see Grammar note below).

> **ANSWERS**
>
> 1 I was told that it was suitable for people with no previous knowledge of car mechanics. <u>But in fact</u> everyone else on the course seems to know a lot already.
>
> 2 ... <u>despite the fact that</u> the lessons generally start with a basic concept, they move very quickly onto more complicated ideas.
>
> 3 I don't blame the teacher. <u>On the contrary,</u> he does his best to explain concepts to me.
>
> 4 They know how an engine works already, <u>whereas</u> I have no background at all in mechanics.
>
> 5 <u>While</u> I appreciate it's not really anyone's fault that this has happened, I hope you will understand how unsatisfactory the situation is for me.

Grammar notes

1 *But in fact* = (but) in reality / the truth is that; note that *but in fact* can join two sentences (as here) or two clauses (e.g. *I was told that it was suitable for people with no previous knowledge of car mechanics, but, in fact, everyone else ...*)

2 We use *despite* or *in spite of* + *the fact that* + clause when joining two clauses and expressing a contrast; we can also use *despite* or *in spite of* + *-ing*. *Although* and *even though* are also used when joining two clauses and expressing a contrast.

3 More formal phrases such as *On the contrary, On the one hand … On the other hand* and *However* are used to join two sentences, not two clauses.

4/5 *while, whereas* and the more formal *whilst* are used to join two clauses.

3b

- Ask students to rewrite the ideas in Exercise 3a using the new linking words and phrases. Let students compare answers in pairs before checking with the class.

> **ANSWERS**
>
> So **although** the lessons start with a basic concept, they move very quickly onto more complicated ideas.
>
> They know how an engine works already. I, **on the other hand**, have no background at all in mechanics.

3c

- Ask students to work individually to complete the sentences with appropriate linking phrases. Let students compare answers in pairs before checking with the class.

> **ANSWERS**
>
> 1 Despite the fact that
> 2 but in fact
> 3 Despite the fact that
> 4 but
> 5 whereas / while
> 6 On the contrary

Grammar notes

Despite the fact that and *Although* are used for real or surprising contrasts. Note that in sentences 1 and 3 above, there is a real contrast.

By contrast, *whereas, while* and *whilst* are used to say two things are different. In sentence 5, the two facts are different.

Compare these examples:

John is tall, whereas his brother is short. (different)

Although John's brother is short, he's great at basketball. (surprising contrast)

It's important to show students that the uses here are not synonymous.

4

- **Optional step** Start with a class discussion. Ask students to suggest possible misunderstandings, e.g. course is the wrong level, (not) an exam course, wrong subject, the age of the other students, teaching room isn't suitable, course not at the place you expected, cost was different, length of course is different.

- Remind students of the courses at the Adult Education centre on page 136. Ask students to spend one minute making notes about what they want to include in their email. Monitor at this stage and help with ideas and vocabulary. You could let students compare their ideas in pairs and ask for help.

- Ask students to write their email. This task could be set for homework.

5

- Ask students to work in pairs and exchange their written work. Ask students to check their partner's work and suggest how to improve it.

- **Optional step** Ask students to revise and rewrite their email based on their partner's suggestions.

Extra activity

Pin the emails on classroom walls or a noticeboard. Ask students to walk round, read the emails and decide whether they would return the students' money or not.

Alternatively, use this as an opportunity to use technology: ask students to write and send an email to another specific student online in class. Once students have received each other's email, ask them to write a reply. Monitor and check what students have written on screen. Alternatively, this activity could be done as homework.

11f Paraguay shaman

Before you watch

1

- Ask students to look at the photo and the caption, and answer the questions. Elicit some ideas from students, but do not comment at this stage (students will find out more when they watch the video).

Background information

Shamanism is carried out by 'shamans'. Shamans claim special powers. They change their state of consciousness, perhaps by dressing in animal skins, singing and dancing, or taking drugs, and this prepares them to communicate with the spirit world.

Key vocabulary

2a

- Ask students to work individually to read the sentences and guess the meaning of the words from context.
- Let students compare their answers in pairs before moving on to Exercise 2b.

2b

- Ask students to match the words in bold in Exercise 2a with the definitions. Let students compare their answers in pairs before checking with the class.

ANSWERS

1 d   2 e   3 a   4 c   5 b

Teacher development

Learning words with personalized examples

One way of making sure that students understand and can use new words effectively is to ask them to write or say their own personalized examples. This also makes language more memorable. Here, for example, ask students to name and describe a nature reserve in their country or an isolated part of their country. Ask them how they would heal a small cut, or what illnesses antibiotics can be used to cure. Ask where you might hear chanting (in church, at a football match, at a demonstration).

While you watch

3 ■◀ [11.1]

- Ask students to watch the video and note answers to the questions. Play the whole video. Let students compare answers in pairs before checking with the class.

ANSWERS

1 a rainforest / nature reserve in Paraguay
2 deforestation
3 plants that will help cure diseases like cancer

Videoscript ■◀ 11.1

0.00–0.20   Somewhere in this forest, maybe in this plant or that herb, there could be a cure for an illness like diabetes, malaria, or even common fevers and colds.

But as the plants disappear, the potential cures disappear with them.

0.21–0.53   The rainforests of Paraguay have been a source of medicinal cures for a long time. Traditional folk healers often show us where to find the plants that provide the medicines. Paraguay's famous healers, called 'shamans', have a deep knowledge of local medicinal plants – the equivalent of the knowledge contained in an entire medical library.

But Paraguay has one of the highest deforestation rates in the world. That's why researchers believe it's a priority to record the shaman's extensive knowledge before the forest disappears.

0.54–1.27   The journey begins in Paraguay's isolated Mbaracayú Forest Nature Reserve and the nearby native community of Tekoha Ryapu, where shaman Gervasio lives.

To reach Gervasio, a group of researchers set out on a long journey through the reserve.

Meanwhile, at the village, Gervasio is using chants and prayers, perhaps to make a spiritual connection with the forest.

When he feels ready, Gervasio and his wife take the group on the search.

1.31–2.03   They are looking for a plant called Suruvi, also known as *Jatropha isabelli*, which is used to treat and cure various illnesses. Scientists are very interested in this family of plants for cancer research. Gervasio brings the root back to the village, where his wife puts it in a pot of water to prepare tea.

Scientists have published a book to help record and transmit Gervasio's forest knowledge. The book helps people to easily identify and study local plants.

2.04–2.24   Recording and studying Paraguayan plants for possible medical cures is urgent business, some may even call it an emergency.

Medicinal plants that were once healthy and multiplying are now disappearing – and the possibility of finding new medical cures is disappearing with them.

4 ■◀ [11.1]

- Ask students to read the statements carefully and note what sort of information might be incorrect.
- When students are ready, play the video again. Students underline the incorrect words in each statement. Let students compare their answers in pairs before checking with the class.

ANSWERS

1 heart disease (colds)
2 shamans (cures)
3 encyclopaedia (library)
4 research facility (native community)
5 dancing (praying/chanting)
6 fever (cancer)
7 local dish (tea)
8 online (in a book)

After you watch

Vocabulary in context

5a ■◀ [11.2]

- **Optional step** You may wish to ask students to look at the glossary at the bottom of the page and check that they understand the words.

UNIT 11   Knowledge and learning

- Explain that students are going to watch some clips from the video which contain some new words and phrases. They need to choose the correct meaning of the words.
- Play the clips. When each multiple-choice question appears, pause the clip so that students can choose the correct definition. You could let students compare answers in pairs before discussing with the class.

ANSWERS
1 c   2 a   3 b   4 b   5 c

Videoscript ■◄ 11.2

1 As the plants disappear, the **potential** cures disappear with them.
   a most effective
   b rare
   c possible
2 The rainforests of Paraguay have been **a source of** medicinal cures …
   a a store or supply of
   b an idea or inspiration for
   c a hiding place or secret home for
3 … it's a priority to record the shaman's **extensive** knowledge …
   a specific and precise
   b wide and detailed
   c special and uncommon
4 Gervasio brings the **root** back to the village …
   a the main body of the plant
   b the underground part of a plant
   c the part of the plant which holds the seeds
5 … published a book to help record and **transmit** Gervasio's forest knowledge.
   a preserve
   b advertise
   c pass on

Vocabulary notes

potential = possible in the future (note that this adjective can only go in front of a noun, so, *a potential cure* but not *a cure is potential*)

source = where something comes from (coal mines are a source of coal, for example)

extensive = very large in amount or degree (extensive damage = damage everywhere; extensive menu = a lot on the menu, covering many different types of food)

root = the root or roots of a plant are under the ground – typical root vegetables include carrots and potatoes

transmit = this verb is usually used to describe how radio waves send signals

5b

- Students work individually to complete the sentences. Elicit one or two ideas for the first sentence to get them started. Let students compare sentences in pairs. Invite a few students to share their sentences with the class.

EXAMPLE ANSWERS
1 *The internet* is the best way to transmit knowledge.
2 *My grandfather* has always been a source of wisdom and learning in my life.
3 A potential disadvantage of drinking too much coffee is *high blood pressure*.

6

- Organize the class into small groups. Ask students to work together to make lists. Remind them to add another problem and cure to their list. Monitor and help with ideas and vocabulary. Encourage students to explain any interesting ideas they may have to group members and to share experiences.

EXAMPLE ANSWERS
1 vitamin C, echinacea (a type of flower), fresh ginger root, eucalyptus essential oil, lemon hot drink, citrus fruits, tea (especially elderflower tea)
2 the same things as for colds and also: androgrhais, boneset, elderberry
3 cloves, garlic, pepper and salt, onion, warm salt water
4 epsom salts, chicken soup, mint, camomile tea, rice water
5 indigestion: ginger, peppermint; sore throat: honey and lemon, warm salt water

7

- Organize the class into groups of four or five. Ask students to discuss the beliefs. In feedback, ask different groups what they think before giving the answers.

ANSWERS
1 T   2 F   3 T   4 F   5 T   6 T

Background information

1 Omega-3 fatty acids are common in many fish and help build brain-cell membranes.
2 Spicy food can irritate existing ulcers, but it isn't the cause. Typically, a bacterium called Helicobacter pylori causes ulcers.
3 Chicken soup speeds up the movement of mucus through the nose, which can relieve congestion.
4 Rhinoviruses, which cause the common cold, are passed on in low temperatures, but you won't get an infection simply because your hair is wet.
5 Eating heavy meals with a high fat content late at night can give you indigestion, which in turn disturbs your sleep, and disturbed sleep often involves more nightmares.
6 Lemon juice helps cut through congestion and honey soothes the throat.

UNIT 11 Review and memory booster

Exercises 3 and 5 are Memory Booster activities. For more information about these activities and how they benefit students, see page 10 of this Teacher's Book.

I can ... check boxes

As an alternative to asking students to simply tick the *I can* ... boxes, you could ask them to give themselves a score from 1 to 4 (1 = not very confident; 4 = very confident) for each language area. If students score 1 or 2 for a language area, refer them to additional practice activities in the Workbook and Grammar summary exercises.

Grammar

1

• Ask students to work individually to choose the correct options to complete the story. Let students compare answers in pairs before checking with the class.

ANSWERS

1 would
2 could
3 was able to
4 were going to
5 would have remained
6 Was he really able

2

• Ask students to work individually to read the story in Exercise 1 again and answer the questions. Elicit answers from the class.

ANSWERS

1 Because the man was seeking asylum in Brazil.
2 That we don't have enough evidence that he can speak as many languages as he says he can, but that even if he only speaks half as many, it's still impressive.

3 >> MB

• Ask students to work in pairs and take it in turns to share information about themselves. At the feedback stage, invite a few individuals to tell the class what they found out about their partner.

Vocabulary

4

• Ask students to work in pairs to complete the expressions about learning with a verb or preposition. Let students compare answers in pairs before checking with the class.

ANSWERS

1 pass; revise
2 from; hard
3 inspire/motivate/encourage; with
4 get/grasp/understand; up
5 take; by
6 walk; run

5 >> MB

• Ask students to work in pairs to look at the photos and discuss the questions. Monitor as students speak and encourage them to use vocabulary items from the unit.

EXAMPLE ANSWERS

1 At the Indianapolis Children's Museum children are encouraged to learn with interactive displays, visual displays and real-life stories. At the Lumiar International School in São Paulo children are encouraged to learn by allowing them to learn in a variety of spaces such as play areas, the hall and the dining room, instead of just in classrooms. Most learning is done through collaborative projects and children can leave a lesson if they want to.
2 Students' own answers

Real life

6

• Ask students to work individually to match the phrases 1–5 with the phrases a–e with the same meaning. Let students compare answers in pairs before checking with the class.

ANSWERS

1 d 2 c 3 e 4 a 5 b

7

• Tell students to work individually to think of five facts in Unit 11 about learning and memory.
• Ask students to work in pairs and take turns to tell each other the facts. For each statement the other student should respond with a different phrase from Exercise 6.

Unit 12 Money

Opener

1

- Ask students to look at the photo and the caption. Discuss the question with your class. Elicit ideas from students in feedback.

> **ANSWER**
>
> Students' own answers

2 🔊 [103]

- Ask students to offer opinions about the statement. You could ask students to discuss their opinions in pairs or threes first.
- Play the recording. Ask students to listen and note whether each speaker agrees or disagrees with the statement. Let students compare their answers in pairs before checking with the class.

> **ANSWERS**
>
> Speaker 1: disagrees
> Speaker 2: agrees (in theory)

Audioscript 🔊 [103]

Speaker 1

No, it does matter, absolutely. Because you end up with a divided society instead of a united one – the haves and the have nots, as some people call it. Apparently in Japan, the income gap between rich and poor is pretty insignificant. That's partly because bosses don't take huge salaries. They understand that that would be socially irresponsible. It'd create feelings of envy and resentment among people who were worse off. The result is that Japan actually has a much more united society than other western countries where there are big differences in pay between top and bottom.

Speaker 2

Well, I think it's OK if the rich are getting richer – as long as everyone else's standard of living is rising too. In other words, if people who aren't earning so much can nevertheless see that their buying power is increasing. Of course that depends on their wages going up faster than the cost of living. But actually, I think it's how people *see* things that's important. If they think their quality of life is good, then they won't mind if the rich have a better standard of living. On the other hand, if they think they're getting a bad deal and that the rich aren't contributing, then they'll complain.

3 🔊 [103]

- **Optional step** Ask students to remember or predict the missing words before they listen again.
- Play the recording again. Students listen and complete the phrases. Let students compare answers in pairs before checking with the class.

- **Optional step** Rather than asking students to define the phrases in feedback, ask them to work in pairs to put the phrases in sentences that show their meaning, or ask them to say what ideas each phrase is connected to, e.g. *standard of living* = the economy; *haves and have nots* = rich and poor.

> **ANSWERS**
>
> 1 living
> 2 nots
> 3 income
> 4 power
> 5 living
> 6 life

Vocabulary notes

the haves and the have nots = a fixed expression meaning the rich and poor; people who can afford to live well and buy things, and people who can't

the income gap = the difference between what different people get paid (a chief executive might be earning millions while the person who cleans her office might be on a few thousand a year); note, we also say *pay gap*

the standard of living = the type of life a person or society has according to the amount of money they have; note *a high/low standard of living*

people's buying power = in economics, how much extra money people have to buy things after paying for essentials

the cost of living = how much it costs to pay for essentials (food, heating, rent)

quality of life = how good your life is regardless of how rich you are – a person in a low-paid job may have a better quality of life than a person in a high paid job because they work fewer hour and have less stress and more freedom to do things they enjoy

4

- Organize the class into pairs or small groups to decide whether the two statements are true or false. In feedback, encourage students to justify their answers with evidence.

> **EXAMPLE ANSWERS**
>
> 1 True – I think we have a better standard of living than a few years ago – many people have smarter clothes and furniture, better cars. However, I also think that people are more careful with their money.
>
> 2 True – people work long hours and they don't feel very secure in their jobs. But having said that, people do try to make the most of their free time – eating out, doing activities, taking weekend breaks away and so on.

Extra activity

Write the following phrases on the board and ask students to work in small groups to say or guess what they mean.

living wage

rising prices

minimum wage

performance-related pay

Christmas bonus

Ask students to look up meanings in dictionaries. Then ask them to say how they relate to their own societies and economies.

12a Saving for a rainy day

Lesson at a glance

- vocabulary: money
- reading: Norway's riches
- grammar: focus adverbs *only*, *just*, *even*
- pronunciation: focus adverbs
- speaking: the economy in your country

Vocabulary money

1

- **Optional step** Start by asking students to explain the title: *Saving for a rainy day*. It means saving money in good times (not spending it all) in case there are bad times in the future. Ask students to say how they would express this idiom in their first language.

- Ask students to work individually to complete the sentences. Elicit the first answer to get students started.

- In feedback, elicit answers and check students understand all the vocabulary. Ask students whether they agree with the statement.

- **Optional step** You could ask students to put the extra verb in a sentence to show its meaning, e.g. *Could I borrow your pen for a moment, please?*

> **ANSWERS**
>
> 1 earn 2 invest 3 lend 4 save 5 spend 6 owe

Vocabulary notes

1 *earn* = to get money for doing a job

2 *invest in (something)* = to put your money in the stock market, or in a company, or in buying property or art or gold, with the idea that you will make more money

3 *lend (money)* = to give money (or an object) to somebody for a period of time to help them (you expect them to *pay* you *back* – give you the money or the object back); the opposite is *borrow*

4 *save (money)* = to keep money in the bank (and not spend it)

5 *spend (money)* = to buy things with money

6 *owe (money)* = to be in debt; if you borrow from a bank or a friend, you owe money until you pay it back; note the pronunciation: /əʊ/

2

- Ask students to work individually to complete the sentences with the correct noun. Elicit the first answer to get students started. Point out that some of the nouns are formed from verbs in Exercise 1.

- Let students compare their answers in pairs before checking with the class. In feedback, ask students whether they agree with the statements.

> **ANSWERS**
>
> 1 income   4 savings
> 2 investment   5 spending
> 3 loan   6 debts

Vocabulary notes

salary = the money you earn annually for doing your job; *salary* is often used with professional jobs (*a £30,000 a year salary*) whereas *wages* is used with jobs paid on an hourly or daily basis

investment = money put in (stocks, a company, etc.) with the hope of financial gain

loan = money borrowed from a person or bank

savings = money you save

spending = money you spend

debts = money you owe

Note that the word *earnings* can be used to mean money you earn – however, it tends to be used in quite specific cases (e.g. when calculating tax – *What are your average earnings?*) or when talking about the economy (e.g. *earnings in the retail sector have fallen*).

Reading

3

- Start by asking students to brainstorm what they know about Norway in pairs. In feedback, elicit and share ideas with the class.

- **Optional step** Organize students' answers on the board by writing words or phrases next to the three headings: Landscape, People, Industry. After students read, you can then ask them to say what ideas they thought of came up in the article.

EXAMPLE ANSWER

The photo shows a traditional Norwegian village of red, wooden houses in a rocky, mountainous landscape – the houses are by a *fjord*, which is, geologically, a long, narrow inlet with steep sides or cliffs, created by glacial erosion.

Background information

Norway has a total area of 385,000 square kilometres and a population of five million. It's part of Scandinavia in Northern Europe and shares a long eastern border with Sweden. It also borders Russia and Finland in the far north.

Norway is long and narrow and much of its population lives by the sea. It has a rugged, granite landscape of cliffs, mountains, fjords and lakes.

Its capital is Oslo. Other major cities include Bergen, Stavanger and Trondheim. Norway is a kingdom and King Harald V is the current King of Norway.

Norway has extensive reserves of petroleum, natural gas, minerals, wood, seafood, fresh water and hydropower. It produces more oil and natural gas than any other country outside the Middle East.

Students may mention some of the following: Vikings, winter sports, the Sami people (who live in the north), Norway's progressive politics particularly with regard to women's rights, Grieg the composer, Ibsen the playwright, A-ha the pop band.

Extra activity

If you think your students will know little or nothing about Norway, write the following words up on the board before they do Exercise 3 and ask students to say whether and why they might apply to Norway: *Vikings, Europe, blond, oil, mountains, skiing, fish, rich*.

4 💿 [104]

- Ask students to work individually to read the article and answer the question. Let students compare their answers in pairs before checking with the class.

- **Optional step** The reading text is recorded. You could play the recording and ask students to read and listen.

ANSWERS

It's one of the wealthiest (richest) countries in the world. Norwegians get a good education and unemployment is low.

People have a good quality of life and the country has invested money for the future.

5

- Ask students to complete the summaries of the four paragraphs. Elicit the first missing words to get students started.

- Let students compare with their partner, and then another pair, before checking with the class.

ANSWERS

1 quality of life
2 their natural thrift; strong work ethic
3 having a balanced life
4 its pension fund

Vocabulary notes

thrift = note that this word is similar to *meanness*, but without the negative connotation – if you are *thrifty*, you are careful and sensible with money so that you don't waste any

work ethic = a strong belief in the value of hard work

Norway is sitting pretty = an idiom meaning that Norway is in a good position

6

- You could discuss this question with the class or in small groups.

EXAMPLE ANSWERS

Students will probably suggest they are right – oil prices might fall, alternative power sources could be developed, supplies could run out, so saving for a rainy day is a good idea.

Grammar focus adverbs: *only, just, even*

7

- Ask students to look at the grammar box and answer the questions. Let students compare answers in pairs before checking with the class.

> ANSWER
>
> b

Refer students to page 178 for further information and practice.

> ANSWERS TO GRAMMAR SUMMARY EXERCISES
>
> **1**
>
> 1 don't think   4 'their biggest fans'
>
> 2 surprised   5 other things, too
>
> 3 less   6 looked
>
> **2**
>
> 1 only   2 just   3 just   4 even/just   5 just   6 even   7 just
>
> **3**
>
> 1 just/only   2 just/only   3 just   4 even   5 even   6 even

Grammar note

Just, only and *even* are called focus adverbs because they come directly before the word or phrase they are emphasizing or 'focusing' on.

Just and *only* are near synonyms – they can be used mostly interchangeably to focus on one particular thing to the exclusion of all others.

Even is used to show something is unusual or surprising.

8

- Ask students to work individually to find other examples of focus adverbs in the article. Let students compare their answers in pairs before checking with the class.

> ANSWERS
>
> *only Luxembourg and a couple of others are richer* (emphasizing Luxembourg and other countries) (line 5)
>
> *unemployment is just 2.5 per cent* (emphasizing 2.5 as a low percentage) (line 8)
>
> *People say even the prisons are quite comfortable!* (emphasizing 'the prisons') (lines 9–10)
>
> *Just last century* (emphasizing 'last century') (lines 11–12)
>
> *But it isn't only Norway's huge reserves that account for its success* (emphasizing Norway's huge oil reserves) (lines 15–16)
>
> *other less successful economies have even greater resources* (emphasizing 'greater') (lines 16–17)
>
> *In fact, in today's digital age where work seems to follow us everywhere – even on holiday* (emphasizing 'on holiday') (lines 23–24)
>
> *They have even said* (emphasizing 'said') (line 29)
>
> *It is one of the only countries to do so* (emphasizing that very few countries make paternity leave compulsory) (line 30)
>
> *not even new schools and hospitals* (emphasizing that new schools and hospitals are an obvious thing to spend money on) (lines 35–36)

9

- Ask students to work in pairs or small groups to discuss the meaning of each sentence first.
- Then ask students to work individually to match the sentences with the clause or sentence that follows it.

> ANSWERS
>
> 1 e (emphasizing visitors rather than locals)
>
> 2 c (emphasizing Norway rather than other countries)
>
> 3 b (emphasizing having visited Norway once)
>
> 4 d (emphasizing having visited Norway, but not Sweden or Denmark)
>
> 5 a (emphasizing that it is a surprise fathers have time off)
>
> 6 f (emphasizing that it is a surprise fathers have time off with older children)

10

- Ask students to work individually to put the focus adverbs in the correct place in the sentences. Elicit the first answer to get them started. Let students compare their answers in pairs before checking with the class.

> ANSWERS
>
> 1 No, thanks. I'm <u>just</u> looking.
>
> 2 <u>Even</u> the most difficult problems have a solution. (Here, we are emphasizing 'the most difficult problems', i.e. it's surprising that difficult problems have solutions.)
>
> 3 I'm <u>just</u> going to brush my teeth, then we can go.
>
> 4 Don't worry. It's <u>only</u> money.
>
> 5 He <u>even</u> lost his own wedding ring once. *or* He lost <u>even</u> his own wedding ring once.
>
> 6 It's <u>just</u> a suggestion – you don't have to follow it.
>
> 7 I'm afraid that's <u>just</u> life, isn't it?
>
> 8 It's <u>only</u> the second time we've met.

Pronunciation focus adverbs

11a [105]

- Play the recording. Ask students to listen to the sentences from Exercise 10 and say whether the focus adverbs are stressed.

> ANSWERS
>
> yes, apart from in sentence 1

Audioscript [105]

1 No, thanks. I'm just looking.

2 Even the most difficult problems have a solution.

3 I'm just going to brush my teeth, then we can go.

4 Don't worry. It's only money.

5 He even lost his own wedding ring once.

6 It's only a suggestion – you don't have to follow it.

7 I'm afraid that's just life, isn't it?

8 It's only the second time we've met.

11b

- Ask students to work in pairs to practise saying the sentences. Remind them to stress the focus adverbs. Point out that it makes sense to stress the focus adverbs because they are working hard to strongly emphasize the words or phrases they are focusing on.

Speaking my life

12

- Ask students to work individually to rewrite sentences. Let them compare answers and discuss the facts in pairs before checking with the class.

EXAMPLE ANSWERS

1 Many people work long hours during the week, so they only/just see their children at weekends.

2 Even people with university degrees are finding it difficult to get jobs these days.

3 For many people a job is only/just a way to make money, not something they particularly enjoy.

4 The rich are only a very small part of the population.

5 You don't see extreme poverty. Even poor people usually have food and somewhere to live.

6 The state pension gives you enough to live on, but only to live a very basic kind of life. or The state pension gives you just enough to live on, but only to live a very basic kind of life.

13

- Organize the class into new pairs to write sentences. If you have a mix of nationalities in your class, you could put people of the same nationality together, or ask them to discuss ideas, but write their own sentences. Monitor and help with ideas and vocabulary.

14

- Organize the class into groups of four by putting pairs together. Ask students to take turns to read and explain their sentences. In feedback, ask students to tell the class what they found out about their group mates' countries.

- As students speak, monitor and listen for errors, noting down any errors you hear which you can write up and focus on in feedback. Write up five or six short sentences containing anonymous errors you heard. Ask students in pairs to correct the errors.

Extra activity

Write the following common expressions on the board:

I was only joking; I was only trying to help; I'm just looking; Even in summer; It's just you and me now; Even my mum doesn't like me

Ask students to work in pairs. Tell them to choose two expressions and write and then act out short dialogues to illustrate their meaning and use.

12b Get someone else to do it

Lesson at a glance

- vocabulary: services
- wordbuilding: *the* + adjective
- listening: the growing service economy
- grammar: causative *have* and *get*
- pronunciation: /ʃ/, /tʃ/, /ʒ/ and /dʒ/
- speaking: getting things done

Vocabulary services

1

- **Optional step** Start by writing *the service sector* on the board and asking students to suggest jobs in which people provide a service. Useful examples would be a hairdresser, a painter and decorator or a plumber.

- Ask students to work in pairs to match words to make services. Elicit one or two examples to get students started. Set a five-minute time limit, then find out which pair has the longest list.

EXAMPLE ANSWERS

car washing, carpet cleaning/fitting, clothes alterations, computer repair, child minding, dog walking, furniture restoring, hair cutting, house painting, party planning, shoe repair/cleaning, window cleaning

Other less common possibilities: house repair, window repair, dog minding, hair restoring

Vocabulary notes

carpet fitting = to fit a carpet means to cut and shape it to the exact size to fit the room (here, we are talking about wall-to-wall carpets commonly fitted in British homes)

child minding = here, to mind means to look after (the term *childcare* can also be used; note that *child minding* refers to the more professional role of looking after pre-school children, in contrast to *babysitting*, which refers to being in the house with children while their parents are out – a typical pocket money job for teenagers)

furniture restoring = if you restore furniture, you clean and fix it to return it to its previous good condition

2

- Ask students to discuss the questions. You could ask students to do this activity in pairs or small groups. In feedback, elicit ideas and personal experiences from individual students.

EXAMPLE ANSWERS

1 Depending on the DIY skills of individuals, all these could be done by people themselves. Equally, all could be done by someone else as a paid service.

2/3 Furniture restoring, computer repair and shoe repair are perhaps the jobs requiring the greatest specialist skill, so they are the services people would be most likely to pay for. After these, carpet fitting and clothes alterations require quite a lot of skill to do well (but are more commonly done at home). Hair cutting is something anyone can do badly, but most people would pay to have it done well. Car washing, child minding, dog walking and house painting don't require a lot of skill. People only pay for them for convenience. They pay for child minding so they can go to work. They pay for house painting to get a quicker, higher quality job than they could do. Party planning depends on the party. If it's a big wedding or celebrity do, then actually this could be a very demanding, expensive, specialist job.

Listening

3 💿 [106]

• Tell students they are going to listen to an interview with an economics professor. Ask them to note answers to the questions. Play the recording. Let students compare their answers in pairs before checking with the class.

• **Optional step** The tasks involves students hearing and noting a series of services. You could write the list of services from Exercise 1 on the board first and ask students to copy them then tick the ones they hear as they listen. This simplifies the task by reducing what students have to write. Alternatively, you could ask students to note down what the speaker actually says as they listen. This encourages them to listen for and notice causative *have* and *get*. However, it's a more demanding task and may involve the need to play the recording more than once.

ANSWERS

1 car washing (*getting someone to hand wash your car*)
  carpet fitting (*fitting a carpet*)
  house painting (*painting their house*)
  window cleaning (*get your windows cleaned*)
  hair cutting (*have your hair done*)
  dog walking (*have someone walk their dog*)
  party planning (*get a professional party planner to organize the party*)

2 He thinks it's a good thing for the economy as it creates employment.

Audioscript 💿 [106]

Note: the uses of *get/have done* are underlined because they are the answers to Exercise 7 below.

I = Interviewer; D = David Stiles

I: Are we all getting lazier or has economic development just meant that there's now someone available to do any job you want? Forty years ago, the idea of getting someone to hand wash your car was unthinkable – except to the very rich. Either you washed it yourself at home on a Sunday morning or you took it down to the automatic carwash at your local garage. Nowadays, you can have it washed inside and out by professional

car washers for as little as £8. David Stiles, Professor of Economics at Cranford Institute, is here with us to try and explain this phenomenon. What's changed, Professor?

D: Well, first of all, hello and thank you for inviting me onto your programme. So, yes, the short answer to your question *is* 'economic development'. As society gets richer, people have more money available to buy services, and to get others to do things that they don't particularly want to do or feel they're not good at doing – like fitting a carpet or painting their house.

I: And I suppose it has to do with time too. We all have much busier lives.

D: Yes, that's true. It saves time and of course the big positive is that it creates a lot of employment. You don't have to be especially rich to have a cleaner tidy your house once a week or to get your windows cleaned every couple of months or have your hair done, for that matter. But I think you made a valid point at the beginning about people getting lazier. There are some rich people who take things to extremes. I'm thinking of people who, for example, employ personal shoppers or who have someone walk their dog every day. When they have a party, they probably get a professional party planner to organize the party. I've even heard of people who get their Christmas tree installed and then have someone else decorate it for them.

I: That's a bit extreme. Decorating the Christmas tree is supposed to be a pleasure.

D: Well, I tend to agree with you but, as I say, I don't think the people who provide the services are necessarily complaining. That's how the economy works – people, particularly the wealthy, pay to have things done for them and the people who provide the services benefit from that.

4 💿 [106]

• Play the recording again. Students listen and make notes about points 1–4. Let students compare their answers in pairs before checking with the class.

ANSWERS

1 The speakers also mention having a cleaner tidy your house, personal shoppers and getting a Christmas tree installed and decorated.

2 We're getting richer and we have less time / we're busy and some people are getting lazier.

3 He thinks it's a bit extreme: *Decorating the Christmas tree is supposed to be a pleasure.*

4 They are not complaining, i.e. they benefit from providing these services.

Vocabulary notes

unthinkable = impossible to imagine, e.g. *Malta? Win the football World Cup? Unthinkable!*

a valid point = a good contribution to the conversation that deserves to be taken seriously

take things to extremes = to do something to the largest possible amount of something; more than is reasonable or usual

Wordbuilding *the* + adjective

5
- Read the information in the box to the class. Elicit other examples, e.g. *the old, the aristocracy, the media, the British*.
- Ask students to work in pairs to make expressions using *the* + adjective. Elicit ideas from the class in feedback and provide answers.

> **EXAMPLE ANSWERS**
> a the elderly / the retired / the over-70s
> b the unemployed / the jobless
> c the homeless
> d the sick
> e the hard-working
> f the young and healthy

Refer students to Workbook page 99 for further practice.

Extra activity

Write the following on the board and ask students to say what groups of people they refer to: the disabled, the visually impaired, the hard of hearing, the working poor, the jet set, the nouveau rich.

Grammar causative *have* and *get*

6
- Ask students to read the information in the grammar box. Then elicit answers to the questions.

> **ANSWERS**
> a all of them
> b sentence 2
> c sentences 3 and 4

Refer students to page 178 for further information and practice.

> **ANSWERS TO GRAMMAR SUMMARY EXERCISES**
> **4**
> 1 Amy is getting/having her hair cut
> 2 We got/had our windows fixed
> 3 'm going to get/have my car washed
> 4 got/had our bags carried
> 5 had/got some food delivered
> 6 get/have your eyes checked
>
> **5**
> 1 repainted   4 check
> 2 stay   5 made
> 3 to bring   6 to fit
>
> **6**
> 1 the little jobs done   4 the ingredients delivered
> 2 your/the house cleaned   5 do the cooking
> 3 to find the perfect gift   6 an information pack sent

Grammar note

***have/get* (something) + *done* (the past participle)**

We use this form when we have asked (and often paid) someone to do work for us (*I had my hair cut*). We don't need to say who did the work, but we can choose to add the agent with *by* (*I had my hair cut by Mrs Sproggs*). *Get* is an informal use and not appropriate in formal situations.

have* (somebody) *do*; *get* (somebody) *to do

The use here is similar to the use above except that we say who we asked. We are more likely to use this form when talking about jobs you give to an employee or family member (*I got my husband to fix the light*).

7
- Tell students to look at audioscript 106 on page 190 of the Student's Book.
- Ask students to find and underli~~~~~~ples of ~~~~~~~~~~~~ et students ~~~~~~~~~~~~~~ king with

> **ANSWERS**
> Examples are underlined in audioscript 106 above.

8
- Ask students to work individually to complete the summary with the correct form of the verbs. Elicit the first answer to get students started. Let students compare answers in pairs before checking with the class.

> **ANSWERS**
> 1 do (*have other people to do* is a possible answer using infinitive of purpose – as in *employ people to do*)
> 2 to help
> 3 done
> 4 cleaned
> 5 to do
> 6 fix (or *to fix*: see 1 above)
> 7 organize/organise (or *to organize/organise*: see 1 above)
> 8 looked

9
- Ask students to complete the sentences with causative forms. Let students compare their answers in pairs before checking with the class.

> **ANSWERS**
> 1 got someone to organize
> 2 have a personal trainer take their children / have their children taken (by a personal trainer)
> 3 have a driver pick their children up / have their children picked up (by a driver)
> 4 have a travel consultant choose their holidays / have their holidays chosen (by a travel consultant)
> 5 get a nanny to look after their children / get their children looked after (by a nanny)
> 6 get someone to pack their bags / get their bags packed

Grammar note

In feedback to this exercise, point out that the causative is the preferred form in this context (talking about what rich people get people to do). This is because the speaker wants to emphasize the action caused rather than the agent. This will help students understand when to use the causative.

10

- Ask students to work individually to prepare ideas. Monitor and correct any errors of form or meaning.
- Put students in pairs to share their ideas.
- **Optional step** Extend this activity into an open class discussion and find out which students would choose to do things themselves and which ones are more likely to get someone to do it for them, and why.

EXAMPLE ANSWER

I usually wash my car myself because it's quick and easy to do, but I'd definitely have my computer repaired in a shop.

Pronunciation /ʃ/, /tʃ/, /ʒ/ and /dʒ/
11a 💿 [107]

- **Optional step** Start by writing the four phonemic symbols on the board and demonstrating to students how to say them (see Pronunciation notes below).
- Play the recording. Students listen and note the pronunciation.
- Ask students to work in pairs to practise saying the words.

Audioscript 💿 [107]

/ʃ/	/tʃ/	/ʒ/	/dʒ/
carwash	chores	decision	change
shelves	richer	garage	college
shopper	watch	pleasure	fridge

Pronunciation notes

/ʃ/

The /ʃ/ sound is unvoiced, meaning you don't use your vocal chords to make the sound, and sibilant, meaning you direct a stream of air with the tongue towards the sharp edge of the teeth when making the sound. To produce the sound, pull your tongue away from your top teeth, allowing a flow of air to hiss through the gap. Words spelt with 'sh' have this sound, but note that it can be represented by other letters (national, official, sure).

/tʃ/

By placing the unvoiced /t/ in front of the /ʃ/ sound, a new sound is made. Students should practise saying /t/ by pressing their tongue behind their top teeth, then /ʃ/ by pulling the tongue away and allowing air to flow over. Words spelt with 'ch' have this sound, but note that it can be represented by other letters (culture, nature, champagne).

/ʒ/

The /ʒ/ sound is a voiced sibilant. With this sound, the speaker produces friction through clenched teeth by directing air flow through a narrow channel formed along the middle of the tongue. Words spelt with 'su' or 'si' may have this sound (measure, vision, conclusion).

/dʒ/

By placing the voiced /d/ in front of the /ʒ/ sound, a new sound is made. Again, get students to practise pressing their tongue against upper teeth to make the first sound before quickly moving into the longer, sibilant sound. Words spelt with 'j', 'ge' or 'gi' may have this sound (job, college, age, religion).

11b 💿 [108]

- Play the recording. Ask students to listen and say which sounds they hear.
- Ask students to practise saying the words in pairs or small groups.

ANSWERS

/ʃ/: fashion, machine, sugar
/tʃ/: cheese, choice
/ʒ/: television, usual
/dʒ/: agent, arrange, general, January

Speaking my life
12

- Start by eliciting that DIY stands for Do-It-Yourself – the activity of making or repairing things for your home instead of paying someone to do them for you. DIY is popular in the UK and there are a lot of big DIY stores selling everything from pots of paint to planks of wood.
- Organize the class into pairs. Give students a few minutes to combine the words to make as many jobs as they can.
- Then ask students in their pairs to talk about places they have lived that have needed a lot of work doing to them. Encourage students to refer to and use the phrases they made.

ANSWERS

1 assemble or put up or fit
2 fit or clean
3 put up
4 fix (fit is also possible, meaning that you put the tap in the correct place in the sink or bath)
5 put up or fit
6 tile or decorate or clean
7 do
8 fix or tile

Vocabulary notes

assemble = to put together from a set of parts

put up = to put on the wall and connect it to the wall

fit (a carpet) = if you fit something, you make it the right size so that it 'fits' a space

fix = to repair (something that is broken)

tile = to put on tiles (ceramic squares that are used in bathrooms and kitchens)

13

• Organize the class into pairs to do this exercise. First tell them to brainstorm a list of things that would need to be done. Go round the class and answer questions about vocabulary.

• Once students have discussed and decided what to do themselves and what to get done professionally, ask students to find another pair in the class and to share their ideas.

• In feedback, point out any errors with causative *have* and *get* that you notice during this exercise.

EXAMPLE ANSWERS

Students may suggest doing the following themselves: picking up the rubbish, cleaning the window, taking things to the dump, getting new curtains, painting walls

Students may suggest getting professional help for the following: getting someone to put up some shelves, having someone paint the room or have a painter decorate/paint the walls, getting a cleaner to tidy the room, getting some curtains made/fitted, getting the carpet cleaned/replaced

---

Extra activity

Ask students to share personal experiences of moving into a new flat or house. Ask: *What did you have to get done? What did you get people in to do? What were the biggest challenges?*

12c Start-up

Lesson at a glance
• reading: a new business trend
• vocabulary: business words
• critical thinking: opinion words
• speaking: new business ideas

Reading

1

• Ask students to look at the photo and discuss the questions. You could ask students to do this in pairs or small groups first.

EXAMPLE ANSWERS

1 It might sell burgers, hot dogs, tacos or pizza, for example.

2 Students may think they make a lot of money because they can go to places where there are a lot of customers, they can charge high prices for cheap ingredients, and they have very low costs (no rent to pay on a building, no personnel to pay, etc.); some may think they don't make a lot of money because it's a competitive business, they may have to pay a licence fee and they have low profit margins.

3 Students' own answers

---

2 ⊚ [109]

• Ask students to read the article and make notes. Let students compare answers in pairs before checking with the class.

• **Optional step** The reading text is recorded. You could play the recording and ask students to read and listen.

ANSWERS

1 to use a mobile kitchen to bring higher quality food at a reasonable price to a new generation of consumers

2 the economic recession of 2008 – people could still find quality food at a reasonable price

3 early use of social media – particularly Twitter – for advertising

4 branding, cheap, sociable

Vocabulary notes

Note that many of the more difficult words in this text are explained in the glossary.

create a buzz around the brand = to make people interested in and talking about the brand (the name or make of the product)

branding = giving a (good) name to a product that will help sell it

viral eatery = an eatery (restaurant) which has become well known because of what people are saying about it through social media

Background information

Today, there are five Kogi Korean BBQ food trucks in Los Angeles.

3

- Ask students to work individually to read the article again and match the subheadings (A–F) with the paragraphs.

- Let students compare answers in pairs before checking with the class. In feedback, ask students to justify their answers with reference to the article.

> ANSWERS
>
> 1 E (*It started as a simple business idea.*)
> 2 B (*the economic recession of 2008 was an excellent opportunity*)
> 3 C (*a growing, $800-million annual industry*)
> 4 A (*exploiting the growing power of social media … to create a buzz around the brand*)
> 5 D (*Branding and a catchy name are very important*)
> 6 F (*There is definitely an important social aspect to this. It may be takeaway food, but it's a shared experience*)

Teacher development

Handling feedback

Consider how you handle feedback to a reading or listening exercise. Taking too long can waste lesson time, but failing to go into enough detail may frustrate students. Here are some suggestions about how to handle feedback:

1. Let students compare answers in pairs before feedback. That way, you can monitor to find out what problems they are having, and it means you can elicit answers from pairs, thus avoiding the possible embarrassment of trying to elicit from an individual who gets the answer wrong.

2. Write up answers on the board (so long as they are short) so that students can see and note them. You could do this as students discuss answers – there is no need to 'deliver' the answers – just be ready to answer queries.

3. Ask students to justify answers by referring to what they read or heard in the text.

4. Use techniques where students give feedback themselves. For example, ask individual students to come up to the board and write up the answers or be responsible for leading a discussion of answers. Alternatively, ask students to say what problems they had with understanding a text and to base your feedback on what they most want to discuss.

Vocabulary business words
4

- Ask students to work in pairs to find and underline the words and phrases in the article. Then ask them to try to work out meaning from the context, and from what they may already know. Ask students to think about what part of speech the words are and what ideas they are connected with.

- Students can check their answers on page 155 of the Student's Book.

> ANSWERS
>
> a trend (n) = a fashion or direction
> b recession (n) = a period of (economic) decrease
> c set up (v) = to establish
> d upmarket (adj) = high quality and more expensive
> e passing (adj) fashion (n) = something which is popular for only a short time
> f loyal (adj) = faithful
> g buzz (n) = excitement and activity
> h catchy (adj) = easy to remember

Critical thinking opinion words
5

- Read the information about opinion words and phrases and elicit examples students can think of, e.g. *In my opinion, Surprisingly, In fact.*

- Ask students to read the article again and underline the words and phrases used to give opinions.

- Discuss what the writer is saying in each situation with the class. You could ask students to discuss in pairs or groups first. In feedback, elicit and discuss answers.

> ANSWERS
>
> 2 The writer thinks this is strange.
> 3 He thinks this is surprising.
> 4 He thinks this is a real achievement.
> 5 He's sure that this is true.
> 6 He doesn't want us to forget this point.

Vocabulary notes

Even more significantly = note how *even* is used here to emphasize the comparative phrase

after all = used for saying that something is true despite what was said or done before

6

- This is an opportunity for students to reflect on and comment on the text, as well as their ability to note the writer's opinion. Discuss in open class and encourage a range of opinions and contributions from different students.

> ANSWERS
>
> Positive: the author thinks they have started a big new trend and that it's the social nature of eating in this way that has made the business such a success.
> Students' own answers

Extra activity

Ask students to imagine a mobile eatery that would be successful in their town. In small groups, ask students to decide on what sort of food to sell, how upmarket it would be, how they would create a buzz and how they would design the van.

Speaking ⟨my life⟩

7

- Start by eliciting a few ideas of what might be done to transform out-dated railway carriages into something modern and practical.

- Organize the class into groups of four or five students. Ask students to talk together to decide how they would transform the railway carriage and to consider the areas listed on the page. Monitor and help with ideas and vocabulary.

- When students have discussed their ideas, ask them to prepare a presentation.

8

- Ask different groups to make their presentation. As students speak, set a task (e.g. to think of two questions to ask the speakers at the end of the presentation) so that other students follow the presentation closely. At the end, have a class vote and decide on the best idea.

- As students speak, use the opportunity to make notes on errors and examples of good language use from your students. In feedback, write up some incorrect or interesting language on the board and ask students to correct or comment on it.

> **EXAMPLE ANSWERS**
>
> Ideas include adapting the railway carriage to be a restaurant, an internet café, holiday accommodation, a small cinema, a party or event venue, a shop, a library, a training centre, a central store room for community-owned tools and equipment to loan.

Extra activity

As an alternative activity, with a mature and creative class, ask students to think of problems or issues in their own cities and to develop a business idea to solve that problem. Students then make a presentation, stating the problem, the solution and why it would be successful.

12d The bottom line

> ### Lesson at a glance
> - real life: negotiating
> - pronunciation: long vowel sounds

Real life negotiating

1

- **Optional step** Start by writing *the bottom line* on the board. Elicit what it might mean in a business context (the bottom line can mean: 1 the amount of money a business makes or loses; 2 the lowest price someone will accept in a business deal; 3 the most basic fact or issue at stake).

- Ask students to discuss the questions and situations. Point out the meaning of *do the chores* (= do the housework jobs). You could ask students to discuss the questions in pairs before eliciting answers from the class.

> **ANSWERS**
>
> Students' own answers

2

- Discuss the advice with the class. In feedback, ask students if they would offer any advice about negotiating (e.g. stick to your principles, look people in the eye, be prepared to lose).

> **ANSWERS**
>
> Students' own answers
> It seems like good advice – the best negotiators never reveal their hand.

3 🔊 [110]

- Read the situation and the questions. Point out that a *lease* is the period of time you are allowed to live in a property you are paying rent for (e.g. *a 99-year lease*).

- Play the recording. Students listen and answer the questions. Let students compare answers in pairs before checking with the class.

> **ANSWERS**
>
> 1 the length of the lease / how long the lease is
> 2 sign a ten-year lease, but with a get-out clause after, say, six years
> 3 The woman decides to call her business partner (to see what he thinks).
> 4 The woman (really) wants to agree the lease; the estate agent isn't so bothered *or* the woman wants to agree the lease more than the estate agent.

Audioscript 🎵 [110]

LA = Letting agent; W = Woman

LA: So, you've had a look at the offices. What do you think?

W: Well, yeah, I think they're absolutely perfect for our needs.

LA: That's great. You'd like to take them then?

W: Well, ideally, yes, I would, but …

LA: But?

W: Well, a key thing for us is the length of the lease.

LA: Umm … It's a ten-year lease. I think that was on the details I sent you.

W: Yes, that's right, but actually I was hoping we could negotiate that down because, if you look at it from our point of view, we're a young business and we don't really know how things are going to go over the next few years. Let's face it, ten years is a big commitment. Do you think your client would be willing to move a bit on that?

LA: I doubt it. I'm sure you'll appreciate that our client's main concern is for someone to rent the property for as long as possible. It gives them security. To tell you the truth, that's why the rent is so low. So I can ask, but I'm not at all sure we'll get a positive response.

W: Umm … isn't there some way around that, maybe?

LA: Not that I can think of. What did you have in mind?

W: Well, perhaps if we could sign a ten-year lease, but with a get-out clause after, say, six years.

LA: No, I don't really see how that helps. We do actually have other people interested in the premises, so I'm pretty sure someone will take it. If I were in your shoes, you know, and I found the terms of the lease difficult, I think I'd just leave it. At the end of the day, it has to feel right for you.

W: But it *does* feel right for me. Hang on a minute. I'm just going to call my business partner and see what he thinks.

LA: OK, no problem.

Background information

a get-out clause = a clause (part) of a contract that agrees to allow someone to end the contract

4 🎵 [110]

• Ask students to listen and complete the expressions in the language box. You may need to play and pause the recording if students have difficulties. Let students compare answers in pairs before checking with the class.

ANSWERS

1 the length of
2 negotiate that
3 young business
4 big commitment
5 move
6 main concern
7 so low
8 leave it
9 feel right

5

• Ask students to work in pairs to categorize the expressions.

• In feedback, go through the phrases, checking meaning and use (see Vocabulary notes below).

ANSWERS

Say what the important thing is: *A key thing for us is …* ,

Be direct and clear: *Let's face it, …* ; *To tell you the truth, …* ; *If I were in your shoes, …* ; *At the end of the day, …*

Talk about an obstacle to the agreement: *Isn't there some way around that?*

Ask the other person to see your side: *I was hoping we could …* ; *If you look at it from our point of view, …* ; *Do you think (your client) would be willing to …* ; *I'm sure you'll appreciate that …*

The phrases *Not that I can think of* and *What did you have in mind?* don't clearly fit these categories. Both are direct and clear. *What did you have in mind?* (= What do you intend to do? or What is your idea?) is being used to talk about an obstacle.

Vocabulary notes

When asking another person to see your side – when trying to gently persuade in a negotiation – English speakers use tentative language. Examples here include using continuous forms (*I was hoping, I was thinking, your client would be willing to*) instead of simple forms, using modals (*could, would*) and using negative questions (*Isn't there … ?*).

a key thing = an important thing

Let's face it, … / *To tell you the truth, …* = I am about to say what the facts are in a clear and direct way

If I were in your shoes, … = If it was my decision to make

At the end of the day, … = this is similar to *after all* (a phrase used earlier in the unit) – it's used to say that this is what is true despite what was said or intended before

6

• Discuss the question with your class. Alternatively, ask students to discuss in pairs or small groups and elicit answers in feedback.

EXAMPLE ANSWER

The letting agent has been clear, direct and professional throughout, and has politely put pressure on the woman to agree.

The woman has tried hard to negotiate and get the letting agent to see her view but, in the end, has given in and agreed to call her partner. Perhaps she could have been firmer, and walked away, or tried to show less enthusiasm. However, in that case she may have just lost the lease.

Pronunciation long vowel sounds

7a 🔘 [111]

- Play the recording. Students listen and repeat.

Audioscript 🔘 [111]

/eɪ/ del**ay** t**a**ke
/iː/ m**e**dium d**e**tailed
/aɪ/ f**i**nal l**i**ne
/əʊ/ l**ow** neg**o**tiate
/uː/ incl**u**de sh**oe**s

Pronunciation note

The long /iː/ sound and the diphthongs /aɪ/ and /eɪ/ are pronounced with lips spread. To make /aɪ/, the mouth starts in the position to make /a/ and stretches to make /ɪ/. To make /eɪ/, the mouth starts stretched for /e/ and stretches a bit more for /ɪ/.

The sounds /əʊ/ and /uː/ are produced with rounded lips. To make /əʊ/, we start with loose lips and tighten them and make them rounded to form the /ʊ/ sound.

7b 🔘 [112]

- **Optional step** Ask students to underline parts of each sentence where they think there is a long vowel sound, and use phonemic script to show how to pronounce the sounds before playing the recording.

- Play the recording. Students listen and underline long vowel sounds.

- Ask students to practise saying the sentences.

Audioscript 🔘 [112] **(with long vowel sounds marked)**

1 A k**ey** thing for us is …

2 I was h**o**ping w**e** could …

3 Let's f**a**ce it …

4 At th**e** end of the d**ay**, …

5 What did you have in m**i**nd?

6 To tell you the tr**u**th, …

8

- Organize the class into new pairs. Ask students to read the situation then decide which role to take. Student A wants to buy a car (see Student's Book page 153) and Student B wants to sell one (see Student's Book page 155). Give students five minutes to read the information about the car and prepare what to say. Encourage them to look back at the expressions box on the page and use the expressions to organize their ideas.

- **Optional step** Instead of preparing individually, ask students to prepare in pairs of As and pairs of Bs. When they are ready, split the pairs so that an A is with a B.

- Ask students to roleplay the conversations. Tell fast-finishing students to swap roles and act out a second conversation.

- As students speak, monitor and note errors and examples of good language use. At the end, provide some feedback on language students have used.

Extra activity

Ask students to create their own negotiation situations. For example, you could ask students to think of three things that they would like to buy second hand. Put them in pairs and find out if that partner has one of the three things they would like. Students then negotiate. You could do this as a mingling activity – students walk round the class and negotiate to buy things from each other.

Teacher development

Practice makes perfect

Encourage students to practise conversations like those above three or four times. Get students to think of roleplay conversation practice as a way of fine-tuning language, both in terms of its accuracy and delivery.

Ideas include giving students lots of time to prepare (by writing ideas and notes, or even the whole dialogue), getting students to practise their dialogues in pairs without being listened to (and only going over to listen, comment and correct when students are ready for you to listen), and getting students to perform their dialogues in front of the class (but only after they have practised enough to be confident in their performance).

12e Get to the point

Lesson at a glance
- writing: a short report
- writing skill: key phrases in report writing

Writing a short report

1
- **Optional step** With books closed, write the following quote from Blaise Pascal (a seventeenth-century French mathematician) on the board: *I'm sorry I wrote you such a long letter; I didn't have time to write a short one.* Ask students to work out what Pascal is trying to say. (He's saying that it's more difficult to be short and concise when expressing what you wish to say.)
- Ask students to read the report and answer the questions. Let students briefly compare answers in pairs before discussing with the class.

> ANSWERS
> 1 to improve public speaking techniques; yes, it was successful (as an introduction)
> 2 It concentrated on drama techniques rather than how to structure a talk.

Vocabulary notes

posture = how you hold your body when standing or sitting or walking

sceptical = if you are sceptical, you question things because you have doubts about whether those things are true or correct

innovative = creative, full of new ideas

2
- Ask students to work individually to complete the notes. Let students compare and discuss answers in pairs before checking with the class.

> ANSWERS
> 1 a public speaking course (first, opening paragraph)
> 2 LeGard School in Paris (first paragraph)
> 3 a great experience (start of second paragraph)
> 4 concentrated on voice control, breathing, posture and movement (second paragraph)
> 5 improved confidence (end of second paragraph)
> 6 how to write a speech (third, concluding paragraph)
> 7 strongly recommended as an introduction to public speaking (third, concluding paragraph)

Writing skill key phrases in report writing
3a
- Ask students to find the words and phrases in the report. Tell them that the phrases they are looking for appear in the same order in the report. Elicit the first answer to get students started. Let students compare answers in pairs before checking with the class.

- In feedback, point out how these key phrases are used in a sentence (see Grammar and vocabulary notes below).

> ANSWERS
> 1 As requested   4 Initially
> 2 Overall   5 Consequently
> 3 specifically   6 To sum up

Grammar and vocabulary notes

As requested = a very formal, written way to say you asked/requested me to do this

In general, these linking words go at the start of a sentence and are followed by a comma. Note that, in the text, *specifically* is used in the middle of a sentence to give specific examples and is followed by nouns or noun phrases, not a clause or complete sentence.

3b
- Ask students to work individually to complete the sentences. Let students compare answers in pairs before checking with the class.

> ANSWERS
> 1 Overall / To sum up
> 2 As requested; specifically
> 3 Consequently
> 4 Initially

4
- **Optional step** Start with a class discussion. Ask students to talk about courses they have taken. Ask: *What was the course? How long was it? How did you learn? How effective was the course and why?*
- Ask students to spend four or five minutes making rough notes about a course based on the headings provided. Monitor at this stage and help with ideas and vocabulary. You could let students compare their ideas in pairs and ask for help.
- Ask students to write their report. Before they do, ask students to think what key phrases they could use to organize their ideas, and how they might organize the ideas.

5
- When students have written their reports, ask them to exchange their written work with a partner. Ask students to check their partner's work using the questions and suggest how to improve it.
- **Optional step** Ask students to revise and rewrite their reports based on their partner's suggestions.

Extra activity

Organize the class into groups of four or five. Tell students in each group to pass round their reports, read them, and choose a course to take. Once students have read the reports, they talk to their group, saying which course they have chosen and giving reasons why.

12f The Farmery

Before you watch

1

- Ask students to look at the photo and the title of the video and answer the question.

> **EXAMPLE ANSWER**
>
> It's something to do with gardening or growing vegetables in a different way.

Background information

A *farmery* is defined in a dictionary as the buildings and yards of a farm. It's not a commonly used word – it's more common to say *farm* or *farm buildings*.

Key vocabulary

2a

- Ask students to read the sentences and guess the meaning of the words from context. Start students off by eliciting the meaning of the first word.

- Let students compare their answers in pairs before moving on to Exercise 2b.

2b

- Ask students to match the words in bold in Exercise 2a with the definitions. Let students compare their answers in pairs.

> **ANSWERS**
>
> 1 d   2 b   3 e   4 a   5 c

While you watch

3 ◼◀ [12.1]

- Tell students they are going to watch the video and tick the things in the list they see. Pre-teach any words students aren't sure of and that don't appear in the glossary (*crops* = things farmers grow). Play the whole video. Let students compare answers in pairs before checking with the class.

- In feedback, discuss what makes Ben's idea original.

> **ANSWERS**
>
> All of the things are seen in the video apart from shops (although we see an artist's representation of an area where people can buy produce) and a street market.
>
> Main points of the business idea:
>
> Creating an urban farming market / To grow and sell on the same site
>
> Customers can see the food growing, cut their own purchases, buy food from the area they live in
>
> Changes the way people look at and buy food

Videoscript ◼◀ 12.1

Part 1

0.00–1.00   When I drive around rural North Carolina I see how this land is used for agriculture, and it makes me think of the complex journey that the food has to take from these fields to the retail store shelves. It has to be harvested; it has to be packed, transported, cooled. And at every step there's massive inventory loss. What if, what if this entire system could be consolidated into one site? What if you grow and you sell at the same site? What would that look like?

1.02–1.40   The Farmery is an urban farming market where we use the entire structure to grow food and the bottom level is used as a retail area where we can sell the food. The Farmery is created from shipping containers and modular greenhouse components. We have these living wall panels that we've developed that hang off the outside of the shipping containers. We grow aquaponic crops on those and inside the shipping containers we grow gourmet mushrooms.

1.41–2.11   My farming methods differ in almost every way from conventional agriculture. For one thing the plants are grown in expanding clay pebbles instead of using soil. I use basically a fifty per cent aquaponic, fifty per cent hydroponic nutrient mix. Aquaponics is the combination of aquaculture – the growing of fish – with hydroponics – which is growing plants in water-based systems.

2.12–2.28   The crops that we primarily focus on at The Farmery are gourmet mushrooms, strawberries, herbs, greens, baby greens, salad mixes, lettuces.

Part 2

2.29–2.52   But then, once you've grown it on a small space, the question is: what do you do with it? And that's really where the magic happens. If you grow it in such a small space to the point that you can locate a retail element to it, then you've created a completely new experience.

2.53–3.15   Customers can walk in there and cut the crops, harvest it, put it in a little baggy and they'll have a story right there – you know, that's what it is. They'll have an intimate connection with their food that they won't experience anywhere else.

3.16–3.52   We'd like to put a Farmery in every city across America, you know, starting with regional growth and hopefully expanding into national. I think we have a lot of different options as far as locating The Farmery. I think two of the most attractive options are: putting it in urban neighbourhoods, where customers can come in and they can see their food growing on the walls, they can have this unique experience that's typically not provided in an urban area for them.

> 'So we grow and sell in the same space is the eventual idea.'
> 'Oh! ...'

3.53–4.14   But I think also on the flip side of not just selling to that higher-end middle class market, I think there's also an argument for lower-income, urban neighbourhoods as well. Having them buying food from the area they live in maybe would make them more proud of themselves. And it's almost like celebrating their identity, you know.

4.15–5.06   I kept pursuing The Farmery because I believe in it. I'm on a mission to create something spectacular, something that I think people could be a part of, really. I hope The Farmery changes the way we look at food, the way we eat food. I hope The Farmery makes us realize that food is about quality over quantity. I want people to be charmed, I want people to be charmed by experiencing the 'Willy Wonka' of agriculture that is The Farmery. That's what I want.

4 ▪️ [12.1]

- Ask students to read the summary carefully and note what sort of information is needed.
- When students are ready, play the first part of the video (0.00–2.28) again. Students complete the summary. Let students compare their answers in pairs before checking with the class.

ANSWERS
1 transported
2 lose
3 consolidate
4 grow
5 sell
6 hang
7 use

Pronunciation note

Note that the speaker on this video is American, so students will have to catch his American pronunciation. They may note that *herbs* is pronounced with a silent 'h', for example.

5 ▪️ [12.1]

- Ask students to read the questions carefully and note what sort of information is needed.
- When students are ready, play the second part of the video (2.29 to the end) again. Students make notes. Let students compare their answers in pairs before checking with the class.

ANSWERS
1 a new experience, a story, an intimate connection with food
2 to every city in America, first regionally then nationally
3 middle-class and also lower-income urban markets
4 proud (that food is grown in their area)
5 that quality is more important than quantity
6 charmed (like visiting Willy Wonka's factory)

Background information

Willy Wonka is a fictional character created by British author Roald Dahl. He appears in the 1964 children's novel *Charlie and the Chocolate Factory*, which has been made into more than one film. He's fun and eccentric and runs a chocolate factory that is a wonderful and exciting place to visit.

After you watch

Vocabulary in context

6a ▪️ [12.2]

- Explain that students are going to watch some clips from the video which contain some new words and phrases. They need to choose the correct meaning of the words.

- Play the clips. When each multiple-choice question appears, pause the clip so that students can choose the correct definition. You could let students compare answers in pairs before discussing with the class.

ANSWERS
1 c   2 a   3 a   4 b   5 b   6 a

Vocabulary notes

Contrast *retail* (selling to the public) with *wholesale* (selling to suppliers or shops).

conventional agriculture = if something is conventional, it's done in a typical or traditional way

pursue = to follow or chase; we talk about pursuing a career or an idea or a dream

on a mission = this idiom comes from the idea of religious missionaries who went across the world to persuade people to believe in their faith

Videoscript ▪️ 12.2

1 ... the **complex** journey that the food has to take.
   a long
   b difficult
   c complicated
2 ... there's **massive** inventory loss.
   a enormous
   b wasteful
   c necessary
3 ... the bottom level is used as a **retail** area ...
   a for selling to the public
   b for selling to other companies
   c for selling in large quantities
4 My farming methods differ in almost every way from **conventional** agriculture.
   a industrial
   b traditional
   c local
5 I kept **pursuing** The Farmery because I believe in it.
   a building
   b continuing with
   c thinking about
6 I'm **on a mission** to create something spectacular.
   a I have an ambition
   b I'm on a journey
   c it's a risk I'm taking

6b

- Students work individually to complete the sentences. Elicit one or two ideas for the first sentence to get them started. Let students compare and discuss their sentences in pairs.

7

- Discuss the questions with your class. Use the opportunity to encourage students to share personal views and experiences.

ANSWERS

Students' own ideas

8

- Organize the class into groups of four or five. Ask students to work together to choose a product and prepare a presentation.
- When groups are ready, ask each group to briefly present their idea.

EXAMPLE ANSWERS

Ideas for making it interesting include:

having an interesting exhibit connected with the shop (e.g. a display of old chocolate advertisements or a museum of shoes through the ages)

allowing customers to visit the place where you make the product (e.g. a viewing area so they can see people putting bikes together or pouring chocolate into moulds)

having guided tours of your whole manufacturing and retail plant

making the shop area look interesting (e.g. make the shop front look like a cake)

letting customers choose the product as it's being made or be involved in the process

UNIT 12 Review and memory booster

Memory Booster activities

Exercises 6 and 8 are Memory Booster activities. For more information about these activities and how they benefit students, see page 10 of this Teacher's Book.

I can ... check boxes

As an alternative to asking students to simply tick the *I can* ... boxes, you could ask them to give themselves a score from 1 to 4 (1 = not very confident; 4 = very confident) for each language area. If students score 1 or 2 for a language area, refer them to additional practice activities in the Workbook and Grammar summary exercises.

Grammar

1

- Ask students to work individually to put the words in brackets in the correct order to complete the article. Let students compare answers in pairs before checking as a class.

ANSWERS

1 than just how

2 to have our car repaired

3 Some communities have even set up

4 have got a roofer to fix

5 might even ask for

6 that is just human nature

7 getting others to help

8 The only thing it doesn't do

2

- Ask students to read the article again if necessary to answer the question. Elicit the answers from the class.

ANSWERS

saves money; builds social connections; reduces waste

3

- Ask students to work in pairs and take it in turns to talk about areas listed. Encourage students to give reasons and ask each other questions.

Vocabulary

4

- Tell students to work individually to look at the phrases about jobs around the home. Ask them to rewrite the phrases with an appropriate verb. Monitor and help individuals where necessary and ensure their phrases are correct.
- Then ask students to work in pairs and discuss which of the things they think they could do themselves. Note that views will depend on each person's level of knowledge and skill.

UNIT 12 Money

EXAMPLE ANSWERS

1 fit a carpet	4 do the garden
2 fix a tap	5 assemble a wardrobe
3 tile the bathroom	6 put up some bookshelves

5

• Ask students to work individually to complete the definitions with five of the words in the box. Let students compare answers in pairs before checking with the class. At the feedback stage, you could ask students to verbally suggest definitions for the words in the box that were not used to complete the sentences (*invest, lend, living, salary*).

ANSWERS

1 save	4 life
2 owe	5 loan
3 earnings	

6 >> MB

• Ask students to work in pairs to write definitions for the words and phrases. When they have written them, tell them to compare their definitions with another pair. Elicit some of the definitions and see if there are any variations.

EXAMPLE ANSWERS

A **debt** is an amount of money that you owe someone, or for example, the bank.

The income gap is the difference between the amount of money that the rich and poor people have in a society.

Someone's **standard of living** is the amount of money, comfort and material goods that are available to that person.

Real life

7

• Ask students to work individually to complete the conversation by matching each of the travel agent's statements (1–4) with the customer's responses (a–d). Let students compare answers in pairs. Check answers by asking students to read out the dialogue in the correct order.

ANSWERS

1 c 2 a 3 d 4 b

8 >> MB

• Ask students to work in pairs to act out the conversation in Exercise 7. They should cover most of Exercise 7, leaving only the first few words of each line visible to prompt them. Tell them to add two more sentences to finish the negotiation.

• Once students have practised the conversation, ask them to change partners and try to repeat it, but without looking at the book.

Photocopiable tests

Unit 1 Test

Vocabulary

1 Use the word given in CAPITAL LETTERS at the end of each sentence to form a word that fits in the gap in the same sentence. Here is an example (0).

0   Danny's nine months old and very _*energetic*_ . He won't sit still!   ENERGY

1   Wendy Surtees is one of our most _____ employees. She's always on time
and completes all her projects.   DEPEND

2   Don't be so _____ ! You only ever think of yourself.   SELF

3   Adam Scott is one of the most _____ businessmen in our region.
He's made millions.   SUCCESS

4   Thanks for your advice. It's been very _____ .   HELP

5   Paul's _____ behaviour is annoying. He gets jealous when he isn't
the centre of attention.   CHILD

6   Jack's very _____ . He'd like to be boss of the company one day.   AMBITION

7   We need to take _____ action to stop the spread of this disease. We mustn't
waste a moment.   DECIDE

8   When she was young, she was very _____ . She never listened to her parents
and joined a punk band.   REBEL

9   The operation was quite _____ . It really hurt. But Bob's feeling better now.   PAIN

10 Our car's _____ . It often breaks down – we got stuck on the motorway last week.   RELY

___ / 10

2 Read the text below and decide which answer (A, B, C or D) best fits each gap. There is an example at the beginning (0).

My Uncle Tim

Of all my relatives, I have a very strong **(0)** ___ with my uncle Tim. He's a **(1)** ___ friend and really
(2) ___ me. Perhaps it's because he's older than me – thirteen years older, in fact – but not so much older to make
him of a different generation. As I was growing up, he was so cool and relaxed, you know, really **(3)** ___ , as if nothing
worried him. And now I'm twenty myself, he's just good fun. He's the kind of person you want to **(4)** ___ just because
he's fun to talk to, and the kind of person you can share problems with because you know he'll always be supportive.
Uncle Tim would always **(5)** ___ by me if things got tough. And I respect his advice because he talks a lot of **(6)** ___ sense.

Uncle Tim works in the city centre, not far from my college, so we meet **(7)** ___ for a coffee and a chat
at least once a week. He always asks me how I'm **(8)** ___ on at college, and we tell each other funny stories.
We share the same **(9)** ___ of humour so it's always a laugh. In the summer, I'm going to travel round Europe,
and I'm trying to **(10)** ___ him to come with me. I hope he can – I can't think of anyone I'd sooner travel the
world with.

0 **A** join	**B** bond	**C** connect	**D** support
1 **A** true	**B** really	**C** main	**D** strong
2 **A** rules the world for	**B** makes the earth for	**C** shows the earth to	**D** means the world to
3 **A** mutual	**B** dutiful	**C** laid-back	**D** considerate
4 **A** hang down from	**B** hang out with	**C** hang away from	**D** hang over
5 **A** go	**B** run	**C** stand	**D** lie
6 **A** common	**B** usual	**C** standard	**D** proper
7 **A** on	**B** in	**C** over	**D** up
8 **A** making	**B** getting	**C** taking	**D** doing
9 **A** fashion	**B** set	**C** feel	**D** sense
10 **A** take	**B** get	**C** go	**D** move

___ / 10

Grammar

3 Complete the text using the correct form of the verbs in brackets. There is an example at the beginning (0).

In the last twenty years, over five million Britons **(0)** _have left_ (leave) home for a new life abroad. More than one hundred thousand **(1)** _____ (move) abroad last year. Today, Australia **(2)** _____ (remain) the most popular destination. Its high standard of living and sunny weather **(3)** _____ (attract) two hundred thousand Britons in the last five years alone, and it **(4)** _____ (continue) to be the dream destination of many 'poms'*. Meanwhile Spain, which **(5)** _____ (be) a favourite among retiring Britons in the 1990s, **(6)** _____ (drop) down the league table of popular destinations in recent years. The Spanish economy **(7)** _____ (struggle) since 2008, and the unemployment rate **(8)** _____ (rise) year on year. The sharp fall in Spanish house prices in 2008 **(9)** _____ (hit) ex-pat houseowners from the UK hard. As a result, Spain **(10)** _____ (become) a less attractive destination.

* pom = a jokey name for an English person in Australia

___ / 10

4 Complete the sentences with the past simple, present perfect simple or present perfect continuous form of the verbs in brackets. Here is an example (0).

0 I _'ve known_ (know) Julia all my life. She's very supportive.

1 All day, everybody _____ (chat) online about that drama serial on TV last night. I keep getting messages in my inbox even now!

2 Jake and I _____ (not get) on during last summer's holiday. He's the least considerate person I know.

3 Some time ago, John and I _____ (decide) to travel round the world together.

4 Ray _____ (buy) a new car. It's outside. Come and have a look!

5 It's about time you got here. It's really late and we _____ (wait) for ages.

6 My brother _____ (move) to Canada. We won't see him so much now.

7 My headache _____ (get) worse all morning. Perhaps I should lie down.

8 So far this year, the weather _____ (be) awful.

9 We first _____ (hear) about our interesting family history when our uncle was here.

10 Amy _____ (not pass) her test yet. She's hoping to take it again in the spring.

___ / 10

5 You are going to read an article about National Geographic's Genographic Project. For questions 1–10, choose from the sections (A–E). The sections may be chosen more than once. There is an example at the beginning (0).

Which section says

  0 which people are carrying out research into the human genome? _B_

  1 that our view of human evolution has changed to some extent? ___

  2 why ordinary people should take part in the project? ___

  3 whether or not other people will have access to an individual's DNA data? ___

  4 how many years the Genographic Project has been going on? ___

  5 whether genetical information from one group of participants may be more important than information from another? ___

  6 how ordinary people can gather and send useable material? ___

  7 what the project most hopes to discover? ___

  8 whether any of the data will be kept secret or not? ___

  9 how an individual's DNA is analysed using technology? ___

  10 whether the quantity of information collected is a concern for the researchers? ___

___ / 10

Reading

National Geographic's Genographic Project

A

It's no secret that we all want to know who we really are and, since its launch in 2005, National Geographic's Genographic Project has been using advanced DNA analysis to help answer fundamental questions about where humans originated and how we came to populate the Earth. Now, cutting-edge technology is enabling the project to shine a powerful new light on our collective past. By participating in the next phase of this real-time scientific research, you will be able to learn more about yourself and your roots than you ever thought possible. You will also help support the Genographic Legacy Fund, which works to conserve and revitalize indigenous cultures around the world.

B

The Genographic Project is a multi-year research initiative led by National Geographic Explorer-in-Residence Dr Spencer Wells. Dr Wells and a team of renowned international scientists are using advanced genetic and computational technologies to analyse historical patterns in DNA from participants around the world to better understand our human genetic roots. As well as aiming to gather research data in collaboration with indigenous and traditional peoples, the project is reaching out to ordinary members of the public to help. Vital as it is to collect data from peoples who have evolved in relative isolation, having as large a database of samples as possible is just as essential to the success of the project.

C

To join this real-time scientific project all you have to do is purchase a Genographic Project Participation Kit, called Geno 2.0. Basically, this is a simple swab that you swipe on the inside of your cheek to collect your own DNA. Although it takes seconds to complete your part in the project, it will be months before you receive the results of the researchers' analysis. However, it will be worth the wait. A technology called single nucleotide polymorphism uses computer chips to probe for 150,000 different mutations in any individual's strand of DNA. Analysing these tiny mistakes, passed down over thousands of years of evolution, is what the project aims to do.

D

Although not a primary aim of the research, an area of study that may fascinate the layman is the extent to which our ancestry may or may not include genes from Neanderthal or Denisovan peoples. Until recently, it was believed that all humans were descended exclusively from *Homo sapiens* who evolved in what is now East Africa. Today, however, it is commonly accepted that modern humans, as they migrated north, west and east from Africa, mated with Neanderthal and Denisovan peoples, who had evolved separately. These peoples died out but their DNA has survived in a surprisingly large number of people today. It will be fascinating to discover the extent to which we are all Neanderthal.

E

Although taking part in National Geographic's Genographic Project has a financial cost, your money won't be wasted. A portion of the proceeds from all Geno 2.0 kit sales will be used to fund further research, and a further portion will go to the Genographic Legacy Fund, which in turn supports community-led indigenous conservation and revitalization projects. The Genographic Project is anonymous, non-medical and non-profit, and all results will be placed in the public domain following scientific peer publication.

Listening

6 🔊 [113] You will hear five short voicemails which Penny received. For questions 1–5, choose the reason why (A–H) each person has contacted Penny. Use the letters only once. There are three extra letters which you do not need to use.

Speaker 1 ___

Speaker 2 ___

Speaker 3 ___

Speaker 4 ___

Speaker 5 ___

A I want to go round to Penny's house.

B I want Penny to do something for me.

C I'm inviting Penny to visit.

D I want to fix something for Penny.

E I'm going on holiday with Penny.

F I'm agreeing to help Penny.

G I'm inviting Penny out.

H I want to return something to Penny.

___ / 10

Writing

7 Read the task below.

> Your classmates from primary school have organized an event to celebrate your 20-year reunion next month. Write an email to a school friend inviting him/her to the party.

Write your email (180–200 words). Make sure you:

- include a greeting and the reason for writing.
- give your news (about work, studies, your marital status and kids, anything interesting you have done in life, etc.).
- ask for their news.
- include good wishes and an appropriate ending.

___ / 10

Speaking

8 Read the task below and give your presentation in class.

> Prepare a two-minute presentation for your teacher and classmates about your family and how someone in your family has influenced you.

In your presentation, include:

- a description of at least three family members – their appearance, personality and relationship to you.
- a description of how one family member has influenced you and why.

___ / 10

Unit 2 Test

Vocabulary

1 Complete the text with the words in the box. There are three extra words which you do not need to use. There is an example at the beginning (0).

character	fast-moving	gripping	heading	key	original	plot	romantic
setting	summit	theme	thought-provoking	~~thriller~~	track		

Everest is a beautifully filmed **(0)** ___*thriller*___ which tells the true story of an attempt by a group of inexperienced climbers to reach the **(1)** _____ of the world's highest mountain. Its **(2)** _____ is, of course, spectacular – partly filmed on the mountain itself in Nepal, some of the aerial shots of steep cliffs and snow-filled canyons are amazing. This sense of realism, however, doesn't extend to the people in the film. The main **(3)** _____ , a well-meaning tour company operator called Rob Hall, is a stereotype, as are all the many mountaineers in the film. At times, it was hard to keep **(4)** _____ of who was who.

The film's based on a true story, but the overall **(5)** _____ is very thin and dull – we know what's going to happen from one scene to the next. I must admit though that the scenes in the mountains are really **(6)** _____ . I carried on watching because they were so exciting. The **(7)** _____ moment in the film, when the climbers **(8)** _____ up the mountain realize that a blizzard is about to reach them, is powerful. In the end though, the film's neither **(9)** _____ – there have been many other better films of this kind – nor **(10)** _____ – it didn't make me think very much at all!

___ / 10

2 Read the text below and decide which answer (A, B, C or D) best fits each gap. There is an example at the beginning (0).

Storytelling

Storytelling is an ancient tradition. Good storytellers know how to **(0)** ___ their audience by **(1)** ___ emotions. They know how to make their stories so **(2)** ___ that people cry, or so **(3)** ___ that people believe them to be true. They know how to **(4)** ___ a story to life. I once witnessed an ancient storyteller in a remote mountain village. He **(5)** ___ the villagers entertained for hours with magical tales. His great strength was the way he impersonated each **(6)** ___ in his stories with different voices. One moment, he was an evil money-lender, **(7)** ___ under his breath in an angry voice you could not hear. The next, he was a young lover, speaking of her lost romance with a sad and painful **(8)** ___ . Many of his stories were really **(9)** ___ – so scary they made the hair on your neck stand on end. I loved listening to him – mind you, his stories went on so long, you really had to **(10)** ___ an eye on the time.

0 **A** tell	**(B)** engage	**C** connect	**D** share
1 **A** sharing	**B** reaching	**C** convincing	**D** bringing
2 **A** gripping	**B** shaking	**C** fast-moving	**D** touching
3 **A** convincing	**B** believing	**C** provoking	**D** moving
4 **A** keep	**B** hang	**C** bring	**D** take
5 **A** went	**B** kept	**C** stood	**D** took
6 **A** theme	**B** plot	**C** character	**D** background
7 **A** muttering	**B** signing	**C** moaning	**D** screaming
8 **A** hurry	**B** moan	**C** mumble	**D** sigh
9 **A** anxious	**B** creepy	**C** fast-moving	**D** original
10 **A** make	**B** get	**C** keep	**D** move

___ / 10

Grammar

3 Complete the text with the correct narrative tense form of the verbs in brackets. There is an example at the beginning (0).

Hans Christian Andersen **(0)** ___died___ (die) in 1875, at the age of seventy. By then, he **(1)** _____ (write) numerous plays, poems and novels. However, today, he's remembered, not for the works he **(2)** _____ (produce) for an adult audience, but for his children's fairy tales.

Although he started writing young, Anderson **(3)** _____ (not find) success until the early 1830s. It was then that, while he **(4)** _____ (travel) through Switzerland and Italy, he **(5)** _____ (complete) his first novel, *The Improvisatore*, to instant acclaim in Denmark.

Real lasting fame, however, **(6)** _____ (not arrive) until 1845 when a London magazine **(7)** _____ (publish) English language versions of the various volumes of fairy stories he **(8)** _____ (write) since 1835. At last, Anderson **(9)** _____ (become) a success and from then on he **(10)** _____ (devote) himself to producing fairy tales, including such timeless classics as *The Snow Queen*, *The Ugly Duckling* and *Thumbelina*.

___ / 10

4 Complete the second sentence so that it has a similar meaning to the first sentence, using the word given. Do not change the word given. You must use between two and four words, including the word given. Here is an example (0).

  0 In these parts, people know Billy Hughes by his nickname 'Whizzer'.

  AS

  In these parts, Billy Hughes _____*is known as*_____ 'Whizzer' – that's his nickname.

  1 Our drama teacher showed a thought-provoking film in class.

  WAS

  A thought-provoking film _____ by our drama teacher in class.

  2 The thieves flew to Cuba before the police reached the airport.

  HAD

  By the time the police reached the airport, the thieves _____ Cuba.

  3 The police refused to name any of the victims.

  COULD

  The police said none of the victims _____ .

  4 For centuries, storytellers have told their wonderful stories.

  BEEN

  Wonderful stories _____ storytellers for centuries.

  5 Sally left her handbag on the bus on the way home.

  SHE

  When she got home, Sally realized _____ her handbag on the bus.

  6 The academy will give the actor an award for his work.

  BE

  The actor _____ an award for his work by the academy.

  7 How much are they paying you to appear in this commercial?

  PAID

  How much _____ to appear in this commercial?

  8 The teacher promised to correct our exams by Friday.

  WOULD

  The teacher said our exams _____ by Friday.

  9 You have to see the documentary to believe it.

  TO

  The documentary _____ to be believed.

  10 Richard was waving through the window moments before the train crashed.

  HAD

  Just before the train crashed, Richard _____ through the window.

___ / 10

Reading

A Quiet Passion reviewed

A Quiet Passion is Terence Davies's biopic of the nineteenth-century American poet Emily Dickinson, author of 1,800 (incredibly wonderful) poems, of which only 10 were published in her lifetime. Who was this woman? She's fixed in our minds as a recluse who would only talk from behind her bedroom door, but was she always a recluse? Is it the truth of her that matters, or the truth of her poetry? Can the two become one?

As a general rule poets do not make the best film characters. Poets are not crime-fighters who are part spider or dress like bats. What a poet does is inward-looking – they sit, and think, and write. By its very nature, a poet's life is uncinematic. Furthermore, films about poets tend to ignore the poetry, in favour of simplifying a character so that they are, for example, an angry or a miserable loner.

So, how well does Davies do? He brings the story to life in a fairly straightforward way. It is chronological, but told in a series of disconnected scenes, and it doesn't simply go from birth to death like an old-fashioned biography. It opens with Emily, played by talented young actress Emma Bell, as a teenager. She's being told off in school for breaking school rules. Time passes, and the film's character grows into adulthood. Cynthia Nixon, well-known for her role in long-running TV series *Sex and the City*, is terrific as the adult Emily. Indeed, at times you feel that she has become the poet.

Emily lives in Amherst, Massachusetts, with her family, and they are her world because she has no other world. In the mid-nineteeth century, or so the film informs us, the lives of women were so controlled that their days were unbelievably dull. You feel it in the film. Clocks tick as women stare into space. They sew. They play hymns at the piano. And that was it, pretty much, for a Saturday night.

The first hour of the film is pure period drama, with beautiful dresses, and horse carriages, and sunlight coming in through windows. Emily is vivacious, sociable and very opinionated. With a script by Davies, she is also sharp and funny, perhaps too much so. Was everything she said brilliant? However, you can also sense her spirit being crushed. She must ask her father for permission to write. She suffers disappointments in friendship and romance, and her love for a married man, who does not show any interest in return, marks the beginning of her decline into bitterness, despair and isolation. The second hour moves as slowly and as disconnectedly as the first, but is more deeply moving.

From his first autobiographical films through to his later adaptations of great novels, Davies has always made highly personal films, and this is a very personal interpretation of Dickinson's life. A number of facts have been changed. Perhaps, because he is more interested in exploring Emily's feelings than her writing, this says more about Davies than Dickinson. And where is the poetry? We see Emily writing at a desk, and placing her poems into little books, but we don't find out much about how she came to write them.

Still, as far as films about poets go, this succeeds more than most, particularly with Cynthia Nixon's terrific central performance. However, what it most made me want to do is get out my copy of Emily's poems. The poetry is where it's at.

5 You are going to read a review of the film *A Quiet Passion*. For questions 1–10, choose the answer (A, B, C or D) which you think fits best according to the text. There is an example at the beginning (0).

0 In the opening sentence of the review, we learn that Emily Dickinson

   A didn't want her poems published in her lifetime.

   B couldn't get any poems published while she lived.

   C had only a fraction of her works published when alive.

   D had to spend her own money to get published.

1 In the first paragraph, the reviewer says she wants to find out

   A why the director chose to make a film about Emily Dickinson.

   B whether our view of Emily Dickinson is accurate.

   C why we no longer remember Emily Dickinson for her poetry.

   D how Emily Dickinson's poetry influenced her life.

2 The reviewer says that poets are poor film characters because

   A their lives lack the action of more typical film characters.

   B they tend to have negative characteristics such as anger.

   C it is difficult to ignore the poetry and focus on their personality.

   D it is important to represent them in a precise way.

3 What do we learn about *A Quiet Passion* in the third paragraph?

   A It contains flashbacks from Emily's adult life back to her childhood.

   B It is old-fashioned because it sets out events in order.

   C It shows both scenes from Emily's youth and her adult life.

   D It begins when Emily is born and shows her life until her death.

4 What's the reviewer's attitude towards the actresses in the third paragraph?

   A She is critical of one of them.

   B She compares their performances.

   C She dislikes both their performances.

   D She compliments one of them more.

5 The reviewer says that Cynthia Nixon's performance is

   A very thought-provoking.

   B totally convincing.

   C extremely touching.

   D not entirely accurate.

6 What do we learn about the film in the fourth paragraph?

A It becomes dull when it shows Emily's daily life.

B It depicts some women's daily life in the nineteenth century.

C It tries to capture the lives of most nineteenth-century women.

D It misrepresents Emily's daily life.

7 What is the review critical of in the fifth paragraph?

A The way the film shows the contradictions of the main character.

B The settings, costumes and style of the film's 'period drama' feel.

C The slow-moving nature of the later part of the film.

D Aspects of the film's dialogue which may not be true.

8 In the film, Emily becomes increasingly isolated after

A she is rejected by someone she has feelings for.

B her father fails to show support for her ambition.

C her spirit is crushed by people in her family.

D she finds it difficult to write under pressure.

9 According to the reviewer, why is *A Quiet Passion* typical of Davies's work?

A It reveals things about the interests and views of Davies himself.

B It adapts a major novel, which is something he often likes to do.

C It changes facts in the story and isn't always true to life.

D It shows a greater interest in the writer's genius than in her emotions.

10 What does 'where it's at' mean in the last line of the review?

A The poetry makes *A Quiet Passion* a good film.

B Emily's poems are what really matter.

C We can see the real Emily Dickinson in her poetry.

D Films about poets are becoming more popular.

___ / 10

Listening

6 🎧 [114] You will hear Janice tell a story. For questions 1–10, complete the sentences with a word or short phrase. There is an example at the beginning (0).

0 At the time of the story, Janice was _nineteen years old_ .

1 Janice took Tommy to a _____ .

2 Tommy's mother is Janice's _____ .

3 Janice says she _____ to help Tommy's mother.

4 Tommy refused to get on the _____ .

5 Janice didn't realize Tommy wasn't with her until she was _____ .

6 When Janice reached _____ she couldn't see Tommy.

7 After losing Tommy, Janice was feeling really _____ .

8 Concerned about Tommy, Janice dropped both bags of _____ .

9 Janice asked a lady selling _____ to help her.

10 When she saw Tommy, he was accompanied by _____ .

___ / 10

Writing

7 You have seen this announcement in an English-language magazine.

> **Stories wanted**
>
> We need stories for our English-language magazine. Your story must include one of these sentences:
>
> → *As I looked out of the window, an old acquaintance was walking up the path.*
>
> → *I knew that I had seen her somewhere before.*
>
> → *That was the moment I realized I was in the wrong place.*

Write your story (180–200 words). Make sure you:

- start the story at a dramatic point.
- use correct past tenses to describe events.
- use some descriptive verbs and adverbs.

___ / 10

Speaking

8 Choose one of the topics below and prepare a short story to tell your teacher.

- a time when you were responsible for someone and something went wrong
- a time when you missed a train or a plane or an important appointment
- a time when you had to act to solve a crisis

___ / 10

Unit 3 Test

Vocabulary

1 Complete the text with the words in the box. There is an example at the beginning (0).

brick   cardboard   concrete   cotton   glass   leather   metal   nylon   plastic   rubber   ~~wood~~

The wonder of materials

How far has civilization in Europe depended on the development of materials? Here is a rough guide.

Houses

Originally, of course, most houses in Europe were made of **(0)** _wood_ from trees. The material was plentiful in forests and easy to cut and use. In the Middle Ages, builders began to use **(1)** _____ to build important buildings. Made from dried clay from river beds, and baked in ovens, this material was long-lasting and resistant to fire. It was at this time that **(2)** _____ started to be used in windows, especially in churches, to let in light. In the nineteenth century, building techniques were revolutionized by the invention of reinforced **(3)** _____ , a material so hard and strong that you could build skyscrapers from it. In more recent times, cheaper or more ecological materials have been used in house building. The wikkelhouse, for example, is a new type of house made from **(4)** _____ , a material made from layers of packed paper.

Cars

Early cars were made from steel, a strong, light, shiny, man-made **(5)** _____ , which had also been used in trains. The material that really revolutionized cars, however, was **(6)** _____ , a material produced by trees in south-east Asia. Its elastic properties made it perfect for tyres.

Clothes

The first clothes were hand-made from natural products. **(7)** _____ from animal skins was used to make coats, boots and jackets, for example. In the eighteenth century, there was an explosion in the use of **(8)** _____ in clothes manufacturing. A white, fluffy material, it was grown in huge amounts on slave plantations and shipped to Europe to be made into shirts and dresses. The invention of man-made synthetic material, commonly referred to with the generic term **(9)** _____ , revolutionized the manufacture of just about everything, from toys to furniture. **(10)** _____ is a synthetic material with the properties required to make clothes, notably stockings and dresses.

___ / 10

2 Decide which answer (A, B, C or D) best fits the gap in each sentence. Here is an example (0).

0 There's a flu ___ spreading across the country. Thousands are ill!
   A starvation   **B** congestion   Ⓒ epidemic   **D** poverty

1 Use this can ___ to take the top off the can and get the food out.
   A key   **B** opener   **C** hook   **D** breaker

2 Don't forget your phone ___ . You don't want the battery to go flat.
   A charger   **B** maker   **C** holder   **D** switch

3 We're out of ink. We need a new printer ___ .
   A case   **B** carton   **C** box   **D** cartridge

4 Buying these boxes was a great idea. It's a ___ solution for all my storage needs.
   A helping   **B** neat   **C** cutting   **D** cute

5 We custom-___ all our cars to the exact demands of people who buy them. That's why they are so expensive.
   A make   **B** manufacture   **C** build   **D** construct

6 The hotel is luxurious and located in the city centre but it doesn't cost the ___ to stay there.
   A world   **B** life   **C** earth   **D** leg

7 We want to find a ___ solution to the problem. We'd like to fix it and never have to worry about it again.
   A long-term   **B** well-made   **C** labour-saving   **D** time-consuming

8 We only use environmentally-___ products.
   A easy   **B** friendly   **C** helpful   **D** pleasant

9 The photocopier is out of ___ again. It seems to have broken down.
   A use   **B** work   **C** order   **D** shape

10 Don't eat those biscuits. They're ___ date.
   A off   **B** away from   **C** over   **D** out of

___ / 10

Grammar

3 Complete the text using the correct future form of the verbs in brackets. There is an example at the beginning (0).

Today we **(0)** _'re going to look_ (look) at the question of climate change. The problem **(1)** _____ (get) more and more serious each day, and may even **(2)** _____ (be) so bad that it is irreversible. This speech has a clear prepared outline. I **(3)** _____ (talk) about ozone layers and about how evidence shows that ice caps **(4)** _____ (melt) if we don't take action. In the next twelve days, I **(5)** _____ (visit) ten capital cities to spread this message – I'm sure you **(6)** _____ (agree) that's a pretty demanding itinerary!

I usually deliver my lecture first, but, actually, today, I think I **(7)** _____ (do) things differently. I think I **(8)** _____ (start) by asking you, my audience, to write on a piece of paper what you think is probably **(9)** _____ (happen) in the next twenty years or so to our climate. We are about **(10)** _____ (face) disaster. Are you ready to act or are you feeling complacent?

___ / 10

4 Complete the second sentence so that it has a similar meaning to the first sentence, using the word given. Do not change the word given. You must use between two and four words, including the word given. Here is an example (0).

0 It's possible that we'll have underground cities in the future.

EVEN

We _____ _might even have_ _____ underground cities in the future.

1 The economy's going to take a hit in the next few weeks.

ABOUT

The economy _____ a hit.

2 We're flying to Cuba at midday tomorrow.

BE

At midday tomorrow, we _____ to Cuba.

3 When will this project of theirs be complete?

COMPLETED

When will they _____ this project?

4 How much longer will your studies on this course take?

STUDYING

How much longer _____ this course?

5 Dad'll fall asleep before the end of the film.

HAVE

By the time the film ends, Dad _____ .

6 Current statistics show a probable future rise in house prices.

TO

According to current statistics, house prices _____ rise in the future.

7 I expect you to feel a lot better by tomorrow afternoon.

MUCH

You'll _____ better by tomorrow afternoon.

8 I don't intend spending the holiday visiting museums – and that's for sure.

DEFINITELY

I'm _____ spend the holiday visiting museums.

9 With no time for lunch between now and the end of the walk, Tom will be bad-tempered.

HAD

Tom will be bad-tempered by the end of the walk because he _____ time for lunch.

10 Do you want a sandwich from the café? I'm just about to go and get one.

GOING

_____ get a sandwich from the café. Do you want one?

___ / 10

Reading

Historic Solar Flight Shows Promise

Completing the first trip around the world exclusively on solar power, the experimental Solar Impulse has shown what may be possible in energy and flight. When it concluded its journey in the summer of 2016, the Solar Impulse became the first aircraft to circumnavigate the globe without a drop of liquid fuel. The flight took seventeen months, and included stops in seventeen cities. Sun power propelled the pilots across approximately forty-three thousand kilometres of sky, and their landing in Abu Dhabi happened one day after the birthday of Amelia Earhart, who was the first woman to fly alone across the Atlantic in 1932.

Although a significant moment in the history of flight, Solar Impulse was always more about energy than aviation. Outlining his vision for the project more than twelve years ago, Bertrand Piccard, one of the pilots on the Solar Impulse, noted that clean energy wasn't being promoted properly. Solar Impulse, then, is an airborne argument for solar technologies. According to the supporters of the project to fly on solar energy alone, it will cut the world's energy consumption in half and protect a warming planet.

Of course, impressive though the flight was, solar-powered commercial air travel at the capacity and speeds the general public would expect isn't yet possible, and probably won't be in most of our lifetimes. Solar Impulse can only carry one person at a time – the pilot – and travels at about the speed of a car, seventy-five kilometres per hour, so it isn't likely to appeal to people keen to fly to the beach for their holidays.

A lot of what the achievement of the Solar Impulse is demonstrating is probably going to be relevant to earth-bound applications before it becomes important to flight. For example, the plane's lightweight materials and other components could be used on the road. Its super-efficient engine ran on electricity generated from 17,248 solar cells. These were special, energy-dense batteries which,

uniquely, stored sun power so the plane could fly at night. It proved that a 24-hour electrical system, powered exclusively by renewable energy, is possible. The project helped develop solar cells that are nearly fifty per cent more efficient than regular ones.

A major supporter of the journey was Masdar, the sustainability testing ground located in Abu Dhabi, Solar Impulse's beginning and ending destination. 'In Abu Dhabi, you can feel the excitement surrounding Solar Impulse,' says Masdar CEO Mohamed Jameel Al Ramahi. 'Being the host city is a source of tremendous national pride.' In particular, he says, the plane's 118-hour flight over the Pacific Ocean 'shattered the myth that solar energy captured by PV panels can't be stored and utilized at night.' Here again is where Solar Impulse stands for advances that will more likely appear first on the ground, as power plants look to introduce more renewable energy while balancing the intermittent nature of the sun and wind.

While much of the technology aboard the Solar Impulse may be better employed on the ground for now, there is one area that seriously interests the aviation industry. Dan Rutherford, program director for marine and aviation technology at the International Council on Clean Transportation, notes that Solar Impulse is not just about the solar power. It's also about using electricity instead of combustion and hydraulics to power flight. 'We've already seen a movement toward more electric aircraft,' Rutherford says, pointing to the Boeing Dreamliner, which has batteries that power its auxiliary system and computers. Between the amazing advancements on the Solar Impulse and the most advanced commercial planes there are similarities. Although it may well be a while before we get on board a plane powered by the sun, it isn't going to be that long before trans-Pacific planes are exclusively using electricity to fly.

5 You are going to read an article about solar-powered flight. Are the sentences true (T) or false (F)? Or is there not enough information (N) to say if the sentences are true or false? There is an example at the beginning (0).

  0 The Solar Impulse set off on its historic journey round the world in the summer of 2016. __*F*__

  1 No source of energy other than that provided by the sun was used during the Solar Impulse's historic flight. ___

  2 The Solar Impulse landed in Abu Dhabi one day later than originally planned. ___

  3 The main reason why Piccard wanted to fly the Solar Impulse round the world was to create aviation history. ___

  4 It's unlikely that ordinary people will go on solar flights in the near future. ___

  5 People designing vehicles may be interested in the technology used in the Solar Impulse. ___

  6 The text suggests that the Solar Impulse used batteries that were better at storing energy than any previously used. ___

  7 Jameel Al Ramahi says that Masdar made a significant investment to get the Solar Impulse to start and finish its journey in Abu Dhabi. ___

  8 Al Ramahi believes that the Solar Impulse's flight proved something about solar energy that people had previously doubted. ___

  9 Dan Rutherford says that the Solar Impulse has increased the likelihood that we will have solar-powered flight in the future. ___

  10 According to the text, advanced commercial planes have already installed aspects of technology learned from the flight of the Solar Impulse. ___

___ / 10

Listening

6 🔊 [115] You will hear people talking in five different situations. For questions 1–10, choose the best answer (A, B or C). There is an example at the beginning (0).

A hotel guest calls reception

0 Which room is the guest in?
   A Room 8
   (B) Room 18
   C Room 80

1 What's the problem?
   A The hotel has given the guest the wrong room.
   B The guest needs a bed for a one-year-old baby.
   C The beds in the room aren't suitable for the guest.

2 How will the receptionist solve the problem?
   A by moving the guests to a different room
   B by changing the furniture layout in the room
   C by getting the right bed for the baby

Two work colleagues are talking next to a photocopier

3 What does the man do?
   A He apologizes for damaging the machine.
   B He blames somebody else for the damage.
   C He asks for help to repair the machine.

4 What does the woman suggest?
   A moving the machine
   B placing the machine elsewhere
   C accessing the machine using a lever

A radio commercial for a vacuum cleaner

5 How does the commercial describe the Dixon 125?
   A as an appliance that won't break down easily
   B as an appliance that costs less than other brands
   C as an appliance that's been on the market for a while

6 What does the commercial say about the appearance and feel of the Dixon 125?
   A It's small for a vacuum cleaner.
   B It isn't difficult to move it around.
   C It's made of cutting-edge materials.

Dan's leaving a phone message

7 What's the relationship between Dan and Jane?
   A They're flatmates.
   B They're brother and sister.
   C They're old school friends.

8 Why has Dan left Jane a message?
   A He's asking her to let him in because he has no key.
   B He's informing her that he's delivering something.
   C He's reminding her about something.

Simon is calling his friend Melissa

9 What does Simon say to Melissa?
   A He tells her that there's been a change of plan.
   B He accuses her of being late.
   C He tells her he's feeling hungry.

10 Where do Simon and Melissa arrange to meet?
   A at the cinema
   B in Simon's apartment
   C at a restaurant

___ / 10

Writing

7 Read the task below.

> You've booked a twin room at a hotel. However, you want to change it to a room with a double bed and a cot for an infant. You also want to book the hotel's restaurant for dinner and find out whether there's parking at the hotel. Write an email to the hotel asking for these things.

Write your email (180–200 words). Make sure you:

- include a greeting and the reason for writing.
- include an apology and request for a change to your booking.
- include a request for dinner and an enquiry about parking.
- include good wishes and an appropriate ending.

___ / 10

Speaking

8 Read the task below and give your presentation in class.

> Prepare a two-minute presentation for your teacher and classmates about your study or career plans and how you think life will have changed for you in the next ten years.

In your presentation, include:

- a description of your plans for courses you plan to do, what you hope to do after completing a course, or what you plan to do next in your career.
- where you hope and/or expect you will be in ten years' time.

___ / 10

Unit 4 Test

Vocabulary

1 Use the word given in CAPITAL LETTERS at the end of each sentence to form a word that fits in the gap in the same sentence. Here is an example (0).

  0 Damien Hirst is one of the country's leading _artists_ .   ART

  1 An actor and a _____ , Ricky Gervais is often on TV.   COMEDY

  2 It was one of the best _____ by a teenager I have seen in a long time.   PERFORM

  3 I never give money to _____ in the street even if they put on a good show.   BUSK

  4 To be a good designer, you have to be _____ as well as dedicated.   CREATE

  5 The fine _____ are on display in all their grandeur in London's greatest galleries.   ART

  6 Melbourne has many places of _____ beauty.   NATURE

  7 _____ , what's important is not art itself but how we experience it.   ULTIMATE

  8 The new _____ at the Tate Gallery was a little disappointing.   EXHIBIT

  9 Davina is very _____ . She is so talented that she has won a place at one of the country's leading art colleges.   ART

  10 My dad was a circus _____ in his youth.   PERFORM

  ___ / 10

2 Complete the text with the words in the box. There are two extra words which you do not need to use. There is an example at the beginning (0).

acting ~~closing~~ exhibiting exposing participating performing protesting
regulating soothing spending (x3) waking

I've always been a big fan of small live venues so when I heard that a historical venue near my home was
(0) _closing_ down, I decided it was time to take action. There are still plenty of arty art galleries in my city
(1) _____ boring artwork, or trendy jazz bars playing dull, barely audible music – **(2)** _____ after
a day at work, I guess, but who wants to relax?! Shockingly though, there simply aren't many venues for new,
lively rock and indy bands. In this digital age, it's easy to forget how essential such places are for new bands.
In my youth, I remember **(3)** _____ with my pretty talentless band in some great (if slightly run-down)
venues in my home city of Sheffield, **(4)** _____ hours setting up our kit, and **(5)** _____ in endless
rows about which songs to play and in which order. On one occasion, the stage we were on fell apart,
(6) _____ all the plumbing and electrical wires beneath, and nearly breaking the ankle of our lead singer.
(7) _____ all our free time doing gigs was fantastic – it gives me goosebumps to remember those great
days. What a shame that today's generation of kids is being denied the same opportunity. Local government
is to blame. Politicians are **(8)** _____ small venues out of business by making them meet strict legal
guidelines. Some venues are **(9)** _____ a fortune on fire precautions and emergency exits, while others
are closing. Disappointingly, few people are **(10)** _____ about the closure of so many venues, but I think
it's time more of us did.

  ___ / 10

Grammar

3 Read the text below and decide which answer (A, B, C or D) best fits each gap. There is an example at the beginning (0).

A decade ago, a decision was made to redesign **(0)** ___ of the National Museum. To do this, **(1)** ___ museums
would have closed down completely, but **(2)** ___ trustees of the National Museum didn't want to follow such
a course of action. Closing the **(3)** ___ museum would have cost a huge **(4)** ___ of money in ticket sales. Consequently,
an alternative solution was needed. The museum asked a **(5)** ___ of leading architectural design companies to propose
a solution. **(6)** ___ company was given the opportunity to submit their plans. Initially, **(7)** ___ company came up
with a solution that met the museum's demands. Eventually, however, two companies were shortlisted to do the work.
(8) ___ had good ideas. One proposed closing down one wing at a time, while the other proposed carrying out work
behind glass barriers to protect the public from any debris. **(9)** ___ option seemed viable. In the end, the museum chose
the latter idea, hoping that by keeping **(10)** ___ gallery in the museum open during the entire refurbishment they would
keep their customers happy.

0	A many	B̄ much	C any	D certain
1	A most	B plenty	C a lot	D much
2	A almost no	B enough	C a lack of	D several
3	A all	B whole	C every	D most
4	A number	B loads	C amount	D plenty
5	A few	B several	C certain	D number
6	A Each	B All	C Whole	D Some
7	A any	B no	C hardly any	D none
8	A Both	B Every	C Either	D Some
9	A A little	B A few	C All	D Either
10	A certain	B every	C both	D all

___ / 10

4 Complete the second sentence so that it has a similar meaning to the first sentence, using the word given. Do not change the word given. You must use between two and four words, including the word given. Here is an example (0).

  0 There aren't any people in the museum at this time of night.
   NO
   There are no people in the museum at this time of night.

  1 All the visitors were searched before entering the gallery.
   EVERY
   _____ before entering the gallery.

  2 Both artists were absent from the awards ceremony.
   NEITHER
   _____ present at the awards ceremony.

  3 We don't have enough volunteers to help put on the show.
   LACK
   There _____ volunteers to help put on the show.

  4 In our band, there are two guitarists, and each plays left-handed.
   BOTH
   In our band, _____ left-handed.

  5 Just about everybody there agreed that the performance was brilliant.
   MOST
   _____ that the performance was brilliant.

  6 Several people in the audience left early.
   NUMBER
   _____ in the audience left early.

  7 All the artists are really talented, which is why the exhibition is amazing.
   EACH
   _____ really talented, which is why the exhibition is amazing.

  8 Hardly any cinemas showed the art film.
   ALMOST
   _____ showed the art film.

  9 All the paintings in the collection were cleaned.
   WHOLE
   _____ cleaned – that's every single painting.

  10 No performances will take place during the holiday break.
   BE
   There _____ performances during the holiday break.

___ / 10

Reading

Cave walls record early encounters between the Old World and the New

Deep inside caves beneath a lonely island that lies about sixty kilometres west of Puerto Rico, archaeologists have discovered a number of underground galleries full of intriguing art. **(0)** _D_ This is something nobody expected to find. There are ancient drawings by the islanders alongside religious symbols made by Spanish sailors from one of Christopher Columbus' ships.

Although barely fifty square kilometres in area, the whole of the remote island of Isla Mona has caves underground. More than two hundred have been discovered so far, but only a few have been explored. **(1)** ___ It is thought that they made these fantastical swirls, lines and figures by dragging fingernails through the soft surface of the walls and ceilings. Representing the most diverse collection of motifs in all the Caribbean, the thousands of designs catalogued so far include humans, animals and geometric symbols. Some span several metres in width, and many overlap to form an illustrated record of repeated visits to the caves.

Research has shown that indigenous people lived on this rocky outpost for more than five thousand years, and that the last century of that period of habitation overlapped with the start of the European colonial era. There is, of course, no written record of their history. **(2)** ___ This event placed the island on what would become a well-travelled route between Europe and the New World. And that's when things get doubly interesting in the underground passages. In one of the same caves that

contain indigenous art, archaeologists have found marks that appear to have been left by early Europeans who visited the island from the Spanish strongholds of Puerto Rico and Hispaniola. The marks include Spanish names, phrases in Latin and Spanish and other symbols. **(3)** ___ The most useful of these symbols, from a historical point of view, were the surprisingly modern graffiti – names and dates, most from the mid-sixteenth century, that people must have scratched onto the cave walls to record their presence.

One name in particular points clearly to a European: Francisco Alegre. Historical documents identify him as a Spaniard who arrived in the West Indies in the 1530s. **(4)** ___ Similarities between his signature and the cave inscription suggest that Alegre himself visited this cave and succumbed to the age-old impulse of leaving his mark.

The juxtaposition of the European and indigenous markings, the lack of images showing conflict, and the fact that Europeans would have needed native guides to find this cave, all suggest a narrative that's very different from the usual saga of the Spanish conquest of the New World. This was one moment in time when two groups of strangers were getting to know each other and sharing ideas. **(5)** ___ It truly is a remarkable discovery and one that will change our understanding of the history of the Caribbean.

5 You are going to read an article about cave paintings that were found on a Caribbean island. Six sentences have been removed from the article. Choose from the sentences A–G the one which fits each gap (1–5). There are two extra sentences which you do not need to use. There is an example at the beginning (0).

A In contrast, there's plenty of evidence that Christopher Columbus stopped on the island in 1494.

B You could say that they were figuring out what this new intercultural connection might mean for the future.

C A number of archaeologists have cast doubt on the latter of these claims, arguing that the images may be of an earlier date.

D Created by both indigenous peoples and early European visitors, the images record the first contact between two very different worldviews.

E Intrigued by such an amazing discovery, the team have set up an international database to process their finds.

F Of those that have, about two dozen have revealed intricate designs reflecting the spiritual beliefs of the indigenous people.

G Based in San Juan, Puerto Rico, he eventually was put in charge of royal estates, which included Isla Mona.

H Many were carved with sharp-edged tools which indigenous people could not have had in their possession.

___ / 10

Listening

6 🎧 [116] You will hear an interview with a journalist called Marion Clark, who's talking about an artist's memory loss and the new discoveries made about the brain. For questions (1–10), choose the best answer (A, B or C). There is an example at the beginning (0).

0 The presenter's aim today is to

  A speak to Marion Clark about her new book.

  B talk about a number of interesting books.

  C discuss fictional works on memory loss.

1 What does Marion say she has been reading this week?

  A a scientific book by an American author

  B a fiction story about memory loss

  C various titles that study how memory works

2 What does Marion say about Lonni Sue Johnson's career before the accident?

  A She worked in the music industry.

  B She was a commercial pilot.

  C She had success as an artist.

3 What information does Marion explain?

  A both where and when Lonni Sue first showed symptoms of the disease

  B how Lonni Sue's family responded when they saw she was ill

  C the reasons why Lonni Sue caught such a serious infection

4 What happened to Lonni Sue right after she got ill?

  A She was looked after at a neighbour's house.

  B She was examined by doctors.

  C She went to her farm to recover.

5 What does Marion say about viral encephalitis?

  A It's a disease that affects a specific part of the brain.

  B A large number of patients with this disease have memory problems.

  C It's a rare disease with small chances of recovery.

6 Which of these memories was the hardest for Lonni Sue to recover?

  A remembering how to play a musical instrument

  B being able to recall her close relatives

  C knowing what her job had been before the infection

7 According to Marion, Lonni Sue couldn't remember

  A how her father had died.

  B who her father was.

  C whether her father was alive.

8 What memories has Lonni Sue completely lost?

  A memories of things that had happened

  B memories of all the people she had known

  C memories of how to do particular things

9 Marion says that Lonni Sue's inability to form new memories

  A may be the most surprising aspect of her condition.

  B occurs less often than other aspects of her condition.

  C is what her friends struggle to deal with most.

10 To Marion, which of the following is most important when it comes to memory?

  A Without it we can't really make plans or decisions.

  B Without it we lose a sense of our identity.

  C Without it we'll forget our loved ones.

___ / 10

Writing

7 You have seen this notice on an English-language website called *Bookworms*.

Reviews wanted!

A book I learnt a lot from

Have you read an interesting book recently that you learnt a lot from? Write a review of the book and send it to us.

The best reviews will be posted on our website.

Write your book review (180–200 words). Make sure you:

- give information about the title, the author and the reason for choosing to review the book.
- if the book is a novel, describe the setting, plot, characters and background.
- if the book is non-fiction, describe the topics it covers and the way the book is organized.
- give reasons why you recommend the book.

___ / 10

Speaking

8 Read the task below and give your presentation in class.

Prepare a two-minute presentation about a show or performance that you have recently seen or taken part in.

In your presentation, include:

- a description of the kind of show it was and the main characters.
- who was in it and a description of their performance.
- aspects you liked or didn't like and reasons why.

___ / 10

Unit 5 Test

Vocabulary

1 Write the word which best fits the gap in each sentence. Here is an example (0).

0 Once great friends, Harry and George haven't spoken since they fell _____*out*_____ .

1 It's a very _____-written book – the author's clearly talented and has a way with words.

2 The car was _____ damaged in the crash. In fact, the garage said they couldn't repair it.

3 Although relatively poor, the island's population is _____ literate. Few can't read or write, and most go on to university on the mainland.

4 We hoped to go away for a few days, but our plans fell _____ at the last moment because Sophie had an emergency at work.

5 I didn't realize you knew so much about the council's plans. You seem very _____ informed. Who's been telling you things?

6 My parents are reasonably well-_____ . That's why they can help me pay my rent.

7 The wedding reception was _____ organized. There wasn't enough food, and there was nowhere for guests to go when it started to rain.

8 Young people tend to do things on the _____ of the moment. They never plan ahead.

9 Now I'm fifty-four, I suppose I have to admit to being _____-aged.

10 When I was a teenager, I fell _____ this Italian guy. I was so in love that I spent all my money on a ticket to Rome.

_____ / 10

2 Read the text below and decide which answer (A, B, C or D) best fits each gap. There is an example at the beginning (0).

Mumbai

Mumbai's a huge **(0)** ___ – indeed, it's the most populous city in India with eighteen million people living there. Today, the city's **(1)** ___ , with new businesses opening every day, and much of the population **(2)** ___ a rise in living standards. As a result, however, developers are beginning to make plans to build in more historical run-down areas. They want to build luxury apartment **(3)** ___ for the wealthy, replace traditional markets with shopping **(4)** ___ , and replace busy roads with car-free pedestrian **(5)** ___ . No doubt the plans will **(6)** ___ the local economy by bringing jobs, new infrastructure and wealthy residents to these poorer suburbs, but many fear that what will be lost is the colour and character of the old communities. There's also the danger that current residents won't be able to **(7)** ___ to live in the expensive new high-rises. If the developers **(8)** ___ to their current plans, despite the campaigns against them, many of the places that once gave Mumbai its unique flavour will disappear. For me at any **(9)** ___ , and I've lived in Mumbai all my life, it doesn't make **(10)** ___ to replace the traditional with the modern, just because the money's there. Mumbai needs a rethink.

0 A consortium	**B** obstruction	**C** strait	**D** metropolis
1 A enhancing	**B** thriving	**C** increasing	**D** rising
2 A adding to	**B** making better	**C** benefitting from	**D** improving to
3 A blocks	**B** rises	**C** areas	**D** parks
4 A halls	**B** spaces	**C** stations	**D** malls
5 A regions	**B** zones	**C** parks	**D** spaces
6 A boost	**B** add	**C** thrive	**D** allow
7 A help	**B** afford	**C** enhance	**D** involve
8 A stay	**B** point	**C** stick	**D** remain
9 A account	**B** state	**C** rate	**D** stage
10 A certain	**B** sense	**C** point	**D** need

_____ / 10

Grammar

3 Complete the text using the *to* infinitive or the *-ing* form of the verbs in brackets. There is an example at the beginning (0).

As part of proposals for a new rail link, developers want **(0)** _to create_ (create) an entire new station alongside the existing Euston Railway Station in London. It's all part of an effort to help **(1)** _____ (make) Euston a more modern and reliable transport hub. The vision is bold. Imagine **(2)** _____ (have) a walkway to connect up the station with Euston Square underground station. It's just one of the many ideas that'll allow visitors to London **(3)** _____ (access) the city with the minimum of fuss. Proposals suggest **(4)** _____ (build) six new platforms which, in turn, will allow train companies **(5)** _____ (operate) more services and passengers **(6)** _____ (travel) to all parts of the country without having to change station. Naturally, if the government decides **(7)** _____ (go) ahead with such a major project, it'll involve **(8)** _____ (spend) a lot of taxpayers' money. However, it's vital that London chooses **(9)** _____ (invest) in its rail infrastructure. The alternative is to risk **(10)** _____ (lose) custom to other transport operators.

___ / 10

4 Complete the second sentence so that it has a similar meaning to the first sentence, using the word given. Do not change the word given. You must use between two and four words, including the word given. Here is an example (0).

0 Please don't forget to write emails.

REMEMBER

Please ___ _remember to write_ ___ emails.

1 I'm sorry I didn't send Jo an invitation.

REGRET

I _____ Jo an invitation.

2 We had no intention of spending the night there.

MEAN

We _____ the night there.

3 The twins have memories of their stay at their grandparents' cottage.

REMEMBER

The twins _____ at their grandparents' cottage.

4 I'd rather read books than go clubbing.

TO

I prefer _____ clubbing.

5 Jamie made no attempt to stop her leaving.

TRY

Jamie _____ her leaving.

6 Despite numerous warnings, homeowners have kept on building unsafe structures.

CONTINUED

Homeowners _____ unsafe structures despite numerous warnings.

7 'I'm really sorry for cracking your phone screen. It was an accident,' Sheila said.

MEAN

Sheila apologized for cracking my phone screen and said she _____ it.

8 After completing his first novel, Wilson wrote eight more.

ON

Wilson _____ eight more novels after completing his first.

9 Simon's father hasn't sent him money since he moved abroad.

STOPPED

Simon's father _____ him money after he moved abroad.

10 I apologize for saying this but I'm afraid you haven't achieved the grade necessary to complete the course.

REGRET

I _____ that you haven't achieved the grade necessary to complete the course.

___ / 10

Reading

The growth of our cities

A

There once was a time when big cities thrilled and amazed people. 'It is the metropolis of the universe, the garden of the world,' Ibn Khaldun, the Arab historian, wrote of Cairo in 1382. English traveller Thomas Coryat described Renaissance Venice as a 'beautiful queen.' French artist Marcel Duchamp, in 1915, called New York City 'a complete work of art.' Since their appearance in about 3,000 B.C., cities have always been the natural centre of everything that mattered: the temple, the court, the market, the university. And for anyone who's slightly ambitious, there's little choice. Shakespeare left Stratford to go to London, after all; not the reverse.

B

Of course, your own city may not immediately inspire words like 'peerless' or 'paradise.' However urban life strikes you, though, there is one thing that can't be denied: cities worldwide have been growing ever more rapidly. Some of this growth has occurred in the developed world – Las Vegas, for example, grew by eighty-three per cent in the nineties. But the most dramatic increase has been in the Third World. Almost all the world's population growth over the next thirty years will take place in the cities of developing countries. By the year 2030, for the first time in history, sixty per cent of the world's people will be living in urban environments.

C

Experts believe this growth is actually good news in some ways. 'Cities are the fundamental building blocks of prosperity,' says Marc Weiss, chairman of the Prague Institute for Global Urban Development, 'both for the nation and for families.' Industrial and commercial activities in urban areas account for between fifty and eighty per cent of the gross domestic product (GDP) in most countries of the world. 'There's the crazy notion that the way to deal with a city's problems is to keep people out of them,' Weiss continued. 'But the problems of rural life are even more serious than those of the city.' For better or worse, urban-watchers are clear on one point: the quality of life for most people in the future will be determined by the quality of cities.

D

Those cities will be bigger than ever. A megacity has more than ten million inhabitants. In 1995 there were fourteen; soon there will be more than twenty. And the ranking will have shifted: the five largest cities today will, in a few years, probably be overtaken by rapidly merging mega-cities in Asia. Of course, population numbers by themselves don't determine a city's prospects, and explosive growth is not necessarily the determining factor. 'City problems,' one authority points out, 'mostly have to do with weak, ineffective, and usually unrepresentative city governments.'

E

According to most social scientists, the optimistic ones at least, none of this is inevitable. Many people today consider slums to be the fate of the Third World, but experts remind us of the horrific lower depths of London, Paris and New York that inspired the great social movements of the 19th and 20th centuries, and novelists Charles Dickens and Victor Hugo and photographer Jacob Riis against the festering tenements, sweatshops, and child labour that blighted these cities. Today, they point out, these cities are now among the First World's proudest metropolises. Solutions have been found before.

F

To discover how people are coping with drastic urban growth, photographer Stuart Franklin and I went to São Paulo, Bangkok, Lagos and Hyderabad. I was prepared to be overwhelmed, and I was. But it wasn't the choking air, the crushing slums and mindless skyscrapers that left the deepest impression. It was the people, so tenacious, ingenious and hopeful. These massive cities are not, as they may first appear, just big, crowded, ugly places. They're full of life. Even in the anonymous parts on the edges of the great cities, I found that what appeared to be each city's greatest problem – all those people – is in fact her richest resource. How to make cities work is the problem.

5 You are going to read an article about cities. For questions 1–10, choose from the sections (A–F). The sections may be chosen more than once. There is an example at the beginning (0).

In which section does the writer

0 define a megacity? _D_

1 express a personal and optimistic view of cities? ___

2 quote historical authors? ___

3 admit that not all cities appear thrilling or amazing to their citizens? ___

4 contrast how cities have changed in recent years in two different parts of the planet? ___

5 say that cities have been viewed in negative terms in the past? ___

6 say why cities are necessary structures in countries around the world? ___

7 say why some modern cities are not successful? ___

8 say that there is an inevitability about the way that people are attracted to cities? ___

9 quote the view that living in the countryside is worse than living in urban environments? ___

10 describe the profile of current city dwellers? ___

___ / 10

Listening

6 💿 [117] You will hear five short extracts in which people are talking about their teenage years. For questions 1–5, choose from the list (A–H) what each speaker is doing. Use the letters only once. There are three extra letters which you do not need to use.

Speaker 1 ____

Speaker 2 ____

Speaker 3 ____

Speaker 4 ____

Speaker 5 ____

This speaker …

A criticizes adults for their lifestyle.

B describes himself or herself as kind.

C blames others for what they are like now.

D draws on a teenage experience in adult life.

E is reluctant to come up with an answer.

F has a positive view of family members now.

G regrets not doing something in adult life.

H is angry with people in their family.

___ / 10

Writing

7 Read the task below.

In your English class you have been talking about life in the countryside. Now, your English teacher has asked you to write an essay.

Write an essay using all the notes and give reasons for your point of view.

'It is better to grow up in the countryside than in the city.'
Do you agree?

Notes
Write about:
1. health
2. entertainment
3. ... (your own idea)

Write your essay (180–200 words). Make sure you:

• start with an example, a quote, statistics or a personal experience and state your point of view.

• give reasons to support your point of view.

• detail any views against your point of view.

• sum up and restate your point of view and your main reason to support that view.

___ / 10

Speaking

8 Read the task below and take part in a debate with your classmates.

The local council wants to build a new shopping mall where currently there is a park. Prepare and present arguments to debate the issue.

___ / 10

Unit 6 Test

Vocabulary

1 Use the word given in CAPITAL LETTERS at the end of each sentence to form a word that fits in the gap in the same sentence. Here is an example (0).

   0 Have you printed off the _boarding_ passes yet?   BOARD

   1 I always take out travel _____ before going skiing.   INSURE

   2 Before going to West Africa you need _____ against various tropical diseases.   VACCINE

   3 We stayed in a _____ apartment. It had a kitchen so we cooked all our own meals.   CATER

   4 We drove along the mountain pass because the _____ up there was magnificent. We took lots of photographs.   SCENE

   5 My favourite activity on holiday is _____ . I don't want to just sit on a beach – I want to go and look at interesting and historical places.   SIGHT

   6 We went on a _____ tour of the castle.   GUIDE

   7 Don't forget your mosquito _____ . You don't want to get bitten.   REPEL

   8 I always claim travel _____ when I come back from business trips.   EXPEND

   9 The Parthenon in Athens is one of the most important _____ monuments in Europe.   CULTURE

  10 _____ is fun. We go for long walks every weekend.   HIKE

                                                                             __ / 10

2 Write the word which best fits the gap in each sentence. Here is an example (0).

   0 I'm in two _minds_ about whether to go to the party or not. I don't know what to do.

   1 I can't remember the last time I had a day _____ . I just work nine to five every day!

   2 How long does it _____ to get to London from here? I have to be in the office by two.

   3 When we're on holiday, we always eat _____ . We never cook at home.

   4 Bring some suntan _____ . It'll be very hot and you'll need it to stop getting burned.

   5 After work, let's head _____ to the beach and go for a swim.

   6 Don't worry. I'll make my _____ way to the centre. I've got a map.

   7 They were thinking of riding a segway around Rome but they _____ their mind when they realized that it was quite dangerous.

   8 Jim's had a lot _____ his mind recently – what with the baby and all the changes at work.

   9 I'm sure you'll come up with lots of great ideas if you just _____ your mind to it.

  10 I'm sorry. I can't remember your name. My mind's gone _____ .

                                                                             __ / 10

Grammar

3 Complete the text with the phrases in the box. There are three extra phrases which you do not need to use. There is an example at the beginning (0).

> can you explain why   can you tell me when   can't I   do they   do you have information about how
> do you know what   don't I   don't they   ~~how do~~   is it OK   is it the case that
> surely not   they can   what's included

Gap year: Frequently Asked Questions

Taking a gap year is a big decision, so you've probably got a lot of questions on your mind! Below are quick-fire answers to some of our most frequently asked questions – if you can't find an answer here then get in touch!

  Q (0) _How do_ I book with Go Gap?

  A You can book online or by phone.

  Q (1) _____ anyone over eighteen can travel with Go Gap?

  A Our programmes are open to anyone over the age of eighteen as long as you have a good level of English. In most cases we can cater for those with special dietary requirements and arrange programmes for those with disabilities.

Q (2) _____ need any special skills?

A All you need is enthusiasm and commitment! Any training necessary will be given when you get there.

Q I'm worried about travelling alone. 'Gappers' do meet people, **(3)** _____ ?

A Most of our gap-year travellers travel alone, but you're likely to meet people going to the same place. Don't worry.

Q (4) _____ the programmes start?

A All projects have set start dates but they are different times of the year – you'll find one that suits you.

Q (5) _____ in the programme price?

A Advice, an information pack and a briefing meeting, as well as transport, transfers and accommodation – you'll also get support from our local coordinator and free meals.

Q (6) _____ everything's included?

A We can't cover your flights, I'm afraid, or visas and vaccinations, travel insurance and any personal expenses.

Q (7) _____ my accommodation will be like?

A You'll be in carefully chosen homestays with local families.

Q If I have problems during my trip I can get home, **(8)** _____ ?

A Of course. We've trained personnel who will be at hand to deal with any issues and provide friendly advice. You'll also be given an emergency contact number.

Q (9) _____ I can change my programme if I don't like it?

A We expect a basic level of commitment to your project, but local coordinators will help you move to an alternative project if there's a serious problem.

Q (10) _____ if I take time off from my project to travel?

A You'll have weekends free to travel, but you can only take longer periods off with notice.

___ / 10

4 Complete the second sentence so that it has a similar meaning to the first sentence, using the word given. Do not change the word given. You must use between two and four words, including the word given. Here is an example (0).

0 We haven't got any luggage to check in.
NO
_____ _We've got no_ _____ luggage to check in.

1 Cynthia's contribution shouldn't be ignored.
LET'S
_____ Cynthia's contribution.

2 Penny decided that staying up late would be a bad idea.
NOT
Penny decided _____ up late.

3 Nobody on the flight complained.
NONE
_____ people on the flight complained.

4 I hate summer because it gets so hot and so does my brother.
EITHER
My brother doesn't like summer because it gets so hot and I _____ .

5 There is no obligation on you to stay. Go if you like.
DON'T
You _____ stay. Go if you like.

6 In my opinion, he won't get here on time.
THINK
I don't _____ get here on time.

7 Will Paul and I get home before nightfall?
WE
Paul and I will get home before nightfall, _____ ?

8 I imagine that Emily has no key, but I'm not sure.
NOT
I don't know if Emily has a key, but _____ .

9 I told Peter to go on without us.
WAIT
I told Peter _____ for us.

10 We wanted a large family room but they didn't have any available.
NONE
We wanted a large family room but _____ .

___ / 10

Reading

Stay at National Geographic Lodges

Do you know where you can find peace and relaxation, luxury and natural beauty, all in one place? You don't? Well, we do! **(0)** _E_ On the one hand, you'll find yourself at the heart of nature at its most stunning; on the other, you'll find yourself staying in a wonderful hotel with all mod cons.

Rosalie Bay Resort

There is a place on the Caribbean island of Dominica where a freshwater river rushes out to a turquoise sea, a jungle filled with life ends at a black-sand beach, and volcanic peaks rise up in the background. **(1)** ___ Created over eight years by a Minnesota native and her Dominican partner, this is a wellness sanctuary infused with local charm that offers discovery of unique ecosystems and vibrant cultures.

Set within the foothills of the Morne Trois Pitons, a UNESCO World Heritage site, Rosalie Bay is an ideal base from which to hike to jungle waterfalls and geothermal lakes, swim in gem-coloured natural pools, find bright birds in the canopy, and inspect a wild array of tropical flora. **(2)** ___ This truly wonderful spectacle takes place thanks to the protection of a thriving conservation programme initiated by the lodge owners.

Why We Love This Lodge

The owners of Rosalie Bay Resort, Beverly Deikel and Patris Oscar, set out to develop an ecolodge that honoured the natural wealth of Dominica, so, on discovering that endangered sea turtles used their beach as a nesting ground, they decided not to rest until they'd secured the turtles' future. **(3)** ___ Important as the design and placement of each lodge was, it was of greater importance that they didn't impede the turtles' route to the sea.

Rosalie Bay Resort may be the world's only high-end hotel to have taken into account the habits of baby turtles. It's just one reason why wildlife lovers from all corners of the globe have taken the place to their heart. **(4)** ___ Since discovering nesting sea turtles in 2002, Beverly and Oscar have established Dominica's first sea turtle conservation programme, and they are keen to involve guests in their work. The energy and friendliness of your hosts will greatly enhance the experience of being there, adding local knowledge and a personal touch to every day's adventure. Rosalie Bay is a textbook example of the positive power of tourism when it's combined with a respect for the natural environment and local people.

Our National Geographic Exclusive Offer

Join a guide for an excursion that's exclusive to guests who reserve their space through National Geographic Unique Lodges. Walk to the friendly village of Grand Fond for a glimpse of everyday life. **(5)** ___ Learn about the local flora and fauna from your knowledgeable guide, and stop for a refreshing dip in a Rosalie River swimming hole on your return to the resort.

---

5 You are going to read an article about Rosalie Bay Resort, a National Geographic Lodge. Six sentences have been removed from the article. Choose from the sentences A–G the one which fits each gap (1–5). There is one extra sentence which you do not need to use. There is an example at the beginning (0).

  A When drawing up the blueprints for the development of the resort, this annual event was uppermost in the couple's minds.

  B Visit typical homes and learn about Dominican customs, meeting residents and farmers along the way.

  C Just here is where you find Rosalie Bay Resort, an intimate collection of Caribbean-style cottages built with heart, by hand.

  D Let's not forget that you can set out with guides to explore the numerous trails on the lodge property, learning about birdlife and exotic flowers.

  E Located among dramatic scenery, National Geographic Lodges offer the best of both worlds.

  F If you too find that experiencing natural wonders at first hand is truly rewarding, this is a unique opportunity.

  G Right on the lodge's beach three species of sea turtle hatchlings make a mad dash to the sea every year.

___ / 10

Listening

6 ⊙ [118] Listen to three photographers, Simon Carter, Nicola Halliday and Joe Clarke, talk about their job. For questions 1–10, choose from the photographers (A, B or C). The photographers may be chosen more than once. There is an example at the beginning (0).

    0 Who mentions where they were born?

      A Simon   Ⓑ Nicola   **C** Joe

    1 Who says that they studied photography at university?

      A Simon   **B** Nicola   **C** Joe

    2 Who thinks that they have an unusual approach to photography?

      A Simon   **B** Nicola   **C** Joe

    3 Who got into photography before going to university?

      A Simon   **B** Nicola   **C** Joe

    4 Who says they don't need to take photos to make a living?

      A Simon   **B** Nicola   **C** Joe

    5 Who was a photographer for other magazines before becoming a wildlife photographer?

      A Simon   **B** Nicola   **C** Joe

    6 Who says how their father and mother helped their career?

      A Simon   **B** Nicola   **C** Joe

    7 Who says that being good at the technical side of photography is very important?

      A Simon   **B** Nicola   **C** Joe

    8 Who became more confident after discovering photography?

      A Simon   **B** Nicola   **C** Joe

    9 Who found it hard to change their career direction?

      A Simon   **B** Nicola   **C** Joe

   10 Who tries to tell stories with photographs?

      A Simon   **B** Nicola   **C** Joe

___ / 10

Writing

7 Read the task below.

> You're a gap-year student who's just returned from a trip to Bangladesh organized by Go Gap. On the trip, you weren't met at the airport, stayed in a hostel and not with a host family as promised, had to buy and cook your own food, and didn't have free time to travel. Write an email of complaint to Go Gap.

Write your email (180–200 words). Make sure you:

- state the purpose of your email.
- detail the problems you encountered.
- say what you would like Go Gap to do.
- use the conventions of a formal email of complaint.

___ / 10

Speaking

8 Read the task below and give your presentation in class.

> Prepare a two-minute description for your teacher and classmates of a holiday or weekend destination you know well.

In your presentation, include:

- a description of the kind of place it is, where it is and how to get there.
- reasons why you go there, how it makes you feel and why it's special for you.

___ / 10

Unit 7 Test

Vocabulary

1 Complete the sentences with the words in the box. There are three extra words which you do not need to use. Here is an example (0).

almond garnish groom lettuce matter niche praise shame ~~snob~~ spoil stag
stomach tune veil

0 The clothes shop in the High Street relies on _____*snob*_____ appeal for its sales. People buy things from there because of the label.

1 The meal was served with a _____ of rosemary and tomato.

2 When she got married, my sister wore a long white dress with a white _____ over her face.

3 This is very tasty. I think it's got nuts in it – I can taste _____ , I think.

4 My brother has a business selling sombreros in Scotland. I suppose you could call it a _____ market – but, believe it or not, he does sell some.

5 I don't think I can _____ any more of Joe's complaining. He's been moaning all day and it's really annoying me.

6 I went to Tom's _____ do at the weekend. He's getting married next month. We went to an Indian restaurant then on to a night club – and Tom dressed up in a chicken costume.

7 Sarah's become a professional comedian. I wish her luck! I know she makes us laugh all the time, but doing it for a living is a completely different _____ .

8 The bride and _____ have already arrived at the reception. They make a lovely couple.

9 I don't think you should _____ children into doing things. They are sensitive and vulnerable, and making them feel embarrassed or wrong is unfair.

10 I know you think my business delivering pizza on a bike is a stupid idea, but when I'm rich and successful, you'll be singing a different _____ .

___ / 10

2 For questions 1–10, read the text below and think of the word which best fits each gap. Use only one word in each gap. There is an example at the beginning (0).

Dear *Family Magazine*,

I've long been an advocate **(0)** ___*of*___ the 'carrot and stick approach' when it comes to bringing **(1)** _____ children. There's no point in giving **(2)** _____ to their demands, or trying to win them **(3)** _____ by handing out sweets all the time. Take my nephews. They have no manners. If there's food on the table, they'll just dive **(4)** _____ and eat all they want before anyone else has had a chance. My sister's always telling her children **(5)** _____ , but they don't take any notice. I've mentioned this to her but, well, let's say we had a difference **(6)** _____ opinion with regard to the matter. Now, if I was in charge, I'd set some strict rules. Staring **(7)** _____ electronic screens would be banned for a start – I'd make sure they switched phones and tablets **(8)** _____ at mealtimes and in the evening. And I would make sure bed time and bath time were fixed times. I recognize that any spoilt child would rebel **(9)** _____ such a strict regime but, frankly, it makes no difference **(10)** _____ me. Being disliked by a child is hardly the worst thing in the world. Don't spoil kids, I say. You have to be cruel to be kind.

Yours,
Arnold Switch (bachelor)

___ / 10

Grammar

3 Complete the text using the correct form of the verbs in brackets. There is an example at the beginning (0).

People used **(0)** ___to eat___ (eat) honey long before refined sugar became widely available. Indeed, the ancient Greeks **(1)** _____ (produce) it in large quantities. Back then, the Greeks **(2)** _____ (buy) and eat honey every day. It was a regular part of their diet. Today, of course, we have got **(3)** _____ (put) sugar in our tea, coffee and cakes, so we don't add as much honey to food as we once **(4)** _____ (use). Many experts are trying to encourage us to change this habit. If we **(5)** _____ (start) eating honey instead of sugar, perhaps we'll all be healthier. It's logical. Generally, things we eat **(6)** _____ (be) better for us if they're produced naturally. And honey is about as natural as you can get. And there **(7)** _____ (not be) any shortage of honey as long as we **(8)** _____ (look) after our honey bees. It's worth emphasizing the product's other benefits too. If you **(9)** _____ (have) a cough, for example, there's nothing more soothing than honey. Of course, we're all **(10)** _____ (hear) how this product or that product is good for you, and we tend to take no notice. When it comes to honey, though, it's about time we all rediscovered it.

___ / 10

4 Complete the second sentence so that it has a similar meaning to the first sentence, using the word given. Do not change the word given. You must use between two and four words, including the word given. Here is an example (0).

0 Susie will come to the graduation party if she doesn't have to make a speech.

LONG

Susie will come to the graduation party _____*as long as*_____ she doesn't have to make a speech.

1 I'll stop at a service station and phone you.

WHEN

I'll phone you _____ at a service station.

2 We won't be able to go on holiday if we don't start saving now.

UNLESS

We won't be able to go on holiday _____ saving now.

3 The moment there's light outside, we'll head off.

SOON

We'll head off _____ there's light outside.

4 The film will start in a minute so I think I'll drive home.

BEFORE

I think I'll drive home _____ .

5 We spent hours outdoors when I was a kid.

SPEND

When I was a kid, we _____ hours outdoors.

6 I'm still not familiar with this new timetable.

GOT

I still _____ this new timetable.

7 Unless something goes horribly wrong, we'll finish on time.

NOTHING

We'll finish on time as _____ horribly wrong.

8 We'll have lunch when Dan gets home.

UNTIL

We _____ Dan gets home.

9 Paul's father owned the butcher's shop in the High Street back in the 1970s.

OWN

Back in the 1970s, Paul's father _____ the butcher's shop in the High Street.

10 It's strange not having Rosie around.

USED

I can't _____ having Rosie around.

___ / 10

Reading

Do whales have culture?

A

If you've ever wondered what you might learn from hanging out with whales, you'll love this story. According to researchers involved in carrying out a recent study into the behaviour of humpback whales, these magnificent animals are capable of an advanced level of behaviour few thought possible not so long ago. We've got used to being surprised at the ingenuity and adaptability of animals – think chimpanzees hunting in packs, or crows breaking open nuts with stones – but this story, based on the long-term observation of a particular group of whales, is truly remarkable. Whales are routinely observed the world over, from the freezing Antarctic to the tropical Pacific, but no other group does what this group does.

B

Whether it's learning a new song, figuring out how to use tools to forage for food, or picking up the local customs, learning from others is an important part of life for many animals, not least human beings. Indeed, having a culture of traditions – that is, behaviour shared by an identifiable group and acquired through social learning – is one of the most fundamental aspects of human society. The idea of such a culture in whales and dolphins, however, has long been controversial among scientists. Many have doubts. That's why this new study is so fascinating. It claims to have found strong evidence that a group of humpback whales is sharing a new kind of feeding behaviour via their social networks.

C

This new kind of behaviour, called 'lobtail feeding', was first recorded in one whale in the Gulf of Maine in 1980. Since then, 278 humpback whales – out of about 700 observed individuals – have employed the strategy, according to the study. Lobtail feeding is a variation on a technique called 'bubble-net feeding', which is used by humpbacks around the world. In bubble-net feeding, a whale blows bubbles into a kind of imaginary net surrounding the prey, forcing the fish together. Then the whale lunges up through the fish with its jaws wide open, scooping up mouthfuls of food. In lobtail feeding, the humpback slaps the surface of the water one to four times with the underside of its tail before diving down and blowing the bubble net.

D

'I've been arguing for over a decade now that cultural transmission is important in cetacean societies,' said study co-author Luke Rendell, a marine biologist at the University of St Andrews in Scotland. Though he wasn't surprised the whales traded information, he was surprised at how strongly his data said the whales learned the new feeding strategy socially, rather than because of other factors like having a genetic predisposition to the behaviour.

E

Experts believe the origin of this group of whales' unique behaviour was strongly associated with the collapse of herring numbers and a boom in the numbers of another type of edible fish – the sand lance. It appears that lobtail feeding came about when humpbacks switched from hunting herring to catching sand lances. By analysing data compiled by trained observers from the Whale Center of New England, Rendell and his colleagues found that the whales who knew how to catch and eat sand lances all had loose social connections. Basically, an inexperienced whale was more likely to start lobtailing if it associated with a whale it knew that already used the new technique.

F

Scientists who specialize in social learning have been quick to praise the sort of data analysis used by Rendell and his team to investigate questions of traditions and social learning in mammals. Previously, this quite complex area of analysis, which involves comparing many different sets of information, had not been shown to work, and some found it hard to believe that it had, at last, proved successful. It is likely that the technique will be applied to many other areas of investigation in the future, some of which may have little to do with whales.

G

Although reaction to the research has been largely positive, there have been some notes of caution. Some have suggested that a behaviour can spread through a population without social learning. Since whales move around together, there's no reason why they might not just pick up the same behaviour at the same time, rather than actually passing it on from one individual to another. And, if that's the case, then that has nothing to do with 'culture'. It would seem that further research is needed before alternative explanations for the spread of lobtail feeding in certain humpback whales can be ruled out. In the meantime, the evidence for social learning remains strong. It seems that whales have 'culture' – just like us.

5 You are going to read an article about the development of culture among whales. For questions 1–10, choose from the sections (A–G). The section may be chosen more than once. There is an example at the beginning (0).

In which section does the writer

0 provide a definition of the word 'culture'? _B_

1 say where the humpback whales in the recent study are located? ___

2 explain why some whales may have changed one aspect of their feeding? ___

3 provide an example of a tool used by an animal to get at food? ___

4 mention something about Rendell's research that surprised others? ___

5 convey doubts about the theories formed against the recent study? ___

6 say how long the leader of the study has believed that whales have 'culture'? ___

7 provide detail about how many hunting whales operate? ___

8 say that Rendell's way of analysing data may be picked up by research teams in other fields? ___

9 suggest that some experts have felt for a long time that whales don't have 'culture'? ___

10 say where an individual scientist involved in the research is based? ___

___ / 10

Listening

6 🔘 [119] You will hear an interview with a writer called Elsie Hain, who's talking about school dinners. For questions (1–10), choose the best answer (A, B or C). There is an example at the beginning (0).

0 What do we find out about Elsie Hain in the presenter's introduction?

A the year she finished school

B the location of her school

C when she started school

1 According to the speakers, what's the difference between school meals today and those in the 1950s?

A There's a greater variety of dishes on offer.

B The food's cooked better.

C Salad has become a more common option.

2 What does Elsie say about the dinner ladies?

A They were employed by the school.

B They were parents of school pupils.

C They had strict rules but were friendly.

3 How does Elsie describe the queue for dinner?

A Nobody ever spoke in the dinner queue.

B The dinner queue was long and slow-moving.

C Nobody ever tried to push in at the front of the queue.

4 What examples does Elsie give of situations when she might be punished while eating dinner?

A not wearing socks at meal times

B speaking while eating

C moving about the dining hall

5 How does Elsie describe the dining hall?

A It was a very large room.

B There were eight or more students on each table.

C There was varnished wood on the ceiling.

6 Who did Elsie sit with at the dining table?

A different pupils every day

B pupils of different ages

C pupils from the same age group

7 According to Elsie, what happened after dinner each day?

A Dinner ladies collected their plates from the tables.

B Pupils had to clear away their own plates.

C Pupils who were noisy had to eat alone.

8 What reason does Elsie give for the quality of the food?

A Schools couldn't afford quality food.

B Things like meat weren't cooked thoroughly.

C Not enough spices were used in the food.

9 What does Elsie say about paying for school meals in the 1950s?

A They were free in all schools in the country.

B In some schools, pupils paid for them.

C Everybody had to pay for school meals in those days.

10 How did Elsie pay for her school dinners?

A by paying the dinner ladies every school dinner time

B by registering to pay for meals each year

C by giving money to a member of the school's staff every week

___ / 10

Writing

7 Read the task below.

> Think of an event that takes place each year in your family. It could be a birthday, an anniversary, a holiday or a get-together. Write a description of it.

Write your description (180–200 words). Make sure you:

• say when and where the event happens, and who attends.

• describe what you do to celebrate the event.

• explain the significance of the event and why.

• sum up and say why it is special.

___ / 10

Speaking

8 Read the task below and give your presentation

> Prepare a two-minute presentation for your teacher and classmates about a typical wedding in your country.

In your presentation, include:

• a description of the sequence of events at a wedding.

• an explanation of their significance.

___ / 10

Unit 8 Test

Vocabulary

1 Use the word given in CAPITAL LETTERS at the end of each sentence to form a word that fits in the gap in the same sentence. Here is an example (0).

0 Ed has some good ideas but he isn't __*ambitious*__ enough to become a politician. AMBITION

1 Our parents often place great _____ on us, which are difficult to live up to. EXPECT

2 My sister works as a _____ for the United Nations. TRANSLATE

3 I asked the _____ to help me find a book about geology. He was very helpful. LIBRARY

4 Brian Cox is one of the leading _____ in the country. PHYSICS

5 My _____ is a real financial expert – he has saved me thousands in taxes. ACCOUNT

6 I was surprised by the _____ beauty of the mountains. MAJESTY

7 I don't really have a _____ when it comes to transport – both the bus and the underground are reliable options. PREFER

8 Our college offers a vocational _____ service to help students decide on their career options. GUIDE

9 I've never felt so _____ in all my life. MISERY

10 My dad used to be a _____ before he gave up his career to travel round the world. LAW

___ / 10

2 Write the word which best fits the gap in each sentence. Here is an example (0).

0 I haven't the faintest ____*idea*____ what you are talking about.

1 I can understand why the twins behave so badly – they're only teenagers – but Tom should know _____ . He's twenty-five and needs to grow up.

2 Do you mind if I _____ a suggestion? I think I have some good ideas that could help.

3 It's your turn to _____ the housework. I cleaned and tidied last weekend.

4 Carrying all this garden waste to the bins really is back-_____ work.

5 I _____ a mistake when I turned down the job. I really should've taken it.

6 What's the matter? Can I _____ anything to help?

7 We were alarmed _____ the news, but fortunately it turned out to be nothing.

8 They decided to close down the factory because it wasn't _____ a profit.

9 We have to _____ the shopping. There's nothing in the fridge.

10 You'd _____ start saving or you simply won't have enough money to pay your bills.

___ / 10

Grammar

3 Complete the text with the correct form of the verbs in brackets. There is an example at the beginning (0).

What would happen to the world if sea levels **(0)** _____rose_____ (rise) by two hundred feet (that's about eighty metres)? Much **(1)** _____ (change), from the shape of our coastlines to the size of our oceans. The entire Atlantic seaboard of the United States **(2)** _____ (vanish), for example, if such a catastrophe **(3)** _____ (occur). Scientists predict that it **(4)** _____ (take) five thousand years for all the ice on the planet to melt but that this could happen if global warming remains unchecked. Imagine the year 7000 – the planet devoid of ice; if any people **(5)** _____ (be) still living then their world **(6)** _____ (look) very different to ours. Much of western Europe **(7)** _____ (disappear) into the sea centuries before and a great inland sea **(8)** _____ (cover) most of what is now Australia. Some experts argue that the damage is already done. If we **(9)** _____ (take) steps in the past to stop global warming, we **(10)** _____ (reduce) the likelihood of the events described above happening. Perhaps it's all too late already.

___ / 10

4 Complete the second sentence so that it has a similar meaning to the first sentence, using the word given. Do not change the word given. You must use between two and four words, including the word given. Here is an example (0).

  0 I didn't apologize because I didn't do anything wrong.

    WOULD

    I _would have apologized if_ I'd done something wrong.

  1 We won't be able to afford the rent because we aren't rich.

    RICHER

    If we _____ be able to afford the rent.

  2 We took a map with us. That's why we aren't lost in the mountains now.

    STILL

    We _____ in the mountains if we hadn't taken a map.

  3 I'm annoyed that you haven't started looking for a job.

    WOULD

    I wish _____ looking for a job.

  4 I wrote this book because people know so little about the subject.

    MORE

    I wouldn't have written this book if people _____ the subject.

  5 Sadly, I can't sing.

    ONLY

    _____ sing.

  6 The neighbours are rude to us all the time – it's very upsetting.

    SO

    I wish the neighbours _____ to us all the time – it's very upsetting.

  7 Please don't make that horrible noise.

    STOP

    I wish you _____ that horrible noise.

  8 There are no fire exits, which is why the council didn't give the venue a licence.

    HAVE

    The council _____ the venue a licence if it had fire exits.

  9 I didn't make a donation because I didn't know about the appeal.

    IF

    _____ about the appeal, I would have made a donation.

 10 Sadly, Susie won't listen to my advice.

    IF

    _____ listen to my advice.

___ / 10

Reading

Are we evolving?

(0) _D_ However, our ability to analyse the human genome has shown that in fact our biology continues to change to suit particular environments.

(1) ___ Our original genetic inheritance, which was carried by these people, was appropriate for the warm climates where we first evolved from early hominins to humans. But a lot has happened since that time, as human populations have expanded around the world. It's only natural that ongoing evolution is the result. Australian Aboriginals living in desert climates, for example, have a genetic variant, developed in the past ten thousand years, that allows them to adjust more easily to extremely high temperatures. The Inuit of Greenland have an adaptation that helps them digest fatty acids in fish far better than the rest of us. If these kinds of changes hadn't taken place, humans wouldn't have been able to populate so many varied environments on the planet.

(2) ___ Prehistorically, most humans, like other mammals, could digest milk only in infancy – we had genes that turned off the production of the milk-digesting enzyme when we were weaned. But around nine thousand years ago, some humans began to herd animals rather than just hunt them. These herders developed genetic alterations that allowed them to continue making the relevant enzyme for their whole lives, a handy adaptation when their livestock were producing a vitamin-rich protein.

(3) ___ For example, in the past fifty years, researchers have uncovered adaptations in Andeans and Tibetans that allow them to breathe more efficiently at high altitudes. Andean populations retain higher levels of oxygen in their blood. Among Tibetans, by contrast, there is evidence that a gene was introduced through interbreeding with Denisovans, a mysterious branch of the human lineage that died out tens of thousands of years ago. These different but equally successful adaptations give indigenous people living at high altitudes an advantage. If only we all had this adaptation. If we did, climbing Everest wouldn't be quite so challenging.

(4) ___ It is culture, and its weaponized cousin, technology. That's because evolution is no match for the speed and variety of modern life. Despite what evolution has accomplished in the recent past, it'll only be of secondary importance from now on. Humans produce a new generation only every twenty-five to thirty-five years or so. At this rate, it can take thousands of years for an advantageous trait to be spread throughout a population. Given genetic evolution's slow-moving way of going about things, it's no surprise technology has superseded it. Technology now does much of the same work and does it far faster, supporting our physical skills, deepening our intellectual range, and allowing us to expand into new and more challenging environments.

(5) ___ If new diseases were to develop, they say, it would be those people that had evolved immune systems that could cope who would survive, and not the most technologically-minded. Undoubtedly, they have a point. Nature could come back and bite us.

In the meantime, however, it would be fair to say that both our culture and our evolution will be the two factors that keep us alive and thriving in the future. Without the first, we will not be able to keep up with our changing world – the one we are making for ourselves. Without the other, we won't have the adaptations needed to make the best of this new world – we won't have the improved intelligence and dexterity we humans will need.

5 You are going to read an article about human evolution. Six sentences have been removed from the article. Choose from the sentences A–G the one which fits each paragraph (1–5). There is one extra sentence which you do not need to use. There is an example at the beginning (0).

    A A number of recent, real-life examples of this process can be found all over the world.

    B In our world now, however, the primary mover for reproductive success isn't genetic evolution.

    C Another fascinating aspect of evolutionary change is our evolving ability to eat different foods.

    D Until recently, it was thought that our species had stopped evolving far in the past.

    E When the chance of survival can be increased, evolution finds a way or various ways to make a change.

    F Of course, not everybody accepts the argument that genetic evolution is no longer of supreme importance.

    G Anatomically modern humans migrated from Africa sometime between eighty and fifty thousand years ago.

___ / 10

Listening

6 💿 [120] You will hear five short extracts in which friends are giving Jo advice about her lifestyle. For questions 1–5, choose from the list (A–H) what each friend says. Use the letters only once. There are three extra letters which you do not need to use.

Speaker 1 ___

Speaker 2 ___

Speaker 3 ___

Speaker 4 ___

Speaker 5 ___

A Do sport or dance to get fit.

B You should consider joining a gym.

C If I were you, I'd give more hugs.

D You should do a training course.

E Reading for pleasure would do you good.

F You definitely need to give up coffee completely.

G Try eating leafy greens at least once a day.

H You ought to drink less of something.

___ / 10

Writing

7 Read the task below.

> You recently saw this post on an environmental blog.
>
> *'Many wildlife species across America are in decline. Today, one third of bird species in North America is in need of urgent conservation action. And yet, cities continue to expand and housing developers continue to build on greenbelt land. It seems that there is no solution to the crisis.'*
>
> Write a comment that will be posted on the blog.

Write your comment (180–200 words). Make sure you:

• start with a reference to the blog.

• write examples that illustrate the problem.

• write a recommendation or request for action.

• sum up the problem.

___ / 10

Speaking

8 Read the task below and take part in a discussion with your classmates.

> Discuss your preferences in the following situations.
>
> 1 It's Friday evening. Do you stay in or go out?
> 2 You want to book a holiday. Where do you choose to go and why?
> 3 You have free time to do an evening course or take up a sport. What do you choose and why?

___ / 10

Unit 9 Test

Vocabulary

1 Complete the sentences using the correct form of the words in the box. Here is an example (0).

admit   astonish   award   beg   blame   charm   encourage   ~~inspire~~   take   warn   word

0 Her speech was ___inspiring___ . It made me feel that I too could rise to the top of my profession.

1 All your hard work has paid off and your company is making a profit. I don't _____ you for celebrating it.

2 I think the new theatre is great, but don't _____ my word for it. Read the reviews.

3 It was very _____ that all my colleagues were in favour of my idea for the new project. It really kept me going.

4 Jenkins was _____ a medal for saving the lives of people trapped in the burning building.

5 I thought Amy Stone's performance was _____ . I was amazed. It was better than anything I have ever seen before on the stage.

6 As we had no money when we arrived in the country, we had to _____ for food from well-wishers.

7 The announcement _____ people to be careful with their belongings. It said that there were thieves operating in the mall.

8 The world champion _____ taking drugs at the press conference. Nobody could believe it. His career was over.

9 The restaurant doesn't advertise – it relies on _____ of mouth to get customers.

10 Although they were both in their eighties, Tom and Marie fell in love at first sight. What a lovely and _____ story – the sort of story that makes you feel warm inside.

___ / 10

2 Read the text below and decide which answer (A, B, C or D) best fits each gap. There is an example at the beginning (0).

Commuters on the rail service between Uckfield and London were **(0)** ___ for words last week when a herd of sixty cows entered a mainline station and stood on the platform as if waiting for a train. Photos of the occurrence shared online are really **(1)** ___ – you just have to laugh; they show morning commuters standing next to the cows!

Some commuters **(2)** ___ the rail service for not having adequate barriers to prevent the cows from entering the station, while others **(3)** ___ legal action, **(4)** ___ that they had lost time and money as a result of the delays. Most, however, saw the funny side. For their part, the rail service was very apologetic but **(5)** ___ doing anything wrong. They said that they had followed all safety procedures, and that their staff could not have done anything to prevent the cows from approaching the track. Indeed, they **(6)** ___ their staff for responding quickly and professionally to prevent any serious accident. Passengers affected on the day will be **(7)** ___ a refund and railway inspectors have **(8)** ___ that changes should be made to the station entrance area, which is very close to the cows' field. All this will cost in the **(9)** ___ of £30,000. The rail service has **(10)** ___ its word that cows will never be allowed near the track again.

0 **A** lost	**B** missed	**C** thrown	**D** spoken
1 **A** inspiring	**B** amusing	**C** engaging	**D** encouraging
2 **A** begged	**B** asked	**C** criticized	**D** praised
3 **A** thanked	**B** accused	**C** blamed	**D** threatened
4 **A** promising	**B** claiming	**C** begging	**D** asking
5 **A** denied	**B** blamed	**C** persuaded	**D** convinced
6 **A** threatened	**B** accused	**C** begged	**D** congratulated
7 **A** begged	**B** swore	**C** offered	**D** complained
8 **A** recommended	**B** persuaded	**C** encouraged	**D** convinced
9 **A** place	**B** region	**C** rate	**D** amount
10 **A** given	**B** made	**C** offered	**D** held

___ / 10

Grammar

3 Complete the text using the *to* infinitive or *-ing* form of the verbs in brackets. There is an example at the beginning (0).

Here's today's news. Campaigners have asked the prime minister **(0)** *to reconsider* (reconsider) proposals to raise corporation tax. They have accused the government of **(1)** _____ (fail) to help small businesses, and have recommended **(2)** _____ (limit) any new tax rises to major businesses and multinationals. A government spokesperson has thanked campaigners for **(3)** _____ (raise) concerns but urged them **(4)** _____ (wait) until the proposals are announced in full. The spokesperson refused **(5)** _____ (say) whether taxes would rise, but said that the prime minister had promised **(6)** _____ (listen) to a wide range of views before making any final decisions. Campaigners refuse **(7)** _____ (believe) that the tax rises won't go ahead, and object to **(8)** _____ (be) advised not **(9)** _____ (criticize) the government. Many are now insisting on **(10)** _____ (take) industrial action in an attempt to make the government think again.

___ / 10

4 Complete the second sentence so that it has a similar meaning to the first sentence, using the word given. Do not change the word given. You must use between two and five words, including the word given. Here is an example (0).

0 'Would you like to stay?' Patrick asked us.

INVITED

Patrick ___*invited us to*___ stay.

1 Hilda said well done to everybody because they played so well.

PRAISED

Hilda _____ playing so well.

2 'I know nothing about the missing laptops,' Louise said.

DENIED

Louise _____ about the missing laptops.

3 I told Emily that she should apply for the job.

ENCOURAGED

I _____ for the job.

4 Scientists know that the ozone layer is getting thinner.

BE

The ozone layer _____ getting thinner.

5 Some think the murderer has left the country.

THOUGHT

It _____ the murderer has left the country.

6 'You must start investing more in the safety of structures,' the architect told the mayor.

URGED

The mayor _____ investing more in the safety of structures.

7 'Don't return to the building,' a firefighter told us.

WARNED

A firefighter _____ return to the building.

8 People believe the company accountant is involved in hiding details of the financial transactions.

BE

The company accountant _____ involved in hiding details of the financial transactions.

9 'He hasn't revealed all the information he has,' many say.

KNOW

He _____ more than he has revealed.

10 The press reports that the police are looking for a red car in connection with the crime.

TO

According to the press, the police _____ looking for a red car in connection with the crime.

___ / 10

Reading

Treasure trove of ancient human footprints found near volcano

Nine miles from the volcano the Maasai call 'the Mountain of God', on the southern shore of Tanzania's Lake Natron, researchers have made an astonishing and very rare discovery. It is reported to be an enormous set of well-preserved human footprints left in the mud between five thousand and nineteen thousand years ago. There are more than four hundred of the footprints, and they are believed to cover an area slightly larger than a tennis court. No other site in Africa has as many ancient *Homo sapiens* footprints, making it a treasure trove for scientists trying to tell the story of humankind's earliest days.

Some of the tracks are believed to show people jogging through the mud. Other prints imply a person with a slightly strange, possibly broken, big toe. Yet more tracks suggest that around a dozen people, mostly women and children, travelled across the mudflat together, striking toward the southwest for parts unknown. The mud has captured it all, including the small bits of mud that fell from their feet with each step.

These new Tanzanian tracks can now be added to an exclusive set of human footprints that have stood the test of time. Laetoli – a site in Tanzania some sixty miles southwest of Lake Natron – has 3.6-million-year-old footprints possibly made by the human ancestor *Australopithecus afarensis*. Australia's Willandra Lakes site has seven hundred fossil footprints made about twenty thousand years ago, and two sites on the South African coast have *Homo sapiens* tracks dating as far back as a hundred and twenty thousand years ago. However, few other places in the world offer as exciting an opportunity to find out about early human history as this new find. The abundance and diversity of prints on the shores of Lake Natron offer a strikingly detailed snapshot of what life was like for our ancestors in Africa.

The newly-discovered site – and the researchers who excavated it – owe a great deal to Ol Doinyo Lengai, the volcano that stands high above Lake Natron. The 7,650-foot-tall peak is a place of pilgrimage for the local tribespeople, the Maasai. It is thought that ash-rich mud from the volcano formed the mudflats on which the ancient people walked, recording their footprints. In a matter of hours to days, the mud's surface dried out, preserving the prints in a cracked crust. Another flow of debris then buried the footprints at least ten thousand to twelve thousand years ago, entombing them for millennia.

Local villager Kongo Sakkae found some of the footprints prior to 2006, but the site didn't reach the attention of scientists until 2008, when conservationist Jim Brett happened to be staying at the Lake Natron Tented Camp, just a few hundred yards from the footprints. Stunned by what he saw, Brett snapped as many pictures as he could and resolved to pass them along to a scientist he knew he could trust. This was geologist Cynthia Liutkus-Pierce, whom he had met when she was a postdoctoral researcher. Several days later, Liutkus-Pierce saw Brett's photographs and was awestruck by the quality of preservation. In short order, she recruited a diverse team of scientists to make further investigations.

Dating exactly when humans walked across the mud near Lake Natron proved to be an enormous challenge. Originally, it was thought that the mud that captured the footprints began as ash that had rained down after Ol Doinyo Lengai erupted. If that were true, the ash would be essentially the same age as the footprints themselves – an approach that initially suggested the prints were about a hundred and twenty thousand years old. The team announced this possible age at a conference in 2011, raising excitement but also stirring up some debate over the interpretation. However, once the team realized that the ash had been carried to the site by water, they changed their method of determining the age of the footprints, and ultimately placed them at a more conservative age somewhere between five thousand and nineteen thousand years old.

The next step is to preserve the site for the long term. For now, the Tanzanian government is protecting the site, but there is always the danger that it might be destroyed by natural elements or by people. Even in the worst-case scenario, however, future scientists will be able to see what the research team saw when they first reached the site. With the help of the Smithsonian Museum, the team has created 3D scans of all the footprints. Essentially, they have the ability to replicate the site with 3D printing.

5 You are going to read an article about the discovery of ancient footprints. For questions 1–10, choose the answer (A, B, C or D) which you think fits best according to the text. There is an example at the beginning (0).

0 Where in Tanzania have ancient footprints recently been found?

    A beneath a lake

    (B) near a volcano

    C to the north of a lake

    D inside a volcano

1 What do we find out about the ancient footprints in the first paragraph?

    A when they were found

    B how many people made them

    C how big they are

    D whether they are in good condition

2 According to the article, the footprints show that

   A many people had foot problems.

   B the people were of different ages and gender.

   C most people were fit.

   D the majority of the people were women.

3 What did the children's footprints indicate?

   A the exact number of children in the area

   B the health problems they suffered from

   C the direction they were heading

   D the relationship they had with their mothers

4 What do we learn about the footprints found in Tanzania in the third paragraph?

   A They are the oldest set of footprints discovered in Africa.

   B They are found at one of many other similar sites around the world.

   C There are more of them than there are at most other sites.

   D They belong to *Australopithecus afarensis*.

5 Which of the following information about the volcano Ol Doinyo Lengai is not revealed in the article?

   A details of its height

   B some aspects of its appearance

   C information about its location

   D reasons why it's called this

6 In the fourth paragraph, the writer explains that the footprints recently discovered

   A were covered by volcanic material within days of being formed.

   B were made in volcanic mud that very quickly stopped being wet.

   C were left open to the skies until today.

   D were preserved because of the lack of rain in the region.

7 According to the article, the initial discovery of the footprints happened

   A as a result of a well-organized scientific expedition.

   B by accident when a conservationist came across them.

   C a couple of years before the scientific community knew anything.

   D during reconstruction of a tented village.

8 How is the relationship between Brett and Liutkus-Pierce described in the fifth paragraph?

   A They'd known each other before the discovery.

   B They were colleagues on the same project.

   C Brett was part of Liutkus-Pierce's team.

   D They were both geologists.

9 What does the article say about how the footprints were dated?

   A It was difficult because of the wet nature of the mud.

   B The first attempt was later revised.

   C A final decision was reached in 2011.

   D It required analysis of the water carrying mud to the site.

10 What does the article say about the future of the site?

   A The Tanzanian government may not wish to protect it.

   B It will inevitably be destroyed according to scientific evidence.

   C Steps have been taken to keep a record of the site in case it is lost.

   D Natural elements have already started to damage many of the footprints.

___ / 10

Listening

6 🔊 [121] You will hear five short extracts in which people are talking about how fundraisers are raising money for cancer charities. For questions 1–5, choose the fundraisers (A–H) each person describes. Use the letters only once. There are three extra letters which you do not need to use.

Speaker 1 ____

Speaker 2 ____

Speaker 3 ____

Speaker 4 ____

Speaker 5 ____

A They raise money through a race for women.

B They didn't raise as much money as hoped.

C They had a birthday during an adventure.

D They went on an adventure on their own.

E They went on a trek with colleagues.

F They currently hold fundraising events in different places.

G They hold a regular event in a city.

H They raised money by selling an amusing product.

____ / 10

Writing

7 Read the task below.

Write a news article using one of these headlines.
CRASH NEAR GOLF RESORT
TRAIN STRIKE INTO TENTH WEEK
SPORTS STAR GETS LIFE BAN
CELEBRITY COUPLE SPLIT

Write your article (180–200 words). Make sure you:
- catch the reader's attention.
- give details.
- include a quotation.

____ / 10

Speaking

8 Read the task below and give your presentation in class.

Prepare to report five pieces of gossip. This could be about people you know, celebrities in the news or things you have read on the internet.

In your presentation, include:
- facts such as date, place, people involved.
- your opinion of what happened.

____ / 10

Unit 10 Test

Vocabulary

1 Use the word given in CAPITAL LETTERS at the end of each sentence to form a word that fits in the gap in the same sentence. Here is an example (0).

    0 Ambition is just one of the common _characteristics_ shared by successful business people.   CHARACTER

    1 Helen's _____ in business studies and management make her the perfect candidate.   QUALIFY

    2 Jason's _____ of the history and geography of the region was remarkable.   KNOW

    3 My dad has poor _____ . You have to shout before he notices you are talking to him.   HEAR

    4 My grandmother was a _____ archaeologist specializing in ancient Egypt.   PASSION

    5 I think you're a really _____ person. You're a professional artist who also keeps a poetry blog.   CREATE

    6 It is important to be _____ in the modern workforce because new technology means that your job is likely to change.   ADAPT

    7 Joe is very _____ . He hopes to be promoted soon.   AMBITION

    8 I was _____ by his negative attitude.   FURY

    9 Princess Beatrice is the rightful _____ to the throne.   SUCCEED

    10 We were _____ to hear that you have given birth to a healthy baby boy.   JOY

___ / 10

2 Read the text below and decide which answer (A, B, C or D) best fits each gap. There is an example at the beginning (0).

Although Sir Frank Whittle died in 1996, his legacy **(0)** ___ . His invention – the turbojet engine – is what powers the aviation industry today. Whittle was born in 1907 and developed an interest in flying at an early age. He decided to **(1)** ___ a career with the armed services, and **(2)** ___ a job with the Royal Air Force as soon as he **(3)** ___ school. However, his application to **(4)** ___ the air force was rejected at first. Determined and **(5)** ___ , Whittle refused to accept this, however, and eventually **(6)** ___ a pilot. He **(7)** ___ in the air force for the rest of his life. His real **(8)** ___ lay, not in being a pilot, but in being an engineer. He was so naturally brilliant that, after **(9)** ___ an engineering course with the air force, he went on to study the subject at Cambridge University and he **(10)** ___ Peterhouse College in Cambridge with a first. By then, he'd already taken out a patent on the turbojet engine. He was well on his way to becoming one of the world's most remarkable engineers.

0 **A** goes away	Ⓑlives on	**C** makes forward	**D** carries after
1 **A** reach	**B** follow	**C** keep	**D** join
2 **A** applied for	**B** wrote after	**C** accepted to	**D** made for
3 **A** lost	**B** went	**C** left	**D** passed
4 **A** become	**B** fly	**C** join	**D** connect
5 **A** self-confident	**B** self-help	**C** self-conscious	**D** self-made
6 **A** was	**B** became	**C** achieved	**D** did
7 **A** passed	**B** went	**C** served	**D** devised
8 **A** talents	**B** experience	**C** background	**D** qualifications
9 **A** making	**B** doing	**C** going	**D** gaining
10 **A** passed after	**B** graduated after	**C** passed from	**D** graduated from

___ / 10

Grammar

3 Complete the text with *a, an, the* or – (no article). There is an example at the beginning (0).

Rosalind Franklin (1920–1958) was **(0)** _an_ English chemist and X-ray crystallographer who made contributions to **(1)** _____ discovery of the molecular structure of DNA. She was born into **(2)** _____ British Jewish family and educated in **(3)** _____ south of England. After working in **(4)** _____ Cambridge and Paris, Rosalind became **(5)** _____ research associate at **(6)** _____ King's College London in 1951 and worked on X-ray diffraction studies, which would eventually help lead to the double helix theory of DNA. In 1962, three male scientists, James Watson, Francis Crick and Maurice Wilkins, shared **(7)** _____ Nobel Prize for their work on the double helix theory. Sadly, Rosalind did not share in **(8)** _____ award. She died in 1958 at the age of thirty-seven from ovarian cancer, and **(9)** _____ Nobel Prize committee do not award prizes to **(10)** _____ people who have died.

___ / 10

4 Rewrite each pair of sentences as one sentence using the word given. Do not change the word given. Include commas where necessary. Here is an example (0).

0 He is a talented student. He has a background in science.

WITH

He is a talented student _____ *with a background in science* _____ .

1 Hilary Grant can solve mathematical problems. They are too difficult for most people.

THAT

Hilary Grant can solve mathematical problems _____ .

2 This is the invention. Jack is famous for it.

FOR

This is the invention _____ .

3 Rosalind Franklin is a scientist I admire. She helped discover the DNA molecule.

WHO

Rosalind Franklin, _____ .

4 Patrick Kelly is an explorer. He has an interesting story to tell.

WITH

Patrick Kelly is an explorer _____ .

5 My grandfather hardly received any formal education. He went on to become an accomplished scientist.

WHO

My grandfather, _____ .

6 My English teacher was an inspiring figure. Her first novel was published recently.

WHOSE

My English teacher, _____ .

7 You have done a lot for us. We are really grateful for this.

WHAT

We are really grateful _____ .

8 Few women have graduated from this college. That's disappointing.

IS

Few women have graduated from this college _____ .

9 My uncle died last week. He had been ill for a while.

WHO

My uncle _____ .

10 The car crashed against a tree. It was being driven at high speed.

WHICH

The car _____ .

___ / 10

Reading

The Science of Superheroes

Most people dismiss the fantastic feats of superheroes and their formidable enemies as mere fantasy. But to Robert Weinberg, an American science fiction writer, superheroes are worthy of scientific study. Along with Lois Gresh, Weinberg has written two books on the subject – *The Science of Superheroes* and his new book, *The Science of Supervillains*. Weinberg's mission is to separate scientifically believable comic book characters from those who are literally incredible. Yet to be convinced of the need for in-depth analysis myself, I have spent the last few days reading Weinberg's books and, I must say, I have found some fascinating insights.

One interesting aspect of superhero fiction is that comic book characters have long been involved in science. Many villains followed a career in biology, physics or chemistry before acquiring some superhuman power that enabled them to create chaos in the world. Take, for example, Lex Luthor, Superman's long-standing enemy. Originally portrayed as a scientific genius at a young age, Luthor was transformed into what Weinberg calls 'the original Dr Evil' after he became exposed to a huge amount of radiation. It seems to me that no comic book hero or villain is ever invented without a story involving the sciences in some way.

In his books, Weinberg is very interested in Lex Luthor. One question he asks is how plausible the scientific methods used by the evil villain to battle Superman really are. In one famous comic strip, for example, Luthor builds a teleportation machine that makes him invisible whenever Superman gets too close. While real-life scientists have successfully teleported photons (particles of light) from one place to another, it is scientifically impossible to beam people from one location to another. The reason for this is that a human body contains too much information to scan and build as replicas. Instead, Weinberg suggests that there may be another explanation – Luthor may have been using a hologram machine to project images of walls, rooms and himself.

In holography, laser light is used to record the light-wave patterns reflected from an object or person. It is a perfectly believable scientific explanation. Weinberg is keen to show that science can explain much of what seems to be fantasy in comic books.

Nowadays, Hollywood filmmakers are striving to make their movies as scientifically realistic as possible, and they have the cinematic technology to make the incredible believable. To my mind, however, it would be wrong to think that just because they look great, today's films are based on science facts to a greater extent than the comics and films of fifty years ago. Weinberg shares a similar opinion. He argues that the comic books from the so-called 'Silver Age of comics' (the late 1950s and the 1960s) were more grounded in science than most of what is being published today. Indeed, he expresses the view that many of today's comic book writers seem to have learned their science from reading comic books and not from studying modern technology. While some comic book writers have suggested that good science means sacrificing an entertaining story, Weinberg points out that many best-selling science fiction books feature accurate science. Personally, I don't see why a good story needs to be grounded in science. Let's face it, *The Invisible Man* is hard to explain in scientific terms – but, on the other hand, I don't see why the science should necessarily get in the way of the story.

Finally, it is worth making the point that Weinberg and Gresh are not alone in studying superhero science. There is one website that reviews movies based on scientific merit, and many senior physics teachers use superheroes to teach science to their students. As one professor put it: 'Talking about how Superman flies, or how Spiderman produces webs, is a fun way of getting students to think about how the physical universe operates.' Next time you are amazed by the abilities of X-Men like Magneto, think about how it might well all be explained by science.

5 You are going to read an article about the science behind superheroes in comics. For questions 1–10, choose the opinion which is expressed. There is an example at the beginning (0).

A = the author's opinion   W = Robert Weinberg's opinion   O = other opinions

0 The abilities of superheroes aren't based on science at all. _O_

1 We should analyse the science behind the powers villains have in comic books. ___

2 The powers of most comic book characters can be explained by science. ___

3 One of Superman's enemies could be described as the first evil scientist in comic books. ___

4 Science appears to feature in the creation of all superheroes in comics. ___

5 We can use scientific theories to explain why teleportation is possible. ___

6 Hollywood superhero movies are scientifically more realistic than they used to be. ___

7 Sixty years ago, comics were often based on good science. ___

8 Some authors successfully manage to combine entertainment and scientific knowledge. ___

9 It isn't always necessary for a good science story to be believable in scientific terms. ___

10 Making a study of the science of superheroes gets students more interested in science. ___

___ / 10

Listening

6 [122] You will hear an interview with a writer called Jake Flynn, who's written a book about Yuri Gagarin. For questions 1–10, complete the sentences with a word or short phrase. There is an example at the beginning (0).

0 Jake Flynn has written Yuri Gagarin's ___*biography*___ .

1 Yuri Gagarin was the first person to go _____ .

2 In his biography, Jake mostly writes about Gagarin's _____ .

3 Around the time he became famous, Jake says that Gagarin felt _____ and _____ .

4 As well as Canada, Gagarin visited _____ and _____ on his world tour.

5 Jake says Gagarin disliked having so much _____ after returning to Earth.

6 Gagarin couldn't go back into space because he was an important _____ for his country.

7 Vladimir Komarov, who was Gagarin's friend, was killed in _____ in space.

8 Apart from training new astronauts, Gagarin also got involved in _____ .

9 In the mid-1960s, Gagarin passed a course in _____ .

10 In 1968, Gagarin died during a _____ .

___ / 10

Writing

7 Read the task below.

> Write a personal profile for a job application or university application.

Write your profile (180–200 words). Make sure you:
- describe your personality.
- describe your skills, talents, experience and background.
- say what your ambition is and how you will achieve it.

___ / 10

Speaking

8 Read the task below and give your presentation in class.

> Prepare a description of three things you aim to achieve in the next five years. These could be related to your studies, your job or your lifestyle.

In your presentation, include:
- a description of your skills, talents and experience.
- a description of your dreams and ambitions.

___ / 10

Unit 11 Test

Vocabulary

1 Complete the text with the correct form of the verbs in the box. There are three extra verbs which you do not need. There is an example at the beginning (0).

> acquire address break cram engage fail get inspire make pass
> revise take (x2) turn

(0) ___*Acquiring*___ a less common language is like being part of a secret club. It allows you to (1) _____ with a culture and a people who would otherwise be strange, and it allows you to (2) _____ what people are saying when all your friends look confused. Moreover, learning one, new, unusual language can (3) _____ you to learn many more. Before long, you'll be a polyglot! When I was at school, studying French, we had to (4) _____ an exam in the subject every term, and if we didn't (5) _____ the exam by getting eighty per cent of the answers correct, we had to spend the entire summer holidays (6) _____ for another exam. I remember (7) _____ for my exams at the last minute, staying up all night to learn lists of words. The problem was that I was never interested in using the language to speak to French people. This was a problem I never (8) _____ while at school, but one that I've dealt with now. I love the idea of learning a less common language because you learn it purely for the love of speaking to people. Of course, learning a new language – especially an unusual one like Tuareg or Thai – is never easy. You have to (9) _____ up for a lot of lessons, and you have to (10) _____ in a lot of information, but it is incredibly rewarding.

___ / 10

2 Complete the second sentence so that it has a similar meaning to the first sentence, using the word given. Do not change the word given. You must use between two and four words, including the word given. Here is an example (0).

0 Graham has learned everything by living his life.
 EXPERIENCE
 Graham has learned ___*everything from experience*___ .

1 Jamie left college without graduating two years ago.
 DROPPED
 Jamie _____ college two years ago.

2 Pamela memorized the words for her Spanish test.
 HEART
 Pamela learned _____ for her Spanish test.

3 Simon needs to learn everything about the job.
 TRADE
 Simon needs to learn the _____ .

4 You can always learn new things despite your age.
 LATE
 It's never _____ new things.

5 Get some experience before doing difficult things.
 RUN
 Learn to walk _____ .

6 I won't make that mistake again.
 LESSON
 I've _____ .

7 I learned by making mistakes.
 HARD
 I learned _____ .

8 Forests are a place where you can find wood.
 SOURCE
 Forests are _____ wood.

9 Doctors can't stop some types of diseases.
 CURE
 There is _____ some types of diseases.

10 Nobody saw Sally at school today.
 TURN
 Sally _____ for school today.

___ / 10

Grammar

3 Complete the short posts using the correct form of the verbs in brackets. There is an example at the beginning (0).

I was about **(0)** ___to start___ (start) a course in Italian when I saw an advertisement for lessons in Albanian. I managed **(1)** _____ (change) onto the Albanian course and I succeeded in **(2)** _____ (learn) the language really well in two years. Of course, I knew people would **(3)** _____ (question) why I'd spent so much time learning a language which is only spoken in one small country, but I don't regret it. It's a fascinating language.   **Jo**

I was going **(4)** _____ (do) Spanish at university until I realized that I could **(5)** _____ (study) similar but much less common languages like Portuguese and Catalan instead. I decided to major in these languages. Of course, I'd **(6)** _____ (take) exams in Spanish, too, but my tutor advised me to just concentrate on two languages.   **Grant**

I was supposed **(7)** _____ (complete) my course in Zulu at the University of Durban in May, but I didn't manage **(8)** _____ (finish) because I was ill. I didn't mind though. I could **(9)** _____ (speak) fluently and I was able **(10)** _____ (communicate) with native speakers, so I didn't really need the qualification.   **Dan**

___ / 10

4 Complete the second sentence so that it has a similar meaning to the first sentence, using the word given. Do not change the word given. You must use between two and four words, including the word given. Here is an example (0).

0 Could Sarah swim that well when she was young?

  ABLE

  _____*Was Sarah able to swim*_____ that well when she was young?

1 Were you able to close the window?

  MANAGE

  _____ close the window?

2 Neither John nor Irene was able to contact the police.

  SUCCEEDED

  Neither John nor Irene _____ the police.

3 I knew that Danny would soon leave.

  ABOUT

  I knew that Danny _____ .

4 We should have gone to Kelly's party but we all felt too tired.

  SUPPOSED

  We _____ to Kelly's party but we all felt too tired.

5 I had intended to stay but I didn't feel well, so I came home.

  WOULD

  I _____ but I didn't feel well, so I came home.

6 Jerry's plan was to paint the front of the house silver until the council told him that it was not permitted.

  GOING

  Jerry _____ the front of the house silver until the council told him that it was not permitted.

7 After a lot of effort, Stephanie stopped the water coming into the kitchen.

  MANAGED

  Stephanie _____ the water coming into the kitchen.

8 I was on the point of calling the rescue services when Mark walked in.

  ABOUT

  I _____ the rescue services when Mark walked in.

9 I couldn't get a job back then because of the high unemployment rate.

  WASN'T

  I _____ a job back then because of the high unemployment rate.

10 We managed to fix the roof even though it was badly damaged.

  REPAIR

  Although it was badly damaged, we were _____ the roof.

___ / 10

Reading

Are you ready to learn a new language?

(0) _C_

It's all very well making the grand New Year's resolution to learn Mandarin. But without realistic, short-term objectives, you're likely to give up before you've barely got going. For example, if the real reason why you want to learn Spanish is to chat to locals in bars, make a learning plan that includes questions and opinions about popular conversation topics like music and football. The key is to break down your language acquisition into achievable milestones and tailor your practice accordingly.

(1) _____

Don't throw away the textbooks just yet, but be aware that there's a world of fun and addictive resources online for you to tap into. Gone are the days when you're supposed to sit in a quiet corner with a vocabulary book, learning lists of words by heart (not that anyone ever felt doing such a thing would be useful!). These days you can combine a language course app, such as Duolingo, with a flashcard app for vocabulary, such as Memrise, and, whatever your level, the opportunities to practise with native speakers on chat platforms, including HelloTalk or HiNative, are endless. Whenever you head abroad, keep Google Translate or iHandy Translator in your digital arsenal.

(2) _____

Despite what many may tell you, living abroad isn't a prerequisite for learning a foreign language; there's nothing 'in the air' that will magically make you fluent. The useful bit — being exposed to everyday language — can be replicated wherever you are through TV, film, radio, podcasts and music. Having a Brazilian soap opera on while you commute or cook, for example, will help tune your ear to the pronunciation of Portuguese. I once managed to turn a wet and windy summer in Scotland into a month on Copacabana beach in Rio simply by surrounding myself with all things Brazilian – and I was able to make great progress in Portuguese at the same time.

(3) _____

Romance languages, such as French, Spanish, Portuguese and Italian, have many words in common with English as a result of shared Latinate sources. 'Action', 'nation', 'frustration', 'tradition', 'extinction', and thousands of other '-tion' words are spelled the same in French (although pronounced differently). Switch that '-tion' to a '-ción' and you have the same words in Spanish. Italian is '–zione' and Portuguese is '-ção'. In any language, loan words are your allies; they should be quick and easy to memorize.

(4) _____

If you're having a hard time getting key words to stick, try to glue them in your brain using a visual mnemonic. Picture the meaning in a dynamic, colourful and weird way that links to its translation. Also, when you come across a new word, try using it a few times right away in different sentences. Studies show using words flexibly activates different parts of your brain. While some words, like cognates, may stick without you having to try too hard, others will soon be lost unless you succeed in bringing them to life in some way.

(5) _____

There may never be a time when you feel 'ready' to begin conversing, so find a conversation partner and jump in, using whatever phrases you know, right from the start. 'I was going to wait until I could say something meaningful in Mandarin before trying to talk to a native speaker,' said Lloyd, a student in his first year of Mandarin studies, 'but getting together with Li twice a week has done me the world of good. And we're close friends now.' Companies such as Conversation Exchange can set up conversation lessons with native speakers. Taking advantage of such possibilities is a sure way of building your confidence in a new language.

(6) _____

Fillers are the words and phrases people say all the time between sentences. In French, an example might be 'alors', in Spanish, 'pues', in Japanese, 'so desu-ne'. They don't always mean much, but peppering your conversation with these flourishes will make you seem as if you've spent much of your life hanging out in Marseilles, Madrid or Osaka. Not only that, but it'll buy you precious, face-saving time to think while formulating your sentences.

5a You are going to read an article about language learning. For paragraphs 1–6, choose from the headings (A–J). There are three headings which you do not need to use. There is an example at the beginning (0).

A Get with the tech
B Use memory techniques
C Have a goal
D Wait before trying to converse
E Keep a vocabulary book
F Try virtual immersion
G Learn to sound more native
H Start with cognates
I Formulate sentences carefully
J Practise speaking early on

5b Read the article again. For questions 1–4, choose from the paragraphs (0–6). You do not need to use all the paragraphs. There is an example at the beginning (0).

In which paragraph (0–6) does the writer

0 quote a language learner to support a point? paragraph _5_

1 refer to how people studied languages in the past? paragraph ___

2 challenge a commonly-held view about language learning? paragraph ___

3 refer to research into language learning? paragraph ___

4 compare phrases from different languages which have similar functions? paragraph ___

_____ / 10

Listening

6 🔊 [123] You will hear an interview with Sophie Watson, who's talking about her job as a museum curator. For questions 1–10, choose the best answer (A, B or C). There is an example at the beginning (0).

0 Before deciding to work in museums, Sophie wanted to be

  Ⓐ a nurse.

  B a holiday rep.

  C an artist.

1 Sophie became interested in museums

  A because a family member worked in one.

  B after she went to one almost by accident.

  C while working in one during the school holidays.

2 In her current job, Sophie

  A works in a museum at a university.

  B is the curator of a city centre museum.

  C works in a university art department.

3 Sophie says the most important part of her job is to

  A put on art exhibitions.

  B publicize her place of work.

  C raise money for projects.

4 Sophie often has to

  A come up with good ideas for art shows.

  B choose how to display art in art shows.

  C interview artists and art lecturers.

5 What does Sophie say she does on a typical day?

  A She works from early in the morning to late in the evening.

  B She starts work early but doesn't work a full day.

  C She's in the office from one or two in the afternoon.

6 During her working day, Sophie says she has to spend a lot of time

  A in meetings.

  B organizing galleries.

  C writing things.

7 When talking about her free time, Sophie says she

  A rarely goes to other art galleries.

  B reads things like magazines to find out about art.

  C keeps a blog about art.

8 Sophie first worked in museums and galleries

  A after she left college.

  B without getting paid.

  C in the fundraising department.

9 Sophie says that she became an art curator

  A after raising funds from her family.

  B while working as a volunteer receptionist.

  C after getting hired by an arts organization.

10 Sophie advises people who want to be an art curator to

  A get the necessary qualifications.

  B learn while doing the job.

  C become an artist first.

___ / 10

Writing

7 Read the task below.

> You recently saw this online advertisement.
>
> **SWAHILI EXPERTS**
>
> *Are you interested in learning Swahili? Join our course and learn this exciting language in less than six months! Our unique course involves a workbook, video and audio disks and online support from a native speaker.*
>
> You bought the course but six months later your Swahili still isn't very good. Write an email of complaint.

Write your email (180–200 words). Make sure you:

- explain what you expected from the course.
- explain how and why it hasn't lived up to your expectations.
- ask for the company to respond in some way and compensate you.

___ / 10

Speaking

8 Read the task below and give your presentation in class.

> Prepare a two-minute description of a course that you have taken. It could be a language course or any other type of course.

In your presentation, include:

- a description of the course, where and when you did it.
- a description of what you learned and how.
- an evaluation of whether it was a successful course or not.

___ / 10

Unit 12 Test

Vocabulary

1 Complete the sentences using the correct form of the verbs in the box. Here is an example (0).

borrow   earn   fit   invest   lend   owe   pursue   save   set   s̶i̶t̶   spend

0 Our house has doubled in price. We're ___*sitting*___ pretty – we can afford expensive holidays now.

1 I'm trying to _____ money each week for a new car. So far, I have about £2,000 but I need more than that.

2 Before lunch, Tom and Harry managed to _____ the new carpet and repaint all the walls in the living room.

3 Joe _____ £30,000 a year. It's a good salary but he's asked his boss for a rise.

4 We _____ up the company in 2010, and it's become more and more successful each year.

5 Could you _____ me £50 until after the weekend? I'll pay you back on Monday.

6 It's important to _____ in infrastructure. If the government doesn't do this, the quality of our road and rail systems will suffer.

7 Jeremy decided to _____ a career in financial services.

8 Last summer, Danny _____ money from his parents to put down a deposit on the flat. He hasn't paid them back yet.

9 Louise booked the tickets and paid online. We each _____ her £30. Let's give her the money tonight.

10 We went to New York and _____ a lot of money – there was so much to do!

___ / 10

2 Read the text below and decide which answer (A, B, C or D) best fits each gap. There is an example at the beginning (0).

The income (0) __ between 'haves' and 'have nots' is growing in the United States. According to a shocking new report, homelessness among (1) __ has reached a new all-time high of two and a half million. As the cost of (2) __ rises, one out of every seven Americans relies on food banks to put food on the table, and people's buying (3) __ has reached rock bottom – meaning that shops can't sell their goods.

DIY is on the rise in the UK. Whether it's (4) __ up shelves, (5) __ a dripping tap or (6) __ new kitchen cabinets from a well-known Swedish furniture store, many of us will be spending this weekend on jobs about the house. And it seems the current (7) __ for DIY is set to continue. Figures show that there has been a ten per cent rise in sales by DIY shops.

Statistics show that many young people are (8) __ to pay their own way through university. As the recession bites, and education costs rise, more and more youngsters are turning to part-time work, ranging from child (9) __ to dog (10) __ in order to make ends meet.

0 **A** space	Ⓑgap	**C** trap	**D** place
1 **A** young	**B** the young people	**C** the young	**D** a young person
2 **A** to live	**B** lives	**C** life	**D** living
3 **A** power	**B** strength	**C** ability	**D** needs
4 **A** helping	**B** taking	**C** putting	**D** making
5 **A** restoring	**B** fixing	**C** cutting	**D** altering
6 **A** assembling	**B** arranging	**C** tiling	**D** setting
7 **A** model	**B** trend	**C** feel	**D** suit
8 **A** on a mission	**B** in a need	**C** on a journey	**D** in a change
9 **A** looking	**B** minding	**C** helping	**D** setting
10 **A** taking	**B** wandering	**C** running	**D** walking

___ / 10

Grammar

3 Complete the text with *only, just* or *even*. In some cases, there is more than one possible answer. There is an example at the beginning (0).

People often think of Europe's great cities as expensive places, but hardly any of them **(0)** _*even*_ make a new list of the ten most expensive cities in which to live. Instead, this is dominated by Asian and African cities. **(1)** _____ Zurich and Geneva make the list. **(2)** _____ London and Paris fail to be listed.

(3) _____ last Wednesday, the list was published. Hong Kong remains the world's most expensive city, where it costs almost $7,000 a month for an apartment with **(4)** _____ two bedrooms. Second place may surprise **(5)** _____ those of you familiar with travelling and living abroad — the monthly rent in Luanda, Angola, will cost you $6,700 a month. Thanks to a booming oil economy in a city with **(6)** _____ a small supply of luxurious housing, some rents are **(7)** _____ as high as those in world cities with more reputation.

Compare Luanda's $6,700 a month with Sydney, where a similar apartment would cost $2,600, or Vancouver, where the monthly rent is **(8)** _____ slightly lower than in Sydney. It seems crazy that prices are so high, especially when you consider that ordinary Luandans don't earn enough to live in such luxury. **(9)** _____ the best paid locals earn less than the rent on these apartments and **(10)** _____ a small number of foreigners can afford to live in them.

___ / 10

4 Complete the second sentence so that it has a similar meaning to the first sentence, using the word given. Do not change the word given. You must use between two and four words, including the word given. Here is an example (0).

0 The repair shop fixed our dishwasher.
   HAD
   We _had our dishwasher fixed_ at the repair shop.

1 They didn't take long to redecorate our kitchen.
   GOT
   We _____ in next to no time.

2 We hope that somebody will take over Jo's responsibilities by the end of the month.
   HAVE
   We hope to _____ Jo's responsibilities by the end of the month.

3 Please persuade Paul to call her.
   GET
   Can you _____ her?

4 Cable TV was installed for no cost.
   HAD
   We _____ for no cost.

5 Did you manage to finish your project before the deadline?
   GET
   Did you _____ before the deadline?

6 I asked Tim if he would help me and he said yes.
   GOT
   I _____ me.

7 A cleaning company did Robert's housework for him.
   DONE
   Robert _____ by a cleaning company.

8 Making Paul work overtime isn't fair.
   GETTING
   The idea of _____ overtime isn't fair.

9 Every summer, somebody cleans Peter's carpets.
   HAS
   Peter _____ every summer.

10 The kids washed Mr Jones' car because he gave them £10.
   TO
   Mr Jones _____ wash his car by giving them £10.

___ / 10

Reading

The journey of humankind: How money made us modern

Since ancient times, humans have utilized all sorts of items to represent value, from large stones to cakes of salt, squirrel pelts and whale teeth. In the ancient world, people often relied upon symbols that also had some tangible value in their own right. The ancient Chinese, for example, were among those who used cowrie shells, which were prized for their beauty as materials for jewellery, to make payments. Even today, many characters in Chinese writing that relate to money include the ancient symbol for the cowrie shell. Durable, easily cleaned and easy to count, the shells defied imitation or counterfeiting.

In the Mesopotamian region of Sumer, about 9,500 years ago, ancient accountants in the region kept track of farmers' crops and livestock by stacking small pieces of baked clay, almost like the tokens used in board games today. One piece might signify a bushel of grain, while another with a different shape might represent a farm animal or a jar of olive oil. The humble little ceramic shapes they used might not seem to have much in common with today's $100 bill, let alone with credit card swipes and online transactions, but the roots of our modern modes of payment almost certainly lie in the Sumerians' tokens. Such early accounting tools ultimately evolved into a system of finance and money itself – a symbolic representation of value, which can be transferred from one person to another as a payment for goods or services.

Civilization existed before money, but probably wouldn't have got very far without it. Ancient humans' invention of money was a revolutionary milestone. It helped to drive the development of civilization by making it easier not just to buy and sell goods, but to pay workers in an increasing number of specialized trades – craftsmen, artists, merchants and soldiers, to name a few.

In ancient times, gold gradually became a universal currency. The gleaming precious metal was stable, yet could also be combined at high temperatures with other metals to create alloys, and was easy to melt and hammer into shapes. It became the raw material for the first coins, which were created in Lydia, a kingdom in what is now Turkey, around 2,700 years ago. Lydian coins didn't look much like today's coinage. They were irregular in shape and size and didn't have denominations inscribed on them. There was a stamped image on each coin, just as now, but it was there to indicate the weight and value of each coin. Unlike modern money, ancient Lydian coins were what economists call full-bodied or commodity money, whose value was fixed by the metal in them. If the gold or silver in them became worth more, people tended to melt them down.

The emergence of money in the form of coins helped connect the world, by enabling traders to roam across continents and oceans to buy and sell goods, and investors to amass wealth. Its convenience made it easier for merchants to develop large-scale trade networks, in which they bought and sold spices, grain and even slaves over distances of thousands of miles. In the ancient Greek city-state of Corinth, banks were set up at which foreign traders could hand in their own coins and get Corinthian ones back. And the Greek historian Herodotus, writing in the fifth century BC, describes Carthaginian traders unloading their wares on beaches and, after setting smoky fires to signal shoppers, accepting the locals' gold as payment.

The hazards of moving money and goods over distances – whether it was from storms at sea or bandits and pirates – led humans to develop increasingly complex economic organizations. In the 1600s, for example, investors who gathered in London coffeehouses began underwriting traders and colonists venturing across the ocean to the New World, financing their voyages in exchange for a share of the crops or goods they brought back. Investors would try to reduce their risk by buying shares of multiple ventures. It was the start of a modern global economy in which vast quantities of products and money flow across borders in the search for profits.

Over the centuries, money has continued to evolve in form and function. The ancient world's stones and shells gave way to coins, and eventually to paper currency and cheques drawn upon bank accounts, physical tokens which, in turn, are gradually being superseded by electronic ones. Ranging from credit card transactions to new forms of digital currency designed for transferring and amassing wealth on the internet, we are currently in the middle of a money revolution. Who knows what shape our money will take in the years to come?

5 You are going to read an article about the use of money throughout history. For questions 1–10, choose the answer (A, B, C or D) which you think fits best according to the text. There is an example at the beginning (0).

0 According to the article, which of the following have people used for money in the past?
A their own teeth
B parts of animals
C sweet snacks
D blocks of wood

1 What does the article say about the cowrie shells?
A The Chinese were the only people who used them for money.
B They had a symbolic rather than monetary value.
C The Chinese considered them attractive enough to wear.
D The more beautiful they were, the bigger their value.

2 Cowrie shells were a useful means of making payments because
A there were vast numbers of them.
B they never seemed to get dirty.
C they were rare and priceless.
D they were durable and hard to copy.

3 What does the writer compare the clay coins of ancient Sumer to?
A bushels of grain
B small baked cakes
C pieces from games
D small animals

4 Why does the writer say that the clay coins of ancient Sumer are important?
A They were the first coins to show animals or other valuable objects.
B They each had a value equivalent to $100 in today's money.
C They were the first coins used in a way comparable to how we use money now.
D Their roots lay in a complex system of finance we no longer use.

5 In the third paragraph the writer uses the phrase 'a revolutionary milestone' to say that money allowed
A the emergence of human civilization for the first time.
B humans to compensate each other for work they did.
C people to sell things they couldn't have sold before.

D a few specialized groups to become wealthier.

6 According to the article, why was gold used so widely as a form of currency?
A It was commonly found across the ancient world.
B Its irregular shapes and sizes made it useful.
C It could be mixed with other metals in natural conditions.
D It could easily be turned into what we now call coins.

7 In what way are Lydian coins comparable to modern coins?
A They had some sort of picture on them.
B Their value depended on how much gold was in them.
C Coins of the same shape and size had the same value.
D They could easily be melted down.

8 What example does the writer provide of how money transformed trade?
A an example of the first large-scale trade network
B an example of an early currency exchange system
C an example of a market selling spices and slaves
D an example of how people traded on beaches

9 How did seventeenth century investors make investing in trade safer?
A They stopped going on long distance voyages themselves.
B They started to finance different trading opportunities at the same time.
C They carefully selected only the safest ventures to invest in.
D They made sure they owned all the shares in one company.

10 In the concluding paragraph, what does the writer say about money?
A Money will never cease to evolve.
B People will possess greater wealth in the future.
C Money as we know it will not change.
D We may return to ancient methods of using money.

___ / 10

Listening

6 [124] You will hear people talking in four different situations. For questions 1–10, choose the best answer (A, B or C). There is an example at the beginning (0).

A customer asks a shop assistant about shoes.

0 What sort of shoes does the customer want to buy?

A summer shoes

(B) smart shoes

C brown shoes

1 What does the shop assistant say about the type of shoes the customer wants to buy?

A They are inexpensive.

B They have a special price.

C They are worth the money.

2 How many pairs of shoes does the customer want to try on?

A just the pair at the front

B the shoes on sale

C two of the pairs he's been shown

An interviewer talks to an expert American economist.

3 According to the interviewer, what has the Federal Reserve done?

A Despite warnings about the economy, it has reduced interest rates again.

B It has increased interest rates for the first time in the last year.

C Not for the first time this year, it has made a change to interest rates.

4 According to the economist, who might benefit because of the changes to interest rates?

A people with houses

B businesspeople

C investors

5 What does the expert say about the value of the dollar?

A It has fallen in value since the Federal Reserve changed interest rates.

B Its value is likely to rise because of interest rate changes.

C It has risen considerably in value since the Federal Reserve changed interest rates.

A seller of kitchen cabinets and a buyer negotiate.

6 The seller says that he won't cut prices because

A it will result in a reduction of the quality of his product.

B the buyer's offer does not justify such an action.

C his company doesn't ever negotiate on price.

7 The buyer feels that the seller should cut prices because

A the quality of the product is not as good as the buyer says.

B sales are going well and the seller is making a large profit.

C her company may make large orders in the future.

A radio interview with a leading economist

8 What does the economist say about his studies?

A He started a degree and then changed to do a different one.

B Before completing his studies, he had a job in the financial sector.

C Before ever working, he got a first degree and a Master's degree.

9 How did the economist feel about economics when he started his studies?

A He preferred another subject.

B He didn't like the way it made him think.

C He didn't think he was very good at it.

10 Which of the following does the economist now find interesting about the subject?

A There are a lot of difficult problems to be solved.

B He enjoys finding solutions to everyday problems.

C He admires the work of different economists.

___ / 10

Writing

7 Read the task below.

Your college would like to start an English-language magazine with articles on a variety of topics. Your teacher has asked you to write a report on one of the following subjects:

- a language course you have completed

- an organized trip or tour you have been on

- an event you have attended

Write your report (180–200 words). Make sure you:

• include an introduction.

• give details.

• include key report phrases.

___ / 10

Speaking

8 Read the task below and give your presentation in class.

You are about to negotiate with your boss for a pay rise and improved working conditions.

In your presentation, include:

• an explanation of the rise and working conditions you want.

• reasons why you deserve the above.

___ / 10

Photocopiable tests: answer key

Unit 1 Test

Vocabulary

1

1 dependable	5 childish	9 painful
2 selfish	6 ambitious	10 unreliable
3 successful	7 decisive	
4 helpful	8 rebellious	

2

1 A	2 D	3 C	4 B	5 C
6 A	7 D	8 B	9 D	10 B

Grammar

3

1 moved
2 remains
3 have attracted
4 continues
5 was
6 has dropped
7 has struggled / has been struggling
8 is rising / has risen / has been rising
9 hit / has hit
10 has become / is becoming

4

1 has been chatting	6 's/has moved
2 didn't get	7 's/has been getting
3 decided	8 's/has been
4 's/has bought	9 heard
5 have been waiting	10 hasn't passed

Reading

5

1 D	2 B	3 E	4 A	5 B
6 C	7 A	8 E	9 C	10 B

Listening

6

1 B	2 F	3 C	4 H	5 A

Unit 2 Test

Vocabulary

1

1 summit	5 plot	9 original
2 setting	6 gripping	10 thought-
3 character	7 key	provoking
4 track	8 heading	

2

1 A	2 D	3 A	4 C	5 B
6 C	7 A	8 D	9 B	10 C

Grammar

3

1 'd/had written	6 didn't arrive
2 produced	7 published
3 didn't find	8 'd/had been writing
4 was travelling	9 'd/had become/became
5 completed	10 devoted

4

1 was shown	6 will be given
2 had flown to	7 are you being paid
3 could be named	8 would be corrected
4 have been told by	9 has to be seen
5 (that) she had left	10 had been waving

Reading

5

1 B	2 A	3 C	4 D	5 B
6 C	7 D	8 A	9 A	10 B

Listening

6

1 shopping mall	6 the other escalator
2 sister	7 anxious
3 volunteered	8 shopping / (Christmas)
4 escalator(s)	decorations
5 halfway up (the escalator)	9 jewellery
	10 a shop assistant

Unit 3 Test

Vocabulary

1

1 brick	5 metal	9 plastic
2 glass	6 rubber	10 Nylon
3 concrete	7 Leather	
4 cardboard	8 cotton	

2

1 B	2 A	3 D	4 B	5 C
6 C	7 A	8 B	9 C	10 D

Grammar

3

1 's/is getting	6 'll/will agree
2 be	7 'll/will do
3 'm/am going to talk	8 'll/will start
4 will melt	9 going to happen
5 'm/am visiting	10 to face

4

1 's/is about to take	6 are going to
2 'll/will be flying	7 (probably) feel / be
3 have completed	feeling much
4 will you be studying	8 definitely not going to
5 'll/will have fallen asleep	9 won't have had
	10 I'm going to

Reading

5

1 T	2 N	3 F	4 T	5 T
6 T	7 N	8 T	9 F	10 F

Listening

6

1 C	2 B	3 B	4 C	5 A
6 B	7 B	8 B	9 A	10 C

Unit 4 Test

Vocabulary

1

1 comedian	5 arts	9 artistic
2 performances	6 natural	10 performer
3 buskers	7 Ultimately	
4 creative	8 exhibition	

2

1 exhibiting	5 participating	9 spending
2 soothing	6 exposing	10 protesting
3 performing	7 Spending	
4 spending	8 regulating	

Grammar

3

1 A	2 D	3 B	4 C	5 D
6 A	7 B	8 A	9 D	10 B

4

1 Every visitor was searched
2 Neither artist was
3 is a lack of
4 both guitarists play
5 Most (people) there agreed
6 A number of people
7 Each artist is
8 Almost no cinemas
9 The whole collection was
10 won't be any / will be no

Reading

5

1 F	2 A	3 H	4 G	5 B

Listening

6

1 C	2 C	3 A	4 B	5 B
6 A	7 C	8 A	9 A	10 B

Unit 5 Test

Vocabulary

1

1 well	5 well	9 middle
2 badly	6 off	10 for
3 highly	7 badly	
4 through	8 spur	

2

1 B	2 C	3 A	4 D	5 D
6 A	7 B	8 C	9 C	10 B

Grammar

3

1 (to) make	5 to operate	9 to invest
2 having	6 to travel	10 losing
3 to access	7 to go	
4 building	8 spending	

4

1 regret not sending
2 didn't mean to spend
3 remember staying
4 reading books to going
5 didn't try to stop
6 have continued to build
7 didn't mean to do
8 went on to write
9 stopped sending
10 regret to say

Reading

5

1 F	2 A	3 B	4 B	5 E
6 C	7 D	8 A	9 C	10 F

Listening

6

1 E	2 A	3 H	4 F	5 D

Unit 6 Test

Vocabulary

1

1 insurance	5 sightseeing	9 cultural
2 vaccinations	6 guided	10 Hiking
3 self-catering	7 repellent	
4 scenery	8 expenses	

2

1 off	5 off	9 put
2 take	6 own	10 blank
3 out	7 changed	
4 lotion	8 on	

Grammar

3

1 Is it the case that	7 Do you know what
2 Don't I	8 can't I
3 don't they	9 Do you have information about how
4 Can you tell me when	
5 What's included	10 Is it OK
6 Surely not	

4

1 Let's not ignore	6 think he'll/he will
2 not to stay	7 won't we
3 None of the	8 I imagine not
4 don't (like it) either	9 not to wait
5 don't have to	10 none was available

Reading

5

1 C	2 G	3 A	4 F	5 B

Listening

6

1 C	2 B	3 C	4 B	5 A
6 B	7 C	8 A	9 A	10 B

Unit 7 Test

Vocabulary

1

1 garnish	5 stomach	9 shame
2 veil	6 stag	10 tune
3 almond	7 matter	
4 niche	8 groom	

2

1 up	2 in	3 over	4 in	5 off
6 of	7 at	8 off	9 against	10 to

Grammar

3

1 produced / used to produce
2 would buy / used to buy
3 used to putting
4 used to
5 start
6 are
7 won't be
8 look
9 have
10 used to hearing

4

1 when I stop
2 unless we start
3 as soon as
4 before the film starts
5 used to spend / would spend
6 haven't got used to
7 long as nothing goes
8 won't have lunch until
9 used to own
10 get used to not

Reading

5

1 C	2 E	3 A	4 F	5 G
6 D	7 C	8 F	9 B	10 D

Listening

6

1 A	2 B	3 C	4 C	5 B
6 B	7 B	8 A	9 B	10 C

Unit 8 Test

Vocabulary

1

1 expectations
2 translator
3 librarian
4 physicists
5 accountant
6 majestic
7 preference
8 guidance
9 miserable
10 lawyer

2

1 better
2 make
3 do
4 breaking
5 made
6 do
7 by
8 making
9 do
10 better

Grammar

3

1 would/could/might/may change
2 would/could/might/may vanish
3 occurred
4 would/could/might/may take
5 were
6 would/could/might/may look
7 would/could/might/may have disappeared
8 would have covered / would be covering
9 had/'d taken
10 would/could/might/may have reduced

4

1 were richer, we would
2 would still be lost
3 you would start
4 knew more about
5 If only I could
6 wouldn't be so rude
7 would stop making
8 would have given

9 If I had known
10 If only Susie would

Reading

5

1 G	2 C	3 E	4 B	5 F

Listening

6

1 G	2 A	3 H	4 E	5 C

Unit 9 Test

Vocabulary

1

1 blame
2 take
3 encouraging
4 awarded
5 astonishing
6 beg
7 warned
8 admitted
9 word
10 charming

2

1 B	2 C	3 D	4 B	5 A
6 D	7 C	8 A	9 B	10 A

Grammar

3

1 failing
2 limiting
3 raising
4 to wait
5 to say
6 to listen
7 to believe
8 being
9 to criticize
10 taking

4

1 praised everybody for
2 denied knowing anything
3 encouraged Emily to apply
4 is known to be
5 is thought (that)
6 was urged to start
7 warned us not to
8 is believed to be
9 is said to know
10 are reported to be

Reading

5

1 D	2 B	3 C	4 C	5 D
6 B	7 C	8 A	9 B	10 C

Listening

6

1 C	2 H	3 G	4 D	5 A

Unit 10 Test

Vocabulary

1

1 qualifications
2 knowledge
3 hearing
4 passionate
5 creative
6 adaptable
7 ambitious
8 infuriated
9 successor
10 overjoyed

2

1 B	2 A	3 C	4 C	5 A
6 B	7 C	8 A	9 B	10 D

Grammar

3

1 the	**2** a	**3** the	**4** –	**5** a
6 –	**7** the	**8** the	**9** the	**10** –

4

1 that are too difficult for most people
2 Jack is famous for / for which Jack is famous
3 who helped discover the DNA molecule, is a scientist I admire
4 with an interesting story to tell
5 who hardly received any formal education, went on to become an accomplished scientist / who went on to become an accomplished scientist, hardly received any formal education.
6 whose first novel was published recently, was an inspiring figure
7 for what you have done for us
8 , which is disappointing
9 , who died last week, had been ill for a while / , who had been ill for a while, died last week
10 , which was being driven at high speed, crashed against a tree.

Reading

5

1 W	**2** W	**3** W	**4** A	**5** O
6 O	**7** W	**8** W	**9** A	**10** A

Listening

6

1 into space
2 life (story)
3 excited and exhausted
4 Japan and Egypt
5 attention
6 symbol
7 1963
8 politics
9 aerospace engineering
10 (routine) training flight

Unit 11 Test

Vocabulary

1

1 engage
2 get
3 inspire
4 take
5 pass
6 revising / cramming
7 cramming / revising
8 addressed
9 turn
10 take

2

1 dropped out of college
2 the words by heart
3 tricks of the trade
4 too late to learn
5 before you can run
6 learned my lesson
7 the hard way
8 a source of
9 no cure for
10 didn't turn up

Grammar

3

1 to change
2 learning
3 question
4 to do
5 study
6 have taken
7 to complete
8 to finish
9 speak
10 to communicate

4

1 Did you manage to
2 succeeded in contacting
3 was about to leave
4 were supposed to go
5 would have stayed
6 was going to paint
7 managed to stop
8 was about to call
9 wasn't able to get
10 able to repair

Reading

5a

1 A	**2** F	**3** H	**4** B
5 J	**6** G		

5b

1 paragraph 1
2 paragraph 2
3 paragraph 4
4 paragraph 6

Listening

6

1 B	**2** A	**3** A	**4** B	**5** B
6 C	**7** B	**8** B	**9** C	**10** B

Unit 12 Test

Vocabulary

1

1 save
2 fit
3 earns / is earning
4 set
5 lend
6 invest
7 pursue
8 borrowed
9 owe
10 spent

2

1 C	**2** D	**3** A	**4** C	**5** B
6 A	**7** B	**8** A	**9** B	**10** D

Grammar

3

1 Only / Just
2 Even
3 Only / Just
4 only / just
5 even
6 only
7 just
8 only
9 Even
10 only

4

1 got our kitchen redecorated
2 have somebody take over
3 get Paul to call
4 had cable TV installed
5 get your project finished
6 got Tim to help
7 had his housework done
8 getting Paul to work
9 has his carpets cleaned
10 got the kids to

Reading

5

1 C	**2** D	**3** C	**4** C	**5** B
6 D	**7** A	**8** B	**9** B	**10** A

Listening

6

1 C	**2** C	**3** C	**4** C	**5** B
6 B	**7** C	**8** B	**9** A	**10** A

Photocopiable tests: audioscripts

Unit 1 Test

 [113]

Speaker 1

Hi, Penny. It's Mum. Are you there … ? Oh … OK … It's that machine thingy, William … I was just calling … I just wanted to get in touch about the holiday. I was wondering whether you wouldn't mind doing the checking in online bit for us. You know, to save us the bother at the airport. We fly on the ninth – for three weeks – so we'll be out of your hair for ages. And we'll send you a postcard. Say you'll help and I'll send our passport numbers and what not. Thanks, sweetie. Your dad would do it but you know he's hopeless when it comes to anything technical. He couldn't fix a light bulb.

Speaker 2

Hi, Penny. Stefan calling. Just got your message. No problem about looking after the cats while you're away. A week in Cornwall, eh? That sounds like a wonderful place for a holiday. Hope you're going with Mark this time, and not your parents. A caravan can be pretty cosy with your boyfriend, but not so great with your mum and dad. Anyway, give me a call about details. I'm in all day tomorrow. Got a repair man coming in to fix the dishwasher. Should be fun.

Speaker 3

Hi, Penny. Adam here. Just back from Barbados. It was amazing. Holiday of a lifetime. I can't wait to tell you all about it. So wish you'd been able to come with me, but, hey, I do know how tough it is to make ends meet these days. And Barbados is, well, so, you know, top-end luxurious. I'm having a little get-together at my place with Greta and Marta from the tennis club tomorrow at three-ish, so come over and say hello. Marta was asking after you the other day. And I have so many photos to show you.

Speaker 4

Hi, Penny. It's Sue. I'm in a bit of a hurry. Off on holiday for a few days – so I need to get on with the packing. Anyway, I've just been around to your house and you weren't in. I dropped a note through the door but I'm a bit worried you might not see it. So I thought I'd call. It's about the hairdryer you left at my place. I thought I'd better get it back before going to Ibiza – it's in your shed round the back. Bye for now. And see you soon.

Speaker 5

Hi, Penny. It's Claire. I was just wondering what you're doing later. I think I need a bit of a chat – you know, a serious one, like old times. It's Max, you see, you know, the electrician guy – brilliant at repairing everything – doesn't say much. Well, anyway, we've been seeing a lot of each other recently, and even planning a holiday together, but he hasn't returned any of my calls since the weekend, and I'm not sure what to do. I don't want to meet up in a café or anything – I think I might cry – but, well, can I come to your place? Just text me if that's OK.

Unit 2 Test

 [114]

P = Philip; J = Janice

P: So, do you have a 'lost in the supermarket' story, Janice?

J: Well not exactly. I've never been lost myself. But something really scary happened to me once. I was only nineteen at the time, and I wasn't in a supermarket. I took my three-year-old nephew Tommy to a shopping mall – it seemed like a good idea at the time, but I'd never really spent a whole day with a kid before …

P: Oh no, I can see where this is going.

J: Yeah. I'd volunteered to look after Tommy because my sister needed help. Anyway, when we got to the escalators, Tommy, well, he just would not get on. I stepped on to show him how easy it was, and then encouraged him to follow me. I was halfway up before I noticed he wasn't coming. I yelled to him to wait for me to come back to get him. But by the time I'd run round to the other escalator, I'd lost sight of him.

P: Oh, no. That must have been awful.

J: It was. You can imagine how anxious I was at that point.

P: Yeah. I would have been in a real state.

J: Anyway, when I got back, he was gone. I was carrying two huge shopping bags full of Christmas decorations. I hadn't had time to buy any clothes by that point. Naturally, I just dropped the bags, and started screaming for him in a panic. Then, as I was telling a lady at the jewellery counter to call the police, along came Tommy, not with the police, or with a security guard, but with a shop assistant. I just burst into tears.

P: Phew! What a relief. You were lucky, I guess.

J: Yeah. Anyway, Tommy is eighteen now and still teases me about the time I lost him in the mall.

Unit 3 Test

 [115]

Situation 1

R = Receptionist; G = Guest

R: Hello. Reception. Can I help?

G: I hope so. My husband and I are in Room 18. And we've got a bit of a problem. We booked a family room with a baby's cot – we've got a one-year-old you see, and, well, the cot's OK, but there are two separate beds here. You know, narrow ones.

R: Ah, I see. And you wanted just the one king-size double.

G: That's right. Yes.

R: Well, it does specify a twin room on your booking. Perhaps you made a mistake.

G: I may have done, yes. But it's not what we intended, you see …

R: Yes, it's no problem. I'm going to sort it out for you. Normally, we'd allocate you another room, but we are booked up right now. We'll send someone along to put the beds together to make a double, if that's OK.

G: Yes. Sure. That's fine if you can do that.

Situation 2

A: Oh, no. I've got something jammed I think.

B: What have you done?

A: Nothing. I just pressed copy and it's broken down on me. I bet the last person to use it left it like this.

B: You're going to have to take the back off. The paper will be stuck in there. It's not easy to get to it because of the wall.

A: Yeah. I wonder who decided the copier should be placed here in the corridor? I'm going to have to pull it out, I reckon.

B: Don't do that. See the lever down there. Press that and you'll be able to get at the paper from underneath.

A: Oh, right. OK. I'll try that.

Situation 3

The Dixon 125 is the latest cutting-edge vacuum cleaner from the name you can trust. Labour-saving and environmentally-friendly, it provides reliability that simply can't be matched by any other leading brand. It's made of light-weight materials which make it incredibly easy to handle despite its size. The Dixon 125. Check it out online today.

Situation 4

Hi, Jane. It's Dan. I'm outside. Anna's lent me a key. Don't worry, I've still got it, but I didn't want to just come barging in without calling you. Anyway, I'm on your answer phone, and you're not picking up, so I'll just come in, shall I? I've just come from Mum's and I've brought your old record collection. All in a big cardboard box. It's seriously heavy. I have to say, these old records bring back memories. I remember listening to them when we were kids. Or rather, I remember you and your mates from school listening to them, and closing the door so I couldn't listen. Anyway, I'll put them in your room. Wouldn't want your flatmate Anna seeing them before you get home and having a laugh at your expense.

Situation 5

S = Simon; **M** = Melissa

S: Hi, Melissa. Are you coming over? Tom and Diana are here.

M: Already? Sorry, Simon. I thought you said seven. I'm still at home. I've only just got out of the shower.

S: Don't worry. Just get yourself to my place as soon as you can. We thought we'd head out a bit earlier than we said. Tom hasn't had much to eat yet, so we're going to try that new Chinese place near the station before we go to the cinema.

M: Oh, OK. I'm a bit hungry myself, to be honest, but it'll be at least half an hour before I can get to your apartment. Perhaps I'll grab something to eat here and see you in front of the cinema.

S: Oh … OK, if you like, but we won't get a chance to talk much once the film starts, and you'll have missed all Tom and Diana's gossip. Tell you what, why don't I order for you when we get to the Chinese, and we'll see you there. It's on the way to the cinema.

M: Sure. That'll work. Right. I'd better get going. Oh, and nothing with prawns in, OK? I'm allergic.

Unit 4 Test

🎵 [116]

P = Presenter; **M** = Marion Clark

P: On *Book Review* today, I'm talking to Marion Clark about several intriguing new books on the market – what have you got for us, Marion?

M: Well, I've been looking at non-fiction this week and, in particular, a number of books that look at the function of memory – why it's important, how it works, and what happens when it doesn't function properly. One book in particular has caught my eye.

P: And what's that?

M: Michael D. Lemonick's book *The Perpetual Now* – it's a book about an American woman called Lonni Sue Johnson, who was quite a remarkable woman in her own right before a serious brain infection changed her life forever. She was a talented amateur musician, and a trained pilot of a private plane. But, above all, she was a successful commercial artist, whose works included illustrations for *The New Yorker* magazine. The book explores what happened to her after catching the infection, and looks at the new discoveries that were made about memory.

P: OK. So, what *did* happen to her exactly?

M: It all started during the Christmas period of 2007, at Lonni Sue's farm outside Cooperstown, New York. It was there that she got ill with fever and headaches. She became incoherent and her neighbours rushed her to hospital. It was there that they found she had viral encephalitis.

P: Which is …?

M: A very serious brain infection that can at times even kill the patient. In many cases, the virus attacks the part of the brain that creates memories and that's what happened to Lonni Sue. After she recovered from the infection, she developed amnesia or, in other words, an inability to remember the past. I mean she could remember some things. She almost immediately recognized her mother and her sister; it wasn't long before she remembered she had been an artist and a pilot; and after about eight months she could read music and play the viola again.

P: OK. So what couldn't she remember?

M: Well, when it came to memories of major events in her life, like the death of her father twenty years earlier, whom she had been very close to, she was astonished. She asked where her father was and they said, 'Well, he died.' 'What do you mean he died? Why didn't I know that? When did this happen?'

P: That must've been terrible for Lonni Sue.

M: Yes, and she didn't recognize old friends either and couldn't supply any details about her life. She could say, 'Yes, I was an artist.' But, who did you work for? Where did you go to school for art? All of these details were gone. When they brought her back to the house in Cooperstown, she didn't recognize it and had no memory of ever having been there before.

P: How awful. And how amazing.

M: True, but amnesia is not only about losing memories. There is another aspect to it, and this is even more startling for most of us to contemplate. She became almost entirely incapable of forming new memories. People would come and see her and say, 'Don't you remember me, I'm your next-door neighbour?' She wouldn't remember. When the person came back the next day, she still would have no idea who the person was.

P: Wow. And I guess memory is so essential because without it we can't really make plans or decisions.

M: Well, yes, but, more importantly, losing it means you lose a sense of who you are. In every situation I'm in, I am calling on my memory to tell me how to act appropriately, how to be myself, if you like. Not consciously, necessarily, but unconsciously. Everything I am today is based on what happened to me throughout my life. If somebody mentions my parents, I instantly have pictures in my mind of them. Both have died, but I remember their voices and the things they told me, the things I loved about them and the things that drove me crazy. All this context we operate in, all day, every day, is tied up with memory. In a sense, you are your memories.

P: Right. Let's turn to how an investigation into Lonni Sue's condition has helped lead to breakthroughs. What do you think the future holds for people of her condition …

Unit 5 Test

 [117]

Speaker 1

Most of my memories are pretty awful, I regret to say. I was actually a nice kid, but I remember feeling inadequate most of the time, and, sadly, I don't think I even got one meaningful kiss in all the years I was at school … But, if you insist on making me say something, I guess the flip side of hating school was the excitement of being free at the end of term. Nothing matches that feeling on the last day, knowing you've got weeks ahead of just doing nothing, and not having to wear that horrible uniform for some time.

Speaker 2

I'm a teenager and the best part has been, well, my mates and all the laughter they bring. Grown-ups think we're all madly in love with ourselves and our phones, and we're dead anti-social, but I look at my parents, you know, and, well, they hardly ever go anywhere or see anyone. The thing about being a teenager is that, like, while our phones

are our lifeline, it's only because they're the way we keep in touch. I can't imagine living without my mates Raphia and Olly – they mean everything to me.

Speaker 3

Most of the time, my two younger brothers made life a misery for me when I was a teenager. They were really close, but they excluded me. Looking back, I blame myself. I was so miserable and uncommunicative, and I spent most of my time making them feel like they were idiots. It's no wonder they played tricks on me. Then, one birthday, I got the most amazing present from them – a kitten – it was so cute and I loved it to bits, and for years after I felt warmly towards my brothers for being so kind and considerate. It was only a couple of years ago that they admitted they'd found the kitten in the park and had only given it to me to avoid having to pay to get me a real present. I tell you, I'm so annoyed I've stopped talking to them again!

Speaker 4

I guess I was your typical risk-taking teenager. I was always out, skateboarding or climbing or whatever, and I never listened to a word anyone told me, which I kind of regret now. Why? Well, it's not that I think I've missed out on any opportunities or anything, it's just that I now think being respectful and stuff to people like your grandfather or your mum is important. And they talked sense, I guess. Anyway, I loved being a teenager 'cause I got to do what I wanted as long as I wanted. Now, I'm working and I don't have a moment to do stuff I like.

Speaker 5

I think my best memory was getting my driver's licence. I was seventeen – just – and I thoroughly expected to fail right up until the moment the instructor told me different. I think adults forget how fragile the self-confidence of a teenager is, and how easily it can be built up or destroyed. That moment made me feel like I could do anything. And I still recall the feeling when I've got to do something that makes me nervous – like a presentation or whatever at work.

Unit 6 Test

 [118]

Simon Carter

I started doing photography because I'm quite a shy person. When I was at university, my aunt gave me a camera for my birthday. The camera gave me a new way to express myself – it was a great feeling. I knew then that I wanted to be a photographer, even though my Maths degree had nothing to do with photography at all!

Anyway, after university, I became a fashion photographer in London. I had some interesting assignments for different magazines and it was fun, but I wanted to do something that involved the natural world more. I wanted to become a wildlife or landscape photographer, but it was hard to change track when people only knew my name in the fashion world. Eventually I got lucky and a newspaper published some photos I took in a remote part of Nepal. Getting those shots was definitely more dangerous than anything I did in London, but it was totally worth it !

Nicola Halliday

I'm an outdoor adventure photographer. I was born and raised in Alaska, but I moved to live here in Colorado a few years ago. I haven't ever really studied photography as a subject – I just started going outside and taking pictures of whatever interested me. I think that's taught me so much.

Luckily, I have a regular job as the editor of a lifestyle blog, which gives me the freedom to enjoy my photography without worrying about my pictures paying my salary. This means I can choose the narrative that *I* want my pictures to tell. My attitude is probably a bit different to most photographers' too. My love for the outdoors and adventure is definitely more important to me than the technical side of photography.

I was so lucky growing up because my parents would take my family camping to national parks every summer. I was able to explore and make my own little adventures. That's when I fell in love with the natural world.

Joe Clarke

I'm often asked how I got into photography. Here's what I did: I borrowed a camera from my dad and started taking pictures for fun. I wasn't very good at it, but I enjoyed it anyway. I majored in photography at university – I was never really interested in studying anything else. I had a part-time job with a local newspaper at the same time and took pictures as much as possible. I think this practice is really important if you ever want to get your work published.

My first real photo job was for a small travel magazine. I learned a lot working there, and eventually became senior photographer. I became really good at making tricky situations work, for example, shooting in difficult light and dealing with other technical challenges. Having that knowledge has been so important throughout my career – as has being able to say a few words in lots of different languages!

Unit 7 Test

 [119]

P = Presenter; **E** = Elsie Hain

P: Hello and welcome to *Thanks for the Memories* – the programme that remembers what things used to be like. Today, we're talking about school dinners, and my guest in the studio is writer Elsie Hain. Back in the fifties, Elsie was a pupil at Coppel School in Wiltshire. Welcome to the programme, Elsie.

E: Hello. Thank you for inviting me.

P: Kids today have a wide choice of what to eat at school, ranging from salad bar choices to hot, well-cooked lunches. In your time, though, things were very different, weren't they, Elsie?

E: Oh, yes. At my school all us children would be given exactly the same plate of food and expected to eat it. It's not like today.

P: I guess not. So, what used to happen at lunch time at Coppel School back then?

E: Well, very clearly, I remember standing in a queue waiting to be served by the dinner ladies. And served 'dinner' by the way, we never called it 'lunch', you know. In my day, the midday meal was called 'dinner'. Anyway, the dinner ladies were volunteers, you know, just ordinary mums of some of the girls in the school. But none of them were very friendly. They'd put the food on your plate and tell you to move along. Quite strict, they were. And talking in the queue wasn't allowed – they'd tell us off if we opened our mouths, not that it ever stopped us whispering to each other. As for jumping the queue, well, that was never heard of.

P: It all sounds pretty strict.

E: Well, as a girl in those days, you got used to the discipline, you see. We didn't know any different. We were punished for just about anything. If we didn't pull up our socks, or if our uniform wasn't tidy, we got punished and, although we could chat over lunch, we'd be in big trouble if we shouted or left our seat or anything like that. Kids today are always running around and shouting at each other in the dining hall – there was none of that in my day.

P: What was the dining hall like?

E: Well, it wasn't all that big, but it had a high ceiling, and I remember rectangular tables of varnished wood, set against the walls, and seating – I think – four on each side and a 'head of table' at the end. We were assigned our tables for a year, and the idea of sitting anywhere else, well, we didn't even think of doing that. I suspect that we were allowed to sit with one particular friend, but I can't remember exactly how this was organized, but otherwise the policy was to mix the years. A member of the sixth form sat at the table head, presumably to keep order, but order was never a problem. I think the mixing of the years worked well for the teachers. It meant that we couldn't sit in a gang, and we didn't have much to talk about with the students we had to sit with.

P: Mmm … I can see the logic of that from the school's point of view, but I can't see kids today putting up with it. What happened after you'd eaten your dinner?

E: Well, after we'd finished eating, we all had to queue to scrape what was left on our plates into bins, and dinner ladies would stand there and watch us do it. Sometimes they'd send us back to the table to finish eating what was on our plates if they thought we hadn't eaten enough.

P: Really? You were forced to eat what was on your plate?

E: Oh, yes. I remember having to eat cold cabbage on my own because I'd been sent back to the table. The food we had to eat was not very nice either.

P: Was it really that bad?

E: Well, it wasn't very tasty, let's say that. I suppose the main reason why school dinners were so awful in the 1950s was the country's austerity. There just wasn't that much money in the country after the Second World War, and things like meat were in short supply. And people didn't use to put on herbs and spices and things like they do now. So a lot of our school dinners were made up of boiled vegetables.

P: What else do you remember of those days?

E: Well, we had to pay for our dinners, but that was because my school was quite middle class – none of us came from poor families, so the government didn't pay for us. The money for school dinners for the whole week was collected by the form teacher on Monday mornings after she had taken the register. It was a simple process, and as far as I remember, involved every girl. Nobody ever came to school without the money. They would've been too embarrassed.

P: Fascinating. Thanks for your memories, Elsie. After the break, we'll be reading out some of our listeners' emails and texts …

Unit 8 Test

 [120]

Speaker 1

Hi, Jo. OK. I know, I know, you've heard this one a thousand times before – from me. But guess what? It works. If you switched to a veggie diet, you'd feel great! Natural, detoxifying, slimming, energizing, and just plain amazing, what's not to like? And you'll save loads of money, too! They boost your immunity and lower your risk of disease. I know that a full cup of kale, rocket, or spinach for breakfast doesn't sound exciting right now, but you'd quickly get used to it!

Speaker 2

You know what I'm going to tell you to do, Jo. You don't get a body like mine without a bit of effort. But I also know that not everybody can be as committed to toning their body as me. I wish they could be. Most people stop doing their routines because they simply don't enjoy them. Believe me. I know. I run the training courses! If they absolutely loved them and looked forward to doing them, how likely would they be to quit? So, if I were you, I wouldn't give up on my body, but, rather than wasting money on gym membership, I would do something like signing up for a salsa or hip-hop class … or figure skating lessons, or rock climbing – anything. Get out there, girl!

Speaker 3

As you know, like you, I'm the world's biggest coffee drinker. I really wish I could cut down a bit. And if I were to go caffeine free, I'd make you do the same. Who wants to take up salsa or spend all their days in a gym if there's a simpler solution to feeling good – cutting down on the black stuff! Of course, I'm not suggesting you should never drink a cup of coffee again – that would be impossible. But, if you replaced a couple of your daily cups with something green and organic – you know what I'm saying – it would do you the world of good!

Speaker 4

If I were you, Jo, the first thing I'd do is switch off that mobile phone of yours for a few minutes, close down your laptop and switch off the TV. You really spend too much time staring at screens, and not enough buried in a good story or two. There are some great novels out there, and I know they used to be your thing back in college. Unlike watching TV, they give your brain a break from the external stimulation you're bombarded with all day long. They allow you to unplug, slow down and lose yourself in your imagination. And that's great for your health, your brain and your happiness!

Speaker 5

Physical affection is amazing for your health, your happiness, and it even helps you lose weight. It's better than a diet! It lowers blood pressure and reduces stress. It's astonishing how it can make you feel happier, calmer and more secure, in next to no time. But, if you want the people you love to start showing the love, you'd better give a bit of love yourself first. So, no shaking hands or air kissing from now on. Next time we meet, whether it's in the gym doing that workout, or in the coffee shop, over a latte, I want to feel some physical affection, first. OK?

Unit 9 Test

 [121]

Speaker 1

After winning her battle against cancer five years ago, Sally Parker decided to thank the doctors at her local hospital for saving her life by climbing Mount Kilimanjaro in Africa with three other friends and former cancer patients. Sally reached the summit of the mountain in Tanzania on her 40th birthday and raised over £5,000. She said she wanted to do something to help raise awareness among women who could easily let small symptoms go unchecked. The climb took a lot of training and mental strength but it was such an adventure and completely worth it.

Speaker 2

Work colleagues Paula Croft and Tom Kelly raised over £6,000 by creating a fun product for bearded men everywhere! It may sound weird but the idea of buying little silvery balls to put in your beard proved a big hit online, and all the money raised went to the pair's chosen cancer charity. They sold out worldwide and their little balls became one of the most Googled search terms worldwide. The project was supported by an Australian charity which promotes growing beards in the summer to protect skin from the sun.

Speaker 3

Every two years, the Great Christmas Pudding Marathon is organized in central London, to raise money for cancer charities. It's a unique event. Teams of six compete against the clock around an obstacle course while trying to keep a Christmas pudding on a plate at the same time! Over £20,000 was raised at last year's event and hundreds turned out to cheer on the competitors. Organizers are hoping to extend the event to other locations around the country next year.

Speaker 4

After losing her father and husband to cancer, Sue Morris decided to go on a long-distance trek across Vietnam to raise money for charity. Sue's friends got involved by sponsoring her. After returning from Vietnam, Sue has continued to raise money, by giving talks about her trek and how she survived all alone for many weeks in tropical forests. Together with colleagues from work, Sue has also organized several events, including concerts, jumble sales, an afternoon tea party, and a raffle to raise money. So far, she's raised almost £3,000.

Speaker 5

The Ladies Tractor Road Run takes place each year in Norfolk, and is organized by a local couple. In the event, ladies drive tractors through the countryside – all of which are painted bright pink with colourful decorations. It's quite a sight and the event's well supported by the local community. Over £100,000 was raised last year. When asked who won the tractor race, it was politely explained to me that racing is not allowed in the road run as all the tractors have to stick to strict speed limits.

Unit 10 Test

 [122]

P = Presenter; J = Jake Flynn

P: Hello and welcome to *People of our Time*. In today's programme, I'm talking to Jake Flynn, who has just written a new biography of Yuri Gagarin, the famous Russian cosmonaut. Gagarin, of course, is famous for being the first person to journey into space. In his book, however, Jake is more interested in the man's life story than in his achievements. Welcome to the programme, Jake.

J: Hello.

P: The world held its breath when Gagarin orbited Earth in his Vostok spacecraft on April the 12th, 1961. But what was this time like for Gagarin himself?

J: It was exciting and exhausting. He became a national hero of the Soviet Union and travelled all over the world. Thousands turned out just to see him in countries as diverse as Japan, Canada and Egypt, and he got used to being cheered in many languages. Fame wasn't easy for him though. It's fair to say that he was a shy man who didn't really enjoy being surrounded by so much attention.

P: Did he ever return to space?

J: No. No, he didn't. He probably would have loved to go back, but he was too important as a symbol of the Soviet Union's technological superiority. You have to remember that the world was in the middle of the Cold War at this time. If Gagarin had died in space, it would have been really bad news for the space programme. In fact, after Gagarin's friend Vladimir Komarov was killed in a space flight in 1963, Gagarin was banned from being a cosmonaut.

P: So, what did he do then?

J: Well, he worked at Star City training new cosmonauts. But, because of his fame and importance, he also had a career in politics, and he was elected to important positions.

P: And was he happy?

J: Well, his first love was flying, and it was during this time that he re-qualified as a fighter pilot. He took a course in aerospace engineering, too, and passed with flying colours. So, yes, this was a happy and successful period for Gagarin – he had a good standard of living and was pursuing his dreams.

P: But, sadly, it was to end in tragedy, wasn't it?

J: Yes, in March 1968, on a routine training flight, he crashed his plane and died. He was cremated and his ashes were buried in the walls of the Kremlin on Red Square. He was only thirty-four. It was a tragic ending, but one that, in hindsight, seems almost inevitable for a man prepared to risk his life to further humankind's ability to explore our limits.

Unit 11 Test

 [123]

P = Presenter; S = Sophie Watson

P: Sophie Watson was always going to be a nurse when she was growing up, but a chance visit to an art museum while on holiday with her family sparked a passion for museums which has shaped her career choices. Sophie is here with me today on *Jobs Now* to talk about her career as a museum curator. Welcome to the studio, Sophie.

S: Hi. Hello.

P: So, how would you describe what you do, Sophie?

S: Well, I'm the art curator at a museum that is part of a small university. On a day-to-day basis, I do a lot of different things. For instance, I provide publicity material for the museum and I also make sure there's enough money to finance projects. But the main thing that I do, that I love most, is organizing exhibitions of contemporary art.

P: What does that entail? What do you have to do?

S: Well, I'm in charge of a team of resident artists and art lecturers who think of ideas for exhibitions – I very much rely on their knowledge and creativity. My job is to select the artworks that will be shown as part of the exhibition and decide where exactly they will go. I also have to research the artworks and, occasionally, I get to interview artists when I can. Before our last exhibition, I managed to interview Theodore Webber, an important local artist, whose work is really exciting. I wrote about his art for the exhibition catalogue and for an online article.

P: What's a typical work week like?

S: I'm in the office typically from quite early – before eight – to lunchtime, but I often have one or two evening or weekend events during busy times like exhibition openings or family day events. I usually have anywhere from one to three meetings a day to talk things through with other staff members. I try to keep them brief – I hate long meetings. Otherwise, I might be in one of our galleries working out how to organize an exhibition or, if I'm lucky, I'll spend part of a day talking to artists or collectors. Actually, a lot of my time is spent writing in all different capacities, from exhibition labels to grant applications to emails.

P: So, are you always at the gallery?

S: Well, no, not really. I have to be there in the mornings but, like a lot of people who have the joy of working in my field, I also spend a good portion of my free time doing things related to my job, like visiting other museums and galleries, or reading about art online or in publications.

P: How did you get started?

S: As you said in your introduction, I've loved going to museums ever since my first trip. In fact, I started volunteering in museums and galleries when I was in high school, and my first job out of college was as a receptionist at a small contemporary art museum. Then I got promoted to work in fundraising for a museum – not something I really wanted to do, but the experience was incredibly helpful in terms of learning how museums raise money.

P: And did you move from that job straight into curating?

S: My career took a few twists and turns after that job, and I took time out to start my family, but I did get a curatorial opportunity eventually. It was organizing a contemporary art show as a freelancer for a local arts organization. I had been volunteering for them already. They actually turned down many of my suggestions for art exhibitions before eventually letting me put one on.

P: A final question. What advice would you offer someone considering this career?

S: I succeeded in seeing hundreds of exhibitions at museums and galleries before I became a curator, so my advice for anyone keen to get into this profession is to do just that. Getting the hang of who presents what kind of work, what is their style in creating exhibitions, and which type of artists the public like to pay to see – those are just some of the things you'll need to master. And learning from experience is the only way to really get good at this job – there are special degrees you can do but they only get you so far.

Unit 12 Test

 [124]

Situation 1

A = Assistant; **C** = Customer

A: Hello. Can I help you?

C: Yes, I'm just looking for a new pair of shoes. Black ones. You know, quite smart. I'm going to a wedding.

A: OK. So, you won't want any of these on sale then. They're our summer stock, so they're a bit too casual for you. Have a look at some of these – they aren't reduced in price, I'm afraid, but, as you can see, they're well-made.

C: Yes. I think these are what I'm looking for – and they aren't all that expensive, are they? I mean, considering.

A: Well, yes. Great value for the quality you get. Which ones would you like to try on?

C: I'm not sure. They're all good. I think I'll try the ones at the end, and could you see if you've got these here at the front in stock too?

A: Sure. I'll go and get them. Any others catch your eye?

C: No, I'll start with those. Let's see if they fit first. I've got wide feet.

Situation 2

I = Interviewer; **E** = Expert

I: America's central bank, the Federal Reserve, last night raised interest rates for the fourth time in six months. What does that mean for the economy?

E: Well, the government has warned consumers and businesses to expect the cost of borrowing to go up. And I think that's likely to happen.

I: So, bad news for everybody then.

E: Not necessarily. There are always winners and losers in these types of situations, and savers will be glad of the higher rates. But, ultimately, it's likely to hit homeowners and small businesses pretty badly.

I: Will it affect the value of the dollar?

E: At one stage yesterday, before the central bank's announcement, the dollar dropped to a record low against the euro – it ended only slightly up in the wake of the decision but, actually, it may even strengthen further in the long run. Now that the raised interest rates have brought clarity.

Situation 3

S = Seller; **B** = Buyer

S: Well, to tell you the truth, we feel that our kitchen cabinets are top quality, both in terms of design and manufacturing quality. So, we're reluctant to cut prices.

B: OK. But, as you know, we have outlets across the UK and, if sales go well, we'll be interested in multiple orders. At the end of the day, we're offering you the potential to make mass sales.

S: True. We get that. But, as I'm sure you'll appreciate, your initial order is not particularly large, and there are no promises that you will make large orders in the future. It is a risk we don't think you should ask us to take.

B: What do you have in mind, then?

S: We were hoping we could agree to an initial sale at our standard price. If things go well, and you return with a bigger order, we'd be happy to renegotiate prices. But not at this stage.

Situation 4

P = Presenter; **E** = Economist

P: Where did you first study economics?

E: At Oxford University. I studied Philosophy, Politics and Economics and later, after a brief period working for a financial institution in the city, I returned to Oxford to do a Master's degree in Economics.

P: And what attracted you to the subject in the first place?

E: I was sceptical about the subject at first – philosophy seemed much more interesting – but I was drawn in by the way it makes you think. I suppose I loved the odd combination of strategic thinking, mathematics and psychology. At undergraduate level, there was a lot of puzzle-solving involved, and I loved that.

P: What keeps you interested in economics?

E: I think it's the sheer range of interesting problems. We'll never crack these economic problems but we'll have fun trying.

Photocopiable communicative activities

Unit 1 Communicative activity A
People in my life

I live with _____ .

I've known _____ for ages.

I've been seeing a lot of _____ recently.

I've been on holiday with _____ a few times.

I text or speak to _____ on the phone most days.

One of my favourite teachers at school was _____ .

I haven't seen _____ since I was about five years old.

A teacher at school that I didn't like much was _____ .

_____ lives near me but I don't see him/her very often.

_____ is helping me with something at the moment.

Fold --

Unit 1 Communicative activity B

Who's your oldest friend?

START	*What's the opposite of 'dependable'?*	In what situation would you really need a friend to stand by you?	Talk about your most considerate friend for one minute.
How ambitious are you? Give examples to explain your answer.	Who's your oldest friend? How long have you known him/her?	*What's the opposite of 'shy'?* **Throw again. Go BACK that number of squares!**	When did a friend last come round to your house? What did you do?
Talk about your most energetic friend for one minute.	How many of your blood relatives do you see more than once a year? When and where do you see them?	Which of your friends do you spend most time hanging out with? What do you do?	Who is the most successful member of your family, and why?
When did you last go round to a friend's house? What did you do?	Who's your closest friend? Why do you get on so well?	Which of your friends or family members has the same sense of humour as you?	*What's the opposite of 'energetic'?* **Throw again. Go BACK that number of squares!**
What's the opposite of 'serious'?	In what ways are you helpful to your friends and family?	How many of your grandparents do you know? What did they do when they were younger?	Describe three forms of behaviour which you think are selfish.
FINISH	*What's the opposite of 'considerate'?* **Throw again. Go BACK that number of squares!**	How decisive are you? Give examples to explain your answer.	How well do the older and younger generations of your family get on? Give examples to explain your answer.

Unit 1 Communicative activity C

How's everything going?

Name: _____

You've been travelling a lot recently.

Where?

What were the best experiences?

What are you going to do next?

You can't really talk – you need to go and buy …

Name: _____

You haven't been out of the house much recently because you haven't been feeling well.

What's the matter?

Why have you come out today?

It's nice for you to see people and have a chat. Everyone you meet looks very well and relaxed. Tell them!

Name: _____

You've just won the lottery.

How much have you won?

How do you feel?

What are you going to do with the money?

You can't really talk – you need to go and meet …

Name: _____

You've just got a new job.

What job?

Do you like it? Why? / Why not?

You can't really talk – you need to go and …

Name: _____

You've been getting ready for an important event.

What event?

How are you feeling about it?

You want to chat to people for as long as you can. What do you want to chat about?

Name: _____

You haven't been doing much recently.

Why not?

Where have you been?

How are you feeling?

You want to hear other people's news. What questions will you ask?

Name: _____

You've been studying hard recently.

What?

Why?

How are you feeling?

You can't really talk – you need to go and …

Name: _____

You've moved house recently.

Where's your new home?

What's it like?

Are you happy there?

You can't really talk – you need to go and …

Name: _____

You've been very creative recently.

What have you made/written/painted?

How do you feel about it?

You want to chat to people for as long as you can. What do you want to chat about?

Unit 2 Communicative activity A

Survival!

Story 1

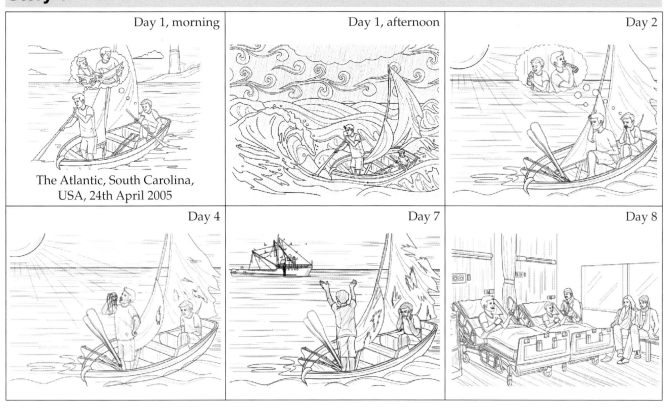

Day 1, morning — The Atlantic, South Carolina, USA, 24th April 2005

Day 1, afternoon

Day 2

Day 4

Day 7

Day 8

Story 2

Day 1 — The White Mountains, Arizona, USA, 31st March 2016

Day 1

Days 2–6

Day 7

Day 8

Day 9

Unit 2 Communicative activity B

Story quiz

1 Which _____ tells the story of _____ ?
   a) _____   b) _____   c) _____

2 The setting of this *funny / gripping / thought-provoking / touching / creepy* _____ is (*place, time*) _____ .
   What's it called?
   a) _____   b) _____   c) _____

3 In which _____ is the hero _____ ?
   a) _____   b) _____   c) _____

4 In which _____ does the main character _____ ?
   a) _____   b) _____   c) _____

5 A key moment in this _____ is when _____ .
   What's it called?
   a) _____   b) _____   c) _____

6 The turning point in this _____ is when _____ .
   What's it called?
   a) _____   b) _____   c) _____

7 This _____ explores themes of _____ .
   What's it called?
   a) _____   b) _____   c) _____

8 This _____ brings the story of _____ to life.
   What's it called?
   a) _____   b) _____   c) _____

Unit 2 Communicative activity C

You're kidding!

I was in the kitchen cutting (*What food?*) _____ with a really sharp knife
and I was talking to (*Who?*) _____ at the same time. The knife slipped
and I felt a sharp pain in the end of my (*Which finger?*) _____ finger.
I couldn't look for a moment, but when I eventually did I saw that I had cut a tiny bit off the top of my finger.
There was blood everywhere. I took the little bit of finger with me to A and E. The doctor said (*What did the doctor
say?*) _____ . If you look at my finger now you can see (*What can you
see?*) _____ .

✂- -

Story B

I've done that thing where you write a (*What?*) _____ and then you send it to the
wrong person. I was (*Where?*) _____ and I wanted to contact (*Who were you intending
to contact?*) _____ because I wanted to tell them that (*What did you intend to say?*)
_____ . But instead of sending it to (*Who?*) _____ I sent it to
(*Who?*) _____ ! Agh!

✂- -

Story C

I was (*Where?*) _____ and I was (*How were you travelling?*) _____
down a big hill really fast. I saw what I thought was a (*What?*) _____ ahead of me but it
turned out to be (*What?*) _____ . Fortunately, (*What was OK?*) _____ ,
but (*What wasn't OK?*) _____ .

✂- -

Story D

This happened when I was living and working in (*Which country?*) _____ . I didn't
speak (*What language?*) _____ very well. I'd been away for the weekend but I needed
to get home for work the next morning. It was late when I arrived at the station. I was (*How were you
feeling?*) _____ . I got on the train but something felt wrong. I soon realized I was on
the wrong train! I got off at the next station and (*How did you travel?*) _____ back to the
town but I'd missed the last train home. I went to a hotel and phoned my boss to explain. She (*How did she
react?*) _____ . I felt very stupid!

✂- -

Story E

I was driving to (*Where?*) _____ but I stopped in town on the way because I needed to buy
some (*What?*) _____ . When I got back to the car, I took my car keys out of my
(*What?*) _____ but I dropped them and they fell down a drain. I had no idea what to do
because they were a long way down and I really couldn't think of any way to get them out again. In the end
I spoke to a (*Who?*) _____ who was passing and they had the really good idea of using a
(*What?*) _____ to get my keys out. I was so grateful to them!

Unit 3 Communicative activity A

How optimistic are you? (Part 1)

1 Which statement about technology 100 years from now do you most agree with?
   a) Scientists will have used it to end problems like pollution, poverty and starvation for ever.
   b) It will have made life safer, more comfortable and more interesting for most people.
   c) The world will be a less varied, creative and interesting place because of it.
   d) The human race will be very much under its control.

2 Will your life be better a year from now?
   a) Of course! I'll have achieved quite a lot and be happier than I am now.
   b) Probably. Things won't have changed much, but I'll be older and wiser.
   c) Not really. I'll just be a year older.
   d) I doubt it. Something bad will probably have happened.

3 What do you think will be true of the natural world seventy-five years from now?
   a) Animals like pandas and tigers will have been saved from extinction.
   b) Governments and other organizations will be much more committed to protecting the environment.
   c) Pollution and global warming will be getting worse.
   d) Many species of plants and animals will be extinct and most places will suffer from bad pollution.

4 What do you think will be true in your country ten years from now?
   a) Most schools, hospitals and businesses will be much better than they are now.
   b) Organizations like the police and health service will be operating better because they will have learnt from their mistakes.
   c) In general, things won't have got any better.
   d) It will have become a much more difficult and dangerous place to live.

5 How do you feel about next weekend?
   a) It's going to be great!
   b) I'm quite looking forward to it.
   c) It won't be much different to any other weekend.
   d) I'll be glad when it's over.

✁ -

☺ Results

Mostly 'a' = You're an optimist. You love making plans for the future and you don't give up when things get difficult. You don't get stressed much and you sleep well at night. Lucky you!

Mostly 'b' = You are pretty optimistic. You look forward to your free time and trust that the future is good, although you sometimes need reassurance. Just keep concentrating on the positive things in life and all will be good!

Good news for optimists!

According to a 2009 report, optimists are likely to have better physical and mental health than pessimists. They are also likely to live longer.

How optimistic are you? (Part 2)

6 What will life be like for you when you're seventy-five years old?

a) It'll be great! I'll probably have lots of grandchildren and I'll be living life to the full.

b) I'll be older and wiser. I'll have had lots of interesting experiences.

c) I won't have as much energy as I do now, and I won't be as fit as I am now. But at least I'll be alive!

d) It'll certainly be worse than it is now. I don't even want to think about it!

7 How will travel be different in one hundred years' time?

a) People will be using amazing forms of transport, like flying cars.

b) It will be safer, cleaner and more efficient.

c) Some new advances will have been made, but congestion and pollution will still be a problem.

d) There will be more vehicles on the road, so pollution and congestion will be even worse than it is now.

8 Do you think people will be living on Mars fifty years from now?

a) Yes, I do. I think there'll be a large colony where people will live safely, peacefully and happily.

b) I think there'll have been some successful missions to Mars and a few people might be living there.

c) Maybe, but they will be facing the same problems as people here, and they'll have other problems, too.

d) No, I don't. It will be too expensive, and there'll be too many problems on Earth that need more attention than space travel.

9 What do you think will be true about our planet two hundred years from now?

a) Scientists will have found ways to solve the problems of starvation and water shortages.

b) It will be a safer and more peaceful place to live.

c) People won't be living on it any more.

d) It won't exist.

✂- -

☹ Results

Mostly 'c' = You're a realist. You get fed up with people saying 'Everything will be all right' because you know that that isn't always true. You know that it's important to face reality so that solutions are in place when problems arise.

Mostly 'd' = You tend to focus on the negative and to worry about what might go wrong in a situation. Keep the motto 'Hope for the best, prepare for the worst!' in mind, as this will help you turn your pessimism into a positive action.

The world needs pessimists

By imagining negative outcomes, pessimists are able to prepare mentally, emotionally and physically for all eventualities. By making sure strategies are in place if things go wrong, they are in a good position to help others who are more optimistic.

Unit 3 Communicative activity B

Name five things

five things that are made of brick
_____
_____
_____
_____

five labour-saving devices
_____
_____
_____
_____

five things that are made of cotton
_____
_____
_____
_____

five materials that can be recycled
_____
_____
_____
_____

five things that are made of plastic
_____
_____
_____
_____

five things that are made of wood
_____
_____
_____
_____

✂ -

five things that are made of leather
_____
_____
_____
_____

five things that are made of cardboard
_____
_____
_____
_____

five things that are made of rubber
_____
_____
_____
_____

five handy gadgets
_____
_____
_____
_____

five things that people hang on coat hooks
_____
_____
_____
_____

five things you can use a paper cup for
_____
_____
_____
_____

Unit 3 Communicative activity C

Is everything OK with your room?

Hotel guest 1

You have these problems with your room:

There's no internet connection.
(*I can't ...*)

The water doesn't go out of the basin.
(*The basin's ...*)

Receptionist A

You started working at seven o'clock this morning and now it's five to six in the evening. It's nearly time for you to go home. You're tired and hungry.

Listen to the guests, but try to sort their problems out with as little effort as possible.

Hotel guest 2

You have these problems with your room:

You can't open the window.
(*The window won't ...*)

You don't have towels in your bathroom and you need some.
(*There aren't ...*)

Receptionist B

You know that standards are not very high at this hotel, despite the very high prices that it charges for the rooms.

Listen to the guests, and be apologetic and helpful.

Hotel guest 3

You have these problems with your room:

There's only cold water.
(*There's no ...*)

The fridge is really noisy.
(*There's a loud noise ...*)

Receptionist C

You've been working at this hotel for six months and you are really hoping to get the hotel's 'Receptionist of the Year' award this year.

Listen to the guests, and be as friendly and as helpful as you possibly can.

Hotel guest 4

You have these problems with your room:

There's a problem with the main light.
(*The main light is flickering ...*)

The bath smells horrible.
(*There's a bad smell ...*)

Receptionist D

It's your last day working at this hotel. You're very happy about this because you're fed up with the very low standards here.

Listen to the guests, and sort out any problems that you can – but you don't need to pretend that everything's perfect at this hotel!

Hotel guest 5

You have these problems with your room:

The air conditioning is much too cold.
(*I can't seem to ...*)

You can't switch on the TV with the remote control.
(*The remote control ...*)

Receptionist E

It's your first day in this job and you don't know where anything is or who to ask for help because nobody has told you.

However, you've heard that this is a very good hotel and you're happy to be working here.

Unit 4 Communicative activity A

Is it true?

Statement 1:

A few people in the class have been to a gig in the last six months.

I think this is True / False.

In fact, …

Statement 2:

About half the people in the class would describe themselves as artistic.

I think this is True / False.

In fact, …

Statement 3:

Nobody in this class has taken a ballet exam.

I think this is True / False.

In fact, …

Statement 4:

Everyone in this room listens to music every day.

I think this is True / False.

In fact, …

Statement 5:

Several people in the class have been to a music festival.

I think this is True / False.

In fact, …

Statement 6:

A few people in the class have played in an orchestra.

I think this is True / False.

In fact, …

Statement 7:

A large number of people in the class spend two hours or more every day watching TV, films or online videos.

I think this is True / False.

In fact, …

Statement 8:

Most people in the class would like to be either a famous singer or a famous actor.

I think this is True / False.

In fact, …

Statement 9:

Several people in the class have been to a musical.

I think this is True / False.

In fact, …

Statement 10:

Everyone in the class performed in a show when they were younger.

I think this is True / False.

In fact, …

Unit 4 Communicative activity B

Spot the difference

Unit 4 Communicative activity C

Likes and dislikes questionnaire

1 What do you think of *abstract art / contemporary dance / electronic dance music* ?

  A I'm really into it. _____

  B It's not my kind of thing.

  _____

  C It gets on my nerves. _____

2 Do you like *seeing circus performers / hearing buskers / seeing living statues* in the street?

  A Yes, very much. _____

  B I don't really notice them.

  _____

  C Not especially. _____

3 How do you feel about *war films / animations / fantasy films* ?

  A I'm really into them. _____

  B They're OK. _____

  C Not my kind of thing at all.

  _____

4 Do you like TV *wildlife documentaries / chat shows / dramas* ?

  A Yes, I love them! _____

  B Not really. _____

  C No, they don't really do anything for me.

  _____

5 What do you think of *graffiti / street advertising / street art* ?

  A I like it. _____

  B Some of it's very good. _____

  C I get a bit tired of seeing it everywhere.

  _____

6 Do you like *classical / folk / country* music?

  A Yes, I'm a big fan of it. _____

  B It doesn't do much for me.

  _____

  C I can't bear it. _____

7 What do you think of *comedians / Disney films / modern art installations* ?

  A A lot of them are amazing.

  _____

  B There are some I'm quite keen on.

  _____

  C Some of them are OK, but there are others I can't bear! _____

8 Do you like *ballet / jazz music / performing on stage yourself* ?

  A Yes, it's great. _____

  B Not particularly. _____

  C I'm not so keen on it. _____

9 How do you feel about *old black and white films / films with lots of CGI (computer generated imagery) in them / kids' films* ?

  A Some of them are brilliant.

  _____

  B I really enjoy them. _____

  C They're not my kind of thing.

  _____

10 And finally, would you like to learn how to *rap / knit / dance* ?

  A I can do that already! _____

  B Yes, I'd love to! _____

  C No, not really! _____

Unit 5 Communicative activity A

How well do you know me?

I really like _____ .

I've never asked anyone _____ .

I can't afford _____ .

I'd like to stop _____ .

I can't decide whether or not _____ .

I'd really like _____ .

I can remember _____ .

When I was young, my parents didn't let me _____ .

I never want _____ .

I regret _____ .

I've never managed _____ .

I've never tried _____ .

I try to avoid _____ .

At school, the teachers used to make me and my classmates _____ .

I don't mind being here but I'd prefer _____ .

I once helped someone _____ .

Unit 5 Communicative activity B

Urban features web search

Student A

What's it called?	What is it?	Where is it?	What's special about it?
1 One Central Park			
2 The 'sinking ship'		Seattle, USA	
3 Il Vulcano Buono		Nola, Italy	
4 Cheonggyecheon			

✂- -

Student B

What's it called?	What is it?	Where is it?	What's special about it?
1 Bosco Verticale			
2 Car Towers			
3 Khan Shatyr		Astana, Kazakhstan	
4 The High Line		New York, USA	

✂- -

Student C

What's it called?	What is it?	Where is it?	What's special about it?
1 Reversible Destiny Lofts		Tokyo, Japan New York, USA	
2 1111 Lincoln Road			
3 Canal City		Fukuoka, Japan	
4 1–5 Colonnade			

Unit 5 Communicative activity C

How should we develop the town?

Our plan for the town

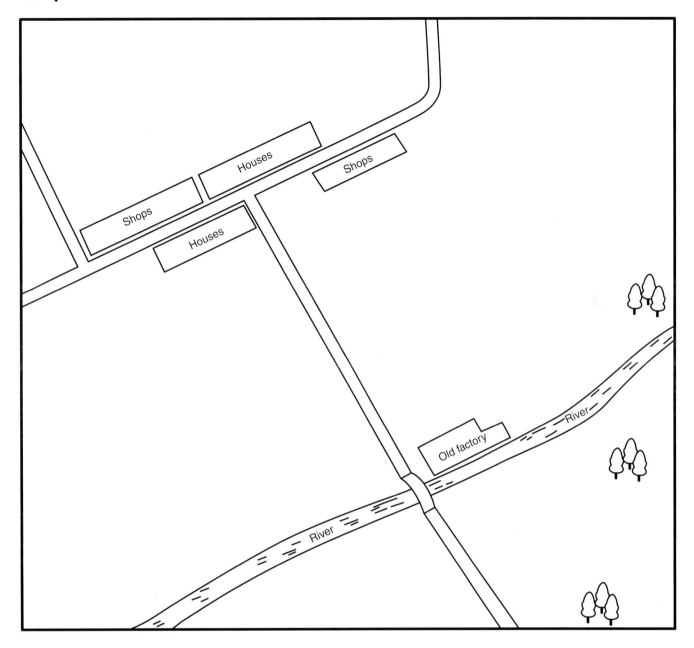

bridge   bus/railway station   business park   car park   cinema

high-rise building   hospital   leisure centre   luxury apartments

office block   park   pedestrian zone   playground   residential area

school   shopping centre/mall   theatre   town hall   town square

Unit 6 Communicative activity A

No way!

Student A

I hope not.	No, I'm not.	Definitely not.
I don't know.	No way!	I don't think so.

✂ -

Student B

No, I can't.	Me neither.	No, thanks.
No, I didn't.	Nobody.	No, I haven't.

✂ -

Student C

I'm not sure.	Let's not!	No, I haven't.
No, I can't.	No, I wouldn't.	None.

✂ -

Student D

No, it didn't.	Never.	I can, but I don't have to.
None.	I don't think so.	Nothing.

Unit 6 Communicative activity B

Holiday pairwork crossword

Student A

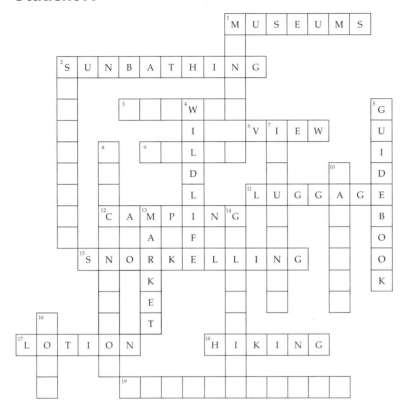

Across:
1. MUSEUMS
2. SUNBATHING
6. VIEW
11. LUGGAGE
12. CAMPING
15. SNORKELLING
17. LOTION
18. HIKING

Down:
5. GUIDEBOOK

✂ -

Student B

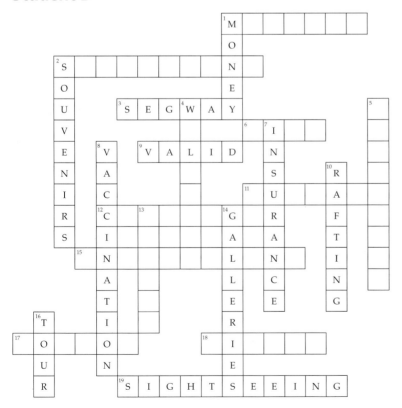

1. M O N E N E
2. S O U V E N I R S
3. SEGWAY
6. I N S U R G A N C E
8. V A C I N A T I O N
9. VALID
10. R A F T I N G
11. C I
12. C
15.
16. T O U R
17.
18. I E
19. SIGHTSEEING

Unit 6 Communicative activity C

Getting around roleplay

NEED 1
Your flight gets in at 10.30 on Friday morning and you will need to get from the airport to the city centre.

NEED 2
You want to go to the beach. You don't know how to get there.

NEED 3
You want to go sightseeing. You don't know where the best place to go is.

NEED 4
You need to eat out this evening. You don't know the best place to go or how to get there.

NEED 5
You need to get to the airport from the city centre. Your flight leaves at 18.30.

NEED 6
You really want to go rafting from the Riverbridge Activity Centre but you have no idea how to get there.

OFFER 1
You're happy to lend your bike to anyone. (It's a very old mountain bike.)

What you know:

- Your friend gives people lifts to or from the airport for £15 and to or from the beach for £5 (but he doesn't have any insurance to operate as a taxi driver).

OFFER 2
You've got an electric bike. You're happy to lend it to anyone as long as they promise to look after it.

What you know:

- It takes about 10 minutes to cycle into the city centre and to the old part of the city.
- There are no buses or trains to the Riverbridge Activity Centre.

OFFER 3
You're very happy to give anyone a lift in your car. (It's new and you love driving it!)

What you know:

- There are lots of good restaurants and cafés in the city centre and at the beach.
- The best place to go sightseeing is in the old part of the city.

OFFER 4
You don't have a car or bike.

What you know:

- The Riverbridge Activity Centre is 25 km north-east from here, on Wild Valley Road.
- It takes 45 minutes to walk to the beach or there's a bus every 10 minutes.

OFFER 5
You've got a car and you're happy to give people lifts in the evening but you're working until 4.30pm every day this week.

What you know:

- There's a bus into the city centre and to the old part of the city every 20 minutes.

OFFER 6
You're usually very happy to give people lifts but your car is at the garage.

What you know:

- It takes about 10 minutes to cycle to the beach and 45 minutes to walk there.
- There's a bus between the town centre and the airport every 30 minutes.

Unit 7 Communicative activity A

I bet you agree with all of them!

It's OK for parents to tell children off sometimes as long as they …
a) praise them a lot, too.
b) don't shame them.
c) give them lots of things, too.

Children used to …
a) be more polite.
b) read more books.
c) play outside more.

People used to …
a) spoil their children more.
b) spend more time with their children.
c) love their children more.

You can get used to anything as long as …
a) you don't mind being flexible.
b) you have a positive attitude.
c) someone pays you enough for it!

If you keep nagging someone to do something, …
a) they'll eventually do it.
b) they'll get really annoyed with you.
c) perhaps you should do it yourself!

It's OK to eat lots of things like crisps and chocolate …
a) as long as you eat plenty of fresh fruit and vegetables, too.
b) as long as you limit how often you do it.
c) because life's too short not to enjoy yourself!

It's rude to …
a) interrupt someone when they're talking.
b) answer your phone during a meal.
c) talk when you've got food in your mouth.

People can have a difference of opinion with someone they know and still get on well …
a) unless it's a disagreement about religion.
b) as long as you treat each other with respect.
c) as long as you never talk about it.

It makes no difference to me …
a) how someone dresses.
b) how someone earns their money.
c) whether someone is polite or not.

Adults should always tell children off when they do something that …
a) harms other people.
b) harms the natural world.
c) damages objects.

When people have children, they usually …
a) become really boring.
b) learn a lot about themselves.
c) become much kinder.

Children usually rebel against their parents …
a) when they become teenagers.
b) because it's an important part of growing up.
c) if the parents are very strict.

Unit 7 Communicative activity B

The same or different?

Student A

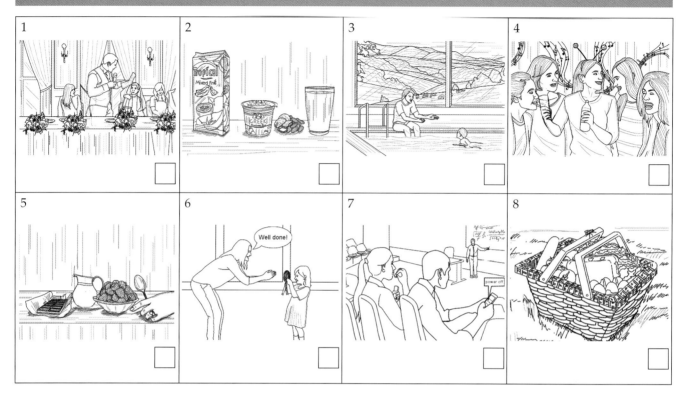

Student B

Unit 7 Communicative activity C

Traditions web search

Student A

	Tradition 1	Tradition 2	Tradition 3
What's it called?	The Quinceañera		
Where does it take place?			
Who is it for?			
What does it mark?			
What happens?			
What does it symbolize?			

✂- -

Student B

	Tradition 1	Tradition 2	Tradition 3
What's it called?		Seijin-no-Hi	
Where does it take place?			
Who is it for?			
What does it mark?			
What happens?			
What does it symbolize?			

✂- -

Student C

	Tradition 1	Tradition 2	Tradition 3
What's it called?			The Bullet Ant Ritual
Where does it take place?			
Who is it for?			
What does it mark?			
What happens?			
What does it symbolize?			

Unit 8 Communicative activity A

Is it a good thing?

YES   NO

← ——————————————————— I'm studying English.

This is an exam. ————————————————→

I can speak English.

I'm a man.

I'm a woman.

I can drive.

I've got a car.

I've got long hair.

I've got brown eyes.

I've got a good job.

I can speak Spanish.

The world is a peaceful place.

I'm not colour blind.

I'm eighteen years old.

I've got children.

I've got a daughter.

I've got a son.

I can fly.

I don't live in a big city.

It's raining.

It isn't snowing.

I feel optimistic about the future of our planet.

I had breakfast this morning.

I haven't been to university.

I was born one hundred years ago.

I was born one thousand years ago.

I didn't study hard enough at school.

I was brought up by people whose first language is English.

I knew when I was a child what job I wanted to do when I grew up.

I didn't grow up with any brothers or sisters.

I was born in the summer.

I learned to ski when I was a child.

Unit 8 Communicative activity B

Define that word!

electrician	back-breaking	delight	decision	ambition	baker
electricity	difficult	happiness	decide	job	bakery
equipment	physical	delighted	conclusion	dream	bread
install	tiring	pleasure	think	want	cake
fix	work	joy	make	ambitious	make

hope	profit	historian	lawyer	housework	bleak
want	gain	history	law	clean	hopeless
wish	money	past	crime	house	miserable
dream	business	study	legal	work	depressing
hopeful	amount	know	illegal	tidy	bad

librarian	regret	astrophysicist	conservationist	wish	geologist
library	wish	physics	conservation	hope	geology
book	only	stars	protection	dream	rock
borrow	sadness	planets	environment	want	Earth
quiet	disappointed	astronomy	wildlife	ambition	history

firefighter	mistake	goal	majestic	receptionist	alarmed
fire	error	hope	beauty	reception	alarm
emergency	wrong	aim	amazing	hotel	worry
danger	accident	football	big	hospital	frightened
dangerous	judgement	target	grand	phone	worried

unique	translator	suggestion	better	economist	calculation
one	translate	plan	good	economics	maths
only	translation	idea	improve	economy	mathematical
unlike	language	suggest	more	production	mathematics
individual	words	think	desirable	country	calculate

explorer	filmmaker	scientist	business	astronaut	geographer
explore	film	science	consultant	spacecraft	geography
travel	make	nature	business	space	land
learn	direct	observation	consult	travel	physical
discover	produce	experiments	advice	moon	Earth

preference	rocket	shopping	money	achieve	superpower
choice	astronaut	do	make	do	ability
prefer	space	buy	spend	succeed	able
like	machine	shop	buy	gain	fly
choose	spaceship	money	profit	goal	invisible

Unit 8 Communicative activity C

What do we have in common?

	Me	Someone with the same answer
Do you prefer talking or listening?		
Do you prefer sunrise or sunset?		
Do you prefer cooking or being cooked for?		
Which do you like more, being indoors or outdoors?		
Would you rather be 15 minutes early or 15 minutes late for things for the rest of your life?		
Would you prefer to only be able to say one word a day, or say as many as you like but you have to shout every word?		
Would you prefer to know everything about the past or a few things about the future?		
Would you rather learn English for the rest of your life or teach English for the rest of your life?		
Would you rather lose all your possessions but keep all the photos you've ever taken or lose all the photos you've ever taken but keep all your other possessions?		
Choose what you'd rather do this evening: • go and watch a film • go for a run • _____ • _____		
Choose where you'd prefer to go for a holiday: • Alaska, to see the Northern Lights • Hawaii, to swim with dolphins • _____ , to see _____ • _____ , to go _____		
If you could choose, where would you rather be right now? • _____ • _____ • _____ • _____		
Which do you like more, _____ or _____ ?		
Would you rather never eat _____ again or never eat _____ again?		
If you were able to choose, would you rather be able to _____ really well or _____ really well?		
Would you rather be famous for _____ or _____ ?		

Unit 9 Communicative activity A

Keep talking!

Can you name THREE objects that are believed by some people in your country to be lucky? **30** ☐	Can you name THREE things that people often promise to do? **30** ☐	Thank someone in the group for something they have done for you recently. ☐	Tell the group what sort of stories you find inspiring. ☐
Can you name THREE things that people often congratulate their friends on? **30** ☐	Talk about a time someone persuaded you to do something you didn't really want to do. ☐	Can you name THREE things that people often promise NOT to do? **30** ☐	Can you name THREE things that people often thank friends, family or strangers for? **30** ☐
Talk about a time you gave your word to someone that you would do something. ☐	Can you name THREE things that parents often have to persuade their children to do? **30** ☐	Can you name FIVE things that people offer to do at home? **30** ☐	Talk about a time someone criticized you or a friend for doing something. ☐
How many things that someone might warn you not to do can you name? **30** ☐	Tell the group what sort of stories you find amusing. ☐	Invite someone in the group to go somewhere with you next week. ☐	How many things that people often apologize for can you name? **30** ☐
Ask someone in the group to do something for you. ☐	Talk about a time lots of people congratulated you on something. ☐	Can you name FOUR things that can be difficult to explain to someone? **30** ☐	Can you think of something that was thought to be true in the past but which is now known not to be true? **30** ☐
How many things that people often complain about can you name? **30** ☐	How many things that people sometimes accuse other people of doing can you name? **30** ☐	Talk about a time you found yourself lost for words. ☐	Tell someone in the group to draw something here: ☐

Unit 9 Communicative activity B

She's asking him to go away!

A: Did you _____ ?
B: No! It wasn't me! I didn't do it! Really, it wasn't me.
　　　　　(**deny** doing something)

A: OK, OK. I'll _____ if you really want me to.
B: Oh good! It will be such a help!
　　　　　(**agree** to do something)

A: I'll _____ , if you like.
B: Oh, thank you. That would be great.

　　　　　(**offer** to do something)

A: Hey! I hear you _____ !
　　That's great news! Well done!
B: Thank you!
　　　　　(**congratulate** someone on doing something)

A: I'm so grateful to you for
_____ yesterday.
B: You're welcome! Any time!

　　　　　(**thank** someone for doing something)

A: Please would you _____ ?
　　Please, please, please?
B: I'm not sure …
A: Please?
　　　　　(**beg** someone to do something)

A: Excuse me.
B: Yes?
A: This _____ isn't cooked properly. It's cold in the middle.
　　　　　(**complain** about something)

A: I think Sam was wrong to
_____ . It caused a lot of problems.
B: Mmm. You could be right.
　　　　　(**criticize** someone for doing something)

A: I'm a bit embarrassed to say this but I'm afraid it was me that _____ .
B: Oh, I see. I'm not sure what to say.
　　　　　(**admit / confess** to doing something)

A: Be careful! Don't _____ !
　　It's dangerous.
B: OK, I'll bear that in mind.
　　　　　(**warn** someone not to do something)

A: Hey, would you like to _____ with us next week?
B: Oh, what a nice idea! That would be lovely.
　　　　　(**invite** someone to do something)

A: Oh dear. How on earth has this happened?
B: Well, it's Peter's fault. He _____ .
　　　　　(**blame** someone for doing something)

A: I'm sorry, I know you want me to
_____ but I simply won't do it, however much you ask me.
B: OK … if you're sure.
　　　　　(**refuse** to do something)

A: I think you should _____ .
B: Really?
A: Yes, I think it would be the best thing to do.
　　　　　(**advise** someone to do something)

A: I'll _____ when I get home.
B: Are you sure?
A: Yes, of course I will, trust me!
　　　　　(**promise** to do something)

A: You did the right thing when you
_____ . Well done.
B: Oh, thanks. I'm glad you think so.
　　　　　(**praise** someone for doing something)

Unit 9 Communicative activity C

Have you heard about James and Vicky?

Gossip cards

1 Local gossip! You heard this from: _____ A friend of yours … _____ _____ _____ _____	**2 Local gossip!** You can't remember where you heard this. Your boss … _____ _____ _____ _____	**3 Celebrity gossip!** You read this in/on: _____ The prime minister / princess / prince of … _____ _____ _____	**4 Celebrity gossip!** You can't remember where you read this. The lead singer of … _____ _____ _____ _____
5 Local gossip! You heard this from: _____ Suzy and Paul … _____ _____ _____ _____	**6 Local gossip!** You can't remember where you heard this. Your neighbour … _____ _____ _____ _____	**7 Local gossip!** You heard this from: _____ One of your neighbours … _____ _____ _____ _____	**8 Celebrity gossip!** You read this in/on: _____ A footballer / footballer's wife … _____ _____ _____

Response cards

Student A	**Student B**
You like and tend to believe gossip about: • money and status • other people's relationships You're not interested in and don't tend to believe gossip about: • celebrities' lives • other people's character and reputation	You like and tend to believe gossip about: • celebrities' lives • other people's character and reputation You're not interested in and don't tend to believe gossip about: • money and status • other people's relationships
Student C	**Student D**
You like and tend to believe gossip about: • other people's character and reputation • other people's relationships You're not interested in and don't tend to believe gossip about: • money and status • celebrities' lives	You like and tend to believe gossip about: • money and status • celebrities' lives You're not interested in and don't tend to believe gossip about: • other people's character and reputation • other people's relationships

Unit 10 Communicative activity A

That's me!

The qualities which appeal to me most in other people are _____ , _____ and _____ .

Of the five senses _____ is the one that's strongest for me, which is probably why _____ .

My _____ , which is a qualification I got in _____ , has helped me _____ .

_____ is someone whose job I'd love to do because _____ _____ .

_____ , who I met when I was _____ , is the most creative person I know.

Something I always have with me is _____ _____ .

What I love doing most is _____ _____ .

I've got a lot of experience in _____ , which has helped to me to _____ .

I _____ , for which I'm really grateful.

My _____ , who's a _____ , really enjoys his/her job.

People who _____ really annoy me.

Becoming an astronaut is something I _____ _____ .

A famous person whose voice I really like is _____ _____ .

I'd love to do a course which would enable me to _____ .

I know someone who serves in the _____ , which is something I _____ _____ .

A subject I was really bad at when I was at school was _____ .

Unit 10 Communicative activity B

Call my bluff

Team A

1 A 'graduand' is someone …

   a) who is about to graduate from university.

   b) who has more than one university qualification.

   c) _____

   _____

2 The word 'self-raising' describes the kind of …

   a) _____

   _____

   b) people who educate themselves.

   c) flour which people use to make cakes.

3 'Synaesthesia' is …

   a) the ability to swim underwater for more than ten minutes.

   b) _____

   _____

   c) a condition which makes people experience strong connections between the senses.

4 A 'jack of all trades' is someone who …

   a) _____

   _____

   b) does lots of different jobs instead of following a career.

   c) has several exceptional talents.

5 People who are 'self-righteous' …

   a) think they are better than other people.

   b) _____

   _____

   c) don't like other people helping them.

6 A 'stickybeak' is someone …

   a) who keeps their mouth closed when other people are sharing their opinions.

   b) who always wants to know what other people are doing.

   c) _____

   _____

Team B

1 The term 'AWOL' is used to describe someone …

   a) who works for a law firm.

   b) _____

   _____

   c) who has left the army without permission.

2 People who are 'self-effacing' are very …

   a) shy, humble and modest.

   b) _____

   _____

   c) confident, loud and arrogant.

3 A 'kaleidoscope' is …

   a) a tube in which there are mirrors and pieces of coloured glass whose reflections make pretty patterns when the tube is moved.

   b) _____

   _____

   c) a large tank of salty water in which people float for a long time in order to relax.

4 A 'monocle' is …

   a) a round piece of glass which was used in the past by people with bad eyesight.

   b) _____

   _____

   c) a glass ball in which some people believe they can see people's future.

5 Having 'self-restraint' means …

   a) _____

   _____

   b) being able to control your actions and emotions.

   c) having a low opinion of yourself.

6 People with 'anosmia' …

   a) _____

   _____

   b) have a very strong sense of feeling in their fingertips.

   c) have no sense of smell.

Unit 10 Communicative activity C

What's your career personality type?

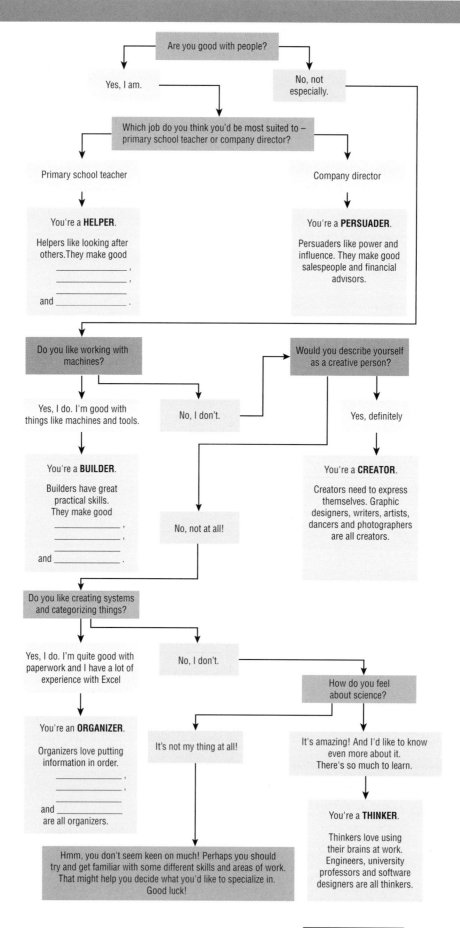

Are you good with people?

Yes, I am.

No, not especially.

Which job do you think you'd be most suited to – primary school teacher or company director?

Primary school teacher

Company director

You're a **HELPER**.

Helpers like looking after others. They make good

_____ ,
_____ ,
and _____ .

You're a **PERSUADER**.

Persuaders like power and influence. They make good salespeople and financial advisors.

Do you like working with machines?

Would you describe yourself as a creative person?

Yes, I do. I'm good with things like machines and tools.

No, I don't.

Yes, definitely

You're a **BUILDER**.

Builders have great practical skills. They make good

_____ ,
_____ ,
and _____ .

No, not at all!

You're a **CREATOR**.

Creators need to express themselves. Graphic designers, writers, artists, dancers and photographers are all creators.

Do you like creating systems and categorizing things?

Yes, I do. I'm quite good with paperwork and I have a lot of experience with Excel

No, I don't.

How do you feel about science?

You're an **ORGANIZER**.

Organizers love putting information in order.

_____ ,
_____ ,
and _____
are all organizers.

It's not my thing at all!

It's amazing! And I'd like to know even more about it. There's so much to learn.

Hmm, you don't seem keen on much! Perhaps you should try and get familiar with some different skills and areas of work. That might help you decide what you'd like to specialize in. Good luck!

You're a **THINKER**.

Thinkers love using their brains at work. Engineers, university professors and software designers are all thinkers.

What's your career personality type?

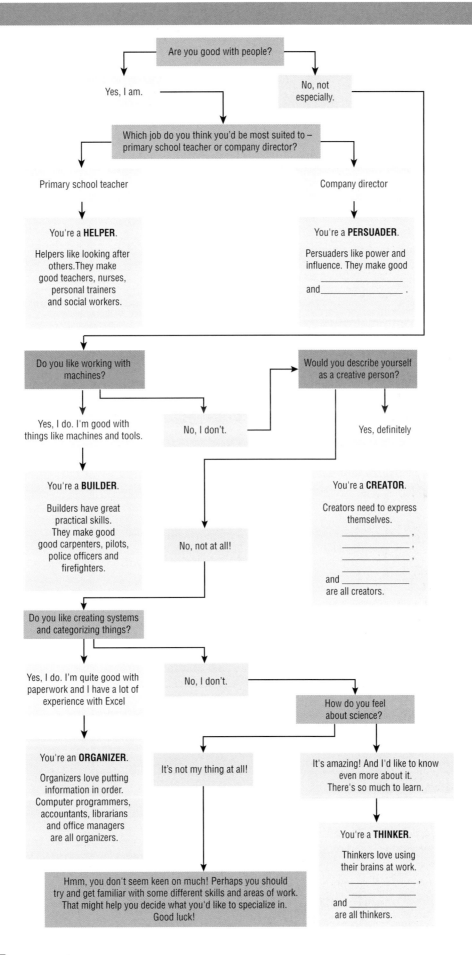

Are you good with people?

Yes, I am.

No, not especially.

Which job do you think you'd be most suited to – primary school teacher or company director?

Primary school teacher

Company director

You're a **HELPER**.

Helpers like looking after others. They make good teachers, nurses, personal trainers and social workers.

You're a **PERSUADER**.

Persuaders like power and influence. They make good
_____
and_____ .

Do you like working with machines?

Would you describe yourself as a creative person?

Yes, I do. I'm good with things like machines and tools.

No, I don't.

Yes, definitely

You're a **BUILDER**.

Builders have great practical skills. They make good good carpenters, pilots, police officers and firefighters.

No, not at all!

You're a **CREATOR**.

Creators need to express themselves.

_____ ,
_____ ,
_____ ;
and _____
are all creators.

Do you like creating systems and categorizing things?

Yes, I do. I'm quite good with paperwork and I have a lot of experience with Excel

No, I don't.

How do you feel about science?

You're an **ORGANIZER**.

Organizers love putting information in order. Computer programmers, accountants, librarians and office managers are all organizers.

It's not my thing at all!

It's amazing! And I'd like to know even more about it. There's so much to learn.

You're a **THINKER**.

Thinkers love using their brains at work.

_____ ,
and _____
are all thinkers.

Hmm, you don't seem keen on much! Perhaps you should try and get familiar with some different skills and areas of work. That might help you decide what you'd like to specialize in. Good luck!

Unit 11 Communicative activity A

Lessons in life

START	What were you able to do ten years ago that you can't do now?	What subjects at school did you get good / bad marks in? Do you like those subjects now?	Can you ski? If so, when and how did you learn? If not, would you like to be able to? Why? / Why not?
What was the last exam you took? How did it go?	Can you remember… two meanings of the word *address*?	How do you revise for your exams?	Name three of your practical skills. How did you acquire them?
Have you got your driving licence? If so, how many times did you take your driving test? If not, are you planning to learn to drive? Why? / Why not?	**FINISH** If you decided to train (or re-train) as a teacher, who would you teach and what would you teach them? Why?	Can you write a simple computer programme? If so, when and how did you learn? If not, would you like to be able to? Why? / Why not?	What sort of things did you have to learn by heart when you were at school?
Talk about a time when you learned by your mistakes. What happened?	Name three areas in which you learnt by experience.	What sport would you like to be able to do really well?	Can you remember… two meanings of the word *date*?
Name three areas in which you have academic knowledge. How did you acquire this knowledge?	Can you remember… two meanings of the word *rest*?	Talk about a time that you finally succeeded in doing something you'd been trying to do for a long time.	What motivates you to study?
What couldn't you do ten years ago that you can do now?	Do you find it easy to pick up other languages?	Can you swim? If so, when and how did you learn? If not, would you like to be able to? Why? / Why not?	What musical instrument would you like to be able to play really well?

Unit 11 Communicative activity B

I was going to come, but I missed the train

10b	1a	1b	2a
but _____ _____ _____ _____ _____ .	I would have come to your party,	but _____ _____ _____ _____ _____ .	I was going to make a speech,

2b	3a	3b	4a
but then _____ _____ _____ _____ _____ .	I was supposed to take the exam on Friday,	but _____ _____ _____ _____ _____ .	It would have been a perfect day,

4b	5a	5b	6a
but _____ _____ _____ _____ _____ .	I was about to take a photo,	but then _____ _____ _____ _____ _____ .	I was about to introduce myself to him,

6b	7a	7b	8a
but _____ _____ _____ _____ _____ .	I would have told you what happened,	but _____ _____ _____ _____ _____ .	I was about to start eating,

8b	9a	9b	10a
but then _____ _____ _____ _____ _____ .	I was supposed to go to Paris this week,	but _____ _____ _____ _____ _____ .	I almost managed to leave the house on time,

Unit 11 Communicative activity C
Which teambuilding day?

Forest Teambuilding Day

09.00   **Foraging in the forest**
Find your lunch! Our experts will help you find edible food* in the forest.
(*For example, leaves, berries and mushrooms)

10:00   **Tug-of-war**
Which team will win this classic test of strength?

11:15   **Bushcraft**
Learn to build a shelter, light a fire without matches, make clean drinking water and other wilderness survival skills.

12:00   **Masterchef**
Each team has 45 minutes to cook lunch from a mystery bag of ingredients and food foraged from the forest. Which team will cook the best meal?

13:00   **Lunch**

14:15   **Woodland adrenalin adventure**
The ultimate outdoor adventure! Climb trees, swing on ropes and jump from tree to tree!

17:00   **End**

City Teambuilding Day

08:00   **Scavenger hunt**
1 _____
_____
_____

10:00   **VAK**
2 _____
_____

11:30   **You're the entertainer!**
3 _____
_____

13:00   **Lunch**
4 _____

14:30   5 _____
6 _____
_____
_____

17:00   **End**

Forest Teambuilding Day

09.00   **Foraging in the forest**
1 _____
_____
_____

10:00   **Tug-of-war**
2 _____
_____

11:15   3 _____
4 _____
_____
_____

12:00   **Masterchef**
5 _____
_____
_____

13:00   **Lunch**
14:15   **Woodland adrenalin adventure**
6 _____
_____
_____

17:00   **End**

City Teambuilding Day

08:00   **Scavenger hunt**
Your team has a list of tasks* and one hour to complete it in. Which team will win?
(*Example tasks: taking a selfie with a stranger, finding a red flower, taking a photo of a glass building)

10:00   **VAK**
A quiz to find out whether you're a visual, auditory or kinaesthetic learner, followed by a talk by psychology expert Dr Helen Marsden.

11:30   **You're the entertainer!**
Learn circus skills like juggling, fire-eating and stilt-walking – then perform them to members of the public.

13:00   **Lunch**
A three-course meal at the Royal Hotel, Regency Street

14:30   **Cool Art**
Each team has a large block of ice, gloves and ice-carving tools. Which team can create the most impressive ice sculpture?

17:00   **End**

Unit 12 Communicative activity A

Find someone who ...

1 ... has had their hair cut in the last three weeks.	2 ... doesn't owe anybody any money.	3 ... is saving money for something special.
4 ... has been earning money for more than ten years.	5 ... can fit a carpet.	6 ... works with the elderly or would like to work with the elderly.
7 ... can fix a tap.	8 ... has their dog walked once or twice a week.	9 ... never gets their car washed.
10 ... thinks job satisfaction is more important than a good salary.	11 ... can put up a picture.	12 ... loves planning parties and would never pay to have a party planned for them.
13 ... has had an item of clothing altered for them.	14 ... likes gardening.	15 ... can put up shelves.
16 ... doesn't mind cleaning the bathroom.	17 ... has had an item of clothing made for them.	18 ... would like to set up their own business.

Unit 12 Communicative activity B

Opinions and attitudes questionnaire

1 I would only have my shoes cleaned if I was completely unable to do the job myself.	Agree ⟵————————⟶ Disagree
2 I often give money to the homeless.	Agree ⟵————————⟶ Disagree
3 The unemployed should try harder to find work.	Agree ⟵————————⟶ Disagree
4 I would never have my computer repaired by someone else.	Agree ⟵————————⟶ Disagree
5 Only I can make my favourite drink the way I really like it.	Agree ⟵————————⟶ Disagree
6 I just want to make other people happy – nothing else is important to me.	Agree ⟵————————⟶ Disagree
7 I only have a few really good friends.	Agree ⟵————————⟶ Disagree
8 The rich should pay more to get their medical problems treated than the poor.	Agree ⟵————————⟶ Disagree
9 I only work because I need the money.	Agree ⟵————————⟶ Disagree
10 Everyone, even the very young, should help with household jobs like cleaning and cooking.	Agree ⟵————————⟶ Disagree
11 You should only borrow money from banks, not friends and family.	Agree ⟵————————⟶ Disagree
12 People who pay to have their children looked after by a childminder are lazy.	Agree ⟵————————⟶ Disagree
13 The elderly should just stay at home and relax every day.	Agree ⟵————————⟶ Disagree
14 Most people only really care about themselves.	Agree ⟵————————⟶ Disagree

Unit 12 Communicative activity C

Would you be willing to move a bit on that?

Student A	Student B

FOR SALE: INFLATABLE TENT

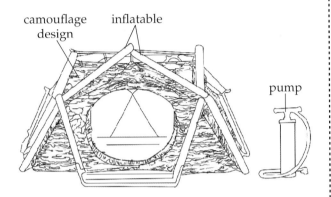

- £600
- Sleeps three people.
- Takes less than one minute to put up.
- Green, with a camouflage design.
- Has only been used once.
- Pump also for sale – £75

FOR SALE: CAMPERVAN

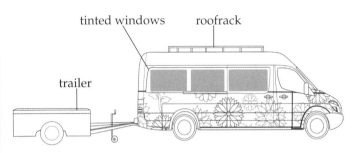

- £7,000
- Sleeps four people.
- Unusual design – blue with pink and yellow flowers
- Twenty years old

Student A: The bottom line (selling your tent)

You paid £700 for this tent and pump a year ago. It's a good tent (though the pump is quite heavy) but you want to sell it so that you can buy a bigger tent. You've advertised it for £600. How much are you willing to accept for it now? £_____

What about the pump? Would you come down on the price? Would you offer it free as part of your negotiation?

_____

Student B: The bottom line (selling your van)

You paid £9,500 for this van ten years ago. You had it decorated by an artist you know. It's a good van but you want to sell it so that you can buy a better one. You've advertised it for £7,000. How much are you willing to accept for it now? £_____

What about the trailer? Would you take some money off the van if the buyer didn't want it? If so, how much?

_____

Student A: The bottom line (buying a van)

- You urgently need a van for next week.
- You need a big van because you need to transport a lot of equipment for your job as a gardener.
- You'd like to be able to cook in it, so you need a sink and oven. (Ask about this.)
- You want to be able to drive fast. (Ask about this.)
- You might sleep in it sometimes.
- Ideally, you'd like a grey / green / blue / pink / yellow / red / white / black van. (circle one)
- You're hoping to spend about £4,000 but you are prepared to pay £5,000.

Student B: The bottom line (buying a tent)

- You urgently need a tent for next weekend.
- It needs to sleep two people.
- It should be quick and easy to put up.
- It needs to be light. (Ask about the weight.)
- You want it to be waterproof. (Ask about this.)
- Ideally, you'd like a grey / green / blue / pink / yellow / red tent. (circle one)
- You'd also like it to be plain / flowery / camouflage / stripy. (circle one)
- You're hoping to spend about £350 but you are prepared to pay £450.

Unit 1A People in my life

AIM: to practise using a range of tenses to talk about people who are, or who have been, significant in your life

LANGUAGE: present simple, present continuous, present perfect simple, present perfect continuous and past simple

GENRE: pairwork

MATERIALS: a copy of the worksheet for each student

CLASS TIME: 30 minutes

PROCEDURE:

- Give each student one worksheet. Give them five minutes to complete the ten sentences by adding a name in each gap. Then tell them to copy their ten names into the shapes below, but in a different order.

- Tell students to fold their worksheets so that only the names in the shapes are showing.

- Ask students to work in pairs. Explain that they are going to find out some information about the people in each other's lives. Students take turns to ask each other about the names. Encourage them to expand on what they say about the people in their lives and to ask each other questions.

- Invite individual students to report back to the whole class on one of the people that their partner told them about.

Unit 1B Who's your oldest friend?

AIM: to practise using vocabulary connected to relationships and character by playing a board game

LANGUAGE: words used for describing character; phrasal verbs (friendships); adjectives formed from nouns; also present simple, past simple, present perfect simple

GENRE: groupwork

MATERIALS: a die and a copy of the worksheet for each group of three or four students, a counter for each student

CLASS TIME: 30 minutes

PROCEDURE:

- See how many different words for family members and friends from Unit 1 students can remember (e.g. *brother-in-law, grandparent, blood relative, flatmate, acquaintance*). Review the meaning of *generation* and check students understand the difference between *close friend* and *old friend*.

- Organize the class into groups of three or four and give one worksheet and a die to each group. Students place their counters on 'Start' then take it in turns to roll the die, move their counter and give an answer to the question on the square that they land on. They should try to talk for about a minute about the personalized discussion questions. *Note:* If they have to roll the die and go back a number of squares, they don't need to answer the question on that square.

- The first player to reach 'Finish' is the winner. As each player finishes they can continue to play by taking their turn and working their way back towards 'Start' until the last player reaches 'Finish'.

- At the feedback stage, invite individual students to report to the class one or two things that they learned about their classmates during the activity.

Unit 1C How's everything going?

AIM: to practise the language used for meeting people by taking part in a roleplay

LANGUAGE: expressions used for meeting people

GENRE: whole class

MATERIALS: a copy of the worksheet for every nine students, cut into role cards as indicated

CLASS TIME: 30 minutes

PROCEDURE:

- Tell the class that they are going to create their own role cards for a roleplay.

- Hand out one role card to each student. Give students five minutes to think of a name for themselves and to answer the questions on their role card. Encourage them to be imaginative.

- Review the language of meeting people by writing some of the expressions from the language box on page 16 of the Student's Book on the board, gapped, and asking students to supply the missing words. See how many other expressions from the lesson students can remember.

- Tell students to imagine they are in town and that they are going to walk around and meet people they know. They should talk to at least five different people.

- At the feedback stage, invite individual students to report back on some of the people they met in the roleplay.

Unit 2A Survival!

AIM: to practise narrative past tenses by telling a story and discussing the similarities and differences between stories

LANGUAGE: narrative past tenses

GENRE: pairwork

MATERIALS: a copy of the worksheet for each pair of students, cut into two storyboards as indicated

CLASS TIME: 50 minutes

PROCEDURE:

- Tell students they are going to prepare and tell a survival story to a partner.

- Divide the class into two groups, Group A and Group B. Give all the students in Group A a copy of the Story 1 storyboard and all the students in Group B a copy of the Story 2 storyboard.

- Organize students within each group into pairs or small groups. Write *This story happened in …* on the board and give students 10 to 15 minutes to prepare and practise telling their story, starting with the words on the board. Monitor as students work, making sure they are using narrative tenses correctly and providing them with any vocabulary they need (e.g. Story 1: *sailing boat, sharks, storm, waves, rough, jellyfish, fishermen;* Story 2: *run out of fuel, cactus, pond, sticks, hunters*).

- Organize the class into pairs with one Student A and one Student B. Allow five to ten minutes for students to tell their story to their partner. They can look at their own storyboard but they mustn't show it to their partner. Explain that when they listen to their partner's story they should think about how the two stories are similar and in what ways they are different.

- When both students have told their stories, tell them to spend five minutes discussing the similarities and differences between the two stories. After five minutes, allow them to look at each other's storyboards to check and find any further information.

- Finally, tell students that the two stories in this activity are based on true stories. Ask: *Which of the two situations do you think was the most dangerous?*

ANSWERS

Similarities:

Both stories are about people being rescued after getting lost for about a week.

Both stories are set in the USA.

In both stories the people were found by other people who happened to be in the same place, not by search and rescue services.

In both stories, something unusual was eaten.

In both stories, the people ended up in hospital but were fine.

Differences:

Story 1 is about two teenage boys. Story 2 is about an older woman.

Story 1 happened at sea. Story 2 happened in a forest and in the desert.

In Story 1, the boys stayed in their boat. In Story 2, the woman left her car.

In Story 1, the boys were rescued on the seventh day. In Story 2, the woman was rescued on the ninth day.

In Story 1, the boys were found by fishermen. In Story 2, the woman was found by hunters.

In Story 1, one of the boys ate a jellyfish. In Story 2, the woman ate plants.

In Story 1, the boys couldn't drink anything. In Story 2, the woman found water she could drink.

In Story 1, the boys didn't make any signals but in Story 2, the woman signalled for help with a sign made from sticks and smoke from a fire.

The situation in Story 1 is probably the most dangerous because the boys couldn't drink seawater and had no shelter from the sun.

Unit 2B Story quiz

AIM: to talk about stories by preparing and doing a quiz

LANGUAGE: describing stories

GENRE: groupwork; whole class

MATERIALS: a copy of the worksheet for each team; access to the internet

CLASS TIME: 50 minutes

PROCEDURE:

- Elicit different ways that stories are told, e.g. films, books, TV dramas, plays, documentaries, graphic novels. Then elicit different kinds of stories, e.g. fairytales, biographies, thrillers, romances, adventure stories, true stories, myths, legends, etc. Write them on the board.

- Organize the class into three teams and tell them they are going to prepare eight questions for a quiz about stories. They should think of books, films, stories and legends that are reasonably likely to be known by the other students in the class.

- Give one worksheet to each team. Give them 10 to 15 minutes to complete the eight quiz questions, including the three multiple-choice answers. Tell them to share knowledge and to use the internet to research anything they're not 100% sure about.

- The first team asks the second team a question (the question is worth two points). If the second team doesn't answer it correctly, it passes to the third team (and is now worth one point). Then the second team asks the third team a question (worth two points), which can pass to the first team (then worth one point), and so on.

- Keep score of the points on the board. If a team has no idea what the correct answer is, they should guess. The team with the most points at the end wins the quiz.

Unit 2C You're kidding!

AIM: to practise telling and reacting to stories

LANGUAGE: reacting to stories; narrative past tenses

GENRE: groupwork

MATERIALS: two copies of the worksheet for every five students in the class, cut into five strips as indicated

CLASS TIME: 45 to 60 minutes

PROCEDURE:

- Write the following on the board: *I was walking* (Where?) _____ *once when I saw a* (What?) _____ . *It was* (What was it like?) _____ . Then elicit different ways of completing the sentences, e.g. *I was walking in the mountains once when I saw a really big snake. It was quite scary. I was walking through town once when I saw a brand new red Ferrari. It was very nice!*

- Tell students they are going to create first-person stories by using their own ideas to complete two story frameworks similar to the one on the board.

- Hand out two different frameworks to each student. Give them 15 minutes to prepare their stories. Monitor, giving help with vocabulary and ideas.

- Review the language of reacting to stories (Student's Book page 28) and make sure students can pronounce the expressions naturally.

- Organize students into groups of five. Tell them to take turns telling their stories. The others should listen and react appropriately. Encourage them to look for links between the stories so that they can use the *Talking about similar experiences* expressions.

- At the end, get some feedback from the class by asking if any true stories were told.

Unit 3A How optimistic are you?

AIM: to practise future forms by completing and discussing a questionnaire about the future

LANGUAGE: future forms; future perfect simple, future continuous

GENRE: pairwork; groupwork

MATERIALS: a copy of the Part 1 worksheet for each student in half the class and a copy of the Part 2 worksheet for each student in the other half of the class, with the Results sections cut off as indicated.

CLASS TIME: 45 minutes

PROCEDURE:
- Draw a picture of a glass half full of water on the board. Ask the class if they see the glass as half full or half empty. Teach the idiom *Is the glass half full or half empty?* (= Are you optimistic or pessimistic?) and ask students if they have a similar expression in their language. Tell them they're going to do a questionnaire to find out how optimistic they are.

- Check students understand *colony* (= a group of people who go to live in a different place but keep their own customs and habits), *the human race* (= all the people in the world, when thought of as a group) and *missions* (= special journeys made by spacecraft).

- Organize the class into pairs, and give a Part 1 worksheet to Student A in each pair and a Part 2 worksheet to Student B in each pair. Ask them not to look at each other's sheets. Give students five minutes to read and complete their own questionnaire. Then, get Student A to ask Student B the questions on his/her sheet, and vice versa. Encourage students to give reasons for their answers. Each student must make a note of their own answers (a, b, c or d). Allow about ten minutes for this stage.

- When all students have finished, tell them to add up how many a, b, c and d answers they've got in total. Get a show of hands for the results and ask students to sit in groups of 'mostly a and b' and 'mostly c and d'. Give 'Results ☺' strips to the groups with 'mostly a or b' answers and 'Results ☹' strips to the groups with 'mostly c or d' answers. Allow a couple of minutes for students to read them.

- Regroup students into new pairs or groups, making sure everyone is working with someone who has a **different** Results strip to theirs. (If this isn't possible, make sure students can at least see the other Results strip.) Give students time to compare their results, the information on their Results strip, their answers to the questions and the reasons for their answers.

- At the feedback stage, ask students whether they think the result of the questionnaire is a fair reflection of how they see themselves.

Unit 3B Name five things

AIM: to practise using vocabulary related to technology and materials by playing a team game

LANGUAGE: vocabulary for describing technology, materials; compound nouns (noun + noun)

GENRE: groupwork

MATERIALS: a copy of the worksheet for every two students, cut into A and B sections as indicated; a stopwatch or mobile phone for each group to use as a timer

CLASS TIME: 30 to 45 minutes

PROCEDURE:
- Prepare a list of five things made of glass, e.g. a bottle, a vase, glasses, a window and a jar. Write *five things that are made of glass* on the board. Tell them you have a secret list of five things and challenge the class to see if they can call out all the things on your list in one minute or under.

- Tell students they are going to play a game like this. Organize the class into groups of six to eight and divide each group into Team A and Team B. Give the Team A section of the worksheet to each Team A and the Team B section of the worksheet to each Team B.

- Give the teams 10 to 15 minutes to write five words for each category without the other team hearing or seeing what they are writing.

- To play the game, a player from Team A reads out one of the categories from their sheet and another member of the same team starts timing a minute. Players from Team B call out words they can think of in that category, and a player from Team A ticks any words that are on their piece of paper.

- Team B scores one point for every correctly guessed word, and a bonus of three points if they get every word on Team A's list. Team A scores one point for every word on their list that Team B doesn't guess.

- Teams take turns to guess words until all the categories have been used. The team with the highest score at the end are the winners.

Unit 3C Is everything OK with your room?

AIM: to practise the language of dealing with problems in a roleplay between hotel guests and receptionists

LANGUAGE: dealing with problems

GENRE: pairwork

MATERIALS: a copy of the worksheet for every ten students in the class, cut into ten role cards as indicated

CLASS TIME: 30 minutes

PROCEDURE:

- Divide the students in the class into hotel guests and receptionists and give them a role card each. With smaller classes, you could give the hotel guests more than one card each (i.e. a longer list of problems!).

- Give students time to think about the language they will need to use in the roleplay. Briefly elicit examples of phrases used for asking for help, explaining problems and responding to a problem (Student's Book page 40).

- Organize students into guest and receptionist pairs to conduct the roleplay. Change the pairs and repeat the activity at least once so that the guests can experience the different attitudes of the receptionists and the receptionists can deal with a variety of problems.

- Ask the students to swap roles, so that guests can try being receptionists and vice versa. Redistribute the role cards accordingly.

- When all the roleplays are finished, invite some of the guests to report back to the whole class on how helpful the different receptionists were and invite some of the receptionists to report back to the class on how polite (or not!) the different guests were.

Unit 4A Is it true?

AIM: to practise using determiners and expressions of quantity by conducting a survey about the arts

LANGUAGE: determiners; expressions of quantity; also word families: art

GENRE: whole class

MATERIALS: a copy of the worksheet for every ten students, cut into strips as indicated

CLASS TIME: 30 minutes

PROCEDURE:

- Write on the board: *Hardly anyone in the class has been to a classical concert.* Take a vote on whether students think the statement is true or false. Then ask: *What question do I need to ask to find out what's true?* and elicit *Have you ever been to a classical concert?*

- Do a quick class survey by asking everyone the question. Keep a tally on the board of students' *yes/no* answers. When you've finished, establish whether the statement on the board is indeed true or false for your class. Write a summary statement, e.g. *In fact, about a third of the students in the class have been to a classical concert.* Ask anyone who answered 'yes' to the question a few follow-up questions, e.g. *What pieces of music were played? Did you enjoy the concert?*

- Give each student one strip. Each student looks at their statement and decides whether they think it's true or false. With smaller classes, students can work with two or more strips.

- Explain that they are going to do a class survey to find out whether each statement is true or not. Give

them a minute or so to prepare the main survey question(s) they need to ask, and any follow-up questions they'd like to add.

- If you have enough space, tell students to stand up and mingle to ask each other their questions. Ask them to keep a record of the answers they get. If space is limited, put students in large groups. Encourage them to ask follow-up questions.

- To finish, tell students to summarize what they found out in a few words in the 'In fact, ...' box.

- Invite individual students to report what they found out to the rest of the class.

Unit 4B Spot the difference

AIM: to practise using vocabulary connected with the arts by describing and comparing pictures

LANGUAGE: the arts, word families: art; also determiners, expressions of quantity

GENRE: pairwork

MATERIALS: a copy of the worksheet for every pair of students, cut into Picture A and Picture B sections as indicated

CLASS TIME: 30 minutes

PROCEDURE:

- Establish the topic by asking how many kinds of artists, performances and venues they can remember.

- Tell students they are going to talk with a partner to find the ten differences between their own and their partner's pictures. Organize students into pairs and ask them to sit facing each other. Give out one worksheet section to each student. Tell students to look only at their own picture.

- Give students 10 to 15 minutes to talk about the pictures to find the differences.

- When students think they have found the ten differences, they can show each other their pictures to make sure they have identified the differences correctly.

- Check the ten differences with the class (see Answers below). Give clarification of any vocabulary that students may have struggled with.

- Close the activity by asking which of the artistic things and people in the pictures they commonly see in their own town.

ANSWERS

1 In Picture A there is an exhibition of **modern artwork** in the art gallery but in Picture B it's an exhibition of **portrait/fine/traditional art**.

2 In Picture A there are **lots of people in the art gallery** but in Picture B there are **hardly any/very few people**.

3 In Picture A there's **a busker** playing in the street but in Picture B **a whole band** is playing.

4 In Picture A there's **an artist** in the street but in Picture B there's **a circus performer**.

5 In Picture A the woman is wearing **arty clothes** but in Picture B the woman is wearing **ordinary** clothes.

---

6 In Picture A there's **a lot of graffiti** on the wall but in Picture B there's **only a bit of graffiti**.

7 In Picture A, people are listening to **a classical concert /performance**, but in Picture B they're listening to **a comedian**.

8 In Picture A there's **an actor** but in Picture B there's **a street dancer**.

9 In Picture A a woman is giving **medicine** to a baby but in Picture B she's giving the baby **chocolate**.

10 In Picture A there are **clouds** in the sky but in Picture B there **aren't any clouds**.

Unit 4C Likes and dislikes questionnaire

AIM: to practise asking about and describing likes and dislikes by interviewing others

LANGUAGE: describing likes and dislikes; the arts

GENRE: pairwork

MATERIALS: a copy of the worksheet for each student

CLASS TIME: 45 minutes

PROCEDURE:
- Check students understand *abstract art, contemporary dance, living statues, animations, fantasy films, advertising, rap, country music, modern art installations.*
- Give each student a copy of the questionnaire and give them five minutes to read it and personalize it by circling the topics they want to talk about. Then ask them to tick and write *Me* or their initials by the answers that are true for them.
- Ask students to sit in two rows opposite each other (or in a 'wheel' formation with an inner circle facing out and an outer circle facing in) so that each student is facing a partner. Students take turns to interview their partner using their questionnaire. They keep a note of their answers by writing their name or initials next to each answer they choose. Encourage students to ask their partner a few follow-up questions to find out more information about some of their partner's answers.
- After about five minutes, ask all the students on one side of the line (or on the outer 'wheel') to move round one space so that everyone has a new partner to interview. Repeat so that each person interviews at least three people.
- At the feedback stage, invite individual students to report back some of the things they've found out, using expressions like *Both Yuri and I think …, Both Maria and Yoshika like …, None of the people I spoke to like …, Most of the people I spoke to don't like … but …, A few people are into …* and so on.

Unit 5A How well do you know me?

AIM: to talk about likes, dislikes, hopes, dreams, regrets, experiences and memories by playing a bluffing game

LANGUAGE: verb + infinitive or *-ing*

GENRE: whole class

MATERIALS: a copy of the worksheet for each student

CLASS TIME: 30 to 40 minutes

PROCEDURE:
- Choose two of the unfinished sentences from the activity and write them on the board. Elicit different ways of completing them. Point out that although some of the sentences can be finished with a noun (e.g. *I really like salsa music*), you want them to think of endings that use a verb (e.g. *I really like dancing to salsa music*).
- Tell students that they are going to be playing a bluffing game (*bluff* = to try to trick people into believing that a false statement is actually true, for fun). Using the sentence beginnings on the worksheet, tell students two things that are true about you and two that are false. Can students can identify the false statements?
- Give each student a copy of the worksheet and give them about ten minutes to complete the statements on the sheet. Tell students to include between five and ten deliberately false statements.
- When students have finished, ask them to stand up and move around the class talking to different students. Each pair should take turns to read out four of their statements. The listener should listen to all four statements carefully before deciding which (if any) they think are true and which (if any) they think are false. Their partner can then tell them how many they got right. After doing this, they can briefly talk about anything interesting that has come up in the conversation before moving on to talk to a new partner. Once students have spoken to three or four partners, ask them to go back to their seats and sit down again.
- To close the activity, invite some students to report to the whole class anything funny/interesting/surprising, etc. that they found out about each other.

Unit 5B Urban features web search

AIM: to practise the use of urban features vocabulary by doing a web search and sharing, comparing and evaluating the findings

LANGUAGE: urban features

GENRE: groupwork

MATERIALS: a copy of the worksheet for every three students, cut into three sections as indicated; access to the internet

CLASS TIME: 45 to 55 minutes

PROCEDURE:
- Tell students that between them they are going to do a web search to find out about twelve unusual urban features around the world. Give Student A worksheets to all the Student As, student B worksheets to all the Student Bs and Student C worksheets to all the Student Cs. If access to the internet is limited, put students in AA BB CC pairs or AAA BBB CCC groups. Tell them they need to research and fill in all the columns on their sheet.

- Allow students 20 to 30 minutes to research the four urban features on their sheets and make notes. Point out that looking for images will help them, as will adding the word *architecture* to their search term. Monitor as students work, making sure they're filling in their sheets correctly (see Answers below).

- When they've completed their worksheets, put students into ABC groups to share their answers. They will discover that they have found information about three different high-rise apartment blocks, three car parks, three shopping malls/leisure centres and three green urban spaces.

- Now give students about ten minutes to decide which high-rise apartment block, car park, shopping mall/leisure centre and green urban space they think is the most unusual; and which they would most like to visit or use and why.

ANSWERS			
STUDENT A			
1	a high-rise apartment block	Sydney, Australia	It has many 'green' features such as vertical hanging gardens, its own water recycling plant and solar panels that move to catch sunlight at different times of day.
2	a car park	Seattle, USA	It's built at an angle that makes it look as though it's sinking into the ground.
3	a shopping mall and leisure centre	Nola, Italy	The architecture is unusual. It was designed to look like the nearby volcano, Mount Vesuvius.
4	a green space	Seoul, South Korea	The park is 10.9 km long and has a stream running through the centre of it. Previously, the stream had been hidden under concrete.

STUDENT B			
1	a pair of high-rise apartment blocks	Milan, Italy	There are 900 trees and more than 2,000 other plants growing on these tower blocks, creating 7,000 m^2 of forest.
2	a car park	Wolfsburg, Germany	The driver leaves their car at the bottom and the cars are taken up robotically to a parking space. Each tower can hold 400 cars and other vehicles.
3	a shopping mall and leisure centre	Astana, Kazakhstan	Everything is contained under a 150-metre high transparent tent, including streets, a river, mini-golf and an indoor beach resort.

4	a green space	New York, USA	It was developed on a disused railway line. It is narrow and runs 2.3 km and is 9 m above ground.

STUDENT C			
1	an apartment block	Tokyo, Japan and New York, USA	They're very colourful, they don't have doors inside between spaces. Lots of objects like TVs and chairs hang from the ceiling. Some of the floors slope and they are designed to keep the people who live in them young and healthy.
2	a car park	Miami Beach, USA	It's famous for the unusual design of its architecture. You can also eat, shop and have parties there.
3	a shopping mall and leisure centre	Fukuoka, Japan	It's a 'city within a city'. It has 250 shops, cafés and restaurants as well as cinemas, a theatre, two hotels and a canal running through it.
4	a green space	Seattle, USA	It's located under a motorway and has trails for mountain bikers to use.

Unit 5C How should we develop the town?

AIM: to practise the language of debating issues by discussing different plans to improve a town

LANGUAGE: debating issues; urban features

GENRE: pairwork; groupwork

MATERIALS: a copy of the worksheet for each pair or small group

CLASS TIME: 45 minutes

PROCEDURE:

- Tell the class they are going to plan some changes to an imaginary town. Their task is to think of ways to make more people want to come and live, work and relax in the town.

- Elicit/teach some verbs connected with changes in towns and cities – e.g. *knock a building down, cut a tree down, build sth, construct sth, expand sth, develop sth, improve sth,* and lack of change, e.g. *leave sth as it is, leave sth unchanged/untouched.*

- Organize students into pairs (or small groups) and give one worksheet to each pair/group. You need to have at least three pairs/groups and at most four pairs/groups. Explain that they should think of how they want to change the town. They can cut down trees and knock down shops but they can't knock down the houses. They can use the urban features from the bottom of the page or their own ideas.

- Give the pairs/groups five minutes to discuss what sort of changes they want to make before they start drawing their ideas on the plan. They should try to agree on what their main priority is – is it developing business in the town, for example, or creating a green and pleasant place to live?

- Tell students to start drawing with a pencil as they might want to make changes as they go along. Allow 15 to 20 minutes for this stage.

- When they've prepared their plans, give the pairs/ groups five to ten minutes to prepare how they are going to present their plans to the rest of the class.

- Explain that each pair/group is going to present their plan to the others. (If you have enough time, you could get students to copy their plans onto larger pieces of paper.) They should look at and listen carefully to the other plans, as they need to think of questions to ask and/or arguments to make against them. Explain that when everyone has presented their plans, there will be a chance for debate and discussion and then students can vote for the plan they like best.

- Point out that although this activity is not a formal debate, students can use much of the language from the 'debating issues' language box on Student's Book page 64. Briefly review this by giving students some key words to see if they can produce the whole phrases, e.g. Teacher: *agree* (Students: *I agree completely*.), Teacher: *not/agree* (Students: *I don't agree*.), Teacher: *point* (Students: *The point is, …*), Teacher: *depends* (Students: *Well, that depends*), Teacher: *accept* (Students: *I don't accept that*), Teacher: *bothered* (Students: *Actually, I'm not too bothered by that*.)

- At the presentation and discussion stage, make sure each pair/group gets roughly the same amount of time to speak and be questioned.

- When all the pairs/groups have presented their ideas and all the ideas have been discussed, take a vote to see which plan is the most popular. (Students can't vote for their own plan!)

Unit 6A No way!

AIM: to practise question forms and negative forms by playing a game

LANGUAGE: question forms; negative forms

GENRE: whole class

MATERIALS: a copy of the worksheet for every four students, cut into four sections as indicated

CLASS TIME: 30 minutes

PROCEDURE:

- Tell students they are going to play a game in which they try and make people say the negative answers on their game card. They will need to ask each other lots of questions, 'hiding' their prompt questions in a natural conversation if possible.

- As an example, write *No, never!* on a piece of paper and turn it face down on your desk. Ask individual students a series of questions, e.g. *Did you ever travel by helicopter as a child? Have you ever seen people parachuting? Would you ever jump out of an aeroplane without a parachute?* in an attempt to elicit the answer *No, never!* If and when someone says the phrase, turn over the piece of paper and show the class.

- Give Student A game cards to all the Student As, student B game cards to all the Student Bs , etc., making sure students don't see each other's sheets.

- Give students ten minutes to look at the negative answers on their sheets and to prepare as many questions as they can which they think might make their classmates say the answers on their sheet. Remind them to use a range of question forms, such as indirect questions, negative questions and tag questions. Point out that they should also prepare to ask additional questions in order to help 'hide' the answers they are trying to elicit.

- When someone succeeds in getting their classmate to say one of the answers on their sheet, they should write that person's name next to it. They can't then use that square again until they have at least one name on all the other squares.

- Ask students to stand up and move around the class starting conversations and asking each other questions. The student with the most names on their sheet after 15 minutes is the winner.

Unit 6B Holiday pairwork crossword

AIM: to practise using vocabulary connected to holidays and travel by working together to complete a crossword

LANGUAGE: holidays, travel, holiday activities

GENRE: pairwork

MATERIALS: a copy of the worksheet for every pair of students, cut into two as indicated

CLASS TIME: 30 minutes

PROCEDURE:

- Organize students into pairs and ask them to sit facing each other. Give out worksheet A to Student As and worksheet B to Student Bs. Make sure students can't see their partner's sheet. Explain that A and B have the same crossword but with different words missing. They have to describe or define words to each other to complete their crosswords. Tell them that all the words are from Unit 6 and are related to the theme of travel and holidays.

- Give students a few minutes to check they know the meaning of the words that are already completed in their crossword, and to think about how they will define them to their partner.

- Students take turns to ask each other for clues to their missing words, e.g. *What's 1 across?* One student must define or describe the word for their partner, who then writes the word in his/her crossword. Students can help each other with clues if necessary, e.g. by giving the first or last letter of the word.

- When students have finished they compare their crosswords to make sure they have the same words and have spelt them correctly.

Unit 6C Getting around roleplay

AIM: to express travel needs and make offers of help by taking part in a roleplay

LANGUAGE: useful language for getting around; travel

GENRE: whole class

MATERIALS: a copy of the worksheet for every twelve students, cut into twelve role cards as indicated

CLASS TIME: 30 minutes

PROCEDURE:

- Copy one worksheet per twelve students and cut into six 'need' role cards and six 'offer' role cards.

- Write *NEED* on the board, and ask students how they can express travel needs and wishes (see Student's Book page 76, e.g. *How do I get to …?, I'm coming in by plane/bus/coach*, etc.)

- Write *OFFER* on the board. Ask students how they can make offers of travel help (e.g. *I can/'ll … give you a lift / come out and get you, You can / could borrow …*) and how they can offer travel suggestions (e.g. *You could just …, Alternatively, you could …, You can hop on …, It's only a ten-minute …, The easiest thing is to …*)

- Give one 'need' or 'offer' card to each student. In classes of fewer than twelve students, make sure you distribute equal numbers of need and offer cards, or give students more than one need or offer card. Ask students to write NEED or OFFER on the back of their card(s).

- Tell students to walk around the room talking to different students. When a student with a need card meets a student with an offer card they should have a conversation. At the end of the conversation, if the person with a need card has received *either* a satisfactory offer of help *or* enough information to enable them to get around independently, the pair can swap their cards. If not, they should keep their cards. In either case, they should then find new partners and start new conversations.

Unit 7A I bet you agree with all of them!

AIM: to practise conditional language by playing a game

LANGUAGE: zero and first conditionals with *unless, as long as*; also *used to, get used to*; vocabulary connected to raising children (verbs)

GENRE: groupwork

MATERIALS: a copy of the worksheet for every group of three or four students, cut into cards as indicated; a piece of paper and a pen for each student

CLASS TIME: 30 minutes

PROCEDURE:

- Organize the class into groups of three or four. Tell each player to write down their groupmates' names on a piece of paper. Give each group a full set of cards and put them face down in the middle of the table. Player 1 turns over the first card and reads out the sentence with the three different endings (i.e. three times). They then put it on the table for everyone to see. The other players then write down how many of the statements they agree with – 0, 1, 2 or 3. Meanwhile, Player 1 writes down next to each of his/her groupmates' names how many of the statements he or she thinks each of his/her groupmates agrees with.

- When everyone's ready, Player 1 must declare his/her guesses, e.g. *I don't reckon you agree with any of them! I think you agree with two of the statements.* He/She gets a point for every correct number he/she says. Students can then briefly tell each other which (if any) of the endings they agree with and why. If a player thinks someone is bluffing they can challenge them to justify their answer.

- It's Player 2's turn next, and the game continues until all the cards have been used up.

- At the end, groups go back through the cards, identifying which statements they all agree on.

Unit 7B The same or different?

AIM: to practise using vocabulary connected to raising children, habits, food and weddings by describing and comparing pictures

LANGUAGE: raising children (verbs), food, weddings

GENRE: pairwork

MATERIALS: a copy of the worksheet for every pair of students, cut into A and B sections as indicated

CLASS TIME: 30 minutes

PROCEDURE:

- Tell students you are going to give them a sheet with eight pictures on. They need to find out which of the pictures are *exactly the same* as the pictures on their partner's sheet, and which of them are *slightly different*. They must talk about the eight pictures without looking at each other's sheet.

- Organize the class into Group A and Group B. Give Student A worksheets to all the students in Group A and Student B worksheets to all the students in Group B. Give them about five minutes in pairs to practise describing the eight pictures.

- Regroup students into AB pairs, making sure they can't see each other's sheet. Tell them to talk about each picture in turn, and then to write S (same) or D (different) in the box next to it when they have reached a decision. Allow about 10 to 15 minutes.

- Then join pairs with other pairs to compare their answers, making sure Student As don't look at the B sheets yet, and vice versa.

- Finally, check answers with the whole class. Elicit the correct answers, and encourage students to describe the pictures as they do so. Pay particular attention to students' pronunciation of the vocabulary, giving feedback as appropriate.

ANSWERS

1 D – In Student A's picture **the groom** is talking but in Student B's picture the **bride** is talking.

2 S – Both pictures show a meal of almonds, yogurt and fruit juice.

3 S – Both pictures show a man encouraging a child to swim. He isn't forcing the child to swim.

4 D – In Student A's picture the woman has got a bottle of **still (not fizzy)** water but in Student B's picture she's got a bottle of **fizzy** water. (They're at a hen do.)

5 S – Both pictures show some chocolate, a jug, a bowl of raspberries and a woman's hand wearing an engagement ring and a wedding ring.

6 D – In Student A's picture the woman is **praising** the girl, but in Picture B she's **rewarding** the girl.

7 D – In Student A's picture the male student **is switching off his phone**, but in Picture B **it's on**.

8 D – In Student A's picture there's a **fly** on the basket but in Student B's picture there's a **caterpillar** on the basket.

Unit 7C Traditions web search

AIM: to practise describing traditions by researching coming-of-age traditions around the world and sharing and comparing the findings

LANGUAGE: describing traditions

GENRE: groupwork

MATERIALS: a copy of the worksheet for every three students, cut into three sections as indicated. Students will need access to the internet. If you have a lot of students from Latin America, Japan or Brazil, you may wish to suggest different coming-of-age traditions celebrated by different cultures.

CLASS TIME: 60 minutes

PROCEDURE:

- Tell students they are going to do a web search to find out about three ceremonies around the world. (Don't tell them they are coming-of-age ceremonies at this stage.)

- Give Student A sheets to all the Student As, student B sheets to all the Student Bs and Student C sheets to all the Student Cs. Tell them they need to fill in all the columns on their sheet. If access to the internet is limited, put students in AA BB CC pairs or AAA BBB CCC groups to do the research.

- Allow students 15 to 20 minutes to research the ceremony named on their sheets and make notes to answer the questions. Monitor as students work, making sure they're filling in their sheets correctly (see Answers below).

- Give students about ten minutes to prepare how they will describe the tradition they've researched to other students in the class. You could remind them to look at the language for describing traditions on Student's Book page 88.

- When they're ready, put students into ABC groups to compare what they've found out by taking turns to describe the tradition they've researched to the others in the group. You could ask students to make brief notes as they listen in order for them to be able to compare and contrast the traditions at the end.

- Ask the whole class: *What do the three traditions have in common?* (They're all coming-of-age traditions.)

- Put students in small groups again to discuss whether coming-of-age traditions in their own country are very similar or different to the traditions they've researched and discussed. Bring the lesson to a close by asking some students to tell the whole class about coming-of-age traditions in their own country.

ANSWERS

Tradition 1	Tradition 2	Tradition 3
The Quinceañera	Seijin-no-Hi	The Bullet Ant Ritual
Mexico, and many other Latin American countries	Japan	the state of Amazonas in Brazil
15-year-old girls	20-year-old men and girls	13-year-old boys of the Sateré-Mawe people
Coming of age	Coming of age	Coming of age
A ceremony at church is followed by a big party with lots of food and dancing. At the party, the girl gives one of her dolls to a younger girl and changes her flat shoes for high-heeled shoes.	The girls wear kimonos (traditional Japanese robes) with long sleeves, traditional sandals, fake fur scarves and flowers in their hair. The men also wear traditional clothes. A speech is given by a local government official and then there's a big party.	The boys have to dance for ten minutes while wearing a glove full of ants that have very painful stings, without crying.
It symbolizes the girl giving up her childhood and becoming a woman.	It symbolizes the fact that when people reach the age of 20 in Japan they can drink, smoke and vote.	It symbolizes the fact that in this culture men are expected to experience pain without tears.

Unit 8A Is it a good thing?

AIM: to practise using conditional language to talk about your life and what you would like to change

LANGUAGE: second, third and mixed conditionals, *wish* and *if only*

GENRE: pairwork; whole class

MATERIALS: a copy of the worksheet for each student

CLASS TIME: 30 minutes

PROCEDURE:

- Draw one smiling and one sad face on the board, with plenty of space around each one. Add a thought cloud above each face and write in each one *I don't have a lot of money.*

- Draw speech bubbles coming from the two faces. Elicit what the first person might be saying, e.g. *I wish I had a lot of money. If I had a lot of money I'd travel round the world* and write this in the speech bubble. Then elicit what the second person might be saying, e.g. *I'm glad I don't have much money* and write it in the speech bubble. Point out that we usually use *glad* instead of *happy* when we are talking about things we don't want to change.

- Check students understand *colour blind* (= a decreased ability to see differences in colour).

- Give one worksheet to each student in the class and ask them to read it and to draw an arrow to 'Yes' if a statement is true for them or to 'No' if it's false. Allow about five minutes for this stage.

- Ask students to reflect on which of the factors on the list they're happy with and why, which they would like to change and why, and what it would mean for them if they could change it. Tell them to write:
  – SIX sentences with *I'm glad*
  – THREE sentences with *I wish* or *If only*
  – THREE second conditional sentences
  – THREE third or mixed conditional sentences.
  Tell them that in order to do this they should make grammatical changes to the sentences on the sheet as needed. Use the first two sentences as examples, e.g. *I'm glad I'm studying English. / I wish I wasn't studying English. / If I wasn't studying English, I'd be studying German. / I'm glad this isn't an exam. / If this was an exam, I'd be feeling really nervous.*

- Put students in pairs to share and compare the sentences they have written. Encourage them to give reasons for what they have written and to ask about and comment on each other's sentences. Also ask the pairs to notice whether they have chosen similar things that they are happy with and that they would like to change.

- Now ask students to move around the class and to compare and discuss their sentences with a few more partners.

- Ask students to return to their original partner and to report back on whether they noticed any patterns in what people are happy with and what they would like to change.

- Close the activity with a group feedback stage focusing on what things on their list different students are happy with and why.

Unit 8B Define that word!

AIM: to practise using vocabulary items from Unit 8 by playing a guessing game

LANGUAGE: noun suffixes (jobs and work), strong feelings

GENRE: groupwork

MATERIALS: a copy of the worksheet for every six to eight students, cut into 42 cards as indicated; 42 blank cards for every six to eight students; a stopwatch or mobile phone for each group to use as a timer

CLASS TIME: 30 minutes

PROCEDURE:

- Write the phrase *bucket list* on the board and underneath it write a list of four words: *experience, die, hope, aim.*

- Now ask the class to think of a definition for *bucket list* that doesn't use any of those four words. Explain that they are going to play a game which works in a similar way: they will be using game cards that each have a main word from Unit 8 at the top and four smaller words below it. They must define as many of the main words as they can for their teammates to guess, but they mustn't use the smaller words in their definitions. First, though, they are going to prepare their own cards to add to the ones given on the worksheet.

- Put students in pairs and give each pair five blank pieces of paper or 'cards'. Give them 10 minutes to prepare their own game cards like the one on the board using vocabulary from Units 1 to 7.

- Organize the class into groups of six to eight students and then divide each of those groups into Team A and Team B. Give each group a set of game cards, face down in a pile. Redistribute the 'home-made' cards so that each group has an equal amount (these should be ones they haven't made themselves). Tell them to *shuffle* (= mix) them into their pile ready for the game to begin.

- Player 1 from Team A has one minute to define as many words from the pile as possible, without using any of the 'forbidden' words below it. Every word his/her teammates say correctly wins a point. A member of the other team should time one minute and monitor to make sure none of the smaller words is used. After one minute, Player 1 from Team B then takes their turn for a minute, then Player 2 from Team A and so on.

- If a player doesn't know what one of the main words means, they can return that card to the bottom of the pile and take another card, but if a player accidentally uses one of their 'forbidden' words in a definition they must discard that card and they mustn't use it again.

- The team that have successfully defined most words at the end of the game are the winners.

Unit 8C What do we have in common?

AIM: to practise language used for talking about preferences by finding out what people have in common

LANGUAGE: talking about preferences

GENRE: groupwork

MATERIALS: a copy of the worksheet for each student

CLASS TIME: 30 minutes

PROCEDURE:

- Write *I prefer …* and *I'd prefer …* on the board. Elicit the difference in use (*I prefer* = talking about preferences in general, *I'd prefer* = talking about a preference on a specific occasion), and some example endings (e.g. *I prefer swimming to running. I'd prefer to walk to the station this afternoon.*) See how many other expressions students can remember (see Student's Book page 100).

- Give one worksheet to every student in the class and give students time to read the sheet and complete the last seven questions with their own ideas. Then tell students to make a note of their own answers in the column headed 'Me'.

- Ask students to stand up and move around the class, asking and answering the questions. Tell students they should use the language for talking about preferences rather than just giving one-word answers. When they find someone with the same answer as them they should write that person's name in the column marked 'Someone with the same answer'. Tell students they can only put the same name four times. This is to ensure that they speak to plenty of different people.

- Stop the activity when a few students have found a name for every question, or after about 20 minutes.

- To close the activity, ask individual students to tell the whole class whether they spoke to anyone with four preferences that were the same as their own. If so, who was it and what preferences did they have in common?

Unit 9A Keep talking!

AIM: to practise using verb patterns with reporting verbs by playing a board game

LANGUAGE: verb patterns, also reporting verbs

GENRE: groupwork

MATERIALS: a copy of the worksheet for each group of three or four students; a stopwatch or mobile phone for each group to use as a timer

CLASS TIME: 45 minutes

PROCEDURE:

- Organize the class into groups of three or four. Make sure each group has a stopwatch or mobile phone to use as a timer.

- Explain that they are going to play a speaking game in which students will take turns to choose questions from a board. The aim of the game is to put their initials on as many of the squares on the board as possible. To do this, they must either talk about a topic for about a minute, perform a task such as thanking another student, or complete a stopwatch challenge. The time limit for a stopwatch challenge is 30 seconds. With a stopwatch challenge, a player can only write their initials if they have named the required number of things for that task. If they haven't successfully listed all the things, another player can choose that square when it's their turn, repeat what has already been said, and then add their own answers.

- Give one worksheet to each group and allow at least 30 minutes for them to play the game.

- To close the activity, ask students *Which questions were easy/difficult to answer? Who was asked to do something in your group? Did they do it? Who was asked to draw something in your group? What did they draw?*

Unit 9B She's asking him to go away!

AIM: to practise using reporting verbs and verb patterns by performing and listening to mini-dialogues

LANGUAGE: reporting verbs, also verb patterns

GENRE: pairwork; whole class

MATERIALS: a copy of the worksheet for every 16 students in the class, cut into sixteen cards as indicated

CLASS TIME: 30 minutes

PROCEDURE:

- Draw a stick woman and a stick man on the board. As an example of the activity, draw a speech bubble coming from the woman's mouth and write the words *Please can you _____ ?* in it. Elicit some different ways of finishing the sentence and choose one to write in the speech bubble, e.g. *go away*, *help me*, *stop singing*. Now ask students to summarize what's happening by using a reporting verb, e.g. *She's **asking** him to go away/to help her/to stop singing.*

- Give one card to every student in the class. Tell them to keep their cards secret for now. Give them a few minutes to look at the reporting verb at the bottom of their card and then to read and complete the dialogue above it. Monitor, giving help and ideas as necessary.

- Put students in pairs (making sure that no two students with the same cards sit together) and give them another five minutes to practise reading their two mini-dialogues together. Encourage them to put expression into what they say.

- Finally, pairs take turns to perform their mini-dialogues to the rest of the class. The other students watch and listen. The first student to call out the appropriate reporting verb completely accurately wins a point for their pair. The pair with the most points at the end of the game are the winners.

Unit 9C Have you heard about James and Vicky?

AIM: to practise reporting what others say by taking part in a roleplay about gossip

LANGUAGE: reporting what you have heard

GENRE: whole class

MATERIALS: a copy of the worksheet for every four students, cut into eight gossip cards and four response cards as indicated

CLASS TIME: 30 minutes

PROCEDURE:

- Write *Have you heard about James and Vicky?* on the board and ask students to think of ways the gossip might continue. Example answers: *Someone told me (that) they've split up. / It seems that they're having some money problems at the moment. / According to my sister, they're engaged.*

- Review the four topics that people commonly gossip about that students saw on Student's Book page 112 (money and status, other people's relationships, celebrities' lives, other people's character and reputation). Tell students they are going to do a roleplay in which they will be gossiping and reacting to gossip in different ways.

- Check students understand *prime minister* and *lead singer*. Hand out two gossip cards to each student. Give students five to ten minutes to read and complete their gossip cards. Tell students that they can change any of the people on their cards if they want to, but celebrity cards must have a celebrity on them. Encourage them to be as imaginative and sensational as they can be. Monitor, giving help and ideas where necessary. When they've finished, ask students to put their gossip card(s) to one side for now, face down.

- Give each student a response card. Explain that it tells them how to act during the roleplay. Before starting the roleplay, review the language of reporting what you have heard (Student's Book page 112).

- Ask students to take their gossip cards, stand up and walk around the room, reporting the gossip on their cards to as many different people as possible. Tell them to listen to each other carefully and react to the gossip they hear according to the information on their response card.

- At the feedback stage, ask: *What was the most shocking piece of gossip you heard? Who was most interested in your gossip? Who wasn't interested? Who didn't seem to believe it at all?*

Unit 10A That's me!

AIM: to practise using relative clauses and articles by completing personalized sentences about people, places and times and using these as discussion points

LANGUAGE: relative clauses; articles; words connected to the senses, careers, personal qualities; verb and noun collocations

GENRE: groupwork

MATERIALS: a copy of the worksheet for each pair of students, cut into 16 cards as indicated. You will also need an envelope or container for each group of six students.

CLASS TIME: 30 minutes

PROCEDURE:

- Choose one of the unfinished sentences from the activity and write it on the board. Elicit different ways of completing it, e.g. *Something I always have with me is … my mobile phone/my house keys/a photo of my children.*

- Put students in pairs and give each pair a set of unfinished sentences. Ask them to spread them out on the table, face down, and to take eight each. Give them 10 to 15 minutes to finish their unfinished sentences in any way they like, but in such a way that the sentences are true. They should not write their names or let their partner see what they're writing.

- Join pairs together to make groups of six. Ask students to fold up their completed pieces of paper and put them in the envelope or container.

- Students now take turns to take a piece of paper and read out what's written on it. The others in the group try to guess who wrote it, giving reasons for their answer. E.g. *What I love doing most is playing computer games. I think that's you, Victor, because you're always talking about the computer games you like.* Once it's been established who wrote the sentences, the writer can briefly say more about their sentence and/or the others can ask them questions.

- Ask students to report to the whole class anything funny/interesting/surprising, etc. that they found out about the others in their group.

Unit 10B Call my bluff

AIM: to practise the use of relative clauses, articles and vocabulary from Unit 10 by playing a bluffing game

LANGUAGE: relative clauses; articles; words connected to the senses, careers; verb and noun collocations

GENRE: groupwork

MATERIALS: a copy of the worksheet for each pair of students, cut into Team A and B sections as indicated

CLASS TIME: 40 minutes

PROCEDURE:

- Divide the class into two. Give half the class a copy of the Team A worksheet and half the class a copy of the Team B worksheet and explain that they are going to use these sheets to quiz the other team.

- Explain that only one of the two definitions given for each word or expression on their worksheet is correct. Organize students into pairs within their teams and give them about ten minutes to guess which the correct answers are. They can check their answers by looking in a dictionary, looking online or asking you. Don't do a whole class check of the correct answers at this stage!

- Give the pairs about 15 to 20 minutes to write a second false definition for each word or expression. Monitor and give lots of help at this stage as this is quite a challenging activity. Make sure their definitions sound natural and convincing, and check that students are using articles and relative clauses correctly.

- Reorganize the class so that students are in groups of four, each made up of one Team A pair and one Team B pair. Explain that the teams are going to take it in turns to read out one of their words or expressions and its three definitions without saying or giving away which is the correct definition. The opposing team must discuss and guess the correct definition.

- Teams score one point for each correct answer and one point if the opposing team believes their made-up definition is correct. The pair with the highest score are the winners.

ANSWERS

Team A

1 a 2 c 3 c 4 b 5 a 6 b

Team B

1 c 2 a 3 a 4 a 5 b 6 c

Unit 10C What's your career personality type?

AIM: to practise describing skills, talents and experience by using a flowchart to roleplay giving careers advice

LANGUAGE: describing skills, talents and experience

GENRE: pairwork; groupwork

MATERIALS: a copy of the Student A worksheet and a copy of the Student B worksheet for every pair of students

CLASS TIME: 30 to 45 minutes

PROCEDURE:

- Raise interest in the topic by asking: *Has anyone been to see a careers adviser? Was it a useful experience? Why/Why not?*

- Tell students they are going to complete a flow chart (show one of the worksheets to the class to show what a flow chart is, if necessary) about career personality types.

- Organize students into pairs. Give Student A worksheets to Student As and Student B worksheets to Student Bs. Ask them to sit facing each other if possible, and tell them not to look at each other's sheet. Explain that they each have the information that is missing from their partner's worksheet. Students look at the different personality types and complete the missing information by asking their partner *What sort of jobs are good for helpers/persuaders?* etc.

- When all the students have finished this information exchange, regroup students into new pairs. Student A in each pair takes the role of career adviser, and uses the

flow chart to interview Student B. Point out that it may be helpful to repeat the process and identify a secondary career personality type during the simulation. Students should also discuss what jobs from the list (if any) might suit them. They then swap roles.

- When the interviews have finished, ask students to stand up and move around the class, comparing their results to find as many different career personality types in the room as possible, and to discuss which (if any) of the jobs on the sheet they think are good for them, giving their reasons why.

- When students have finished and returned to their seats, they can tell their partner what they found out about their classmates.

- At the feedback stage, find out who are the helpers, persuaders, organizers, etc. in the class. You could also ask: *Can you identify what career personality types members of your family are? Do you like doing personality tests like these? Why not? How useful do you think they are?*

Unit 11A Lessons in life

AIM: to practise talking about learning, education, skills, experience and memory by playing a board game

LANGUAGE: *could, was able to, managed to, succeeded in*; also words connection to education; homonyms

GENRE: groupwork

MATERIALS: a copy of the worksheet for each group of three or four students; a die for each group; a counter for each student

CLASS TIME: 30 minutes

PROCEDURE:

- Review the vocabulary from the unit by writing the key words *learn, take, acquire* and *get* on the board and circling them. See how many education-related collocations and expressions students can make by adding words around them.

- Organize the class into groups of three or four and give one worksheet and a die to each group. Students place their counters on 'Start' then take it in turns to roll the die, move their counter and give an answer to the question on the square that they land on. They should try to talk for a minute about the personalized discussion questions.

- The first player to reach the 'Finish' square is the winner, but they have to throw the exact number in order to reach it.

- At the feedback stage, invite individual students to report to the class one or two things that they learned about their classmates during the activity.

Unit 11B I was going to come, but I missed the train.

AIM: to practise future in the past clauses by playing a game of dominoes

LANGUAGE: future in the past + *but*

GENRE: groupwork

MATERIALS: a copy of the worksheet for each pair of students and a pair of scissors for each group of two to four students

CLASS TIME: 30 minutes

PROCEDURE:

- Draw a picture of a few traditional domino playing pieces on the board and elicit/teach the word *dominoes*. Check students know how the game works. Explain that they are going to play a game of 'future in the past' dominoes but that they have to prepare the cards first.

- Write *I would have come to your party, but …* on the board and elicit different ways of finishing the sentence, e.g. *I wasn't feeling well, I lost the invitation and I don't know your address or phone number, I had to work that evening, I fell asleep in front of the TV.*

- Point out that after *was going to, would have* and *was/were supposed to* we use *but …* . However, after *was about to* and *almost managed to* we usually use *but then …* .

- Organize the class into pairs and give one copy of the worksheet to each pair of students.

- Point out the way the dominoes are arranged and explain that they are numbered on the worksheet to show which parts of a sentence are connected to each other. In pairs, students must complete the clauses in squares 1b, 2b, 3b, etc. so that they logically follow the clauses in 1a, 2a, 3a, etc. While students do this, monitor each pair, making sure their sentences are correct. If the sentences are not grammatically correct at this stage, the game will not work. Offer help and ideas if needed.

- When they have completed the worksheet, ask pairs to join with another pair. If there are an uneven number of pairs, ask three pairs to work together. Give each pair or group a pair of scissors and tell them to cut the dominoes out as indicated. Make sure they cut the numbers off the dominoes.

- Each group should shuffle their two sets of dominoes together and pass them to another group. They then play the game. To do this, they take four dominoes each and leave the rest in a pile face down. Player 1 puts down any of their dominoes face up. Player 2 puts down one of their dominoes at either end of the first domino so that a sentence is made which makes logical sense, if they are able to. The players take turns to add their dominoes. If a player can't go because they can't make a sentence which makes sense, they take a domino from the top of the pile and put it down if they can. If students think a sentence sounds wrong, they can challenge it, and the player who made it must try to explain why it makes sense. Other players can vote on whether the sentence is acceptable or not. The first player to get rid of all their cards is the winner.

- When all the groups have finished playing, they can shuffle their cards and play again or pass their cards on to another group.

Unit 11C Which teambuilding day?

AIM: to practise language used for getting clarification by describing and discussing two teambuilding days

LANGUAGE: getting clarification

GENRE: pairwork; whole class

MATERIALS: a copy of the worksheet for every pair of students, cut into two sections as indicated

CLASS TIME: 30 minutes

PROCEDURE:

- Write: *I don't understand, Slow down, I can't hear you* and *I didn't hear you* in speech bubbles on the board and see how many ways students can remember to express these four ideas politely (Student's Book page 136).

- Find out if anyone in the class has been on a teambuilding day. Ask *What sort of activities did you do? Did you enjoy it? Why?/Why not?*

- Write *Forest Teambuilding Day* and *City Teambuilding Day* on the board. Tell students they are going to work in pairs. They each have information about one of the teambuilding days, but they need to ask their partner questions to find out more about the other day. As they do so, they should try to use as much of the 'Real life' language for getting clarification as they can. Point out that students should say as little as possible when they are in the 'giving information' role so that their partner has to work harder to get the clarification they need.

- Hand out Student A worksheets to all the Student As and Student B worksheets to all the Student Bs. Make sure students don't look at each other's worksheets. Allow about 15 to 20 minutes for this information exchange stage. Monitor students, encouraging them to ask for clarification (including examples) if you don't hear them doing so.

- When the pairs have exchanged all their information, give them a few minutes to discuss which of the two days they'd rather do and why.

Unit 12A Find someone who …

AIM: to practise using vocabulary connected to money, services and work by asking and answering questions

LANGUAGE: vocabulary connected to money, services; also causative *have* and *get*

GENRE: whole class

MATERIALS: a copy of the worksheet for each student

CLASS TIME: 30 minutes

PROCEDURE:

- Write: *Find someone who finds it easy to save money.* on the board. Elicit the question *Do you find it easy to save money?*

- Show the class the worksheet but don't hand it out yet. Tell them that they are going to see how many *yes* answers they can get from different people. To do this, they need to move around the class and ask people questions. When they get a *yes* answer they must write that person's name on the sheet and then move on to talk to a different person.

- Assign each student a number between 1 and 18 and tell them that's the question they should start with and then give a worksheet to every student in the class. Give students about five minutes to read through the sheet and think about the questions they need to ask, then get them moving round the classroom and talking.

- Stop the activity after about 15 to 20 minutes, or when someone has got a name in every square, or when someone has run out of people to ask.

- Run the feedback stage as a whole class discussion by asking questions such as *So, Ahmed, did you find anyone who can fix a tap? Does anyone have a different name for that question?* and also asking follow-up questions like *How did you learn to fix a tap? What sort of business would you like to set up? Why don't you ever have your car washed?*

Unit 12B Opinions and attitudes questionnaire

AIM: to practise using focus adverbs, causative *have* and *get* by completing and discussing a questionnaire about various aspects of life, work, money and society

LANGUAGE: focus adverbs: *only, just, even*; causative *have* and *get*; also vocabulary connected to money and services

GENRE: pairwork

MATERIALS: a copy of the worksheet for each student

CLASS TIME: 30 to 40 minutes

PROCEDURE:

- Give each student a copy of the questionnaire and give them ten minutes to read it and complete it by marking their opinions with a cross somewhere on each *Agree / Disagree* line. The more strongly they agree or disagree with a statement, the closer to *Agree* or *Disagree* they should put their cross. If they don't have a strong opinion either way, they should put their cross in the middle of the line.

- Put students in pairs to compare their answers, giving reasons for their opinions. Tell students to feel free to move their cross if their partner changes their opinion about something.

- Join pairs with other pairs, and ask them to once again compare and discuss their opinions but this time as a group of four (or six).

- Finally, bring all the groups together and facilitate a whole discussion for five to ten minutes by asking a few questions such as *Which statements did most people agree on? Which statements did people have very different opinions on? Why? Did anyone change their mind about anything? What? Why?*

Unit 12C Would you be willing to move a bit on that?

AIM: to practise the language of negotiation by roleplaying the sale/purchase of a campervan and a tent

LANGUAGE: negotiating

GENRE: pairwork

MATERIALS: a copy of the worksheet for every pair of students, cut into six sections as indicated

CLASS TIME: 45 to 50 minutes

PROCEDURE:

- Write *I want you to change your offer* on the board and elicit the formal way of saying it in a negotiation (= Would you be willing to move a bit on that?). Supply the first two or three words if students are struggling.

- See what other expressions students can remember (Student's Book page 148), again giving the first few words as a prompt.

- Tell students they are going to act out two negotiation roleplays – one in which they're a buyer, and one in which they're a seller.

- Put students into AA and BB pairs or groups to prepare. Give Student A worksheet cards to all the Student As and Student B worksheet cards to all the Student Bs. Give the pairs five to ten minutes to prepare what they're going to say and to decide what information they strategically want to AVOID revealing. Encourage students to be imaginative in what they can say or offer as part of the negotiation. Monitor and make sure all students have completed the missing information on their 'selling card' and that they have prepared questions and circled their choice(s) on their 'buying' card.

- Regroup students into AB pairs. All the pairs should start by doing the tent roleplay. Tell them they can now show each other their 'For Sale' advert but they must not show their other two cards. Encourage students to take their time over the negotiation and to try to reach a deal if they possibly can. Allow five to ten minutes for this stage.

- When they've finished, regroup students into new AB pairs (by moving all the Student As around) to do the campervan roleplay. Again, allow five to ten minutes for this.

- When all the pairs have finished, ask students to go back to their original pairs/groups to compare how successful they were in their negotiations.

- At the whole class feedback stage, ask some individual students *Are you happy with the result of your negotiations? Why? Why not? Do you think you're a good negotiator? Why? Why not?*

Grammar summary: answer key

UNIT 1 (page 157)

1a
1 are becoming
2 has bought
3 have known
4 I often meet
5 She's staying
6 is always
7 It's raining
8 I'm learning

1b
a 6 b 4 c 7 d 8 e 1 f 5 g 2 h 3

2
1 are/'re
2 he's been going
  or he goes
3 haven't seen
4 doesn't like
5 's looking
  or he's been looking
6 have moved
7 'm
8 's ringing

3
1 've been waiting
2 've had
3 's been
4 've been working
5 have they been
6 've been looking
7 've seen it

4
1 from 2012 to 2014
2 twice this week
3 in 1998
4 for a few days
5 since
6 over the last few months
7 for

5
1 have been arguing
2 I've tried
3 's not spoken
  or hasn't spoken
4 helped
5 have given
6 didn't teach
7 've been working

UNIT 2 (page 159)

1a
1 e 2 i 3 b 4 g 5 a 6 f 7 d 8 h 9 c

1b
'd left – e
had completely forgotten – b
had – a
was sitting – c
'd been waiting – d

2
1 it had been raining all night.
2 he hadn't been sleeping well.
3 We hadn't been waiting for long …
4 I had been studying all morning …
5 Had you been looking for a new job for a long time …
6 he had been trying to pass the exam for years.
7 I had been singing all morning.
8 Had Maria been working at the company for long …

3
1 was reading
2 saw
3 decided
4 received
5 had received
6 didn't understand
7 had printed
8 wrote
9 developed
10 had sent

4
1 It can be seen in the British Library in London.
2 It was written and performed by Pharrell Williams.
3 In 2024, they will be held in Paris.
4 It had been stolen two years earlier from a gallery in Oslo.
5 They were never found …
6 While you're reading this sentence, about 1,000 messages are being sent every second.

5
1 was made
2 being read
3 has been downloaded
4 had already been taken out
5 be seen
6 to be awarded

UNIT 3 (page 161)

1
1 won't
2 going to
3 might
4 it's about to
5 isn't going to
6 we might not
7 I'll

2a
1 I'm flying to Canada next month!
2 I'll have some coffee, please.
3 We're going to visit Tom's parents some time next month.
4 I'll make you a sandwich.
5 They're eating out tonight.
6 … so she's going to look for her own place soon.

2b
a 3,6 b 1,5 c 2,4 d 4

3
1 are you going to come or are you coming
2 're going
3 'm meeting or 'm going to meet
4 'll call
5 'll pick
6 's going to come

4
1 will have increased
2 will be using
3 will have started
4 will be producing
5 will have become
6 will be selling
7 will be using

5

1 won't be sitting; will have started
2 'll be teaching; won't have finished
3 won't be driving; will have stopped
4 'll be passing; won't have got
5 Will you be using; won't have fixed

6

1 will have started
2 won't have finished
3 'll be having lunch
4 won't be talking
5 will be working out
6 will have been

UNIT 4 (page 163)

1

1 All the
2 either
3 certain
4 Most
5 Some
6 any
7 no
8 Neither

2

1 each
2 all
3 an
4 any
5 every
6 most of

3

1 any
2 The majority
3 The whole
4 certain
5 both
6 each
7 Either

4

1 plenty of, loads of
2 much, a lot of
3 a lack of, almost no
4 any, a huge amount of
5 a small number of, a few
6 hardly any, almost no

5

1 hardly any
2 too much
3 loads of
4 several
5 a little
6 no/not any

6

1 a 2 b 3 b 4 a

UNIT 5 (page 165)

1

1 to go
2 to help
3 making
4 building
5 work
6 watching
7 to come

2

1 to drive
2 driving
3 drive
4 to exercise
5 exercise
6 exercising
7 working
8 to work
9 work

3

1 to expand
2 to make
3 to take
4 fly
5 queueing
6 hiring
7 write

4

1 b 2 b 3 a 4 b 5 a 6 b

5

1 to calm down
2 to inform
3 drinking
4 living
5 to tell
6 coming

6

1 to organize
2 to talk
3 leaving
4 making
5 to eat
6 sightseeing
7 to join

UNIT 6 (page 167)

1

1 not
2 not wait
3 doesn't think it's
4 not to be
5 Don't
6 don't have to
7 mustn't

2

1 Let's not
2 We don't believe (that)
3 don't have to book a table
4 Don't forget to lock
5 'm afraid not
6 not to spend

3

1 None of
2 neither
3 no
4 either
5 no
6 neither

4

1 Didn't you like
2 Wasn't
3 Isn't he coming
4 Haven't you eaten
5 Don't you have to
6 Shouldn't

5

1 where the station is
2 what time the museum opens
3 what time you're leaving
4 where you were yesterday evening
5 they're not/they aren't going on holiday again (, are they)
6 who that man is

6

1 aren't you
2 is he
3 could they
4 didn't you
5 are we
6 did she
7 have you
8 hasn't he

UNIT 7 (page 169)

1

1 If you ~~won't~~ **don't** book a ticket before you go, you won't get a seat at the concert.
2 If I ~~was~~ **am** late to my lesson, the teacher gets angry.
3 It's dangerous to drive when it ~~will snow~~ **snows** hard.
4 When I finish working, I'll call you.
5 You ~~did~~ **'ll do** better in your exams, if you study hard now.
6 The football match will be cancelled, if the weather is bad.

2

1 You won't get the job unless you practise for your interview.
2 You can borrow my car as long as you promise to be careful.
3 You can go out as long as you finish all your homework.
4 Unless she works hard, she'll never be successful.
5 You can borrow my umbrella as long as you remember to give it back.
6 Unless you practise every day, you won't get better at playing the piano.
7 We can go out for a picnic as long as it doesn't rain.

3

1 g – Please call me as soon as you **get** this message.
2 a – Before they go out for a walk this morning, they**'ll have** something to eat.
3 b – I'll wait with you at the station until your train **arrives**.
4 d – While you're cleaning the house, I**'ll take** the dog out for a walk.
5 e – You'll never be able to run the marathon unless you **start** training.
6 f – After he finishes work, he**'ll join** his friends at the gym.
7 c – I always get a headache when I **don't drink** enough water.

4

1 I would cook with my mother a lot when I was young.
2 We used to live in the town centre until two years ago.
3 He didn't use to like drinking coffee before a long run.
4 When they were little, their grandma would take them to the cinema once a month.
5 Did you use to have a best friend at school?
6 For years, I would visit my aunt in Lima every summer.
7 Our football coach would make us run for twenty minutes before each session.

5

1 'm used to making speeches
2 'm getting used to commuting
3 wasn't used to eating
4 Are you used to wearing
5 got used to living
6 's not used to cooking

6

1 used to dream
2 wasn't used to seeing
3 get used to living
4 got used to taking
5 I'm not used to waking up *or* I haven't got used to waking up
6 I'm used to trying *or* I've got used to trying
7 get used to doing

UNIT 8 (page 171)

1

1 had; 'd/would take
2 'd/would have worn; 'd/had known
3 'd/would go; had
4 wouldn't have chosen; hadn't encouraged
5 spent; wouldn't be
6 'd/would have done; 'd/had practised

2

1 d (ii) 2 a (i) 3 b (ii) 4 f (i) 5 c (i) 6 e (ii)

3

1 hadn't left; wouldn't be
2 spoke; 'd/would have understood
3 'd/would come; hadn't; seen
4 lived; 'd/would have gone
5 would be; hadn't met
6 weren't/wasn't; 'd/would have been able

4

1 were/was
2 didn't have to
3 lived
4 could
5 weren't
6 saw/could see

5

1 I'd had
2 didn't have to
3 had taken
4 there were
5 wouldn't make

6

1 wouldn't keep
2 'd/had learned
3 wouldn't shout
4 'd/would clean
5 hadn't left
6 'd/had bought

UNIT 9 (page 173)

1

1 b 2 f 3 a 4 d 5 c 6 e

2

1 recommended visiting
2 threatened to leave
3 apologized for being
4 invited me/us
5 advised her to go
6 encouraged me to learn

3

1 eliminating
2 to watch
3 to stop
4 to recycle

5 to do
6 to introduce
7 starting

4

1 It is believed that two prisoners have escaped.
2 It is known that the journalist **is** to be arrested.
3 The director is expected **to** resign.
4 The photos are thought to **have** been taken in 1990.
5 She is said to **be writing** a book at the moment.

5

1 to arrive, to be arriving
2 to have found
3 to be living
4 to be
5 to cause, to be causing, to have caused
6 to have been caused

6

1 is understood (that) the high street is being closed.
2 is believed to have spent a lot of money on it.
3 is reported that there will be live music, a fairground and food stalls.
4 is said to have been really crowded and badly organized.
5 is thought that the organizers have made some improvements.
6 are expected to be offering free food on the first day.

UNIT 10 (page 175)

1

1 ✓
2 ✗ She hasn't found **a** job yet.
3 ✗ I'd like to live in ~~the~~ Paris.
4 ✓
5 ✗ They're going to the museum in **the** morning.
6 ✓
7 ✗ That's probably **the** best film I've ever seen.

2

1 I had a long chat about gardening with **a** man …
2 Oh, it's **the** man over there.
3 That's Thomas – he's **a** lovely neighbour.
4 Yes, he showed me **a** picture of it on his phone.
5 Well, he seems very ordinary, but he's actually **a** famous mountaineer!
6 And he takes tour groups up mountains three or four times **a** year.
7 He also gives talks about it all around **the** world.
8 We only talked about **the** best flowers to plant in spring.

3

1 *the*
2 zero article
3 *the*

4 *The*
5 *the*
6 *the*

---

7 *a*
8 *a*

9 zero article
10 *a*

4a

1 c – that/which
2 a – where
3 f – who/that

4 b – what
5 d – that/when
6 e – whose

4b

1 and 5

5

1 That's the woman (who) I played tennis with last week.
2 Is this the shop where you bought your new coat?
3 This isn't the same airport that/which we flew to last year.
4 Are you the person (that/who) I spoke to when I called earlier?
5 Please show me the credit card (that/which) you paid with.
6 This is the kind of music (that/which) I always listen to when I'm driving.

6

1 We live in Salto, which is in the north west of Uruguay.
2 I went to the cinema with Igor last night, which was fun.
3 My friend Louis, who is a doctor, has just started a new job.
4 The museum was closed when we went there, which was disappointing.
5 You should speak about this to my sister Lena, who knows a lot about this kind of thing.
6 DDT bank, which employs over 20,000 people, has serious financial problems. *or* DDT bank, which has serious financial problems, employs over 20,000 people.

UNIT 11 (page 177)

1

Sentences 2 (*couldn't*) 3 (*could*) 5 (*couldn't*)

2

Correct forms:

1 was able to, managed to
2 couldn't
3 succeeded in
4 managed to, was able to
5 couldn't, weren't able to
6 was able to, could

3

1 f – to run
2 a – use
3 e – increasing

4 c – to paint
5 b – to visit
6 d – make

4

1 was about to go
2 would have called
3 weren't going to be,
  wouldn't be

4 would definitely be
5 would improve
6 was supposed to use

5

1 were going to
2 was about to
3 wouldn't

4 was supposed to
5 would have

6

1 was about to go
2 was going to go
3 was supposed to be

4 you'd/you would never
  borrow
5 'd/would have bought

UNIT 12 (page 179)

1

1 don't think
2 surprised
3 less

4 'their biggest fans'
5 other things, too
6 looked

2

1 only
2 just
3 just
4 even/just

5 just
6 even
7 just

3

1 just/only
2 just/only
3 just

4 even
5 even
6 even

4

1 Amy is getting/having her hair cut
2 We got/had our windows fixed
3 'm going to get/have my car washed
4 got/had our bags carried
5 had/got some food delivered
6 get/have your eyes checked

5

1 repainted
2 stay
3 to bring

4 check
5 made
6 to fit

6

1 the little jobs done
2 your/the house cleaned
3 to find the perfect gift
4 the ingredients delivered
5 do the cooking
6 an information pack sent

Workbook: answer key

Unit 1

1a (pages 4 and 5)

1

b

2

1 b 2 b 3 b 4 c 5 a 6 a

3

1 truth (line 6) 2 strength (line 9) 3 warmth (line 18)
4 length (line 25) 5 depth (line 36)

4

1 is dying out (line 1–2), France is changing and perhaps becoming (line 29–30)
2 we work with (line 3–4), we chat to (line 4), they reserve (real intimacy) (line 32)
3 friendships have lost (line 9), you have ever visited (line 17)
4 have been declining (line 12)

5

1 have you spent *or* have you been spending
2 Do you consider
3 do you have
4 is still increasing
5 Have you made
6 have you known
7 do you see
8 do you look for

6

1 intimate, close, strong 2 strong 3 close, true
4 complete 5 casual

7

1 student 2 companion 3 acquaintance 4 flat
5 blood 6 passing

8

1 serious, good fun 2 laid-back 3 unreliable
4 energetic 5 shy, outgoing 6 considerate

9

1 out with 2 up with 3 on 4 round 5 by 6 up with 7 up

1b (pages 6 and 7)

1

1 T 2 F 3 T 4 F 5 T 6 F

2

1 rate 2 boom 3 retirement 4 lifestyle
5 expectancy 6 developed

3

1 has declined, was
2 have improved, did
3 've also learned
4 has made, didn't have
5 have increased, was
6 has risen, 've been spending *or* are spending

4

1 have raised, hasn't been
2 has been encouraging, have reduced
3 have gone, was
4 had, has been going
5 has been looking, has had

5

1 last year 2 all morning 3 yet 4 before
5 since the age of sixteen 6 in the past 7 so far 8 just

6b

1 A: **Have** you finished using the computer yet? I need to check my emails.
   B: Yes, I **have**. But the internet connection **has** been a bit funny.
   A: What do you mean? **Have**n't you been able to connect or **has** it just been slow?
2 A: How **has** your visit to Scotland been? **Have** you had a good time?
   B: Well, the weather **has** been terrible, but apart from that, it's been wonderful.
   A: No, it **has**n't been a very nice summer, but I'm afraid that's pretty typical.

7

1 I think my parents' generation has been quite lucky.
2 My parents worked hard all their lives, but they both retired when they were sixty and they've been given good pensions. So now they can relax and enjoy themselves.
3 They've said that they don't want to be a burden on us, and that they don't expect us to look after them when they get old.
4 Considering that my husband and I will probably have to work until we are 68, I'm glad they said that.

1c (page 8)

1

c

2

1 F 2 T 3 T 4 T 5 F 6 T 7 F 8 F

3

1 a 2 a 3 c 4 b 5 b 6 c

4a

1 dy<u>na</u>mic 2 fan<u>tas</u>tic 3 eco<u>no</u>mics 4 gene<u>ra</u>tion
5 re<u>stric</u>tion 6 tra<u>di</u>tion
Rule: The penultimate syllable is always stressed.

4b

spe<u>ci</u>fic i<u>tal</u>ics ter<u>ri</u>fic scien<u>ti</u>fic characte<u>ris</u>tic
im<u>pre</u>ssion re<u>la</u>tion inter<u>rup</u>tion transfor<u>ma</u>tion
compre<u>hen</u>sion

1d (page 9)

1

1 – 2 for 3 – 4 – 5 about 6 – 7 on 8 from 9 in
10 with

2a

1 PPS 2 PPC 3 PPS 4 PPC

2b

1 present perfect continuous
2 present perfect simple

3

1 been wondering   2 been working   3 decided
4 been helping   5 finished   6 lost

4

a Fancy bumping into you here
b What a nice surprise
c it obviously suits you
d how's it all going with you
e Do give her my best regards
f great to see you
g Good luck with the job

5a

1 are things
2 I'm doing fine
3 're looking very well
4 's been ages
5 should probably get back
6 I've got to rush

6

Students' own answers.

1e (page 10)

1

1 g   2 c   3 f   4 e   5 a   6 d   7 b

2

1 you're able to **get by** (manage)
2 I **got** a letter (received)
3 I'm trying not to **get** too excited (become)
4 to **get** a job (obtain)
5 Eva is going to **get** married (be)
6 when you **get** a moment to write (have)

3

1 understand   2 put down or stop speaking on
3 bought   4 arrive at or reach   5 take or catch
6 recover from   7 won   8 find or bring or fetch

4

1 received or got   2 am   3 arrived or got   4 sounds
5 have had or have been having   6 were or got
7 hope   8 have recovered
9 hasn't become or hasn't got / doesn't become or doesn't get
10 sounds   11 don't think   12 have ever experienced
13 has happened   14 am trying or have tried or have been
trying   15 haven't been   16 find or get   17 helped or has
helped or has been helping   18 don't really understand or
don't really get

Wordbuilding / Learning skills / Check! (page 11)

1

-*ful*: respectful, helpful, successful (also 'careful')
-*ish*: foolish, childish, selfish
-*ive*: sensitive, decisive, supportive
-*ious/-ous*: ambitious, adventurous, humorous
-*ent/-ant*: dependent, confident, patient
-*al*: practical, emotional, traditional
-*ing*: caring, controlling, loving
-*ate*: considerate, fortunate, passionate

2

Possible answers:
1 dependent   2 caring   3 traditional   4 patient
5 controlling   6 practical   7 humorous   8 fortunate
9 successful   10 ambitious

3

1 decisively   2 take   3 indecisive   4 conclusion

4

Students' own answers.

5

1 b   2 a   3 a and c   4 c   5 b

Unit 2

2a (pages 12 and 13)

1

b

2

1 b   2 c   3 c   4 c   5 a

3

1 a   2 b   3 b   4 c   5 b

4

1 drove   2 made   3 arrived   4 was getting   5 climbed
6 had gone   7 were hanging   8 put   9 moved   10 trapped
11 stood or was standing   12 had crushed or was
crushing   13 hadn't told   14 had already been waiting
15 had decided

5

1 b   2 a   3 c

6

1 had been cycling   2 had left   3 started
4 was shining   5 checked   6 cut

7

1 crashed   2 top   3 stuck   4 cat   5 sung   6 drunk

8

1 drama   2 background   3 main   4 key   5 setting
6 theme   7 moving   8 touching   9 funny   10 filmed

9a

The tenses used to describe the film are: present simple,
present continuous and present perfect.

9b

1 gives   2 begin   3 reaches or has reached
4 grow or are growing   5 are getting

2b (pages 14 and 15)

1

1 That they walk hundreds of miles (across Antarctica) to
  reach their breeding ground.
2 The struggle between life and death.

2

1 have chicks   2 their young   3 dramatic
4 predictable   5 in such hard conditions

3

1 are left, is described
2 was made, was (also) inspired, was impressed
3 haven't (really) been approached
4 will not be fed
5 can be (easily) predicted

4

1
was also **inspired** by the incredible beauty of Antarctica,
the action **is described** by a narrator
They **haven't** really **been approached** by humans before
I **was** really **impressed** by that
2
are left (by the females)
will not be fed (by their mothers)
where the film was made (by the director)
can be easily predicted (by us / by the filmmakers)

5

1 The original French version of *March of the Penguins* was
   released in 2005.
2 In 2006 it was given the award for best documentary by the
   Academy of Motion Arts and Sciences.
3 The film can be seen in over twenty different languages.
4 In the English version, the penguins' voices had been
   changed to the voice of a narrator.
5 The film has been praised for its interest and beauty by
   critics all over the world.
6 Comparisons between the lives of penguins and humans
   have also been made.

6

1 I am often asked that question
2 All of them have been challenged by difficult situations.
3 You are not bothered by the cold so much. *or* You are not
   bothered so much by the cold.
4 So (your) movement must be kept to a minimum.

7a

1 were   2 been   3 will   4 are   5 is   6 was, been

8

1 engage, tell   2 present   3 expressed *or* summed up
4 share   5 brought   6 express *or* sum up

9

1 setting for; thought-provoking book
2 characters are you and me and every other typical passenger
3 book is based on conversations that the author had
4 The idea behind it; can portray modern civilization

2c (page 16)

1

1 T   2 T   3 T   4 F   5 F

2

1 children; adults   2 fairy tale   3 sadness   4 moved
5 moral lessons

3

1 a fine-looking   2 watches closely   3 stops to rest on
4 asks   5 people   6 days   7 becomes ill   8 destroy

4

1 a   2 b

5

1 kept their promise
2 kept an eye on
3 keep him company
4 keep track of
5 keep a record
6 keep a secret

2d (page 17)

1

1 tore   2 broke   3 stuck   4 made   5 froze   6 burst

2

a What a
b That was
c How *or* That was
d How *or* That was
e What
f How
g Poor
h What a *or* That must have been
i How *or* That must have been
j What a *or* That must have been a
Possible answers:
1 a *or* c   2 a *or* j   3 a *or* c *or* i   4 c   5 a   6 a *or* j

3

1 Hannah's passport was out of date.
2 She went to the passport office in London to get a new
   passport.
3 Very stressed.

4

1 Poor   2 awful   3 luck   4 stressful   5 sympathize   6 same

6

Students' own answers.

2e (page 18)

1a

whispered, replied anxiously, moaned, muttered, cried

1b

1 c   2 b   3 g   4 d   5 e   6 a   7 f

2a

1 He said, 'What a surprise!'
2 'I know,' she said, 'that you don't like eating spicy food.'
3 'Do you agree?' he asked.
4 'I don't agree,' he said.

2b

'I don't think this is going to work,' Christopher
sighed. 'We've been trying to build this canoe for three days
and it still looks like a lump of wood. The wood's too hard,'
he added. 'Actually, Christopher,' said Jen encouragingly,
'we are making some progress. What we really need to do is
find some better tools.' Just then Tom screamed, 'I've got it!
Instead of using our penknives directly on the wood, why
don't we make some better tools using our knives?'

3

Model answer:
'Look out,' screamed Fergus, 'I think he's angry now.' The two friends edged nervously backwards as the snake turned its head to face them. Josh had thrown a large rock at it, hoping that this would frighten it, but it seemed that it had had the opposite effect. Now Josh was looking around for something else to hit the snake with. 'Where's a stick when you need one?' he muttered. 'Too late for that,' said Fergus. 'Let's get out of here.' And with that, he leaped towards the trees and started running.

Wordbuilding / Learning skills / Check! (page 19)

1

1 made 2 take 3 shared 4 paying 5 catch 6 take
7 get 8 telling 9 expresses 10 catch 11 committed
12 do 13 give 14 makes

2

1 b 2 a 3 a 4 b 5 b 6 a

3, 4 and 5

Students' own answers.

6

1
a a documentary
b a children's story *or* fairy tale
c a fantasy film

2
a film director *or* producer
b author *or* writer
c racing driver

3
a keep
b nightmare
c flames

Unit 3

3a (pages 20 and 21)

1

c

2

1 rich 2 increase 3 more 4 look after them 5 8.3
6 there are three ways

3

1 rises 2 boost 3 grown 4 increase 5 peak
6 decrease *or* decreasing 7 fall 8 go down
9 lessening 10 reduce

4

1 reduce 2 grow *or* increase *or* rise 3 fall *or* go down
4 reduce *or* lessen 5 increase *or* boost 6 increase

5

1 will have, will be
2 will rely
3 I'll tell, I'll be, doesn't start
4 won't solve

5 is going to
6 I'm going, begins

6

1 Are you going *or* Are you going to go
2 are you getting *or* are you going to get
3 'll probably drive *or* 'm probably going to drive
4 'll go
5 'll give
6 are you leaving *or* are you going to leave
7 starts
8 'll finish *or* 'll be finished

7

1 etcetera 2 contributed 3 lot 4 fifteen 5 years
6 powerful 7 motives 8 meet 9 secretly 10 years

3b Smart technology (pages 22 and 23)

1

Items mentioned: kitchen gadgets, water use,
sound-proofing, visual media, lighting

2

1 a 2 b 3 c 4 c 5 c 6 b

3

1 b 2 f 3 a 4 c 5 e 6 d

4

1 will be hearing 2 will be making 3 will all be
using 4 will have become 5 will be using
6 will be cleaning 7 will be installing 8 will have become
9 will be launching

5

1 will be doing 2 will be cleaning 3 will have developed
4 will be doing 5 will have been 6 won't have acquired

6

1 cardboard 2 brick 3 Cotton 4 leather 5 concrete
6 rubber

7

1 d 2 e 3 c 4 f 5 a 6 b 7 g 8 h

8

1 information age, information overload, information
  technology
2 data security, data storage
3 computer games, computer graphics, computer
  programmer

9

1 data security 2 information age 3 computer graphics
4 data storage 5 information overload

10

1 The weekday edition of *The New York Times* contains more
  information than the average person in 17th-century
  England learned in a lifetime.
2 Around a thousand books are published internationally
  every day and the total of all printed knowledge doubles
  every five years.
3 More information has been published in the last thirty
  years than in the previous 5,000.

3c (page 24)

1

1 b   2 c   3 c   4 b

2

1 2007; 6,000   2 99.9%   3 6   4 700   5 30   6 2010

3

1 works   2 provides   3 contains   4 lasts   5 weighs   6 run

4a

1 /ɪ/   2 /ɪ/   3 /aɪ/   4 /ɪ/   5 /aɪ/

5

1 neat   2 appropriate   3 consuming   4 handy
5 cutting   6 fix

3d (page 25)

1

1 blocked   2 loose   3 stuck   4 broken   5 cracked
6 squeaking   7 blank   8 faulty

2

Possible answers:
1 blank, cracked, faulty
2 loose, squeaking, stuck
3 broken, faulty
4 blocked, cracked
5 broken, faulty, loose, squeaking

3

1 ceiling fan
2 it doesn't look very safe or may have become loose
3 use the desk fan
4 TV
5 the screen is blank
6 switch the monitor on separately *or* use the on/off button
  on the screen (rather than the remote control)

4

1 wonder, look
2 seems to be
3 working, may
4 supposed, won't
5 get, whatever
6 tried
7 try

5

The two verbs which do not fit the stress pattern are: *highlight*
and *open*

3e (page 26)

1

1 Please can/could I pick up my bicycle on my way home from
  work tonight? *or* Can/Could I please pick up my bicycle on
  my way home from work tonight? *or* Can/Could I pick up my
  bicycle on my way home from work tonight, please?
2 I wonder if you can/could help me.
3 Do you have any idea I can find a battery charger for my
  old phone?
4 Could you send me an instruction manual for my washing
  machine, please? *or* Could you please / Please could you
  send me an instruction manual for my washing machine?

5 Please can/could you advise me how to … *or* Could you
  please advise me how to …?
6 Do you know what the phone number for Apricot
  Computers is?
7 Would you mind showing me how to use Powerpoint?
8 Could/Can you please tell me what number I should call to
  get technical advice?

2

a interest   b practice   c business   d print   e date
f order   g way   h luck

3

1 g   2 a   3 e   4 d   5 h   6 c   7 b   8 f

4

Model answer:

Hi Jim

I hope all is well with you. I tried to call you earlier, but I
couldn't get any answer. I wonder if you could help me.
I've just bought a new hi-fi system, but I can't set it up.
The speakers aren't working, but I don't understand the
instructions. Would you mind calling me some time? I'll be
at home this evening.

Many thanks

Sam

Wordbuilding / Learning skills / Check! (page 27)

1

address book
battery life
credit card
data protection
information technology
news story
instruction manual
travel agent

2

1 estate, travel
2 office, kitchen
3 bottle, can
4 video, board
5 coffee, lunch
6 ironing, message

3

1 travel agent, credit card
2 information technology, instruction manual
3 news story, video game
4 credit card, coffee break *or* lunch break

4

Students' own answers.

5

1 gadget   2 lazy   3 overpopulation   4 by
5 Appropriate   6 luck
Word: global

Unit 4

4a (pages 28 and 29)

1

1 In the first photo, the graffiti has been drawn on public walls. In the second photo, the graffiti is part of a piece of artwork.
2 Students' own answers.

2

1 being put in jail
2 shouldn't
3 the property owner

3

1 c   2 b   3 c   4 c   5 a   6 a

4

1 every member of the club
2 either method works *or* either method would work
3 any celebrities at the opening night
4 all our money
5 countries have their own laws and rules
6 whole world is waiting to see what will happen

5

1 each, all   2 no   3 both   4 any   5 Every   6 no
7 whole   8 Either

6

1 no   2 all the   3 the whole   4 each   5 Both

7

1 artwork   2 exhibition   3 artist   4 gallery   5 street
6 artistic   7 fine   8 arty

8

1 The message was clear: is this how far we have come since the Stone Age?
2 Often it carries a political or social message, but in an amusing way that ordinary people can relate to.
3 Despite not calling himself an artist, his work has been shown in galleries and has sold for thousands of dollars.
4 Banksy, who is based in the UK, is perhaps the world's best-known graffiti artist.
5 Banksy loves to surprise. In 2005, a picture showing a primitive human being pushing a shopping cart appeared in the British Museum.

The correct order is: 4, 3, 2, 5, 1

4b (pages 30 and 31)

1

1 show, performer   2 gig, venue, band   3 exhibition, gallery   4 buskers, halls   5 play, musical

2

1 Batman Live, This is Design
2 The Alternative Village Fete, Notting Hill Carnival
3 The Alternative Village Fete, Notting Hill Carnival
4 The Alternative Village Fete
5 The Floating Cinema
6 Notting Hill Carnival
7 Batman Live
8 The Alternative Village Fete

3

1 communal   2 float   3 eye candy   4 mundane
5 take for granted   6 workshop

4

1 a little   2 enough   3 a lot of, A large number of
4 plenty of, no   5 a lack of   6 many   7 hardly any
8 a bit of

5

1 number   2 no   3 several *or* some   4 plenty *or* loads *or* lots
5 any   6 few

4c (page 32)

1

1 country music   2 dance music   3 (punk) rock (music)
4 hip-hop (music)

2

Suggested answers:
a 3   b 1   c 1   d 4   e 2   f 2

3

1 Country; real
2 influences
3 teenagers; rock
4 sounds; technology

4

1 be connected to   2 escape   3 seem true   4 discover
5 think of   6 (not) be important

5

1 He spends a fortune on clothes every month.
2 I spent two hours trying to find their house.
3 She spends money like there's no tomorrow.
4 We haven't spent much time together recently.
5 They spent £20,000 on renovating their house.
6 See how you manage, but don't spend ages on it.
7 Why don't you spend the night with us on Tuesday?
8 She has spent her whole life trying to help people.

4d (page 33)

1

1 the Amazon River (and the people who live and work around the river)   2 He likes the presenter.

2

1 X   2 X   3 X

3

1 kind of thing   2 feel particularly inspired   3 a big fan of
4 got on my nerves   5 listen to him   6 a bit tired of

4

1 I could listen to Bach all day.
2 Documentaries don't really do anything for me.
3 I'm not really into TV.
4 I'm not particularly keen on the presenter.
5 I get a bit tired of reality TV shows.
6 I don't generally watch much TV. *or* I don't generally watch much TV.

5

1 documentary   2 everywhere   3 specifically   4 interest
5 separate   6 restaurant   7 listener   8 general

6

Students' own answers.

4e (page 34)

1

a I, we and you; it   b active; passive   c contracted;
uncontracted   d formal   e Avoid   f furthermore   g Share

2

Possible answers:
¹ I've got to admit that ² I'm ³ not a big fan of stand-up
comedy. ⁴ I always think that it's a rather unnatural
thing. The comedian ⁵ stands up in front of an audience who
stare at him or her as if to say, 'Come on, then, make me
laugh.' The comedian then has a few minutes to make them
laugh or the audience will start to get restless. It's all a bit
too aggressive for me. ⁶ So when ⁷ I went with an old school
friend to see new British comedian Spencer Brown last
Tuesday night at the Bristol Comedy Club, ⁸ I wasn't really
looking forward to it.

1 contraction
2 contraction
3 personal details
4 share your feelings
5 active verb
6 conversational linking phrase
7 active verb
8 share your feelings

3

Possible answers:
1 But   2 weren't   3 the rest of the audience seemed to like
his act   4 start   5 you think at first   6 then or after that
7 that's   8 putting together   9 in fact or actually

4

Model answer:
The secret of the show's success is that Spencer Brown
really understands his audience and what people find
funny. Not only that, but he comes across as a nice guy too.
If you are in Bristol, I'd definitely recommend going to see
him. He'll be at the Bristol Comedy Club until Saturday
10th December. You'll be smiling for weeks afterwards!

Wordbuilding / Learning skills / Check! (page 35)

1

1 bookshop   2 book club   3 booking   4 fully booked
5 bookish   6 booking office   7 bookkeeper   8 bookmark
9 do things by the book   10 booklet

2

1 fully booked   2 bookkeeper   3 bookmarks   4 booklet
5 booking   6 bookish

4

1 No, not really.
2 /ˈkʌmftəbl/
3 You use *either* + singular noun, but *both* + plural noun.
4 Yes, 'it gets on my nerves'.
5 American
6 Yes, it's quite direct.

5

1a full   b Melbourne   c such
2a a few   b folk   c fine (art)
3a an impersonal tone   b a lot of luck   c spend a fortune
4a gig, busker   b gallery, arty   c play, musical

Unit 5

5a (pages 36 and 37)

1

1 F   2 T   3 T   4 F

2

1 back to normal   2 floods or flood waters, winds   3 resettle
4 co-ordinated   5 depressed   6 safe   7 imaginative or
innovative   8 practical

3

1 to be   2 seeing   3 to hold   4 to return   5 to resettle
6 building   7 seeing   8 wondering

4

verb + *to* + infinitive: ask, help, hope, want
verb + *someone* + *to* + infinitive: allow, ask, get, help, want
verb + *-ing*: carry on, enjoy, imagine
verb + *someone* + infinitive: help, make

5a

verb + *to* + infinitive: choose, learn
verb + *someone* + *to* + infinitive: force, teach
verb + *-ing*: avoid, finish, involve, (not) mind
verb + *someone* + infinitive: let

5b

1 to visit   2 rebuild or to rebuild   3 to participate   4 doing
5 to work   6 learning   7 to do   8 meeting

6

1 pedestrian   2 centre   3 residential   4 luxury   5 spaces
6 blocks   7 park   8 centre

7

1 knock down   2 turn into   3 spoil   4 modernize
5 redevelop

8a

The fact that most people have returned says a lot about how
special this city is. The people who live here can't imagine
living anywhere else.
I'm a musician and making a living in New Orleans has
always been a challenge. We hoped to see more investment
in jobs and tourism after the hurricane.
But since Hurricane Katrina, life has definitely become
harder. I love this city, but these days, I'm forced to go out of
town to find work.

Answer: Yes, the resident is happy living in New Orleans.

8b

1 can't imagine living   2 hoped to see   3 'm forced to go

5b (pages 38 and 39)

1

Sentences a and b are true of Monterey today.

2

1 T   2 N   3 F   4 T   5 T   6 T   7 F   8 T

3

1 dynamic   2 join (in) the party
3 just like that   4 old-timers   5 set up   6 sample

4

1 dynamic   2 industrial   3 attractive   4 preserved
5 regulated   6 essential

5

1 NC   2 NC   3 C   4 C   5 NC   6 NC   7 C   8 C

6

1 going   2 putting   3 catching   4 to say *or* saying
5 fishing   6 to make   7 to go   8 eating

7

1 to visit   2 to see   3 to open   4 to do   5 having

8

China – minor   placed – taste
found – drowned   rule – tool
front – hunt   way – weigh
meant – sent   whale – they'll
ocean – motion   where – share

5c (page 40)

1

1 in later life   2 things   3 talk   4 technology   5 three

2

1 language ability, overall development and success (in life)
2 in, off
3 seeing the child as a true conversation partner or having a
  conversation with your baby/child
4 that babies respond to what you are saying a long time
  before they can speak
5 digital media
6 thirty million

3

1 key   2 spatial awareness   3 commentary
4 facial expression   5 interacting   6 statistic

4

1 behind   2 for   3 through   4 apart   5 out   6 over *or* off

5b

<u>c</u>ommentary   <u>d</u>ominate   <u>em</u>pathy   <u>in</u>fluence   <u>p</u>owerful
a<u>bi</u>lity   de<u>ve</u>lopment   tech<u>no</u>logy

5d (page 41)

1

1 d   2 e   3 g   4 a   5 c   6 f   7 b

2

1 public   2 local   3 green   4 pedestrianized
5 leisure

3

Conversation 1: b
Conversation 2: e

4

1 I find it
2 I agree completely
3 The thing is
4 absolutely
5 For me,
6 make much more sense
7 understand
8 you also need to consider
9 I'm more concerned
10 Not necessarily.

5

1 I <u>know</u> and I agree <u>completely</u>.
2 The thing <u>is</u>, it's our <u>taxes</u> they're <u>spending</u>.
3 For <u>me</u>, that would make <u>much</u> more <u>sense</u>.
4 I <u>understand</u> why you <u>say</u> that.
5 But <u>actually</u>, you <u>also</u> need to <u>consider</u> all the <u>old</u> people.

6

Students' own answers.

5e (page 42)

1

1 B   2 D   3 A   4 C

2

c quoting what someone (often famous) has said about this
problem

3

Possible answers:
(giving a dramatic example) You used to be able to drive
from Washington to Boston, a distance of 450 miles, through
rich, green landscape. Now the only green you see is the
paint on people's houses!

(giving some statistics) In the United States, the area between
Boston and Washington DC, a distance of 450 miles, is now a
massive urban region with a population of about fifty million
– that's almost 17% of the US population on 2% of the US
land area.

4

1 In addition
2 Because of this; As a result
3 on the other hand

5b

1 … three acres of land, the house comes with a swimming
  pool. *or* … coming with three acres of land, the house has a
  swimming pool.
2 … rising crime, people have moved out of the centre. *or* …
  a rise in crime, …
3 … a good bus service, we have excellent roads into the city
  centre. *or* … having a good bus service, we have excellent
  roads into the city centre.
4 … restrictions on building on green spaces, we are starting
  to redevelop city centres.

Wordbuilding / Learning skills / Check! (page 43)

1

1 badly, well
2 short-term, long-term
3 newly, well
4 highly, well

5 quietly, highly
6 poorly, cleverly
7 culturally, socially
8 reasonably, extremely

2

1 long-term unemployed
2 reasonably well-off
3 quietly confident
4 cleverly designed
5 badly prepared
6 culturally mixed
7 highly educated
8 newly built

4

Possible answers:
• It doesn't say who wrote it, but it doesn't seem to be a travel article. The interest seems to be from an urban development perspective.
• The main argument is that a fantastic city has grown up in a place you would not expect it, because of one person's dream and ambition.
• The writer doesn't say whether he/she likes what has happened to Dubai or not, but he/she seems uncertain that it will be a long-term success.
• I agree with the writer's argument. It seems an unsustainable development.

5

1 c   2 c   3 c   4 a and c   5 b

Unit 6

6a (pages 44 and 45)

1

Speaker 1: c
Speaker 2: e
Speaker 3: f
Speaker 4: b
The two extra items are a and d.

2

Speaker 1: d   Speaker 2: f   Speaker 3: b   Speaker 4: a
The two extra activities are c and e.

3

1 a   2 b   3 b   4 b   5 c

4

1 Let's not pretend
2 Don't answer
3 You don't have to do
4 not to go
5 I don't think it's extravagant
6 I hope not
7 not to let the children know
8 you really mustn't let

5

1 I'm afraid not, sorry.
2 I don't think it's a great idea.
3 Let's not do anything to upset them.
4 I hope I didn't give her the wrong impression.
5 You don't have to give the book back to me immediately.
6 Try not to be late, please.
7 You mustn't take food into the library.
8 None of them (there) knew the answer, not even the teacher.

6

1 off or holiday   2 catering   3 scenery   4 view
5 airlines   6 luggage or baggage   7 journey or drive or way
8 countryside   9 took   10 suitcase or bag

7

1 sunbathing   2 guided   3 souvenirs   4 snorkelling
5 sightseeing   6 riding   7 eating out   8 beachcombing

8

1 In tough economic times, people will try not to spend so much on luxuries and that includes holidays.
2 However, they don't want to go without a holiday altogether, because holidays are an important break from the stresses of work and daily life.
3 You don't have to go abroad to go on holiday. You can have a staycation instead. These have increased in popularity in recent years.
4 I don't think it's a bad trend because it means that people discover more about their own country, and at the same time, they boost the local economy.

6b (pages 46 and 47)

1

1 print off boarding pass
2 buy guidebook and suntan lotion
3 check travel insurance is up to date
4 write down contact details or write contact details down
5 get vaccinations before travelling
6 check passport is valid

2

1 consultancy-type roles   2 highly skilled professionals
3 four to six months   4 no costs

3

1 c   2 b   3 a   4 c   5 c   6 b

4

1 rewarding   2 tough   3 lasting   4 fresh   5 suited to
6 flexible

5

1 do you   2 wouldn't it   3 is it   4 didn't you
5 mightn't there   6 wouldn't I

6

1 me what kind of expenses you cover
2 it would harm my future career to take time away from work to volunteer
3 Wouldn't you like to use your skills to help others
4 if there are organizations which offer long-term volunteering jobs for inexperienced people
5 It's a bit selfish to volunteer just because you want to travel, isn't it
6 Surely it's more interesting to see another country as a volunteer rather than as a tourist

7

1 F   2 F   3 R   4 R   5 R   6 F   7 R   8 F

6c (page 48)

1

Items on *NG Endeavour cruises:* a swimming pool, a library, professional photographers, kayaking trips, wildlife excursions, expert guides

2

1 fishing   2 sun   3 fitness   4 lounge   5 Islands
6 kayaks   7 naturalist   8 $1,000   9 day   10 Ecuadorian

3

1 comfortable   2 educational   3 adventurous   4 expensive

4

1 sleek   2 cranes   3 base   4 unique   5 remote

5

1 **If you had a cruise in mind**, try one of Lindblad's expedition.
2 **If you don't mind a bit of danger and excitement**, Lindblad cruises are perfect.
3 I meant to book this holiday, but **I've had a lot on my mind** (lately).
4 **Bear in mind that** these are not typical cruises.
5 I used to think that cruises were for the retired, but **I've changed my mind** now.
6 **I'm in two minds about going** on one of their cruises.

6b

1 Don't   2 No   3 It doesn't   4 No   5 Don't   6 It doesn't

6d (page 49)

1

1 in   2 up   3 to   4 on   5 out   6 on   7 up   8 out *or* down

2

1 He's working. *or* He's at work.
2 He'll get a bus, then walk.
3 At Steve's office.

3

1 The easiest thing is to take the bus.
2 Alternatively, I can (just) take a taxi.
3 I can make my own way.
4 It's only a fifteen-minute bus ride.
5 I'm coming in by train.
6 If I get held up, I'll let you know.

4

1 drive   2 flight   3 ride   4 walk   5 ride   6 crossing

5a

1 d   2 b   3 a   4 e   5 c

6

Students' own answers.

6e (page 50)

1

1 She had to pay £30/extra charges to carry her coat onto the plane.
2 She wants a refund and she wants the airline to investigate the matter.

2

1 Oxford   2 customer – company   3 formal

3

1 register a complaint   2 unjust   3 stated   4 informed
5 placed   6 attempted   7 wished   8 opted
9 these circumstances   10 investigate

3b

Model answer:

Dear Sir/Madam

I am writing to **register a complaint** about the meal we **were served** on our flight home last week – flight UZ332. On the booking confirmation it **stated** that we **would be given** breakfast and lunch. **However**, breakfast **only consisted of** a cup of tea and lunch a tuna sandwich. By itself, this would not have been a problem, but **I regret to say that** my husband and I both **suffered** food poisoning from the sandwich.

4

Model answer:

Given the circumstances, I would ask you to do two things. Firstly, please ensure that in future communication with passengers you make it clear what kind of meal will be served. Secondly, please ensure that the food which you provide is fresh and has not been stored in the wrong conditions.

Yours faithfully

Thomas Garcia

Wordbuilding / Learning skills / Check! (page 51)

1

1 in   2 out   3 out   4 in   5 out   6 in   7 in   8 out
9 up   10 in

2

a fall out (with)   b take in   c drop in (on)   d look in (on)
e fall in (with)   f look out   g give in (to)   h take out
i drop out (of)   j give up

3

1 reason for writing   2 link the ideas   3 examples
4 spelling

4

1 Because it's a letter of complaint to a person you don't know.
2 Reason for writing; details or facts about the incident; action wanted
3 At the time (that); consequently; Otherwise; Given these circumstances
4 formal
5 She didn't want to delay other passengers; it's not unreasonable to wear a coat onto a plane

5

1 She took a Japanese holiday in her own city (New York).
2 voluntourism
3 in a prison hotel
4 in an art hotel, e.g. Propeller Island City Lodge, in Berlin
5 couch surfing

Unit 7

7a (pages 52 and 53)

1

Speaker 1: e
Speaker 2: d
Speaker 3: a
Speaker 4: c

2

a 2 b 4 c 2 d 1 e 3 f 4

3

1 b 2 a 3 a 4 c 5 b 6 a

4

1 are, provide
2 don't, are
3 don't, decide, will make
4 try, will end
5 are, have

5

1 'll feel, manage
2 promise
3 'm going to reserve or 'll reserve, is
4 will get, returns or has returned
5 'll just read, 'm waiting or wait
6 hear or 've heard, 'll let
7 wins, 'll take
8 find or 've found
9 'll cook, get
10 won't have or doesn't want to have, 's living

6

1 brought 2 spoil 3 punished 4 tell 5 disobey
6 nagging 7 rebelled 8 give 9 reward

7

Everything depends on what you see as the future role of
your children. In other words, what is it that you are raising
them to do?
Do you want them to be good members of society? If so,
you will teach them values such as obeying the law,
co-operating with others and generally being good citizens.
Or do you want them to be successful individuals? If so, you
will help them to be free thinkers and to be independent.
Or is it important that they are good family members? Then
you will teach them to respect their elders and to follow
family traditions.

7b (pages 54 and 55)

1

b

2

1 b 2 c 3 a 4 a 5 c

3

1 used to eat 2 weren't used to seeing 3 would use
4 would have 5 are used to eating 6 have got used to
eating 7 usually eat out 8 are used to seeing 9 used to
eat 10 usually eat

4

1 didn't use to cook 2 used to cook 3 wanted
4 used to hang or would hang 5 was 6 had
7 used to cook or would cook 8 were used to doing or
used to do

5a

/uː/: blue, lunar, rude, suit, truce
/juː/: consume, fortune, humanity, humour, menu,
used, usually

6

1 P, SF
2 D, F
3 F, P or S, SD
4 P, SD or D

7c (page 56)

1

1 F 2 F 3 T 4 F 5 F 6 T

2

1 d 2 b

3

1 rather 2 Unlike 3 little 4 such 5 At worst

5

1 all the same   5 a difference of opinion
2 the same coin   6 no difference
3 a different matter   7 a different tune
4 the same thing   8 the same boat

7d (page 57)

1

1 honeymoon 2 reception 3 stag 4 veil 5 engagement
6 groom or bridegroom 7 fiancé(e)

2

1 It's a sign of wealth and social status.
2 Because the bride didn't go out to work (so this was her
  financial contribution to the marriage).
3 the bride's family
4 the groom's family
5 They bring gifts.
6 clothes and jewellery

3

1 symbolizes 2 rule 3 customary 4 marks 5 occasion
6 place 7 traditional 8 On

4

1 /z/ 2 /s/ 3 /z/ 4 /s/ 5 /s/ 6 /z/ 7 /s/ 8 /s/
9 /z/ 10 /s/ 11 /z/ 12 /z/

5

Students' own answers.

7e (page 58)

1

1 e 2 c 3 a 4 d 5 b

2

1 romantic
2 magnificent
3 bright red
4 spectacular, colourful, magical

3

1 takes place 2 marks 3 begin 4 highlight 5 gathers
6 dancing

Wordbuilding / Learning skills / Check! (page 59)

1

1 bits and pieces	7 life and soul
2 bride and groom	8 plans and arrangements
3 husband and wife	9 pomp and ceremony
4 food and drink	10 singing and dancing
5 friends and family	11 suit and tie
6 fun and games	12 time and trouble

2

1 pomp and ceremony   2 time and trouble   3 bits and pieces   4 life and soul   5 friends and family   6 suit and tie

5

1 in   2 out   3 at   4 of   5 up   6 to   7 with   8 off

Unit 8

8a (pages 60 and 61)

1

1 target   2 come   3 live   4 aim   5 have   6 achieved

2

Speaker	Their ambition	What they were doing before
1 Rhea	to help children get a good education	working for a big insurance company
2 Sasha	to work in the art world	(went to art college) painting as a hobby working as a waiter / working in bars

3

1 a   2 c   3 b   4 b   5 c   6 c

4

1 b   2 b   3 a   4 a   5 b   6 b

5

1 had felt, would have carried
2 hadn't told, wouldn't be
3 were still learning, would probably be
4 was, wouldn't have moved
5 hadn't found, wouldn't have been
6 hadn't had, probably wouldn't be receiving

6
Suggested answers:
1 If she were/was a (more) ambitious person, she would have applied for the job of director.
2 If I hadn't met my (German) wife, I wouldn't be living in Germany now.
3 If I were/was a risk-taker, I would invest my own money in the business.
4 If she had received more encouragement, she would have become a pilot *or* she wouldn't have given up her plan of becoming a pilot.
5 If I were/was worried about the situation, I would have said something about it.
6 If he hadn't left college and become a ski instructor, perhaps he wouldn't be so happy with his life.

7

1 C   2 W-W-C   3 C-C   4 W-C   5 W-C

8

1 make   2 do   3 did

9

1 make, do
2 doing, made
3 made, do
4 doing, make

8b (pages 62 and 63)

1
b

2

1 N   2 T   3 T   4 N   5 T   6 N   7 T   8 F

3

1 legacy   2 passing (her) by   3 excuse   4 alternative
5 unlikely   6 support

4

1 would stop   2 could   3 had travelled   4 were
5 hadn't   6 would change   7 hadn't started   8 didn't have

5

1 'd left (= had left)
2 'd stop (= would stop)
3 had
4 were *or* was
5 would take
6 would turn

6

1 match   2 ship   3 chew   4 Swiss   5 shock   6 bass

7

I am very suspicious of bucket lists now. They started out as a good idea, but like a lot of things they have become too commercial. In bookshops you now find titles like *100 Places You Must Visit Before You Die* or *100 Films You Should See*. And if your dream is to hold a baby tiger, there are even websites you can go on where they can make your wish come true.

8c (page 64)

1

1 forest, Cancún, no   2 giraffe, yes   3 tree, Britain, yes

2

1 F   2 T   3 T   4 N   5 N   6 F

3

1 rotting   2 classic   3 sale   4 victims   5 heroic
6 wonderful   7 small   8 rarest

4

1 classic   2 a victim   3 buried   4 for sale   5 rotting

5

Emotive words: back-breaking, desperate, majestic

6

1 rescue   2 deprived   3 giant   4 exploit   5 wonderful
6 most threatened   7 over-developed

8d (page 65)

1

1 d   2 a   3 f   4 b   5 e   6 c

2

They mention: b, d, e

3

1 rather not do   2 'd prefer to do   3 mind helping
4 someone else did   5 'd probably be better   6 like doing

4

1 'd prefer not to do   4 'd be better
2 'd rather do   5 'd rather go
3 be happy to help   6 prefer doing

5

1 Would you prefer   2 Shall we take
3 Would you rather we went   4 Do you like

8e (page 66)

1

1 Speaking loudly on mobile phones is anti-social.
2 No, he doesn't agree. He says speaking loudly is social, not
  anti-social. It encourages people to be more open with each
  other.

2a

1 a call to someone to get up, a reminder to buy something
  from the shops, asking someone to get out of the bathroom
2 when people speak loudly on their mobile phones just to
  show off

2b

Example answers:
1 shops or restaurants
2 shops or restaurants
3 the train or the underground
4 what they are doing or where they are or how long they are
  going to be or what they're going to eat for dinner
5 what they are doing or where they are or how long they are
  going to be or what they're going to eat for dinner

3

a (ought to know better)

4

1 be better   2 go one better   3 know better   4 be better off

Wordbuilding / Learning skills / Check! (page 67)

1

1 plumber   2 florist   3 translator   4 banker   5 pharmacist
6 librarian   7 accountant   8 specialist   9 surgeon
10 consultant   11 inspector   12 optician

2

1 a salesperson   2 a police officer   3 a fire fighter
4 an actor   5 a flight attendant

4

1 Globalization <u>helps</u> <u>people</u> in <u>rich</u> <u>countries</u>.
2 They can have goods out of <u>season</u>.
3 But to be <u>honest</u>, I don't <u>need</u> <u>flowers</u> imported
  from Africa in De<u>cem</u>ber.

6

Across: 2 rocket   5 lemur   6 girl   7 been   9 to   10 if only
11 invisible
Down: 1 goal   3 target   4 ambition   8 noise

Unit 9

9a (pages 68 and 69)

1

Across: 2 criticize   5 urge   6 begs   7 ask   8 deny
Down: 1 accuse   2 complain   3 threaten   4 suggest

2

1 cover, 1982
2 photo, magazine or Magazine

3

1 F   2 T   3 F   4 T   5 F   6 F   7 T   8 F

5

1 of manipulating reality.
2 altering the image. or that they had altered the image.
3 doing anything wrong. or that they had done anything wrong.
4 modern technology for making it easy to alter images.
5 their designers (that it is OK) to alter images for covers.
6 about being given a false impression. or that they had been
  given a false impression.
7 not to trust a photo if there's anything important
  depending on it.

6

1 for invading   2 (for) taking   3 for manipulating
4 to alter   5 using   6 to add   7 for making   8 to accept

7

1 recommends using an analogue camera
2 encourages you to look at the preview before you take a
  photo; keeps you in the moment
3 that with a digital camera you need more time to edit the
  images after they've been taken
4 you can make them look like the image as you saw it

9b (pages 70 and 71)

1

1 b   2 d   3 a   4 c

2

a 3   b 2   c 3   d 4   e 1   f 1 (or 3)

3

1 donations   2 zimmer frame   3 brainchild   4 brighten up
5 plunged   6 speeding

4

1 it is estimated that rioters (story 1)
2 The café owner was reported to have put (story 2)
3 It is believed that (story 3)
4 He is not thought to have been speeding (story 4)

5

2 is known
3 used to be believed
4 has been estimated
5 was thought
6 was said

6

2 was hoped that
3 used to be thought that
4 isn't recommended
5 is expected that, will carry on
6 was said to have prevented
7 was considered to be *or* was considered to have been
8 has been reported that

7

1 charming
2 amusing
3 inspiring
4 engaging
5 astonishing
6 optimistic

8

a optimistic
b amusing
c astonishing
d engaging, charming
e inspiring

9c (page 72)

1

b

2

1 a particular   2 two experts   3 man-made   4 both views
5 working for tobacco companies   6 amount of real evidence

3

1 biased   2 fundamental   3 overwhelming
4 distorts   5 proportionate

4

1 b   2 b   3 a   4 a

5

1 word of mouth
2 eat my words
3 one person's word against another's
4 don't take my word for it
5 gave his word
6 From the word go
7 was lost for words
8 have the last word

9d (page 73)

1

1 take (D)   2 gets (B)   3 believe (B)   4 exaggerate (D)
5 surprise (B)   6 take (D)

2

1 He was seen/spotted by a theatrical agent and they want to work with him / sign him up.
2 Kate
3 Not to tell anyone. Patrick wants to keep quiet about it.

3

1 about   2 apparently   3 reckons   4 pinch
5 to   6 heard   7 gossip   8 seems, supposedly

4

1 comedy   2 festival   3 apparently   4 reckon   5 according
6 difficult   7 agency   8 theatrical

5

Students' own answers.

9e (page 74)

1

The correct order is: C, A, D, B

2

1 C   2 A   3 D   4 B

3

1 Whatever the reason
2 The problem is that
3 What is more
4 It is hoped that
5 But now
6 at the same time

4

1 One resident described his life in Bama. 'I have everything I want here,' he said. 'I can go fishing when I want to. I don't have any stress.' And then he added, 'Why would I want to go and live in the city?'
2 'Some people come here to take wedding photos,' said another resident, 'which is fine. But when they leave their rubbish behind, I get very angry.'
3 A health tourist said, 'Before I came here I could hardly breathe or speak, because the pollution in my city was so bad. Now I sing every day,' he said with a big smile on his face.

Wordbuilding / Learning skills / Check!(page 75)

1

1 worrying   2 confusing   3 refreshing   4 charming
5 inspiring *or* touching   6 depressing   7 touching *or* inspiring   8 tiring

2

1 inventive   2 persuasive   3 creative   4 competitive
5 productive   6 talkative   7 protective   8 attractive

3, 4 and 5

Students' own answers.

6

1
Possible verbs:
a agree, offer, refuse, swear
b advise, beg, convince, invite, persuade, recommend, urge, warn
c accuse (... of), blame (... for), congratulate (... on), praise (… for)
2
a iconic   b ageing   c zero
3
a mouth   b good   c gossip   d headline(s)

Unit 10

10a (pages 76 and 77)

1

1 small village in Illinois
2 radio broadcaster; (an) actor (in films and television)
3 the Soviet Union
4 read the lines/words he was given by his advisors
5 listen to people *or* make people feel special
6 (great) economic growth

2

1 b 2 a 3 a 4 b 5 b 6 a

3

1 graduated 2 worked 3 follow *or* pursue 4 joining
5 did 6 become

4

Countries: the United Arab Emirates, the Netherlands
Places: the Amazon River, the countryside, the Moon
Times: the weekend, (the) spring
Others: the police, the poor
All the other nouns take zero article.

5

1 the 2 the 3 the, the 4 a 5 the 6 –, the
7 –, – 8 –, –, – 9 the, the 10 –

6

1 /r/ 2 /j/ 3 /w/ 4 /j/ 5 /r/ 6 /r/ 7 /j/
8 /w/ 9 /w/

7

1 I guess I was lucky to do a subject that not many other people at college did. I studied plant sciences and after my course, I got a job as a research assistant at the Institute of Botany.
2 It's not easy to be an artist and make a living from it. You are always wondering if it would be better just to get a job with a regular income.
3 I was always told that having good qualifications and the right degree opens doors, but actually it's good communication skills that help you advance in an organization.

8

1 background 2 experience 3 qualifications
4 qualities 5 knowledge 6 talents

10b (pages 78 and 79)

1

1 My mission is to find simple, inexpensive ways to monitor health
2 these medicines can cause liver damage
3 The small piece of paper is a low-tech tool
4 to attend university
5 I want all women to believe in themselves and know they can transform society *or* to encourage young women who attend university abroad to bring their skills back to their homelands

2

1 c 2 b 3 c 4 a 5 b 6 b

3

1 a 2 b 3 c 4 b 5 c 6 c

4

1 … could be a medical breakthrough **that will save millions of lives.**
   … millions are dying from the same drugs **that are supposed to cure them.**
2 … is a low-tech tool **which detects disease by analysing bodily fluids.**
3 … does not surprise people **who know her.**
4 A new foundation **she has launched** …
5 Positive results, **which show up in less than a minute,** …
6 she prepared for her college entrance exams, **for which she studied for up to twenty hours a day.**
7 no one monitors patients to see **what** is working and **what** isn't.

5

1 where *or* in which 2 which 3 who 4 what
5 that *or* who *or* no pronoun 6 that *or* which *or* no pronoun
7 with whom 8 whose

6

1 The piece of paper, **which** is the size of a postage stamp, could save thousands of lives. *or* The piece of paper, **which** could save thousands of lives, is the size of a postage stamp.
2 The charity 'Diagnostics for All', **which** was co-founded by Sindi, produces the tool. *or* The charity 'Diagnostics for All', **which** produces the tool, was co-founded by Sindi.
3 The tool will be used in developing countries **where** it is difficult to find clinics.
4 People say things about existing drugs, which I agree with. *or* People say things about existing drugs, with which I agree. *or* I agree with the things (that) people say about existing drugs.
5 The results show up on the paper, **whose** colour changes if there is a problem.
6 Sindi went to England **when** she was a young woman.
7 Sindi, **who** was the first Saudi woman to study biotechnology at Cambridge University, later went to Harvard. *or* Sindi, **who** later went to Harvard, was the first Saudi woman to study biotechnology at Cambridge University.
8 Sindi has become an inspiration for other women **who** want to follow her example.

7

1 She believes that new technology **which was created** at Harvard University will make it possible. *or* She believes that new technology **which has been created** at Harvard University will make it possible.
2 The first thing I ask the children **who are attending** the class is to draw a picture of a scientist.

8

1 suffering 2 living 3 designed 4 determined
5 wishing 6 launched, wanting

10c (page 80)

1

Things to tick: an anti-slavery campaigner, a spy, a nurse, an army officer, a mother, a writer, a public speaker

2

1 b 2 b 3 c 4 a 5 b 6 c

3

1 next door *or* bordering
2 a wonderful place
3 strong-willed, wanting to succeed in something very much

4 the money you get (from a company or the state) when you retire
5 the right for women to have a say in who is elected for public office

4a

1 e<u>ffec</u>tive oOo
2 im<u>pres</u>sive oOo
3 su<u>pport</u>ive oOo
4 <u>pos</u>itive Ooo

5 per<u>sua</u>sive oOo
6 <u>sen</u>sitive Ooo
7 de<u>ci</u>sive oOo
8 <u>talk</u>ative Ooo

4b

Rule for words that end with vowel + -*tive*: 1st (or antepenultimate) syllable is stressed. For other words, the 2nd (penultimate) syllable is stressed.

5

1 conscious
2 control
3 interest

4 made
5 help
6 confident

10d (page 81)

1

1 in   2 with   3 at   4 of   5 to   6 with   7 on   8 about

2

A job to lead outdoor activities and expeditions for young people.

3

1
Applicant 1: very good with children
Applicant 2: canoeing, water sports and outdoor activities; good organizational skills
Applicant 3: good at a number of different sports; experienced PE teacher

2
Applicant 1: hasn't got experience working with this age group
Applicant 2: hasn't got experience of mountaineering
Applicant 3: hasn't got experience of leading expeditions

4

1 participating   2 to leave   3 travelling   4 doing
5 to work *or* on working   6 to find out *or* in finding out

6

Students' own answers.

10e (page 82)

1

a 4   b 1   c 2   d 3

2

1 which has
2 with an interest in
3 with an ambition to work
4 who has a passion for
5 who has specialist knowledge of
6 with experience in
7 with limited access
8 who loves teaching

3

1 c   2 f   3 e   4 b   5 a   6 d

4

Possible answers:
1 enthusiastic, creative, flexible, adaptable, etc.
2 with
3 specializes
4 aim, goal, ambition, passion, interest
5 which *or* that
6 can
7 have

Wordbuilding / Learning skills / Check! (page 83)

1

The verbs which do not collocate are:
1 do   2 make   3 get   4 make   5 acquire   6 win   7 own
8 work   9 earn   10 take on

2

1 took   2 follow   3 get *or* do   4 had   5 get *or* gain
6 joined *or* set up   7 got *or* gained   8 acquire *or* learn

3

1 d   2 f   3 h   4 b   5 e   6 a   7 c   8 g

4

1 felt   2 definite article   3 acquire *or* get   4 yes
5 semi-formal

5

1 a a mahout   b Daniel Kish *or* the 'real-life' Batman
2 step, mankind
3 a the Atlantic Ocean   d the USA   e the Moon
4 a which is also used (= a defining relative clause)
   b where it is often key (= a non-defining relative clause)

Unit 11

11a (pages 84 and 85)

1

c

2

1 b   2 c   3 c   4 a   5 c   6 a

3

1 aim   2 extinct   3 record   4 diversity   5 centuries
6 express   7 huge   8 understand

4

1 succeeded in discovering
2 were able to help
3 managed to build
4 was able to help
5 could bring
6 couldn't save

5

Possible answers:
1 managed to find *or* was able to find *or* succeeded in finding
2 could speak *or* was able to speak
3 didn't manage to convince *or* didn't succeed in convincing *or* weren't able to convince
4 couldn't understand *or* wasn't able to understand
5 could express *or* was able to express
6 managed to get *or* succeeded in getting; could only remember *or* was only able to remember

6

1 take   2 acquire   3 unaware   4 engage   5 get   6 inspire

7

1 picked up
2 inspire *or* motivate *or* engage with *or* connect with
3 unaware of
4 get *or* understand
5 get *or* understand
6 take in *or* understand

8a

1a Munichi   b Wappo
2a Swarthmore   b Pennsylvania
3a Arunchal   b Koro
4 chary
5 floccinaucinihilipilification

8b

a 5   b 2a   c 4   d 1b   e 3b

11b (pages 86 and 87)

1

a 2   b 1   c 3

2

1 T   2 F   3 F   4 N   5 F   6 F   7 F   8 T   9 T

3

1 block (something) out   2 ran into   3 came up (to)
4 turned out (that)   5 come across   6 get away with

4

Text 1
1 My sister and I **were just about to go** to bed … *or* **were just going to go** to bed …
2 My sister **was going to say** goodnight … *or* **was about to say** goodnight … *or* **would have said** goodnight.

Text 2
3 I **would have asked** his name … *or* **was going to ask** his name
4 I **was supposed to know** …

Text 3
5 who **was going to give** evidence in court … *or* **was supposed to give** evidence in court … *or* **was about to give** evidence in court …
6 her neighbour **wasn't going to get away with** it …

5

1 was going to write *or* would have written
2 was just about to book, would be full
3 would speak
4 would have lasted *or* was supposed to last, were about to finish *or* were going to finish
5 was going to take *or* would have taken *or* was supposed to take
6 was just about to ask *or* was just going to ask

6a

1 I was <u>going</u> to <u>email</u> him, but I decided it would better to speak face to face.
2 He was <u>supposed</u> to get here <u>early</u>, but he's already ten minutes late.
3 I <u>would</u> have come by <u>train</u>, but there's a strike on at the moment.

4 She said she would be <u>pleased</u> if I talked to him, but she seemed really angry.
5 I was <u>about</u> to <u>buy</u> a flat, but Katie said I could rent hers for six months while she was away.
6 Liz was <u>going</u> to be in charge of the project, but now she's just acting as an advisor.

6b

1 I was going to email him, but I decided it would better to speak <u>face to face.</u>
2 He was supposed to get here early, but he's already <u>ten minutes late.</u>
3 I would have come by train, but there's a <u>strike</u> on at the moment.
4 She said she would be pleased if I talked to him, but she seemed <u>really angry</u>.
5 I was about to buy a flat, but Katie said I could <u>rent hers</u> for six months while she was away.
6 Liz was going to be in charge of the project, but now she's just acting as an <u>advisor.</u>

7

1 c   2 d   3 a   4 e   5 b

11c (page 88)

1

1 border collie   2 crow   3 dolphin   4 Bonobo monkey
5 scrub-jay

2

a 3   b 4   c 1   d 5   e 2

3

a 2   b 3   c 5   d 1   e 4

4

1 smart   2 inventive   3 playful   4 expressive
5 mischievous

5

1 walk   2 late   3 mistakes   4 tricks   5 lesson   6 live
7 way   8 heart

11d (page 89)

1

1 mean   2 speak   3 explain   4 'm   5 saying   6 give
7 take   8 catch *or* hear

2

1 Greek and Roman history
2 He doesn't have as much background knowledge as the other students.
3 Reading some history *or* a book by Herodotus.

3

1 what the course is going to be about
2 no previous knowledge of ancient history is needed
3 stories like the war at Troy and so on
4 a book I could read now, outside class
5 Herodotus

4

1 me   5 me   6 me
The other sentences don't need an indirect personal object.

6

Students' own answers.

11e (page 90)

1

1 c 2 e 3 d 4 b 5 a

The writer's application for a course has been rejected even though he/she applied before the deadline.

2

1 While we sympathize with your situation, it is too late to do anything about it now.
2 Although you sent your form in before the deadline, we had already received too many applications.
3 You say in your letter that we have no right to do this, but in actual fact, the college has the right to close the application process early.
4 We don't 'make up the rules as we go along' as you suggest. On the contrary, we are very careful to follow the rules.
5 Whereas most colleges would keep your application fee, we are refunding it to you.

3

Model answer:

Dear Sir/Madam

I am writing to inform you that I will be unable to attend the accountancy course (B102) this term owing to a misunderstanding.

When I enrolled for the course, I had assumed it was an evening class. In actual fact it turns out to be on Tuesdays between 10 a.m. and 12.30 p.m. I have asked my employer if it would be possible to release me for this period each Tuesday. Although they would like to do this, they say that the timing makes it impossible.

While I realize that this is probably my fault for not reading the timetable carefully enough, I hope you will be sympathetic. I hope to enrol on a future course, but for the moment I would be grateful if you could refund the course fees I have paid.

I look forward to hearing from you.

Yours faithfully

Mark Riley

Wordbuilding / Learning skills / Check! (page 91)

1

1 point 2 company 3 tip 4 spare 5 room
6 value

2

1 b 2 a 3 b 4 b 5 a 6 a

3, 4, 5 and 6

Students' own answers.

7

1 succeeded 2 engage 3 managed 4 late 5 experience
6 reality
Character 1: SEMLER
7 catch 8 clever 9 heart 10 explain
Character 2: ALEX

Unit 12

12a (pages 92 and 93)

1

1 savers and spenders
2 No, these characteristics are too simplistic.

2

1 b 2 a 3 c 4 a 5 b 6 c

3

fund (v) – finance (v)
prudent – careful
transaction – deal (n)
wages – salaries
wasteful – extravagant

4

1 cost *or* standard 2 haves, nots 3 income
4 standard *or* cost 5 power 6 quality

S	H	A	V	E	S	B
Q	U	A	L	I	T	Y
U	N	I	T	C	A	P
N	G	I	H	O	N	A
O	R	N	E	S	D	S
T	Y	C	Y	T	A	T
S	P	O	W	E	R	E
N	O	M	I	N	D	N
Y	D	E	L	I	V	E

5

1 Let's **just** consider ~~just~~ people's attitude to money at its simplest level.
2 Of course, savers spend ~~only~~ money, but **only** when they can afford it.
3 People in these countries ~~even~~ would have to work longer hours, pay more taxes and **even** accept lower wages.
4 You ~~only~~ don't **only** risk losing the money, but you also risk putting the borrower in a difficult situation.
5 We need both types of person, but **only** if they lend and borrow ~~only~~ responsibly.

6

1 Some people believe that if you go through life ONLY saving money, you will never have any fun. *or* Some people believe that if you ONLY go through life saving money, you will never have any fun.
2 Some people carry on spending money EVEN when they can't afford to.
3 You can protect yourself against bad times by putting aside JUST a small amount of money each week.
4 If ONLY a few people save money, the banks won't have any money to lend to others.
5 It's not JUST me who has debts; other people have them too.
6 Some people say that your attitude to money is JUST to do with your upbringing. *or* Some people JUST say that your attitude to money is to do with your upbringing.
7 Most people are ONLY careful with money when times are hard.
8 Some borrowers admit that sometimes EVEN they borrow money irresponsibly. *or* EVEN some borrowers admit that sometimes they borrow money irresponsibly.

7

1 payments   2 spending   3 investment   4 loan   5 savings
6 borrowing   7 debts   8 earnings

8

I think that people often get into debt because they want a lifestyle that they can't really afford.

It's a lifestyle which is sold to them constantly through advertisements, for example on TV and in magazines.

This desire to have a better lifestyle can affect some governments too. They want to improve their citizens' standard of living so that people will vote for them again.

12b (pages 94 and 95)

1

a

2

1 NG   2 T   3 F   4 NG   5 T   6 T   7 T   8 NG

3

1 dominant   2 mass production   3 profitable   4 wages
5 consumed   6 call centres   7 outsourcing   8 harm

4

1 have people work
2 get their work done
3 have their clothes made
4 get their tuna processed
5 get most questions answered, get them to put
6 get anyone to do, have your own employees do

5a

/ʃ/: machine, revolution
/tʃ/: cheap, richer
/ʒ/: decision, usually
/dʒ/: major, wages

6

1 fit   2 put   3 decorate   4 assemble   5 fixed   6 tiled
7 do   8 cleaned

7

1 b   2 f   3 a   4 d   5 c   6 e

12c (page 96)

1

b

2

1 c   2 b   3 b   4 c   5 a

3

1 passing   2 buzz   3 trend   4 catchy   5 loyal   6 upmarket

4

1a is running hard
1b is hardly running
2a hardly works *or* is hardly working
2b works hard *or* is working hard
3 hardly know
4a thought hard
4b hardly thought
5a hardly tried
5b tried hard

12d (page 97)

1

1 h   2 a   3 e   4 b   5 d   6 f   7 c   8 g

2

1 a leaving party for a colleague
2 a reduction in the price

3

1 honest   2 mind   3 hoping   4 would   5 face   6 shoes
7 appreciate   8 key

4

1 L   2 L   3 S   4 L   5 L   6 L   7 L   8 S

5

1 I'm afraid that would be difficult for me.
2 Would you move a bit on the price?
3 Would you be willing to negotiate?
4 I would need to have some kind of guarantee.
5 When would you need to know?
6 I wouldn't want to put you to any trouble.

6

Students' own answers.

12e (page 98)

1

1 As requested   2 Overall   3 specifically   4 Consequently
5 Initially   6 To sum up

2

1 b   2 c   3 a   4 a   5 e   6 c   7 d

3

Possible answers:
1 here is my feedback *or* here are my comments
2 was an excellent course *or* was a very good/useful course
3 some small and large company websites
4 it is very important to know what kind of design is suitable for different purposes *or* it was very useful to do this comparison
5 to use them, even for someone with no previous experience of design
6 would recommend this course
7 time to practise and a bit more guidance with my own work

Wordbuilding / Learning skills / Check! (page 99)

1

1 the rich   2 the unemployed   3 the poor   4 the homeless
5 the elderly   6 the famous   7 the adventurous
8 the hard-working   9 the lazy   10 the sick *or* the ill

2

1 P   2 N   3 N   4 N   5 X   6 P   7 P   8 P   9 N   10 N

3 and 4

Students' own answers.

5

1 rainy   2 income   3 catchy   4 have   5 end   6 saving
Word: RICHES

IELTS Practice test

Listening Test answer key

1 C   outside in the grounds
2 B   just the morning or the afternoon would suit me fine
3 A   you'd have to sign up like anyone else, and there's a monthly fee
4 A   tips on how to put a CV together
5 D   a seminar led by one of the big recruitment agencies
6 JAYNES   J.A.Y.N.E.S
7 Business Studies   M: So which faculty's that? Economics? F: Business Studies actually
8 technical translations   But this time, she's doing technical translations
9 construction industry   he's going to be talking about openings in the construction industry
10 Geology   He's working in the Geology department
11 C   provides opportunities to meet the scientists who work at the Observatory
12 B   an adult single ticket would cost £6.50 in the summer months and £5.50 at other times of year, whereas a family ticket would cost either £24 or £20.
13 C/D   explore the universe using hands-on activities
14 D/C   the glass-walled café with outside terrace
15 Botany   It wasn't the Astrophysics department that bought it, though, but the Botany department
16 meteor shower   installed just in time to observe a meteor shower
17 1947   in 1947, the 218-foot Transit Telescope
18 Mark 1/One/I   This was named the Mark One Telescope
19 solar system   a scale model of the solar system
20 World Heritage   to place Jodrell Bank on the UK shortlist for consideration as a site with World Heritage status
21 A   how you balance these two aspects is up to you
22 C   I hadn't even chosen a specialty – so that made it tough.
23 B   I'd have done better with a straight four-week split.
24 A   talk to people ... That's how I found the one I went with
25 emergency   I went for emergency
26 beach   photos ... of the beach that drew me to Belize
27 300,000   with only 300,000 people
28 (the) north   up in the north where I was
29 Cuban   a lot of the doctors working there are actually Cuban
30 teaching (the staff)   I'd rather think of teaching the staff
31 One/1 metre/meter   that grows to around one metre
32 Dark brown   The male ... being a dark brown
33 Silver(-)grey/grey   the female is distinguishable by its silver-grey skin
34 (Dense) undergrowth   has a preference for dense undergrowth
35 Lizard(s)   tends to rely on lizards as its main source of food
36 Bird   Bird Island – the place where one was eventually spotted
37 (six-week) survey   They commissioned a six-week survey
38 100   supporting a racer population of around 100 individuals
39 B/C   The right kind of habitat is not found over a wide area
40 C/B   although the snake's habitat does remain vulnerable to hurricane damage

Reading Test answer key

1 TRUE   start by identifying the appropriate granting body to contact
2 TRUE   check ... the deadline for the submission of applications
3 FALSE   Your proposal should be written out in the format stipulated
4 FALSE   It's a good idea to propose only those objectives that you feel relatively confident of achieving within the grant period
5 NOT GIVEN   (there is no mention of whether this is advisable or not)
6 TRUE   cover what is already known about the problem in the scientific literature
7 FALSE   In addition, many forms now have a section ... required to describe how the research is likely to contribute to economic development
8 NOT GIVEN   (there is no mention of whether they do this or not)
9 TRUE   state clearly that you're aware of the limitations of your approach
10 FALSE   describe briefly any particular strengths of your laboratory
11 iii   like to see a concise description of the results of any work you have already carried out
12 v   your application should include latitude and longitude, elevation, vegetation ...
13 vii   Describe how you plan to find people to take part in experiments
14 ii   laboratory procedures ... a brief description of the various analytical techniques that you will carry out
15 vi   how it will be entered on a computerized database and what software will be used
16 viii   the partners with whom you intend to work
17 C   evidence for at least 15 separate occasions when it acted as a home
18 B   predate other known instances of plant matting by approximately 50,000 years
19 A   a tree whose foliage contains chemicals that kill biting insects. Dr Wadley thus thinks ... mattresses on which the inhabitants slept
20 A   a range of hitherto unknown artefacts ... pictograms
21 C   a range of hitherto unknown artefacts ... arrows
22 D   a range of hitherto unknown artefacts ... needles
23 (a/the) tree(s)   They probably settled in trees at night
24 climbing   they still retained features useful for climbing, such as curved fingers and long arms
25 chimpanzees   just as chimpanzees do today
26 fire   once hominids learned how to control fire they discovered they could sleep on the ground
27 grass   Neanderthals were also building grass beds
28 YES   a group of more than sixty cognitive psychologists and neuroscientists signed a document stating that the brain training industry took advantage of people's anxieties and was not supported by sufficient research.
29 NOT GIVEN   (There is no information in the text regarding the attitudes of the participants in the study towards the results.)
30 YES   In a 2015 survey of the general public, the majority of respondents believed that memory was a natural element of brain function, but in reality, the brain is programmed to forget information in case it becomes overloaded.
31 NO   It recognizes six key types of memory – including remembering words and faces – all of which are equally significant
32 NO   The Clinic conducted a study on elderly subjects who all carried the gene for Alzheimer's disease (APO-E4) but were otherwise in good physical health.
33 NOT GIVEN   (There is no information in the text regarding the number of subjects in the study.)
34 driving   Driving is another such commonplace skill that studies show has been enhanced by Merzenich's techniques.

35 injury   those who have suffered a serious head injury appear to respond positively.

36 prison   these techniques might be used with offenders who have been sent to prison

37 medication   conventional medication is ineffective for treating many of the symptoms she observes

38 motivation   it can be difficult for them to maintain sufficient motivation

39 nutrition   there are also other factors involved, notably the role of proper nutrition

40 doctors / Doctors   doctors seldom see the value in her techniques … the benefits of brain training could be experienced much more widely

How to mark the Writing Test
Task 1

There are four criteria for marking the Part One tasks, which are equally weighted.

Task achievement

This is an assessment of how well the student has fulfilled the task.
A successful task will:
- include at least the minimum number of words
- have a text structure appropriate to a letter
- be relevant to the context established in the input material
- achieve the writer's intended purpose
- cover the functions indicated in the bullet points

Coherence and cohesion

This is an assessment of how clear and fluent the writing is.
A successful task will:
- be appropriately organized
- successfully link information and ideas
- contain logical sequencing
- make effective use of cohesive devices

Lexical resource

This is an assessment of the use of vocabulary.
A successful task will:
- include a range of relevant vocabulary
- use vocabulary accurately
- use vocabulary in an appropriate way

Grammatical resource

This is an assessment of the use of grammar.
A successful task will:
- use an appropriate range of grammatical forms at sentence level
- use grammatical forms accurately

Task 2

There are four criteria for marking the Part Two tasks, which are equally weighted.

Task response

This is an assessment of how well the student has responded to the task.
A successful task will:
- make clear the writer's position on the issues raised in a question or statement
- develop arguments to support that position
- support the arguments with evidence and examples
- include at least the minimum number of words

Coherence and cohesion

This is an assessment of how clear and fluent the writing is.
A successful task will:
- be appropriately organized
- successfully link information and ideas
- contain logical sequencing
- make effective use of cohesive devices

Lexical resource

This is an assessment of the use of vocabulary.
A successful task will:
- include a range of relevant vocabulary
- use vocabulary accurately
- use vocabulary in an appropriate way

Grammatical resource

This is an assessment of the use of grammar.
A successful task will:
- use an appropriate range of grammatical forms at sentence level
- use grammatical forms accurately

How to mark the Speaking Test

The speaking test is an assessment of how effectively students can communicate in English.
There are four criteria for marking the Speaking Test, which are equally weighted.

Fluency and coherence

This is the ability to:
- talk at a consistently normal speed
- link ideas and language together in logical sequences
- use the language features which create coherent, connected speech

Lexical resource

This is the ability to:
- use a range of relevant vocabulary
- use words appropriately to convey meaning
- use paraphrase strategies when required

Grammatical range and accuracy

This is the ability to:
- use a range of grammatical forms appropriately
- use grammatical forms accurately

Pronunciation

This is the ability to:
- use a range of phonological features to convey meaning
- produce intelligible individual sounds
- use stress, rhythm and intonation effectively

Listening Test audioscript

[104]

PRESENTER: In this test you'll hear a number of different recordings and you'll have to answer questions on what you hear. There will be time for you to read the instructions and questions and you will have a chance to check your answers. The recording will be played once only. The test is in four sections.

Now turn to Section 1 on page 100 of your book. You will hear a student called Martin telling his friend about a careers day which is being held in the city where they are studying. First you have some time to look at questions 1 to 5. You will see that there is also an example which has been done for you.

Now we shall begin. You should answer the questions as you listen, because you will not hear the recording a second time. Listen carefully and answer questions 1 to 5.

WOMAN: Hi, Martin. Did you hear about the careers day that the college is holding? My tutor was just talking about it.

MARTIN: Yeah, apparently there's something on the notice board about it, or so my flatmate was saying.

WOMAN: Well, it's probably this leaflet he saw pinned up there. Look, it's got all the details.

MARTIN: Great. Is it being held in the college then? I heard they were going to hire space in the Town Hall.

WOMAN: Really? I think you must be thinking of some other event. Our college is actually sharing the day with the technical university, and they're putting the day on at their campus. It's going to be outside in the grounds if the weather's nice.

MARTIN: Look, it goes on all day from ten till five. I wouldn't want to hang around that long though, just the morning or the afternoon would suit me fine. I start getting bored after a couple of hours at these things.

WOMAN: Well, look at the programme of talks – it'll help you decide which.

MARTIN: Anyway, there's a website with all the talks on, so it doesn't matter if you miss some of them.

WOMAN: Well, the event is free to students enrolled at the college, but the website isn't: you'd have to sign up like anybody else, and there's a monthly fee. But then you do see stuff from other similar events around the country too.

MARTIN: Sounds good. There are some sessions on in the lunchtime too. Look. And it's not the usual talks by old students or videos about voluntary work in other countries either. You can get tips on how to put a CV together or go to a seminar led by one of the big recruitment agencies.

WOMAN: Right. My careers advisor was recommending those when I met her for my one-to-one advice session the other day.

MARTIN: Should be good then.

PRESENTER: Before you listen to the rest of the conversation, you have some time to read questions 6 to 10.

Now listen and answer questions 6 to 10.

MARTIN: So what are the main talks on the programme, then?

WOMAN: Well, each faculty's put up one speaker. Our college in the morning and the technical university in the afternoon. But the speakers aren't only talking about stuff relevant to those subjects.

MARTIN: Sure. So let's see. It starts at ten and the Law faculty is putting up Professor Jaynes.

Woman: The famous judge?

MARTIN: No, you're thinking of James. This is Jaynes, J . A . Y . N . E . S. And he's talking about contracts of employment.

WOMAN: Oh right. Could be interesting though.

MARTIN: Maybe. But eleven o'clock you've got Professor Smith talking about internships – that should be more interesting. She lectures in accountancy, apparently. So which faculty's that? Economics?

WOMAN: Business Studies actually.

MARTIN: Oh yes, of course. Then Dr Wentworth is representing the Languages faculty at eleven. I heard her give a really good talk on cross-cultural misunderstandings last term – you know gestures and stuff you can get wrong – it was brilliant. But this time, she's doing technical translations.

WOMAN: Oh right. Yeah, she's a good speaker.

MARTIN: Then after lunch, there's Dr Shah from the Engineering faculty. It says here he's an expert in computer modelling, but he's going to be talking about openings in the construction industry.

WOMAN: Shame, I'd rather hear about the models.

MARTIN: Me too. Then there's Dr Bellucci from Sports Science – she's doing something on the Olympic Games which should be interesting – all the different jobs from different disciplines that are involved.

WOMAN: Right. And then it's our old friend Dr Fulton doing interview techniques. He's working in the Geology department at the technical university now, and they've put him up for this. Though when he was here, he was in the faculty of Geography.

MARTIN: Still he's a great speaker – always gets a laugh.

WOMAN: So what do you think ...

PRESENTER: Now turn to Section 2 on page 102 of your book. You will hear some information about Jodrell Bank, a famous radio telescope, which is part of the University of Manchester. First you have some time to look at questions 11 to 14.

Now listen and answer questions 11 to 14.

MAN: Good evening. I'm here to tell you about the Jodrell Bank Observatory, which has been a world leader in radio astronomy since the second half of the twentieth century. The site is part of the University of Manchester and there's also an arboretum with over 2,500 rare trees. A visitor centre provides information about both the famous radio telescope and the trees.

The giant Lovell Telescope that stands on the site is an internationally renowned and awe-inspiring landmark. This is a radio telescope so visitors cannot look through it directly. The observatory buildings are also still in use for operating the telescope, so are not usually open to the public. But the visitor centre provides a good view of the telescope and visitors can walk along a pathway not far from the base, where they will find plenty of notices providing information about the history of the telescope and how it works. The centre also provides opportunities to meet the scientists who work at the Observatory.

The visitor centre also provides activities for visitors of all ages. Admission prices at the centre vary according to the type of ticket and the season in which the visit is made. For example, an adult single ticket would cost £6.50 in the summer months and £5.50 at other times of year, whereas a family ticket would cost either £24 or £20. An annual ticket is available for individuals at £19.50 and for families at £60. Concessionary tickets are available at all times for children, students and retired people.

In terms of facilities available at the visitor centre, these are divided between two buildings: the Planet Pavilion, where you'll find the entrance as well as the glass-walled café with outside terrace – you get amazing views of the telescope from there. There's also a gift shop and a small exhibition space where visitors can learn about the planets. The second building is the Space Pavilion, which is the main exhibition area. Here visitors can find answers to the wonders of the universe, listen to the sound of the Big Bang and explore the universe using hands-on activities. As many returning visitors are aware, our planetarium was demolished in 2003, along with the old visitor centre. But we are looking to secure funding to restore this feature in the not-too-distant future.

PRESENTER: Before you hear the rest of the presentation, you have some time to look at questions 15 to 20.

Now listen and answer questions 15 to 20.

MAN: Next, a bit about the history of the telescope. It's named after Sir Bernard Lovell, who was a pioneer in the study of astrophysics in the twentieth century. The site itself, which is about fifteen miles south of the other university buildings in Manchester, first came into the university's possession in 1939. It wasn't the Astrophysics department that bought it, though, but the Botany department who were looking for a place to cultivate wild plants. In 1945, Bernard Lovell was given some equipment to use in his work, including a radar. But because of electrical interference from trams passing the university buildings, it didn't work properly in central Manchester, so he asked to move it to Jodrell Bank instead. It was installed just in time to observe a meteor shower that was visible that year.

Over the next few years, Lovell installed other equipment on the site, including an aerial on a searchlight mount in 1946, and in 1947, the 218-foot Transit Telescope – at the time the largest in the world. This telescope was superseded by a larger and more up-to-date model in 1957. This was named the Mark One Telescope, later

upgraded and eventually renamed the Lovell Telescope in honour of Sir Bernard. This telescope became famous in the 1960s for tracking manned and unmanned space missions, as well as providing information about astronomy itself. And the telescope remains a world leader in this field.

Further developments followed in the 1960s and 1970s, including a teaching telescope for use by undergraduates, and the creation of the arboretum in 1972. This features national collections of various rare trees and other plants as well as a scale model of the solar system.

More recent developments at the site have included the opening of a new Discovery Centre in 2011, an event which coincided with a decision to place Jodrell Bank on the UK shortlist for consideration as a site with World Heritage status. In July that year, the site also hosted a rock concert called 'Live from Jodrell Bank'. These are excellent examples of how the scientists at Jodrell Bank have always worked hard to engage with the wider community and increase the impact of their science.

PRESENTER: Now turn to Section 3 on page 103 of your book. You will hear an interview with a medical student called Damian, who is talking about his elective, a period of work experience he did overseas as part of his degree course. First you have some time to look at questions 21 to 24.

Now listen and answer questions 21 to 24.

WOMAN: Hi, Damian.

DAMIAN: Hi.

WOMAN: Thanks for coming to talk to college radio about your elective. Now that's a period of work experience in a hospital you do in your final year as a medical student, isn't it?

DAMIAN: That's right. The idea is that being a doctor is about understanding the psycho-social factors involved in each patient, as well as the medical ones. You do an elective in a speciality, to explore it in greater breadth and depth, and that's especially interesting when the placement's abroad.

WOMAN: So is it a sort of working holiday really?

DAMIAN: No. I wouldn't say that. But electives do also give you the opportunity to travel and have fun. How you balance these two aspects is up to you. Whilst in Belize, I learned to scuba dive, climbed Mayan ruins and explored the jungle, not something you can say about every medical placement!

WOMAN: And it's up to you to organize the whole thing, isn't it?

DAMIAN: That's right. Many students have problems when it comes to organizing an elective. For some it's the first time they've travelled alone or the first experience of being exposed to different cultures. I was cool with all that, but it's important to choose your speciality well. I had no idea where I wanted to go because I hadn't even chosen a speciality, so that made it tough.

WOMAN: Do you have to spend the whole period in one place, or can you split it up?

DAMIAN: You can choose. I chose to divide mine into a six-week placement abroad and a two-week placement at home in the UK. Many people would argue that a two-week placement doesn't give you enough time to fit into a team and gain relevant experience, and I'd go along with that. With the benefit of hindsight, I'd have done better with a straight four-week split.

WOMAN: And where can you go for help with these decisions?

DAMIAN: Well, many companies will organize elective placements for you, as well as providing cover and support ... at a price! But there are lots of companies out there, and I've heard that if you're willing to hunt around, you can find some reasonably priced deals. It's always worth asking round though. If you can talk to people about companies they've used, you can check whether those companies are any good or not. That's how I found the one I went with and I've no complaints.

PRESENTER: Before you hear the rest of the conversation, you have some time to look at questions 25 to 30.

Now listen and answer questions 25 to 30.

WOMAN: So Damian, tell us about your placement in Belize.

DAMIAN: Well, having been undecided for a long time between specializing in surgery or emergency medicine, I went for emergency, because I thought it would give me a broader experience than surgery would. My first choice of country would've been Jamaica, but they only had places for dermatology and obstetrics, so that's how Belize came up. I'd never really heard of the country before.

WOMAN: And was it a company that helped you?

DAMIAN: Yes, they provided photos of medical and non-medical facilities in a couple of different countries in the Caribbean and Central America. In the end, it wasn't the photos of the hospital but those of the beach that drew me to Belize – perhaps I shouldn't admit to that!

WOMAN: So tell us a bit about working there.

DAMIAN: The health system in Belize is a mixed one of both public and private. The government subsidizes a significant proportion of health care for the average Belizean, although there's a limited number of hospitals with in-patient facilities. Belize has an area of 22,000 square kilometres with only 300,000 people spread sparsely around it, and a big town is one with about 20,000 inhabitants. It means that a significant percentage of the population is rural based and nowhere near a free national hospital.

WOMAN: Right.

DAMIAN: I was one of three British students placed by the company: the two others were in the south of the country and I think they had a different experience, but up in the north where I was, the biggest frustration was that, despite Belize being an English-speaking country, the default language was Spanish, because a lot of the doctors working there are actually Cuban. I speak French, but not Spanish, so when

consultations weren't in English, I needed the doctor to explain what had been said.

WOMAN: Would you go to Belize again?

DAMIAN: Yes. And people do sometimes get jobs in the places they've been to on electives. But next time I wouldn't go with the idea of being a hospital doctor, I'd rather think of teaching the staff. But I think I could've made better use of my clinical experience if I'd learned basic Spanish – so that would be a priority before I went back.

WOMAN: Damian. Thanks.

PRESENTER: Now turn to Section 4 on page 104 of your book. You will hear a student giving a presentation about the Antiguan Racer Snake, a rare species living on a Caribbean island. First you have some time to look at questions 31 to 35.

Now listen and answer questions 31 to 35.

WOMAN: In my presentation today I want to talk about the rarest snake in the world – the Antiguan Racer Snake – an animal that has been rescued from the brink of extinction by the efforts of conservationists.

The snake is one of the racer snake family that is found in various regions across the Americas. It's a small harmless snake that grows to around one metre, with the female being slightly longer than the male.

Many of the racer snakes found in the Caribbean region, and especially those in the southern states of the USA, are black in colour, whereas the Antiguan Racer is lighter. The male is closer in colouring to the black racers, being a dark brown, whilst the female is distinguishable by its silver-grey skin.

The Antiguan Racer is found in various habitats, including sandy beaches and rocky ridges, but has a preference for dense undergrowth, which is one of the reasons why it's relatively rarely seen.

In terms of diet, the Antiguan Racer is very choosy. Other racer snakes feed on small mammals and amphibians such as frogs, but the Antiguan sub-species tends to rely on lizards as its main source of food. Maybe this is one of the reasons why it's an endangered species, although there's little evidence that its prey has ever been in short supply.

PRESENTER: Before you hear the rest of the presentation, you have some time to look at questions 36 to 40.

Now listen and answer questions 36 to 40.

WOMAN: By the end of the twentieth century, it was feared that the Antiguan Racer, which was once common on the large island of Antigua after which it's named, had indeed become extinct. And this was probably the case. The snake had once been common on the neighbouring island of Barbuda too, but hadn't survived the human development of these large islands. But the local inhabitants were convinced that the snakes might be surviving on one of the smaller islands off the Antiguan coast, such as Rabbit Island or Crump Island, or on Bird Island – the place where one was eventually spotted in 1995.

The tiny island was uninhabited and looked after by the Antiguan Forestry Unit, which was keen for scientists to establish how many snakes might be living there. They commissioned a six-week survey, to be carried out by one of the conservationists who had made the discovery, Mark Day, who later went on to work for the conservation body, Fauna and Flora International.

What was established by his work was that the small island, only measuring some 18,000 square metres, was supporting a racer population of around 100 individuals. The rarest snake in the world was alive and well, but seriously endangered. In 1996, a conservation project was set up to ensure its survival.

And with the current population standing at around 500 snakes, this project has been hailed a success. A captive breeding programme has been effective in increasing numbers, even though it was adversely affected by disease at first. Reintroduction to other nearby islands, and to the mainland of Antigua, has meant eradicating the rats that had decimated the snake population in the twentieth century – a programme that has worked, although the snake's habitat does remain vulnerable to hurricane damage. Now that the species is officially protected, there are unlikely to be further incursions of tourist development into its natural habitat, another cause of its earlier decline. The right kind of habitat is not found over a wide area, though, and this will eventually limit the extent of the snake population. So before I go on to ...